A DICTIONARY

OF

SLANG, JARGON & CANT

British Library Cataloguing-in-Publication Data
A catalogue record for this book is available from the
British Library

A DICTIONARY

OF

SLANG, JARGON & CANT

EMBRACING

ENGLISH, AMERICAN, AND ANGLO-INDIAN SLANG
PIDGIN ENGLISH, GYPSIES' JARGON
AND OTHER IRREGULAR
PHRASEOLOGY

COMPILED AND EDITED BY

ALBERT BARRÈRE

*Officier de l'instruction publique; Professor R.M.A. Woolwich
Author of "Argot and Slang," &c. &c.*

AND

CHARLES G. LELAND, M.A., Hon. F.R.S.L.

*Author of "The Breitmann Ballads," "The English Gypsies
and their Language," &c.*

VOL. II. L—Z.

1897

A DICTIONARY

OF

SLANG, JARGON, AND CANT.

—⊷—

L

LABELS (American), postage stamps.

Lace (popular), spirits.

He got royally blind, showed a liking for *lace.—Bird o' Freedom.*

Laced (old cant), sugared, as *laced* coffee.

Laced mutton, used by Shakspeare (Two Gentlemen of Verona). *Vide* MUTTON.

Lacing (popular), a beating.

Ladder (common), "can't see a hole in a *ladder*," said of one who is intoxicated.

Ladies' grog (common), hot, strong, sweet, and plenty of it (Dickens).

Ladies' Mile (society), Rotten Row.

Ladle, to (theatrical), to speak the text in a pedantic and pretentious manner, *i.e.*, to "*ladle* it out."

Lad of wax (thieves), shoemaker.

Ladroneship (nautical), literally a pirate, but it is the usual epithet applied by the Chinese to a man - of - war (Admiral Smyth).

Lady (old cant), a misshapen woman.

Lady-bird (common), a specially nice or dainty kept mistress. (Popular), a wanton or lewd girl.

Lady-caller (American), explained by quotation.

A *lady-caller* is a cultivated and presentable woman nicely dressed, who takes a salary for distributing cards for fashionable folk, and, as we presume from the accomplishments demanded of her, even occasionally makes actual calls instead of the lady who employs her, and who, by a social fiction, is supposed to be calling.— *St. James's Gazette.*

Lady - fender (popular), a lazy woman who gives herself airs. Chiefly used by servants in reference to a mistress who likes to sit by the fireside doing nothing.

Lady Green (prison), the prison chaplain.

Lag (thieves), a prisoner, convict. *Vide* To LAG.

Asking . . . what improvement there was in the grub at Brixton; was there going to be a war with Russia? If so, was it likely they would want the *lags* for soldiers.—*Evening News.*

An old *lag*, one who has been through penal servitude.

To start, I, a confirmed old *lag* myself, think I may say that there isn't a prison in London that I haven't seen the inside of.—*Greenwood: Dick Temple.*

(Westminster School), a fag.

Every morning the *lag* junior prepares and brings to hall the "list," which is the rota of duties for the day.—*Everyday Life in Our Public Schools.*

Lage (old cant), wash water, thin drink. Probably from the Gaelic and Irish *lag*, weak, feeble.

I bowse no *lage*, but a whole gage
Of this I bowse to you.
—*Brome: A Jovial Crew.*

This term is still used by the low class of actors. It is curious to note that *laigue*, in old French argot, signifies water, from the Spanish *agua*, with the article prefixed. But there is no evidence that the English term is from the French *laigue*.

Lager (American). In German *lager* means a resting-place, a camp; from the root *legen*, lay a place. Hence a warehouse where goods lie, a stock or deposit. *Lager bier* in Germany is stock beer, as one says stock ale in Anglo-Saxondom. It was in America that the word *lager* was most incorrectly applied, for the first time about 1847, in Philadelphia, to German beer, to distinguish it from American and English malt drinks. All German beer is not *lager*, any more than all English beer is Indian pale ale or "bitter."

Und is mein sabre sharp and true?
Und is mein war-horse goot?
To get one quart of *lager* bier,
I'd shpill a sea of bloot!
—*Ballads of Hans Breitmann.*

Lage, to (old cant), to wash. *Vide* LAGE.

Lagger (thieves), a sailor. Possibly from his way of walking. Also one who gives evidence; an informer. *Vide* To LAG.

Lagging (thieves), a term of imprisonment or hard labour. *Vide* To LAG.

Now the whole of the difference between passing a comfortable *lagging* and a hard *lagging*, is to give no trouble to the officer. I always make it a rule—don't trouble me and I'll not trouble you.—*Evening News.*

Lagniappe (Creole American), a trifling commission or discount.

All New Orleans grocers give to every purchaser a *lagniappe*. If child or servant buys five cents' worth, *lagniappe* is expected and given rigidly, as though so nominated in the bond. It may be sugar, or spice, or candy. If the purchaser demand quartee (two and a half cents' worth) rice and quartee beans, two *lagniappe* are given. There are groceries in the French quarter where the chief business of the supplemental small boy is the rolling of brown paper sheets into cornucopias, and the filling of these horns of plenty with *lagniappe.*—*American Newspaper.*

This system is getting general now in London for grocers to give presents to all purchasers. The higher the purchase the greater the present. The practice is usual in France, and probably in most countries.

Lags (American), layers of leaves of tobacco. Dutch *laag*, a lay, a row layer.

Lag, to (thieves), formerly to transport or cause to be transported; now to send to penal servitude or to prison.

They'll ask no questions after him, fear they should be obliged to prosecute, and so get him *lagged.*—*Dickens: Oliver Twist.*

A day or two after Bill returns alone. The girl asks him where her sweetheart is. "He's *lagged*," says Bill.—*Sims: How the Poor Live.*

To *lag*, which, it is conjectured, originally came from "lagging," or tying the prisoners together, is curiously allied to *lagan*, the right of the lord to take goods cast up on the shore of his manor. Also goods *tied* to a buoy and then sunk in the sea. In gypsy and Hindu *lagar* or *lugarna* has the same meaning. Compare the French cant word "fagot," for a convict, *i.e.*, tied up like a bundle of sticks. Hotten suggests the derivation from the old Norse *lagda*, laid, laid by the leg. To *lag*, which formerly had also the meaning of to steal, seems to be connected in the sense with the German *lagern*, to lay, to put away.

(Old cant), to *lag*, to void urine. A *lagging gage*, a chamber-pot. The expression is still common among showmen and strolling actors. *Vide* LAGE.

Laid in lavender. *Vide* LAVENDER.

Laid out (American), also English, but more extensively applied in "the States." Beaten, flattened out.

Mr. M—— is horizontally *laid out*. Nevertheless, the war taxes must go. *Boston Herald.*

Laker. Although applied as a term of derision to Wordsworth, Southey, and their famous friends, because they lived in the Lake country, the word had been in use from time immemorial in Yorkshire and Lancashire, in another sense, with reference to players. The dictionaries give "*Lake*, to play, to sport," hence *laker*, or derisively, "lazy *laker.*" *Lake*, a north-country word for play, is from Danish *lege*, to play.

One of the delicate pleasantries invented at the expense of the players in the last century, runs as follows. When the drum announced their advent in the rural districts of Yorkshire, the farmers' dames were wont to say—"Get the shirts off the hedge, wench, for here comes the *lakers.*"

In the year 1750, Gentleman Holman, a famous actor and author, and the recipient of high honours from his *Alma*

Mater at Oxford, was fulfilling an engagement at Leeds. He had dressed at his hotel for Beverley, in "The Gamester," and was attired in his court suit, with powdered hair and bag, chapeau bras, diamond buckles, &c. On his way to the theatre, in a sedan chair, the porters were stopped on Leeds Bridge, and overhauled by a gang of roughs of the period, who demanded to know who was inside. On being informed that the gentleman in court dress was a play-actor, the ringleader said to his friends — "Oh! it's nobbut a *laker ;* chuck him in t' river, lads." Before they could carry out this laudable intention, the *laker* stepped out, confronted them with his rapier, which he slipped into them, right and left, sending the ruffians howling in every direction.

La-li-loong (pidgin-English), a thief, thieves.

The barber complained he had been called a *la-li-loong*, the pidgin-English for a thief.—*Celestial Empire*, 1876.

Just t'hen he savvy *la-li-loong*,
Same tief-man muchee bad,
Hab wantchee kill one foleigna'
An' catchee állo had.
—*Wang-ti.*

L ā l l - s h r a u b (Anglo-Indian). English-Hindu, *lāl-shrāb*, red wine. The name for claret in India. In English gypsy, *lāl* or *lulli-moll*.

Lamb (old), name given formerly to a dupe, now a "pigeon," "mug," or "juggins." (Popular), an elderly person who dresses and makes up like a young one. *Vide* LAMBS.

Lamb and salad (popular), to give one *lamb and salad*, to give a sound thrashing. Also *lamb-pie*, a flogging. From *lam, vide* LAMM.

Lambasting (popular), beating, thrashing. *Vide* To LAMB.

L a m b d o w n (Australian up-country), to beat. *Vide* To LAMM.

He saw the publican . . . narrating with coarse glee to a fellow-poisoner how he had copped the old —— on the hop and *lambed him down* to rights.—*A. C. Grant.*

Lamb, lam, to (popular). *Vide* To LAMM.

Lambs (common), the roughs at an election employed to create a disturbance and break up the meetings held by and in favour of an opposing candidate. Also roughs of any kind.

The bold Bendy, who until the past year or two was notorious as the foremost "bully boy" amongst the *lambs* of Nottingham.—*J. Greenwood : Low-Life Deeps.*

Lame duck. *Vide* DUCK.

Lammie Todd (tailors), a phrase used by tailors, meaning "I would if I could."

Lamm, to (popular) to beat, strike. From the Icelandic *hlemma*, to beat, bruise; Anglo-Saxon *lama,* Irish *lamh*, old Norse *lamr*, Hotten deriving it from the old Norse *lam*, hand. *Lam* is originally to strike with the hand.

Compare *smack*, to slap, and Irish *smac*, the palm of the hand. This word is old English, and is now used only by slang-talking people.

> Dauber, to beat, swindge, *lamme.*—
> *Cotgrave.*

> De vellers ash *lam* de Romans dill dey roon mit noses plue.
> —*Charles G. Leland: Breitmann Ballads.*

> But forty-nine more were wanted, and I was getting mad,
> For I hadn't done what I wanted, which was, I'll now expound,
> To *lamm* the ball to a certain and distant part of the ground.
> —*Bird o' Freedom.*

Lamm it on, lay it on, hit hard.

Lammy (thieves), a blanket. An allusion to lamb and wool.

Lamp country (military), walking out at night without money in one's pockets. The soldier's hours of recreation are generally after dark, when the lights are lit, and if he has no funds to defray entrance to places of amusement, or pay for refreshments at other houses of call, he has to be content with *lamp country*.

Lamp-post (common), a nickname for a tall lanky individual, much in vogue among schoolboys. A synonym is "sky-topper."

Lampresado, defined in the New Canting Dictionary as one who comes into company with but twopence in his pocket! An impostor, an informer.

Lamps (thieves and others), the eyes. The synonyms in French

argot and Italian furbesco are *quinquets* and *lampante*. *Vide* GIG-LAMPS.

Landed (popular). A man is said to be *landed* when he has amassed a fortune large enough to keep him for the rest of his life.

(Thieves), to be *landed*, explained by quotation.

> When I fell this time I had between four and five quid found on me, but they gave it me back, so I was *landed* (was all right).—*Horsley: Jottings from Jail.*

Land-grabber (common), farmer who rents a farm from which another has been evicted.

> Oh, those dreadful Irish! Fiendish affair reported in *Banner*. Goose belonging to Nationalist deliberately allowed to wander about meadow rented by a *land-grabber*, and eat up grass. *Land-grabber's* horse consequently has to go short of green food, poor starved thing! The Coercion Bill must be pressed on at all hazards.—*Funny Folks.*

Landlubber (nautical), a useless long-shorer; a vagrant stroller. Applied by sailors to the mass of landsmen, especially those without employment (Admiral Smyth).

Landsharks (nautical), crimps, pettifogging attorneys, shopmongers and the *canaille* infesting the slums of seaport towns (Admiral Smyth). Also lawyers.

Land, to (common), to hit, to place a blow, to fall.

> And he *landed* the P. P. to rights, and he dodged his redoubtable digits,
> And Grimthorpe cried, Go for him, G. G. !
> —*Punch.*

To Mitchellise him till he couldn't hit half an ounce, or *land* within half a mile of a haystack.—*Punch.*

(Common), to *land a kick*, to bring one's foot in violent contact with a person's breech. Also "to hoof, hoof one's bum, to root," &c. (Popular), *landing it hot*, hitting hard ; *land*, to strike.

> Her fingers so lovely and taper, ah, yes,
> No hand e'er had fingers like those ;
> But the way she has got of just clenching the lot,
> And *landing me hot* on the nose !
> —*Song: Poor Mr. Coppit.*

Lane, Harriet (military), preserved or tinned meat. A modern epithet on a ration now much used in campaigns, and obviously derived from the unfortunate girl *Harriet Lane*, who was murdered by Wainwright, and put by in a box with chloride of lime, which preserved instead of destroying the body.

Lane, red (popular), the throat.

Lane, the (legal). Chancery Lane is always spoken of by lawyers as *The Lane*. (Theatrical), a colloquial abbreviation among the employés of Drury Lane for the theatre. (Popular and thieves), Petticoat Lane. (Thieves), *the Lane*, represented, in the slang of the criminal classes, Horsemonger Lane Gaol.

Lanthorn, dark (old cant), a servant or agent in a court who receives a bribe.

Lan-tun (pidgin), London. "Hab muchee man in *Lan-tun* town, but flom dat tim I know."

Lap (old cant), tea. (Popular), liquor, drink. *Lap* is a term invariably used in the ballet-girls' dressing - room for gin (Hotten).

Lap ears (American University), students of a religious turn of mind are so called ; also donkeys.

Lapland (popular), the society of women, an expression derived from the female sex being called "cats."

Lapper (popular), a rare *lapper*, a hard drinker. (Thieves), drink.

Laprogh (tinker), a goose or duck ; a bird of any kind.

Lap, to (common), to drink. (American), this word still retains many old meanings among American thieves and gamblers, or has taken new ones, such as to pick up, to take, steal, wipe out, put out of sight, drink, and buttermilk, which, like *lap*, is also a term for gin. A "*lap-tea*" is where there are so many guests that girls sit in one another's laps, or in those of the men, or where it is done for pleasure. A "*lap*-ride," where the same thing is done in a vehicle. "*To lap* a girl." "Do you let George *lap* you ?" "No, we only sit sideways as yet." *To lap* the gutter, *vide* GUTTER.

Lardy-da, lah-de-dah (common), a word borrowed from the refrain of a song which was popular some twenty years ago. Applied to a fop or dandy.

At the bar, forming the central figure of a group otherwise composed of *lah-de-dah* youths (now known as imitation dudes), stood a short, stocky-built man of about thirty-five years of age.—*American Newspaper.*

Lardy - dardy toffs (popular), effeminate swells.

Large blue kind, the (American). This very eccentric expression, signifying magnitude and intensity, seems to have been suggested by blue bottle flies, which are larger and more disliked than any others. A particularly bad humbug or lie is sometimes described as being one *of the large blue kind.*

Large order. *Vide* ORDER.

Largo, largey, largo (*g* soft like *j*) (pidgin), much, great, magnanimous, loud. Expresses magnitude or extent of all kinds.

My *largo* man, my have catchee peace, my have catchee war.—*Points and Pickings of Information about China* (London, 1844).

Lárkin (tinkers), a girl. This is curious as indicating an affinity between the Hindustani *lárki*, a girl, and the gypsy *rakli.* (Anglo-Indian), a very strong spiced punch.

Lark rig. *Vide* RIG.

Larks (American thieves), boys who steal newspapers from doorsteps.

"Boy, why don't your father take a newspaper," said a man to a small *lark*, whom he had just found *larking* his morning *Tribune.*

"He generally does," was the reply, "but this mornin' he sent me to take one wherever I could snap it."—*Tribune.*

Larky subaltern's coach, the (military), a carriage which used to be attached nightly to a goods train, starting from the Nine Elms Station at 2.30 A.M. for Aldershot, put on for the convenience of military officers who had from various causes got benighted in London, and missed the ordinary train. *Larky,* as used here, is probably from the phrase, "up with the lark."

Larn-pidgin (pidgin), learn-pigeon; an apprentice, a boy admitted by favour of the upper servants to a house that he may learn English and domestic duties.

Larrikin (common), a rough, a wild fellow.

And yonder yelling fools contrive
To lend some truth to Mammon's text.
The laziest *larrikin* alive,
With babbling tongue and brow perplex'd,
Can help do that.   —*Punch.*

Imported from Australia, where it is sometimes abbreviated to *lary.*

In your article on "Our *Larrikins*" of June 2nd, you invite an explanation of the origin of this Colonial synonym for "rough." If the common account be correct, it arose out of a misunderstanding. An Irishman, on being brought up for unruly behaviour before an Australian magistrate, excused himself by saying that he was only "larkin'." Any one familiar with the peculiarities of the Irish brogue will easily realise how the two-syllabled participle was mistaken for a three-syllabled noun.—CELT in the *Spectator*.

Lascar (Anglo-Indian), originally meaning a soldier, "lashkari." It has now become a generally used term for a Malay sailor. In the French army the term is applied to a bold, devil-may-care fellow.

Lashins (Irish), large quantities.

Lashool (tinker), nice. Irish, "lachool."

Lass, to (American, Western), to catch with the lasso, lariat, or reata.

It don't pay to have fellows blazing off their revolvers, and stampeding the cattle, and spurring their horses on the shoulders, and always going on a lape, and driving cattle at a lape too, and *lassing* steers by the fore feet on the trail, and throwing 'em head over heels, just for the satisfaction of hearing the thud they make when they fall.—*F. Francis : Saddle and Moccasin.*

Last of the Barons (legal), a nickname given to the "Baron of Exchequer" last appointed, since afterwards the Court of Exchequer was done away with, and merged in that of Queen's Bench, and no more barons would therefore be appointed.

Last run of shad, the (American). To say that a man looks as if he had come in *the last run of shad*, is equivalent to declaring that he has a very thin, wretched, forlorn, or "played-out" appearance. To be "in the last of pea-time," signifies a hard-up and poverty-stricken condition.

Latchpan (popular), the lower lip.

Late-play (Westminster School), a half-holiday, or holiday beginning at noon.

Lather, to (popular), to beat, thrash.

My father is a barber,
And is unkind to me,
So I'd rather *lather* father,
Than father *lather* me.
—*Popular Song.*

Latty (theatrical), a bed. *Vide* LETTY.

Launch, to (Winchester College), to pull a bed over a "man."

Lavender-cove (popular), a pawnbroker. So called because property is there laid up "in lavender."

Lavender, in (turf), is said of a man or horse to denote that he is ill, unfit, out of the way.

Most people are tired of waiting for the Beaver, who was put down as certain to win one of the early spring handicaps, but so far has been *in lavender.*—*Bird o' Freedom.*

(Common), laid *in lavender*, put away, pawned, or left in lodging for debt. From the practice of placing lavender in drawers in which clothes are kept.

(Thieves), hidden from the police.

Lawful time (Winchester College), at the end of "log-time," or preparation on a "remedy" or holiday, the prefect on duty calls out *lawful time*, as an announcement that all may leave study.

Lawn, the (sporting), Ascot Lawn.

Lay (thieves and roughs), particular business, line of work, pursuit, enterprise.

Kept a leaving shop—a sort of unlicensed pawnbroker's, you know . . . that wos his *lay* for years.—*J. Greenwood: Dick Temple.*

A dodge, swindle.

To a constable he told the misadventure of the day,
But the man in blue responded, "It's a very common *lay*,
Did she talk about a child, sir?" Said the innocent, "She did."
"I thought so," said the officer—"but, bless you, that's her kid!"
—*Sporting Times.*

Alas, that writer kept it, too,
Reminded me of debts long due,
Then lodged me safe in Holloway
The victim of a heartless *lay*.
—*Bird o' Freedom.*

On the *lay*, at work.

Dodger! Charley! It's time you were on the *lay*.—*Dickens: Oliver Twist.*

In America (north-east coast), a *lay* is a share in a venture.

(Tailors), a good *lay*, an economical method of cutting, or when a man is doing anything that will be beneficial to himself or others.

Lay down the knife and fork, to (common), to die.

Layer. *Vide* To LAY.

Lay for, to (American), to lie in wait for, to ambush. Also "to lay by for."

There's a cat in the garden
A *layin for* a rat,

And a boy with a catapult
A *layin for* the cat;
The cat's name is Susan,
The boy's name is Jim;
And his father round the corner
Is a *layin by* for him.
—*American Ballad.*

Lay it on, to (common), to exaggerate.

The member who moved an amendment throwing responsibility upon the employé as well as the employer was told he was "*laying it on* too thick," and the amendment was defeated.—*Funny Folks.*

Lay one out, to (roughs and thieves), to kill one.

Several of the prisoners were with him. Galletly was saying, "I've *laid one out*" to the other prisoners. . . . Witness also saw the knife, and there was blood on it half way up the steel.—*Evening News.*

Lay out (American), a turn. "It's my *lay out*," i.e., it's my turn.

"Boys, yer got me this time. They've called her 'Utella!' as near my name as they could get, and it's my *lay out*. What'll ye hev?"
The glasses clinked merrily, and Mr. Bill beamed with happiness.—*New York Star*

Lay over, to (American), to defeat, excel, surpass. Probably derived from wrestling.

"Can you write?"
"Well, I've seed people could *lay me over*, thar."—*Mark Twain: A Tramp Abroad.*

"In scolding a blue jay can *lay over* anything human or divine." — *Mark Twain: A Tramp Abroad.*

Lay them down, to (thieves), to play cards.

Lay, to (turf), to bet for or against.

He overheard one noble penciller tell another ominously that "he could *lay* the favourite."—*Bird o' Freedom.*

To *lay* the field, *vide* FIELD. (Common), to *lay* one's shirt on a horse, to *lay* all one's money on a horse.

Lead (theatrical), the most important part in a play.

Miss ——, who returned from abroad yesterday, has, we learn, refused to entertain an offer to play "the *lead*" in the old English comedies at the Strand Theatre. *Daily News.*

(Thieves), *lead*, or friendly *lead*, a collection made for one "in trouble."

I was landed without them getting me a *lead* (collection). — *Horsley : Jottings from Jail.*

Lead or **leader** (Australian mining slang), a vein of gold.

The *leader* is the vein or deposit of gold in an Australian gold mine : said always to run north and south, which if it be true is a phenomenon of magnetism. In size, form, and value, the precious metal within a certain area will present great diversities. Sometimes the *leader* from which the gold is presumably discharged could be identified if it were not that specimens of an entirely opposite character embedded in greenstone, sometimes combined both with greenstone and quartz, sometimes with quartz alone. Often it is as fine as flour, again it will range from "colours" to nuggets of several ounces. It may be worth only £2, 18s. per ounce : it may and does assay £3, 18s. and £4.—*Queenslander.*

Leading juvenile (theatrical), the expression explains itself. Corresponds to the *jeune premier* of the French.

Hamlet is the "lead," Laertes the *leading juvenile*, and Horatio, though an excellent pal, is known as the walking gentleman.—*Globe.*

Leafless tree (old cant), the gallows.

Oh ! there never was life like the robber's
   —so
Jolly, and bold, and free ;
And its end—why, a cheer from the crowd below,
And a leap from a *leafless tree !*
   —*Lord Lytton : Paul Clifford.*

Lean (printers), this is a metaphor used to indicate solid or bad paying work in contradistinction to "fat" or good work.

Leanaway (slangy Australian), one who is tipsy. The metaphor is of course from the drunkard's reeling.

Leap the book (common), a false marriage, or one which is illegal.

Leary (popular and thieves), wide-awake, knowing, wary. *Leary*-bloke, a knowing or artful man.

But mummery and slummery
  You must keep in your mind,
For every day, mind what I say,
  Fresh fakements you will find.
But stick to this while you can crawl,
To stand till you're obliged to fall ;
And when you're wide-awake to all,
You'll be a *leary* man.
   —*The Leary Man.*

From *lear* or *lere*, to learn, obsolete or provincial English.

On that sad book his shame and loss he leared.   —*Spenser.*

Leary cum Fitz (theatrical), a vulgar, impudent minor theatre actor, is usually described as a regular *Leary cum Fitz.*

Leather (American thieves), a pocket-book.

He burst out into a grin, when the magistrate, who was up to his little game, suddenly asked him if he remembered how a certain elderly gentleman had been robbed of his pocket-book while going on board a steam ferry-boat. "Don't I just remember," he cried, "how we 'lifted' the old bloke's '*leather*.'"—*American Newspaper.*

(Football), the *leather*, the football.

Leather-head (Canadian), a swindler.

Now the Senator is only a *leather-head*, who made his pile by such and such a swindle, and the parson is a gospel-shark, or devil-dodger.—*Phillipps-Wolley: Trottings of a Tenderfoot.*

Leather-hunting (cricket), this term is sometimes used to mean fielding. A *leather-hunting* game is one in which there is much fielding to be done.

Leather-necks (naval), a term for soldiers; from their leather stock, which to a sailor, with his neck free of any hindrance, must appear such an uncomfortable appliance.

Leathers (popular), the ears, otherwise "lugs."

Leather, to (popular), to beat.

Leaving shop (thieves and others), an unlicensed pawnbroker's establishment.

Led captain, a fashionable sponger or "swell," who by artifice ingratiates himself into the favour of the master of the house, and lives at his table (Hotten).

Leer (old cant), a print, a newspaper; old English *lere*, to learn.

Leet jury (popular), explained by quotation.

The meddlesome fellows who had caused the disagreeable exposure were called a *leet jury*, whose business it was to pounce on evil-doers whenever they thought fit, once in the course of every month.—*J. Greenwood: Seven Curses of London.*

Left forepart (tailors), the wife.

Left-handed wife (common), a mistress. *Left*, or sinister, is in all languages applied to that which is doubtful or bad. In gypsy *bongo* means left-handed, crooked, or evil. Compare the French "mariage de la main gauche."

Left, over the. *Vide* OVER THE LEFT.

Leg (turf), abbreviation for black-leg, a bookmaker or ring-man.

Leg-bail, to give (common), to run away, or decamp from liability.

Leggings (popular), a name for stockings.

Leg it, to (popular), to run.

Legs (American cadet), a nickname given to a tall lanky man, one who is sparely and angularly built.

Legs and arms (tailors), beer without any "body" in it.

Lel (gypsy), to take, to arrest. Not uncommon among the lower orders in London. The writer has heard "Look out, or you'll get *lelled*," said by one young girl to another within a few steps of Regent Street. It is from the third person indicative present, *lela;* first person, *lava,* I take. This use of the third person for all the others is usual in *posh an' posh* (half and half), or corrupted Romany, and it occurs in Hindustani.

Length (theatrical), an arbitrary division of a part into so many components, after this fashion. Hamlet is thirty-seven lengths, and seventeen lines. Each length is forty-two lines.

Actors do not learn their parts, they "study" them, and they measure each part by *lengths.—Globe.*

(Thieves), six months' imprisonment.

Let her flicker (American), said of any doubtful issue, the simile being that of a flame flickering in a draught of air, when it is doubtful whether it will be blown out or not. It may be remarked that in American slang there is more metaphor than in that of any other country.

Let her up! Let 'er up! (American), stop there, be quiet for an instant, hear what I have to say. This agrees exactly with the Dutch *Let 'er op! Let 'er op wat ik se zeg!* "Mark what I say to ye."

Let his marbles go with the monkey, to (American), an eccentric phrase derived from a story of a boy whose marbles were carried off by a monkey.

But my sanguinary hearers—let 'em try it. Dey'll find dat Yankee Doodle ain't de boy *to luff his marbles go wid de monkey*—not by a free (three) pint-jug full —for he's bound to go ahead and let 'er rip.—*Brudder Bones's Complete Entertainment.*

Let in, to (society), to cause to lose money by not very upright means; it is a common expression in society. *To let in* a friend is a low trick, and means to deceive, defraud, trick him.

It is their friends and acquaintances who are *let in* by them. — *Saturday Review.*

(American), to attack, beat, abuse.

"I *let in to* the coot about east, I can tell yer," remarked Jake. "I gave him my opinion of himself, and threw in a character, gratis, of all his relations, all the way down to his aunt's sisters."— *Fireplug Moses.*

Let it slide (American, of English origin), leave it to chance, leave it alone, do without it. The metaphor is of course that of watching a thing slip without attempting to save it.

Let on, to (English and American), to appear to know or to show any acquaintance with a subject with which one may be quite familiar.

Now, if I wanted to be one of those ponderous scientific people, and *let on* to prove what had occurred in the remote past, by what had occurred in a given time in the recent past, or what will occur in the far future by what has occurred in late years, what an opportunity is here! Geology never had such a chance, nor such exact data to argue from.—*Mark Twain.*

Also to admit, as, he never *let on* he knew me.

Letter perfect (theatrical), knowing one's part perfectly.

Let the band play (American), equivalent to calling out for anything to begin, to start anything up, commence. A common cry to an orator to begin, or an exhortation to a speaker, actor, or any other person to let himself out, or make an effort (C. Leland Harrison's MS. Collection of Americanisms).

In England it is common to say, when anything reaches a climax, " Then the band played."

Tableau, and *the band played.—Bird o' Freedom.*

Letting down, or out, tucks (American), a phrase referring to making preparations, for example, in a building, with a view to future alterations. It is borrowed from the custom of making the trousers of rapidly growing boys or the dresses of girls with *tucks*, so that they may be let out or lengthened.

In England, *let down* easily, means not taking advantage, or being lenient with one in difficulty.

Letty (thieves), a bed; from the Italian *letto*. Used in the form "latty" by strolling actors, with whom the term originated.

Let up (Stock Exchange), a term to express the sudden disap-pearance of artificial causes of depression in the money-market, thus causing money to become "tighter" and loans more difficult to obtain.

Let up on, to (American), to cease, to pause, rest, give over for a time.

You can't be mum—you cannot sing,
You cannot always smile,
You must *let up on* everything
From time to time awhile.
—*A Poem : Susan of Poughkeepsie.*

L e v a n t e r (common), a card-sharper, or defaulting gambler, who makes himself scarce. *Vide* To LEVANT.

No prelusive murmurs had run before this wild *levanter* of change.—*De Quincey.*

Levant, to (common), to go to the *Levant*, that is, to run away from one's creditors, to abscond; to throw or run a *levant*, to play or stake and leave without paying in case of loss.

Never mind that, man (having no money to stake), run a *levant* . . . but be circumspect about the man.—*Fielding : Tom Jones.*

To *levant*, run a *levant*, originated in a pun on the words *leave* (provincial *leve*), and *Levant*. Compare with the French "faire voile en *Levant*," to purloin or steal, and the Italian "andare in *Levante*, venire di *Levante*," to carry away, steal, which are respectively from a play on *lever* and *levare*, to raise, lift. These phrases belong to the numerous class of jocular expressions coined in the same way with allusions to some locality, as to be off to *Bedford-shire* or Land of *Nod*, to feel sleepy; to go to *Peckham*, feel hungry, formerly *Hungarian*; those in bad circumstances are made to live in *Queer* Street, &c. In French we meet with punning phrases of the same class, " aller à *Niort* (nier)," to deny, the name of this town being suggested to the pedlars (who so much contributed to argot language) by the frequency of their visits to Niort, formerly famous for its fairs. " Aller à *Versailles* (verser)," to be upset ; "aller à *Cachan* (se cacher)," to conceal oneself; "aller à *Rouen* (ruine)," to be ruined, a bankrupt ; " voyager en *Cornouaille* (être cornard)," to be made a cuckold (same metaphor in Italian) ; " envoyer à *Mortagne* (mort)," to kill; "aller à *Patras* (ad patres)," to die, &c. In Italian, "andar in *Picardia*, a *Longone*, a *Fuligno*," to be hanged, &c.

Level best (American), when a man does the best he can, plainly, squarely, and fairly, not extravagantly, but by his average ability.

> Let this be put upon his grave,
> He done his *level best*.
>   —*Newspaper Poems.*
>
> Saying this he drew a wallet from the inner of his vest,
> And gave the tramp a dollar which it was his *level best*.
>   —*The Ballad of Charity.*

Level-headed (American), a man of plain, practical commonsense is said to be *level-headed*.

The phrase has become universal within a few years.

Levite (clerical), a term sometimes used by beneficed divines of humble brethren whom they hire. The origin is to be found in the story of Micah and the young man of Bethlehem-Judah in Judges xvii. 7–13.

Levy (Liverpool), a shilling. A term taken in all probability from the American *levy*, *i.e.*, an abbreviation of elevenpenny bit, also commonly called a shilling. Hotten suggests that it is derived from *levy*, a term used among labourers for a sum of money advanced to a workman before he has earned it. There is a very great number of American terms current in Liverpool owing to its intimate commercial relations with New York.

Libb, libbege (old cant), a bed. " Mill the cull to his long *libb*," kill the man. From the Irish *leaba*.

Liberties (Eton), an immunity from all fagging for the first ten days.

Liberty (Eton School), the first six Oppidans, and the first six Oppidans in Fifth Form, who work with Sixth Form under the Head Master. (Nautical), *liberty*-man, a man on leave ; *liberty*-ticket, a pass.

Libkins, lipken (old cant), house, lodgings. From *lib* or *lip*, to sleep, and *ken*, a general term for house, dwelling.

I will not conceal aught I win out of *libkins*, or from the ruffmans, but will preserve it for the use of the company.— *Bampfylde-Moore Carew.*

Library-cads (Winchester College), two juniors who have to keep the library in order, that they may set off other fagging.

Lib, to (thieves), to sleep.

Lick and a promise (popular), a wash of an imperfect nature. " I'll just give my face a *lick and a promise*," *i.e.*, will do it more thoroughly later on. Also in general use to signify a cheap temporary remedy and repair for anything. Miss Baker in her " Glossary of Northamptonshire Words " erroneously claimed this as a provincialism.

Licker (popular), " that's a *licker* to me," that " licks " me, is above my reach, beyond my conception.

Lickety split (American). This means headlong, or at full speed. It also implies sometimes go fast by exertion. There is an old English expression "to put in big licks," to do one's best, also to lick, to beat, which probably gives the origin of this expression.

Lickety split is synonymous with the equally elegant phrase "full chisel." He went *lickety split* down hill. *Lickety cut* and *lickety liner* are also used.—*Bartlett: Dictionary of Americanisms.*

Lick into fits, to (common), to give a good thrashing.

Lickspittle (common), a parasite, a cringing fellow. The French *lèche-bottes.*

Lie low, to (American), to keep to one's bed.

Lie off, to (turf), to make a waiting race by keeping some distance in rear of the other horses. A jockey is said to "lie out of his ground" when he pushes the lying-off tactics to excess, and gets so far behind that he has little or no chance of making up the lost ground.

Lifer (thieves), a man sentenced to penal servitude for life.

They know what a clever lad he is; he'll be a *lifer*. They'll make the Artful nothing less than a *lifer*. —*Charles Dickens: Oliver Twist.*

Miss —— would make it up with the comic villain if she could, but his comicality is too much for her, so he probably gets "a *lifer*."—*Referee.*

Till recently there was a distinction between being sentenced to penal servitude for life and for natural life. Good conduct might cause the release after some twenty-four years of a person sentenced for life, *e.g.*, Constance Kent. The writer has had under him in prison a man who had endured a life sentence, got out, and got in again.

Lift (football players), a kick at football.

Lifter (old cant), a thief. Used by Shakspeare in " Troilus and Cressida." The word survives in shop-*lifter*, one who steals from a shop, but does not apply to one who steals in a shop by false weight and measure, and adulterated goods. Also a crutch.

Lift, to (thieves), to steal.

At one time I had a very pleasant companion whose speciality was stealing cattle. He was a Newcastle man, and had done three "laggings" for *lifting* cattle.— *Evening News.*

This should be naturally understood in the sense of taking off, removing, just as in French slang *soulever*, to raise, to lift, means to steal; but the Rev. A. Smythe Palmer's "Folk Etymology" says, "It has nothing to do with *lift*, raise, but is (like *graf-t* for *graff*), an incorrect form of *liff*, cognate with Gothic *hliffan*, Latin *clepere*, Greek *kléptein*, to steal. Klepto-mania is a mania for *lifting*."

And so whan a man wold bryng them to thryft,
They wyll hym rob, and fro his good hym *luft.*
    — *The Hye Way to the Spyttel Hous.*

A *lift* or *lifter* is an old word for a thief or shop-lifter; it now means a theft.

Is he so young a man and so old a *lifter?—Shakspeare: Troilus and Cressida.*

Women are more subtile . . . than the cunningest foyst, nip, *lift.* — *Greene: Theeves falling out.*

(Sport), *to lift* in a walking race is *to lift* your knees unduly into a run or shamble, to break into an unfair walk or trot.

Light (popular), though a popular slang term to a certain extent, it is specially used by printers, being usually applied to credit at a public-house. While a man can obtain this he is safe from having his *light* put out.

Light bob (military), light infantry soldier.

Light feeder (thieves), a silver spoon.

Light frigate (old cant), a woman of loose morals.

Lightmans (old cant), night.

Or else he sweares by the *lightmans*
To put our stamps in the Harmans.
    —*T. Dekker: Lanthorne and Candle-Light.*

Light - master (printers). This term is applied to the man who acts as a "go-between" between the landlord of the house of call and the workmen that avail themselves of it. He is generally one of the workmen of a large establishment, and introduces new clients, and arranges matters, and gives the landlord the "tip" in case the indebted one should be leaving his situation, and thus probably avoiding payment.

Lightning (common), a name for gin.

The man holds out a tin mug in his dirt-begrimed hand. According to his views, this is the first step of hospitality. She sniffs cautiously.
"Don't like its smell."
"It's *lightning.*"
The child takes a gulp of the raw spirit, chokes, coughs, and bursts into angry sobs.—*Savage London.*

A flash of *lightning*, a glass of gin.

Lightning changers, shifters (American), women thieves who can in a minute, by adroit and ingenious manipulation, change their dress in a most extraordinary manner. The process is fully described in the following extract from the *Chicago Tribune:*—

She was arrayed in the garments of a *lightning change* artist, and could, without the removal of an article, change her dress into four distinct styles. When arrested she wore a black cashmere dress, a tight-fitting bodice of the same colour and material, and a hat with a wide brim. A swift displacement of hooks, eyes, and buttons, a deft adjustment of unseen fastenings here and there, a crushing squeeze of the hat, and the woman stood with a brown woollen dress with corded front bodice, and a neat little turban upon her head. Another set of manipulations and the dress was transformed into a gown, the turban gave place to a coif, a chaplet fell from the girdle, and the woman stood arrayed as a brown nun. Once more a tug of the skirt, a yank at the coif and waist, a flash of the hands, everywhere at once, and the nun was transformed into a young lady of aspiring fashion, in bright-coloured alpaca and the original wide-brimmed hat.

There is also a dress worn by women of this class in Paris, consisting of all the garments in one, so made that in a few seconds the whole may be slipped off, and the wearer be left *in cuerpo.*

Lights or **top-lights** (popular), the eyes.

Like bricks (popular), quickly, with energy.

VOL. II.

Charley Dix, cut his sticks, *like bricks.*
—*Punch.*

This morning did my laundress bring
My shirt back in a stew,
Says she, " If I wash this again,
I shall wash it into two."
" Into two ! " I cried, " you don't mean that?
Go, wash away *like bricks*,
For you'll be doing me a service
If you'll wash it into six."
—*Popular Song.*

Like one o'clock (popular), rapidly. "She tipped off her twopen'orth *like one o'clock.*"

Lil (gypsy and common canting), a book, a paper or document or letter, a five-pound note. In American gypsy a *lil* is a dollar, also a bad bank-bill. In canting, a pocket-book. Gypsies call a purse a *kissi* or *gunno.*

Lily Benjamin (popular), a long white coat, such as worn by umpires at cricket.

L i m (university), from Dr. Limeon of King's; an evangelically-minded student, a "piman." (American), a funny fellow or clown.

Limb, an angry epithet applied to an ill-tempered child or woman. An abbreviation of *limb* of the devil.

" Now listen, you young *limb*," whispered Sikes, drawing a dark lantern from his pocket, and throwing the glare full on Oliver's face, " I'm a going to push you through there."—*Dickens: Oliver Twist.*

A young or obscure lawyer is vulgarly called a *limb* of the law, or a *limb* of Satan. The word, according to Halliwell's " Archaic Dictionary," generally

B

seems to imply deterioration; a *limb* was even held to signify a determined sensualist. A man overmuch addicted to a thing was anciently said to be a *limb* for it.

Limburger, the real (American), used grotesquely in many ways, especially to anything actually or genuinely German. The Limburg cheese has a strong smell, which is intolerable to those who are not accustomed to it, for which reason it is sometimes called "knock me down at forty rods."

Lime basket (popular), as dry as a *lime basket*, very thirsty.

Mr. Chitling wound up his observations by stating that he had not touched a drop of anything for forty-two mortal long hard-working days; and that "he wished he might be busted if he warn't as dry as a *lime basket.*"—*Charles Dickens.*

Lime juicer (nautical), a nickname given by Americans to English vessels and seamen on account of the compulsory practice of serving out *lime juice* as an anti-scorbutic.

Line (tailors), a job *line* is an occasional clearance; a bargain. (Common), on the *line*, a picture is said to be hung on the *line* at the Royal Academy when it is in the best position, that is, at the height of the spectator's eye.

Lineage (journalistic), contribution to a newspaper paid at so much a line.

He was a struggling young writer, already engaged on two weeklies, at a rate of remuneration yclept *lineage*, sufficient to provide him with whisky and cigarettes.—*Bird o' Freedom.*

Linen, the curtain in a theatre. In Ireland they say, "Up with the *linen* and make a beginnin'."

Linen arbours (American cadet), the dormitories.

Liner (studios), a picture hung up high at the exhibition. (Journalistic), a casual reporter. Diminutive of penny - a - *liner* (Hotten).

Lines (theatrical), an actor's own part which he has to learn. It may happen that an actor will know nothing whatever of the play in which he is taking part beyond his own *lines* and the cues which guide him. (West America), explained by quotation.

Without stopping the coach-horses or his own, Billy scrambled upon the vehicle with his post-bags, and relieved the driver of the *lines.*—*H. L. Williams: In the Wild West.*

Lines, on (printers), an expression used by compositors to intimate that the companionship is in full swing. Mostly used to indicate the resumption of business after "cutting the *line*." A reference to the fact that their earnings depend on the number of lines composed.

Line, to get in a (popular), to hoax.

Lingo (popular), language, speech, slang. Latin, *lingua*.

Lint-scraper (medical), a young and inexperienced medical man. Applied by Mr. Batchelor to Mr. Drencher, M.R.C.S.I., together with other expletives, as pestle-grinder, &c., in Thackeray's "Lovel the Widower."

Lintys (theatrical), a name associated with sprites. Possibly from the French *lutins.*

Lionesses (Oxford), ladies visiting an Oxford man.

Lip (popular), talk, impudence.

Lipey (popular), a common mode of address among the lowest class. "What cher, *lipey*, if you see my Rachel, slap her chops, and send her 'ome." Possibly from the German *liebe.*

Lip-lap, a vulgar and disparaging nickname given in the Dutch East Indies to Eurasians, and corresponding to the Anglo-Indian *chee-chee* (Anglo-Indian Glossary).

Lip, to give (nautical), to chatter, to prattle.

Liquor up (common), a drink. To *liquor up*, to partake of alcoholic drink, generally at a bar. Of American origin, but the expression has become very common in all English-speaking countries.

I had a thirsty neighbour next door, and so I accepted the offer of a *liquor up.* —*Evening News.*

The report of his mission included that he had passed the portals of the "Three Stoats" and "had *liquored up*" with the worthy landlord.—*J. Greenwood: Dick Temple.*

Lispers (old cant), the lips. The derivation is obvious.

Lissum (popular), pliant, supple.

List, on the (popular), in disfavour. An abbreviation of the well-known "on the black *list.*" It was introduced in a popular opera, "The Mikado," and since that time has been very general.

Listening backwards (common), or as in Ireland, "walking *backwards.*" Those who do these things are regarded as having the "evil eye," and also the misuse of any faculty or talent.

Listening and walking *backwards* is considered unlucky in Ireland, and children are cautioned carefully to avoid both, on the ground that God has given them faculties to be rightly used, and not contrary to the manner for which these were designed. I have often seen the children of the peasantry severely reprimanded, and not unfrequently punished, for breaches of the direct natural law of the sense of hearing and the order of motion.—*Notes and Queries.*

Little ben (thieves), a waistcoat.

Little church round the corner (American), a slang term for a drinking-place.

Little end of the horn (American), an expression first made popular in the Jack Downing Letters. Bartlett defines "coming out at the *little end of the horn*" as being said when a ridiculously small effect has been produced after great effort and much boasting. It would be more correct to define it as failing or coming to loss, grief, or poverty in any way. Probably derived from old drinking customs. He who missed at guessing riddles was obliged to drink from the little end or tip of the horn while the victor drank from the brim. The *horn* seems in popular parlance to be connected with evil, contrary to old folk-lore, which made it a symbol of abundance and a protection against evil. " In a *horn* " is a refusal, or a qualification of falsehood. *Horns* denote a cuckold, and *horn-swoggle* means mere nonsense or humbug.

Little England (West Indian), Barbados. The inhabitants of this island rightly or wrongly are credited with egregious self-complacency and esteem. The following is the incident which led to this sobriquet being given to the miniature island in the Caribbean Sea, which to tell the truth is intensely British in everything compared to the other islands. Charles II. was in exile; he had lost his throne, and there seemed little chance of his ever recovering it. The plucky Brins, who were royalist to the backbone, then sent a humble address to the exiled king, "bidding him be of good cheer and stout of heart, reminding him in his exile that all was not lost, for, although all the world might be against him, Barbados was ever at his back." In consequence of this grandiloquent assurance the island has ever since been satirically called *Little England*.

Little go (Cambridge University), a public examination held early in the course, "which," says Lyell, "from its being less strict or less important in its consequences than the final one, has received this appellation."

. . . whether a regular attendance on the lecture of the college would secure me a qualification against my first public examination ; which is here called the *little go.—The Etonian.*

Also called at Oxford "smalls."

You must be prepared with your list of books, your Testament for responsions (by undergraduates called *little go* or "smalls"), and also your certificate of matriculation.—*Collegians' Guide.*

Little Hell, explained by quotation.

There are few worse places in London than certain parts of Cow Cross, especially that part of it anciently known as Jack Ketch's Warren, or *Little Hell*, as the inhabitants more commonly designate it, on account of the number of subjects it produced for the operations of the common hangman.—*Greenwood: Seven Curses of London.*

Little man (Eton), a footman.

He called the footman (or *little man*, as was the generic term for this class of domestic at my tutor's), and bade him reach down the obnoxious placard. To hear in this case was, unfortunately, not to obey. *Little man* visited the roof, reconnoitred the position, felt his own weakness, and, coming down, confessed to the tutor that he "dursna do it !"—*Sketchy Memoirs of Eton.*

Little off, a (American, also English), slightly incorrect or erroneous, insane, poor, reserved. From a term used by dealers in diamonds, "off colour."

Your reply to "three *Tribune* subscribers" in this morning's *Tribune* in regard to private secretaries of United States Senators is *a little off.*—*Chicago Tribune.*

After that he was always a *little off,* as he had no money left, or friends to help him. He was a queer fellow, that old man, and he had a gait in walking I shall never forget.—*Chicago Tribune.*

(Common), *little off* colour, unwell, slightly intoxicated.

Little side (Rugby), a term applied to all games at Rugby organised from a "house" standard, *e.g., little side* football.

Little snakesman (thieves), a young thief who is passed through an aperture to let in the others.

Live (American), not only alive, but also intelligent, vigorous, and progressive. "A *live* Yankee." In the Western newspapers "a *live* man" seems to generally signify one who is vigorous and intelligent but uneducated, in accordance with a popular belief that an individual who has never been to school, or at least who has had only the simplest education, must naturally be far better qualified for positions requiring culture and knowledge than any other. The writer has before him a number of one of the most widely circulated journals in America, in which it is editorially asserted that to fill diplomatic appointments in Europe, what is required is not a man who "knows French," or who has been to college, or moved in society, but a "*live* practical man," plainly indicating that in the mind of the editor in question there is a direct antagonism between education and capacity to fill responsible offices. Of late *live,* extended from America to England, has begun to signify excellence, even in inanimate objects.

So Maria and me goes to a big 'ouse in a fried fish and whelk-stall sort o' neighbourhood. We goes up ever so many stairs till we gets into a enormous attic at the top, when you 'as to pass mysterious like through a big curting. The attic had all its walls covered with noosepapers in foreign languages, and proclamations was stuck up with big borders, as reminded me of the big posters of "a wholesale grocery store will open on Saturday night. A real *live* glass milk-jug and a splendid pair of plated tongs given to every lady that buys one pound of our two-shilling Bohea."—*Fun: Murdle Visiting.*

Livener (military), an early morning drink.

Liverpool tailor (tailors), one who sits with his hat and coat on, ready for the road.

Live to the door, to (popular), to live up to one's means. A variant is, to live up to the knocker (which see).

Living gale (nautical), a fearful storm.

Liza (popular), generally used in the injunction, "Outside, *Liza!*" that is, be off, addressed to any person.

Loaded for bears (American). This expression signifies that a man is slightly intoxicated, enough to feel ready to confront danger. Equivalents for it are, a little shot, soothed, a little set up.

Loaded to the gunwales (American), intoxicated, full.

Sis said she was afraid you'd come home and make it lively for em, but Sis' beau said he guessed you wouldn't come home and make any trouble, as he saw you at a sample-room *loaded to the gunwales.* What did he mean?—*St. Paul Globe.*

Load on (American). A man who walks unsteadily, owing to intoxication, is said to have a *load on,* "to be loaded," "to have a turkey on his back," *i.e.,* to have more than he can carry. Also "He walks like he was carrying a pig, and a darned discontented one at that." Also English.

Load up, to (American), a term peculiar to the Stock Exchange, meaning to obtain or accumulate.

The few men who make money in Wall Street speculation sell when the crowd is clamouring to buy, as they have been the last week, and the many who lose always rush in on such occasions to *load up* to the extent of their ability.—*Stock Report.*

Loafer (military), a soldier employed on the staff, or in any capacity that takes him from his regular "sentry-go" duty. *Vide* OUTFITTER.

(American), originally a pilfering vagabond; now applied to idlers and hangers-about of every description. The term is now recognised and in common use in England. There have been many suggestions as to the origin of this now familiar word. Bartlett declares, rather boldly, that it came into the United States "probably from Mexico or Texas, and derives it from the Spanish *gallofero,* or *gallofo,* a vagabond." But this would imply the first Mexican war, at least, as the date of its advent. The word *loafer,* however, was common in New England and Philadelphia in 1834, 1835, but it was generally applied by boys to "pilfering." They would say in jest, "Where did you *loaf* that?" *Loafer,* merely as a drunken, thievish bummer, succeeded this.

At this time all the sketches of the genus *loafer* represented him as a petty pilferer, one who carried a gimlet and tube with him to steal whisky from the barrels, and who was popularly regarded as a lazy sponger of food and garments. In the first year of the *New York Herald,* and in the sketches of J. C. Neal as well as in other "life pictures" of the time, the *loafer* is always a pilfering bummer of the lowest class. It was several years before the word was extended to mean a *flâneur* of any kind whatever. Bartlett says that "the origin of this word is altogether uncertain. Two etymologies have been suggested for it; namely, the German *laufer,* a runner (compare the Dutch *leeglooper* and *landlooper*, a vagrant), and the Spanish *gallofero*, abbreviated *gallofo*, whence the Italian *gagloffo* (?), a wandering mendicant, a vagabond. The Spanish *gallofa* means what was given to the *galloferos*, alms, vegetables, &c." It may here be observed that *laufer* in German thieves' slang is the abbreviate of *landlaufer*, which means exactly and precisely a tramp or *loafer* in its later American sense. As regards the Dutch, there is in its low slang the word *loever*, from *loeven*, to go (*gaan*), to stroll about ; but with the sense of going astray or out of the course. Compare (says Teirlinck) with *loeven, op zee van den koers ofwijken, op side sturen* (to go aside out of the course— to luff). *Loever* is pronounced almost like *loafer*, and meaning the same, that is, one who idly strolls here and there, allows but little room for doubt as to its New York derivation. In old English cant *loaver* was the same with *loure*, to steal, as well as money. It would seem as if it had kept an unnoticed place in English slang, and then in America been influenced by or combined with the Dutch *loever*, or *loefer*, *f* being synonymous with *v*.

Loaf, to, an Americanism which has become a recognised word, to idle about.

Shoeblacks are compelled to a great deal of unavoidable *loafing;* but certainly this

one *loafed* rather energetically, for he was hot and frantic in his play.—*H. Kingsley : Ravenshoe.*

(American University), to borrow anything, generally without any intention of returning it.

Loaver (popular), money. From the gypsy *louver*, specie, or coin.

Lob (thieves), a till ; properly something heavy. *Lob*-sneaking, stealing the contents of tills. To pinch a *lob* has the same signification. *Lob*-crawler, a thief who crawls into a shop, and behind the counter, to rifle the till.

Poor old Tim, the *lob*-crawler, fell from Racker and got pinched.—*Horsley : Jottings from Jail.*

Also a box, snuff-box. (Pugilistic), the head. Properly a large lump.

Lobber or **looper** (American), run, curdled, coagulated, run together. A New York term, from the Dutch *loopen*, to run ; *hy heft de loop*, he has a looseness ; *een loopend water*, running water. Bartlett says very correctly that the proper term is *loppered*.

Loblolly boy, a derisive term for a surgeon's mate in the navy. *Loblolly* is water-gruel, or spoon meat.

Lobster (popular). Sailors dressed in blue were vulgarly called raw lobsters in the first five decades of the present century, and soldiers were called boiled lobsters from the colour of their coats. Soldiers were sometimes and are still called crabs. The name of *lobster* has been in later times transferred to the policeman.

Lobster-box (popular), a barrack.

Lobster, to (Winchester College), to weep, which makes the eyes and face red.

Lock (jailors), "on the *lock*," attending to prisoners. (Old cant), a receiver of stolen goods.

That woman they spoke to is a *lock*, *alias* receiver and buyer of stolen goods. —*Hitchin: A True Discovery, &c.*

Abbreviated from "*lock* all fast," which had the same meaning. The *lock*, the magazine or warehouse whither the thieves carry stolen goods. *Lock*, also chance, means of livelihood. "He stood a queer *lock*," he stood an indifferent chance. "What *lock* do you cut?" how do you get your livelihood? In this sense it seems to be the same word as *lurk*, which has the same meaning. It must be remembered that in many canting dictionaries distortions of words constantly occur.

Lockees (Westminster School), lock-house.

Locker (old cant), explained by quotation.

I am a *locker*, I leave goods at a house and borrow money on them, pretending that they are made in London.—*Hitchin: A True Discovery, &c.*

Vide LOCK.

Lock, stock, and barrel (American). Bartlett says of this phrase that it means the whole, a figurative expression borrowed from sportsmen and having reference to a gun. Sometimes we hear horse, foot, and artillery used in the same phrase. It is also very commonly used to say that anything has been so renewed that nothing of the original is left, from the story of a fine gun which had belonged to General Washington or some other great man, and of which certain portions were new, such as the *lock, stock, barrel*, and ramrod. Also used in reference to a knife which had a new blade, and then a new handle, and again a new blade, and so on for many restorations, but which "was still the same old knife."

Lock-ups (Harrow School), detention in study.

Loco-foco (American). Bartlett defines this, as "1. A self-igniting match (or cigar); 2. the name by which the Democratic party was (till within a few years) extensively distinguished throughout the United States." He also gives the history of the match, and how its name came to be applied to the Democrats, all of which the writer can confirm from memory. It is very doubtful, however, whether the matches took their name from "locomotive." The wild flash which the first matches made when "snapped off" was greatly admired. They were sold in combs of about twenty matches in the piece, 144 matches costing 12½ cents (6d.). This was in 1834, 1835. Boys regarded them as a kind of fireworks. The writer was the first to introduce them to his school, and to a large rural neighbourhood, where they excited as much astonishment as they now do among savages. He has always been under the impression since early boyhood that the name is derived from a barbarous combination of *loco*, the Spanish for "mad," and *foco* (*i.e. fuego*), "fire," literally wild-fire. Marck, the inventor or patentee, had in all probability the German word *irrlicht*, as well as the English "wild-fire," to guide him in the name.

Locomotive (American), a drink made of half of the yolk of an egg, a tablespoonful of honey, a dash of curaçoa, a flavouring of cloves, all whisked thoroughly together in a quarter of a pint of hot Burgundy. A winter drink.

Locomotive tailor (tailors), one who travels by train.

Loddomy, luddemy ker (gypsy), a lodging-house; *lodder*, to lodge; *baro loddomy ker*, a hotel, *i.e.*, a great lodging-house; *loddomengro*, a lodger; *loddomengro rye*, a landlord.

Loge (old cant), a watch; from the French *horloge*.

Logie (theatrical), an ornament made from zinc. So called from one David Logie, who invented it. At one period these ornaments were made as large as saucers, and were in great vogue in transformation scenes, and halls of enchantment, in which they dazzled and delighted the eyes of the rising generation.

Log-rolling (American), explained as follows by the *Cornhill Magazine*: "*Log-rolling* is a somewhat rare term in England, but is well understood at Washington. When a backwoodsman cuts down trees, his neighbours help him to roll them away, and in return he helps them with their trees; so in Congress, when members support a bill, not because they are interested therein, but simply to gain the help of its promoters for some scheme of their own, their action is called *log-rolling*." A *log-rolling* in America, where neighbours meet to bring logs together to build a house, is generally made the occasion of a frolic.

Logy (American), dull, slow, awkward; "he's a regular *logy*." Also loggy, *i.e.*, like a log. It would seem also to be derived from the Dutch *log*, heavy, slow, unwieldy. *Een log verstand*, a dull wit (Jewel).

John Clossen was a real *logy*,
Heavy, bungling, dull old fogy,
Yet he had his startlin' flashes,
Now and then like flames from ashes,

And it made the people stare
To think that embers still were there.
—*Sunday Courier.*

Loll (American), a favourite child,
the mother's darling.

Loller (American), usually applied to a lively, sportive damsel,
or "bit of muslin."

Oh, if she is a *loller*,
I would like to be her loll !
And if she is a scholar,
Let me turn into a schol !
Or whate'er she scholarises
Or whate'er she tries to do,
Or what kind of game arises,
So she'd only put me through !
—*A Song: Poor Jones.*

Lolly (pugilistic), the head.

**Lone ducks, lone doves, quiet
mice.** Women who hire their
apartments, where they receive
gentlemen visitors, or who go
with them to houses of assigna-
tion. A woman without a *sou-
teneur*, one who tries as much
as possible to evade observation,
and to keep up a respectable appearance. This class of women
has increased incredibly within
a very few years in London, as
in all the larger American cities.

Long (University), explained by
quotation.

"Last *Long?*" "Hem ! last protracted
vacation."—*Charles Reade: Hard Cash.*

Long bow. *Vide* DRAW.

Long ear (American University),
a sober, religiously - minded
student. The reverse is called
a short ear.

Long-faced one (army), a horse.

Long feathers (army), straw.
In French argot *plume de
Beauce.* La Beauce, formerly
a province, is renowned for its
wheat, and consequently straw.

Long firm (common), an association of swindlers who pretend
to be a solvent firm of traders.
It is called *bande noire* by the
French.

The Austrian Consul-General in London
having informed the Vienna Chamber of
Commerce that Austrian merchants have
repeatedly incurred heavy loss by giving
credit to *long firms* in England, the
Chamber has issued a notice warning
traders of the risk of opening accounts
with foreign customers, without first obtaining satisfactory information respecting
their position.—*Standard.*

The police reports give us occasional
glimpses of what are called *long firms,*
but glimpses which are for the most part
deceptive. They show us small bands of
disreputable people taking premises in
busy quarters, starting sham businesses,
and obtaining goods from manufacturers
for which they never intend to pay, and
which they dispose of as quickly as possible at any price they will fetch. The
reports go on to show us how this kind of
thing lasts until one or other of the vic-
timised manufacturers sets the police upon
the track of the swindlers, who are invariably hunted up and arrested, when the
business collapses.—*Thor Fredur: Shady
Places.*

Long-ghost (common), a tall,
thin person.

Long-haired chum (tailors), a
young woman, a young lady
friend.

Long-knife (American), a white
man, so called from the swords
which the first settlers wore.
The term came from the Algon-

kin Indians. In Chippeway to this day the term for a white man is *chee-mókomon, i.e.,* great or *long-knife.* The writer once knew a very refined and beautiful young lady, a Miss Foster, of Philadelphia, and also an old Indian whose name meant "He who changes his position while sitting," but who was termed Martin "for short." Martin usually smoked a very handsome *poaugun,* or pipe mounted with silver, but one day he appeared with a miserable affair, made of freestone, not worth a sixpence. On the writer's asking him what he had done with the fine calumet, he replied, "I sold it yesterday to the *chee-mókomon ikweh,*"—to the *long-knife* woman. The " *long-knife* woman" referred to was Miss Foster.

Long-oats (army), fork or handle of a broom used to belabour a horse with.

Long paper (Winchester College), paper for writing tasks on.

Longs (Fenian), rifles.

Longs and "shorts" for rifles and revolvers were familiar enough names to those who followed the Fenian trials a score of years ago.—*St. James's Gazette.*

Longs and shorts (gambling cheats), cards contrived for cheating.

Long-shore butcher (nautical), a coastguardsman.

Long shots (turf), to take the *long shots* is to back a horse which is not in popular favour

at the moment, and against which the bookmakers therefore give a larger rate of odds. It is in fact a form of speculating for the rise.

Button Park and Bonnie Lassie, at 33 to 1 each, seem fairly well backed ; but the outsiders that smack of business amongst the *long-shot* division are Ten Broeck and Althorp.—*Bird o' Freedom.*

How oft at morn we've laughed to scorn
  A *long shot's* chance to win ;
How oft at eve we've had to grieve
  O'er our departed tin.
We've had the tip, and let it slip,
  What's done we can't retract,
And we have to pay on the settling day,
  O'er the winner we might have backed.
      —*Sporting Times.*

Long-tailed one (thieves), a bank note for a large amount.

Long tails (sporting), pheasants, greyhounds.

Long ton (miners), twenty-one hundredweight. In the coal trade they usually reckon twenty-one tons as twenty.

Long trot (popular), explained by quotation.

We was 'bliged to shoot the load afore we could begin ag'in. Sometimes we had to do the *long trot* (go home) with it, and so sp'iled a whole arternoon. —*Greenwood : Seven Curses of London.*

Lonsdale's nine-pins (political), the nine boroughs for which Lord Lonsdale used to send up members to St. Stephen's. A repartee connected with them is attributed to Burke.

Loo (common), for the good of the *loo,* for the benefit of the company or the community.

Loocher (Anglo-Indian), a low and especially a lascivious blackguard. Hind. *luchcha*, a lecher; the being one, *luchchi pana*. In English gypsy *luchipen* or *lutchipen*, lustfulness.

Loo'd, looed (English and American), beaten or defeated. "A term borrowed from the game called 'loo'" (Bartlett). In a list of imaginary last words attributed to notorious Southern characters, Bella Boyd, a celebrated fast woman and female spy, was represented as saying, "I'm *looed*." In provincial English, *looed* means supplanted.

Looking-glass, ancient slang for a chamber utensil, derived from the usual examination made by medical men, for diagnosing the probable ailments of their patients. In Ireland the necessary article is often, if not commonly, called a "Twiss," because the portrait of that once noted politician appeared as an ornament at the bottom, produced for ready sale by a satirical and patriotic earthenware manufacturer in Coleraine to perpetuate the name and fame of Mr. Twiss, for having slandered the women of Ireland by a baseless accusation of unchastity. The accusation was denied, but the penalty remained, by the operation of the principle sarcastically recommended by Douglas Jerrold in all cases of doubt: if you do not know the rights of a thing, believe the worst.

Looking on (turf), one of the many terms which imply that a horse is not intended to do his best in a race.

Look nine ways for Sundays, to (nautical), to squint.

Look-see pidgin (pidgin), mere sham, hypocrisy. "This is all *look-see pidgin*" (Anglo-Chinese newspaper), religious humbug.

My tink he cat he makee chin-chin Fo,
My tinkee puss-cat be Joss-pidgin-man
Who no can *chow-chow* meat—*hai-yah!*
ph'hoy!
Dat cat hab cheatee, cheatee, cheatee
my;
My tink he 'hood—he all too bad—*maskee!*
He Joss-pidgin be all *look-see pidgin*,
My wish dat cat be dam—wit' evely-ting ι
For àllo worl' be bad, an' all be bad,
An' evely side hab pizen—cats an' tlaps,
My no can do make tlust one man no
more.
　　　　　　　　　—*The Cat.*

Loon - flat (old cant), thirteenpence halfpenny.

Loose-box, a term sometimes applied to a brougham.

Loose ends (common). When a business is neglected, or its finances are in a precarious condition, it is said to be at *loose ends*.

Loose, on the (common), out carousing.

At the same fair, Jem Moor was about three-quarters and an eighth towards being tight through having been out *on the loose* all the morning with the governor.—*Hindley: Adventures of a Cheap Jack.*

Also getting a living by prostitution.

Looter (gypsy), to steal from. Anglo - Indian *loot*, plunder, booty. Hind. *lūt*, from Sanskrit *lotra*, root ; *lūp*, rob, plunder. *Lūter* and *lour* are English gypsy terms for the same word, and are also used as verbs.

Lop, horse (army), puddings of suet without plums.

Loppers, lobbes, loppus (American). The writer has never seen this word in print, but he has often heard it in Pennsylvania. An awkward, shambling fellow, a hobble-de-hoy. Dutch *lobbes*, a clownish fellow, also a shaggy dog. This is nearly allied to the English *lob*, a lubber or clown.

Lord (popular), a hump-backed man.

That a deformed person is a *lord* . . . after a painful investigation of the rolls and records under the reign of Richard the Third, or "Richard Crouchback," as he is more usually designated in the chronicles . . . we do not find that that monarch conferred any such lordships as here pretended, upon any subject or subjects, on a simple plea of conformity in that respect to the "royal nature."—*C. Lamb : Essays of Elia.*

She invariably wound up at night with a mad fighting fit, during which my *lord*, vulgar slang for hunchback, was always thrashed unmercifully.—*Standard.*

Probably thus called in ridicule from the self-importance and air of complacency supposed to be generally assumed by hunchbacks. Wright suggests the Greek *lordós*, bent forwards, and Smythe A. Palmer the old English *loord*, *lordain*, *lurden*, or *lourden*, heavy, clumsy,

sluggard. French *lourdaud*, old French *lorde*, Low Latin *lurdus*.

Lord Mayor (burglars), a large crowbar or jemmy, used for breaking open safes.

Numerous are the names given to crowbars. There is "the *Lord Mayor*," "the Alderman," "the Common Councilman," and so on. These are principally used for breaking into safes.—*Tit Bits.*

Lords (Winchester College), the first eleven are thus called.

Lose the combination, to (American), to miss the meaning or point of anything. One often hears such an expression in conversation as "Hold on there. I've missed the combination."

"Did you see the butchers' parade?" asked the snake-editor of a casual caller yesterday afternoon.

"Yes."

"See that man throwing sausages at the crowd?"

"Yes."

"Well, I never sausage a thing before."

"Ha ! ha ! Pretty good. I'll surprise my wife with that when I get home."

When the casual caller arrived at home he said to his wife :

"My dear, in the butchers' parade to-day there was a man throwing sausages to the spectators."

"Was there?"

"Yes ; and I never saw anything like that done before."

"Neither did I."

He waited five minutes for his wife to laugh, and then went out to wonder how he *lost the combination.*—*Pittsburg Chronicle.*

The "snake-editor" mentioned in this anecdote is supposed to be the writer specially employed on a newspaper, to invent or discover wonderful "yarns" of snakes, mosquitoes, enormous pumpkins, extraordinary instances of instinct in animals, and similar marvels. He is "the big gooseberry man" of the English provincial press.

Lost and gone poetry (American). The wailing, feeble-minded rhyming over "lost Edens and buried Lenores," imaginary griefs and sham sorrows, so characteristic of all beginners in poetry, has not escaped the notice of American newspaper wits, who often turn it into ridicule.

Lotion (popular), a drink. "What's your *lotion?*" what are you drinking?

Loud (common), flashy, "pronounced," extravagant, whether in manners or colours, dress or demeanour. Originally English, it has been very much extended in America.

A much more loquacious, ostentatious, much *louder* style. — *Carlyle: Life of Sterling.*

Husband—"Now, Mrs. B.'s dress, I suppose, is what you would call a symphony?"
Wife—"Yes, a Wagnerian symphony."
Husband—"Why Wagnerian?"
Wife—"Because it's so *loud.*"—*Detroit Free Press.*

Lounce (sailor's), a drink. Generally a pint of beer, probably a corruption of allowance.

Lounge (university and public schools), a term of Etonian origin. It means a treat. In the West of England a *lounge* is a large lump of bread.

Lour, loure (old cant), money. From the gypsy.

To strowling ken the mort bings then
To fetch *loure* for her cheats.
　　　　　— *The English Rogue.*

Louver, lovva, lovo, lovvy, lover (gypsy), money, *i.e.*, specie, or coin. *Vide* LOUR.

Lovage (popular), tap droppings. Properly a plant which possesses diuretic properties.

Love (common), in scoring of any game equals nought, or nothing.

I have seen those lose the game that have had so many for *love.* — *Bailey's Erasmus.*

I sometimes play a game at piquet for *love.*—*C. Lamb : Essays of Elia.*

Love is here the antithesis of money. "To play for *love* (of the game) and not for money." French, "pour l'amour de l'art," "gratis pro Deo."

Love apples, explained by quotation.

Love apples, the latest name which the dynamiters have given to their bombs, affords another illustration of the love of conspirators for euphemistic terms.—*St. James's Gazette.*

Tomatoes were generally called *love apples* in Australia about sixty years ago. In France *pommes d'amour.* It may be remarked, *en passant*, that the terms *love apples* and *pommes d'amour* are mistranslations of Italian *pomi del mori* or *Moors' apples*, mala Æthiopica.

Low-down (common), out of sorts, out of money, and out of luck ; also mean, underhand.

That's just the way; a person does a *low-down* thing, and then he don't want to take no consequences of it.—*The Adventures of Huckleberry Finn.*

Lowie (Scotch thieves), money; a form of lour, or the common gypsy *lowy* or *lovvy.*

A good deal of talk afterwards took place about the *lowie,* which he believed signified money.—*Scottish Newspaper.*

Low in the lay (thieves), in want of money, "hard up."

Fighting Attie, my hero, I saw you to-day
A purse full of yellow boys seize;
And as, just at present, I'm *low in the lay,*
I'll borrow a "quid," if you please.
—*Lytton: Paul Clifford.*

Low-pad (old cant), a footpad.

Low-water-mark, at (common), without funds.

I'm *at low-water-mark,* myself, only one bob and a magpie.—*Dickens: Oliver Twist.*

Lucky (popular), to make or cut one's *lucky,* to escape, run away.

That was all out of consideration for Fagin, 'cause the traps know that we work together, and he might have got into trouble if we hadn't made our *lucky.*—*Dickens: Oliver Twist.*

Lug chovey (popular), a pawnbroker's shop.

Lug, in (popular), in pawn. Scotch *lagd,* laid by, put away

Lullaby cheat (old cant), a child.

Lüller (gypsy), to vanish, disappear.

Lully (thieves), linen, a shirt; *lully* prigger, a thief who steals linen off hedges or lines.

Lumber (old cant), a room.

Lumberer (turf), a swindling tipster, who works his business *vivâ voce* instead of by advertisement. His happy hunting-grounds are the bars of fashionable restaurants, though he may be also encountered on racecourses. His method is either to be introduced by a confederate, or to force acquaintance with raw youths (*vide* JUGGINS), and by pretending to intimacy with jockeys and familiarity with owners of horses to persuade his victim that he is willing, from sheer good-fellowship, to part with valuable information; and, provided a commission is entrusted to him, to insure success on some impending race. The name of the horse is given or withheld as may suit the circumstances of the case, but once he has secured the money or credit of the "juggins" the result is the same. Should the horse win (a most unlikely contingency), there are twenty excellent reasons why the stake has not been invested; if beaten, as he usually is, the *lumberer* urges some impossible combination of rascality on the part of owner or jockey as an excuse for present defeat and in proof of future infallibility. (Common), a man who goes about public-houses sponging on acquaintances. From to *lumber,* to loiter, stroll lazily.

So I pulled out my flask, and my two *lumberers* drained it, and, with a "Lord luv us, Bill, I feels er nu'un," and with the other saying, "Them's my sentiments," began chaffing me—"Are yer agoing to have another game er nap?"—*Bird o' Freedom.*

Lummox (American), a fat, unwieldy, stupid person. From provincial English *lummock*, a lump.

Lummy (popular), first - rate, clever, jolly.

To think of Jack Dawkins—*Lummy* Jack—the Dodger—the Artful Dodger going abroad for a common twopenny halfpenny sneeze-box.—*Dickens: Oliver Twist.*

Lump (popular), a party, association; to go in the *lump*, means to go to the parish workhouse.

Lump hotel (popular), the workhouse. Termed also the "pan."

Lump on the thick un's, to (turf), to make a heavy bet in sovereigns.

Lump, to (popular), used in the phrase "if you don't like it you may *lump* it," *i.e.*, get rid of it by swallowing it. "M. Oliphant regards the word as a corruption of old English *lomp*, Anglo-Saxon *gelamp*, it happened; and so to *lump* would be 'to take what may chance'" (A. Smythe Palmer). (Thieves), to *lump* the lighter, to be transported. In this case to *lump* signifies to load. (Turf), to put weight on.

Not content with *lumping* him in the handicap.—*Bird o' Freedom.*

Lumpy (booksellers), costly; *lumpy* books, costly books. (Popular), intoxicated, pregnant.

(Cricket), applied to rough ground.

The wicket was unsatisfactory, and the batsmen complained that it was *lumpy*.—*Evening News.*

Lunan. Hotten declares that this is gypsy for a girl. It is common in canting, but the writer has never been able to determine that it is Romany. Probably from the Swedish or Danish *luns*, a slatternly girl.

Lung-box (popular), mouth.

My tar, if you don't close your *lung-box* I shall run you in. — *Brighton Beach Loafer.*

Lunka (Anglo-Indian), a strong cheroot from the Bengal Presidency, so called from being made from tobacco grown in the islands, the local term for which is *lanka* of the Godavery Delta (Anglo-Indian Glossary). They are becoming known in London.

Lunkhead (American), a horse of inferior breed and appearance.

Our new Minister to France is studying the art of politeness and elegance of diction prior to his advent into Parisian society. He calls our worthy Secretary of State (Mr. Fish) a "fossilised *lunkhead*." The term *lunkhead* is usually applied by sporting men to a very sorry style of horse, but never, we believe, to a horse mackerel.—*New York Herald.*

From the Swedish *lunk*, a very slow, heavy horse.

Lunk-headed (American), idiotic senseless.

We shall go armed, and the *lunk-headed*, overgrown calf had better keep out of our sight if he values his miserable, worthless life.—*Estelline (Dakota) Bell.*

Luny (popular), a lunatic. "Go along, you *luny*," is a common phrase.

Combining business with pleasure, he chartered a horse and trap, and drove the *luny* to the asylum, intending to wind up with a pleasant drive on his own account. On the road, however, the *luny* saw in the master's pocket the order for admission to the asylum, and he quietly abstracted it. When they arrived he got down from the trap, and told the officials that he had brought them an inmate, a very quiet man, whose only madness was an idea that he was the master of a suburban workhouse.

The master vehemently protested that the other man was the lunatic, and that he himself was really the master of the workhouse. "I told you so," said the lunatic pityingly; "but this will settle the matter; here is the order for his admission." The unlucky master was violently removed, and the lunatic got up in the trap, and drove away.—*Ross: Variety Paper.*

Lur, loure (gypsy), to rob; booty, plunder. This word passed into canting at a very early period.

Your'e out ben morts and toure !
Look out ben morts and toure !
For all the Rome coves are budged a beake,
And the quire (queer) coves tippe the *loure.*
    —*S. Rowlands,* 1610.

That "Rome coves" means gypsies here, as well as "good men," is apparent enough. Stealing linen from hedges, &c., has always been regarded as a speciality of the Romany. *Loure* is still commonly used among gypsies. "Do you pen mandy'd *loure* tute?"—"Do you think I'd rob you?"

Lurk (tramps and others), a swindle; specially applied to obtaining money by a false begging petition. An occupation.

Then says Pudding-faced Ned, with a grin on his phiz,
"It's no one but horses and asses that work ;
Now Larry's got his fancy, Jerry's got his,
And so I've got mine, and it's cadging's my *lurk.*"
    —*J. Greenwood: A Night in a Workhouse.*

Formerly *lurch.*

The tapster having many of these *lurches* fell to decay.—*Peel's Jests.*

(Tinker), eye. This word, in the sense of looking about, observing where work may be got, or anything stolen, &c., possibly suggested the old canting word *lurk*, which was used for every kind of "lay," trick, swindle, or "game." To keenly observe forms the first part of the education of a young thief, and to this his eyesight was regularly trained by observing mingled objects thrown up together, &c. —an exercise which might be with great advantage applied in all schools to develop quickness of perception.

Lurker (tramps and others), an impostor who goes about with a false begging petition.

Lurries (thieves), money or jewellery. From the gypsy *loure*, plunder.

Lurry (old cant), valuables. *Vide* LUR.

The fifth was a glazier, who, when he creeps in,
To pinch all the *lurry* he thinks it no sin.
    —*From A Pedlar's Pack of Ballads and Songs, collected by W. H. Logan.*

Lush (Eton), dainty. Shakespeare uses *lush* with the meaning of luxury. It is a provincial term for rich, succulent. (Common), drink ; more especially drink to excess. Applied equally to beer, wine, or spirits.

I boast not such *lush*, but whoever his glass
Does not like, I'll be hanged if I press him.
—*Lytton: Paul Clifford.*

Though it once was our game when the chucking time came,
'Tis a fact that I freely allow,
When in search of a *lush* to the "Spoofs' we would rush,
But the sharps do the "rushing" just now.
—*Sporting Times.*

Suggested to be from *lush*, full of juice, traced by Wright to *luscious, lushious, luxurious.* Drink seems, in most languages, to be synonymous with "juice." Thus in Scotland whisky is called the "barley bree," or juice of the barley. The French have "jus de la treille" for wine, and the slang term "jus d'échalas." French sailors call rum of the best quality "jus de botte premier brin." But more probably from the gypsy *lush* or *losher*, to drink ; or German *löschen.*

Lush-crib (popular and thieves), a public-house or tavern.

Lushington (popular), a low, drunken fellow, a sot. Up to recent date, there was, or may be now, a tap-room in a certain hostelry, in the immediate vicinity of Drury Lane Theatre, famous for being a favourite haunt of Edmund Kean. Here that ill-starred genius and his parasites were wont to turn night into day, in making their followers free of "the City of *Lushington.*" Other times, other manners.

Lush, to (common), to drink, or drink to excess. *Vide* LUSH.

. . . piece of double Glo'ster ; and to wind up all, some of the richest sort you ever *lushed.*—*Dickens: Oliver Twist.*

Lushy or **lushey** (popular), intoxicated.

It was half-past four when I got to Somerstown, and then I was so uncommon *lushey* that I couldn't find the place where the latch-key went in.—*Dickens: Pickwick Papers.*

Lyesken chirps (tinker), telling a fortune.

Lying in (Royal Military Academy), is said of a cadet who stops at the Royal Military Academy, in his room, on a Sunday when he is supposed to have left on leave.

Lylo (Anglo - Chinese), come hither (Hotten).

Lypken, a word used by tramps in the fifteenth and sixteenth centuries, and probably at an earlier period, for a house where vagrants and thieves could procure a night's lodging. From the Gaelic *leaba,* a bed ; and *cean* (ken), a house.

M

MAB (American), a harlot. Possibly from the canting *Mab*, "a hackney coach," which is common to all who will pay for a passage in it. So the French call a *fille de joie* an omnibus. In the north of England a *mab* is a loose, slatternly girl.

Mabbed up (old cant), dressed carelessly, as a slattern.

Macaroni (thieves), pony (Ducange Anglicus). Formerly a swell, fop. "The Italians are extremely fond of a dish they call *macaroni*, . . . and as they consider this as the *summum bonum* of all good eating, so they figuratively call everything they think elegant and uncommon *macaroni*. Our young travellers, who generally catch the follies of the countries they visit, judged that the title of *macaroni* was very applicable to a clever fellow; and accordingly to distinguish themselves as such, they instituted a club under this denomination, the members of which were supposed to be the standard of taste. The infection at St. James's was soon caught in the city, and we have now *macaronies* of every denomination" (Pocket-book, 1773).

Mace (thieves), to give it on the *mace*, or strike the *mace*, to obtain goods on credit without any intention of paying for them; to sponge an acquaintance, beg or borrow money. Formerly *mace* grieffs were men who wittingly bought and sold stolen fish. Several Yiddish words may have contributed to this term, such as *masser* or *meser*, a betrayer, hence "massestapler," which see; *més-chomet*, a blackguard. Also *moser* or *möser*, a cheat; *mös*, money, hence to make money. Man at the *mace*, explained by quotation.

The following people used to go in there : toy-getters (watch-stealers), magsmen (confidence-trick men), men at the *mace* (sham loan offices), &c.—*Horsley : Jottings from Jail.*

To *mace*, to cheat, swindle in any way.

Maceman, macer (thieves), a man who conducts a sham loan office, a welsher, swindler. *Vide* MACE.

Màchin (pidgin), a merchant. "Allo dot go doun blongy one numpa-one *machin*, he catchee too much dolla'."

Macing the rattler (thieves), travelling in a railway train without paying one's fare. *Vide* MACE.

A rough shock head was obtruded from under the seat, and a gruff voice cried : "J'yer, guv'nor, does your dog bite?" "Great heaven!" gasped the little man, "what in the name of all that's holy are you doing under there?"

"Same as your dog. *Macing the — rattler.*"—*Sporting Times.*

Mackarel, mackawl (old cant), a bawd. French *maquereau, maquerelle.*

Madam (thieves), a pocket-handkerchief.

One day I went to Lewisham and touched for a lot of wedge. I tore up my *madam* (handkerchief), and tied the wedge in small packets and put them into my pockets.—*Horsley: Jottings from Jail.*

(Old cant), *Madam* **Van**, a prostitute.

Made (Winchester). A prefect is said to be *made* when he has received full power from the head-master.

Made beer (Winchester), a beverage compounded of college small-beer, raisins, sugar, nutmeg, and rice, so as to give it some sort of a "head."

Made his Jack (American), got what he aimed at, attained his point, got into office, or became somebody of consequence. Old English, "Jock with the bush." "This phrase," says Wright, "occurs in Barclay's 'Eclogues,' 1570, and seems to mean a Jack-in-office." Dutch, *een groot Hans*, a great Jack or person, "a swashing blade;" German, *prablhans*, a "swell."

Madza (thieves and costermongers), half; from the Italian *mezza*, used as in *madza* saltee, a halfpenny; *madza* poona, half a sovereign, &c. Also *medza*, in low theatrical slang; *medza beargered*, half drunk.

Mafoo (pidgin), horse-boy, groom. "Talkee *mafoo* to come chopchop." (Mandarin), *mah*, a horse; *mah-tung*, a stirrup.

Mag (thieves and popular), a halfpenny; in ancient cant a "make."

You has not a heart for the general distress—
You cares not a *mag* if our party should fall,
And if Scarlet Jem were not good at a press,
By Goles, it would soon be all up with us all!
—*Lytton: Paul Clifford.*

If he don't keep such a business as the present as close as possible, it can't be worth a *mag* to him.—*Dickens: Bleak House.*

In society, "not a *mag*" is equivalent to "not a sou."

And the staff, going and downing it on Indian Ocean and Atlantic, are still broke to a man and a *mag.*—*Sporting Times.*

(Literary and printers), a magazine.

And now of Hawkesbury they talked,
Who wrote in *mags* for hire.
—*Wolcot (P. Pindar).*

Maggots (popular), whims, fancies. Hence "maggotty," fanciful, fidgety. It was once a popular belief that small *maggots* were generated in the human brain, so that the fretting of these insects produced odd fancies and foolish notions. Hence probably the origin which may perhaps also be traced to the fact that crazy sheep have a worm in the brain.

Magistrands. *Vide* BEJANT.

Magistrate (Scotch slang), a herring.

Magpie (popular and thieves), sixpence.

I'm at low-water-mark myself—only one bob and a *magpie.*—*Dickens: Oliver Twist.*

Also the black and white circles in a target.

Magsman (common slang), the *magsman* is at the very head of the profession of roguery. He is the great man, the Magnus Apollo among thieves and swindlers, or what the French call *de la haute pègre.* He is a first-class confidence man who selects his victims in the street, in the smoking-rooms of hotels, in stylish bars. "*Magsmen* are wonderful actors. Their work is done in broad daylight, without any stage-accessories, and often a look, a wink, a slip of the tongue, would betray their confederacy. They are very often men of superior education. Those who work the tidal trains and boats are often faultlessly dressed and highly accomplished" (Hotten).

He has not the slightest sympathy with evil-doers, and fifty guineas would not tempt him to permit on his premises the hilarious celebration of bold Toby Crackitt's release over a bowl of punch, by a select circle of admiring *magsmen.*— *Greenwood: In Strange Company.*

Probably from the Yiddish *machas* or *magas* (to which *mann* may be arbitrarily added), meaning a great swell, a great man or highly honoured lord; or from to *mag*, to talk persuasively. It is curious to note that *meg*, in French cant, which Victor Hugo derives from *magnus*, means master, head of a gang (more probably from Italian cant, *maggio*, lord). It may be these words have a common origin, or this is mere coincidence. Compare old cant *dabe*, head of a gang, and French *dab*, same meaning; the latter probably from *dam*, low Latin for lord.

Mag, to (thieves), to talk, to talk persuasively; a provincialism meaning to chatter. In the quotation *mag* signifies talk. Probably from "magpie."

Oh! if you have any *mag* in you we'll draw it out.—*Madame D'Arblay: Diary.*

Mahmy (up-country Australian), the white commander of a troop of native police.

The troopers were, of course, delighted at the prospect of a collision with their countrymen, and an unusual degree of activity prevailed in the camp, so much so that next morning before sunrise, while Stone and his guest were getting through their hasty breakfast, the corporal of the troop made his appearance at the door, and stiffening himself into an erect military attitude saluted gravely, reporting at the same time, "Every sing all righ, *mahmy.*" —*A. C. Grant.*

Mahogany (society), table; to have one's feet under another man's *mahogany*, to sit at his table, be supported on other than one's own resources (Hotten). *Vide* AMPUTATE YOUR TIMBER.

In a casual way he mentioned the days when his father, the J.P., sat for somewhere or other, and of the dainties that nightly graced his hospitable *mahogany.* —*Sporting Times.*

(Popular), *mahogany* flat, a bug.

Maiden (turf), a horse which has never won a race open to the public. Therefore the winning of one or more matches does not disqualify a horse from being entered as a *maiden* for subsequent events.

Maidstone jailer (rhyming slang), a tailor.

Mails (Stock Exchange), Mexican Railway ordinary stock.

Mailyas, maillhas (tinker), fingers. Gaelic, *meirlach,* stealers, as "pickers and stealers," hands. Possibly the real origin of "maulies," influenced by "maul."

Mai-pan (pidgin, Cantonese), *compradore,* steward.

Maistry, mixtry, sometimes **mystery** (Anglo-Indian), properly a foreman, a master-workman, but used for any artisan, as *rajmistri,* a mason or bricklayer, *lohar-mistri,* a blacksmith. From the Portuguese *mestre,* a skilled or master-workman.

Make (old cant), a penny or halfpenny. (General), to be "on the *make,*" to be always intent on the main chance, seeking to make money. It generally implies unscrupulousness and cleverness.

The English doctors can earn their living in their own country. They haven't gone to Germany on the *make.—Referee.*

While the word is unquestionably derived from the English *make,* as "to *make* money," it is worth pointing out its resemblance to the Yiddish *makir,* one who knows, who is intelligent in anything. Nothing is more remarkable in slang than the manner in which words mutually form and help one another into currency. It is said also of one who asks too high a price for his goods. "On the *make*" is of American origin; a *make* is a successful swindle.

Make a bolt of it, to (common), to run away.

And he has been suspected, detected, has *made a bolt of it,* and has been discovered and brought to justice. — *The Graphic.*

Make a kick, to (common), to raise an objection. French *regimber,* said of a horse that backs and kicks, and figuratively of an unwilling person.

Make a small war, to (American), to amass a small fortune. In reference to a man who had amassed a fortune during the civil war, and of whom it was said that he would like to *make a small war* of his own simply to "finance" it.

Many scores of these philanthropists who have spent their lives in looking for men to enrich whilst anxious only to *make a small war* for themselves, have I encountered.—*F. Francis : Saddle and Moccasin.*

Makee (pidgin), to make, do, cause, effect. "Supposy you *makee* buy-lo!" It is in pidgin generally prefixed to verbs to make them active, *e.g.*, "I *makee* stlike dat too-muchee bad boy."

Make hay (*vide* HAY), to put in disorder, to mix in utter confusion. The expression explains itself.

Some of the warders, full of the irrepressible spirits of Old Erin (we do not mean whisky) had *made hay* with the drugs in the infirmary, with the result that liniments were taken as medicines, blisters applied in lieu of linseed plasters, and in one instance laudanum administered instead of black draught.—*Funny Folks.*

Hay-bag is an old word for a noise, riot, mess.

Make no bones, to (popular), *to make no bones* about doing anything, is to do it without demur or difficulty. Of very ancient origin, Erasmus in his Paraphrase (1548) using it—"He made no manier bones ne stickyng but went in hande to offre vp his onely sone Isaac in sacrifice" (Luke, f. 15). Its derivation is obscure unless it be an allusion to the habit of some people, in eating fish and small birds, to eat bones and all.

Make, to (popular and thieves), to appropriate to one's personal use ; to *make* clocks, to steal watches.

Making clocks was too risky, and guying warn't no catch after I fell in the river at 'Ampton, with a countryman as could swim like a bloomin' duck a throttlin' me.—*Sporting Times.*

(Freemasons), to initiate.

Make tracks, to (American), to decamp, to run away ; in allusion to one who leaves traces behind him, without intending to do so.

He was one of those unpleasant people who keep firearms on the premises, and handy for use. We *made tracks*, as you may suppose, and quickly too. The other two got clear off. As for myself, a snap-shot caught me in the calf of the leg as I tumbled anyhow over the garden wall, and thus put an end to my "crib-cracking" for one while.—*Thor Fredur : Sketches in Shady Places.*

Make - up (theatrical), materials used for making up the face, hands, &c. Soap and water, cold cream, pomatum, or vaseline, pearl powder, Indian ink, rouge, vermilion, blanc de perle, rose water, crêpé hair, spirit gum, wigs, and grease paint of every description. The latter, though a recent discovery in Europe, has been known and used in China for ages. The use of it was first introduced here by the distinguished actor, Hermann Vezin, who, before it became an article of commerce, manufactured it for his own use.

A little girl at the back of the dress circle cried :
"See, ma, he's been kissing the maid, and her *make-up's* come off on his face!"—*Bird o' Freedom.*

This term also refers to the personal appearance assumed by

an actor impersonating a character.

Mr. —— took the part of the aged diplomatist, Sir Henry Craven. His *make-up* was admirable, and his acting worthy of all praise.—*Sporting Times.*

It has the general sense of appearance produced by dress, habits, &c.

Perhaps he owed this freedom from the sort of professional *make-up* which penetrates skin, tones, and gestures. — *G. Eliot: Daniel Deronda.*

Making a pitch (street performers, cheap Jacks, circus, &c.), selecting a locality for a performance of any kind, stopping at any place to perform.

Five times did we *make a pitch* in the wind and the deadly-cold sleet, playing over three times.—*Greenwood: In Strange Company.*

Making a song (thieves), explained by quotation.

Only a purse, with four shillings and a railway ticket in it. What makes me remember the ticket? Why, when I got home—I was still staying at the lodging-house in George Street—a pal told me of a lark he had seen at the market; some poor chap had lost all his money and his return railway ticket, and was *making a song* (telling everybody) about it. —*J. Greenwood: Gaol Birds at Large.*

Making up the log (tailors), putting down the wages. In the stock trade it is taking the number of garments cut, and in some cases where they pay "day work," if the quantity does not come up to the specified number of garments, the deficiency is deducted per ratio from the men's wages.

Malleko (gypsy), a sneaking spy, an informer, a mischief-maker. This is old gypsy, and it recalls the "miching Mallecho" of Shakspeare.

Malley (Anglo-Indian), a gardener.

Malt (popular), beer.

When the purchase-money was paid over, the farmer invited the dealer, as is the custom, to have a glass of *malt* before parting, and they entered a neighbouring public-house.—*Tit-Bits.*

Malt, to (popular), to drink beer.

Malum (Anglo-Indian), a sailing-master.

"In a ship with English officers and a native crew, the mate is called *malum sahib.* The word is, in Arabic, *mu'allim,* literally 'the instructor,' and is properly applied to the pilot or sailing-master" (Anglo-Indian Glossary).

Mammy (West Indian), an elderly negress; generally an old nurse. Sometimes corrupted into *Maumer.*

Manablins (popular), broken victuals (Hotten).

Man a-hanging (common), a man in difficulties (Hotten).

Man at the duff. *Vide* DUFF.

Manchester silk (tailors), thread.

Manders (thieves), "remands."

One promising little lad of about twelve, and who really had some claim to being regarded as an "old offender," overdid it by endeavouring, in the enumeration of his numerous convictions, to palm off a couple of *manders* . . . as genuine magisterial sentences to imprisonment.—*J. Greenwood: Dick Temple.*

Man-handle, to (thieves), to use a person roughly, as to take him prisoner, to turn him out of a room, or give him a beating (Hotten). Properly, *to man-handle* is a nautical term, meaning to move by force of men, without levers or tackles.

Man-man (pidgin-English), slowly, gradually, little by little. Italian *mano mano*.

Man-man one peach-tlee flowery become
   one piecy peach,
Man-man one littee chilo get wise an' all
   men teach,
You catchee one piece can-do; some day
   it make you gleat,
Ahong hab larn this lesson—to fightee,
   shave an' wait.
     —*The Ballad of Ahong and the Mosquito.*

Man of the world (thieves), professional thief.

Man of the world. . . . He so loves to style himself, not from any resemblance to the similarly designated personage of polite society, but from the fact of his accomplishments being such that he can follow his profession anywhere.—*Michael Davitt: Leaves from a Prison Diary.*

Man-trap (common), patches of cow dung in the fields. Also a widow. This old term, still used habitually among American thieves, recalls the bright boy in the New York school who, on being asked the meaning and derivation of the word "virgin," replied, "*vir*, a man; *gin*, a trap; *virgin*, a man-trap."

Manual subscription (American), a blow with the fist. In England "a sign manual."

Want me to subscribe to a Life of Grant, do ye? I'll grant ye yer life ef ye clar out from hyar 'n less 'n a minit, ye scum! General Grant's soldiers stole all my hens, an' shot my second cousin's brother's arm off, and now ye want me to subscribe for his life! I'll give ye a *manual subscription* in the face with my knuckles, ye hellion of a Yankee book-pedlar!—*Trials of a Book Agent.*

Man with no frills (American), a plain person, a man without culture or refinement. An amiable term to express a vulgar fellow. The *Nevada Transcript* describes a blackguard who, because he was worth a million, insisted on being allowed to sit at a *table d'hôte* in his shirt-sleeves, as *a miner millionaire with no frills.*

Map (printers), a dirty proof, heavily marked all over by the reader in consequence of blunders and errors in composing—likened to a geographical drawing with many references.

Marble (American), also *marvel.* To bound, bounce, or run along. From a boy's marble thrown along a sidewalk, which, if properly propelled, will proceed to an incredible distance. Marbles are also vulgarly called *marvels* in Philadelphia, as in Suffolkshire.

Marbles (common), furniture, movables.

I can't git the 'ang of his lingo; his patter's all picter somehow,
And wot he quite means by Calf, mate, I dunno no more than a cow.

But the Scapegoat, that's him, I suppose,
and he looks it; it's rough, as he says;
No *marbles*, no lodging, no grub, and that
sort o' thing for days!   —*Punch.*

Margery prater (thieves and gypsies), a hen, from its constant clucking. So called by association with *margery-howlet*, an old word for an owl, and *margery daw*, jack-daw; *margot*, in French, is a nickname for a magpie.

Maria, for Black Maria, which see.

Although I had no motive for evading her,
'Twas but lately that I came across her
    track,
And two stern-faced men were forcibly
    persuading her
To enter a conveyance, painted black.
Aghast at conduct seemingly so cruel, base,
    And wicked, I its meaning did inquire—
Quoth a gamin, "She's been lifting some
    cove's jewel case,
And she's going for a ride in the *Maria*."
                    —*Sporting Times.*

Marinated (old cant), transported.

Marine (nautical), an empty bottle.

Mark (pugilistic), the pit of the stomach.

Gretting (1724–34) had the nearest way
of going to the stomach (which is what
they call the *mark*) of any man I knew.—
*Captain Godfray: Useful Art of Self-
Defence.*

(Swindlers), one marked by thieves or swindlers as easy to dupe or rob.

" Buy a watch-ticket, John?" cry one
    did—
" Will you bid?—take a quid;"
" In for eight guineas!"   "Oh, nay, you
    don't kid
    This young man," said I, "from the
    North!"

Whispered to me a mock-auction shark—
Thought me a *mark*—"keep it dark."
            —*J. A. Hardwick: Up from the
            Country.*

(Popular), "to come to the, or be up to the *mark*," to be satisfactory. When one is dissatisfied and says that a thing is not up to the *mark*, does not come up to the *mark*, one is still using the metaphor of a measure not filled up to the rim or proper *mark*.

Marked up (tailors), to have one *marked up*, is to know all about him.

Marketeer (turf), a betting-man who devotes himself, by means of special information, to the study of favourites, and the diseases incident to that condition of equine life (Hotten).

Market - horse (turf), a horse simply kept in the betting-lists for the purpose of being betted against (Hotten). The "market" is the Turf Exchange, which is held at Tattersall's, in the betting clubs on the racecourse, or at any great centre where ringmen congregate.

Marking (thieves), watching or picking out a victim.

Marmalade, true (common), excellent. Also "real jam."

Marm puss (tailors), the master's wife, or the wife of any other man.

Marooning (nautical), explained by quotation.

In the good old times when punishments were heroic, when floggings were every-day occurrences and keelhaulings frequent, *marooning* was a well-known term. It consisted of putting a refractory seaman ashore on a desert island and leaving him there to wait for the next ship, which very often never arrived.—*Globe.*

Admiral Smyth says *marooning* was a custom among former pirates, of putting an offender on shore on some desolate cape or island, with a gun, a few shot, a flask of powder, and a bottle of water. The French *marron* (English "maroon") was an epithet applied to run-away negroes, or to an animal which has become wild, as "un cochon marron," from the Spanish *cimarron*, wild.

Married on the carpet and the banns up the chimney (popular), living as man and wife, though not married.

Marrow, local in the North of England for a mate or fellow-workman. The word, though almost obsolete, survives in a variety of applications in the sense of one thing being like another; as in the Scottish phrase, "thae shoon are nae *marrows*," these shoes are not pairs; "his een are no *marrows*," eyes are not alike—*i.e.*, he squints; "my winsome *marrow*," my dear "mate," my love, my sweetheart, my wife. The word is used by Shakspeare in a phrase hitherto unexplained by his numerous critics and commentators. Mark Antony, speaking of the as-sassination of Cæsar, says that he was "marr'd " with traitors —*i.e.*, likened with traitors—as if he himself had been a traitor.

Marrow - bones (popular), the knees; to go by *marrow-bone stage*, to walk.

Marrowskying, *vide* MEDICAL GREEK.

Mary (printers), an expression used to indicate "nix" or "nought," in throwing with the nine quadrats, should it happen that not a single one is turned up with the nick upper-most.

Mary Ann (popular), an effemi-nate youth or young man, known in America as a Molly. Latin *cinœdus*. Also a designation among the secret societies who govern and make rules for Trades Unions and associations of workmen in Great Britain, France, Germany, and the United States, of which the ob-jects are to shorten the hours of labour, maintaining and increasing the rate of wages, &c. "La Marianne," in 1848, was the name of a secret Re-publican Society in France. The Republic has been thus nicknamed.

Marygold (turf), one million ster-ling.

Marylebone stage (popular), the legs. "To go by the *Marylebone stage*," *i.e.*, to walk.

Mash (common), elegance, woo-ing.

> They hint that such a niggard *mash*
> They wouldn't very much like;
> They'd look for 'kerchief, scent, or sash,
> Gloves, jewellery, or such like.
> " 'Tis thus the green-eyed one appears,"
> Says Mary Ann, with laughter;
> " You see I have the *mash*, my dears,
> The presents may come after."
> —*Fun.*

To be on the *mash*, to be making love to; to go on the *mash*, to go about in search of amourettes; to *mash*, to make love to.

> A Johnny . . . *mashing* a young lady behind the counter of a large Boulogne Chemisier, received an abrupt check.
> "Avvy voo, sivvoo play, un necktie—un scarf—of the colours of petite chère mam'selle's eyes—bleu ! "
> "Ve have not, m'sieur—vare sorree—but ve have ze scarf of ze same colaire as m'sieu's nose—rouge ! "—*Sporting Times.*

To make an irresistible impression on girls, to make a girl in love with one.

> My name it is Bertie, the little pet page,
> At court I'm considered the go.
> My carriage and grace, my angelic face,
> Quite *mashes* the ladies, you know.
> —*Bertie the Masher.*

About the year 1860 *mash* was a word found only in theatrical parlance in the United States. When an actress or any girl on the stage smiled at or ogled a friend in the audience, she was said to *mash* him, and "mashing" was always punishable by a fine deducted from the wages of the offender. It occurred to the writer that it must have been derived from the gypsy *mash* (*masher-ava*), to allure, to entice. This was suggested to Mr. Palmer, a well-known impresario, who said that the con-

jecture was not only correct, but that he could confirm it, for the term had originated with the C—— family, who were all comic actors and actresses, of Romany stock, who spoke gypsy familiarly among themselves.

Mashed (common), in love.

> He was *mashed*, so was she, they were married—though sure
> They were each minus oof of their own.
> —*Sporting Times.*

Also *mashed* on.

> He also took charge of the saddle-bags, which contained a cake of tobacco and a love-letter, or, as he styled them, "a chunk of baccer and some durned gush from a gal who's got *mashed* on the owner."—*F. Francis : Saddle and Moccasin.*

Masheen (tinker), a cat.

Masher (common), an exquisite, a swell, a dandy. Imported from America. For origin *vide* MASH.

> "Out of the way, fellow ! " cried a *masher* the other evening, "or I will give you a dressing ! " " I shouldn't try it on," answered the fellow, as he exhibited a shoulder-of-mutton fist, "or you'll still be the better dressed of the two."—*Ally Sloper's Half-Holiday.*

Formerly termed "flasher, blood, Jack-pudding, macaroni, buck, top-sawyer," &c. Girls call their lover their *masher* or "mash."

> So, friends, take my dear-bought advice,
> On girls don't waste your cash,
> If you instead of dark are fair—
> You'll never be their *mash*.
> The darling creature you adore—
> Don't fancy you're her "mark,"
> Or think you e'er her love will gain,
> Unless you're "tall and dark ! "
> —*Bird o' Freedom.*

Mashery (common), explained by quotation. *Vide* MASHER.

> A mass of conceit from the head to the feet,
> A blending of "cheek" and a bashery,
> A hat awry set, and a mild cigarette,
> Appear as the symptoms of *mashery?*
> —*Moonshine.*

Mashing, *vide* MASH. In the quotation this has the meaning of elegant and overwhelming.

The Government's prisoner apparently thought that the time had arrived when a little fresh air would be desirable, and hey presto! a new suit of clothes by some extraordinary means or another was conveyed into the prison, and when the Governor went to see Mr. O'Brien that gentleman was seated by his bedside arrayed in quite the "latest" and most *mashing* suit of tweeds.—*Ally Sloper's Half-Holiday.*

Maskee (pidgin - English), the commonest interjection in pidgin, meaning all right. In the Chinese "Vocabulary of Words in Use among the Red-Haired People" (*i.e.*, Europeans), it is spelt *ma-sze-ki*, and defined to mean "all good." The authors of the Anglo-Indian Glossary say it is a term meaning "Never mind," *n'importe*, which is indeed the way in which it is generally used. It is also used for "anyway," or "anyhow," and very often in an indeterminate manner.

> They talk all same they savvy you—they all can do, *maskee,*
> Such facey man in allo-tim my nevva hab look-see.
> My tinkee muchee culio—he allo be China-man,
> But állo hab he head cut off, and holdee in he han'.
> —*The Ballad of Captain Brown.*

> That mightey-time being chop-chop,
> One young man walkey, no can stop,
> *Maskee* snow, *maskee* ice,
> He cally flag wit' chop so nice,
> Top-side galow!
> —"*Excelsior*" in Pidgin.

Maskin (old cant), coal.

Mason's maund (old cant), sham sore, counterfeiting a broken arm by a fall from scaffolding.

Masoner (old cant), explained by quotation.

> *Masoners* are a set of people that give paper for goods. There are generally three or four of them that go to a fair or market together, where one appears like a farmer or grazier, and the other two as vouchers.—*The Discoveries of J. Poulter alias Baxter.*

Masse-stapler (old cant), a rogue disguised as a woman.

Ma-ta (pidgin), mother.

> "*Ma-ta* hab got one-piecee chilo. Joss-pidgin-man hab makee dat chilo Clistun (Christian)."

Matches (Stock Exchange), Bryant & May Shares. (American cadet), a stripling of a youth. A tall lanky cadet will often be accosted with "Hulloa, Matches!"

Matching for keeps (American), matching coins or marbles, odd or even, &c., with the condition that the money won is to be kept.

Ever since that time he has been working industriously, accumulating wealth and fame, and gliding swiftly for office, office of all kinds, and abstaining scornfully from juggling with such youthful pranks as *matching for keeps.* All his leisure time was spent in the exhilarating sprint for fame.—*Daily Inter-Ocean.*

Matriarchs (American), old dow-
agers. The analogy between
this word and patriarchs is obvious.

Matspeak (church), sixpence from
every one for the seats in the
cathedral.

Mauks (popular), a term of opprobrium for a woman among the
lower classes, a prostitute.
Provincial, *mawks*, a slattern.

Mauld (popular), very drunk. Old
provincial, *mauled* up, tired and
dirty.

Mauley (pugilists), fist. Also
" mawlers," " mawleys."

Professor Sloggins, the eminent artist
with the *mauleys*, will deliver a series of
instructive experiences.—*Sporting Times.*

Also a signature.

Mauleys, handy with his (pugilistic), clever at boxing.

" Now," said the Corinthian, " we shall
see whether this supposed 'slogger' is as
handy with his mauleys as my old friend
Mr. Jackson."—*Punch.*

Maunder (old cant), a beggar, a
tramp.

Nor will any go to law,
With a *maunder* for a straw,
All which happiness, he brags,
Is only owing to his rags.
—*History of Bampfylde-Moore
Carew.*

From *maund*, a basket, as
beg from bag. Reference to a
basket occurs in several cant
terms used by the mendicant
tribe, as bawdy basket, ballad
basket. Webster gives *maunder*,
to beg, from the French *mendier;*
in German cant *mumsen*.

Maundring broth (old cant), a
scolding.

Mavorick (West American), an
unbranded motherless calf.

Nowadays you don't dare to clap a
brand on a *mavorick* even; and if they
catch you altering a brand—hell ! that's a
penitentiary job. — *F. Francis : Saddle
and Moccasin.*

Maw (popular), mouth.

Mawworm (common), a hypocrite. From Bickerstaff's play
of the " Hypocrite " (Hotten).

Max (popular and thieves), gin ;
said to be an abbreviation of
maxime, meaning properly the
best gin.

I bes' the cove—the merry old cove,
Of whose *max* all the rufflers sing ;
And a lushing cove, I think, by Jove,
Is as great as a sober king !
—*Lytton : Paul Clifford.*

But ere they could perform this pious duty,
The dying man cried, " Hold ! I've got
my gruel !
Oh ! for a glass of *max !* "
—*Byron : Don Juan.*

Max it, to (American cadet), to
say one's recitation with readi-
ness and style. From *maxime*.
Sometimes " to make a cold
max."

Mazarine (popular), a common
councilman, from his wearing a
mazarine blue cloak.

I had procured a ticket through the
interest of Mr. ——, who was one of the
committee for managing the entertainment,
and a *mazarine*.—*Annual Register.*

M.B. waistcoat, a name said
to have been invented by an
Oxford tailor for the cassock-
waistcoat which the clergy

began to wear in the earlier days of the Tractarian movement. It meant *Mark-of-the-Beast waistcoat*.

Mealer, in temperance lingo, is a partial abstainer who pledges himself to drink intoxicating liquor only at his *meals*.

Mean (American). The word is most peculiar in its application to bad quality.

The night was dark and stormy, about as *mean* a night as was ever experienced in Washington.—*Philadelphia Post.*

(West American), inferior, savage.

There ain't a drop of *mean* blood in him.—*F. Francis : Saddle and Moccasin.*

Meant (turf), short for *meant* to win.

Mean white, formerly a term of contempt among negroes for white men without landed property (Hotten).

Measly (popular), mean, miserable-looking.

Measured for a funeral sermon, to be (American), to be near death's door. The allusion is obvious.

He had been *measured for a funeral sermon* three times, he said, and had never used either one of them. He knew a clergyman named Braley who went up into that region with Bright's justly celebrated disease.—*New York Mercury.*

Meat and drink (West Indian), a swizzle or cocktail, in which an egg—both white and yolk—is beaten up.

Med. (medical students), an abbreviation of medical student.

Common cads, who, it is well known, describe themselves as *Meds.* when in a scrape.—*Sporting Times.*

Medes and Persians (Winchester College), jumping on another "man" when he is in bed.

Medical Greek, the slang used by medical students at the hospitals.

Medicine-Joss (pidgin), the god of medicine, Jöh-Uong.

No hab got Jöh-Uong-Chü-Su, he *Medicine-Joss* outside China-side.—*Captain Jones and his Medicine Chest.*

Medico (common), physician.

"Give him," said the worthy *medico*, "plenty of champagne and oysters." A week or so passed by and the doctor looked in again, finding his patient considerably better. He said to the wife, "I suppose you've been following my advice?" "Well," she replied, "we're not very well off. Can't afford much in the way of champagne and oysters, but I've done the best I could for him with gin and cockles."—*Bird o' Freedom.*

Megs (Stock Exchange), Mexican Railway 1st Preference Stock. (Old cant), guineas.

Mei-le-kween-kwok (pidgin, Canton), American, 'Melican.

Melt, to (old cant), to spend money.

Melthog (tinker), under or inner shirt. This word has given the theatrical slang term *milltog*, a shirt, mostly used by strolling actors.

Melton (tailors), dry bread. A reference to Melton cloth.

Mem-sahib (Anglo-Indian), the (English) lady head of a family. Ma'am, madam.

"This singular example of a hybrid term is the usual respectful designation of an European married lady in the Bengal Presidency" (Anglo-Indian Glossary).

Menagerie, the (theatrical), the orchestra. So called from the infernal discord occasioned by the tuning of instruments.

Menavelings, odd money remaining after the daily accounts are made up at railway booking-offices. *Menavelings* is properly applied to very small sums, as pence or sixpences. From *menave*, an old provincial word for a minnow, as if the money were small fry, and perhaps because all is fish that comes to certain nets.

Mend fences, to (American), to mend or repair fences for a man is to attend to his interests. A story of a political agent for a man who was candidate for the governorship of Rhode Island, and who succeeded in dexterously obtaining the vote of a community by paying for the restoration of their place of worship, is described in a Western newspaper as "A judicious emissary—how he repaired fences both of the church and his candidate."

Men on the fence. *Vide* FLOATERS.

Mephisto (tailors), the foreman.

Mess (army), to lose the number of one's *mess*, to die. In nautical parlance, "to slip one's cable." The corresponding French slang terms are, "descendre la garde, passer l'arme à gauche, défiler la parade ; " and " casser son câble, déralinguer, virer de bord."

Mess, to (popular), to play with a woman lewdly, to interfere unduly. Costermongers, says Hotten, refer to police supervision as "messing."

Mesty, mustee, mestez (Anglo-Indian), a half-caste.

Metallician (turf), a racing bookmaker. Bookmakers use metallic books and pencils (Hotten). Little used now.

Metal rule (——) (printers). This is a polite way of expressing a vulgar word or oath. *Metal rule* in speech, and "——" in print would be used. Thus a man in irritation would say, "You be *metal-ruled.*"

Mets (American). In sporting circles the members of the Metropolitan or New York baseball club are called *Mets*. The term is extending, so that probably ere long a New Yorker will be generally known as a *Met*. (Stock Exchange), Metropolitan Railway Ordinary Stock.

Met, the, common abbreviation among East-enders for the Metropolitan Music Hall.

Mew-mew (tailors), a derisive ejaculation meaning tell it to some one else, "tell that to the marines."

Mia-mia (up-country Australian), a bed, pronounced *my-my*, rest. *Mia-mia* or *gunyah* is the hut the Australian blackfellow constructs for himself by making a sloping screen of leafy branches. It has passed into white men's slang. Australians say, "I'm going to my *mia-mia*," meaning "I'm going to bed" or "going to rest."

Within our leafy *mia-mia* then we crept,
And ere a man could fifty count we slept.
—*Keighley Goodchild: On the Tramp.*

Mickey (American), a common word for an Irishman, the same as Paddy.

Micky (up-country Australian), a term for a wild bull, said to have originated in Gippsland, Victoria. Probably from the association of *bulls* with Mickeys or Irishmen. *Micky*, by the way, has nothing in common with Michael, as generally supposed, but is derived from *mike*, which see.

The rope after passing through two or three pulleys is fastened round the barrel of a windlass outside. It tightens, the *micky* feels the strain, and gives a great leap.—*A. C. Grant.*

Middies (Stock Exchange), Midland Railway Ordinary Stock. Middy is a common term for a midshipman.

Middle, an old cant term for finger. *Vide* Breton's "Court and Country," 1618.

Middleman (thieves), explained by quotation.

And what is worse, there doesn't seem to be any *middleman* in these degenerate days, who can get stolen property back for you, as in days of yore.—*Bird o' Freedom.*

(Tailors), the immediate employer of workmen, who contracts for others.

. . . The hot haste with which they were stitching away, so as to be able to earn at the rate of a shilling a day of the *middleman*, who paid them the magnificent sum of sevenpence for making a pair of gentleman's trousers.—*J. Greenwood: Shadows on the Blind.*

Middle pie (popular), the stomach.

Middling (tailors), I don't think so, I don't believe what you say.

Midgic (tinker), a shilling.

Miesli, misli (tinker), to go, to come, to send. The origin of "mizzle," begone. It is not generally, or in fact at all, known how extensively Shelta is understood among vagrants even in London. It has probably been the medium by which many Celtic words have passed into English. *Misli* means in Shelta not only to go, but to transfer by going or transit, hence to send, and also to send a message or write. E.g., "*Misli* to my bewer," write to my woman, or wife; "My deal is *mislin* to krady in the kiena," I am going to stay in the house. Also to rain.

Mike (tailors), to do a *mike*, to pretend to be working or hang

D

about. The term is also used as a verb. A corruption of old English *mich* (still used by printers), to skulk or shirk work.

Mild (common), inferior, applied to a feeble attempt. *Vide* DRAW IT MILD.

Mild bloater (popular), weak young man who has pretensions to being horsey.

Miles' boy (tailors), a very knowing lad in receipt of much information.

Miles' boy is spotted (common), a saying addressed to any one in a printing-office who begins to spin a yarn. "Miles' boy" was a young gentleman attached to the last coach which started from Hampstead, and was celebrated for his faculty of diverting the passengers with anecdotes and tales. *Miles' boy is spotted*, we know all about Miles' boy.

Milestonemonger (common), one who likes roaming, a tramp.

Of all men I should be the last to utter a harsh word against the most inveterate *milestonemonger* that ever fled from his family to enjoy the sweets of freedom.—*J. Greenwood: Tag, Rag & Co.*

Mile, to (society), to ride on the Ladies' Mile in Hyde Park.

At six o'clock within the Park,
Midst beauty, rank, and style,
I canter on my bonny bay,
Adown the Ladies' Mile.
I *mile*—I *mile*—
When riding down the Mile.
—*Ballad: The Ladies' Mile.*

Milk hole (Winchester), the hole formed by the rush of water through lock gates.

Milk horse (racing), a horse entered at a race to make money on, and always scratched before the affair comes off. *Vide* To MILK.

Milk shake (American), explained by quotation.

The latest craze in New York is the use of milk in numerous ways, and the dairy trade is enjoying a boom in consequence. The greatest calls for the lacteal fluid are from physicians and their patients, and from saloons and drug stores, where the *milk shake* has become a favourite beverage.—*Sporting Times.*

Milk, to (popular), to bleed, to obtain money from by coaxing, &c. (Turf), to lay against a horse fraudulently, *i.e.*, when the bettor has full knowledge that the horse is not meant to win, or has the power and intention of preventing him from so doing.

Milky ones (popular), white linen rags.

Mill (popular and thieves), the treadmill.

Was you never on the *mill?*—*Dickens: Oliver Twist.*

(Common), a fight.

Quite cautiously the *mill* began,
For neither knew the other's plan.
—*Ainsworth: Rookwood.*

The *Mill* was the old Insolvent Debtors' Court.

Mill, to (popular), to fight; to pound with the fists, as beating corn with a stone.

My Lord related all his feats in London . . ." how he had *milled* a policeman. —*Thackeray: Shabby-Genteel Story.*

From *mall*, to hammer, stamp or beat ; *malle*, a hammer ; Latin *malleus ;* Aryan root *mar.* (Thieves and vagabonds), to kill, as "to *mill* a bleating cheate," to kill a sheep.

Mill a ken, to (thieves), to commit burglary.

To *mill* each *ken* let Cove bing then, Through Ruffmans, Jague, or Laund. —*The English Rogue described in the Life of Meriton Latroon.*

Also to steal. Probably the old gypsy *mill* or *miller*, to convey away, to take. "Old Ruffler *mill* the quire-cuffin," *i.e.*, the devil take the Justice of the Peace.

Mill-clapper (old cant), a woman's tongue.

Milled (thieves), a reference to the treadmill.

I shouldn't have been *milled*, if it hadn't been for her advice . . . and what's six weeks of it ?—*Dickens: Oliver Twist.*

Miller (old cant), a murderer, housebreaker. (Common), to drown the *miller*, is, according to Bartlett, to put too much water in the flour in making bread, which he says is "doubtless an English expression." At all events, he adds, that "putting the *miller's* eye out " is a phrase used when too much liquid is put to a dry or powdery substance. As water-mills are far more common in the United States than wind-mills, Mr. Bartlett might easily have found an apter illustration for the saying than that which he has adopted, and left both England and the baker out of the question. The water is said to "drown the *miller*" when the mill-wheels are rendered useless for work in flood time by superabundance of the fluid. The saying was exemplified by the American miller, whose wife in his opinion was a great poetess—who, seeing that the useful mill-stream had become a raging, 'useless torrent, looked up to it, her eye in a fine frenzy rolling, and exclaimed—

" This here water Comes down much faster than it ought ter ! "

A gentleman had mixed his toddy, when a teetotaller sitting beside him said, in a deep voice :
" There's death in that glass ! "
" What did you say ?" replied the other.
" There's death in that glass ! " repeated the cold-water man, in a still more sepulchral tone.
The gentleman looked at his toddy inquiringly, ladled some out, sipped it slowly to taste it better, and at length said :
" You're right—you're right. I believe I have *drowned the miller*," and at once proceeded to strengthen his liquor.—*Scraps.*

To give one the *miller*, to engage a person in conversation till a sufficient number of persons have gathered together to set upon the victim with stones, dirt, garbage, &c. *Vide* To MILL. Generally to hoot at, to handle roughly, to ill-treat.

The special correspondent of the *Evening News* appears to have been brutally maltreated at Exeter. Future generations of correspondents will do well to reflect upon his "two lovely black eyes," and to pause ere working up ultra-sensational matter about this city, whose inhabitants are of the rough and ready order. Upon one occasion they did not spare their bishop—the present Bishop of London—who fairly " got the *miller*" whilst addressing a meeting at the Victoria Hall.—*Bird o' Freedom.*

Miller, to (old cant), to rob or steal. (Gypsy), to convey away, remove, involving stealing. *Miller* in gypsy means also to mix; mingle, add up, count, colour, adjust. Hindu, *milana. Vide* To MILL A KEN.

Milling (popular), fighting.

With Tommy Sayers, too, I've felt
To box I would be willing;
I should have won his cups and belt—
I stand A1 at *milling.*
—*Bill Sykes: The Coiner's Song.*

(West America), explained by quotation.

He plunges into the fray with as much mastery of himself as possible, singling out the finest-conditioned head, wasting no balls, and, instead of keeping the frightened game on the run, executing the cowboy's device to check a stampede of cattle, namely, *milling.—H. L. Williams: In the Wild West.*

Milling cove (popular), prize-fighter.

Two *milling coves*, each vide avake,
Vere backed to fight for heavy stake.
—*Ainsworth: Rookwood.*

Mill, in the (army), to be a prisoner in the guardroom.

Mill-ken (old cant), housebreaker.

Mr. Wild, with much solemnity, rejoined "that the same capacity which qualifies a *mill-ken*, a bridle-cull, or a buttock-and-file to arrive at any degree of eminence in

his profession, would likewise raise a man in what the world esteems a more honourable calling."—*Fielding: Jonathan Wild.*

Mill-lay (thieves), burglary. *Vide* To MILL A KEN.

Mil-mil (Australian bush slang), see. *Mil-mil* is a blackfellow's word that the whites have incorporated into their slang, principally in the pidgin-English in which the whites carry on their conversation with the blacks.

" Here, Mahmy," said one to his chief, " here that been cut him head off. You *mil-mil* blood."

I shuddered. There, now that it was pointed out to me, on the very stone I had sat down on when stripping to search for the body, the blood-stains were plain. They spattered the dead leaves and stained the grass stalks.—*A. C. Grant: Bush Life in Queensland.*

Mill the glaze, to (thieves), break the window. *Vide* To MILL A KEN.

Mill the quod, to (thieves), to break away from jail.

Milltog (theatrical), a shirt. From the tinker *melthog.*

Millwash (tailors), vest canvas.

Mimming mugger (theatrical). From obsolete to *mime*, to mimic, play the buffoon. "A buffoon, who attempts to excite laughter or derision, by acting or speaking in the manner of another, a mean and servile imitator" (Ogilvie). Of this class are the ape-like animals who, in burlesquing the strongly marked peculiarities of eminent artists, hold them up to derision and contempt. "In the country of the blind, the one-eyed man is king," and amongst mimics, the monkey is legitimate monarch.

Mind your eye (popular), take care.

Mind your p's and q's (popular), observe the details of etiquette. Of *mind your p's and q's* Mr. Edward Fitzgerald, in the Australian Printers' Keepsake, writes, "This advice has a most distinct smack of its origin and extraction, and is now in general use in society which is probably unaware of the source of its obligation. Most unmistakably it originated in the pardonable confusion with which a beginner is likely to treat 'characters' so much alike as *p* and *q*, when first making their acquaintance in a reversed form. It is a near relation of 'to speak by the card,' to which it has a preferential claim on those who endeavour to fulfil the ceremonial law of politeness—etiquette."

Mingo (Harvard University), a chamber-pot. An amusing story in this connection is told of Harvard. Many years ago, some students wishing to make a present to their tutor, Mr. Flynt, called on him, informed him of their intention, and requested him to select a gift which would be acceptable to him. He replied that he was

a single man, that he already had a well-filled library, and in reality wanted nothing. The students, not at all satisfied with this answer, determined to present him with a silver chamber-pot. One was accordingly made of the appropriate dimensions and inscribed with these words :—

" Mingere cum bombis
Res est saluberrima lumbis."

On the morning of Commencement Day this was borne in procession, in a morocco case, and presented to the tutor. Tradition does not say with what feelings he received it, but it remained for many years at a room in Quincy, where he was accustomed to spend his Saturdays and Sundays, and finally disappeared about the beginning of the Revolutionary War. It is supposed to have been carried to England.

Minor (Harvard University), a water - closet. This term is peculiar to Harvard and is of classical derivation, from *minor*, smaller, "house" being understood.

Minor-clergy (popular), young chimney-sweeps.

Mint (old cant), gold. Also a sanctuary in Southwark for those who fled from their creditors. Hence "minters," the inhabitants there.

Miserere seats, in many churches and chapels seats so constructed that if the occupier went to sleep when sitting on one of them he tumbled off.

Misfit (tailors), said of an awkward man, badly built.

Mish (thieves), a shirt. From "commission," which see.

Mish it them (tinker), hit it hard!

Mishtopper (thieves), a coat. *Vide* MISH.

Mislain (tinker), rain, to rain. *Mislain* (or *miesli*, *misli*), in the Shelta or tinkers' dialect, also means to go. *Vide* To MIZZLE.

Miss (printers). In printers' parlance a *miss* is an omission to lay on a sheet in feeding a printing machine.

Miss Baxter (American), a person occasionally referred to in New England in reference to those who are "too previous," or too prompt in love-making, &c.

There was a nice young lady named *Miss Baxter*,
Refused a fine young man before he axed her.

Miss one's figure, to (common), to miss a chance, to make a mistake.

Miss the tip, to (circus), to fall short of an order, suggestion, intention, or object. This is used generally in slang, but in exhibitions it has a special application to the performer not understanding or catching the tip or word which indicates that he must act.

Missy baba (Anglo-Indian), a young lady; a term borrowed from the natives, *baba* being meant for baby. "Is Miss Smith at home?" was asked of a native servant by a visitor. "No, *Missy baba* in tub eating mango," was the answer.

Mistura God help 'em (medical), the title of an *omnium gatherum* of medicines, generally the collected dregs of several bottles, said to have been given as a last resource on the off-chance of some one of the many drugs having a beneficial (!) effect. From a story that a certain man who had a valuable mare apparently dying, gave her all the old odds and ends of medicine in his garret, labelled "*Fiat mistura, God help and cure her!*" The mare recovered, but, "singular to relate," every disease for which the medicines were intended came out on her one after the other!

Mitten (American), to give the *mitten*, to dismiss as a lover. Hotten confines the word to Canada. In Germany a discarded suitor is said to get a basket.

Had I only got her glove—
Without a g—— I'd have her love.
But the lilting jilting kitten,
Has bestowed on me a *mitten*.
　　　—*The Sorrows of Sam.*

Possibly from the old custom of throwing the glove down as a sign of defiance, or derisively bestowing a *mitten* instead of a glove as a keepsake. M. E.

Cobham Brewer, in *Notes and Queries*, suggests the Latin *mittere*, to send about your business. There is an obsolete adjective *mittent*, sending forth. Webster gives the phrase as colloquial English.

Mittens (pugilistic), boxinggloves.

Mivies (popular), landladies.

A lot of old *mivies* gone queer with the greens.
—*Punch.*

Mizzler or **rum mizzler** (popular), one clever at effecting an escape, or getting out of a difficulty. *Vide* To MIZZLE.

Mizzle, to (common), to go away, decamp, vanish.

"Come, come," the Saint answer'd, "you very well know,
The young man's no more his than your own to bestow—
Touch one button of his if you dare, Nick—no! no!
Cut your stick, sir,—come, *mizzle!* be off with you! go!"
The Devil grew hot—"If I do I'll be shot!
An' you come to that, Cuthbert, I'll tell you what's what,
He has asked us to dine here, and go we will not!"
—*Ingoldsby Legends.*

From the Shelta or tinkers' dialect (Celtic), *miesli, mislain,* to go. In the same tongue *needy mizzler,* a tramp.

" To *mizzle*—synonymous with drizzle—thick, fine, persistent downfall of moisture from a foggy sky. About George IV., and afterwards William IV., the vulgar punsters of the time indulged themselves in the punning witticisms that pleased the unfastidious public of the time : 'First they reigned, and then they *mizzled.*' The point of the joke consisted in the double meaning of the word *mizzle,* which signifies to disappear silently, to vanish. Thomas Hood used the word in the same sense."

. And then one *mizzling* Michael night,
The lout he *mizzled* too.
—*Laughter from Year to Year.*

Mob (thieves), gang.

Being with the nice *mob* (gang) you may be sure what I learned. I went out at the game three or four times a week, and used to touch almost every time.—*Horsley: Jottings from Jail.*

(Up-country Australian), a herd, a flock.

Occasionally they passed through a *mob* standing on the roadside, and John was greatly amused at seeing some of the young calves and steers advancing boldly to them with many airs of assumed anger.—*A. C. Grant: Bush Life in Queensland.*

(Popular), a young woman, a corruption of *mab.*

Mobs (thieves), companions.

Mobsman (thieves), pickpocket. Getting obsolete.

My cousin's a fence, with a crib in the Mint ;
My sister goes out with a *mobsman* so smart.
—*J. Greenwood: A Night in a Workhouse.*

Mockered (common), dirtied, defiled. Hotten defines this as "holey, marked unpleasantly." It is the gypsy *mŭkkado,* often pronounced *mockerdo,* or *mock-*

ered, meaning smeared, defiled, dirtied, spotted, and sometimes "painted."

Mods, short for Moderations, the intermediate examination at Oxford.

Mofussil (Anglo-Indian), the provinces, or the country stations and districts as distinguished from the Presidency, or the rural localities of a district as contradistinguished from the Sudder or chief station. The word (Hind. from Arab.) *mufassal*, means properly "separate," and hence provincial (Anglo-Indian Glossary).

Moging (tailors), telling an untruth.

Moisten.   *Vide* CHAFFER.

Moke, the costermonger's name for a donkey, first given in anger or contempt, or as an objurgation to urge the animal to go on ; but now more commonly used in affection for the useful beast. "It originally signified a pig, from the Gaelic *muich*, but has long ceased to have the objectionable meaning among the class who use it." Another derivation is from Swedish *moka*, quarrelsome, obstinate, sullen. Also *mocka*, dung ; both terms of abuse.

What the horse is to the predatory Arab, the donkey is to the costermonger—his all-in-all. The "coster" would sooner sell his wife in Smithfield, if the law would permit, than "swap" his *moke* at the cattle market.—*Diprose: London Life*

Moko, a name given by sportsmen to pheasants killed by mistake during September, before the pheasant-shooting season comes in. They pull out their tails, and roundly assert that they are no pheasants at all ; but *mokos* (Hotten). *Moko* is probably from "mock," or a humorous corruption of *macaw*.

Moles (up-country Australian), moleskin breeches.

Though our pants are *moles*, and apparently made
With the aid of a tomahawk ;
Though we are not in fashion's garb arrayed,
We can revel in tea and talk.
—*Keighley Goodchild: While the Billy Boils.*

Moll (thieves), a girl, woman.

At the head of the letter the following was written across the page : " Poison the *moll*."—*Greenwood: Seven Curses of London.*

A female companion, wife, or mistress.

The party congratulated him that his *moll* would be in good hands.—*Evening News.*

This word, from its resemblance to the nickname for Mary, is assumed to be the same. Compare with "poll," "polled up." It has been suggested that it owes its form to the gypsy Hindu *māl*, which means a female friend or ally.

Moll-sack, a reticule.

Molled (popular), in company with a woman.

Moll-hook (thieves), a female pickpocket.

Moll-rowing. Hotten says that this means "out on the spree in company with so-called 'gay women,' in allusion to the amatory serenadings of the London cats." It may be derived, and probably was, from *Moll*, and *row*, a noise. There appears to have been also, nearly a century ago, a very noted woman named Moll Roe, who is often alluded to in the "fast" literature of the time, and who formed the subject of a song; but whether this was not a pseudonym borrowed from the term, we are not informed.

Or whistle Moll Roe to a pig.
—*Irish Song.*

Moll-slavey (old cant), maidservant.

Moll, to, molling (common), to go with women, to act effeminately. To coddle up or cuddle. Dutch, *mallen*, to play the fool, to behave one's self wantonly. *Malloot*, a foolish girl or wench.

Molly (printers), "Mary." Practically a blank in jeffing with the nine quadrats, when no nicks appear uppermost in the quadrats thrown ; hence no count. (London slang), a young sodomite.

Molly Cotton-tail (American), a she-rabbit.

"Which of the girls did the Rabbit marry?" asked the little boy dubiously.

" I did year tell un 'er name," replied the old man, with a great affectation of interest, "but look like I done gone en fergit it off 'n my mine. Ef I don't disremember," he continued, "hit wuz *Miss Molly Cottontail*, en I speck we better let it go at dat."
—*Uncle Remus.*

Molocher (popular), a cheap hat.

Molo-man (pidgin), *i.e.*, *moro*, a Moor, a negro.

Molto cattivo (circus, theatre, Punch and Judy, &c.), very bad, doing badly.

Molungeon (American). Mr. Henry A. Wise once said, in the Legislature of Virginia, that a mulatto was the offspring of the young gentleman heir-apparent of an estate with one of the family or house servants, but that the child of a female field-labourer by a Yankee pedlar was a *molungeon*.

Monarch (popular and thieves), a man's signature or name. Literally the king, number one. Evidently a term suggested by exalted ideas of one's self-importance. This explanation is supported by the Italian cant term *monarco*, signifying I, myself, which has given the French *monarque*, same meaning. Also *montagna, mia madre*.

Mondayish (popular), disinclined for work, Monday being a day for amusement among workmen. (Clerical), used up, tired. A phrase that has its origin in the clergyman's supposed state of fatigue on Monday, after the work of Sunday.

Moniker, monacher (popular, thieves, and tinker), a man's signature or name. A corruption of "monarch," which see.

When the "box-man" reached out the tools, the new comer seized a pick-axe, which was immediately claimed by another man. The new arrival quietly said, "There's my *moniker* upon it."—*Evening News.*

Monk (printers). Mr. Edward Fitzgerald, in "The Australian Printers' Keepsake," writes:— "Sometimes a *monk* is the object of solicitude, an unsightly blackness caused by ' furniture ' showing, or undistributed ink. It is a saying manifestly originating with the venerable Caxton himself, and evidently alluding to the unwelcome intrusion of the gentlemen of the Scriptorium, near which portion of Westminster Abbey Caxton commenced his English labours." *Monk* is also applied to a proof which is too black, and "friar" when it is too light or grey. From the respective colours of their garments. *Vide* FRIAR.

(American), abbreviation of *monkeying*, trifling with. *Vide* TO MONKEY.

Monkery (tinker), the country. Adopted into common canting, and used especially by Punch and Judy men, itinerants, &c.

Monkey (turf), five hundred pounds. The cry not unfrequently heard in the ring of "The field a *monkey*," means that the layer is willing to bet 500 even against any one horse in the race.

Later on 400 to 500 was accepted, and finally seven *monkeys.*—*Sporting Times.*

(Common), to get one's *monkey* up, to rouse his anger. Hotten says " a man is said to have the *monkey* up, or the *monkey* on his back, when he is out of temper." Probably in allusion originally to the evil spirit which was supposed to be always present with a man. A variant in some parts is "to stroke the black dog down." *Monkey*-board, the step behind an omnibus on which the conductor stands. (Legal), *monkey* with a long tail, a mortgage. (Popular), a short jacket, a hod for mortar or bricks.

'Pon me sowl, I was sick, sore, and tired of goin' up and down the latther wid that ould *monkey* on me shoulder.— *T. Browne: Gilligan's on the Spree.*

(Nautical), the vessel in which a mess receives its allowance of grog. Sucking the *monkey*, explained by quotation.

" Do you know what sucking the *monkey* means?" "No, sir." "Well, then, I'll tell you; it's a term used among seamen for drinking rum out of cocoa-nuts, the milk having been poured out, and the liquor substituted." — *Marryat: Peter Simple.*

Also drinking generally, or abstracting liquor from a cask by sucking with a straw.

Her late lamented was only a low customs' officer, who had been bowled out sucking the *monkey.*—*Sporting Times.*

Monkey catcher (West Indian). Amongst the Jamaican negroes this signifies a cute, shrewd, and level-headed individual— one not too scrupulous in his methods, and who adds a spice of cunning to his cleverness. If a piece of work, or any matter requires special care and attention in its execution, they say, "Soffly *catch monkey*," meaning, take care, exercise tact, don't go blundering, that matter requires finesse and judgment to carry it through. Looked at in any light, the phrase is a curious one. In the first place, it is a good illustration of a certain rough and elementary shrewdness in the negro character; and further, is an example of the hold which the memory of African life still retains upon them, inasmuch as there are no monkeys indigenous to Jamaica, and the phrase is most likely of African origin.

Monkey on one's back, to get a (popular), to get out of temper.

Monkeys (printers), another expression used by pressmen to denote a compositor by way of retaliation for calling them "pigs."

Monkey shines (popular), eccentricities, queer actions.

How can human beings be guilty of such *monkey shines.—Detroit Free Press.*

Monkey, to (American), to play tricks, to trifle, to fool with, to tamper with, obviously from the mischievousness and trickiness of these animals.

It had on it, "Please don't *monkey* with this Indian-rubber trunk. It has loaded guns and pistols, and it won't stand any *monk."—New York Mercury.*

Also to make, effect, execute in any way. Used jestingly or sarcastically.

Andrew Jones he wuz er artis'
    On he high an' lofty scale,
Fo' he *monkeyed* wid de ceilin'
    An' de white-wash brush an' pail.
            —S. Keller.

"Wall, old hoss," I says to Meissonier, "how much do you git a squar' yard fer *monkeyin'* such a pictur as thet ar'?"— *The Hoosier in Europe.*

Monopolises the macaroon (masher), a new way of saying it takes the cake.

"Devilish fine gal, deah boy."
"Yaas, quite takes the cake, Cholly."
"Bah Jove, yass, *monopolises the macaroon*, don't cher know." — *Conversation Overheard in a Theatre.*

Mon. os. (Westminster School), abbreviation of *monitor ostii*, the Queen's scholar of the second election, who announces the hour in Latin at the close of school.

Mons (Winchester College). From the Latin *mons*, a mountain, a heap or crowd, a pile of anything.

Month (city), "a bad attack of the end of the *month*," in the city, is to have run through one's funds about the 20th, and to have to borrow for the remaining ten days.

Mooch (common), the robbers' *mooch* is that peculiar well-known step or striding walk of the brigand or bravo in a melodrama. On the *mooch*, *vide* To Mooch.

Mooch, mouch, to (general), to sponge, to slink away and allow others to pay for your entertainment, to look out for any articles or circumstances which may be turned to a profitable account; also for scraps of food, old clothes, watching in the streets for odd jobs, horses to hold. Loafing about in quest of anything that may turn up in the shape of amusement, strolling about to look at the girls. Also begging, explained by quotations.

He may while away the tedium of the tramp by *mooching*. *Mooching* is the art of getting what things you want to eat at different houses. A successful moocher must be a man of some imagination who can not only lie, but lie in a logical and plausible manner; that is not to be caught by the most rigid cross-examination.—*Detroit Free Press.*

Here I assume the proper *mouching* pose—stoop my head, bend my shoulders, . . . to look at, I am the incarnation of all that is forlorn; and I tell you I cannot get to the end of Bishopsgate Street without being stopped by a dozen people, all of whom thrust something into my hand.—*Thor Fredur: Sketches from Shady Places.*

To *mooch* is from old English *mooch*, *mich*, to creep softly about, to skulk, stroll, idle about, pick while strolling.

Moocher, moucher (popular), a street thief, a beggar.

My friend, the tramp, admitted with some excusable pride that he was considered in the profession a successful *moocher.*—*Detroit Free Press.*

Also one who "sponges" on acquaintances; one who slinks away and allows others to pay for his drink.

Moochy (Anglo-Indian), a man who works in leather in any way. The name of a low caste. Hindu, *mochi.* In English gypsy, leather is called *morchea* or *mortchy.*

Moolvee (Anglo-Indian), a judge or doctor of the law. Arabic *maulavi*, from the same root as *mūllā* (Anglo-Indian Glossary).

A pundit in Bengal or *molavee*
May daily see a carcase burn;
But you can't furnish, for the soul of ye,
A dirge *sans* ashes and an urn?
—*N. B. Halhed: Anglo-Indian Glossary.*

Moon (thieves), a month or month's imprisonment.

They ask the reeler if I was known, and he said no, so I was sent to Maidstone Street (prison) for two *moon.*—*Horsley: Jottings from Jail.*

Moonack (West Indian), probably of African origin. A mythical animal known to negroes only. To meet it, is to be doomed to madness or some lingering disease.

Moon-curser (old cant), a linkboy or one that under colour of lighting people robs them. Also termed a "glim-jack."

Mooney (nautical), not quite intoxicated, but sufficiently so to be unfit for duty.

Moonlight (American University), to make a rush for *moonlight* is to attempt to get the prize for elocution.

Moonlight flitting (common), leaving a house by night to avoid paying the rent. *Vide* FLY-BY-NIGHT.

Moonlighters (common), men in Ireland who carry out sentences of secret societies against individuals and perform their work of violence by night.

The road on either side is bounded with a low wall composed of ragged little slabs of stone, loosely laid and loopholed to an extent that would delight the heart of an Irish *moonlighter.—J. Greenwood: Tag, Rag, & Co.*

Moon-rakers (nautical), sails above the sky-sails.

Moonshee (Anglo-Indian), a secretary, a reader, an interpreter, a writer. It is commonly applied by Europeans specifically to a native teacher of languages, *i.e.*, Arabic, Persian, and Urdu.

Its authenticity was fully proved by Persian *moonshee*, who translated.—*Mill: History.*

Moonshine (common), deception, nonsense, humbug. (Old), gilded *moonshine*, sham bills of exchange.

Moonshiner (American), a smuggler, illicit distiller.

As both brothers had now escaped to the mountains, which are filled with *moonshiners*, it was thought that the Burrows had made good their escape.—*Chicago Inter Ocean.*

Moonshiny (common), deceptive.

The *National* publishes an extraordinary, and, of course, a very *moonshiny* summary of General Boulanger's programme as confided by the deputy for the Nord to a friend on Sunday night.—*Sporting Times.*

Moose-face (American thieves), a rich, ugly-faced man.

Mop (common), an habitual drunkard. From an obvious metaphor. On the *mop*, continually drinking. It may be interesting to remark that *mop* in its proper sense is from old French *mappe*, Latin *mappa*, a napkin. "Some suppose *mop* to be of Celtic origin, as we have Welsh *mopa* and *mop*, Irish *moipal;* but it is probable that these are from the English" (Skeat). It may be added that there are a great many Celtic words which have Aryan roots, and, of course, a resemblance to Saxon or English.

Moper (popular), a deserter. From *mope*, a spiritless person.

Mopped the floor (American), a common slang phrase, signifying that one man has thrashed another so completely as to have taken him like a broom or a mop, and swept or cleaned the floor with him. In speaking of Charles A. Dana, of the *New York Sun*, who is noted for the severity and savageness of his attacks, an admiring Western editor wrote, "Uncle Dana proceeded to mop the floor with his opponent."

When Smith
Came on to fight, he took him by the heels,
And *mopped the stage* with him until 'twas clean.   —*Brand New Ballads.*

At last the crisis came, when one fine day,
For some imagined fault, the boarder said
Unto the waiter, that unless he stirred
A little quicker, he would bung his eye,
And take him by the legs, instanterly,
And *wipe the floor* with him.
          —*Est Modus in Rebus.*

Moppy (common), tipsy. From "to mop" or "mop up," which

see. Some of the numerous synonyms are, "slewed, queer, tosticated, so so, been in the sun, muggy, murky, muzzy, fresh, glorious, bright in the eye, dull in the eye, overtaken, overshot, overdone, done over, lushy, tight, foggy, hazy, swipey, lumpy, obfuscated, groggy, ploughed, bosky, buffy, in liquor, far gone, sewed up, mooney, half seas over, disguised; drunk as an emperor, as a wheel-barrow, as David's sow, as a fish, as a lord, as a piper, as a fiddler," and the old expression "has a drop in his eye." "Boozy" and "hoodman" are now much in vogue among "mashers." The writer has seen a collection of nearly 300 synonyms for drunkenness, mostly American.

Mops (provincial). Statute fairs or "statties" are held, where servants seek to be hired. After the statute fair, a second is held for the benefit of those not engaged. This is called a *mop*, as it *mops* or wipes up the refuse of the statute fair, carrying away the dregs of the servants left.

There is hardly a clergyman or a schoolmaster in the Northern and Midland Counties who is not able to make out the strongest of cases against *mops*, "roasts," and "statties"—fairs or quasi-fairs, which were formerly very useful for the opportunities they afforded to farmers and housewives for annually hiring labourers and domestic servants.—*Daily Telegraph.*

Mop up, to (nautical), a metaphor, to drink or empty a glass. Also to whisk up, as wiping up with a mop.

The fourth I hooked but lost, and by that time the rest of the capricious tribe simultaneously ceased rising, and refused to be tempted. Had I been there earlier, I might possibly have *mopped up* the entire row.—*Sir Henry Pottinger: Trout Fishing.*

Mopusses (popular), cash, coin, money.

> He that has the *mopusses*
> May buy diamonds and topazes.
> —*Punch.*

Possibly a corruption of "mops," grimaces, faces. Compare with French slang *faces*, for coin. This is, of course, mere conjecture.

Mora (Anglo-Indian), a stool. In common use among the English in India.

Moral (popular). "That's a *moral*," equivalent to "that's a certainty." Short for a *moral* certainty.

> They must come a cropper soon,
> They muttered—*that's a moral.*
> —*Punch.*

Morfydite (American), a maritime pronunciation for hermaphrodite, generally applied to the so-called hermaphrodite brig, a vessel between a brig and a schooner.

Morris, to (old cant), to hang dangling in the air, to be hanged. (Theatrical), to make oneself scarce. Alluding in both senses to the quick motions of the legs in the *morris* (or Moorish) dance. Also used by tailors with a like signification.

Mort (canting), a woman. The same in old gypsy. Hindu,

mahar, a wife, woman. It is not improbable that the French word *motte* (*pud. mul.*), which has long been common in England for a woman, and that which the French word expresses, has caused the gypsies to add the *t*. The gypsies very commonly use *minj* for a woman. Tissot, in his work on Hungary, innocently mentions that *gali ming* (English-gypsy *kālo minj*) means a dark girl! This derivation is more probable than that from the Welsh *modryb*, a matron ; and *moryun*, a virgin, given by C. J. Ribton Turner in his " History of Vagrants and Vagrancy " (1887).

Mortar-board (University), the square cap forming part of the academical dress of all members of the university. Said to be a corruption of the French *mortier* cap worn by Presidents of Courts.

"And as your skill," resumed Mr. Tozer, "has been exercised in defence of my person . . . I will overlook your offence in assuming that portion of the academical attire, to which you gave the offensive epithet of *mortar-board*."—*C. Bede : Verdant Green.*

It may seem strange that an educated gentleman prefers to wander in the streets of Oxford in the evening, clad in horsey "checks" or bookmaker's stripes, in preference to the tattered gown and battered *mortar-board*, constituting the costume of an undergraduate.—*Bird o' Freedom.*

Also *mortar.*

Some of them wore a *mortar* on their heads.—*Fuller : Pisgah.*

'Mos (printers), an abridgment of the word "animosity," very often used by printers. " To show no '*mos*," is to express no grudge against a companion.

Moses, a man that for a consideration declares himself to be the father of another man's child. Grose says, " A man is said to stand *Moses* when he has another man's bastard child fathered upon him, and he is obliged by the parish to maintain it." This may be connected with a phrase given by Cotgrave, " Holie *Moses*, whose ordinarie counterfeit having on either side of the head an eminence or luster, arising somewhat in the forme of a horne, hath imboldened a prophane author to stile cuckolds *parents de Moyse* " (Hall). The *Moses* of Michael Angelo has decided horns, probably based on the head of Jupiter Ammon.

Mosh, to (thieves), dining at an eating-house, and leaving without paying. Also doing the *mosh* on the quiet. A corruption of " mooch," which see.

Moshkeneer, to (common), to pawn an article for more than it is worth. There are watches and articles of jewellery made for the special purpose of swindling, and which appear to be of solid gold or silver, but which are only covered with thin rolled metal. Probably from the Yiddish or German-Hebrew *mos*, money, and *kenner*, one who knows, one who is " fly," as in the word *kenner-fetzer,* a thieves' butcher. The word *moss,* it may be observed, has in slang taken a wide range, and is quite applicable not only to money or gold coin, but also to any kind of valuables.

Mosque (old cant), a church.

Moss-backs (American), old fogies, "fossils," men behind the times. People who are "groovy," and slow to learn or advance.

The Dodo didn't exsight as much curiosity as might have been expected ; but when I cum to look into the matter, I found a dozen or more county offishels with *moss* on their *backs* an inch an' a half long, and they had sorter promted the populace (out of jealousy) to look koldly upon my great livin' kuriosity.—*Detroit Free Press : Letter by Professor Brown Whyte.*

Mot (general), a harlot. Turner ("History of Vagrants and Vagrancy") says, "*Mot huys* is a brothel in Dutch, but *mot* is not a word of Dutch origin." It is, however, an old Dutch slang word, whatever its origin may be. In the "Wordenboek van Bargoensch," *mot* is given as *hoer.* "Te *mot* gaen." *Motkasse* is the true Dutch slang for a brothel.

Mot-cart (popular), a mattress. *Vide* MOT.

Mother Shawney (theatrical), a rude offshoot of the Mary Anne. An institution to compel a new member of a company to pay his footing. It was the custom for the novice to be served with a formal notice, usually written in a feigned hand, and running after this fashion :

"Whereas it has come to our knowledge that Joseph Greenhorn is an aspirant to Thespian honours, it is our good will and pleasure that the said Greenhorn shall provide on Saturday next, at the hour of nine, for the delectation of his brethren, my children, in their respective dressing-rooms at the Theatre Royal, Slumstone in the Mud, one bottle of brandy, one of whisky, one of gin, two dozens of soda, and a gallon of beer. Whereupon the boys shall drink said Greenhorn's jolly good health, and wish him luck in all his undertakings, present, and to come. The said Greenhorn is warned that disobedience to our commands will be attended with pains and penalties of the most stringent character. Given under our hand and seal at our Palace of Slumstone.

(Signed)
Robin Goodfellow,
Hon. Secretary.
Shawney × Mother,
Her Mark."

If the neophyte failed to obey this mysterious mandate, the following week he received a more peremptory one, the week after one more imperative still. If he still remained obdurate, he would find his dressing-case rifled and upset, his properties destroyed, his wardrobe ransacked, the sleeves of his dress-coat cut and tied in knots, his hat smashed, his boots filled with filth, &c. Of course, he met with an abundance of affected sympathy ; and, of course, no one ever knew who perpetrated these playful practical jokes. Puck, or Robin Goodfellow, was ubiquitous. There was nothing for it but to grin and bear, and pay.

This institution flourished for a considerable period, until a quarter of a century ago, when, one night at Liverpool, a young actor, who afterwards attained considerable celebrity, refused to obey *Mother Shawney's* behests, and catching Robin Goodfellow *in flagrante delicto* (*i.e.*, tampering with his dressing-case and wardrobe), gave the tricksy sprite a sound licking, and intimated that the dose would be repeated, if necessary. It never was necessary. From that time this charming institution frizzled away until it died out altogether, and *Mother Shawney* rests in peace in the lumber-closet of antiquity.

Mouchey (popular), a Jew.

Mouch, on the (common), strolling about in quest of amusement ; at Oxford, strolling about to watch the girls. For other meaning *vide* To Mooch.

But when once or twice she remained out
    so late,
That her people all night her return had
    to wait ;

And when *on the mouch* in the park she
    was met
While supposed to be "churching," they
    thought it, you bet,
      Somewhat strange !
      —Bird o' Freedom.

Moulder (pugilistic), a lumbering boxer who fights as if he were moulding clay.

Mouldy (naval), purser's steward, or assistant.

Mouldy grubs (popular), travelling showmen, mountebanks who perform in the open air.

Mouldy pates (street), servants in livery with hair powder.

Mouldy 'un, a contemptuous term for a penny.

The chief verger informed him that the fee was eighteen *mouldy 'uns* for maimed ladies.—*Sporting Times.*

Mount (thieves). Applied not only as in England to men who will swear falsely, but also to those who hire clothes out for disguise ; also to those who wear second-hand clothes even honestly. (Old cant), a bridge ; "stall on the *mount*," stop on the bridge.

Mountain - pecker (popular), a sheep's head.

Mounter (thieves), a false swearer. *Vide* Mount.

Mount, to (theatrical), to "get up" a piece, *i.e.*, to provide scenery, costumes, &c.

Mourning (common), a full suit of *mourning*, two black eyes ; half-*mourning*, one black eye.

Mourning shirts (common), flannel shirts, that do not require washing so often as others.

We say *mourning shirts*, it being customary for men in sadness to spare the pains of their laundresses.—*Thos. Fuller: Pisgah.*

Mouse (pugilistic) a black eye, now a common expression.

Poor Chinnery, our favourite "pug,"
    I fear came off but ill ;
He has a blister on his foot,
    'Twould take a pint to fill.
His "dexter ogle" has a *mouse*,
    His "conk's devoid of bark,"
The off-side of his "kissing-trap"
    Displays an ugly mark.
            —*Atkin: House Scraps.*

Mouse digger (Winchester College), a small pick-axe used for digging up fossils, &c., in chalk pits.

Mousetrap (turf), a sovereign. From the resemblance of the crown and shield to a set trap.

" No hunter in England can clear that water," replies the earl. "It's even betting—it's five to two on him—it's a monkey to a *mousetrap!*" rejoins the excited girl. "Don't be so slangy, Julia," remonstrates her father. "Papa, the *mousetrap's* mine."—*Daily Paper.*

(Old cant), marriage.

Mouth (old cant), an ignorant person, a dupe, one that gapes with mouth wide open ready to swallow anything. In French *gobe-mouches.*

One shall lead a horse about, and another shall look for a *mouth* that has a horse to sell or change.—*The Discoveries of John Poulter.*

Mouth-almighty (popular), a very talkative, noisy person.

Mouth-bet (American), when a man in gambling gives only a verbal promise to pay it is called a *mouth-bet.*

"Then, governor, I see you ten dollars and raise you the whole State of Vermont." The game ceased. *Mouth-betting* was not a success.—*Detroit Free Press.*

Mouthpiece (thieves), a counsel.

" You come from ' Brum' (Birmingham), don't yer ? "
" Yes ; I have got seven 'stretch' for a ' burst.' "
" Had you a *mouthpiece?* "
" No, I pleaded guilty. I expected to get off with a ' sixer.' "
" What did you get ? "
" Seven stretch and supervision."—*Evening News.*

Mouth, to have a (popular), to feel the effects of drinking alcohol; an abbreviation for having a dry mouth. One of the most general effects in the morning of taking too much alcohol overnight; another expression for this is, having "hot coppers" or "the coppers." This produces a burning thirst, for which a " brandy and soda " or a " Hock and soda-water," are the most approved remedies.

Move (common), a cunning trick or device ; up to a *move* or two, cunning, experienced.

Mow-beater (old cant), a drover.

Mower (old cant), an ox, cow.

Mozzy (Punch and Judy), Judy. Punch being known as " Swatchell."

M's and w's (printers). A man in a drunken state walking through the streets would be said to be making *m's and w's*, owing to his uncertain and zigzag gait, likened to the shape of these particular letters.

M. T. (railway), an empty carriage.

Muchee (pidgin-English), much, very; intensified as *muchee-muchee*.

My catch one spirit tell my all, but he can no be heard,
Some notha spilit hab got heah—he no can talkee word,
They makee *muchee* bobbely—too *muchee* clowd aloun',
They wantchee *muchee* bad one time to chin-chin Captin Bloun.
—*The Ballad of Captain Brown.*

"Massa he *muchee*-goody, Mississee she *too-muchee* goody—yunki Missee (young Miss) she *too-muchee-muchee* goody galaw —she givee my one dolla' cumshaw fo' time."

Muck (old cant), money.

Mucker (army), a term for commissariat officer, nearly obsolete. (Common), to go a *mucker*, to fail, to come to grief.

To go a fearful *mucker* . . . bad dash at anything and fails, whether he is thrown from his horse when taking a leap, or making "confusion worse confounded" of his college examination.—*C. Bede: Notes and Queries.*

From *muck*, dirt. It has been suggested that it comes from "run amuck."

Muck forks (common), a low term for the hands or fingers. "Keep your *muck forks* off me."

Mucking-togs (popular), clothes worn when mucking about in rain and mud. Possibly a play on macintosh.

Muck-out, to (gambling), to clean out. *Mucked-out*, ruined. The more modern synonym is "stony broke." *Vide* MUCKER.

Mucks, mux, to (American), to disarrange, discompose, to make a muddle or a failure of anything. "He made a regular *mux* of the whole business." "Don't *mux* my collar!" Provincial English *mucksen*, to dirty.

Muck-snipe (gamblers), one who has been cleaned out.

Muck, to (popular), to beat, to excel.

Muck train (army), an obsolete term for commissariat.

Mud crusher (military), name given to infantry men. In French *pousse-caillou*.

Mudding-face (popular), equivalent to muffin-face, or stupid. A muff.

She oped the lattice, and I saw that form of queenly grace,
And heard her very softly say, "Goodnight, *old mudding-face!*"
—*Ballad: She was True to Somebody Else.*

Muddler (turf), a clumsy horse, one who gets in a "muddle."

Mr. ——, who had the offer of the mount, declined it, thinking the horse was too much of a *muddler* to have any chance. —*Bird o' Freedom.*

Mud-hook (nautical), an anchor.

Mud-lark, a phrase applied to those who wade or paddle in the slush left on the shores of tidal rivers that run through great towns, in search of articles of little but still of some mercantile value, brought down by the drains and common sewers. The word is metaphorical, derived from the flocks of birds that sometimes come down to the shore on a similar errand in search of nutriment, and the fragments of waste food that sometimes reward them. A conveyer; other meaning explained by quotation.

He . . . became what is called a *mud-lark;* that is, a plunderer of the ships' cargoes that unload in the Thames.—*Mrs. Edgeworth: Lame Jervas.*

Mud-major (army), an infantry major, one not mounted, who commands a company on foot, on parade. The term dates from the recent addition made to the number of majors in an infantry battalion, which was increased from two to four.

Mud-pickers (garrison towns), garrison military police.

Mud pipes (popular), any kind of boots or shoes, but more specially applied to riding-boots or gaiters.

Mud player (cricketers), one who plays best when the ground is soft.

Mud plunger (streets), explained by quotations.

That rascal and his wife are street-singers and cadgers of the sort known as *mud-plungers.* Fine weather don't suit them; they can't come out strong enough.

Give 'em a soaking wet day, with the mud over their naked toes.—*J. Greenwood: Low Life Deeps.*

Except for professional *mud-plungers*—beggars whose harvest-time is when they can wade in the middle of the road, and in the pouring rain, with an agonising display of saturated rags, and mire-soddened naked feet—wet weather is unfavourable. —*J. Greenwood: In Strange Company.*

Mud-salad market (common), Covent Garden Market, so called from its filthy condition when vegetable refuse and slush prevail.

Mud-salad Market again. Not content with drawing a princely income from his toll on London's food supply, the Duke of Bedford actually refuses to pay for the sweeping-up of the thoroughfares, rendered necessary by their use as a part of "his" market.—*The Star.*

Mud-student, a farming pupil. The name given to the students at the Agricultural College, Cirencester.

Muffin (Canadian), explained by quotation. In reference to *muffins* lying warm and close.

If any young lady, not previously engaged, of course, found favour in your sight, you were at liberty then and there to constitute her your *muffin*, which, being interpreted, signified that by entering into such an arrangement, you might walk, ride, or drive *tête-à-tête* with her; that you had the *entrée* of her parents' house, those parents at the same time keeping obligingly in the background ; that at balls, no ill-natured remarks were made by even the most virulent old maids when you danced every dance together, . . the usual English winding up of such an extensive flirtation was by no means a necessity.—*Once a Week.*

Muffin-cap (popular), a flat cap similar to those of charity-boys.

Muffin face. *Vide* MUDDING FACE.

Muffin-worry, an old lady's tea-party (Hotten).

Mufflers (pugilistic), the old vernacular for boxing-gloves, the "mittens." They are supposed to have been invented by Jack Broughton. The *Daily Advertiser*, in February 1747, announced that "Mr. Broughton proposed, with proper assistance, to open an academy at his house in the Haymarket . . . and, in order that persons of quality and distinction might not be debarred from entering into a course of those lectures, they will be given with the utmost tenderness and regard to the delicacy of the frame and constitution of the pupil; for which reason *mufflers* are provided that will effectually secure them from the inconvenience of black eyes, broken jaws, and bloody noses."

Muffling cheat (old cant), a towel.

Muff, to (society). To *muff* a thing is to spoil it, make a mess of it, *i.e.*, to do it like a "muff."

You were *muffing* your birds awfully.— *Saturday Review.*

Mufti, in (common), in civilian's clothes. Originally Anglo-Indian, from a word signifying a priest. This is now a recognised term.

Blessings flow
From your bold eyes and brown moustache so tufty;
But why, sweet Benedictine, choose to go
So much in *mufti?*—*Punch.*

Mug (general), mouth, face.

His *mug* wore a confident smile, which some might esteem a bit bounceable :
These big 'uns are apt to be cocky, but even a Titan is trounceable.
—*Punch.*

It has been suggested that *mug* is from the old form *munkh* or *mugh* of the gypsy *muï* or *mooe* (mouth and face), but it probably originated in an ordinary slang simile. Another suggested derivation is from the Scottish *murg*, French *morgue*, a solemn, sour face ; Languedoc *murga*, a snout. Formerly mugs or jugs were made which exhibited distortions of the human face, but there is no evidence to show that the term *mug* arose from this circumstance, or *vice versâ. Mug*, a simpleton, a person easily imposed upon. Also a "jug," formerly a "mouth." In French, *cruche, bête comme un pot.*

Any man who is *mug* enough to take a 100-guinea watch to the Derby, does so at his own risk.—*The Globe.*

It might have been the jug—I know I was the *mug*,
That's why I seldom talk about it now.
—*Sporting Times.*

That man must be a maudlin dunce,
What wise men term a *mug.*
—*Punch.*

In turf parlance there is but little difference between the *mug* and the "juggins," except that the former is rather the more hopeless case of the two, the "juggins" being almost invariably a neophyte who may in time develop into a sharp, or, at any rate, into a being reasonably able to take care of himself on the turf; while the true *mug* seldom, if ever, emerges from mughood. Also a stupid financier who finds money for rotten speculations, and is not infrequently swindled by the knave who has led him into a fool's paradise.

Mugging (Winchester and other schools), staying and studying indoors. *Vide* To Mug.

Mugging hall (Winchester College), the hall where boys "mug," that is, prepare their lessons and exercises. *Vide* To Mug.

Muggins (popular), one easily taken in, a simpleton. Variant of "mug," as "juggins" of "jug."

Must ha' thought me a *muggins*, old man,
To ask such a question of 'Arry—as though
  grubbing short was his plan.
      —*Punch.*

Muggy (popular), half-intoxicated. *Vide* To Mug, to get tipsy.

Mug-hunter (thieves), one of a wretched horde (chiefly of women) who infest the streets at night to pick up and rob those who are made foolish (mugs) by their drunkenness.

Mug, mugged (Winchester College). A thing is said to be *mug* or *mugged* when it has a pleasant appearance to the eye, like a bat which has been well *mugged*, that is, well oiled and polished, entailing much labour. *Vide* To Mug.

Mugs (American), roughs and thieves.

"See 'em," said the man at my side; "there's *mugs* for you—look at 'em." "*Mugs?*" said I. "What are *mugs?*" "Hard characters," said he. "Those are thieves from the First Ward, the fellows that rob immigrants, steal cotton from the bales, go through the trunks that stray down by the riverside, and empty pockets on the ferries and excursion boats."—*Philadelphia Press.*

Mugster (Winchester College), one who works hard. *Vide* To Mug.

Mug, to (Winchester College), to work hard. From early English *mog*, to sit over in a discontented way, as of a boy sitting over his books. Also to rub oil well into a bat.

In one corner of school some one may be discovered *mugging*, *i.e.*, oiling his own or prefect's bat.—*Everyday Life in our Public Schools.*

(Popular and thieves), to strike in the face, to thrash, to swindle, that is, make a fool of one. *Vide* Mug. *To mug* oneself, to get tipsy. In this sense it is derivable from *mug*, a drinking vessel, in the same way as the French *gobeloter*, to indulge in drink, from *gobelet*. An ale-house was formerly termed a *mug*-house. Again, it may be due to a metaphor, as of one in a *mug*, provincial for mist. Compare with its synonyms, "in a haze," and "foggy," "muzzy," for intoxicated.

(Common), to criticise keenly, to examine in a minute and teasing manner. Possibly from slang *mug* for face, in which case *to mug* would nearly correspond in one of its applications with the French *dévisager*.

Mug up, to (theatrical), to paint one's face, or dress specially to impersonation. From the slang *mug*, for face. (Army), to work hard or "cram" for an examination. *Vide* To MUG.

Mugwump (American), explained by quotation. "*Mugwump* is an Indian word, and means a captain, or leader, or notable person. From this genuine original meaning it was an easy transition to the signifying a man who thought himself of consequence; and during the last contest for the Presidentship the name had a political meaning attached to it, by its application, in derision, to those members of the Republican party who, rejecting Mr. Blaine, declared that they would vote for his Democratic opponent, Mr. Cleveland, the late President. Such is the explanation, doubtless correct, given by Mr. Brander Matthews of New York. The name is now generally applied to those who profess to study the interests of their country before those of their party " (*Cornhill Magazine*).

Mull (common), failure. (Obsolete English), rubbish; to make a *mull* of it, to spoil it, to bungle, fail through awkwardness. *Vide* MULLOCK.

In *seats,* p'r'aps, her crew have the pull
o'er their rivals ;
But what if the pullers make *mulls ?*
—*Funny Folks.*

The public, how he bores or gulls,
This buzzing busy B.,
Starts maudlin' " Leagues," that end in *mulls,*
And pure fiddle-de-dee!—*Punch.*

Mulligrubs (popular), colic. From provincial English *mull*, to rub, squeeze, rub about ; and *grub*.

Peakyish you feel, don't you, now, with a touch of the *mulligrubs* in the collywobbles.—*C. Bede : Verdant Green.*

Also low spirits.

Mullock (mining slang), rubbish. From obsolete English *mull*, dirt, rubbish. *Mullock* is literally the moraine, the heaps of earth and other rubbish accumulated by glaciers ; from this it is applied to the refuse of mines, the heaps of earthy rubbish which remain after crushing, washing, and the other processes have been gone through. It also means type in bad condition, in Australian printers' slang. The metaphor here is from the mining refuse.

The Boss had got a set on him to set
The *mullock* of the whole establishment.
—*The Australian Printers' Keepsake :
The Legend of Lonely Gully.*

(Anglo-Indian), a nickname applied to members of the Madras Presidency service, as Bengal people are called " Quihis," and Bombayans, " Ducks."

It is ane darke Londe, and ther dwellen yᵉ Cimmerians whereof speketh Homerus Poeta in his Odesseia, and to this Daye thei clepen Tenebrosi or yᵉ Benighted ffolke. Bot thei clepen themselves *mullys* (*mulls*), from Mulligatawnee wh^{ch} is ane of theyr goddys from wh^{ch} thei ben ysprong.—*Anglo-Indian Glossary: Lately Discovered MS. of Sir John Maundevile.*

Multee kerteever (coster-mongers), corruption of *molto cattivo*, which see.

Mumble mumper (theatrical), an old, sulky, inarticulate, unintelligible actor.

Mum-glass (common). "A cant word for the monument in Fish Street, near London Bridge, in commemoration of the dreadful fire in 1666, which consumed the greatest part of the city" (Dyche and Pardon's English Dictionary).

Mummer (theatrical). This term, which properly signified a *mime*, buffoon, is now used in the slangy and deprecatory sense of strolling or inferior actor.

Stage slang is a thing of art, just as turf slang is. Every one knows what "the ghost walking" means, and there are a dozen and more phrases peculiar to "the" profession in England. Over here the same thing exists among the "cabotins," which word corresponds exactly with the English *mummers.*—*Bird o' Freedom.*

According to the best authorities, mummery is described as "low buffoonery" (Nuttall), or, "a low contemptible amusement, buffoonery, farcical show; hypocritical disguise, and parade, to delude vulgar minds" (Ogilvie and Webster).

The *mummery* of foreign strollers.—*Fenton.*

The same authorities describe a *mummer* as one who masks himself, and makes diversion in disguise, literally a "guiser," one of those village bumpkins who from time immemorial have gone from house to house, at Christmas and other festivals, spouting scraps of the old mysteries handed down by oral tradition. A guiser is described by Mitchell as "a person in disguise, a *mummer;*" and by Ogilvie as "a person in disguise, a *mummer* who goes about at Christmas."

The term *mummer* is also frequently applied derisively to a certain class of players. The application of the word in this relation is directly to be attributed to the feud between the equestrians and the actors.

About half a century ago certain players from the minor theatres were engaged by Ducrow to act at Astley's in the "Battle of Waterloo," "Mazeppa," and pieces of a similar character. These gentlemen gave themselves great airs when the equestrians came "'twixt the wind and their nobility," and were regarded by the horse-riders as highly objectionable interlopers. As a natural consequence, when the equestrians were compelled to officiate as supers for the glorification of the vainglorious players, considerable friction occurred, and much ill-blood ensued. The players affected to look down upon the equestrians with contempt, and had the good taste to dub them "mountebanks, horse dung, and sawdust gentry." The equestrians, nothing loth, responded to the compliment by christening the actors "cackling coves and —— *mummers.*" Recently, certain journalists, irritated, doubtless, at the social distinction accorded to eminent actors and actresses, have sought to degrade them in public estimation by stigmatising the entire fraternity, from the highest to the lowest, as *mummers.* It is indisputable, that from the time of the master upwards there have been so-called actors, and popular ones too, who are, and have been, neither more nor less than buffoons.

Mumming (old cant), explained by quotation.

At Abingdon fair there was a person named Smith who was the proprietor of a *mumming, i.e.,* a theatrical booth.— *Parker: Variegated Characters.*

Mummock, mummick (American), to handle any object. To handle or feel the person. "Don't *mummick* me that-a-way, Billy, or I'll tell my ma!" From the Dutch *mam*, the breast.

Mumper (popular), a beggar. *Vide* To **Mump.**

Mumpish, to feel (common), to feel dull, miserable, like one who has the mumps.

Mums (old), lips.

Why, you jade, you look so rosy this morning I must have a smack at your *mums.—Foote: The Minor.*

Mum, to (theatrical), to act; specially applied to strolling actors. In the quotation the word is used figuratively.

A nice stake for Mr. J. A. Craven, for whom the colt *mummed* successfully again in the Double Trial Plate yesterday. *—Sporting Times.*

Munches (tinker), tobacco.

Munds, muns (thieves), the mouth. German, *mund.*

The guests now being met,
The first thing that was done, sir,
Was handing round the kid
That all might smack his *muns*, sir.
—Parker: Variegated Characters.

Mundungus (popular), trashy, coarse tobacco. Spanish *mondongo*, black pudding (Hotten), seldom heard.

Mungarly (hawkers, strolling actors, &c.), explained by quotation.

Now, a lot of us chaps propose to assist you to-night, as it's the last one, in getting you up a rare full house, to help you and your school to some dinarly and *mungarly, i.e.,* money and food.—*Hindley: Life and Adventures of a Cheap Jack.*

Mungarly casa, a baker's shop or eating-house. *Mungarly* is derived from the Italian *mangiare*, to eat.

Mung news (American), news which has been heard before. Now obsolete. In its time it was equivalent to the more modern term "chestnut." From obsolete English *mung*, past of *ming*, to speak of, mention.

Munlee (pidgin), money.

Muogh (tinker), pig. Irish, *muck.*

Murerk (tinker and tramps), the mistress of a house, a lady. Perhaps it has a common origin with Spanish cant *marca*, a woman; Italian furbeschi *marcona;* French argot *marque.*

Mush (common slang), an umbrella. An abbreviation of mushroom, which an umbrella is supposed to resemble.

> He'll shelter "Floss" beneath his cape if
>   she hasn't got a *mush*,
>   When the tart is young.
> —*Song: When the Tart is Young.*

(American), stuff, nonsense, indifferent, uninteresting matter. From provincial English *mush*, dusty refuse.

> Great Jee-rusalem! a sweet time he'll have. Just fancy her making him slick up to the music of slow church bells Sunday mornings and marching him off, 'stead of having a good time at the gardens, to a straight-backed pew to listen to Gospel *mush!*—*Cleveland Leader.*

Mush-head (American), a stupid, witless fellow. Soft like *mush*, *i.e.*, rye, or Indian (maize) meal, boiled to a pap with water.

Mushroom - faker, mush - faker (tinker and popular), umbrella-maker or mender.

Music. *Vide* FACE THE MUSIC.

Mutiny (nautical), explained by quotation.

> Some, of course, were planning how they could get a bust-up of *mutiny* (grog) for the occasion.—*Tit-Bits.*

Mutton (common), used in the phrase "a bit of *mutton*," a woman. The term is used also in America. Also a woman of bad character, otherwise laced *mutton.* In French *veau.*

Muttoner (Winchester College), a hard knock on the thumb from a cricket-ball.

Mutton - fist (common), a large hand. The French call it *épaule de mouton.* (Printers), an index hand (☞) is generally called thus, probably from the fact of its being somewhat fat and shapeless.

Muttongosht (Anglo-Indian), the common English-Hindu for mutton, *i.e.*, "mutton-flesh."

Muttons (Stock Exchange), Turks 1873.

Mutton-walk, the saloon at Drury Lane Theatre (Hotten).

Muzz, to (Westminster School), to read.

Muzzler (pugilistic), a blow on the mouth.

Muzzle, to (popular), to get, to take.

Muzzy (popular), drunk, properly bewildered.

> Lord Frederick Foretop and I were carelessly sliding the Ranelagh Round picking our teeth, after a damned *muzzy* dinner at Boodle's.—*Foote: Lame Lover.*

> Excuse me, you've made a mistake, sir!
>   Not the first one you've made, I suppose.
> I'm a lady, that's straight, and I'm only
>   out late
>   'Cause it's late when the May Meetings close.
> None the less, I'm a bit wideawake, sir—
>   Taking care of one's self's only right—

And you can't make too free with a lady
   like me,
Though you are a bit *muzzy* to-night !
     —*Sporting Times.*

My (pidgin), I, me, mine. Sometimes we or ours.

Myall (up-country Australian), one of the wild blacks in the North of Australia. The name *Myall* is generally applied to those Northern tribes who in physique and ferocity are far more formidable to the white man than the feeble natives of the southern colonies. Many of them probably have a considerable mixture of the Papuan blood, a much more powerful and warlike strain.

The blackfellow now put his feet together and jumped about, imitating the action of a hobbled horse, upon which light at once dawned on the Englishman, who provided the delighted *Myall* with the articles in question.—*A. C. Grant.*

Mycetal duffer (theatrical), a "howling" or great duffer, so called after "a genus of the largest-sized monkeys of America, commonly called the howlers, from the loud sounds of their voices" (Nuttall).

My-deal, correctly *mo-diéle*, myself, I, us. In gypsy, *my-kokero*, myself, is often used for I, and in old canting men said "my

watch," for me. "That is beneship to our watch," that is very good for us. "The same system," says Turner, "prevails in the North Country cant at the present day, 'my nabs,' myself ; 'his nabs,' himself." This word, probably derived from nab (old cant), or nob, meaning head, is in theatrical slang "nibs." *Mo-diele* occurs in the following verse (Shelta or tinker) :—

" Cosson kailyah corrum me morro sari,
  Me gul ogaly ach mir,
  Rahet mãnent trasha moroch
  Me tu soste *mo-diéle.*"—

" Coming from Galway tired and weary
  I met a woman,
  I'll go bail that by this time to-morrow
  You'll have had enough of me."

Me tu soste is gypsy.

Mysteries (popular), sausages ; so called because no one is supposed to know what they are made of.

The peelers I scorn and defy,
While strings of these *mysteries* I wave
  round my head,
And then to the people I cry,
"Sassidges, oh, sassidges ! Oh, beef and
  pork and German !
Little gee-gee, little donkey, newly made
  to-day !
Sassidges, oh, sassidges ! oh, beef and pork
  and German !
Pussy, mi-aow ! doggy, bow-wow ! and
  beautiful sassidges, oh ! "
    —*G. Horncastle : Sassidges, oh!*

N

NAB (old cant), the head, in modern slang "nob." Explained by quotation.

There were particularly two parties, viz., those who wore hats fiercely cocked and those who preferred the *nab* or trencher hat, with the brim flapping over the eyes. —*Fielding: Jonathan Wild.*

I crown thy *nab* with a gag of benbouse, And stall thee by the salmon into clowes.
—*J. Fletcher: The Beggar's Bush.*

Scandinavian *nabb*, beak or bill, once a synonym for face and head.

Nabcheat (old cant). *Vide* CHETE.

Nab-girder (old cant), a bridle.

Nab, to (old English), now used in a slangy sense, properly to take, seize. In thieves' lingo, to receive or take in stolen goods. It is possible that as the "fences" or receivers were once generally Jews, the word in this sense is derived from the Yiddish *nepp.* (French thieves use the word *nep* for a rascally Jew, a receiver, or dealer in sham jewellery.) *Nepp-handel* is cheating by having false or inferior wares, a trade or place in which the goods are all "dickey." *Vide* RUST.

Nag drag (thieves), explained by quotation.

Detective-Sergeant Garner, I Division, stated that when the prisoners were removed to the cells, he went into the passage and heard them calling to one another. Hill said, "This will be a *nag drag.*" Mr. Chance: "What is that?" Witness explained that it was a slang term for three months' imprisonment.—*Daily Telegraph.*

Nag, to (popular), to scold or reprove, or "keep at" any one continuously. *Nagging* implies annoying or vexing one all the time, a "following-up" more than anything else. Probably from the Swedish *nagg,* to prick, *i.e.,* to spur or goad, as in the gypsy *chiv, chivvy.*

She's always, *nag, nag, nagging,*
And keeping up the game,
No matter where we go to,
She always is the same.
—*Ballad by G. Horncastle: Are You Coming.*

My mother-in-law has come to stay
For ever.
It's ten to one she goes away
For ever.
She's always on the *N.A.G.*
And makes a perfect show of me,
I'll chuck her out, I will, you see!
For ever!
—*Ballad by C. Williams: For Ever.*

Naggy is provincial English for irritable.

Na-hop (pidgin), *i.e.,* "no-hab" or "no have." This is given as meaning "without," *i.e.,* "deprived of," or "wanting," in the Chinese-English or Pidgin Vocabulary, according to the idea that not to have is (to be) without. "One piecee man *no-hop* dolla' dat man so bad inisy as *no-hop* lifey"—"He who is without money is as miserable as if he were dead."

Nail-box (printers), the place where printers would assemble to " nail " (which see) or " back-bite " any one. Very often re-fers to a neighbouring " pub." or other rendezvous.

Nailer, nailing (common), terms expressing excellence in any way; a *nailer* at football, riding, &c., a *nailing* shot. It is said of a handsome, clever, or fashion-able lady that she is a *nailer*. At school a *nailer* is a clever, good student. (Turf), a horse which cannot be shaken off, that keeps pace with his an-tagonists.

Still, she had some difficulty in getting rid of the attentions of Theodore, who is evidently a *nailer* when the going is a bit soft.—*Sporting Times.*

Nailing good thing (popular), a thing which is good and dur-able.

The Commander - in - chief inspected Ducker's portable hospital hut. . . . It is a *nailing good thing*, with ne'er a nail in it, nor even a loose screw.—*The Sun-day Times.*

Nail, to (common), to take, seize, detect. (Thieves), to arrest, catch in the act, steal.

"I see," said Mouldy, sagaciously nodding his head. "What was it that you *nailed?*"

"*Nailed?*"

"Ay, prigged, don't you know? Did they ketch it on you, or did you get clean off with it?"—*The Little Ragamuffins.*

(Winchester College), to de-tect, perceive, catch, secure. " To *nail* a man " is to go and

tell him to "sweat" or fag for some prefect; also to "watch out" or field at cricket, and to keep in balls at football, that is, to throw the ball back when it goes beyond a certain line. The *nail* is a nail planted in the middle of the wainscoting un-der "aut disce" in "school," under which any one *nailed* or detected telling a falsehood was placed for punishment. (Printers), to *nail* or "brass *nail*" any one is to "backbite." " No *nail* " would be an expres-sion of apology, or " I am sorry, but it is true."

Namo (costermongers), girl; back slang for woman.

Nammus (thieves and coster-mongers), look out, beware. " If a stranger should advance, the cry is given, *nammus*," and all signs of gambling are out of sight instanter. Also be off, let us be off. Said to be a corrup-tion of Spanish *vamos*, let us be off, which has given *vamose*, which see.

"Done!" said Aaron, and each held up their hands in fighting attitude, when, after sparring a bit for an opening, and not fancying the fellow, Aaron suddenly exclaimed *nammus*, thereby meaning, cut, run, take care of yourselves.—*Hindley.*

Nancy (military), the behind.

Nancy Dawson (popular), a name for a molly, an effeminate youth, apathetic, &c. A recent sketch of the characteristics of the mashers of the pre-sent day, which appeared in a leading magazine, represents two of the fraternity, who are very intimate, as always calling one another by girls' names.

I'll tell you of a fellow who's a very heavy swell,
Who fancies he's the idol of each fashionable belle,
And they call him *Nancy Dawson*,
And isn't he a caution!
Oh, Mr. *Nancy Dawson*, what a tricky man you are!
Oh, *Nancy Dawson*, can't you do the la-di-dar?
      —*Ballad: Nancy Dawson.*

The original *Nancy Dawson* was a noted prostitute, on whom there is a song still current among sailors. Proverbially a finicky, effeminate man is called a Miss Nancy.

Nanny (common), a prostitute. Probably from *nun*, meaning the same. *Vide* ABBESS.

Nanny shop (common), a brothel.

Nantee, nanty (showmen, itinerant actors, &c.), no, not any. Also be quiet, hold your tongue; from Italian *niente*, nothing. *Nanty* dinarly, no money, poor receipts, doing badly.

Nanty parnarly (low), used in Clerkenwell, King's Cross, and Leicester Square, and where there are a number of Englishmen and foreigners. If two men are talking confidentially and a third joins them who is not desired to overhear their conversation, one will say to the other *nanty parnarly*, meaning be careful. This is a corruption of the Italian *niente parlare*.

Napkin (common), a nap. "To be buried in a *napkin*," to be half asleep, not to have one's wits fully about one.

Nap nix (theatrical), one who plays for nothing. *Nap*, to take, receive; and *nix*, nothing.

Nap, nob, or **nopper**, the head. "One for his *nob* or *nopper*," pugilistic slang for a blow on the head. *Nappy* was a once favourite epithet for strong ale, equivalent to the French *capiteux*, heady, affecting the head from below. Derived apparently from the old English *knob*, a protuberance; German *knorpe*, a button, a swelling, a bud before its expansion into a flower. A picturesque mountain in the vale of Grasmere in Westmoreland is named Nab Scaur (*nab*, rising ground), and is more than once mentioned in Wordsworth's poems. Burns uses the word in his admirable poem of "Tam o' Shanter."

" Sit bouzing at the *nappy*,
   An' gettin' fu' an' unco happy."

Nap one's bib, to (popular), to cry, *i.e.*, to catch up one's *bib*.

Nap the regulars, to (thieves), to share the booty. *Vide* TO NAP.

And ve vent and fenced the swag that wery night, and afterwards *napped the regulars.—Lytton: Paul Clifford.*

Nap the slap. *Vide* KNAP THE SLAP.

Nap the teaze, to (prison), to be whipped. From *tees* or T's, the iron holdfasts to which criminals are tied when whipped in prison. From the shape of a T. *Vide* To NAP.

Nap, to (popular), to catch, receive. *Napp*, Danish, Swedish, to catch, snap, bite, &c.

While to another he would mention as a fact not to be disputed, "You *napp'd* it heavily on your whisker-bed, didn't you?" —*C. Bede: Verdant Green.*

Also to steal. To go *nap*, to take, sweep the whole. Probably from the game of *nap*.

Men raise bubble companies others to trap,
And when they're bowled out in it, don't care a rap.
But what is the reason? well, you can go *nap*.
It pays them much better than work!
　　　　　　　—*Music Hall Song.*

Nark, or **copper's nark** (thieves), a man or woman who is a police spy upon his comrades or class.

He had a *nark* with him, so I went and looked for my two pals, and told them to look out for S. and his *nark.*—*Horsley: Jottings from Jail.*

This seems to have some connection with the Dutch *narruken*, to follow about, spy, and *narrecht*, information. German, *nachrichten*.

Nark, to (thieves), to watch, observe, look after or into closely. *Vide* NARK.

Narrow squeak (common), just escaping or avoiding anything by the merest chance.

"Not exactly in danger," murmured Gommy, "but once, if I had not been possessed of great presence of mind, I might have had a *narrow squeak* for it." —*Sporting Times.*

Nash, to (old cant), to run away, default. Gypsy, *nasher*, to run away, to lose, hang, forget, spoil, injure, in all their variations; *nashered, nasherdo*, hanged on the gallows, executed, utterly ruined; *mandy nashered lis avrī my sherro*, I forgot it (lost it out of my head); *tiro wongurs sār nasherd avrī*, your money is all spent. Hence *nass!* away! *Nashermengro*, policeman. Hindu, *násána*, to destroy; *nash*, destruction.

Nask (old cant), a prison.

Nasty (common), spiteful, ill-tempered.

"But couldn't you get rid of them?" "Not without being *nasty.*"—*Pall Mall Gazette.*

Nazie (old cant), drunken; *nazie cove*, a drunken man; *nazie mort* a drunken woman. From the German *nass*, wet. The English lower classes use "wet" in the sense of drink, as in the well-known phrase "heavy *wet*" for porter or beer. "*Wet* the other eye," take another drink. "*Wet* the whistle," drink, or moisten the throat. "*Wet* Quaker," one who drinks on the sly. To make *nase nabes*, literally to make the head drunk.

Now I towr that ben bouse makes *nase nabes.*—*Harman: Caveat.*

Ndaba (South African), explained by quotation.

Ndaba, a pure Zulu word, meaning affair or business, is in frequent use even among the whites. With the natives, it has a most elastic signification, and *ndaba* may mean a wedding, a beer-drinking bout, a quarrel, a trial at law, or a hanging.—*G. A. Sala: Illustrated London News.*

Neap, nip (Suffolk), a turnip, is commonly used to denote a big watch. In French slang *oignon.*

Neat, spirits without water, &c. Liquor or spirit unmixed is "plain, straight, bald-face, reverend, pure, out of the barrel, bare-footed, naked, stark-naked, primitive, raw, in the state of nature, *in puris naturalibus,* unsophisticated, without a shirt, ah, don't mingle, aboriginal, unalloyed, untempered, cold-without, *neat* as imported, or *neat, simplex e munditiis,* uncorrupted, unmarried, virgin, and clean from the still." Stonefence is a drink of whisky plain, a raw recruit is a glass of spirits without water.

Neckcloth (common), the halter.

For the *neckcloth* I don't care a button,
And by this time to-morrow you'll see
Your Larry will be as dead as mutton.
—*Burrowes: The Death of Socrates.*

Neck, to (popular), to swallow; *neck-*oil, drink. Not to be able *to neck* it, not to have the moral courage to do or ask.

Neck-verse, chap. li. ver. 7 of the Psalms in the Vulgate, commencing *miserere mei domine.* The test of clerkship in those claiming benefit of clergy. The record was indorsed in such cases: "Po. se. cul. pet. lib. leg. u. cler. u. i. m. delib. or."—"Posset se (super patriam) culpabilis petit librum legit ut

clericus ustus in manu deliberatus ordinario." Puts himself on the country, asks for the book, reads like a clerk, is branded on the hand, and delivered over to the bishop; in later times, *deliberatur secundum statutum.* Such were branded with a hot iron on the brawn of the left hand. Ben Jonson escaped in this way. Sometimes it ran *cog. indict.,* &c., pleads guilty, &c.

The record of Ben Jonson's conviction for killing Gabriel Spencer in a duel in Toggeston Fields, has been found by Mr. Cordy Jeaffreson, whence it appears he saved his neck by these means :—

Letter or line I know never a one
Wer't my *neck-verse* at Harribee.
—*Scott: Lay of the Last Minstrel.*
The judge will read thy *neck-verse* for thee here.—*Clobery Div. Glimpses,* 1659.

Neddy (thieves and popular), a life-preserver or loaded cane whereby life may be taken. A donkey.

Needful, the (common), money.

Was ordered to pay a fine and costs. . . . Not having *the needful,* Pat went into retirement at the expense of the country.—*Scraps.*

Needle, the (general), vexation, stinging annoyance.

And it gives a man *the needle* when he hasn't got a bob,
To see his pals come round and wish him joy.
—*Song: You should never Marry.*

(Turf), "to get *the needle,*" or "cop *the needle,*" is to be so goaded by "the slings and arrows of outrageous fortune" that the bettor loses his self-control and "plunges" wildly to recover his money. (Athletics), to get *the needle* is to feel very nervous and funky.

Needle, to (common), to annoy.

Needy-mizzler (tinker), a tramp.

Negotiate, a modern slang expression often employed by sportsmen and the writers who chronicle their achievements to signify any attempt to surmount the difficulties they may meet with in the hunting-field.

They aspire to *negotiate* awkward fences.—*Bird o' Freedom.*

Neither buff nor bum (popular), neither one thing nor the other.

Nerve (Eton), impudence.

Nestor (Winchester College), a boy small for his age.

Netgen (coster), half a sovereign; from back slang for ten, and *gen*, a shilling.

Never hit the use (pidgin English-Chinese). 'M. Chung-yung *not hit the use*, *i.e.*, was idle, useless, or all in vain.

One night Wang-ti go walkee—he feel like lonely goose,
How all he study 'M. Chung-yung—he *neva hit the use.*
How some man pass an' catch deglee while he stick fass' behind,
Like one big piecee lock while waves fly pass' him on the wind.
—*Wang-ti.*

Never, never country, the (Australian), the Ultima Thule of civilisation. "*The never*, *never country* means in Queensland the occupied pastoral country which is furthest removed from the more settled districts" (J. S. O'Halloran, Secretary Royal Colonial Institute).

There is no such thing as an "Australian cow-boy." There is as much difference between the real *never*, *never* stockman and the Earl's Court article as there is between the real shell-back of the forecastle or the British tar in "Ruddigore." —*Globe.*

Never too late to mend shop (tailors). *Vide* HAND ME DOWN PLACE.

New-bug (Marlborough College), a contemptuous term to signify a new boy.

New chum (Australian), a new comer, a fresh arrival in the country.

More than once on the road, meeting these fellows tramping along, my driver or companion has recognised them as *new chums* by the cut of their pack.—*C. T. : Blackwood's Magazine.*

This expression is simply the English "chum" with a "new" prefixed to it. It is often used rather contemptuously.

Newgate fringe (thieves), collar of beard worn under the chin.

Newgate hornpipe (common), hanging.

And we shall caper a-heel-and-toeing
A *Newgate hornpipe* some fine day.
—*W. Maginn: Vidocq's Slang Song.*

Newgate knocker (costermongers), the mode of wearing the hair curled in the shape of the figure 6 over the ears. In vogue about 1840 to 1850.

Newgate-ring (popular), moustache and lower beard worn as one, the side whiskers being shaved off.

Newy (Winchester College), a " cad," that is, a fellow who was paid to take care of the canvas tent in " commoner " or school field.

N. F. (printers). This term is very largely used by printers in abbreviation of the words "no fly," to indicate an artful companion—one who is only cognisant of what suits him, and feigns ignorance of matters that apply to him.

N i b (American thieves), the mouth. *Nib* or *neb* is old English for mouth, snout, beak. Anglo-Saxon *nebb*, head, face. Icelandic *nebbi*, beak of a bird, nose. Swedish *snabel*, beak. Probably the origin of "his *nibs*," self, face, and mouth, being synonymous. In French cant *mon gniasse*, *son gniasse*, &c., mean myself, &c., and seem to be abbreviated from *ma tignasse*, my hair, that is, head. (Printers), an expression generally applied to indicate a silly person, otherwise a " mouth," which see.

Nibbler (popular), a petty thief.

Nibble, to (popular), to take or steal.

Nibble, to have a (tailors), to have the best of the bargain, or an easy, well-paid job.

Nib-like (thieves and costermongers), gentlemanly. *Vide* NOBBY.

Nibs. *Vide* HIS NIBS.

Nickers, wild young fellows or mohawks who, in the eighteenth century, when the watch of London was composed of old and feeble men, amused themselves by traversing the streets howling and shouting.

Nick, to (thieves), to steal. " He that *nicks* and runs away will live to *nick* another day," inscribed in a prison cell.

That there cove wot you're a-speaking of . . . what had he been *nicking?—J. Greenwood: Dick Temple.*

Originated from *nick*, to cut, *i.e.*, cutting away pockets. Also to apprehend, arrest.

" Well, ' Jones,' I see you are Robinson this time. What have you got ? "
" Ten stretch and my ticket."
" What did you get *nicked* for this time ? "
" Me and my pal were buckled by the —— coppers as were going to the —— fence with the —— swag."—*Evening News.*

Nigger spit (popular), the lumps in Demerara sugar.

Nightshade (popular), or deadly *nightshade*, a shameless prostitute of the very lowest class.

Nimmer (thieves), thief.

Nimshod (popular), a cat. The allusion is obvious.

Nim, to (thieves), to steal; old English slang *nim*, to take;

same root as the German *neh-men.* Anglo-Saxon *niman.*

Ninepence, right as (popular), means perfectly correct, apparently a corruption from "right as ninepins," which are carefully set up in proper rhomboidal disposition (A. Smythe Palmer).

Nine shillings (colloquialism), cool audacity. Said to be from French *nonchalance,* but it must be noted that *nine,* one of the mystical numbers (three, trinity, represents a perfect unity, twice three is the perfect dual, and thrice three is the perfect plural), occurs in many phrases as indicating an exhaustive plural, perfection or completion, as a *nine* days' wonder, *nine* tailors make a man, dressed up to the *nines,* &c.

Ning-nang (horse-coupers), a worthless thoroughbred.

Nip (old cant), a pickpocket.

One of them is a *nip.* I took him in the twopenny gallery at the Fortune.—*Roaring Girl.*

Nip and tuck (Cornwall), a close contest. An old term in wrestling. *Nip,* to seize, and *tuck,* to chuck or throw.

Speaking of bust-ups, it appears to be *nip and tuck* between Ed. Wolcott, Scott Lee, and the Cincinnati banks. As the score stands now it is a dead tie.—*The Solid Muldoon, Otway, Colorado.*

Also "nip and go tuck."

I've had a terribul fit of the ager since I writ yer last, and one time I thought it was about *nip and go tuck* wether the ager or natur wud whip.—*Major Jack Downing.*

Nip-cheese (nautical), purser's steward. Also a miser.

Nipper (popular), a baby, a child. Also a small draught. One who goes in for sharp practice. The metaphor is in *nipping,* grasping or squeezing a man more than the bargain purports.

"Like enough," returned Stone. "That accounts why he has the credit of being such a *nipper.*"—*A. C. Grant: Bush Life in Queensland.*

Also a pickpocket; formerly a cut-purse. (Marlborough College), a little cad. (Costermonger), the youngest of lads employed by costermongers. (Popular and thieves), explained by quotation.

"Dowse the glim! here come the *nippers.*"

That a *nipper* was a policeman, I well knew.—*The Little Ragamuffins.*

Nip, to (old cant), to take, seize, steal, apprehend.

Meanwhile the cut-purse in the throng, Hath a fair means to *nyp* a bung.
—*Poor Robin,* 1740.

If we niggle or mill a bousing ken,
Or *nip* a bung that has but a win,
Or dup the giger of a gentry cofe's ken,
To the quier cuffing we bing.
—*T. Dekker: Lanthorne and Candlelight.*

Nix or nicks (thieves), nothing. The German *nichts.*

In a bright check suit with staring squares,
And a "topper" of striking grey,
The magsman fly to the course repairs
In quest of "mugs" as prey.
In his "exes" being nil our friend confides,
His "brief" he snatches and for *nix* he rides.

—*Bird o' Freedom.*

It won't do, I say, to stand here for *nicks.—Parker: Variegated Characters.*

Used by French thieves. Spanish cant *nexo ;* Italian *niba, niberta.*

Nix my dolly (thieves), never mind.

> *Nix my dolly*, pals, fake away !
> —*Ainsworth : Rookwood.*

Niz priz (legal), a writ of *nisi prius.*

Nizzie (old cant), a fool.

Nob (common), the head, originally pugilistic. From *knob* or *nub*, the nape of the neck.

> The coachman he not likin' the job
> Set off at a full gal-lop,
> But Dick put a couple of balls in his *nob*
> And prevailed on him to stop.
> —*Romance from Pickwick Papers.*

> I went jest for a lark, nothink else, and
>   wos quietly slinging my 'ook,
> Wen a bit of a rush came around me, a
>   truncheon dropped smack on my *nob*,
> And 'ere I ham, tucked up in bed, with a
>   jug of 'ot spruce on the 'ob.
> —*Punch.*

To scuttle your *nob*, to break your head.

> Soon I'll give you to know, you d——d
>   thief,
> That you're cracking your jokes out of
>   season,
> And scuttle your *nob* with my fist.
> —*Burrowes : The Death of Socrates.*

A great swell, a man of high position. Abbreviated from great *nob* (*nob*, head). In Parisian popular slang *grosse tête.*

> I came to London—p'rhaps I'd better say
>   how I begun,
> For no nabob was half such a *nob*,
> As the Shallaba'lah Ma'rajah.
> —*Punch.*

Vide ONE FOR HIS NOB.

No battle (printers), no good; not worth while.

Nobba saltee (costermongers), ninepence. From *nove soldi.*

Nobber, nobbler (pugilistic), a blow on the "nob" or head.

Nobbet, nobbing, to collect, or collecting money. "A term much used by buskers," says Hotten.

Naubat, in the language of the Hindu Nāts, or musical gypsies, signifies, time, tune, and instruments of music sounding at the gate of a great man at certain intervals. *Nobbet*, which is a gypsy word, well known to all itinerant negro minstrels or tavern singers, means to go about with music, to get money, or to take it in turn. It is manifestly enough of Indian origin. "To *nobbet* round," means to go about by turns to collect.

Nobbing slum (showmen), the bag for collecting money. This is specially used by Punch and Judy men.

Nobbler, thus described by Hindley:—"In my young days there used to travel about in gangs, like men of business, a lot of people called *nobblers*, who used to work the thimble and pea rig, and go 'buzzing,' that is, picking pockets, assisted by some small boys. These men travelled to markets, fairs, and races, and dressed for the most part like country farmers, in brown top-boots, &c. The race of *nobblers* is now nearly extinct, as the old ones have died out, and the younger hands have either turned betting-men or burglars." (Australian), a glass of spirits, literally that *nobbles*, *i.e.*, throttles, kills you.

The other proceeded in the most correct bush style. Every now and then uttering a wild cry, and dashing his spurs into his nag's sides, he would fly along at his top-most speed, only to pull up again at the nearest public-house, to the verandah of which his horse's bridle was hung until he had imbibed a *nobbler* or two. — *A. C. Grant: Bush Life in Queensland.*

(Rodfishers), the *nobbler*, the gaff, *i.e.*, that which gives the finishing blow, that kills.

Then after one alarming flurry on the top of the water, my left hand slips the landing-net under him, and his final struggles are shortly ended with a single tap of the *nobbler.—Sir Harry Pottinger: Trout Fishing.*

Nobble, to (turf), to incapacitate a horse from starting or from winning a race by previously drugging, laming, or otherwise injuring him.

It is no use blinking the matter. The horse was *nobbled*—by whom it does not concern us to conjecture.—*Bird o' Freedom.*

From old word *nobble*, to beat or rub ; also *nubble*, to strike, bruise with fist, or to *nub* (which see), to hang, throttle.

(Popular and thieves), to cheat, outwit, overreach, *i.e.*, to beat.

Don't you fancy the hunemployed bunkum has *nobbled* me: not such a mug ! —*Punch.*

Also to throttle, kill.

There's a fiver in the puss, and nine good quid. Have it. *Nobble* him, lads, and share it betwixt you.—*J. Greenwood: Dick Temple.*

Nobby, nobbish (popular and thieves), fine, stylish ; derivable from *nob*, great *nob*, which see.

Yah, pitch us over yer red slang ! Take orf that ere *nobby* coat !—*Punch.*

"Look here, mate," said another, "they've reformed all that now. The old Jew in Dudley Street has got the sack. You know it ain't a year since I 'chucked up' and I got my duds at the society in Charing Cross, and a real *nobby* suit they were until a shower of rain came on and then you should have seen what a scarecrow I looked."—*Evening News.*

Nob thatch (popular), the hair.

Nob thatcher (popular), a peruke-maker.

Noddle (popular), the head. Probably from *nod.* Used by Shakspeare. *Vide* "Taming of the Shrew," act i. scene 1.

Doubt not, her care should be
To combe your *noddle* with a three-legg'd stool.

Noffgurs (London), prostitutes.

Wrong 'uns at the "Wateries,"
Noffgurs at the Troc,
Schiksas at the Umperies,
Pastry in a frock.
Parties fines at Purfleet,
Petites in the "Square,"
Coryphées by Kettner,
Tartlets anywhere.
—*Bird o' Freedom.*

No flies. *Vide* FLIES.

No kid. *Vide* KID.

Nommus or **namous** (costermongers), be off.

No moss (tailors), no ill-feeling or animosity.

No name, no pull (tailors), signifies if names are not mentioned there can be no libel, or if I do not mention his name he cannot take offence, unless he likes to apply the remarks to himself.

Nonsense (Eton School).

The present Provost of King's, then Lower Master at Eton, on reading over the names of boys who had gained their remove, I remember, quite impressed us with his regal position when he announced that King-Harman was monarch of *Nonsense*. All old Etonians will remember that *Nonsense* was a small division of the third form.—*Standard.*

Noodle (common), simpleton.

The chuckling grin of *noodles.—Sydney Smith.*

In society a foolish man is called *noodles. Noodle* is probably from "nod," like "noddle" and "noddy," because a person who constantly nods to assent is looked upon as being foolish.

Noras (Stock Exchange), Great Northern Railway Def. Ord. Stock.

No repairs (common), said of a set-to or struggle, where the parties rush heedlessly into the fray ; neck or nought.

Norping (theatrical), quoting pathetic, thrilling phrases that will "fetch" the gallery; termed also "piling it up."

North (common), too far *north* for me, too clever, knows too much.

In reference to Yorkshiremen and Scotchmen. The French say of a person who is confused, perplexed, "il a perdu le nord."

Nose (thieves), a spy or detective, *i.e.,* one with his nose on the scent like a bloodhound.

How would they know that there wasn't a *nose*—that is, a detective p'leceman—there in disguise.—*J. Greenwood: Dick Temple.*

Nose-bag (waiters), a visitor at a house of refreshment who carries his own victuals.

Nosender (popular), a blow on the nose. Originally pugilistic.

"You see, sir," said the Pet, "I ain't used to the feel of it, and I couldn't go to business properly, or give a straight *nosender,* nohow."—*C. Bede: Verdant Green.*

Noser (popular), a blow on the nose.

It was a *noser,* and no mistake about it, and the ruby spurted in all directions.— *Hindley: Life and Adventures of a Cheap Jack.*

Nose, to (thieves), to give information to the police, to turn approver, to watch.

Nose warmer (common), a very short black pipe. In French *brûle-gueule.*

Noter (Harrow School), a notebook.

Not for Joe, or **Joseph,** used to intimate that one does not intend or care to do, or have anything requested.

Not half bad, an expression of approval.

Joking apart, *"l'Aine"* is *not half a bad piece.—Punch.*

The French say similarly of a man, "il n'est pas la moitié d'un sot," meaning he is no fool.

Notions (Winchester College), words, phrases peculiar to the "men" of Winchester College.

Not much of a shower (American), a popular phrase, used whenever a political opponent or "any other man" makes light of a great defeat.

Not much of a shower.—With all their efforts, and with many political circumstances in their favour, the Republicans have been unable to create a reaction of any consequence whatever. — *Richmond Whig.*

It is said that while Noah was building his ark a certain man used to visit him daily and laugh at his "fad" of constructing such a boat. But when the rain began, and the flood rose till the scoffer's chin was just above water-level, his tone changed, and he humbly entreated to be taken on board. To this Noah would in nowise assent, when the man, turning his back indignantly, walked off exclaiming, "Go to thunder with your old ark. I don't believe there's going to be *much of a shower !*"

Nowhere (common), to be *nowhere*, to be in a state of utter (comparatively speaking) inferiority or insignificancy for the time being. From a racing phrase ; horses not placed in a race, that is, which are neither first, second, nor third, are said to be *nowhere.*

The brave panther when he has once crossed the threshold of that splendid damsel (who, by the way, is a thief, and addicted to drinking brandy by the " bumper ") is, vulgarly speaking, *nowhere.—J. Greenwood : Seven Curses of London.*

Nozzle the bottoms, to (tailors), to shrink the front of trousers. Also to pawn them.

Nubbing chit (old), the gallows.

When he came to the *nubbing chit,*
He was tucked up so neat and so pretty.
—*R. Burrowes : The Death of Socrates.*

Nub, to (thieves), to hang ; from *nub,* the nape of the neck.

All the comfort I shall have when you are *nubbed* is that I gave you good advice. —*Fielding: Jonathan Wild.*

Nuff (soldiers), to have one's *nuff,* means to have had more drink than is good for one, *i.e.,* enough.

Nursery (turf), a race for two-year-olds only, and almost always a handicap. (Billiards), when all three balls are close together, and the player, by cannoning, scores several times without materially altering the position of the balls, these scores are termed a "*nursery* of cannons."

In this latter run the balls touched when he had made 42, but he soon got them together after they had been spotted, and made a run of 23 *nursery* cannons.—*Evening News.*

Nurse, to (billiards). *Vide* NUR-SERY. (Omnibus people), to *nurse* an omnibus, to try and run it off the road. This is done by sending a rival omnibus close behind, or two omnibuses are placed, one before, the other behind an opposition omnibus to prevent it picking up any passengers.

Nut (general), head. *Noisette* (nut), for head, occurs in the French slang phrase "avoir un asticot dans la noisette," to be off one's *nut*, *i.e.*, crazy. Chaucer has *not*-hed, a head like a *nut*.

A *not*-hed hadde he, with a broune visage.
—*Canterbury Tales.*

Nut-cracker (popular), sharp blow over the head.

Nuts on (popular), partial to, very fond of.

Nutted (popular), deceived by a person who professed to be "nuts on you."

I ain't *nuts on* sweaters myself,
And I do 'ate a blood-sucking screw,
Who sponges and never stands Sam,
And whose motto's "all cop, and no blue." —*Punch.*

From the phrase "that's *nuts* to one," *i.e.*, a great treat, a thing one is partial to. *Nut* has here the sense of a dainty morsel, from *nut*, a sweetbread, or the lump of fat called the Pope's eye ; the *nut* of a leg of mutton (*noix* in French, same meaning, hence *la noix*, the best part, dainty morsel).

Nutty (old), nice.

Who on a lark with black-eyed Sal (his blowing),
So prime, so swell, so *nutty*, and so knowing.
—*Byron : Don Juan.*

O

O (printers), abbreviation for word "overseer." Generally used as a note of warning on his approach.

Oak (University). An undergraduate's rooms at college are enclosed by double doors. The outer one is called his *oak*, being made of extra strength to meet the rough usage usually in store for it. A man is said to "sport his *oak*" when he locks his outer door. The expression has become common for to be "not at home" to visitors.

Oar (nautical), "to shove in an *oar*," to intermeddle, or give an opinion unasked.

Oat (popular), used in the phrase "I never got an *oat* of it," I never got an atom of it. From the small size of an *oat*. Compare with the French "n'y voir *goutte;*" "point," not at all, from *punctum;* the old *mie*, same meaning, from *mica*, a crumb ; and the Latin *ne-hilum*, which became *nihil*, nothing, from *hilum*, a black dot in a bean.

Oats (American), "to feel his *oats*," to be lively and full of spirits. An expression taken from the stables. When a horse is well fed and in good condition, he feels his *oats*.

Oat stealer (popular), an ostler.

Ob (Winchester College), for *obit*.

Obfuscated (common), drunk.

She is scarcely for a moment off the stage, and she appears in half a dozen different disguises; she climbs up a ladder; she gets *obfuscated* by drinking a bottle of *liqueur*.—*Daily Telegraph*.

Observationist (thieves), one who looks out tempting objects for the skilful thief to steal, &c. Generally pedlars, hawkers, &c.

Ochives (old cant), bone-handled knives. *O chiv*, the knife, in gypsy.

Ochre (roughs), money. From the colour of gold.

Sport your *ochre* like a man,
I'm the cove that keeps the tater can.
—*Old Song*.

O'clock (popular and thieves), to "know what's *o'clock*," to be wide awake. Synonymous with "up to the time of day."

Our governor's wide awake, he is. I'll never say nothin' agin him, nor no man; but he knows what's *o'clock*, he does, uncommon.—*Charles Dickens: Sketches*.

October (pugilistic), jocular for blood, being short for *October* ale, the body being the beer-barrel.

While to another he would mention as an interesting item of news, "Now we'll tap your best *October*."—*C. Bede: Verdant Green*.

Oddment (printing), said of a book that ends on an odd leaf. (Linen-drapers), short pieces left from rolls of stuff, linen, cloth, &c.

Odds (turf), an imaginary scale of arithmetical chance, arbitrarily fixed by the bookmakers in respect of the prospects of any horse winning any future event on which their customers may wish to bet. (Common), "what's the *odds*," what is the consequence; "it's no *odds*," it's of no consequence.

Odno (roughs and thieves), back slang for *no do*. Riding on the *odno*, travelling in a railway train without paying the fare. *Vide* DUCK.

Off colour (society), out of health, out of form, not oneself, unable to do things as well as usual. Alluding to a pale face, or a phrase borrowed from the lapidary, who speaks of diamonds as being *off colour*.

When a man has not slept a wink for over a week it is not remarkable that he should look a little *off colour*, but when a constant and not-to-be-escaped brain jangle is added to insomnia, as was the case with the famous Q.C., great ravages are worked at the double.—*The World*.

The arbitrator listened to both sides separately, and soon found that each was a bit *off colour*. Said Billy to the German Sheenie, "You know you cannot show a clean bill of health."—*Sporting Times*.

Mr. —— struck me as a bit *off colour* in his acting on that particular evening. It was, however, an anxious time, no doubt. —*Fun*.

(Printers), a term frequently used by pressmen when they

feel like "St. Monday," and desire a "miche." Derived probably from the fact that a man thus shirking work would be off from inking, &c., the type for printing. It is now used in the United States to indicate any kind of inferiority or defect in men or objects.

Off his base (American), out of his mind, insane, queer.

A Brooklyn professor has been investigating cats and dogs, and he finds just as many cranks and fools among them as among human beings. He says that every fourth cat is *off her base*, while every ninth dog is a sort of fanatic.—*Detroit Free Press.*

Off his cocoa-nut (popular), crazy, mad.

Off his dot (popular), crazy, mad.

Off his kadoova (Australian popular), off his head, insane. *Off his kadoova,* "off his head," "off his chump," or simply "off," all convey the same idea—as a train being off the rails, or a man off his play.

And at the very chapel-door began a free fight, because a man had tried to prove a man wrong who said he was *off his kadoova.—New South Wales Paper.*

Off his nut (common), weak in the head, crazy, mad. (American), illogical, cracked. Also applied to any one who behaves eccentrically or obstinately, or who presses his opinions on others in an asinine manner.

Off his onion (costermongers), imbecile, cracked.

I've a chap on the book now for a hundred and twenty who's gone clean *off his onion* betting.—*Sporting Times.*

Off his own bat (common), by his own exertions; same as on his own hook.

Off his saucer (Australian), tired, not in the humour, out of sorts.

Office (general), giving or tipping the *office,* warning; giving a hint dishonestly to a confederate.

And then, in a word or two that none of the outsiders can understand, the conductor gives the *office* to his driver, who sets the picter of good behaviour, you may depend, till the point of danger is passed.—*J. Greenwood : Low-Life Deeps.*

Information.

Good old Baron, I will still stick to thee. Eurasian has gone up, and has gone down, the *office* having been given that John Hammond was going for Quicksand.—*Evening News.*

They gives the public the *office,* and the public believes 'em, bust 'em !—*J. Greenwood : Seven Curses of London.*

Office is a provincial corruption of *efese* (Anglo-Saxon), the *eaves* of a house ; old English, *ovese.* Hence, perhaps, the phrase, "to give the *office*," as of a person who gives information, the result of *eaves*-dropping.

Office sneak (common), one who sneaks into offices to steal coats and umbrellas.

Offish (common), distant, not familiar (Hotten).

Off its feet (printers), a reference made by printers when type does not stand square through bad workmanship or "locking up."

Off one's chump (common), crazy. *Vide* CHUMP.

"Young man," said the littérateur, as a light dawned in upon him, "you're *off your chump*. I don't want a razor to shave with, I want a raiser that will take me upstairs to bed without having to walk."—*Bird o' Freedom.*

Then I got ill, an' know'd nothing for weeks. They said I was *orf my chump.* —*Fergus W. Hume : The Mystery of a Hansom Cab.*

Off one's feed (common), unable to eat, having no appetite. Originally stable slang.

Off one's rocker (popular), crazy, mad.

Off the reel (nautical), at once, without stopping. In allusion to the way in which the log-line flies off the reel when a ship is sailing fast.

Off the spot (popular), out of form, silly, imbecile. The metaphor is from billiards *off* or *on the spot—off* or *on* the spot stroke, the most paying stroke at billiards. To be *off the spot*, therefore, is strictly to be "out of form," whence it gets an implied meaning of silly, imbecile. To be "off one's dot," which has this latter meaning, is perhaps only a variation of *off the spot.*

Ogle (thieves and pugilistic), eye.

And we shall caper a-heel-and-toeing, With the mots their *ogles* throwing, And old Cotton humming his pray. —*Burrowes.*

That'll raise a tidy mouse on your *ogle*, my lad.—*C. Bede : Verdant Green.*

Oh, after you (tailors), that will do, cease talking.

Oh, dummy! (popular), humbug, nonsense.

Yes, last night I had been making a speech outside the old spot, when a little fellow came up to me and said, "*Oh, dummy!* governor, I've just heard that speech of yours, and I'll lay you had something when you're at home."—*Broadside Ballad : The Second Fiddler of the Band.*

Oh, Moses! (popular), a vulgar expletive expression of surprise or incredulity, like "Oh, Heavens!" "Oh, Jupiter!" "Oh, Jehoshaphat!" and the like.

Thy face "the human face divine!"
Oh, Moses!
Whatever trait divine thy face discloses, Some vile Olympian cross-play pre-supposes.
—*J. B. Stephens : To a Black Gin.*

Oh my! (common). Application gathered from quotation.

The upper crust of Nassau has, as a rule, very little sense of humour, therefore jokes have been voted ill-bred. Venture on one before a Conch lady and she will make a painstaking and conscientious mental effort to discover whether she ought to laugh or not. If her inner consciousness answers this question in the affirmative, she will venture on a smile; if she is in doubt she will probably compromise the matter by exclaiming, *Oh my!* This is a favourite expression with them on all occasions. If they hear a friend has bought a new dress, or is going to be married, they exclaim, *Oh my!* or if the friend has died, or had his house burnt down, they exclaim, *Oh my!* all the same. —*St. James's Gazette.*

Oh swallow yourself! (popular), hold your tongue! don't bother!

Oil of palms (popular), a money bribe, a tip. To *oil* the palm, to bribe, give a gratuity; "to *oil* the knocker," to fee the porter. The French have "graisser le marteau."

Ointment (medical student), butter.

O.K. (American telegraph), all correct, used to denote the line is clear, also to express anything very nice. An expression first attributed to President Jackson, who was said to have written *O.K.* for "all correct."

Old boots! like (popular), a silly simile, like anything, "as cheeky as *old boots*," "as quick as *old boots*."

Old clo'! (popular), anything exhausted, played out, behind the time.

Ole clo'! Ole clo'! any old hats I'll buy 'em,
They say the Tories are no good, well, let
    the nation try 'em,
Gladstone was a statesman, some thirty
    years ago,
But now his line of business ought to be
    Ole clo'!
        —*Catnach Press Broadside.*

Old crow (American), a drink.

I don't tip very often, but when I'm feel-
    ing low,
Life seems a bit to soften when I try a
    good *old crow.*
        —*Broadside.*

    Wherever I go they say hullo,
    Hip, hurrah for a jolly *old crow!*
    —*Francis Bros.: Jolly Old Crow.*

In the United States *Old Crow* is the name of a choice brand of Bourbon or corn whisky.

Old dog (prison), meaning gathered from quotation.

One of the greatest delicacies were large white or black slugs which crawled out in numbers after a shower of rain. I must confess to being shocked upon my march out to labour to find that the men were looking eagerly for those slugs, and as soon as one was seen it was pounced upon by a prisoner and swallowed in an instant while the officer was darting about to see if it was an *old dog*, as the bowls of the tobacco pipes were called.—*Evening News.*

Old doss (New York thieves), the Tombs, the city prison, a sombre building in the gloomiest style of Egyptian architecture.

Old ebony (journalistic), a slang title formerly given to *Blackwood's Magazine*—in allusion to the publisher's name.

Old gentleman (cardsharpers), a card longer than the rest in the deck used by sharpers.

Old gown, smuggled tea (Hotten).

Old Harvey (nautical), the large boat (the launch) of a line-of-battle ship.

Old horse (American), a slang term applied by sailors to salt beef, especially when it does not please them. On such occasions they sometimes repeat the following "grace:"

"*Old horse! old horse!* what brought
    you here?
From Sacarap to Portland Pier
I carted stone for many a year
Till slain by blows and sore abuse
They salted me down for sailors' use.
The sailors they do me despise,
Turn me over and damn my eyes,

Eat my meat and pick my bones,
And pitch the rest to Davy Jones."

Also "salt horse."

Old hoss (American), a term of endearment, equivalent to "old cock." Used also in England.

Old iron (nautical), clothes worn when on shore. A sailor will sometimes say, "I am going to work up my *old iron,*" *i.e.,* he means to say, " I'm going ashore."

Old man (common), the ridge found between two sleepers in a featherbed; also the southernwood tree. In misses' phraseology a blanket used to wrap a young child in. An old name for a species of bird somewhat like a cuckoo, and called otherwise a rain-fowl. (Up-country Australian), an old male or buck kangaroo.

In bush parlance the old male kangaroo is called an *old man;* the young female "a flying doe," and the young one till eight or ten months old a "joey." Some of the *old men* reach to an immense size, and I have often killed them over 2 cwts. —*Bush Wanderings of a Naturalist.*

> Ringed by the fathers of the tribe,
> Surrounded yet alone,
> The Bossaroo superbly posed
> Upon a granite throne—
> A very old *old man* who had
> Four generations known.
> —*J. B. Stephens: Marsupial Bill.*

(English and American sailors), the *old man,* the captain or master.

> Now this is pretty bad,
> Yet it's nothing to what's a-coming,
> But I hear the *old man* a-bawling like mad
> So I guess I will stop my humming.
> —*The Ballad of William Duff.*

Old pelt (printers). This is applied to old and worn-out pressmen—referring to the old ink pelts used in olden times by these individuals for distributing the ink.

Old pie (American), an expression equivalent to a note of admiration or of approval.

" Sir," sed he, turnin' as red as a biled beet, "don't you know that the rules of our Church is, that I the Profit may hev as many wives as I wants?"
" Jes' so," I said. "You air *old pie,* ain't you?"—*Artemus Ward.*

Old pod (American), an old man. Probably associated with limping along or walking slowly. "*Pod,* to put down awkwardly, to go afoot" (Wright). *Podager,* gout in the feet. Latin *podagra.*

Old pot and pan (popular), a familiar form of addressing any one.

> To be called an old man, or *old pot and pan,*
> Is quite the thing, as you know,
> By your servant-maid, a saucy young jade,
> When your wife's in the kitchen below.
> —*C. Sheard: Betsy.*

Old rats (American), equivalent to "one of the boys," a thoroughgoing one, a buck, a hearty old fellow.

She then lade her hed over onto my showlder and sed I was *old rats.* I was astonished to heer this obsarvashun, which I knowd was never used in refined society, and I perlitely but emfattercally shoved her hed away.—*Artemus Ward.*

Old Scratch (common), the devil.

A proper degree of this organ furnishes the possessor with a reasonable foresight of consequences, and a tendency to avoid their evils. Witness an example, on the part of ladies, who choose female servants as ugly as *Old Scratch*—bless the matrons' wisdom — I don't blame them for their prudence, as a charming domestic is apt to be mistaken for the mistress, and the error not found out until the fat's in the fire.—*Stump Orations.*

Old shoe (cant), good luck. Probably alluding to shoes and slippers thrown at a newly-married couple.

Old six (common), old ale at sixpence a quart.

Spoken—Look what I've got to do to-night ! There's fourteen "pubs" on my beat, and I've got to see that every one on 'em is closed at half-past twelve. That means that I've got fourteen pints of *old six* to get down me. Course you're not obliged to drink it, but you don't like to see good stuff wasted. I often thinks of the 'ardships of our perfession.—*Popular Song: As I Walks by my Beat.*

Old son (Australian popular), my fine fellow. An expression of patronage or contempt. One often hears, "I had you there, *old son*," "Steady, *old son*," and such expressions.

Ha ! they've fired the stable. Don't stir ! Have patience. I have you covered, you see, *old son. — New South Wales Paper.*

Old stager (common), one well initiated in anything.

Old, the, death. Sometimes "*the old* man" or master is spoken of as *the old.*

Old time, high (American), to have a *high old time* of it is to amuse oneself prodigiously, to be at liberty to act as one

pleases, to have it "all to one-self."

"The boys" had a *high old time* of it at the Epsom Drag Hunt Meeting last Wednesday. Enraged at the oofless state of the visitors, these merry men proceeded to cut through the refreshment tent.—*Bird o' Freedom.*

Old timer (American), a man who has been in California, or in the mining regions of the adjacent States, since they were first settled.

Coming from the barren deserts of Nevada and Western Utah—from the land where the irreverent and irrepressible *old timer* fills the air with a sulphurous odour from his profanity, and where nature is seen in its sternest aspect, and then suddenly finding oneself literally surrounded by flowers, and conversing with beauty about religion, is enough to charm the heart of a marble statue.—*T. Stevens: Around the World on a Bicycle.*

Old Toast, Old Poger (American thieves), the devil.

Old Tom (common), gin.

Old Tom, he is the best of gin ;
Drink him once, and you'll drink him again !
    —*Lytton: Ernest Maltravers.*

Dr. Brewer says, "Thomas Norris, one of the men employed in Messrs. Hodges' distillery, opened a gin palace in Great Russell Street, and called the gin concocted by Thomas Chamberlain, one of the firm of Hodges, *Old Tom*, in compliment to his former master." But, according to Bee's Slang Dictionary, 1823, the term is properly applicable to the cask containing the liquor.

There are two side-aisles of great casks, . . . bearing such inscriptions as *Old Tom*, 549 ; Young Tom, 360 ; Samson, 1421, the figures agreeing, we presume, with gallons understood.—*Sketches by Boz.*

Old 'uns (turf), horses that are more than three years old.

Of seven horses that were in front at the finish six were *old 'uns.*—*Sporting Times.*

Old 'un, the, or **fool's father** (theatrical), the pantaloon.

Old whale (nautical), a term for a sailor. Also " sea-boy, shell-back, old shell."

Old women (prison), for those prisoners who, being unfit for physically hard work, are employed in knitting stockings.

Ole Virginia never tire (American), a time-honoured expression applied to the Old Dominion State, or the Mother of Presidents. It is generally heard, however, as a negro expression.

In ole Kentuck in de arternoon
We sweep de floor wid a bran-new broom,
An' arter dat we form a ring,
And dis de song dat we do sing :
Klar de kitchen, ole fo'ks, young fo'ks,
Ole Virginny nebba' tire.

Oliver (thieves), the moon. From its colour. It may be conjectured, however, that it is possibly from the Danish *ulf* or *ulfa,* a wolf. The moon (or night) was one of Odin's wolves.

Now *Oliver* puts his black nightcap on,
And every star its glim is hiding ;
And forth to the heath is the Sampsman gone,
His matchless cherry-black prancer riding.
—*Ainsworth : Rookwood.*

Omee (roughs and thieves), a man. From the Italian *uomo.*

Oh, donnys and *omees*, what gives me the spur
Is, I'm told by a mug (he tells whoppers)
That I ought to have greased to have kept out of stir
The dukes of the narks and the coppers.
—*The Referee.*

(Theatrical), " *omee* of the carsa," master of the house. Itinerant actors are accustomed to inquire at a new theatre for the manager, or at their lodgings for the landlord, thus, " Who's the *omee* of the carsa ? "

On (popular), tipsy.

Henceforth when door-exploring Jones,
Who reaches home a little *on,*
Observes, in somewhat husky tones,
" Hulloa, I shay, the keyhole's gone ! "
We must not hasten to cry " Shame ! "
For it's the climate that's to blame.
—*Funny Folks.*

(Sporting), to get *on* a man or horse, to make bets on him or it. (Common), to try it *on,* to make an attempt generally with a view of deceiving. (Winchester College), a call by any prefect to announce that the " men " may enter chapel.

On a string (American). " To send a person to look for something that you are sure is somewhere else is putting him *on a string.* Humbugging, deceiving in any way. When a girl flirts with a sucker she has him *on a string* " (New York Slang Dictionary). Derived from billiards, as when a man gets a " run," or from anything with a view to one's advantage, as, for instance, two ducks in a line.

On doog (costermongers' backslang), no good.

One (popular), a fib or lie. "Don't tell me *one*" is constantly in the popular mouth. Also a blow.

One, &c. (legal), an attorney, being an abbreviation of One of the Attorneys of Her Majesty.

Onee soldi or win (low theatrical), one penny. *Vide* SOLDI. *Win*, old cant, is from a different source.

One-eyed town (theatrical), a disparaging term for some small town or theatre which somebody has visited to his sorrow.

One five (common), hand.

When a "Bobby" apprehends any one, he asks to look at his hands, and judges from the "palm" of *one five* as to the honesty of his prisoner.—*Topical Times.*

One for his nob (popular), a blow on the head.

A snatch was made at the tray, whereon the man with the broken nose dealt the snatcher *one for his nob* with his knuckly fist, coolly remarking, as he did so, "That's wot I'm here for!"—*Daily Telegraph.*

(Cards), when the knave of trump is held at the game of cribbage, the holder cries *one for his nob!*

One-horse (American), anything small or comparatively unimportant. A *one-horse* bank, a *one-horse* town, a *one-horse* insurance company, a *one-horse*

candidate, are depreciatory epithets that are thoroughly understood. When it was said by an opponent that General Grant was a *one-horse* candidate for the Presidency of the United States, the *New York Herald* declared, on the contrary, "that he was a 'whole team' and a big dog under the waggon."

He returned rather out of breath, just as the captain was giving the signal for departure. "A *one-horse* little place, I guess," said a companion. "Well, no," said the explorer frankly; "I guess not. I stole a pair of socks in the market. I was tried, convicted, and publicly whipped in twenty minutes. I call it an uncommonly smart little place."—*Daily News.*

One nitch (printers), a vulgarism applied to infants of the male sex.

One of the Lord's own (American society), a dandy; one who is eminent as regards form, style, and *chic*. Also a "daisy, a stunner, or first-classer" (MS. Americanisms by C. Leland Harrison).

One out of it (tailors). This phrase signifies, "I don't care to be mixed up in it," "I will have nothing to do with the business."

Oner (pronounced wunner), an emphatic rendering of the word "one"—as of a person super-eminent, or greatly distinguished for strength, agility, or prowess of any kind. A heavy blow is also called a *oner*; "one for his nob," or a "*oner* for his nob," are pugilistic elegancies of speech that have survived pugilism itself, in popular usage.

I gave him a *oner* on the nose.—*Punch.*

The watcher is generally hanging about, and he'll "down" you with a *oner* in the back or side (he won't hit you in the face, for fear of spoiling it).—*Greenwood: Seven Curses of London.*

Also a blow, a shilling. Hence perhaps the slang term "blow" for shilling.

One side to his mouth (sporting), is said of a horse that only feels the bit on one side of his mouth. The horse has then a right-handed or left-handed mouth.

One under your arm (tailors), getting in an extra job.

One who makes the eagle squeal (American), said of any grasping, avaricious, or mean man, that when he gets hold of a coin squeezes it so closely that the eagle impressed on it utters a scream or squeal. The expression has been in use for at least forty years. *To make the eagle squeal* is also used in a very different meaning when applied to anything which provokes national indignation (MS. Americanisms by C. Leland Harrison).

On his lines (printers), an alternative expression for "on the piece," or work paid for according to scale, and not by weekly wages or "'stab."

On his uppers (tailors), in very reduced circumstances.

Onion (popular), the head. *Vide* OFF HIS ONION.

Onions (thieves), watch seals.

When his ticker I set a-going,
With his *onions*, chain, and key.
—*W. Maginn: Vidocq's Slang Song.*

On it (American). This eccentric expression meant originally that a man was decidedly engaged in anything. It implied determination. "I'm *on it*," I understand it. It came into very general use about 1860.

On the batter (popular), a bout of low debauchery, riotous living, principally said of a street walker. "It is of Anglo-Irish origin, and signifies on the street, on the road; from the Irish word *bóthar*, a road (originally a road for cattle, from *bo*, a cow), in some parts of Ireland pronounced *batter*, as in the place names Batterstown, Greenbatter, Stonybatter, Booterstown" (A. Smythe Palmer).

As for the word *bater*, that in English purporteth a lane bearing to an highwaie, I take it for a mere Irish word that crept unawares into the English.—*Stanihurst: Description of Ireland.*

On the booze. *Vide* BOOZE.

On the burst, bust. *Vide* BUST.

On the cross. *Vide* CROSS.

On the dead (American), gratis, free. Probably derived from "dead head" (which see).

So we followed him into the chamber as soon as these words were said,
To get those beautiful presents all gratis and *on the dead.* —*Song.*

G

On the dead quiet (common), in secret. A variant is " on the strictest Q. T."

" Why did you sacrifice your beard?" asked a young man yesterday of a friend whose honeymoon was barely over. *"On the dead quiet* I'll tell you," replied the Benedict.—*Sporting Times.*

On the fly (popular and thieves), getting one's living by thieving or other dishonest practices. Also out drinking.

On the forty-ninth ballot (American). When an election is repeated many times before a candidate can be elected, it may be prolonged until it equals that of a Pennsylvania senator which required forty-nine ballottings. Hence the expression as applied to a very long contest of any kind.

Miss Jennie, mindful of her Texas nativity, " went for " a hickory club and the " sarpent " at the same time, tucking her skirts in genuine Amazonian style and attacking by echelon. In spite of his repeated efforts to fasten his fangs in the brave girl she got away with him *on the forty-ninth ballot* and left the field with the slimy varmint dragging behind her triumphant car. His snakeship was the proprietor of sixteen rattles, which makes him nineteen years of age—a regular octogenarian in the reptile kingdom.—*Dallas News.*

On the ground-floor (American). Those who are the very first in any scheme to make money, or the original " promoters " of a speculation, are said to be *on the ground-floor.* It is a common trick to take investors in by assuring them that they are among the first and will have the best chance.

So in Amsterdam Herr Ganef paddled out his Glory bonds ;
And to all he slyly whispered, " I will let you in de first.
On de ground-floor—sell out quickly—for you know de ding may burst."
—*Rise and Fall of Gloryville.*

On the half-shell (American), a very peculiar phrase, derived from an oyster thus served. It is applied to anything prepared and ready for use. When Page's picture of Venus, naked and standing in a shell, was exhibited in New York, the " boys " described it as a girl *on the half-shell.* Also a part of, or by retail, by half-dozens.

I don't intend this essay for laffing in the lump, but for laffing *on the half-shell.* —*Josh Billings on Laughing.*

On the job. *Vide* JOB, ON THE.

On the lay (thieves). *Vide* LAY. *On the lay* conveys the same metaphor as lying in ambush, or lying in wait.

On the ledge (popular), in a predicament, or in danger or trouble.

And now my mother's made a vow,
If he don't take the pledge,
The next time that he gets run in,
She'll leave him *on the ledge.*
—*Geo. Horncastle: The Frying-Pan*

On the loose (popular), free, at liberty, out of prison.

I'd rather have 'arf a bellyfull *on the loose,* than roast meat and baked taters all day long in the steel (prison).—*Greenwood: In Strange Company.*

Also applied to any one engaged in a course of immoral indulgence, in drink or dissipation of any kind.

On the make. *Vide* MAKE.

On the nod (common), speaking to everybody, and claiming or making acquaintances by mere impudence.

> I've found out a secret to live without work,
> Which has proved a good fortune to me,
> I am now *on the nod*, and I find that it pays,
> For I tap every one that I see.
> —*T. W. Barrett: The Strand-rushing Masher.*

(Theatrical), getting trust—particularly at public - houses. Also applies to passing in at theatres.

(Turf), to bet *on the nod* is to bet on credit, each party to the wager merely registering it in their books, and settling on the following Monday. So called in contradistinction to ready-money betting, where the backer hands over his cash to the book-maker at the time of making the bet, and if a winner, receives payment immediately after the race.

Since the suppression of the piquets there has been a good deal of betting *on the nod*, and there is hardly a penciller who has not a few thousands of dead money on his head.—*Bird o' Freedom.*

Also silent bidding at auctions.

On the nose (thieves), watching. *Vide* NOSE.

On the pounce (common). If, as is thought, a word or phrase becomes legitimatised when it has once been used in Parliament, then *on the pounce*, meaning to be on the look-out for attacking, is no longer slang, as appears by the following extract from the report of the proceedings in the House on September 13–14, 1887.

> "I shall not resume my seat," he shouted in tones of passion, waving his arms the while. "You, Mr. Speaker, have been *on the pounce* for me ever since I rose, and I claim my right to speak. I have not transgressed your ruling. You have been *on the pounce* waiting for me all the evening, and I again claim my right to speak."—*Standard.*

On the prigging lay (thieves), out on a thieving expedition, picking pockets, &c.

> As from ken to ken I was going,
> Doing a bit *on the prigging lay*,
> Who should I meet but a jolly blowen.
> —*W. Maginn: Vidocq's Slang Song.*

On the road (theatrical), explained by quotation.

> Companies in the provinces are *on the road*, another relic of the past.—*Globe.*

On the scent (showmen and circus), on the road, travelling about.

On the shallow (beggars), going about half-naked to excite compassion. Apparently from *shale*, a husk, as of anything husked or stripped. Provincial English, *shalligo*, scanty, applied to dress.

On the sharp (American thieves). A man who is familiar with all the mysteries of gambling and not to be taken in is said to be *on the sharp*.

On the shelf (old), transported.

On the slate (printers), waiting for something to turn up.

On the square (popular), of masonic origin, and borrowed from the symbolism of operative masonry. To "act on the square," is to act honourably; the square is one of the most important working tools, perfection of detail and accuracy being impossible without it. Hence the metaphor which has now passed into universal acceptance as synonymous with probity, truth, and honour, or more probably used in contradistinction to "on the cross," or "crook," the reverse of straightforward.

On the stairs (tailors), the usual answer when a job is called for.

On the strict Q.T. (common), on the quiet; a phrase much in favour with the flirting servant girls when they meet their soldiers round the corner, or the cook treats Robert to the traditional cold mutton.

On the swing (American), going, acting, or being employed well enough but only temporarily. Thus a "swing-station" is one where a man only rests, or has a short swing of rest—not "a full swing," till the horses are changed. Probably through New York, from a Dutch phrase. *Jemand op den schopzetten* means to put any one on the swing, that is, to employ him temporarily, with the understanding that he may be summarily dismissed at any time. *Vide* To Scoop. It may here be observed that to

scup for "to swing" is common in New York (Bartlett).

On the tiles (common), out all night carousing. Alluding to cats.

On the win (American), winning or making money. This form of expression is now applied to an endless number of verbal nouns, *e.g.*, "on the walk," "on the borrow," "on the preach," "on the steal," &c.

The coffee ring were *on the win*. They confidently expected to see coffee selling at sixty cents.—*Detroit Free Press.*

On toast (American), anything nicely served. Hence a man who is served out, or at one's mercy. Probably the metaphor is from the way small birds, such as snipe, quail, larks, &c., are eaten *on toast*, trussed and spitted. To have an adversary *on toast*, therefore, means to have him, as it were, trussed and spitted at one's mercy.

Oodles (American), plenty. "Plenty of money" (Bartlett). Possibly from "out deal;" German *austheilen*, to deal out.

Oof (common), the most recent slang term for money. A word brought into vogue by the *Sporting Times*, and now very common.

They quickly sought a neighbouring bar—
They had not far to search—
And there she told him that her pa
Was pastor of a church.
He knew not that the game was spoof,
Or he had held aloof.

" I love but thee—dost need a proof?"
And echo answered *" Oof!"*
　　　　　　—Sporting Times.

O Goschen, mighty king of *oof.*
　　　　　—Funny Folks.

Said to be of Yiddish or Hebrew origin, but a punning joke on the French *œuf*, with reference to the goose with the golden eggs, may have contributed to the term, the more so as mention of the " oof bird " (which see) is often made. The word *œuf* seems always to have tickled the fancy of Englishmen.

Said one young 'Arry to the other young Arry, " Wot blooming fools these Frenchmen are ! Why, they atcheley call eggs money." " 'Ow's that?" says the other. "Why," says the first, " they call a hegg 'day's *oof.*'"*—Scraps.*

Oof bird (common), funds, source from which comes the money. *Vide* OOF. It is sometimes said of a man who marries a wealthy lady that he has found the *oof bird*, or the *oof bird* has come to him.

" Good evening, mein herr,' said the lady in white,
To the Johnny who seemingly looked rather tight,
For the *oof bird* was somewhat remote on that night,
And his fingers with diamonds were gaily bedight.
And the Johnny divined as he looked at that sight,
　　　She was German.
　　　　—Sporting Times.

The " *oof bird* on the job " means that money is plentiful. (Cashiers and clerks), " to make the *oof bird* walk," to make the money circulate.

Oofless (common), poor, without money. *Vide* OOF.

He was loyal, did his painting in a hue that shouldn't fade,
At the Jubilee she must of course rejoice ;
Still the peelers couldn't sanction every playful escapade,
And he found himself compelled to make a choice
'Twixt a month's incarceration and pecuniary amends.
Being *oofless* 'twas a case of lock and key.
He found it most convenient on returning to his friends,
To say he paid a visit to the sea.
　　　　—Bird o' Freedom.

Ooftisch (common), a variation of " oof," money (which see).

If my *ooftisch* disappears before my screw has fallen due,
He's the boy who lets me have a bit ;
Of the Johnnies I'm acquainted with he numbered 'mongst the few
Who'll help me in the matter of a writ.
To whom it is I'm wont to trust my golden watch and chain,
My diamond ring, and wifey's silver plate ;
My demands, however frequent, our relations do not strain,
For he charges me, for love, a heavy rate—
　　　　Does my uncle.
　　　　—Bird o' Freedom.

Open the occurrence, to (police), to make an entry in the books at a police - station of a new case.

Opening his mouth too wide (Stock Exchange), is said of one who gets excited, and in consequence bids for large amounts of stock which is adjudged to him.

Opera buffer (theatrical), one who performs in " opera bouffe."

Opposite tacks (nautical), cross purposes.

Optic (pugilistic), eye.

> Casting my *optics* on the bruisers an gluttons of the past.—*Punch.*

> You will see to what I refer if you will cast your "*hoptic* over the enclosed cutting."—*Sporting Times.*

Orchid (Stock Exchange), explained by quotation.

> A young sprig of nobility, who was admitted to the House as the unauthorised clerk of a dealer in the American market, was once heard to tell a friend that when he was in the House he felt like an "*orchid* in a turnip-field." It is almost needless to say that he very shortly had cause to regret his speech, as ever afterwards he and his friends were known as *orchids.* . . . By degrees an *orchid* has become the nickname for any member who has a "handle" to his name.—*Atkin: House Scraps.*

Order (common), a large, big *order,* a great, difficult, or arduous undertaking.

> For a three-year-old to beat Oberon at even weights at first seems a "large *order.*"—*Sporting Times.*

Orders (theatrical), free admissions. Although the system of indiscriminately giving *orders* has been at various times the ruin of half the theatres in London and the country, yet many good plays which at first were failures have been nursed into great successes by judiciously "papering the house." Managers, however, frequently throw good money after bad, and bolster up bad pieces night after night by filling the house with "dead heads." It is astonishing with what shameless effrontery people of all classes, from the peerage downwards, levy blackmail upon managers by demanding free admissions.

During the Italian Opera, and the performances of certain Italian tragedians ten years ago, it was the custom on the "off" nights to send out *orders* to impecunious members of the aristocracy, and others, to admit three persons free, with the object of inducing a fourth person to pay for admission. It was rarely, however, that the fourth person did pay. A certain manager who was perpetually pestered by cadgers of this description, upon receiving a letter from a soda-water merchant requesting an *order,* sent an answer to this effect: "Sir,— In reply to your solicitation for an *order,* I beg to order a dozen of soda-water, and one of seltzer, for which my servant will pay you on delivery, less five per cent. for cash." Upon receiving a modest request from the head of an "alarming sacrifice" firm for fifty or a hundred *orders* for the ladies and gentlemen of his establishment, the same manager replied by enclosing an *order* for two to the gallery, with the addenda that on this occasion evening dress was indispensable, and that the ticket was inadmissible after half-past seven.

Once upon a time one or two disreputable theatres managed to keep their doors open by flooding the house with paper on what is called the overflow and plunder system. *E.g.,* the unsuspecting auditor has an order for the pit; he goes there, and finds the pit crammed to suffocation by people who have not paid. Upon payment of sixpence he goes to the upper boxes, they are also crowded; sixpence more takes him to the dress circle. Before he can obtain a seat he is bled of another sixpence for his greatcoat, another for his umbrella, and another for a programme. The performances in these places were as disreputable as the management, and, as a rule, would disgrace a show at a country fair.

(Eton), explained by quotation.

While we were in early school our beds had to be made and. our rooms tidied; after that the *orders, i.e.,* rolls, butter, and milk had to be served round.—*Brinsley Richards : Seven Years at Eton.*

Order your name to (Winchester College), an unpleasant intimation. When a master wishes a "man" to taste the sweets of a flogging he tells him to *order his name to.* The culprit then goes to the "Bible clerk" (which see), and asks him to take his name down, giving the reason.

Organ, carrying the (military), carrying pack or valise at defaulters' or marching order drill. The dead weight is compared to that carried by an Italian organ-grinder. (Printers), a man that lends out money to his fellow-workmen at an exorbitant weekly interest.

Any one applying to him for a loan would be said to be "playing on the organ."

Organ-pipes (trade), explained by quotation.

. . . to find that the dress-improver is really banished at last. A little artificial fulness is still introduced.into the back of dress-skirts by means of folds of starched muslin, "their mission being to gloss over the reactionary moment, and avert a distressing sense of suddenness." We are much mistaken if there is not the making of a great diplomatist of the old school in the author of this happy periphrasis for the arrangement known in the trade as *organ-pipes.—Globe.*

Or out goes the gas (popular), a threat to put an end to whatever is going on.

More drink and less talk, *or out goes the gas,*
Be stopping your blethering ways.
—*Broadside.*

O. T. (printers). These initials are used largely by printers and stand for "overtime," *i.e.,* work beyond the ordinary amount of hours calculated as a day's work.

Otta, otter (Anglo-Indian), flour.

Otter (costermongers), eightpence. Italian *otto.*

Out (popular), a dram-glass.

Out-and-out (popular), excellent, beyond measure, true, surpassing, thorough; in the quotation it means quite a man, just like a man.

"Won't he growl at all, when he hears a fiddle playing ! And don't he hate other dogs as ain't of his breed !" "Oh, no ! He's an *out-and-out* Christian."—*Dickens: Oliver Twist.*

Out-and-outer (society), first-class.

> Pretty Polly Pouter
> Is a reg'lar *out-and-outer.*
> —*Punch.*

(Popular), used as a substantive and an adjective, one that excels, surpasses, genuine.

> "They were burglars, then?" "*Out-and-outers,* sir."—*Greenwood: Odd People in Odd Places.*

Out-cry (Anglo-Indian), an auction.

Outfit (American), "the whole *outfit,*" or "the blooming *outfit,*" the whole party. Termed also "all the boiling *outfit.*" Refers also to company, household, caravan, trading expedition.

> The waggon master had the presence of mind to gallop his team out into the prairie, whilst the entire *outfit* made for the best cover it could find.—*O'Reilly: Fifty Years on the Trail.*

Outfitter (military), a term used by officers of the Royal Artillery for one who is not fond of change from home to foreign service or from regimental to staff employment, and who is always getting an "outfit" for the purpose.

Out for an airing (turf), said of a horse that is backward or of a horse not meant to win.

Out here (Australian). An Australian, no matter if he and his parents and grandparents have been born in Australia, and have never left Australia, and own not a sixpence outside of Australia, always speaks of the British Isles as "home," and of Australia as *out here.* Making the voyage to England is "coming or going home," and the voyage to Australia coming or going "out."

> That is my Nellie—she's *out here* and Mrs. Cupid Foote :
> We came to Melbourne late last year, I could not bear the thought
> Of snow, and sleet, and slush, and rain, and yellow London fogs,
> An English winter I maintain is only fit for frogs.
> —*D. B. W. Sladen: The Squire's Brother.*

Out of collar. *Vide* COLLAR.

Out of kilter. *Vide* KILTER.

Out of register (printers). An inebriated person that could not walk straight, but "wobbly," is thus termed, from the fact that pages *out of register* in printing a sheet would be "out of the square," "out of truth."

Out of sorts (printers), a term used when any letter runs "short" or is deficient, and hence the common figurative expression meaning melancholy, annoyed, or slightly indisposed.

Outs (printers), an omission of a part of the copy composed is said to be an "out." The meaning is obvious.

Outside old-river (pidgin), the Yang-tse-kiang. Cantonese, Ngoi-kong-lo.

Outsider (turf), a horse which does not stand high in the public estimation, and is therefore noted in the betting "outside" the circle of "favourites." There is also a human species of *outsider*, viz., any person whose liabilities to the bookmakers cause the inside of the ring to be too hot for him, and who if he goes racing at all is obliged to remain "outside" the sanctuaries of the solvent.

Out, two or three (popular), when a quartern of gin or spirit is divided into two or three glasses.

Over at the knees (stable), said of a horse weak in the knees.

Two of the warrant officers of the court, who have had experience of horses, examined the animal, and reported that it was in very poor condition, and *over at the knees.—Globe.*

Overdraw the badger. *Vide* BADGER.

Over goes the show (popular), a sudden change of resolution, an upset of any kind physical or moral, a catastrophe. Simile from the upsetting a Punch and Judy schwassel-box, or blowing over an exhibition-tent.

It's all very well to say you won't
  Go wrong again—but oh !
When a pretty little widow winks at you,
  Why—*over goes the show!*
I formed a resolution once
  I'd never swear in vain,
If I felt a good swear coming on,
  I bolted it again.
I was so good I kept it up
  For quite a week or so ;
Then I sat down on a piece of glass,
  And—*over went the show!*
                              —Ballad.

Overland-man (colonial), a man driving a flock of sheep, or mob of horses or cattle, overland. The term has another signification, which is the really slang one, a man looking for work in the bush, and who manages to arrive at a station (sheep) about sundown, or after working hours, where he obtains a night's lodgings and rations, and goes on in the morning, doing the same again at sundown. This man is also called a "sun-downer."

Overland trout (American cowboys), bacon.

Over one (common), to come *over one*, to try to intimidate or compel.

Overplush, thus explained by the *Globe:*—"Is it right to give the *overplush*, or is it not ? Probably most people would answer that question by asking another, and inquiring, in the first place, what is *overplush?* Well, according to the testimony of a Midland Boniface, it is the 'long pull'—not the long pull so largely and honourably associated with after-dinner oratory; not the long pull which is indissolubly connected with the strong pull and the pull all together ; but a wholly different pull, namely, the publican's. It is not given to everybody to know everything, or even very much, about the business of the beer-seller; but those who do know something about it will tell you that, in the drawing of beer, there is both a long pull and a short pull, nearly allied to those characteristic pulls on which the precise proportion of froth to liquor so much depends, and which Mr. Arthur Roberts is in the habit of illustrating nightly in his *rôle* of innkeeper of the time of Napoleon. Now, about the short pull there can be no question. Beer-drinkers, and, indeed, other stern moralists, will tell you that it is quite indefensible. You have no business to give short measure—unless you are a teetotaller in disguise; and even then it is not strictly equitable. For his twopence or threehalfpence a man should have his twopenceworth or his threehalfpenceworth. But can the long pull be supported? Ought a publican to give the *overplush?* The legal representative of an official receiver says it seems strange that an innkeeper should sell beer at a loss—supplying more of it than he is paid for. But the particular innkeeper under discussion replied that he had adopted this policy by way of attracting custom. He proposed to win the public by giving over-measure, and then, the public gained, to give only full measure. And surely it is permissible to grant *overplush*, if thereby one can generate an *overplush* in the exchequer."

Overrate it (theatrical), to over-do one's part.

Overs (bank), the odd money remaining after the accounts are made up.

Overshot (popular), intoxicated.

Overtaken (popular), intoxicated.

He was temperate also in his drinking, . . . but I never spake with the man that saw him *overtaken.—Hacket: Life of Williams.*

Over the left (common), explained by quotation.

At this inquiry Mr. Martin looked with a countenance of excessive surprise at his two friends, and then each gentleman pointed with his right thumb over his left shoulder. This action, imperfectly described in words by the very feeble term of *over the left* . . . its expression is one of light and playful sarcasm.—*Dickens. Pickwick Papers.*

Overtoys box (Winchester), a box like a cupboard to hold books, &c.

Owl (American), "drunk as a biled *owl*," very favourite simile for intoxication.

Wanted, a man who can go to Mexico on Government business without getting drunker'n a biled *owl*. Address State Department, Washington, D. C. — *St. Louis Globe-Democrat.*

Oxford clink. A play upon words is called an *Oxford clink* by Leicester in Strafford's Let. i. 224. (Theatrical), free tickets of admission.

P

P's and Q's. *Vide* MIND YOUR P'S AND Q'S.

Pace, to go the (common), to live extravagantly.

He is the son of a famous racing man who *went the pace*, and cut his throat in Newmarket.—*The Tattler.*

Pack (old cant), a gang.

No hooker of another *pack.*—*Oath of the Canting Crew.*

Padding (literary), the light articles in the monthly magazines. Also extraneous matter inserted in any literary work for the sake of quantity.

Padding ken (tramps), a low lodging-house. One on the *pad* or road.

Paddle, to (American), to go or run away.

Paddy, to come Paddy over one (American), to bamboozle, humbug.

"Oh, you infernal, lying, blackguardly rascal," said the devil, who had been improving his language of late by reading the New York Sunday papers, "do you think *to come Paddy* over me in that style?"—*American Story.*

Paddy's hurricane (nautical), up and down the mast, *i.e.*, no wind at all.

Pad the hoof, to (thieves and tramps), to walk, to tramp. It would be more correct to say, "to hoof the pad," *i.e.*, to tramp on the *pad* or road. French,

fendre l'ergot. Literally to split the spur (of birds).

In bus or brougham, city merchants roll to
    villas snug,
While city arabs *pad the hoof*, to where a
    "shoddy" rug,
In some cold gloomy casual ward, will
    cover them to-night,
Well! such is life in London now, but
    say—is it quite right?
    —*J. A. Hardwick: London Bridge.*

Pad, to stand (street), to beg with a piece of paper on the breast bearing the words "I am starving." Literally to stand on the *pad*, obsolete English for footpath, road.

Paint a town red, to (American), explained by quotation.

To paint a town red is, I ought to explain, a Western expression, and signifies the height of reckless debauch; and when a cowboy, having drunk his fill of whisky, has let daylight with revolver shots through the hats of those who have ventured to differ from him, and has smashed all the glasses in the drinking saloon with his stock whip, and gallopped with a wild whoop down the principal street to the danger and consternation of the inhabitants, he may fairly be said to have done his part towards *painting the town red.*—*Cumberland: The Queen's Highway.*

Also *to paint the town.*

One of these chaps from Texas came in there *to paint the town*, and got his tank full.—*F. Francis: Saddle and Moccasin.*

Paint, to (popular), to drink, alluding to a red nose caused by over-indulgence.

The muse is dry,
And Pegasus does thirst for Hippocrene,
And fain would *paint*—imbibe the vulgar
    call—
Or hot, or cold, or long, or short.
       —*Kingsley : Two Years Ago.*

Pair off, to (American). In order
to avoid the trouble of voting
a man will agree with some one
of the opposite side that neither
shall vote. Then both will *pair
off* with as many others as they
can induce to do the same. It
is said that in a Western town
this was carried to such an
extent that at an election not
a single vote was "deposited."

The vast majority of strong-minded
women wouldn't care so much about voting if they could only get a chance *to pair
off.*—*New Haven News.*

Pair, to (parliamentary), formerly
to *pair* off, to go in couples ; my
pair, my companion.

Pal (gypsy), brother, friend. Till
within fifty years this word
existed among English gypsies
as *prala*, which is the common
Romany form all over the Con-
tinent, derived directly from the
Hindu and Sanskrit *brat*. The
accent of a word is called *pal
of a lav, i.e.,* its brother ; *pala !*
oh, brother !

    " Mat, hav akai ! ma pūr ajā ;
       Sār 'shan tu, kūshto, puro púl ;"—
" Mat, come here ! don't turn away !
How are you, good old friend ?"—*E. H.
Palmer.*

    Paleskro, brotherly. "The
geero kaired mandy sar *paleskro,*
as tacho as you'd kam "—" The
man treated me brotherly, as
well as you'd wish."

The term has become general.
In society it means a great
friend of either sex. When used
with regard to a man as being
a great *pal* of a lady, it means
more than mere friendship. The
lower classes and thieves use it
with the sense of companion,
friend, comrade, accomplice.

Ned was a wide-awake villain. It was
not the first time he had been "in trouble,"
and he was properly alive to the advantage
of having a trustworthy *pal* at liberty.—
The Little Ragamuffins.

A prisoner inscribed in one of
his library books, "Good-bye,
Lucy dear, I'm parted from
you for seven year—Alf. Jones."
Beneath this a sour sceptic who
subsequently used the book
added—

    " If Lucy dear is like most gals
      She'll give few sighs or moans,
    But soon will find among your *pals*
      Another Alfred Jones."
       —*Horsley : Jottings from Jail.*

Palaver, conversation ; from
Spanish *palabra.*

His Highness last year met the Crown
Prince on the Riviera. They had several
conversations together ; they dined at
Pegli, they breakfasted at Savona, and
their *palaver* meant peace and nothing
but peace.—*Evening News.*

Palaver, to (general), to talk.
Vide PALAVER. The expression
is common among tramps,
itinerant vendors, strolling actors, &c. Nantee *palaver,* cease
talking.

Pall, to (popular), originally
nautical, to stop. From *pall,* a
small instrument which is used
to stop the windlass or capstan

in a ship. I am *palled*, I cannot or dare not say any more; I am nonplussed, confounded.

Pallyard (old cant), a beggar with manufactured sores. From the French *paillard*, a dissolute fellow; properly and originally a poor person who sleeps on the straw, such as mendicants, tramps. Du Cange says, "palhardus, homo nihili et infimæ conditionis."

Palm grease (common), a bribe. In French slang *graisse*. Also *palm* oil. French *huile*.

In England a bribe is commonly known as *palm oil.—Standard.*

Palmer (thieves), a thief who steals articles in a shop, jewellery, for instance, by making them adhere to his palm.

Palmer's twisters (medical), the name given to strychnine pills, which were the medicine employed by Palmer of Rugeley in getting rid of Cooke.

Palming (thieves), exchanging spurious articles, *e.g.*, watches, rings, diamonds, coins, for real ones. From the term in legerdemain.

Pal, to (popular), to associate.

And we *pals* on with Dukes, Lords, and Markisses,
Which our manners is strictly O.K.,
And they don't make no nasty remarkeses
Respectu-ing Botany Bay.
—*Blueskin : A Lay of Lag.*

Panel-crib (American). The New York Slang Dictionary gives the following explanation:—"*Panel-crib*, a place especially fitted up for the robbery of gentlemen, who are enticed thereto by women who make it their business to pick up strangers. *Panel-cribs* are sometimes called badger-cribs, shake-downs, touch-cribs, and are variously fitted for the admission of those who are in the secret, but which defy the scrutiny of the uninitiated. Sometimes the casing of the door is made to swing on well-oiled hinges which are not discoverable in the room, while the door itself appears to be hung in the usual manner, and well secured by bolts and lock. At other times the entrance is effected by means of what appears to be an ordinary wardrobe, the back of which revolves like a turnstile on pivots. When the victim is ready the thief enters, and picking the pocket-book out of the pocket, abstracts the money, and supplying its place with a small roll of paper, returns the book to its place. He then withdraws, and coming to the door raps and demands admission, calling the woman by the name of wife. The frightened victim dresses himself in a hurry, feels his pocket-book in its proper place, and escapes through another door, congratulating himself on his happy deliverance." A *panel-crib* was formerly termed a *panel-house*. Hence the word *panel* for a prostitute, an inmate of such an establishment; abbreviated from *panel-girl.* Compare with *panel-thief,* which see.

Panel-thief, one who extorts money by threats of violence in a panel-house or panel-crib, which see.

Pannum (costermongers and thieves), bread, food. From the Italian *pane.*

Panny (thieves), a house ; flash-*panny,* a public-house or lodging-house frequented by thieves. Doing a *panny,* committing a burglary.

Ranting Rob, poor fellow, was lagged for doing a *panny!—Lytton : Paul Clifford.*

Panny is probably a corruption of the old *panel*-house (same as panel-crib, which see), with extended meaning.

Panny-man (thieves), a burglar. Also " buster," " cracksman."

Pan on (printers). A person with a fit of the " blues," or " down in the dumps," is said to have a *pan on.*

Pan out, to (American), to pay well, to prove profitable.

I am afraid that, to use a miner's expression, we did not *pan out* as well as was anticipated.—*F. Francis : Saddle and Moccasin.*

From " panning," the process which gold-diggers employ to separate the precious metal from the earth and other substances with which it is usually found associated.

Pantile (nautical), biscuit. (Popular), a hat. More common as " tile." Properly the mould into which sugar is poured.

Pap (thieves), paper; especially in the form of bank-notes.

Come on, we have had a lucky touch for half a century in *pap* (£50 in paper, *i.e.,* notes).—*Horsley : Jottings from Jail.*

Paper-maker (popular), a rag gatherer.

Paper-mill, the office in the old Court of Queen's Bench where the Crown Records were deposited.

Paper, to (theatrical), *to paper* a house, *i.e.,* a theatre, is to fill it with orders. A *paper*-house is a theatre so filled. " There's a good deal of *paper* in the house," is a common expression.

Paper-worker (popular), a vendor of street literature.

Papoose (American), a baby, derived from the aboriginal language of the Virginian Indians.

Paralytic fit (tailors), a very badly fitting garment.

Pard (American), a corruption of partner. Gold-miners, &c., usually work and live in couples, whence the term.

Say, old *pard,* do you want to stake me with fifty dollars?—it's real good investment.—*F. Francis : Saddle and Moccasin.*

Parentheses (printers), a pair of *parentheses* applies to bandy legs.

Parishes (Rugby), explained by quotation.

The victims stand on one of the old wooden bedsteads, flanked by two small boys, each holding one of those tin sconces called at Rugby *parishes.*—*Everyday Life in our Public Schools.*

Park railings (popular), the teeth. A neck of mutton.

Parliamentary press (tailors), an old custom of claiming any iron, which happens to be in use, for the purpose of opening the collar seam.

Parlour-jumping (thieves), robbing rooms, usually by getting in through the window of rooms seen to be unguarded.

This time I palled in with some older hands at the game, who used to take me a *parlour-jumping.* — *Horsley : Jottings from Jail.*

Parter (sport), a liberal man.

Particular, a special mistress, one belonging particularly to one man. A term much in vogue in the time of George IV., but which is seldom heard now. Also "peculiar." In French *particulière* has the meaning of wife or mistress.

Part, to (sport), to pay willingly, *i.e.*, part with one's money.

Party-rolls (Winchester College). On the last Friday but one of the Half after dinner when the tutors had gone out, men used to call out "once, twice, thrice, *party-rolls,*" three times. The custom arose from the coaching days when the students left the school in different parties.

Pass in one's chips, to (West American), to die.

It was not until the following morning that I overtook Lone Wolf, when I found that thirty-two of his band had *passed in their chips,* and over forty-five were wounded.—*O'Reilly : Fifty Years on the Trail.*

Chips are counters in games of faro. (American newspaper), items of news.

Pass the compliment, to (popular), to give a douceur or tip to a servant.

Past mark of mouth (society), expresses that a lady or gentleman is getting on into middle age, borrowed from horse-dealing. After seven years old you cannot tell for certain the age of a horse by the marks on his teeth, and he is called *past mark of mouth.* The French have the vulgar phrase, applicable to a woman past her prime, "elle ne marque plus."

Paste (printers), a synonym for brains, referring to the "paste and scissors" class of editorial gentlemen.

Paste and scissors (printers). Matter borrowed from other sources is from an editorial point of view termed thus— especially that which is appropriated without acknowledgment.

Pasteboard (society), a visiting card. To "shoot a *p. b.,*" to leave a card.

Pasteboard customer (trading), one who takes long credit.

Pasteboard, to (society), *to paste-board* a person is to drop a card at an absent person's house.

Paste-horn (popular), the nose; originally shoemaking expression. From the receptacle used by them for paste.

Pastry. In the language of young men about town, *pastry* is the demi-monde, composed of "tarts" and "tartlets."

Oh, beaks so stern and peelers proud,
You know the whole of the *pastry* crowd.
Their tricks are trite, their graces old,
And they never will go home when they're told.
When we get in the Brighton or Margate train
We're all right—but the tarts remain,
They are left to skulk at their end of town.
—*Sporting Times.*

Pasty (popular), a bookbinder.

Patchey (theatrical), harlequin; so called from the triangular-spangled patches on his dress.

Patch upon, not a (common), not to be compared to. A *patch* ought to match the stuff upon which it is placed—therefore *not a patch upon* signifies literally "not to be matched with," "not fit to hold a candle to."

She's *not a patch upon* the duchess.—*Punch.*

Whatever at the time had been
Her satisfaction at fourteen
When Ted had petted her, she now
Felt to herself inclined to vow
That it was *not a patch upon*
That which she just had undergone.
—*D. B. W. Sladen: A Summer Christmas.*

Patent Frenchman (tailors), an Irishman.

Patrico or **pater cove** (old cant), a vagabond, a degraded friar, monk, or priest, afterwards in Protestant times called a *hedge-parson*, who associated with tramps or thieves, and gave his services to them for a fee in mock marriages. It was customary, according to Grose, on these occasions for the man to stand on one side of the carcase of a dead beast and the woman on the other, and on shaking hands they were bidden by the priest to live together till death did them part, meaning apparently that they were parted by death as soon as the ceremony was ended. This was an old gypsy-Hindu custom.

But alas! 'tis my fear that the false *patricoe*
Is reaping those transports are only due to me.
—*Retoure, my dear Delle.*

Patrico is termed *patriarkeo* in the "Fraternity of Vagabondes," 1575.

Patter (popular and thieves), talk, conjuror's talk to his audience, puffing speech. French *boniment*.

Mavor's Spellin' and Copybook motters is all they can run to. But slang?
Wy, it's simply smart *patter*, of wich ony me and my sort 'as the 'ang.
Snappy snideness put pithy, my pippin, the pick of the chick and the hodd,
And it fettles up talk, my dear Charlie like 'ot hoyster sauce with biled cod.
—*Punch.*

You've got the *patter* all right, Billy, but you've on'y got it in the rough. . .
You'll have to put it in perliter langwage, Billy.—*J. Greenwood: Under the Blue Blanket.*

To *patter* flash, *i.e.*, to talk cant, is old canting.

I *pattered* in flash like a covey knowing.
—*W. Maginn.*

Has been derived from *paternoster*, but it is the old gypsy *pat*, or *patterava;* Hindu *bat*, which means slang or secret language. It is possibly allied in Romany to *pat-serava*, corrupt *patter*, to trust or confide in, hence to speak secretly.

The true origin of the word *patter* occurred to the writer in a strange way. "It was in Brighton, when at a corner I saw a tramp with a few ferns in a basket. "' *Shelkin galopas?* ' I casually said in the curious Celtic dialect known as Shelta. *Shelkin galopas* means ' selling ferns.'

"' That one word,' replied the tramp gravely, ' indicates that you, sir, are a gentleman who knows the world. Indeed, your knowledge of it is more than unusual—it is unique.'

"I at once saw that the tramp had been educated. I asked him if there were any gypsies in town.

"' I have just seen old Lee, the tinker,' he replied. ' And if you will come with me you may see him.'

" We went along to a small public, and entering found old Lee. He had known me of yore. Once, three years before, I had promised to give him a treat. It took the form of rum-hot sweet with a bit o' lemon, if

you please. Then contrary to our express compact that the treat was not to exceed drinks, the needy knife-grinder asked for sixpence. And I replied-- 'I give thee sixpence! I will see thee damned first.'

" On seeing me again he burst out into Romany—*he treated;* the tramp spoke to me in Shelta. The landlord glanced at me unfavourably. I asked for a private room. Drinks and cigars were provided. Mr. Lee had three hot rums, the tramp three whiskies. The tramp was a pale man and seemed to grow sober as Lee got drunk.

"' I don't think,' he remarked, ' that the gypsies are of Hindoo origin. I rather think that they come from the *Jángála*, the hill tribes.'

("Heyday!" I thought. "He doesn't call them jungle men, but uses the vernacular.")

"' For I always observed,' he resumed, ' that while the Hindoos only talk Hindustani, the Jángálas use that and have the *Bàt* among themselves.'

"' Great Dictionary!' I cried, ' why, that's Hindoo slang for slang itself. *Bat* or *pat*, and *patter*, are Romany for the *jib*.'

"' That's true!' exclaimed Lee. ' But *patter* is cantin' now.'

"' Lee,' I answered, ' your great-great-great-grandfather used *patter* for talk. It was old Romany. Then your people dropped it when it got blown. *Patter's the lav.*' And turning to the tramp, I added—'With your permission I will incorporate that observation of yours into the next paper which I propose to read before the Oriental Society. Don't you think that the gypsies came from the Dom ?'

" ' I used to see a great many of the Domes when I was a soldier in India. I always thought they were real gypsies.' " People sometimes ask me, ' How did you learn gypsy ?' Well, for every word learned, ' bang went a saxpence ' for rum or beer."

Patter is, however, very old English for to mutter.

Ever he *patred* on theyr names fast.
—*How the Ploughman Learned his Paternoster.*

The old English to *patter*, to mutter (a paternoster), probably combined with the Romany meaning merely slang.

Patteran, a gypsy trail, made by throwing down a handful of grass occasionally (Hotten).

Patter - crib (thieves), a public-house or lodging - house frequented by thieves.

Patterer (streets), one who cried last dying speeches in the streets, &c.

Paul's pigeons (school), the scholars of St. Paul's School have been so called from time immemorial.

Pav. (London), the Pavilion Music Hall.

The Dalston Colosseum has an animated Cirque ; The Moore and Burgess Minstrels are, as usual, at work ; And if you're fond of music halls, the Empire and the *Pav.* Will give you just about the utmost you could wish to have.
—*Fun.*

Pawnee, Pāni (Anglo-Indian and gypsy). In the latter also *parny*, water. " The word is used extensively in Anglo-Indian compound names, such as *bilā-gāti-pāni*, soda-water ; *brandy-pawnee*, brandy and water ; *kush-bo-pāni*, European perfumes (in gypsy *kūshto-pāni*, or *kushto-sūmeni-pāni*, &c." (Anglo-Indian Glossary). In both Hindustani and English gypsy the ocean is known as the *kāla*, or *kālo-pāni*, " the black water," a term of terror in reference to transportation to penal settlements. In German cant water is termed *bani*.

Pax (Winchester), cease talking, be quiet. Also a chum.

Pay-away (common), go on with your discourse. Originally nautical ; from the. phrase to *pay-away, i.e.,* to allow a rope to run out.

Pay dirt (American). When the soil of a place afforded indication of gold in sufficient quantities to render mining profitable, it is called *pay dirt.* The term probably came from the Chinese diggers. The first story in which it occurs is one of a Chinaman who, having been employed to dig a grave, and finding *pay dirt* or gold while so employed, "pre-empted" the ground, and was shot for so doing. The prefix *pay* is to be found in several pidgin-English words.

As their eyes remarked the symptoms, thus their tongues responsive spoke :
" In this undiscovered section there is *pay dirt*, sure as smoke."
—*The Rise and Fall of Gloryville.*

Pay for one's whistle, to (common), to pay extravagantly for any fancy.

Some, though round them life's expenses bristle,
Are not opposed to *paying for their whistle!*
—*Funny Folks.*

Pay, to (popular), to punish, beat.

Her father once said he would kill her mother, and once or twice he *paid* her — *Standard.*

Pay with a hook, to (Australian thieves' patter), to steal. An expression probably imported into New South Wales in the old convict days. *To pay with a hook* signifies to obtain the article, not by payment, but by hooking it, or running away.

You bought them? Ah, I fear me, John, You *paid them with a hook.*
—*J. Brunton Stephens: My Chinee Cook.*

P. D. (trade), a substance which is sold to grocers for mixing with, and thus adulterating, pepper. It is known in the trade by this rather enigmatical appellation.

Peach (English and American), a very complimentary epithet for a young lady. Also "plum."

(Drivers), an informer against omnibus conductors and drivers. From *to peach,* to reveal a secret, inform against ; corrupted from *impeach.*

Peacock engine (railway), a locomotive which carries coals and water in a separate tender, as distinguished from a tank engine, which carries engine, fuel, and water all on one frame.

Peacock horse, amongst undertakers, one with a showy tail and mane.

Pearlies (costermongers), pearl buttons sewn down the sides of the costermongers' trousers in the East End.

Pear, to (thieves), to take money from the police for information, and then from thieves for telling them how to escape. *Pear-making,* the act of drawing supplies from both sides. Evidently from "pair," and to "pair off."

Pebble - beached (London), *i.e.,* high and dry, or very poor. Explained by quotation.

He had arrived at a crisis of impecuniosity compared to which the small circumstance of being *pebble-beached* and stony-broke might be described as comparative affluence.—*Sporting Times.*

Pec (Eton), money ; from the Latin *pecunia.*

Peck (popular), food. *Peck* and *booze,* food and drink ; *peckish,* hungry ; a good *pecker,* a good appetite. *Peck-alley,* the gullet.

A holiday at Peckham, having nothing to eat. *Peck* is probably derived from the action of a hungry bird *pecking* at seed, and from its beak, which it has to open for the purpose. (Old cant), *pek*, meat (Harman). *Ruff-pek*, bacon. *Pek* or *pekker* means in gypsy to roast or bake, and is commonly applied to roast meat. It is found in all gypsy dialects. Mr. Turner derives *pek* from *pecus*, cattle ("Vagrants and Vagrancy," p. 474).

Peck-alley (common), the throat.

Pecker (Oxford), appetite. (Common), a rare *pecker*, a hearty eater. From *to peck*, to eat voraciously. Keep your *pecker* up, take heart, do not be discouraged, never say die; literally keep your beak or head up, do not be down in the mouth.

Keep your *pecker* up, old fellow! and put your trust in old beans.—*C. Bede: Verdant Green.*

Peckish (common), hungry.

Peck, to (common), to eat voraciously. Also "to wolf."

Ped (sporting), a pedestrian—usually a professional one.

These well-known Birmingham *peds* have joined in a sweepstakes of £5 each to run 120 yards level.—*Referee.*

Pedlar's French and **St. Giles' Greek**. The English commonalty, not understanding the secret jargon of tramps and beggars, different from what was called "flash," or ordinary vulgar slang, were accustomed to call it either "French" or "Greek," which two languages were equally unintelligible to them. The "cant" words of tramps, pedlars, and beggars were thus designated as "French," and the Gaelic words spoken to a large extent by the Irish, who in the seventeenth and eighteenth centuries, and up to the third decade of the nineteenth, inhabited the rookeries of St. Giles', London, through which New Oxford Street has been driven, was designated as "Greek." Shakspeare speaks of the phrase *duc-da-me*, used in the sport, called Tom Tiddler's ground, as a Greek invocation to catch fools into a circle. There was a district in the slums of Westminster, inhabited chiefly by the disreputable classes, who spoke in a cant unknown to the other and less vulgar inhabitants of the metropolis, known as "Petty France."

Pedlar's news (Scotch popular), stale news.

Pedlar's pony (American), a walking-stick.

Peel eggs with, to (common), to stand on ceremony. "He's not one you would stand to *peel eggs with*," *i.e.*, stand on ceremony with.

Peeler (general), a policeman; derived from Sir Robert Peel, who first started the metropolitan police in the place of the Bow Street runners.

Bobby too open to the furtive " tip "?
How can the world malign in such a
manner?
Although self-offered to the *Peeler's* grip,
'Tis plain a " Copper " will not take a
" Tanner."
—*Punch.*

Some years ago policemen
were still called "Bobby Peelers."
Vide BOBBY.

Peel, to (common), to strip, take
off, expose, or show.

Peepers (common), the eyes.

The next question was how long they
should wait to let the inmates close their
peepers. — *Reade: Never too Late to
Mend.*

. . . Or would amiably recommend another that, as his *peepers* were a-goin' fast,
he'd best put up the shutters, because the
early-closing movement ought to be fol-
lered out.—*C. Bede: Verdant Green.*

Peepers in mourning, bruised,
black eyes.

His *peepers* are just going out of
mourning.—*Bird o' Freedom.*

Peeping Tom (old cant), still in
use.

A man who is mighty particular in
peering, peaking, and prying about, especially to perceive maids undressing
or undrest, when they, poor innocents,
deem themselves unseen.—*The Comical
Critick.*

The term is derived from
Peeping Tom of Coventry, who
was struck blind for thus offend-
ing.

So *Peeping Thomas* lost his sight.
The world cries out, "It served him right,
For looking at my Lady G."
But oh, if every soul of us,
Who've done the same were punished
thus,
How many blind men there would be !
—*Ballad of Peeping Tom.*

Peepsies (Punch and Judy), the
pan pipes.

Peg (general), a drink, generally
brandy and soda. Hard drinkers in India, every time they
have a drink, are said to add a
peg to their coffin. The latter
is synonymous with " to add a
nail to one's coffin." (Thieves).
a shilling.

Peg, on the (military), to be
under arrest, as a non-commissioned officer. The expression
is also used when a soldier is
put under stoppages. A very
common synonym in the army
is to be "roosted."

Peg out a claim, to (Australian),
properly to mark out for one's
possession. The miner who
wishes to claim a certain piece
of ground had to mark it out
with *pegs;* so has the free selector (*q.v.*) when taking up
land. Therefore *to peg out one's
claim* means to mark out for
one's possession, and is used
figuratively in ordinary conversation, as well as technically.

She is haunted by viscounts and barons,
With aristocratical names,
Fitzgerald, Fitzjames, and Fitzclarence,
All anxious to *peg out their claims*
On her heart, and her hand, and her
portion
Their broken estates to renew,
Long emaciate with the extortion
Of lawyer, and broker, and Jew.
—*Douglas B. W. Sladen: A Bush
Flower.*

Peg out, to (common), to die.
Like a man who strikes his tent
to take his departure.

There is every reason to believe that the unfortunate woman *pegged out* because a remarkably enlarged liver interfered with the natural play of other internal apparatus.—*Fun.*

Peg, putting in the (military), taking a pull at one's self ; being on the sober or quiet tack, voluntarily, or by superior orders.

Pegs (popular), legs.

Peg, to (common), to drink frequently. *Vide* PEG.

Pelter (nautical), the small ten-gun ship of old. (Popular), out for a *pelter*, means in a very bad temper.

Pelt, to (tailors), to sew thickly.

Pempe (Winchester College). When a new " man " comes, he is asked whether he has his *pempe* (which in reality is an imaginary object, but is represented as being a book). Of course, the answer is in the negative, whereupon he is assured that it is quite indispensable, and is sent from one man to another, each telling him that some one else has it in his possession. The joke ends by his being sent to some master, who gets him out of his difficulties. The derivation is πεμ-πεμψον προτερον, that is, " send the fool further." A kindred joke, perpetrated on a raw recruit in the French army, is to send him on a fool's errand after the " clef du champ de manœuvres," or "le parapluie de l'escouade."

Pen (colonial), a threepenny piece.

Penang lawyer (Anglo-Indian), the name of a handsome walking-stick from Penang and Salampore. " The name is popularly thought to have originated in a jocular supposition that lawsuits in Penang were decided by the *lex bocalinum* (club-law). But *pinang liyar* (wild areca), may almost certainly be assumed to be the real name " (Anglo-Indian Glossary).

Pencil-fever (turf), this imaginary disease sets in when, despite the efforts of the " marketeers," a horse can no longer be kept at a short price in the lists (Hotten).

Penciller (sporting), a bookmaker's clerk.

Penny gaff. *Vide* GAFF.

Penny starver (popular), a penny roll.

Pepper-box. *Vide* COFFEE-MILL.

Peppered (turf), used in reference to a man who has laid large stakes on a horse.

He was *peppered* in one dangerous quarter alone to the extent of three or four thousand pounds, simultaneously with a large outlay on Jerry.—*Sporting Times.*

Perchera (Winchester College), a mark put against a " man's " name who has been " late " for chapel.

Perfectly demmy (American cadet). A man who is dressed in perfectly good taste—stylishly so—is said to be *perfectly demmy*.

Probably from association with Mr. Mantalini of "Nicholas Nickleby."

Periodicals (American), men who go at regular intervals on sprees, or who get drunk only at certain times, are said to have their *periodicals, i.e.,* periodical dissipations.

" Mr. Featherly," inquired Bobby from across the table, " are you in the book business ? " " I ? No ; I'm in the dry-goods business. You know that very well, Bobby." " Yes ; but ma and pa were talking last night about your having your little *periodicals,* and I thought perhaps that you had made a change."—*New York Times.*

Perks (common), perquisites.

To first-class passengers I speak
In accents soft and bland,
To second-class, though quite polite,
No nonsense will I stand ;
But the third-class I'm down upon,
I treat them just like Turks,
The reason is, you understand,
From them I get no *perks.*
—*T. Russell : The Railway Guard.*

Pernicated dude (Canadian), a dandy who assumes a highly swaggering manner.

Pernicketty (American), fastidious, mean, and over-particular.

The Comptroller of St. Louis must be very *pernicketty.* He objects, it seems, to paying out of the City Treasury for carriages to take aldermen home at night. —*Detroit Free Press.*

Perpendicular (London), a lunch taken standing at a bar.

Persuaders (common), pistols.

" The *persuaders ?* " " I've got 'em," replied Sikes.—*Charles Dickens : Oliver Twist.*

Also spurs.

I have known a coster get a month for inflicting upon his donkey half the pain which the poor mare suffered from the jockey's *persuaders.*—*Daily Paper.*

Persuading plate (thieves), an implement used by burglars. It is an iron disk, revolving on a pivot with a cutting point.

Detective - sergeant now produced a quantity of property found on the prisoners, including a *persuading plate* used for the purpose of forcing safes.—*Daily News.*

Pesky (American), an adjective used in detraction, as " the *pesky* horse ! " " This is a *pesky* sight too bad." Probably from the Dutch *pestje !* Pest on it ! was a well-known English oath a century ago, but was still commoner in Dutch and German. *Ein poitchen* (dialect, *Pestche').*

Pete Jenkins (circus), a character introduced in the ring as one who has friends in the audience. Sometimes it is an imaginary old aunt from the country, who is delighted at recognising her long lost nephew, yet horrified at seeing him risking his life by his daring feats on horseback. Peter assures her that there is no danger, and finally persuades her to take a ride. She, of course, tumbles off, and " makes business," to the delight of all lookers-on. Anon some apparent rustic greets him, inquires if the circus-business pays, and is also persuaded into the ring. The original *Pete Jenkins,* a small man with a large nose, was in Dan Rice's troop, or

"Great Show," in America about 1855. *Pete Jenkins* now means a variation on the clown.

Peter (thieves), a parcel.

So while I was looking about I piped a little *peter* (parcel).—*Horsley: Jottings from Jail.*

A cash-box.

After we left the course, we found a dead 'un, and got a *peter* with very near a century of quids in it.—*Horsley: Jottings from Jail.*

Also a very old word for portmanteau. This was the original word. (Australian prison), punishment cell. (Poachers), a partridge.

Peter-claimer (thieves), one who steals boxes, portmanteaus, bundles.

Peter Collins (theatrical), a gentleman never to be found. In towns there are generally young aspirants who want to act, who apply at the theatre, and are told to call in the afternoon. If he does he is sent in search of *Peter Collins*, "that's the man to give him a job," by one of the stage men, or any one who knows the game, and "will you take this up to him," a sack with something heavy in it, counterweights, and an old pantomime mask generally. So the youth is sent from the roof to the cellar, and, finally, is generally let down a trap and left to get out as best he can.

The same trick is practised at circuses, but the password is the "green-handled rake," which the youth is requested to ask for. He is generally settled with a pill of horse-dung when they have had enough of him.

Peter out, to (American), a California mining expression meaning to give out, be exhausted, or come to an end. "To go through St. Peter's needle," (English provincial), to be beaten, or incur loss. Hence perhaps the expression.

Peter Funk (American). In New York city for nearly a century all kinds of petty humbug, deceit, and sham, especially in business, has been characterised by a mythical character named *Peter Funk*. Bartlett ingeniously conjectures that this was a fictitious name given in at the mock-auction shops, where Peter is employed as a by-bidder to run up prices and swindle the ignorant. But there is much in the term "to funk out," or to disappear mysteriously, and in the associations with funk, a stench, or a smoke, which suggest humbug and foul dealing. *Peter Funk* is very fully described in an amusing old American novel called "The Perils of Pearl Street."

Peter Rugg (American). "He'll get home as soon as *Peter Rugg.*" "He's like *Peter Rugg*, the missing man." "He brings weather like *Peter Rugg.*" The writer has often heard these and similar sayings in his youth, in Massachusetts. They are founded on the following legend. About the end of the seventeenth century one *Peter Rugg* and his daughter left Roxbury in a chaise to get to their home in Boston. A friend remarked that a storm was coming up which would prevent his getting home. To which *Peter Rugg* replied with a dire oath, "I will get home to-night or may I never get home." For a hundred years whenever a storm was coming it was always preceded by *Peter Rugg* in his old chaise, asking the way to his house. He was always in great distress, seeming to be bewildered. At last one day when his house had just been sold by auction and passed into the hands of a stranger and was no longer legally his home, *Peter Rugg* drove up, and then disappeared. His penance was at an end.

Petticoat pensioner (common), a man who lives on a prostitute's earnings. Also "Sunday-man, ponce, prosser, Kaffir."

Pew-opener's muscle (medical), a muscle of the palm of the hand so called by the late Sir Benjamin Brodie because it helps to contract and hollow the palm for the reception of a gratuity.

Pewter (common), money.

Philadelphia Catechism (nautical), the name by which the following couplet is known.

"Six days shalt thou labour, and do all thou art able,
And on the seventh—holystone the decks and scrape the cable."

Philip (thieves), a policeman. Obsolete. Also a warning cry.

Philiper (thieves), a thief's accomplice who keeps watch and calls out *Philip !* as a warning cry.

Phiz (common), face, countenance.

Proves as 'Arry is well to the front wen sech higperlite pens pop on him.
Does me proud and no herror, dear pal ; shows we're both in the same bloomin' swim.
Still, they don't cop my *phiz* quite ker-rect ; they know Gladstone right down to the ground ;
But I ain't quite so easy 'it off, don'tcher see, if you take me all round.
—*Punch.*

Piccadilly crawl, a languid walk much affected about ten years ago.

Pickers (popular), a very old term for hands.

Picker-up (Stock Exchange), a man who tries to get members to make a wrong price, and then deals with them.

Pick flies off it, to (tailors), to find fault with it.

Picking out robins' eyes (tailors), side-stitching a black cloth or fine material.

Picking-up (popular), explained by quotation.

There, it seems, the girls of the working class go out *picking-up*, just as the boys go out "mashing." They go by twos or threes, each little party of the same sex ;

the girls looking in the shop windows and giggling, the boys sauntering along, cigarette in mouth and hands in pocket. Presently the latter jostle up against the former. They apologise. No apology, they are told, is needed. "Going to market?" asks the lad. "Yes," is the reply. "May we come along?" "Very well." Thus is the ice speedily and satisfactorily broken!—*Globe.*

Pickle jar (popular), a coachman in yellow livery.

Pick-me-up (popular), a stimulating draught before dinner, or after a debauch.

Pick off, to (Winchester College), to hit somebody with a stone.

Picture, not in the (turf), not placed.

In the Hardwicke Stakes he was fully fifty yards behind Bendigo, who, in turn, was *not in the picture.—Sporting Times.*

Pie (printers). Almost technical. Different kinds of type mixed up together, either through accident, as when a forme not tightened enough falls to pieces when being carried away, or through negligence. German and French printers use respectively the expressions, *zwiebelfisch*, literally fish with onions; and *pâté*, or pie, "faire du pâté," to distribute such mixed up type.

Bacon was a highly educated man, and an expert linguist; yet the foreign in the folio may be summarised as a mass of *pie.* Thus "Dictisima;" "vemchie, vencha, que non te vnde, que non te perreche." These are copied from the quartos. Then we have the French : "il fait for chando, Ie man voi a le Court la grand affaires."—*Standard.*

"We've had an accident, sir," said Old Pleasure, the foreman; "the whole of 'Bits of Turf' has fallen into *pie.*"

"Pick it up," said the great man, "and head it 'Musings at the Cheshire Cheese.'"—*Bird o' Freedom.*

(Booksellers), the miscellaneous collection of books which have been pulled out of the alphabet during the day, and have to be replaced at night. It is always the last job of the day to put the *pie* away.

Piece (common). Hotten says that this is "a contemptuous term for a woman—a strumpet." It occurs in Elizabethan writers in this sense. It is now generally heard in such phrases as "she is a nice *piece*," "a good *piece*."

Piece brokers (thieves), explained by quotation.

As he comes along, bringing your new suit home, he would think it no sin to call at that repository for stolen goods, the *piece broker's*, and sell there a strip of your unused cloth for a shilling.—*Greenwood: Seven Curses of London.*

Piece of calico (American), a girl or woman. "The *calico*," or "the muslin," women in general.

Piece of pudding (popular), a piece of luck, or a welcome change.

Piece of thick (popular slang), a piece of Cavendish, or pressed cake tobacco.

> Never again!
> Will I attempt a pipe to smoke,
> Never again!
> I've tried it once but 'twas no joke,
> I got a clay and *piece of thick*,

Thought I'd do a clever trick,
But crikey, didn't I feel sick,
Never again !
—*Ballad* (*Francis & Day*).

Pieces (thieves), money.

Rêve d'Or should be the mare to go,
Unless you boldly strike for Freedom,
Concerning *pieces* thus to show
The heartless bookies that you need 'em.
—*Bird o' Freedom.*

The flash terms for *pieces* are : "brown, copper, blow," a penny; "bit," threepence; "lord of the manor, pig, sprat, downer, snid, tanner," sixpence; "bob, breaky-leg, deaner," shilling ; "alderman," half-a-crown ; " bull, cartwheel," crown ; " half a quid," half a sovereign ; " sov., quid, couter, yellow-boy, canary, foont," sovereign ; " finnup, fiver," five-pound note; " double finnup, tenner," ten-pound note; "pony," twenty pounds ; "monkey," fifty pounds ; " century," hundred pounds ; " plum," £100,000 ; " marygold," one million.

Pieman (streets), he who is tossing at pitch and toss.

Pie, to put into the (auction). At book sales, to put into a large lot, to be sold at the end.

Pig (thieves and popular), a policeman or detective. (Trade), sometimes cold *pig*, but more often the former. A term by which goods returned from any cause are known.

Pigeon (common), a dupe whose fate it is to be "plucked" by blacklegs and others. The French use *pigeon* in the same sense. In Spanish cant *palomo*, pigeon, is a gullible person.

Pigeon, blue. *Vide* BLUE PIGEON.

Pigeon holes (Winchester College), small studies. (Printers), matter widely and badly spaced. This is a recognised expression amongst compositors and readers, owing to the amount of white between the words, likened to a nest of *pigeon holes.*

Pig, pork (tailors), garments spoiled, cut wrong, not the right material, or any error which precludes the possibility of alteration.

Pigs (Cambridge University), members of St. John's College are called *pigs.*

The Johnians are always known by the name of *pigs ;* they put up a new organ the other day, which was immediately christened " Baconi Novum Organum."— *Westminster Review.*

(Printers), a term of contempt applied by compositors to pressmen. When pressmen entered the composing-room they would be received with grunts. A compositor would not dare to do this out of his own particular department. So " Savage's Dictionary," 1841, says.

Pig's ear, pig's lug (tailors), a name given to a lappel collar or flap too heavy for the size of garment.

Pig's foot (American thieves), a "jimmy," or thieves' short crowbar, cloven at one end like a *pig's foot.*

Pig-sticker (army), sabre.

Pig-sty (printers), a press-room is thus somewhat inelegantly described.

Pig's whistle (American), according to Bartlett, who gives it as a synonym for an instant, "In less than a *pig's whistle.*" As there exists an old English equivalent for this in "less than a pig's whisper," and as there is a well-known old tavern sign called the "Pig and Whistle," it is easy to see how one term might be derived from another. It seems to be a fact and not a mere philological guess, that "pig and whistle" was originally *pigen wœshœl!* Hail to the Virgin! an amusing instance of bathos.

Pigtails (Stock Exchange), Chartered Bank of India, Australia, and China.

Pike (American), a name applied in California to the migratory poor whites, said to have originated, according to Bartlett, from the supposition that they came from *Pike* County, Missouri. "The true *pike*," says Mr. Fraahoff, "is the wandering gypsy-like Southern poor white who lives in a waggon." As the term *pike* and *pikey* have been used for at least a century in England, and probably much longer, for a gypsy or a tramp, the term is evidently enough

not derived from "*Pike* County, Missouri." (Thieves), turn-pike.

Pikers (Australian), wild cattle which cannot be got out of the bush. From English slang to *pike*, to run away.

Pike it, to (popular and thieves), to run away. From taking to the *pike* or turnpike road, as applied to a discontented person, "if you don't like it you can *pike it.*"

Pikey (popular), a tramp or gypsy.

Pile (American), now used in England.

In the course of conversation it was very remarkable to notice the variety of occupations which a rich American has filled before he has "made his *pile.*" He may have been a bootblack, a messenger boy, the editor of a newspaper, the captain of a ferry-boat, a lawyer, or a murderer, but somehow he has "done the trick."—*Pall Mall Gazette.*

To have made his *pile,* is generally supposed to be a term of Californian origin referring to a *pile* of gold dust, or to have come from the gambling tables, meaning a quantity of heaped-up gold. Bartlett has, however, indicated that the term seems to be the revival of an old one used by Dr. Franklin in his "Poor Richard's Almanac" for April 1741, where he says—

Rash mortal, ere you take a wife,
Contrive your *pile* to last for life.

Piler is obsolete English for one who accumulates money, and this supports the above derivation (also the French *amasser*, to hoard).

"In Dutch *peyl*, a certain mark, as a water-mark; *boven de peyl*, above the set mark; *peyler*, one that sounds the deep, hence *peyllood*, a sounding lead, and *peyloot*, a pilot. Hence a man who had made his *pile* would be one who had attained his determined mark or limit, certainly a much more definite expression than that of a mere heap. It is true that about twenty-five years ago an Indian tribe in the West, when the Government offered them an indemnity for certain losses, in their ignorance of the art of counting, could only keep repeating, 'Want heap money—heap big.' At last one of the chiefs set an arrow in the ground and stipulated that there should be as much specie given as would quite cover it. It is curious that the word pronounced *pile* in Dutch should—apropos of this story—mean both a set mark and an arrow, and also in English, a heap" (Chas. G. Leland: Notes).

Pile in, to (American), a common form of invitation to take part in anything, as a meal, or to come into a house, make one of a party in a vehicle or a dance, &c.

They gave us a friendly hail, and whether they fancied we looked hungry or not, kindly asked us to sit down with them and *pile in*, which being interpreted signifies "Pitch in and eat."—*M. Roberts: The Western Avernus.*

To *pile out* means to come forth.

Pile of mags (conjuring), a pile of "faked" coins, or of coins so distributed as to move freely one above the other. This is a very old term, which must have been long in the profession, as the *mags* are generally gold, real or apparent; and in the so-called Gypsy Vocabulary of Bampfylde Moore Carew (but which has hardly a gypsy word in it), *meg* is a guinea. The ancient cant form of the word was *make*. Also *make*, a halfpenny; "Brummagen macks," counterfeit halfpence, according to Dekker.

Pile on the agony, to. *Vide* AGONY.

Pile on, to (American), applied to excess or intensity in any form.

" In acting you should go and see
Our friend *pile on* the agony."

Pile on the lather, Mr. Jones—do! Tell me that I am a twenty-five horse-power angel, 'iled with ottar of roses. It won't tire me much, and it may relieve you.— —*How Jones told his Story.*

Pill (common), a doctor; *pill-driver*, an itinerant apothecary.

Pill-box (popular), a soldier's cap.

Pilled (common), synonymous with "black-balled."

Mr. Jubilee Plunger Benzon was *pilled* for the Southdown Club.—*Bird o' Freedom.*

Pill, to (University), to talk twaddle, or in platitudes.

Pillow-sham (American), a cover for a pillow. "Outwardly I was as decorous as a clean *pillow-sham*," a quaint and slightly sarcastic phrase to express an appearance of decorous gravity assumed for the occasion.

Pimple (popular), the head.

Pimp, to (University), to do little, mean, petty actions, to curry favour.

Pinchbeck villas (journalistic), small cheap houses, mostly in the suburbs of cities, bearing pretentious names, such as "The Oaks," "The Gables," &c.

Our correspondent in Paris informs us that "there is a growing tendency to dub even the *pinchbeck villas* which are springing up all round the metropolis with the pretentious title of château."—*Daily Telegraph.*

Pinch-board (American thieves or gambling), a swindling roulette-table.

There's the *pinch-board*. That's dead crooked. A sucker sees the wheel and the numbers all straight enough, and the little arrow in the middle. The owner tells him his chances are two to one if he bets on the odd or even numbers, and twelve to one if he puts his money on any one of the twelve. That's all muck. The owner has a brass tube running from the arrow to the edge of the board. There's a rod run through that, and a button on to the end of it. His capper stands next to the button, and by pressing his leg against it he can make the arrow stop (or point to) where he wants it. Sometimes the crowd think that the man that's working the wheel is playing them, and they tell him to stand away from the table. He says, "Certainly, gentlemen; anything to oblige!" and steps back a foot or two; but the capper he's there just the same,

and nobody suspects him, 'cause he keeps losin' his money just like the rest of 'em.—*Confidence Crooks : Philadelphia Press.*

It may be remarked that the roulette-tables, spin-boards, dice, teetotums, in short, all the games seen at fairs and races, are swindles. The rifles for firing at a mark for prizes cheat by having false sights or curves in the barrels. The writer at one of these places once succeeded in hitting the mark many times by aiming six inches below it.

Pinch, to (thieves), to arrest, to steal.

Pink (common), the height of perfection. Used by Shakspeare in this sense. (American cadet), being reported for some infraction of the regulations. "He's got a hefty skin of a *pink* for that jollification," *i.e.*, "He's got a severe report against him."

Pinked (tailors), beautifully and carefully made.

Pinked between the lacings, a very old term, from *pinked*, stabbed, still current among criminals and detectives in New York. It signifies convicted by reason of perjury. Also when an honest man is convicted of a false charge by treacherous advantage being taken of some weak point. To question a witness (as is very commonly done by unscrupulous counsel) as to all the sins of all his past life, which have no reference to the case whatever, is to *pink him between the lacings.*

Pinked or **skinned, to get** (American cadet), to get reported.

Pinker (pugilistic), a blow that draws the claret or blood.

Pinky (American), an old New York term for the little finger, from the provincial English *pinky,* very small. A common term in New York, especially among small children, who, when making a bargain with each other, are accustomed to confirm it by interlocking the little finger of each other's right hands, and repeating the following:

> *Pinky, pinky,* bow-bell,
> Whoever tells a lie,
> Will sink down to the bad place,
> And never rise up again.
> (Bartlett.)

Pinnel (thieves), corruption of penal servitude.

Pinners-up (tramps), the sellers of wall - songs, that is, songs printed on small sheets and pinned on a canvas stretched on a wall for display.

Pins (common), legs.

Pint (tailors), "my *pint* for him," I commend him.

Pinto (American cowboys), a piebald horse. From the Spanish *pinto,* painted or coloured (MS. Americanisms by C. Leland Harrison).

Pints round (tailors), an expression used in places where there are a number of cutters employed and one drops his shears on the floor. Then the cry comes as from one man, *pints round,* and means that the unfortunate individual will have to pay for a pint of ale for every man in the shop. It is said that it was customary to enforce this rule, but it is not so now.

Pipeclaying it over (tailors), hiding the faults.

Pipe-laying (American), making arrangements to procure fraudulent votes. It is said to have been first used about 1835, in connection with a plot to import voters to New York from Philadelphia. Extensive works in connection with laying croton water-pipes were then in progress, and hence the phrase acquired its accepted significance. The Whig leaders were actually indicted for the alleged attempt at fraud, but were acquitted by the jury by whom they were tried. (Police), taking measures for the detection of a suspected criminal.

Pipe one's eye, to (popular), to weep.

> Why, what's that to you, if my *eyes I'm a piping,*
> A tear is a comfort, d'ye see, in its way.
> —*Charles Dibdin.*

Piper (London), a spy on omnibus conductors. (American police), a spy. *Vide* To PIPE.

Pipers (pugilistic), the lungs.

Piper's news (Scotch popular), stale news.

Pipe, to (old cant), to cry. (Thieves), to see. In this sense a corruption of "peep," the eyes being termed "peepers."

If I *pipe* a good chat, why, I touch for the wedge,
But I'm not a "particular" robber;
I smug any snowy I see on the hedge,
And I ain't above daisies and clobber.
— *The Referee.*

Also to follow and spy. (Popular), to talk.

"You see," said the barber, "we help one another here, and I have fetched you out this last two nights so as to get you alongside this y'ere chum, who has got fourteen stretch and his ticket. Now then, *pipe* away, red 'un."—*Evening News.*

Pip, to (card-players), to take the trick from your opponent.

Pirates (London street), omnibuses in which extravagant prices are charged for fare.

Did Mr. Shillibeer, when he started the London omnibus on its prosperous career of useful activity, ever foresee a time when a bold bad 'bus, called a *pirate*, would invade the streets?—*Daily Telegraph.*

Pit (thieves), explained by quotation.

I had developed a special aptitude for "buzzing" (pocket-picking) from the *pit* or inside breast coat pocket.—*Tit-Bits.*

Pitch (circus, strolling players, itinerants, &c.), a place suitable for a performance of any kind, sale of goods, &c. In certain towns, some sixteen years ago, actors could not work without getting permission from the mayor or justice of the peace, else they were liable to imprisonment as rogues and vagabonds.

Showmen are agreed that there is no better *pitch* in the world than London.—*Daily Telegraph.*

A performance.

His "fakements" or "properties" were costly and tasteful, and, in short, the entire *pitch* was a complete triumph.—*Daily Telegraph.*

Doing a *pitch*, doing business.

Being at Plymouth fair, and doing a good business, there stood among the crowd a youth who bought a great many lots of me, so that when I had done my *pitch*, and got down from the stage . . .—*Hindley: Life and Adventures of a Cheap Jack.*

To "queer the *pitch*," to spoil the *pitch*, or performance, a theatrical and circus phrase, meaning to stop, spoil a performance in any way.

He was never "loose in ponging," nor did he ever "miss his tip." His equestrianism was emphatically "bono," and there was nothing to "queer his *pitch*."—*Daily Telegraph.*

Used also figuratively, to mar, spoil one's plans, business.

When my *pitch* you endeavoured to queer,
Wasn't friendly at all, so I look for a share
In her merry ten thousand a year.
— *Sporting Times.*

(Popular), a short interval for sleep.

Pitched (tailors), acquaintance cut. No intercourse of any kind.

Pitcher (coiners), one who utters base coin.

Pitching it strong (common), exaggerating, overdoing it.

"Well, I am thinking the *'Tiser* is *pitching it* rather strong."
" My love, what an expression."—*Reade: Hard Cash.*

Pitch in, pull out, to (tailors), to work with a will.

Pitch into a person, to (common), to castigate him, to revile him severely.

Pitch the fork, to (popular), to tell a pitiful tale.

Pitch the hunters, to (fairs), explained by quotation.

When Elias was at a pleasure fair, he would *pitch the hunters*, that is, put up the three sticks a penny business.—*Hindley: Life and Adventures of a Cheap Jack.*

Pitch the nob. *Vide* PRICK THE GARTER.

Pitch, to (coiners), to utter base coin. (Popular), to have a short sleep.

Pitch up (Winchester College), a clique or party, a set of chums. A Winchester boy's *pitch up* are his friends at home.

Pitch up with, to (Winchester College), to associate with. *Vide* PITCH UP.

Pit circlers (theatrical). The expression explains itself.

It is, however, so magnificently put on and so splendidly acted that it is no wonder the stallites, not to mention the *pit circlers*, crowd nightly to see it.—*Bird o' Freedom.*

Pit-pat's the way (popular), trot along, go on, don't stop!
VOL. II.

Wire in and go ahead, like fashionable Fred,
Pit-pat's the way and sharp's about the word.
—*Ballad: Fashionable Fred.*

Pit riser (theatrical), a burst of powerful acting which evokes an enthusiastic acclamation from the pit. Derived from the well-known anecdote of Edmund Kean.

On returning home, after his first appearance at Drury Lane, while describing his triumph to his wife, Mrs. Kean interrupted him by inquiring what Lord Essex thought of the little man's Shylock?
"Damn Lord Essex! The *pit rose* at me!" replied Kean.

Pittsburg grip (American), explained by quotation.

The *Pittsburg grip*, a throat disorder that troubled singers in the smoky city for years, has disappeared with the introduction of natural gas.—*American Humorist.*

From the French *grippe*, influenza.

Place (tailors), "a breast-pocket kind of *place*," or "a one-eyed kind of *place*," is a small shop.

Placebo (medical), "I will please," a dose of coloured water, or something equally harmless, given to a patient with an imaginary malady.

Plain as a yard of pumpwater (tailors), a quaint phrase, meaning very plain.

Plain-headed (society), a term to express that a lady is not good-

I

looking; it is borrowed from house language.

Plain statement (tailors), an indifferent meal, or an easy, simple, and straightforward garment to make.

Plank, to (American and old English), to pay down money. "To *plank* the pewter." In old cant, both shillings and Spanish dollars were called boards.

Now then, ye noble sportsmen, if you can find anything to beat him for a shop, *plank* down your spondulicks.—*Sporting Times.*

To *plank* it down, to lay money on a horse.

This is a better bloomin' game, I give you my vord, than *plankin' it down* to Kempton!—*Sporting Times.*

Plant (thieves and various), a preconcerted swindle, robbery, or burglary, in which sense the term explains itself as being a metaphor taken from planting cuttings or seeds in a garden.

"What have you got to say for yourself, you withered old fence, eh?" "I was away on a *plant.*"—*Dickens : Oliver Twist.*

Hence any dishonest trick, dodge, device.

"He should have tried mustachios, and a pair of military trousers." "So he did, and they warn't of no more use than the other *plant.*"—*Dickens : Oliver Twist.*

"Have they got the requisite coin—you know what I mean—the money?" inquired Mr. Laggers. "It isn't a *plant?*"—*J. Greenwood : Dick Temple.*

You have really no idea
What an artful bird it is,
Fly to trap and up to biz,
Twigs a *plant* in half a minute.
　　　　　—*Punch.*

A *plant*, a decoy, one who keeps watch for burglars to warn them. In this sense it literally means one *planted* there, like the French *planton*, orderly in waiting. Also hidden money or valuables ; to spring a *plant*, to unearth such a hidden hoard.

Plant, to (thieves and various), to mark a person out for robbery or a swindle. It is curious to note that the French have *jardinier* for a confederate in a confidence trick swindle, whose duty is to prepare the victim, foster and nurse him as a gardener would a plant. Also to conceal, hide. In this sense common in Australia.

Why, they stuck up Wilson's station there, and murdered the man and woman in the kitchen; they then *planted* inside the house, and waited until Wilson came home at night with his stockman ; then they rushed out and knocked old Wilson on the head, and drove a spear through the man's side.—*A. C. Grant : Bush Life in Queensland.*

Not being able to send my gold down to the escort office for security, I was forced to content myself with *planting* it, which I did just inside my tent.—*Australian Story.*

To *plant* the job, to arrange and prepare, generally in reference to a robbery.

It was not found necessary to *plant* the job by squaring the servants beforehand, nor to invent any elaborate ruse, for it was considered that the more natural the mode of attack the better would be the chances of success.—*Daily Telegraph.*

(Coiners), to *plant*, to pass spurious coin, intrusted to them by the "dandy master," or manufacturer of base sovereigns and half sovereigns. A bottle of spirits is the ordinary purchase, and the smasher receives it and seven and sixpence as a commission.

It is a two-handed job, and two women, generally an old and a young one, manage it. The former carries the base coin, and the latter *plants* it.—*J. Greenwood: Rag, Tag, & Co.*

Also *plant* the sour.

Although the tradesman on whom "her poor old man" had tried to "*plant* the sour" had sent for a constable, Mr. Maloney in the interim had contrived to put down his throat such evidence of his being a "regular hand" as he happened to have about him.—*J. Greenwood: Rag, Tag, & Co.*

(Conjurors), to place an object to be afterwards magically discovered by the conjuror in the hands or pockets of a conscious or unconscious confederate among the spectators.

(Cardsharpers), to *plant* the books, to place the cards in the pack unfairly, for the purpose of cheating at play, or deceiving by legerdemain.

(Football), when a football is kicked against a person he is said to be *planted*. Is used more specially with reference to a hit in the face. The blow itself is called a *planter*.

Plasterer (sporting), explained in the following extract.

Worse, if it be possible, than this desolater of hares is the "masher" or "chappie" of modern England who prides himself on quick shooting, and cuts down his birds before they are well on the wing. Mr. Bromley-Davenport calls him the

plasterer—one who thinks nothing of the lives and eyes of the men who surround him on all sides, and blows his pheasant to a pulp before the bird is seven feet in the air.—*Daily Telegraph.*

Plaster, to (popular), to flatter.

He'd go out and get as drunk as a fiddler, and then he'd come rowlin' home and begin *plasterin'* myself over, calling me his colleen jhas and lovin' me the same as if we'd been married only fifteen minutes. — *T. Browne: My Husband's Toddy.*

Plate it, to (London), to walk. *Vide* PLATES OF MEAT.

An adipose gentleman *plates it* on to the stage, and chirrups the soul-stirring anthem, "You shan't wipe your nose on the flag."—*Sporting Times.*

Plates of meat (popular), the feet.

As I walk along my beat,
You can hear my *plates of meat.*
—*Music Hall Song.*

They recognise their favourite comedian, and anticipate his lines by numerous gags, and inquiries having reference to "what cheer" he is enjoying, and how his *plates o' meat* are.—*Sporting Times.*

Platform (common). "The word *platform*, when used for the programme of a political party, is often classed as an Americanism, but it is really a revival of a use of the word that was very common in English literature in the sixteenth and seventeenth centuries, though less common, perhaps, as a noun than as a verb, meaning to lay down principles. For instance, Milton, in his 'Reason of Church Government,' says that some 'do not think it for the ease of their inconsequent opinions to grant that church discipline is platformed in the Bible, but that it is left to the discretion of men '" (*Cornhill Magazine*). It is used as a noun in Cromwell's letters.

A standpoint in an argument, a statement of opinion.

Mrs. Anthony presented the following *platform*, which was unanimously adopted, "That the present claim for manhood suffrage sugar - coated with the words equal, impartial, universal, &c., is a fraud so long as woman is not permitted to share in the said suffrage." — *Report of the Great Woman's Demonstration, New York*, 1867.

Pastor Chignel has set aside Dr. Barham's Liturgy and has taken the most advanced *platform* known to modern Unitarianism."—*Nonconformist.*

Platter (common), broken crockery.

Play board (Punch and Judy), the stage.

Play booty, to (theatrical), to play badly, and with malice prepense, for the purpose of flooring a play, or a player.

Play dark, to (popular), to conceal one's true character.

"Look here," said Smithers, wiping the mess from his mouth, "you've been *playing dark*, and I'm out of training, and——."—*Moonshine.*

Play for, to (American), to deal with generally, with an idea of deceiving. *Vide* JAY.

Play Hell and Tommy, to. This expression is thought to be a corruption of "Hal and Tommy," the allusion being to Henry VIII. and his unscrupulous minister,

Thomas Cromwell, who seized and rifled the religious houses, and turned out their occupants to starve. This is, however, a very doubtful derivation. In some parts of England it is very common for an angry man to threaten another that he will *play Hell and Tommy* with him.

Playing it low down (American), an expression signifying that a man has been too unprincipled, mean, or rapacious in an act.

I ain't over particular, but this I *do* say, that interducin' a feller to your sister, and availin' himself of the opportunity while you're a kissin' her to stock the cards, is a *playin' it mighty low down.*—*Newspaper Story.*

Playing the sovereign (American). Office-seekers who, shortly before an election, put on shabby clothes, drink whisky, and shake hands with everybody, and make themselves generally agreeable to all of inferior social position whom it is to their interest to conciliate, are said to be *playing the sovereign*, the object being to secure their good graces and obtain their votes. Probably derived from the common phrase the "sovereign people."

Play old gooseberry, to (popular), to do a person a mischief, to "kick up a row," to behave in a violently inimical manner. *Vide* GOOSEBERRY.

Please the pigs! (common), if you are willing, if all goes well —a form of assent providing no obstacle crops up. Edwards says the phrase, ludicrous as it is in its present shape, had its origin in a deep religious feeling. It was formerly "please the pyx." The pyx was the box which contained the consecrated wafer, and was held in the greatest veneration as the symbol of the Almighty. The phrase therefore, "If it please the pyx," was equivalent to "If it shall please God," or, in modern form, "D.V.," *i.e.*, *Deo Volente*, or, God being willing. This derivation is, however, much more ingenious than probable.

Plebe (American cadet), a new cadet; a military synonym for the freshman of the universities.

Plebs (Westminster school), a tradesman's son. From the Latin *plebs*, populace.

Pledge (Winchester College), to give away. "*Pledge* me" means after you.

Ploughed (common), drunk.

Plough, to (university). A man is *ploughed* when he fails in an examination. Probably this word was suggested by the harrowed feelings of the candidate.

Well, the "gooseberry pie" is really too deep for me; but *ploughed* is the new Oxfordish for "plucked."—*C. Reade: Hard Cash.*

Pluck, to (common), an Oxford term now in general use, to reject a candidate for examination. "When the degrees are conferred," says Cuthbert Bede, "the name of each person is read out before he is presented to the Vice-Chancellor. The proctor then walks once up and down the room, so that any person who objects to the degree being granted may signify the same by pulling or *plucking* the proctor's robes."

Plug (university), explained by quotation.

Getting up his subjects by the aid of those royal roads to knowledge, variously known as cribs, crams, *plugs*, abstracts, analyses, or epitomes.—*C. Bede: Verdant Green.*

(American), a high hat.

Plug a man, to (Royal Military Academy), to kick one behind.

Plugged money (American). Silver money is often treated by rogues who bore pieces out and fill the holes with lead or amalgam. The term is applied also to men with moral defects, *e.g.*, "He is clever but there is a *plug* in him." "You are not up to his *plugs.*"

"Young man!" shouted the retail tobacconist, "didn't I caution you to keep your eyes peeled for *plugged* silver coins?"—*Detroit Free Press.*

Plugs (American), people who assemble on the side-walks and stand there chatting, to the great inconvenience of the passers-by, or who, as any one may see for himself in Bond Street, London, love to stand with their backs to shop windows to exhibit themselves.

Oh, stand on the side-walk—do !
That the world may look at you !
You think you're so complete
And are dressed so very neat,
  Oh, *plug* on the side-walk, do.
Oh, stand in the doorway, do !
To hinder passing through,
  'Tis so very *distingué*
  To be standing in the way ;
Oh, *plug* up the doorway—do !
  —*Newspaper Ballad.*

Plug-teaching (American), teaching trades and arts in casual or evening lessons.

A good deal of boy (and girl) labour in America is brought into existence by what is called *plug-teaching.* "Two young men will be taught engraving in the evenings on easy terms." Telegraphy, typesetting, dress-cutting, and designing are among the businesses thus "taught ; " and as a rule the teaching is the merest swindle.—*St. James's Gazette.*

Plug-ugly (American), the name given in Baltimore to roughs and rowdies, now common.

One that shall devote as much space to literature as to "sport" (of the dog-fighting, rat-baiting kind) ; one that shall give a dead *plug-ugly* a line (if it is in the way of news), and a dead man who has done something in the world, for the world, many lines.—*New York World.*

Plum (common), £100,000.

The next day they disposed of their **swag**
  for a *plum*,
And invested the proceeds in Spaniards
  and Turks.   —*Punch.*

Plums, money.

Daddy's *plums* in the bank, or daddy's dear, delightful daughter, which ?—*Toby.*

It is curious to note that in Spanish *pluma,* and in Italian *pennes,* meaning properly feather, have the slang signification of money.

" It is possible to trace the slang term *plum* for £100,000 to *pluma,* a feather, the idea being that a man who had accumulated this sum had feathered his nest " (*Standard*).

Plum or **plumb** (common), direct, exactly, quite. "The original signification of this word is ' as the plummet hangs, perpendicularly,' hence its secondary meaning of straightforward, directly " (Bartlett).

Tom said she was going to get one of us, sure, before we got through. We got her half way ; and then we was *plumb* played out, and most drownded with sweat.—*The Adventures of Huckleberry Finn.*

Plum duff (sailor), plum pudding.

Plummy (popular), satisfactory, profitable. *Vide* PLUM or PLUMB.

They do manage their things so *plummy.*—*Mayhew : London Labour and the London Poor.*

Plummy and slam (thieves), all right. *Vide* PLUM or PLUMB.

Plumper (racing), all one's money laid on one horse.

The Fitzwilliam Plate was won by Lord Randolph Churchill's colt by Retreat out of White Lily, for which I gave a *plumper,* and he started at 7 to 1.—*Truth.*

(Election), *vide* TO PLUMP. (American), explained by quotations.

A device for puffing out to smoothness the wrinkles of the cheeks, called *plumpers,* has been introduced.—*New York Paper.*

Milo Morgan was yesterday charged with feloniously taking one "palpitating bosom," the property of Emile Horner, who keeps a fancy store, and Milo Morgan stole from it a *plumper*, an article used for artificially rounding out the female bust, palpitating with it.—*Hartford (Connecticut) Times.*

Plump, to (election), to give all one's votes to one single candidate.

"Another election term, which will not be so common in the future as it has been in the past, is the expression to *plump*, and its opposite to 'split.' With the increase of single-membered constituencies these phrases must fall into disuse, and a 'floater' will no longer be able to say with Mr. Chubb, in 'Felix Holt'—'I'll *plump* or I'll *split* for them as treat me the handsomest and are the most of what I call gentlemen; that's my idea'" (*Cornhill Magazine*).

(Racing), to lay one's money on one single horse.

But I shall *plump* for Lord R. Ch.'s L'Abbesse de Jouarre, who has been well tried.—*Truth.*

Plum, to (popular), to deceive; *plum* him up, *plum* the public, &c. Cheating costers fix three large plums at the bottom of a measure. They are so tightly wedged as to be immovable, and though they are in the measure they are not passed on to the purchaser.

Plunder (American), the personal luggage of travellers.

"Help yourself, stranger," said the landlord, "while I take the *plunder* into the other room."—*Hoffman: Winter in the West.*

They'd put in so much *plunder*, two trunks, bandboxes, &c.—*Bartlett: Major Jones's Courtship.*

In Lower Canada packmen call luggage "butin," that is, *plunder*, booty. French soldiers also use the word "butin" for equipment, belongings.

(Common), profit. (American), luggage.

Plunge (society), a heavy and reckless bet.

We did not altogether like Mr. ——'s *plunge* on Martley, and are not surprised to hear that the horse is struck out.—*Sporting Times.*

> Now my soul the question worries,
> Which to *plunge* on—which to back,
> Friday—though the market flurries,
> Shall the colt a backer lack?
> —*Bell's Life.*

Plunger (society), a wealthy man who bets in a reckless manner, who takes large bets at any odds.

The current week has served to introduce us to a new *plunger*, who up to the present has given strong evidence of possession of more money than brains. He is said to have attained his majority only a few days since, and having come into upwards of half a million "ready," has been showing "who's which" in rare style.—*Sporting Times.*

Also a heavy dragoon. A Baptist.

Plush (nautical), from *plus.* The overplus of the gravy, arising from being distributed in a smaller measure than the true one, and assigned to the cook of each mess, becomes a cause of irregularity (Smyth).

Poach, to (sporting), to get the best of a start.

Poacher (Stock Exchange), a jobber who deals out of his own market. The term is also applied to a broker who is continually changing his market.

Pocket mining. *Vide* FOSSICK.

Pockettes (conjurors), pockets worn by some conjurors in addition to the *profondes*. From *poke*, or French *pochettes*.

Pod, in (popular), in the family way, *i.e.*, run to seed. *Pod* is provincial for belly. (American), *pod*, intimate, old-fashioned ways; an old *pod*, an old-fashioned man. Also old *pod*, a man with a prominent stomach.

Poet's walk (Eton), when cricketers get leave of absence from roll-call, and have tea under the trees, they are said to go to *poet's walk*.

Poge (thieves), purse; a corruption of "pouch," or "poke."

I went out the next day to Maidenhead, and touched for some wedge and a *poge* (purse), with over five quid in it.—*Horsley: Jottings from Jail.*

Poggle, puggly, porgly, &c. (Anglo-Indian), a madman, an idiot, a dolt. Hindu *pŏgal*. Often used colloquially by Anglo-Indians. A friend belonging to that body used to adduce a macaronic adage which we fear the non-Indian will fail to appreciate: "Pogal et pecunia jalde

separantur," *i.e.*, a fool and his money are soon parted (Anglo-Indian Glossary).

Point (Stock Exchange). Points are the bases of speculative operations. When a man has a *point*, it generally means that he has secret information concerning a particular stock, which enables him to deal with it to considerable advantage.

Pointer (American), a hint; the same as "straight tip" in English.

She fell into a cogitation on the Irish banshees who came to give one *pointers* on approaching death.—*Chicago Tribune.*

Point rise (American), the rise of one dollar, *e.g.*, as an unit in the value of a stock.

Poke (thieves), purse. Properly a pocket.

Kit, from Seven Dials, remanded innocent on two charges of *pokes*, only out two weeks for a drag, expects to get fulled or else chucked.—*Horsley: Jottings from Jail.*

"The thieves of London," said Dr. Lathom, "are the conservators of Saxonisms." So *poke* is from the Saxon *pocca*, a bag, which otherwise survives in its diminutive "pocket," *i.e.*, a little bag, in "buying a pig in a *poke*," in the noun and verb "pouch," &c.

Poke bogey, to (popular), to play nonsense, to humbug. "Now, don't you *poke* none of your *bogey* at me." From *bogey*, a hobgoblin bugbear, and probably connected with *puck* and *puckle*, old provincial English for spirit or ghost. Icelandic *puka*; Welsh *pucca*, a bugbear; Celtic *bucan*, a ghost.

Poke fun, to (common), to make jokes, to laugh at one.

Little he deems that Stephen de Hoagues,
Who "his *fun*," as the Yankees say, every-
where "*pokes*,"
And is always too fond of his jokes,
Has written a circular note to De Nokes,
And De Stiles, and De Roe, and the rest
of the folks,
One and all, great and small,
Who were asked to the Hall.
—*Ingoldsby Legends.*

Poke him fly (tailors), show him how. *Vide* FLY.

Poker (university), an esquire bedell who carries a large mace before the Vice-Chancellor when engaged in his official capacity. (Fencing), a disorderly, un-courteous, rough fencer. "Un ferrailleur, tirailleur."

He was no better than a "tirailleur, jeu
de soldat"—Anglicised a *poker.*—*Angelo's
Reminiscences, in his account of the bouts
with Dr. Keys.*

Pokerish (American), doubtful, or of dubious safety, an expres-sion implying something dan-gerous or alarming, but not used very seriously. From to *poke*, to feel in the dark.

I knew by the *pokerish* hole in the ground
Which yawned at my feet that a mud-
hole was near,
And I said to myself, "If there's dirt to
be found,
The man who is humble may roll in it
here!"
—*Newspaper Parody.*

Poking drill (military), aiming drill in the course of musketry instruction, so called because the rifle is being constantly poked or pushed to the front so as to accustom the soldier to the weight, and to get his eye quickly along the sights.

Pole (printers). This term is ap-plied to a man's weekly bill, probably from the fact that the more he earns the taller or higher the *pole.*

Pole, to (American university), to study hard. Probably allud-ing to the exertion in climbing a greasy pole; *poler*, one who studies hard; *poling*, close ap-plication to study.

Pole, up the (military), thought well of by your superiors. Also applied to strict, strait-laced people, who are or like to be considered "goody-goody."

Poley (Australian up-country), with the horns off. Though spelt differently, probably con-nected with "to poll." "Polled" or "pollard" trees, willows, limes, &c., are those which have their tops or polls cut off, and are trimmed down. "Polled" animals are often mentioned in the Bible.

When he is jogging along, and not in exciting chase, he sits loosely in his sad-dle, his feet hanging anyhow from sheer laziness; but his keen eye darts this way and that in search of some stray beast—that *poley*-cow that got out of the yard, or Bleny, the strawberry bullock that bolted down by Sandy Creek.—*The Globe.*

Policeman (popular), a fly, especially the " blue - bottle " fly, which has given its name to a *policeman*. Also a sneak, a mean fellow. (Tailors), a man deputed to remind a new-comer that it is customary for new hands to contribute a certain sum of money to enable the men to drink his health; in other words, to pay his " footing." The custom is dying out. It also means " spy " or tale-bearer.

Poll (university), a contraction of *polloi* (πολλοί), a term applied to the ordinary examination for the B.A. degree, as distinguished from the honour examinations at Cambridge. (Society), a prostitute, one of the *demi-monde.* It is derived from sailors, who always christen women Polly.

Polled up (popular), living with a mistress.

Poll, to (printers), to vanquish in competition. (Sporting), to distance, beat in a race. (Thieves), is said of a thief (*poll* thief) who robs another of his share of the booty. From *to poll,* to plunder, pillage, strip. Used by Spenser and Bacon.

Polty (cricketers), easy ; *polty,* or dolly catch, an easy catch.

Pompadours, the 56th Regiment of Foot (Hotten).

Ponce (popular and thieves), a brothel bully, or one who lives on prostitutes.

After he and his wife had entered, the constable came in and said to him, " You come here along with me, you —— *ponce.*" —*Standard.*

Ponce shicer (theatrical), an odious epithet, invented by the actors to stigmatise the most infamous of adventurers, creatures who lay themselves out to captivate actresses, and to live upon their earnings. Crapulous scoundrels who live by *chantage.*

Poncess (thieves), a woman who supports a man by prostituting herself. The feminine of *ponce,* which see.

Pond (common), abbreviated from herring *pond,* the ocean.

We trust Colonel Cody and Mr. Salsbury's plucky venture—for it requires pluck to cross the *pond* with such a show—will meet with a well - deserved reward. — *Bailey's Monthly Magazine.*

Poney (racing), £25. An arbitrary denomination like "monkey" and others.

So there was much plunging on Blanch of Lancaster—*ponies,* tenners, fivers, even quids were being dumped down enthusiastically.—*Sporting Times.*

(American), a *petit verre* of brandy. Hence *poney* brandy, the best. Also a very little woman.

Poney up (American), pay up ; said to be from the German *poniren,* to pay. In Dutch slang *poen* is money.

Pongelow, pongellorum (general), beer ; also used in the army.

Pongelow, to (London), to have some beer.

Pong, ponge, to (theatrical), to vamp through a part in a play in ignorance of the text, substituting the actor's own words for those of the author. (Circus), to perform.

Pongo (circus and showmen), a monkey.

Pon my sivey, a corruption of "asseveration," upon my word.

Pon my sivey, if you were to see her picking you'd think she was laying on pounds' weight in a day instead of losing it.—*J. Greenwood: Tag, Rag, & Co.*

Ponte (showmen), a sovereign; Italian *pondo*, pound.

Ponto (college), explained by quotation.

During a chorister's life in college he had to put up with such a thing as a wooden trencher, or a *ponto* (a much softer missile) thrown at his head [Note.—A *ponto* was the crumb of a new roll kneaded into a ball] and sundry cuffs.—*Sporting Life.*

Poodle (popular), facetiously applied to any kind of dog.

Pool (American), a combination, clique, gang, association, or syndicate formed by all the dealers in a certain article, to force up the price of it.

A window-glass *pool* follows swiftly after the hard and soft coal *pools*, as these had been preceded or accompanied by monopolies for the control of other essential articles.—*New York World.*

Pool, to (common), to form an association, to club together.

So we *pooled* our wealth together, and bought spring traps, and started off to try our luck with the beavers.—*O'Reilly: Fifty Years on the Trail.*

Poona (costermongers), a pound; a corruption of this word.

Poop downhaul (nautical). Russell gives this as "an imaginary rope"—a seaman's jest, like "clapping the reel athwart ships," and other such sayings.

Pootly-nautch (Anglo-Indian), a puppet-show. Hindu, *kath-putli-nāch*, a wooden-puppet dance.

Pop (society), champagne; ginger *pop* is ginger beer. The derivation is obvious. (Eton School), the aristocratic club at Eton, originally a debating society, now a fashionable and exclusive lounge. (American), papa.

It seems that American children know not "dad," and are in the habit of calling their fathers *pop*. On this side of the Atlantic we only associate the word with our "uncles."—*Funny Folks.*

(London), Monday popular concerts.

Passing over the *Pop.* on Monday, as containing nothing remarkable, I come to the performance of the "Rose of Sharon" on Tuesday.—*Referee.*

Pop off the hooks, to (popular), to die.

He stirr'd not,—he spoke not,—he none of them knew,
And Achille cried "Odzooks! I fear by his looks,
Our friend, François Xavier, has *popp'd off the hooks!*"
    —*Ingoldsby Legends.*

Pop off, to (common), to die.

But should I be *popped* off, you, my mates
  left behind me,
Regard my last words, see 'em kindly
  obeyed.
    —*Davey: Will Watch.*

Popped (tailors), annoyed, in a temper.

Popped as a hatter (tailors), very much annoyed.

Popping (American University), getting an advantage.

Poppy - cock (American), bosh, nonsense, idle talk. It has no such meaning as "sound or fury," as the English edition of Artemus Ward declares, but refers rather to the display which appeals to and humbugs, or dazzles.

I venture to say that if you sarch all the earth over with a ten-hoss power mikriscope you won't be able to find such another pack of *poppy-cock* gabblers as the present Congress of the United States of America.—*Artemus Ward.*

From "pop-peacock," as in poppin-jay, influenced by peacock.

Pops (thieves), pistols.

"Are you armed?" asked Ginger.
"I have a brace of pistols in my pocket," replied Thorneycroft.
"All right, then—ve've all got *pops* and cutlashes," said Ginger. — *Ainsworth: Auriol.*

Pop-shop (common), pawnbroker's.

As to the other cloak and shawl, don't be afraid; they shan't go to the *pop-shop.*
—*Lord Lytton: Ernest Maltravers.*

Pop, to (common), to pawn.

And that he meant *to pop*
  It round at "Uncle's" shop,
I never had the shadow of a doubt.
  —*Song: Many Capers I have Seen.*

(Society), *to pop* the question, to propose marriage. Also *to pop.*

Pop your corn (American), "now, then, *pop your corn,*" say what you have to say, speak out. Pop-corn is a variety of maize, of a small grain, sometimes of a dark colour. When roasted it pops or expands suddenly. It is often eaten with milk.

"Juliana!" he said to me in a tremorous voice. "I've some *corn* that I want to *pop*—will you acknowledge that *corn.*"
And I said I would. That was the way he *popped.*—*Newspaper.*

P. P. (racing), play or pay.

Porridge disturber (pugilistic), a blow in the pit of the stomach.

Porterhouse steak (American), a large steak with a small bone.

Porter's knot (common), the large bob of hair at the back of the head worn by women in 1866. Also known as a "waterfall," "cataract," &c.

Portrait (common), a sovereign.

Posers (Winchester College), two men who come down from New College at election. They examine for the Winchester and New College scholarships and exhibitions. From *poser,* an awkward question.

Posh (society), modern term for money, originally used for a halfpenny or small coin. From the gypsy *pash* or *posh*, a half. In Romany *poshero*, the affix *ero* being corrupted from *hāro*, copper, *i.e.*, a copper or a penny. *Posh an' posh*, half and half, applied to those who are of mixed blood, or half gypsy. Also a dandy.

Possum-guts (Australian bush), a term of contempt.

Two bushmen walked into the bar of an hotel which an enterprising Frenchman had just set up in the principal Riverina township : not finding any one to serve them, they pursued their rambles into the house until they were confronted by a glass door with Salle-à-manger painted on it. Sandy was " stuck." " What's that ? " he said, with a storm of expletive words to his mate, an Irishman. " You *possum-guts !* Why, it says if you want anything, sound for the manager."—*D. B. W. Sladen.*

" I'll teach you to whistle when a gentleman comes into the hut, you *possum-guts !*"—*H. Kingsley : Geoffrey Hamlyn.*

Possum, to (American), to feign, to dissemble, to sham dead—a slang phrase almost equivalent to the old English "sham Abraham" (*q.v.*). "The expression," says Bartlett, " alludes to the habit of the opossum, which throws itself on its back, and feigns death on the approach of an enemy."

As one who counterfeits sickness, or dissembles strongly for a particular purpose, is said to be *possuming.*—*Flint : Geography of the Mississippi Valley.*

Also to play *possum.*

You see, the first grizzly I caught in a trap *played 'possum* with me. After the first or second shot I went up to him, sup-posing him to be dead. But I will never allow another grizzly to play that racket. —*Cincinnati Enquirer.*

Post-and-rails (Australian), wooden matches as distinguished from wax vestas. The ordinary Australian has a great contempt for wooden matches, very likely because safety-matches, such a necessary precaution in the bush, are generally made of wood.

" Alf," said a great friend of mine to a companion who was engaged with us on a shooting expedition down in Bulu-Bulu, one of the eastern provinces of Victoria, " Have you got a match ? "

" Only a *post-and-rails,*" was the deprecating reply, responded to with a patronising " Never mind."—*D. B. W. Sladen.*

Post-and-rails tea, coarse tea with stalks and leaves floating in it. The metaphor is obvious. The tea supplied to the station-hands is proverbially bad. It gets its name from the stalks, leaves, &c., floating about when it is decocted.

He brought us some black damper and a dry chip of cheese (for we were famished), together with a hot beverage in a tin pot, which richly deserved the colonial epithet of *post-and-rails tea,* for it might well have been a decoction of "split stuff," or " iron bark shingles " for any resemblance it bore to the Chinese plant.—*D. B. W. Sladen.*

Posted (American), informed as to anything, *posted* up. This term was first used in this sense and made popular by Mr. David Stearns Godfrey of Milford, Massachusetts. (Cambridge University), to be *posted* is to be rejected in an examination.

Fifty marks will prevent one from being *posted*, but there are always two or three too stupid as well as idle to save their *post*. These drones are *posted* separately, as "not worthy to be classed," and privately slanged afterwards by the master and seniors. Should a man be *posted* twice in succession, he is generally recommended to try the air of some small college, or devote his energies to some other walk of life.— *Hall: College Words and Customs.*

Post-horn (popular), the nose. From the noise when blowing one's nose. In French slang *trompette* means face.

Postman (legal), one of the barristers in a common law court is so called from the privileges he enjoys. The expression is well understood.

Postmasters (Oxford University), scholars on the foundation at Merton College.

The *postmasters* anciently performed the duties of choristers, and their payment for this duty was six shillings and fourpence per annum.—*Oxford Guide.*

Post-mortem (Cambridge University), the second examination after failure.

Post the coin, to (sporting), to make a deposit for a match. Generally to pay.

Post, to (university), to put up a man's name as not having paid for food supplied by the college, which precludes him from having any more till he does pay. (Common), *post* the cole, *vide* COAL.

Pot (common), short for *pot* hat.

Nice lads, very nice ; always like Eton boys when they haven't got *pots* on.— *Punch.*

(Sporting and American), the amount of stakes on a horse.

On receiving the list of winning numbers the ticket was at once placed in the hands of the First National bank and yesterday the full amount of the prize, less a small sum for collection, was paid over by the bank to Mr. Poppendick and the *pot* duly divided with his pard.—*Omaha* (Neb.) *Bee.*

Also an adept, a swell, the favourite in the betting for a race.

The prospects of respective cricket *pots.* —*Punch.*

To put on a *pot*, to lay a large sum of money on a horse.

(Winchester College), the *pot*, the canal ; *pot*-cad, a workman at the sawmills ; *pot*-gates, lockgates ; *pot*-houser, a jump into the canal from the roof of a house called *pot*-house.

Potate (American), signifying to drink ; an abbreviation from potation, as the kindred but more permissible vulgarism *orate*, from oration. The last word has already been naturalised in English, but *potate* remains an alien.

Potato-trap (common), the mouth.

That'll damage your *potato-trap!*—*C. Bede: Verdant Green.*

Pot-boiler (studios), an appellation given by artists to a picture painted only for the sake of the pecuniary advantages it brings. French artists term "faire du métier" painting such pictures for the trade. (Journalistic), any production written for money not glory.

It is a strange coincidence that the writer of these lines was actively engaged with Archie M'Neil in collaborating on a *pot-boiler.—Topical Times.*

Pot-fair (university), the name given to the midsummer fair held at Cambridge.

The fair on Midsummer Green, known by the name of *Pot-fair*, was in all its glory. There were booths at which raffles for pictures, china, and millinery took place every evening, which were not over till a late hour.—*Gunning: Reminiscences.*

Pot, go to (common), be off, you be hanged. Explained by quotation.

Isn't saying of a man who's come to grief through beer, that he's "gone *to pot*," a pewter-ful sort of ale-legory?—*Funny Folks.*

To *go to pot*, to die. This expression refers to broken metal placed in the melting-pot.

Pothouse, *i.e.,* Peterhouse, or St. Peter's College, Cambridge.

Pot-hunter (sporting), a man who goes round to small athletic meetings with a view of getting as many prizes as he can. *Vide* POTS. (Fisher), one who fishes only for the sake of the catch, not for the sport.

But ordinary mortals have a natural dislike to returning with empty baskets, and some people not necessarily *pot-hunters* like to eat trout.—*Sir H. Pottinger: Trout-Fishing.*

Pot-hunting (sporting), a sport greatly favoured by amateurs since the abolition of the gentleman-amateur qualification—

e.g., the crack expert arranges on Whit-Monday with his more formidable rivals not on any account to clash with them, but to farm a meeting a-piece. In the old days gentlemen would go any distance to meet a rival and have it out with him, but nothing is further from the thoughts of the present "crack."

Potlash (Canadian), explained by quotation.

Roughly speaking, it seems a *potlash* is an entertainment lasting any time from a week to three months, provided by one tribe for another, and entailing on the tribe so entertained the duties of receiving their hosts in like manner on some future occasion, generally at the same date in the succeeding year.—*Phillipps-Wolley: Trottings of a Tenderfoot.*

Pot on, to put the (trade), to overcharge. (Common), to exaggerate.

Pots (sporting), prizes for athletic sports, generally given in the shape of mugs. (Stock Exchange), North Staffordshire Railway ordinary stock. (Nautical), name for the steward on board passenger-boats. From the pots or basins he provides for sick persons.

Pot-shot (common), a shot from a hole or ambush.

But when you turn in your hounds and wait till the deer come like dumb driven cattle to the water, beside which you have sat till you have got cold and cramped, there is none of the credit due to the quiet *pot-shot* which a quick snap-shot at a buck on the jump might earn.—*Phillipps-Wolley: Trottings of a Tenderfoot.*

Potted fug (Rugby), boys thus term potted meat.

Potted, to be (common), to be snubbed or suppressed.

Pot, to (common), to shoot.

Poisoners of hounds, and enemies of all sport save the *potting* a fellow-creature from behind a fence, can and should be dealt with in no other way.—*Bird o' Freedom.*

(Racing), to lay a large sum on a horse.

Two of these accomplished gentry, who had severally gone for the crack and the field, that is, had systematically and regularly backed the one and *potted* the other. —*Sporting Times.*

(Billiards), to *pot* a ball, send it in the pocket.

Pot, to put on the big (sporting), to bully, arrogantly patronise. A *big pot* is a great swell, an adept, a favourite in racing.

Pot-walloper (elections), thus explained in the *Cornhill Magazine* :—

"One can well imagine what influence the 'man in the moon' had in days gone by with voters of the class known as *pot-wallopers.* The bearers of this melodious name were electors whose sole title to the possession of the franchise was the fact of their having been settled in the parish for six months, the settlement being considered sufficiently proved if the claimant had boiled his own pot within its boundaries for the required period—*wall* meaning to boil. The *pot-wallopers*, with many

other electoral anomalies, were abolished by the passing of the great Reform Bill ; but a cognate abuse, that of 'faggot-voting,' survives in some constituencies."

(Common), a low parasite. (Theatrical), a tap-room talker.

Pouch through, to (American), a post-office term, meaning to convey mail matter in a *pouch.*

Till Special-Agent Death came by one day,
And *pouched* the old man *through* the
  graveyard town.
He lay quite still, when suddenly he cried,
" Mail closed ! " and drew his salary, and
  died.
  —*Robert J. Burdette.*

Pouf (theatrical), an epithet applied by the actors to a silly fellow, who imagines himself to be an actor.

Poulderlings (old), students of the second year at St. John's, Oxford.

The whole companye, or most parte of the students of the same house mette toogeher to beginne their Christmas, of wch some came to see sports, to witte the seniors as well graduates as vnder-graduates. Others to make sports, viz., studentes of the seconde yeare, whom they call *Poulderlings. — Christmas Prince.*

Poulterer (thieves), one who gets letters from post-boxes, opens them, steals the money which they contain, seals them, and drops them again into the box. The receiver naturally supposes that the sender omitted to enclose the money.

Poultice wallah (military), a man of the staff corps ; one whose business it is to attend on the surgeon, carry out treatment, give medicines, apply poultices, and so forth. Hence the expression.

Pound, to go one's (military), applied to a man with a good appetite, is evidently derived from the weight of the soldier's ration ; the pound of bread and of meat which the hungry man can easily devour.

Powerful nerve (tailors), a great amount of impudence.

Pow-wow (American), a conference. Properly the sorcery and ceremony of the Red Indian conjurors. From the Algonkin *bo-öin*, a magician.

And everybody was whooping at once, and there was a rattling *pow-wow.—The Adventures of Huckleberry Finn.*

Poz (popular), certain, positive.

That's *poz*, dear old pal, and no flies.—*Punch.*

Practitioner (popular), a thief.

It is only fair to state, however, that his lordship was not personally responsible for his startling statements. He had them from a *practitioner*, from a thief, that is to say.—*Greenwood: Seven Curses of London.*

Prad (common), a horse.

Just send somebody out to relieve my mate . . . he's in the gig, a-minding the *prad.—Dickens: Oliver Twist.*

Prairie-schooner (American), an emigrant waggon.

I am not long out before meeting with that characteristic feature of a scene on the Western plains, a *prairie-schooner*, and VOL. II.

meeting *prairie-schooners* will now be a daily incident of my Eastward journey.—*Stevens: Around the World on a Bicycle.*

Prat (popular), the buttock, behind.

Prater (old cant), a hen. Also margery *prater*.

Prat, to (thieves), to go, to enter.

I *pratted* into the house.—*Horsley: Jottings from Jail.*

Press (American sporting). When a man wins a bet, and instead of taking away his winnings he adds to the original stake and the winnings also, it is called a *press.*

Pretty horse-breaker, a fashionable and good-looking young woman of immoral life and bad reputation, sometimes called an "anonyma."

Prex (American student), the president of a college, equivalent to the pro-rector of a German university.

I used to think our *prex*
Was great as any rex,
In my green freshman-nual days.
—*Student Song.*

Prick the garter (thimble-riggers), a swindling game. The bet is made that you can't, with a pin, prick the point at which a *garter* is double.

Prig (thieves and popular), a thief.

Prim (American sporting), a handsome woman. Possibly from *prima*, i.e., *prima donna.*

K

Primed (common), on the verge of intoxication. (Students), crammed for an examination.

Prime flat (thieves), an easy dupe. Vaux, in his "Memoirs," says: "Any person who is found an easy dupe to the designs of the *family* is said to be a *prime flat.*"

Printer's devil (printers), a printer's boy. Moxon, 1683, attributes this term to the fact that the boys used to "black and bedaub themselves," whence the workmen jocosely called them "Devils." The real origin, it is believed, was that Aldus Manutius, the Venetian printer, had a negro boy, and in those days printing was ignorantly supposed to be a "black art," hence the term.

Passing for the nonce the itinerant "paper boy," the "errand boy," and the *printer's devil*, which last *genus garçon* machinery is fast driving from his stool, come we to the Arabs of the town.—*J. Diprose: London Life.*

Private stitch, to (tailors), to stitch without showing the mark.

Pro (popular), one of the profession, an actor. (Theatrical), an actor.

Actors are astonishingly fond of abbreviations, and herein lies most of their slang. They love to call themselves *pros.* —*Globe.*

Procession (circus), the parade or public show is always called the *procession.*

Profondes (conjurors), the pockets in the tails of a conjuror's dress coat. French slang.

Prog (common), food of any kind.

What other fellows call beastly *prog*
Is the very stuff for me.
—*Punch.*

Prog, according to Skeat, is from *prog*, to go about begging victuals. Middle English *prokken*, to beg or demand; Swedish *pracka.*

Proggins (university), proctor. The proctors and their subordinates, the pro-proctors, are the magistrates of the university.

Prog, to (printers), an abbreviation much used by printers for the word "prognosticate." "To *prog* the winner of the Derby," &c.

Promossing (Australian popular), talking rubbish, playing the fool, mooning about.

Prompter (school), a member of the second form at Merchant Taylors' School.

Proms (London and American), promenade concerts.

They go to the *Proms*, to a tartlet they'll speak,
Stand one drink, the reason is not far to seek,
For all this is done on a sovereign a week!
'Tis the way of the world, of the age.
—*Bird o' Freedom.*

They have for several years tried to abolish the *proms*, because it adds heavily to many students' expenses.—*Chicago Tribune.*

Prop (thieves), a breast-pin. Probably from *proper* (Cornwall), pretty, ornamental. (Pugilistic), a blow. (Punch and Judy), the *prop*, the gallows.

Proper crowd (Australian up-country), particular friends, a circle, a clique, dependants. An Australian would describe Harcourt, Childers, Labouchere, Conybeare & Co., as Gladstone's own *proper crowd;* Lord Carrington, the Duke of Sutherland, Mr. Christopher Sykes, &c., as being the Prince of Wales's *proper crowd;* and would talk of Lord Wolseley's *proper crowd* as Englishmen talk of his "gang," or apply the term to the Browning Society, &c.

Insolent and overbearing, his own *proper crowd* detested him.—*A. C. Grant.*

Proper first class (popular) denotes excellence.

Prop-nailer (thieves), a thief who devotes his attention to scarf-pins in a crowd.

Props (theatrical), properties. All the inanimate objects or articles used in a play, viz., stage carpet, baize, sea cloth, furniture, anything to eat or drink, books, pictures, vases, statuettes, lamps, fire-irons, fireplace, kettle, pens, ink, paper, swords, foils, guns, pistols, powder, blue fire, thunder, lightning, purse, money, table-cloth, dinner or breakfast service, &c. Certain animate objects, such as horses, pigs, dogs, and babies.

Props include everything kept in the theatre for use on the stage.—*Globe.*

Propster (theatrical), the property master. The man whose business it is, not only to provide ordinary properties for the stage, but to prepare new ones, to make and ornament banners, to model masks, &c.

Prop, to (pugilistic), to strike.

His whole person put in Chancery, slung, bruised, fibbed, *propped*, fiddled, slogged, and otherwise ill-treated.—*C. Bede: Verdant Green.*

Pross, to (theatrical), to sponge. Doubtless derived from the Romany *prass.* The actors, however, affect to derive this detestable word from a line in Otway's play of "Venice Preserved," in which that "dashing, gay, bold-faced villain" Pierre says, "The clock has struck, and I may lose my proselyte." The wealthy proselyte of dogma is always under the thumb of the prose-lytiser, who invariably makes his pupil "shell out" for the good of the cause. Similarly, the lowest class of players have, from time immemorial, been accustomed to sponge upon their proselytes, to bleed them in money or malt. The handsome but infamous "Scum" Goodman, the actor, the *amant de cœur* of the notorious Barbara Castlemaine, bled that lubricous lady almost as freely as the illustrious Jack Churchill, or as she herself bled that anointed scoundrel, old Rowley, who in his turn bled the nation. There is a restaurant, not a hundred miles from a certain fashionable theatre in the Strand, known to the initiated as "Prossers' Avenue." At certain times of the day this place is infested by impecunious loafers, consisting of the outcasts of all professions—actors, journalists, disbanded soldiers, unfrocked parsons, and broken-down adventurers of every description, all of whom make it their business to *pross* for anything, from a fiver down to a glass of gin or beer. The attentions of these enterprising gentry are not restricted to their own immediate circle; they are superior to vulgar prejudice, and will *pross* anything from anybody, more especially from "the stranger at their gates."

This term is common among workmen and others. Are you one for a *pross?* Will you stand a drink?

But now I've grown to man's estate, for work I've never cared,
I've *prossed* my meals from off my pals, ofttimes I've badly fared.
　　　　—Music Hall Song.

Prosser (popular and thieves), a degraded creature, one who sponges, a male prostitute. Said to be from *prostitute.*

Prov. (printers). "On the *prov.*" signifies that a man is out of work and reaping the benefit of the Provident Fund of his Trade Society—a fund established to compensate the unemployed.

Provost (military), garrison or other cells, where the penalty

of imprisonment for a week and under is inflicted, without relegation to a military prison.

Prowl, to (theatrical), waiting for one's pay.

Pruff (Winchester College), explained by quotation.

But deprive a Wykehamist of words in constant use, such as "quill," meaning to curry favour with; *pruff*, signifying sturdy, or proof against pain; "spree," upstart, impudent; "cud," pretty, and many more, and his vocabulary becomes limited.— *Everyday Life in our Public Schools.*

Psalm-smiler (popular), one who sings at a conventicle.

Pub (common), public-house.

Public patterers (popular), swell mobsmen, who pretend to be Dissenting preachers, and harangue in the open air to attract a crowd for their confederates to rob (Hotten).

Puckah (Anglo - Indian). The word is applied in various ways; *puckah* in Hindostani means properly red brick. So a *pucka* house is a red brick house, and in opposition to a "kutcha" house, one built of earth, it is a good, comfortable house. Hence the meaning of good, best, attached to the word. A *pucka* spin is a young lady who is not engaged, a *pucka* officer is a senior officer; should an officer in command go on leave, his deputy is not *puckah.*

But I believe that marrying
An "acting" man is a fudge;

And do not fancy anything
Below a *pucka* judge.
—*Aleph Cheem : Lays of Ind.*

Pucker (military), the best of anything, as the *pucker* colonel, the senior. *Vide* PUCKAH.

Pucker up, to (popular), to get in a bad temper.

Pudding (thieves), liver prepared with a narcotic drug and used by burglars to silence house-dogs.

When I opened a door there was a great tyke lying in front of the door, so I pulled out a piece of *pudding* and threw it to him, but he did not move. So I threw a piece more, and it did not take any notice ; so I got close up to it, and I found it was a dead dog stuffed, so I done the place for some wedge and clobber.—*Horsley : Jottings from Jail.*

Pudding club (popular), a woman in the family way is said to be in the *pudding club.*

Pudding-snammer (popular), one who robs a cookshop.

Pud, to (popular), to greet affectionately, familiarly. *Pud,* the hand.

Puff (common), a favourable notice or praise of any kind in a newspaper, usually incorporated in general reading matter. (Tailors), never in your *puff,* never in your life.

Puffer (boating), a small river steamboat, a steam launch.

These are the lolling idlers in those comfortable floating hotels, which are called steam-launches by the literate, and *puffers* by the river folk.—*Daily Telegraph.*

(Popular), a steam-engine.

And under we went, one on each side, intending to get out again, as usual, as soon as the *puffer* began a-taking us along again.—*Sporting Times.*

(Cheap Jacks, &c.), the special slang meaning is explained by quotation.

We bid or praised up his goods ; in fact, often acted as *puffers* or bonnets to give him a leg up.—*Hindley: Life and Adventures of a Cheap Jack.*

Pug (common), a prize-fighter. Abbreviated from "pugilist."

He insisted, with a smile serene and smug,
That he'd gain distinction later as a fistic gladiator,
Or, in plainer phraseology, a *pug.*
—*Sporting Times.*

A portion of Highgate Cemetery, where Tom Sayers, Knacker-Atcherly, and other pugilists lie buried, is called "*Pugs'* Acre."

Puke, to (schools), to vomit. A variant of "spew."

Puker (Shrewsbury), a good-for-nothing fellow.

Pull (society), to take a *pull* means to stop, check, put an end to, and is very commonly in use. It is borrowed from racing parlance, to take a *pull* at a horse.

But it is like the will-o'-the-wisp, which is pretty sure to lead them to their destruction if they have not the moral courage to "take a *pull*" when they are getting out of their depth.—*Saturday Review.*

(Cricketers), to make a *pull* is to hit a straight ball crookedly. This is generally done intentionally. (Popular), the *pull,* the advantage. To have the upper-hand in pulling a rope gives an extra grip, whence the expression.

> Sharpers try to pick him up,
> Thinking they've a flat in tow,
> But at pool he cleans them out,
> All the *pull's* with Oxford Joe.
> —*Music Hall Ballad: Oxford Joe.*

Pull a horse's head off (racing), to check a horse's progress so as to prevent him from winning. Pulling is done by a man leaning back and pulling at the horse's head.

> The witness, pressed to explain what the meaning of *pulling a horse's head off* was, said that pulling must be intentional on the part of a jockey.—*St. James's Gazette.*

Pull down your vest (American). A few years ago, when trousers were not made quite so high as at present, and waistcoats were shorter, it often happened that a portion of the shirt became visible from the latter garment "rising." Hence the frequent admonition of *pull down your vest* from careful mothers to their sons, or of wives to careless husbands. The phrase soon became general, and took the obvious application of "make yourself look decenter," "attend to your personal appearance," and "mind your own affairs!"

Pulled trade (tailors), secured work.

Pulled up, to be (popular and thieves), to be taken before a magistrate.

Pulley (old cant), a girl. A variation of *pullet*, a girl. *Pullet-*

squeezer, a man who is always fondling young girls.

Pulling a kite (popular), making a face, looking serious. Literally, looking like a *kite* or fool, or alluding to the fixed expression in the face of a person flying a *kite*. Again, perhaps, from a filthy simile.

> My mug, mate, was made for a larf, and you don't ketch it *pulling a kite.*
> —*Punch.*

Pulling in the pieces (popular), to make money, get good wages, or be successful in speculation.

Pull off, to (popular), to achieve, make.

> The burglar is flush of money, and each of his comrades knows that a big job has been *pulled off.*—*Evening News.*

Pull one's self together, to (common), used as a metaphorical expression for collecting one's thoughts, or cooling one's self down from a previous state of excitement. To "pull up," to cease, to refrain. These phrases are constantly used by lady novelists, though not by any writer of high or deserved repute.

> That Lord Hartington's speech outdid the utmost expectations of his friends, in regard to its matter and its fearless outspokenness, is everywhere acknowledged. Here and there it was delivered admirably, and with something of the large manner demanded by his great position. But, truth to say, this was not by any means maintained uniformly, and he frequently seemed only by an effort to *pull himself together.*—*The World.*

Pull out, to (sporting), in athletics, is being thoroughly "extended"—usually by a friendly pacemaker. (American), to leave, depart.

For a minute or two they stood looking at one another, and then Doc *pulled out.* —*F. Francis: Saddle and Moccasin.*

Pull the leg, to (society), to impose upon, to cram one.

Pull the long bow, to (common), to tell falsehoods, cram.

"Don't it strike you, Billiam, that chaps about to be hanged generally do *pull the long bow* a bit?"

"It does, Alexandry," replied the Red-Handed One. "If they had kept Percy Lefroy bottled up much longer, he'd have sworn he murdered Maria Martin, Abraham Lincoln, Harriet Lane, and the Mystery at Rainham."—*Ally Sloper's Half-Holiday.*

Pull the string, to (tailors), to make use of all your influence to obtain the desired result. (Popular), to do well.

Pull, to (common), to drink. (Turf), to prevent a horse from winning by pulling at the reins.

Pumped (common), exhausted.

Pump sucker (popular), a teetotaller.

Puncher (American), a cowboy, one who punches and brands cattle.

Perhaps you find it impossible to bring yourself to eat with "aw—cow-servants, you know," as certain young Englishmen, but newly come from college to New Mexico, and unpurged as yet of old world prejudices, found it not long ago. The title "cow-servants" so delighted the gentle *puncher* that it has become a standing quotation in New Mexico.—*F. Francis: Saddle and Moccasin.*

Pun-paper (Harrow), specially ruled paper for *puns* or impositions.

Punting-shop (common), a gambling house.

Pupe (Harrow), pupil-room.

Pure cussedness. *Vide* CUSSEDNESS.

Pure-pickers (street), pickers up of dogs' dung, which is sold to curriers.

Purge (popular), beer, from its peculiar effects.

Comrades, listen while I urge, Drink yourselves and pass the *purge.* —*Barrack Room Poet.*

Purko (military), beer; possibly from Barclay & Perkins, the great brewers.

Purl, purler (schools), a jump into the water head foremost. (Sporting), a heavy fall from a horse.

Purser's grins (nautical), hypocritical and satirical sneers.

Purser's name (nautical), an assumed one. During the war, when pressed men caught at every opportunity to desert, they adopted aliases to avoid discovery if retaken, which alias was handed to the purser for entry upon the ship's books (Smyth).

Push (prison), a gang associated in penal servitude labour.

Most of these pseudo-aristocratic impostors had succeeded in obtaining admission to the stocking-knitting party, which, in consequence, became known among the rest of the prisoners as the "upper ten *push*."—*Michael Davitt : Leaves from a Prison Diary.*

(Thieves), a crowd ; an association for a robbery or swindle. "I am in this *push*," I intend to participate. (Shopmen), to get the *push*, to be discharged. (Popular), to get the *push*, to be set aside, rejected, discharged.

The girl that stole my heart has given me the *push*.
—*Ballad : I'll Say no More to Mary Ann.*

Pusher (popular), a high-low or blucher boot. Also a female. A square *pusher* is a girl of good reputation. (American), a bit of bread held by children in the left hand to be used as a fork.

Push your barrow (popular), go away.

Puss, an appellation given by Woolwich cads to gentlemen cadets of the Royal Military Academy, formerly called *pussies*, when their uniform coats were short jackets with a pointed tail in rear, as may be seen in old pictures at the R.A. Institution, Woolwich.

Put a down upon a man, to (Australian convicts), is to inform against him. Probably introduced into Australia by the transportees.

"*To put a down upon a man* is to give information of any robbery or fraud he is about to perpetrate, so as to cause his failure or detection" (Vaux's Memoirs).

Put a head on, to (American), to beat a man on the head. To make one's head swell.

Und he gets madt und says he *put some heads on me* if I doan' gif oop dot twenty. Vhell, I vhas a greenhorn und a fool, you know.—*Detroit Free Press.*

Put-away, to (prison), has the same sense as the foregoing ; it means to split or peach, or so act that a man is discovered through the information given.

Put in a hole, to (thieves), to defraud an accomplice of his share of the booty. Also "to put in the garden," possibly an allusion to "plant," meaning swindle. (Common), to defraud any one for whom you are acting confidentially, to victimise.

There was a class of people who if they were advised to put £10 on a horse which won thought the man a good fellow who told them, but if they lost thought they had been robbed or *put in a hole.*—*St. James's Gazette.*

Put in the well, to (thieves), to defraud an accomplice of his share of the booty, or to defraud any one for whom one is acting confidentially.

Put it up, to (American), to spend money, to gamble.

"Bully for you, Squito !" cried Joe. "When it comes to gambling he's a thoroughbred ; he *puts it up* as if it was bad."—*F. Francis : Saddle and Moccasin.*

Put me in my little bed (American), one of many current slang expressions signifying that the

one addressed is beaten or dis-
tanced, or has no more to say.
Also the name of a "fancy"
drink.

Putney, oh, go to (popular),
equivalent to go to Jericho,
Ballyhock, or any other of the
numerous milder modifications
of the place of eternal punishment. Sometimes improved by
adding "on a pig."

> Sarah's gone and left me,
>   Her love for me was sham,
> She can *go to Putney on a pig*,
>   Along with her cat's-meat man !
> —*The Cat's-Meat Man.*

Put one's back into it, to (common), to act with energy.

> It seems to me that if I only hit hard
> enough I must do something. I *put my
> back into it*—that's his expression, not
> mine—and two balls disappear into two
> pockets.—*Ally Sloper's Half-Holiday.*

Put one's back up, to. *Vide*
BACK.

Put on, to (common), to initiate.

> Once on the course he will undertake
> To *put you on* should you be
> Green at the game, but the quids you stake
>   Never again you'll see.
> Or perhaps near a bookie like a clerk he'll
>   stand,
> And gonoph any tickets that may reach
>   his hand.   —*Bird o' Freedom.*

Putter up (thieves), a spy in the
interest of burglars, whose business it is to collect and impart
information to the gang with
which he is connected as to
the general condition and domestic arrangements of houses that
may be most easily robbed, and
that offer the greatest chances
of plunder. The *putters up* are
commonly men of glib tongues
and agreeable manners, who
endeavour to ingratiate themselves with the female servants.
They seldom endanger their own
necks by active participation in
the burglaries they recommend,
but are content to receive a
portion of the booty, trusting
to the validity of the well-
known axiom of "honour among
thieves" for the reward which
they have earned. They are
worse, but not very much worse,
than the professional detectives
who do similarly dirty work for
people who are not burglars or
criminals, but who do not scruple
to employ such disreputable
agents.

Put the kibosh on, to (popular),
to put a stop to. *Vide* KIBOSH.

Put the pot on, to (popular), to
punish, to extinguish.

> And Damon Tubbs, who loved in vain
>   The self-same damsel, lots
> Of times declared with racking brain
>   He'd *put the pot on* Potts.
>   —*Fun.*

(Turf), to lay heavily on a
horse.

Putting a nail in your coffin
(tailors), talking ill of you.

Puttun (Anglo-Indian), a regiment.

**Putty and plaster on the Solomon
Knob, the** (masons, &c.), an
intimation that the master is
coming, be silent !

Putty walla (Anglo-Indian), "the
one with a belt," a term in

Bombay for a messenger or orderly attached to an office. Called in Bengal a *Chuprassy*, and in Madras a *Peon* (Anglo-Indian Glossary).

Put up, betrayal. Hotten limits this simply to inspecting or planning a robbery, or obtaining information in regard to projected theft. But this is very far from the true meaning of the word as used in both England and America. It is thus explained in the "New York Slang Dictionary:"—

"*Put up.* This refers to information given to thieves by persons in the employment of parties to be robbed, such as servants, clerks, porters, &c., whereby the thief is facilitated in his operations. A job is said to be *put up* if the porter of a store should allow a 'fitter' to take an impression of the keys of the door of a safe; or when a clerk sent to the bank to make a deposit, or to draw money, allows himself to be thrown down and robbed, in order to have his pocket picked."

It may be observed that it is quite in this sense that Dickens uses the word in "Oliver Twist," and not at all in that of obtaining information.

Put-up jobs (burglars), explained by quotation.

We often hear that these burglaries are what are called *put-up jobs*; that is to say, they are the result of long and careful study on the part of the criminals, combined with information supplied to them by persons familiar with the inmates and contents of the house marked down for plunder.—*Daily Telegraph.*

Put upon, to (American and English), to impose upon, to ill-treat.

The Pike's Peak gold fever was raging (1859, &c.). He went to the mines and took a claim, but was much *put upon* by bullies because he was the youngest man in camp.—*H. L. Williams : In the Wild West.*

(Common), to sham.

Put up your forks, or, **bones up** (popular), a challenge to fight.

Put up your hands, to (thieves), to submit to being handcuffed. One of the *family* who has been in prison before, and knows the penalties of resistance, will say when a policeman comes for him, "All right, I'll *put up my hands,*" meaning that he will hold out his hands to be handcuffed without a struggle.

Put your forks down, to (thieves), to pick a pocket. *Vide* FORKS.

Put your name into it (tailors), get it well forward.

Pyah (nautical), weak, paltry.

Pyke (military), a civilian friend by whom the soldier on the prowl and impecunious is treated and entertained; some good-natured creature who likes to hear military yarns, and is proud of the privilege of paying for a gallant man's drink. Probably from French slang word *pékin*, civilian, heard by English soldiers in the Crimea.

Q

Q. C. (common), a Queen's Counsel.

I am a barrister elect,
 I try my best to please;
Attorneys pay me great respect—
 I wish they'd pay my fees.
 Of business I get my share,
 As much as some *Q.C.'s;*
But, oh ! what drives me to despair—
 I cannot get my fees.
 *—Bill Sykes: The Barrister's
 Song.*

Q. H. B. (naval), Queen's hard bargain, *i.e.*, a lazy sailor, a "lubber."

Q. T. (popular), quiet. *Vide* ON THE STRICT Q. T.

The essence of 'Arry, he sez, is high
 sperrits. *That* ain't so fur out.
I'm " Fiz," not four 'arf, my dear feller.
Flare-up is my motter, no doubt.
Carn't set in a corner canoodling, and do
 the *Q. T.* day and night.
 —Punch.

Quack (common), a duck.

" Dear madam, your daughter
 Being very much better,
Instead of a call I write you a letter,
 Saying as a regular doctor
No longer she lacks,
 I send her herewith a couple of *quacks.*"

A splendid couple of ducks accompanied
this cheerful letter.—*Bird o' Freedom.*

Quad (printers) is the abbreviated form of the word " quadrat," a piece of metal used by printers to fill up short lines, &c. From Latin *quadratus*, square.

Quadding (Rugby), the triumphal promenade of the chief football players round the cloisters at calling over time before a match.

Quail (thieves), an old maid. Quails are supposed to be very amorous. Le Roux gives *quail-ler*, evidently from *caille* (quail), for to have carnal connection.

Quarron (old cant), the body ; allied to carrion. Old French, *carongne.*

Quarter-deckish (naval), severe, punctilious.

Quartereen (shows, strolling actors), a farthing. The slang expressions for money, used specially by Punch and Judy showmen, and probably by others, are " mezzo," halfpenny ; " solde," penny ; "dui, tri, quarto or quatri, chickwa, sei, sette, oddo, novo, deger, long deger soldi. Beone," a shilling ; " ponte," a sovereign. From the Italian.

Quart-pot tea (Australian). The following passage is fully explanatory of this Irish phrase for tea.

Quart-pot tea, as tea made in the bush
is always called, is really the proper way
to make it. A tin quart of water is set
down by the fire, and when it is boiling
hard a handful of tea is thrown in, and the
pot instantly removed from the fire. Thus
the tea is really made with boiling water,
which brings out its full flavour, and it is
drunk before it has time to draw too much.
—Finch-Hatton: Advance Australia.

Quay (American thieves), unsafe, not to be trusted. Dutch *kwaed*, bad, &c.

Queen's bus (thieves), the prison van. A crazy inmate of Clerkenwell was about to be sent away. To quiet him the warder said the Queen had sent one of her own carriages for him. " One of them with We R. on the side ? " " Yes, one of her carriages." " Wot's We R. stand for ? " " Why, Victoria Regina, of course." " No, it don't ; it stands for Wagabones Removed," said the prisoner. The V.R. on the van is also interpreted by its habitual occupants as standing for Virtue Rewarded.

Queer bail, fraudulent bail ; insolvent persons who made it a trade to bail out persons when arrested. Also called " Jew *bail*." Sometimes also "mounters," as the mounted borrowed clothes for the occasion so as to look respectable.

Queer bit (thieves), spurious coin. *Queer*, in old cant, means anything wrong, counterfeit, or illegal. Possibly allied to the German *quer*, across, athwart, contrary to.

Queer cuffin(old cant), magistrate.

The gentry cove will be romboyled by his dam, . . . *queer cuffiy* will be the word yet, if we don't tout.—*Beaconsfield: Venetia.*

Cuffin is synonymous with *cofe*, cove.

Queer money (thieves), spurious coin.

That town had been worked with a rush by a gang and $20,000 in the *queer*

money had been left there inside of two days.—*Detroit Free Press.*

Queer rooster (American thieves), a man that lodges among thieves to pick up information for the police.

Queer soft (thieves), bad notes.

Queer street, in (common), in a difficulty.

Queer the stifler, to (thieves), avoid the gallows.

I think Handie Dandie and I may *queer the stifler* for all that is come and gone.—*Scott: Heart of Mid-Lothian.*

Queer, to (popular), to ridicule, sneer at.

A shoulder-knotted puppy, with a grin, *Queering* the thread-bare curate, let him in.
    —*Colman: Poetical Vagaries.*

To spoil, mar.

But over the doorstep she happened to trip,
And *queered* the ingenious crime.
        —*Sporting Times.*

To upset arrangements.

The Briton threw a five-franc piece into the machine, stopping the ball, and utterly *queering* the calculations of the numerous systematicians.—*Bird o' Freedom.*

To *queer* a flat, fool, impose upon a simpleton.

Who in a row like Tom could lead the van, Booze in the ken, or at the spelken hustle ? Who *queer* a flat?
        —*Lord Byron: Don Juan.*

To outwit.

He came back in great glee at having *queered* the bobbies on this side the Channel, and " bothered the gendarmes " on the other.—*Punch.*

To *queer* the pitch, *vide* PITCH.

Quencher. *Vide* MODEST QUENCHER.

Qui (printers), an abbreviation of the Latin term *quietus*, an old expression equivalent to the "billet" or "sack," to denote a man has notice to leave his situation.

Quiblets (American), a kind of witticism much in vogue in negro minstrelsy. A man makes a remark which calls forth a question, and the reply involves a jesting equivoque.

Quick (society), explained by quotation.

Young Prince Albert Vic., it would seem, is most *quick*
(That's the new word for dapper and clever). —*Fun.*

Quick, slick, to cut (popular), to start off hurriedly.

Quick upon the trigger (American), very acute to observe, quick to perceive and act, wide-awake, prompt, "fly." A significant expression derived from seeing game the instant it appears, and being quick to shoot it. It occurs in the Crockett Almanacs, 1838, 1840, but is much older.

He's as big and may be bigger,
    That's all the same to me ;
But I'm *quicker on the trigger,*
    And hit twice as hard as he.
For I've lived among the Crows and the Kaws,
And the Soos and the Kroos and the Daws,
And can make a bully Injun take a tree !
    —*Circus Song.*

Quid (general), a sovereign. *Quids*, money in general ; this corresponds to the French *de quoi* and *quibus.*

Oh, well, I thought I wouldn't star, but wait a year or two ;
I know your party's solid, so I'll try and go with you.
A modest forty *quid* a week, you pay all train fares, eh ?
Your offer is an insult and I'll leave you, sir. Good day.
            —*Bird o' Freedom.*

'Tis the last *quid* of many
    Left sadly alone,
All its golden companions
    Are changed, and are gone ;
No coin of its kindred,
    No "fiver" is here,
To burn in tobacco,
    Or melt into beer.   —*Fun.*

Quiff (military), the small curl on a soldier's temple just showing under his glengarry or forage cap. Close-cropped hair is one of the indispensable conditions of military smartness, but the curl used to be allowed, or in lieu of it a false curl which was gummed inside the forage cap so as to lie on the forehead. This *postiche* was especially in favour with men just released from military prison.

(Tailors), a word used in expressing an idea that a satisfactory result may be obtained by other than strictly recognised rules or principles.

Quiffing in the press (tailors), changing a breast-pocket to the other side.

Quiffing the bladder (tailors), drawing the long hair over to hide a bald pate.

Quill-driver (common), a writer. (Turf), a bookmaker.

The annual cricket match between the Press and the Jockeys will be played to-day on the Queen's Club Ground, West Kensington, and my information is to the effect that the *quill-drivers* are likely to have the best of the willow-wielding and leather-flapping engagement with the knights of the pigskin.—*Sporting Times.*

Quiller (common), a parasite ; a person who sucks neatly through a quill, says Hotten.

Quill, to (Winchester College), to curry favour with, to flatter.

Quilster (Winchester College), a flatterer. *Vide* To QUILL.

Quilt, to (popular), to thrash. Much used by tailors. Probably originally a tailor's phrase.

Q u i n t (American cowboy), a whip (Spanish).

Quisby (popular). Hotten defines this as bankrupt. According to a song " sung with terrific success by Miss Kate Constance " it appears to have a slightly different meaning :—

When tars have been away on a voyage o'er the sea,
They're glad to get home again to have a jolly spree,
But when they kiss and cuddle you and won't let you be,
Don't it make you feel *quisby* in the morning ?

Quite too nice (society), expression much used by the æsthetic female portion of society, meaning much the same as " awfully jolly," æsthetic conversation being largely composed of many adverbs and adjectives strung together. " He is really *quite too nice,*" applied to some die-away gentleman with long hair and black velvet coat, who dabbles in art, and who worships a sunflower, regarding it in the light of the most artistic production of nature.

Quius kius (low theatrical), hush ! cease ! A warning.

Quiz (legal), among American law-students a weekly examination in reading is so called. It is equivalent to coaching.

Quod (thieves), prison. Probably from the Hindu gypsy *quaid,* prison. Also said to be from "quadrangle," within four walls.

Here I have been in and out of *quod* for the last five-and-twenty stretch, and 1 have a right to get a good billet if anybody has one.—*Evening News.*

Quodded (thieves), imprisoned.

Quodger (legal), a corruption of *quo jure.*

Quot (old slang), a man who interferes in household affairs, especially in the kitchen.

R

RABBIT (American), a very rough, raging rowdy. Generally heard as "dead *rabbit.*" From a gang of roughs who paraded New York in 1848, carrying a dead rabbit as a standard, the dead rabbit meaning a conquered enemy. Also "dead duck." "A very athletic rowdy fellow; an extinct political party." *Rabbit-suckers,* young spendthrifts, fast, licentious young men.

Rabbit-pie (popular), a low word for a woman in a sensual or carnal sense; a prostitute.

Rabbit-pie shifter (roughs), a policeman. Probably an allusion to his impeding prostitutes' trade. *Vide* RABBIT-PIE.

Never to take notice of vulgar nicknames, such as "slop," "copper," *rabbit-pie shifter,* "peeler."—*Music Hall Song.*

Rabbit-skin (University), by synecdoche, is the academical hood adorned both at Oxford and Cambridge by the rabbit's white fur. To "get one's *rabbit-skin,*" is to take the B.A. degree.

Rabid beast (American cadet), a term applied to a new cadet who is impertinent, *i.e.,* according to the views of those who have been longer in residence.

Rabitter (Winchester College), a blow on the head with the wide of the hand, so called from the way of killing a rabbit.

Rack (Canadian), on the *rack,* constantly moving about, travelling; "always on the *rack*" is synonymous with "always on the move." *Rack* is an abbreviation of "racket," a Canadian snow-shoe.

Racket. Originally meaning in England a dodge, manœuvre, or desire, it has within a few years been greatly extended in the United States, so that one can rarely look through certain newspapers without finding it.

You know all the safe-workers arrested here last season were lodging-house bums, and they were up to that *racket.*—*Chicago Tribune.*

The place was pretty full of all the blackguards in creation then on the same *racket.*—*O'Reilly: Fifty Years on the Trail.*

Raclan, racklaw (tramps), from the gypsy *rākli,* a girl.

Rads (common), for radicals. "The *Rads* have a name of more modern political application, for the term 'Radical,' as a party name, was first applied to Major Cartwright, Henry Hunt, and their associates in 1818. The Americans have many more or less strange nicknames, and one of the last invented has reached this country, only to be in various ways misapplied and misunderstood, we mean the euphonious word *mugwump*" (*Cornhill Magazine*).

He turned him round and right-about
    All on the Irish shore,
Said he, " We'll give P–rn–ll a shake,
    And make the *Rads* to roar,
        My boy !
    And make the *Rads* to roar ! "
                        —*Punch.*

Rafe, ralph (popular), a pawnbroker's duplicate (Hotten).

Raft (American), a great number
or quantity of anything or of
any kind of objects. It is derived from the *rafts* or vast ac-
cumulations of floating timber,
driftwood, &c., which sometimes form in Western American rivers.

Rag (popular), the green curtain.
Hence the gods shout " Up with
the *rag.*" (Common), a contemptuous term for a newspaper
of the inferior sort. The French
call this " feuille de chou."

A writer in a penny *rag*, who has himself failed far more lamentably than Mrs.
———, and in the same attempt, viz., to
entertain the public.—*Sporting Times.*

(Thieves), a bank-note.

Rag-fair (military), kit inspection,
at which all the necessaries,
shirts, socks, underclothing, the
" rags," in short, are displayed.

Ragged brigade, the 50th Irish
regiment of foot.

In his youth he did good service abroad
with the Carabineers, the *ragged brigade*,
and the Springers.—*The World.*

Rag off (Americanism), explained
by quotation.

Well, if that don't " cap all ! " That beats
the bugs ; it does fairly take the *rag off.*—
Sam Slick : The Clockmaker.

Abbreviated from " it takes
the *rag off* the bush."

Rag out, to (American), to dress
up well.

Wall, don't make fun of our clothes
in the papers. We are goin' right straight
through in these here clothes—we air.
We ain't agoin' *to rag out* till we get to
Nevady.—*Artemus Ward.*

Rag proper, to (cowboys), to
dress well.

Rags (American), bank-bills.
Before the war, when there was
no uniform currency, the bills
of the innumerable banks of
the " wild cat," " blue pup," and
" ees' dog " description often
circulated at a discount of 50
or 60 per cent., and in a very
dirty and tattered condition.
These were familiarly called
rags, a word still used now and
then as a synonym for paper-
money.

Oh, times are hard ! folks say,
    And very well too we know it ;
And therefore the best way
    Is while you're young to go it.
The banks are all clean broke,
    Their *rags* are good for naught,
The specie's all bespoke,
        So certainly we ought
To go it while we're young.
                    —*Song of* 1840.

(Common), to go *rags*, to
share.

Rags and sticks (travelling showmen), explained by quotation.

When old Sawny Williams, the proprietor, came later in the morning, he was
horrified at finding his *rags and sticks*,
as a theatrical booth is always termed,
just as he had left them the overnight.—
*Hindley : Life and Adventures of a Cheap
Jack.*

Rag-shop (thieves), a bank. *Vide* RAG.

Rag-splawger (thieves), a wealthy man. *Vide* RAG.

Rag stabber (common), a tailor.

Rag tacker (popular), a dressmaker.

Rag, the (London), explained by quotation.

There is not a single music-hall, from the vast "Alhambra" in Leicester Square, to the unaristocratic establishment in the neighbourhood of the Leather Lane, originally christened the "*Rag*-lan," but more popularly known as the "*Rag*," that I have not visited. And I am bound to confess that the same damning elements are discoverable in one and all.—*Greenwood: Seven Curses of London.*

Rag, to (American University). Hall quotes a correspondent of Union College as follows:—

"*To rag* and 'ragging' you will find of very extensive application, they being employed primarily as expressive of what is called by the vulgar thieving and stealing, but in a more extended sense as meaning superiority. Thus if one declaims or composes much better than his classmates, he is said *to rag* all his competitors."

(English provincial), to abuse, slander. At English universities to annoy, hustle. For other signification *vide* BALLYRAG, its synonym.

Rag trade, the (tailors), the tailoring business. Also the mantle-making trade.

Rain napper (popular), an umbrella. To *nap*, to take, seize, receive.

Raise a bead, to (American), to aim at, to make sure of. The sight of a rifle is called a bead, hence the term. "*To raise a bead* on him," to take aim at him. Bartlett defines the same phrase as to bring to a head, to succeed, and adds that the figure is taken from brandy, rum, or other liquors which will not *raise a bead* unless of the proper strength.

Raised bill (American), a bankbill which has had the value raised or increased by pasting over it slips cut from other and worthless bills.

A couple of young men entered M. Levin & Co.'s saloon, Jefferson and Bardell Streets, called for drinks, and tendering what appeared to be a $20 bill in payment received the change and left. After they had gone the bill was found to be a clumsily-raised $10. The numbers of a Confederate $20 bill had been pasted over the figures in the corners, while a strip of paper stuck across the "X" on the back gave the bill the appearance of having been pasted together and partially concealed the fact that there was only a single "X."—*Chicago Tribune.*

Raise the wind, to (common), an almost recognised phrase. To procure money by borrowing, pawning, or otherwise.

In lieu of a calf! It was too bad by half!
At a "nigger" so pitiful who would not laugh
And turn up their noses at one who could find
No decenter method of *raising the wind?*
    —*Ingoldsby Legends.*

Raising an organ (tailors), clubbing clips together to raise a shilling's worth.

Rake (popular), a comb.

Rake an X, to (American University), to recite perfectly.

Rake in, to (American), to acquire, win, conquer, make one's own. From the very obvious simile of using a rake of any kind to draw objects together.

"Yes," said Tim, with a mournful shake of the head, "Pug's converted. I suppose you've been to the revival meetings of Goodman and Worship. No! Well, you've met Mike Ratagan on Groghan Street? Don't know Mike! Well, they've *raked him in* too."—*Luke Sharp.*

Raker (turf), a heavy bet.

It is said the "new plunger" is standing the favourite for a *raker.*—*Bird o' Freedom.*

To go a *raker*, to make a heavy bet.

Rake the pot, to (American), to take the stakes at gambling.

The artist sat and drew :
No view of frozen Arctic shores,
Where icy billow sweeps and roars ;
Nor Southern desert, Western plain,
Nor colours of the Spanish Main—
Nor vision of celestial spot—
He drew an ace, and *raked the pot!*
—*St. Louis Whip.*

Rally (common), a row, a fight, a spill. (Theatrical), the *rally*, the movement by clown, pantaloon, harlequin, and columbine after transformation scene.

Ralph (printers), the mischief-monger or "spirit" that is said to haunt men when they will not conform to chapel rules. (See Dr. Franklin's "Waps," 1819, p. 56.) A man is "sent to Coventry" if he dares to defy the decision of the chapel, and many tricks are played on him by his companions in consequence. *Vide* RAFE.

Ram (American University), a practical joke, a hoax.

Rama Sammy (Anglo - Indian), used as a generic name for all Hindoos, like Tommy Atkins for a British soldier. A twisted roving of cotton in a tube used to furnish light for a cigar. The name Ramo Samee was popularised in 1820 in England by a Hindoo juggler, who first exhibited swallowing a sword.

Ramcat or **rancat cove** (thieves), a man dressed in furs.

Ramjam (American), the last morsel eaten after which one is filled to repletion.

R a m p (common). This word, when applied to swindling and cheating, *e.g.*, "rampage," thieving and taking in, is evidently of a different origin from *ramp*, to rage, rear up, and act with violence. It is possibly in the former sense allied to the Yiddish *rame*, a deceiver or cheat ; Chaldaic *ramons*, deceit. *Ramp*, to rage, occurs in several old English writers, *e.g.*, Jonson.

These, it is only fair to say, were mostly *ramps*, or swindles, got up to obtain the gate-money, and generally interrupted by circumstances arranged beforehand by those who were going to "cut up" the plunder.—*George R. Sims: How the Poor Live.*

(Thieves), the hall mark on plate. From the rampant lion which is one of the marks.

They told me all about the wedge, how I should know it by the *ramp.*—*Horsley: Jottings from Jail.*

Vide ON THE RAMPAGE.

Ramper (common), a low fellow, a swindler or ruffian who frequents racecourses, generally on welshing expeditions.

Hardly a day passes without some miscreant being charged at police courts, and being recognised by constables as a "welsher," *ramper*, or "ticket snatcher." These are criminal trades, belonging essentially to the racecourse.—*Sporting Times.*

Ramping (thieves), explained by quotation.

George Stamper was charged, on remand, with felony, technically known as *ramping, i.e.,* calling at the houses where parcels had just been delivered from tradesmen to customers, and obtaining possession of them under various pretences.—*Standard.*

(Sports), a swindle, a conspiracy.

The *ramping* of the Jubilee Plunger at pigeon shooting at Brighton is still the principal topic of conversation. Whether Mr. —— will pay up and look pleasant, or repudiate, or prosecute the different parties for conspiracy is more than I can say.—*Sporting Times.*

Also *vide* TO RAMP.

Ramp, to (thieves), to steal forcibly from the person. (Sporting), to swindle, but more especially to bet against one's own horse. Also to levy black-

mail in a brutal manner. From *to ramp*, to spring with violence.

Ramping mad (old), uproariously drunk.

Rampoman (thieves), one who plunders by force. In Mayhew's "Criminal Prisons of London," but obsolete now.

Rams, the (American), the *delirium tremens.* "To have *the rams*," to be extremely eccentric.

Ram, to (American), to *ram* one's face in, or on; to intrude, to force oneself into any company.

Rance sniffle (Texas), mean and dastardly malignity. Peculiar to Georgia.

Randlesman (thieves), silk pocket handkerchief, green ground with white spots.

Random, three horses driven in a line;—"Harum-scarum" being four horses driven in a line (Hotten).

Ranker (military), an officer who has risen from the ranks.

Rank outsider (common), a vulgar fellow, a cad. From a racing term applied to a horse outside the rank.

A *rank outsider* might possibly drop from the clouds—just at the bell—but it is hardly possible that Grandison, or Lovegold, or Lourdes, or Florentine, or Stetchworth, or any other "ranker" can be the horse.—*Sporting Times.*

Ranks (printers). A compositor that has been promoted to the position of overseer or reader is said to return to the *ranks* again should he be reduced. Attributed by Savage, 1841, to the fact that compositors' frames are placed in ranks or rows. More probably from a military term.

Ran-tan (popular), to be on the *ran-tan* (originally American) is to " be on the big drunk," to be in a fit of drunkenness extending over several days, or it may be weeks, after a period of enforced abstinence. Possibly from provincial *ranter*, a large beer jug. The word appears in the works of Taylor, the Water-poet, in 1630. Also "ran-ran," frolic, drunkenness.

My second son's been made a Buff, and goes on the *ran-ran.—Broadside Ballad.*

On the *ran-tan* also means drunk.

Rapparee (old slang), a Tory.

Rap, to (thieves), to talk, to say. From " rap out."

So I said, " All right;" but he *rapped*, " It is not all right."—*Horsley: Jottings from Jail.*

To swear.

D—— me ! I scorn to *rap* against any lady.—*Fielding: Amelia.*

Raspberry (coachmen), explained by quotation.

One gentleman I came across had a way of finding out the cussedness of this or that animal by a method that I found to be not entirely his own. The tongue is inserted in the left cheek and forced through the lips, producing a peculiarly squashy noise that is extremely irritating. It is termed, I believe, a *raspberry*, and

when not employed for the purpose of testing horseflesh, is regarded rather as an expression of contempt than of admiration. —*Sporting Times.*

The allusion is to a grating noise like that produced by rasping.

Raspberry tart (American), a nice dainty girl.

Raspberry tart, with a little poke bonnet,
And a great big bunch of thingamies upon it,
With a pinafore dress that was just the thing,
And a little pug dog at the end of a string.
—*Broadside Ballad.*

Rasper (Stock Exchange), a big " turn," *i.e.*, a large profit on a bargain.

Raspin (old cant), the bridewell. So called from the task there of rasping wood.

Rasping shorter (cricketers), a ball which swiftly slides along the ground when knocked off by the bat, instead of rebounding.

Rat (old cant), a clergyman. " Ratichon " is a very common slang name for a priest in France. (Common), a sneak, informer, turncoat. Also an abbreviation of water-*rat*. (Nautical), an infernal machine for blowing up insured ships for the purpose of defrauding ship insurance companies.

There are two species of *rats*. One species is intended to operate upon iron ships, the other upon wooden ones.— *Times.*

(Printers), a workman that accepts work or wages at unfair rates—not paid according to the existing scale of prices recognised in the locality.

Rat house, rat shop (printers), an office where unfair wages are paid—the employés being called "rats," or "furry tails."

Rats (popular), to "give a person green *rats*" is to backbite him. "To be in the *rats*," to be suffering from drink; to have or see *rats*, the incipient stage of *delirium tremens* (see Zola's *L'Assommoir*). (Common), "to have *rats* in one's garret," to be soft-brained, silly, or idiotic.

"Say, mimmaw," Miss Arethusa remarked, "what's gettin' into you lately. You've got *rats* in your garret, haven't you?"
"No, I haven't anny *rats* in me garret, ur in me brain, aither, me foine lady," said the widow indignantly —*New York Mercury.*

(American), "to have *rats*," to have wild or eccentric fancies; a synonym for "rams," or other animals seen by men with *delirium tremens.*

The word *rat* stands as an opprobrious epithet applied to persons suddenly changing their opinions. Hence the term "ratted," which has become so common in late years. Sir Robert Peel seems to have been the first noted person to whom the term *rat* was applied, and he brought the epithet upon himself by changing his opinions on Catholic Emancipation. Some of our Western editors use the word *rats* in a way unknown to M. Barrère. For example, if one editor takes a flippant view of what another regards as a grave question, the latter at once declares that "our contemporary has *rats*;" and sometimes it will be added that "he has got them bad." Dennis Kearney, of Sand Lots fame, wrote, some years ago, of a certain California capitalist whom he described as a "slab-sided, bung-eyed hyena," and he said also that the capitalist had *rats.*—*C. Leland Harrison: MS. Collection of Americanisms.*

Ratted (common), applied to a "rat," *i.e.*, a turncoat.

Rattled, to get (American), to become nervous, shaky, to lose presence of mind.

Anarchist August Vincent Theodor Spies was the next witness. Spies was a failure. He got *rattled.* He was nervous and fidgety while trying to be smart, and both in his manner and in his damaging admissions he was the worst witness the defence has yet called.—*Chicago Tribune.*

She lifted up another shovelful, but the exertion caused her to slip, and she got *rattled.*—*Detroit Free Press.*

Rattler (old cant), a coach. (Thieves), a railway train.

As soon as he got round a double, I guyed away to Malden, and touched for two wedge teapots, and took the *rattler* to Waterloo. —*Horsley: Jottings from Jail.*

(American), a neck-tie. It is a very curious coincidence that so far back as 1831 a comic writer spoke of a very great swell as one who

"Is on fashion leading-tattler,
And his tie's a real *rattler*,"

and that recently in America cravats are made of rattlesnakes' skins.

Rattle, to give the (American thieves), to talk to a man so as to divert his attention, as, for instance, while robbing him. To confuse by talking.

"*Give him the rattle* with your mouth all the time you're working him," said Mr

Sutton. "Tell him he mustn't fall asleep in a public place."—*Confidence Crooks: Philadelphia Press.*

Rattling (general), jolly, excellent, smart, as *rattling* bait, first-class food, excellent eating.

That's my plan. Give 'em bumping weight (with the little finger in) and shout, "There you are, all that lot for tuppence, it's *rattling* bait !" and they swallers it like jam.—*S. May: Hurrah for a Coster's Life!*

Rattling gloke (old cant), a coachman.

Rat-trap (popular), a woman's bustle.

Rawg (tinker), a waggon.

Raw lobsters (common), a nickname at one time applied to policemen. It was originated about fifty years ago by the *Weekly Despatch,* and was derived from the blue coats of the then new force. Soldiers had previously been called, and were then known, as *lobsters,* from their red coats, and as when caught and previous to boiling a lobster is of a dark bluish hue, the policemen were called *raw lobsters* to distinguish them from soldiers.

Rawnie. This word, according to Hotten, is the gypsy for a young woman. It has, however, no such meaning in Romany, where it is invariably applied to a lady. From the Hindustani *rānee,* a queen.

"Dui Romany chals were bitchadey pardel, Bitchadey parlo boro pānī.

Platos for kaurin,
Lasho for chorin,
The pūtsī avrī a boro *rawnee* "—
"Two gypsies were transported, transported across the great water, Plato for pilfering, Lewis for stealing the pocket from a great lady."

Rawniel, runniel (tinker), beer. *Tripo-rauniel,* a pot of beer.

Razor (American University), a pun.

Many of the members of this time-honoured institution, from whom we ought to expect better things, not only do their own shaving but actually make their own *razors.* But I must explain for the benefit of the uninitiated. A pun in the elegant college dialect is called a *razor,* while an attempt at a pun is styled a sick *razor.* The sick ones are by far the most numerous ; however, once in a while you meet with one in quite respectable health. —*Yale Literary Magazine.*

Reacher (pugilistic), a blow.

And our pugilistic hero felt his courage go to zero;
When the stranger started making matters snug,
By landing sundry *reachers* on our hero's classic features—
Or, in plainer phraseology, his "mug." —*Sporting Times.*

Reach-me-downs, hand-me-downs (common), clothes bought at second-hand shops. In French "décrochez-moi ça." The phrase has now the more extended meaning of ready-made articles as opposed to those made to order.

Read and write (thieves' rhyming slang), flight. Also to fight.

Reader (thieves and tinker), a letter, book, newspaper.

He rubbed his hands so strongly on a man's body that anything in the shape of a piece of thread, a pencil, or a bit of *reader* (newspaper) could be discovered, but he never looked at the handkerchief which was dangled loosely between the thumb and forefinger.—*Evening News.*

Also a pocket-book.

"Agreed," replied the tinker; "but first let's see wot he has got in his pockets." "Vith all my 'art," replied the sandman, searching the clothes of the victim. "A *reader!*—I hope it's well lined."—*Ainsworth: Auriol.*

(Tinkers), "you're *readered* sooblee," you are put in the *Police Gazette,* my man; there is a description of you published.

Read, to (Stock Exchange), to try to ascertain by the expression of a man's features what his intentions are.

Ready (common), money. Also *ready* stuff.

While limiting expenses in this true Arcadian way,
He borrowed all the *ready* which at her disposal lay,
Promising the loan he would infallibly repay—
    Sm'other time.
        —Bird o' Freedom.

Ready-gilt (thieves and popular), money. *Vide* GILT.

Readying (turf), explained by quotation.

Do you mean to say that you don't know what was meant by *readying* Success?—Of course I know what it means. It means pulling.—*Standard.*

Ready-reckoners, the Highland regiments of the British army (Hotten).

Ready thick 'un (thieves and others), a sovereign.

To his appetite still royal, he soon stormed the Café Royal,
Where he blewed a *ready thick 'un* on some dinner.
        —Sporting Times.

Real jam. *Vide* JAM.

"She's *real jam,* she is, by Jove!"—so said the Johnny, as he strove
To make the very most of his position;
For though he in the front row sat, his opera-glass was levelled at
The tasty choregraphic exhibition.
        —Sporting Times.

Ream (theatrical), good. From *ream,* cream, a synonym for anything unusually good.

Swetter than ani milkes *rem.* — *Leg. Catholic,* 13th century.

"Reaming," getting on well.

Reckoning up (common), talking of, usually in a slanderous manner.

It was in the dressing-room, and they were *reckoning up* an absent friend in a manner peculiar to the profession.
"How anybody can consider her an actress," sneered Tottie, "I'm sure I can't imagine. And yet she has the temerity to call herself an artist!"
"And why not, dear?" said Lottie "I'm sure she paints very nicely!"—*Sporting Times.*

Red (stage, thieves, &c.), gold. Same in Icelandic. In French cant *jaune.* In furbesche or Italian cant *rossume,* literally redness. (American), a cent. In French slang, a sou.

Red eel (West American), an abusive term.

"Stranger," said I, "you're a *red eel!*"—*Crockett's Almanac.*

Red flannel (popular), the tongue.

Red fustian (popular), port wine.

Redge, ridge (thieves), gold. Probably from *red*, which see.

Red herring (popular), a soldier. "The terms," says Hotten, "are exchangeable, the fish being often called a soldier."

Red kettle. *Vide* KETTLE.

"What did you earn on an average by your trade as a thief?"

"Generally from two to three pounds a week clear. You see, I laid myself out for picking pockets, and I generally got two or three 'red kettles' a week."

"What is a *red kettle*?" I inquired, feeling ashamed of my ignorance.

"A *red kettle* is a gold watch."—*Evening News.*

Red lane (common), the throat.

Red liner (beggars), an officer of the Mendicity Society.

Red rag (popular), the tongue, also "red flannel." In French slang "le chiffon rouge."

Bah, Peter! your *red rag* will never be still.—*Beaconsfield: Venetia.*

Redraw (prison), back-slang for warder.

Oh, I know now! It was for shying a lump of wet oakum at the *redraw.*—*J. Greenwood: Low Life Deeps.*

Red ribbon (thieves), brandy.

Red 'un (thieves), a sovereign.

She observed, "You'll give me something—won't you, kid?"

So the youth, her wish obeying, placed a coin down—gently saying—

"There's a *red 'un*—or in other words 'a quid!'"

—*Sporting Times.*

Also a watch.

Reefing (thieves), drawing with the fingers. "*Reefing* up into work," is drawing up the pocket until the portemonnaie or purse is within reach of the fingers.

Reeler (thieves), a policeman. From his rolling gait when sauntering about.

One of my pals said, "There is a *reeler* over there who knows me, we had better split out."—*Horsley: Jottings from Jail.*

Reesbin (tinker), prison.

Refresher, a fee paid to a barrister daily in addition to his retaining fee, to remind him of the case intrusted to his care (Dr. Brewer).

Regimental fire (military), some particular regimental custom carried out after drinking a toast, generally on great occasions.

The usual loyal toasts were drunk with much enthusiasm and honoured with *regimental fire.*—*Standard.*

Regulars (thieves), a thief's share of the spoil.

They were quarrelling about the *regulars.*—*Times.*

Reign, to (Australian prison), to be at liberty. "A wire never *reigns* long," a pickpocket is not long without being apprehended.

Reliever, a coat worn in turn by any party of poor devils whose wardrobes are in pawn (Hotten).

Relieving officer (University), a father.

Religious (Texas), quiet, good. It is amusing to hear a Texan ask when about to purchase a horse, "Is he *religious?*" Generally a mustang is anything but that. It means, Is he free from vice? and as Texan horses are notorious for sulking and kicking, the inquiry seems a trifle superfluous.

Remedy (Winchester School), (quasi dies remissionis), on Tuesday or Thursday. If there was any reasonable excuse, prefect of hall used to go up to the doctor after chapel and asked if they might have a *remedy.* If this was granted the doctor gave him a ring (*remedy* ring), and there was a half-holiday, except that all who had not studied had to sit in hall from 9 to 11 A.M. There is still a *remedy* every Thursday in cloister time. There used formerly to be a *remedy* every Tuesday and Thursday, now there is only a half *rem.*

A holiday at Winchester is termed a *remedy* . . . "remiday," *i.e.*, remission day.—*Pascoe: Our Public Schools.*

Remi (Westminster School), remission from tasks.

Renovator (tailors), one who does repairs.

Rent (old cant), to collect the *rent,* to rob travellers on the highway. A *rent* collector, a robber of money only.

Reptile (American cadet), a new cadet.

Re-raw, to be on the (popular), to be on a prolonged drunken spree.

Respun (tinker), to steal.

Resurrection (tailors), the warming up of some previous leaving.

Resurrection pie (common), a pie supposed to be made of scraps and leavings.

Ret (printers), a pressman or machine-minder terms the second side of a sheet or "reiteration" thus.

Retree (printers), a term derived from the French *retrié,* picked again, and used by printers and stationers to denote outside or bad sheets in a ream. An equivalent perhaps to the old term "Cassie" paper, quoted by Moxon, 1683. The term is indicated by stationers by two crosses (× ×).

Returned empty (clerical), uncharitable name for retired colonial bishops of the class that the late Bishop Blomfield described as forming the "Home and Colonial" Episcopate.

Revelation (American), to have a *revelation,* to take a drink. A phrase invented by C. F. Browne.

Smith did a more flourishing business in the prophet line than Brigham Young does. Smith used to have his little *revelation* almost every day—sometimes two before dinner. Brigham Young only takes one once in a while.—*Artemus Ward: Brigham Young.*

Will you have a *revelation*, Mr. Jones, an outpouring of the spirit—Monongahela or brandy—I've got 'em both?—*S. Courier: Hard and Fast.*

Reviver (common), a drink, a "pick-me-up" or stimulant.

It was but twelve o'clock, and therefore early for *revivers* of any sort.—*The Golden Butterfly.*

Reward (kennel), dogs' or hounds' supper. Also the blood and entrails of the objects of chase.

R'ghoglin, gogh'leen (tinker), to laugh.

Rhino (common), money,

> Why gold and silver
> Should be christened *rhino*,
> As I'm a sinner,
> Blow me tight if I know.
> —*Punch.*

If my *rhino* had lasted longer I might have got into worse company still.—*Greenwood: Odd People in Odd Places.*

The word *rhino* can be traced back to the restoration of Charles II. The Seaman's Adieu, an old ballad dated 1670, has the following :—

> Some as I know
> Have parted with their ready *rino*.

Dr. Brewer suggests that it came from the German *rinos*, a nose, alluding to the Swedish nose-tax. Other suggested derivations are the Scottish *rino* and the Spanish *riñón*, meaning kidney ; "tener cubierto el riñón" signifies to be wealthy. Again it may have been coined from the phrase, "to pay through the nose," *i.e.*, to pay a high price.

"Probably as a Yorkshire and

Northern word from the Scandinavian or Danish *ren* or *reno*, fine, brilliant, shining ; a common synonym in every language for money, as the 'shiners.' In the Icelandic Skaldespraket, or poets' language (a part of the Edda), the word *Rhine* (Rhenfloden) is, however, given as one of the twenty terms for gold, because the great treasure of the Nibelungen lies in it " (C. G. Leland : Notes).

Rhinoceral, rich. *Vide* RHINO.

Thou shalt be *rhinoceral*, my lad, thou shalt.—*Shadwell: Squire of Alsatia.*

Rhyme-slinger, a vulgar term for a poet.

" Poetic license," said Doss Chiderdoss, " is all very well, but you have to pay for it now and again."

" Exactly," observed Miss Park Palings. " I suppose you have to take out a license the same as you do for dogs."

But the highly indignant *rhyme-slinger* had rushed off to Yaughan's to get a stoup of liquor.—*Sporting Times.*

Rib (popular), a wife ; of Biblical origin.

Rib bender (pugilistic), a violent blow in the ribs.

If it had killed the man, he deserved it, the rough fellow. I afterwards heard that it was some time before he recovered the *rib-bender* he got from the fat show-woman. —*Hindley: Life and Adventures of a Cheap Jack.*

Ribbers (pugilistic), blows in the ribs.

> Yet, sprightly to the scratch both buffers came,
> While *ribbers* rung from each resounding frame.
> —*Thomas Moore: Works.*

Ribbon (popular), gin or other spirits. *Vide* RED RIBBON.

Ribbons (common), the reins; to handle the *ribbons*, to drive.

Rib-roaster, colloquially a rap across the body at singlestick. Much resorted to in the old cudgelling or "backswording" play for the purpose of trying to bring the opponent's guard down, and thus obtain an opening at his head. An old term.

And he departs, not meanly boasting
Of his magnificent *rib-roasting*.
—*Hudibras.*

(Pugilistic), a smart blow in the ribs.

There's a regular *rib-roaster* for you !
—*C. Bede: Verdant Green.*

Rice-bags (popular), trousers.

Richard (schools), a dictionary. From the abbreviation *dic* (Dick) of dictionary.

Ricochet (American cadet), gay, splendid.

Ridgecully (old cant), a goldsmith. From *ridge*, gold, and *cully*, man.

Riding on the cheap. *Vide* DUCK, DOING A.

Riding the donkey (thieves), cheating in weight.

Rig (booksellers). H. J. Byron says a *rig* is a term which signifies in the book trade a sale by auction, where the lots are "missed" by the proprietor or proprietors. And a leading bookseller says that these rigs have now (1868) become a re-cognised feature in the business. *Rig* is good English for sportive trick, lively frolic, bit of mischief. The *rig* in auction sales is a trick by which the dealers agree not to bid against one another, buy low, and resell by a mock auction called "knock out." A man is said to have the *rig* run upon him when he has to undergo a number of false imputations.

Right as rain (popular), quite right, safe, comfortable.

There was six of us took the rattler at King's Cross by the first train in the morning, and we'd got three briefs and a old 'un with the date sucked off—*right as rain* we was ! We got a kerridge all to ourselves, nice and comfortable.—*Sporting Times.*

Right man (tailors), the workman who makes the right forepart, and finishes the coat.

Right smart (American), a "*right smart* of work," a large amount of work; the phrase is further explained by the following quotation.

Mayor Hewitt has laid out what they call in the far West "a *right smart* of work," and it will be interesting to see what the less energetic aldermen are going to do about it.—*New York Times.*

Right smart chance, many, much, a good occasion.

Rights, to (thieves), to have one *to rights*, to be even with him. "You are *to rights* this time," there is a clear case against you.

Right up to the handle (American), thoroughly; "he is a good fellow *up to the handle.*"

Rigs (popular), clothes. From the expression "to rig out," "to rig up," which see.

I fancy that the style is neat,
Look at my tile, and twig my feet,
With *rigs* like mine you seldom meet,
Eh! Rather!
—*H. Ross: The Husband's Boat.*

Rig, to (Stock Exchange), to unduly inflate a security by fair means or foul. (Mercantile), to *rig* the market, to play tricks so as to defraud purchasers. (Popular), "*to rig* out," "*to rig* up," to dress. From a sea phrase. Given as good English by some dictionaries, but chiefly used by slang-talking people.

Tom and I sent out all our own clothes to pawn, so as to *rig up* a seedy toff (handle to his name and all) and send him in to bet, while we ourselves spent the day in bed without a pair of breeches between us.—*Sporting Times.*

Rikker, rik (gypsy), to carry, keep, retain. *Rikker adré o sherro*, to remember.

"*Rikker* lis adré tīro kŏkerŏs zi te kekno'll jin lis"—"Keep it in your own soul and nobody will know it."

Rikker yer noki trushnees"—"Carry your own baskets."—*Gypsy Proverbs.*

Rinder (University), an outsider. Used at Queen's.

Ring (American), a combination of financiers, manufacturers, or politicians, formed to advance their own interests, and very often to rob the public. Thus the object of the great whisky *ring*, a coalition of distillers, was to evade the revenue laws.

Take the case of New York City, with its enormous revenues, by way of illustra-

tion. The political *rings* and gangs year after year despoil that revenue so that there is little or nothing to show for it. The helpless taxpayers are systematically robbed, and the financial administration of the city and county is rotten with corruption.—*American Newspaper.*

This term is now common in England. Formerly to go through the *ring*, to take advantage of the Insolvency Act, or to be "whitewashed."

Ring-dropper. *Vide* RING-DROPPING.

Tom's evil genius did not . . . mark him out as the prey of *ring-droppers*, pea and thimble-riggers, duffers, louters, or any of those bloodless sharpers.—*Dickens: Martin Chuzzlewit.*

Ring-dropping (thieves), offering for sale to a passer-by a brass ring, or other spurious article, alleged to have been found just in front of the intended victim, or scraping acquaintance with a stranger by asking him if he is the owner of a ring which the sharper pretends to have picked up.

Ringing the horse-shoes (tailors), a welcome to a man who has been out boozing or drinking.

Ring in, to (American), *to ring in*, to force or insinuate oneself into company where one is not wanted, or to which one does not belong. It is applied to getting the better of in almost every sense. Probably from the English "ringing the changes." Also to *ring into*. The term was about 1845 generally associated with Beau Hickman, a notorious low adventurer who made it popular. (Cardsharpers), *to ring in*, to add surreptitiously or substitute cards in a pack.

The gang disappeared with "the spoil," and when the cards were counted sixty over the usual number were found to have been *rung in.*—*Sporting Times.*

To *ring in* a cold deck, to substitute a fresh pack, in which the cards are prearranged.

One day he got half-a-dozen tinhorn gamblers together, and between them they *rung in* a cold deck in a faro-box.—*F. Francis : Saddle and Moccasin.*

Ringster (American), a member of a noisy clique, political or otherwise, whose object is to profit its members at public expense.

The Coast Survey Bureau . . . has been a nest for *ringsters* for the last four or five years.—*American Newspaper.*

Ring-tail (military), a recruit.

Ring-tailed roarer (American). At first a "coon" was a great compliment to a pretentious, or brave, or indomitable man, then ring-tail, from the rings of light grey and grey black which are so prominent on the tail of the racoon.

You're the *ring-tailed squealer*—less
Than a hundred silver dollars
Won't be offered you, I guess."
—*Ben Gualtier.*

Ring, to (thieves), to steal, by changing such articles as coats, saddles at fairs and markets, &c. "*Ringing* the changes," changing bad money for good, or defrauding by means of a trick. Explained by quotation.

The prisoner went into Simpson's and called for a glass of sherry, in payment for which he gave Miss R—— a half-sovereign. She handed him 9s. 6d., whereupon he said that he had some silver, and adding a sixpence to the change asked her to give him a sovereign for that and the ten-shilling piece, which she did. Late in the evening he came again, and calling for a glass of whisky, tried on the same trick, but the lady gave him into custody. —*Daily Telegraph.*

(Conjurors), to substitute one object for another. From the slang phrase "ringing the changes." (Up-country Australian), to patrol round and round cattle.

You'll have *to ring* them. Pass the word for all hands to follow one another in a circle.—*A. C. Grant.*

(American), to make a noise, to burst out with turbulent conduct.

Next time you *ring* I am coming for you.—*F. Francis : Saddle and Moccasin.*

Ring up, to (up-country Australian), to patrol round, to keep riding round and round a herd, which has to be done when they are unsteady, and inclined to make a bolt or stampede. It cows the cattle, who imagine that they are surrounded, and enables the stockmen to see where mischief is brewing.

Gradually they drop into a steadier pace, and at last with panting chests, lolling-out tongues, and glaring eyes, are driven into a mob of quiet cattle, which are found feeding handy. *Ring them up.* Mix them well with the quiet ones, and let them stand a little.—*A. Grant : Bush Life in Queensland.*

Rinkeno rinkni, ránkini (gypsy), pretty, beautiful. (Hindu, *rángini,* gaily coloured),

Rinse (society), drink.

I suggested that something ambrosial we'd quaff,
(The *rinse?* Do you cotton to phiz?)
'Twas Arcadia for nearly a day and a half.
(Goodwood winnings squared the biz.).
—*Bird o' Freedom.*

Rip (old cant), "a poor devil." Dutch slang, gone, lost. J. Teirlinck remarks that "*hij is rip*"—"he is *rip,*" or "gone," comes naturally from the R. I. P. of the tombstones. (Common), a rake. Corruption of reprobate, according to Hotten.

Ripe (old), drunk.

Rip, let it (society), let matters follow their course, go to the deuce. From an American phrase in reference to a steamship, "*Let her rip,* I'm insured," *i.e.,* let her burst, &c.

Rip out, to (American), impatiently giving vent or expression to one's feelings or opinions, to "rap out."

When brought face to face with his opponent, his smarting sense of injustice caused him *to rip out* what he thought of the whole matter.

Ripper (common). A *ripper* may be a really good fellow, a very fast horse, a good play or part, in short, it is applied to any one or anything superlatively good. From an Americanism "to rip," to go at a great pace, the metaphor being in an asso-

ciation of ideas between speed and excellence.

Ripping (common), a popular superlative of the present day. An emphasising term to express excellent, pleasant, amusing, charming, elegant, &c. *Vide* RIPPER.

Why, I've been a thinkin' on yer as bein' dead lots and lots of times, old Smiff, since the last time we seed you, and here you are dressed *rippin'.* — *The Little Ragamuffins.*

"Did you enjoy the Easter festivals much?" asked the poetess of the widower. "*Ripping,*" responded the bereaved.— *Bird o' Freedom.*

Ripping and staving along. *Vide* FULL DRIVE.

Rip, to (American), to tear along headlong. "Ripping and tearing along like all possessed." Commonly heard as "Let her *rip!*" As it implies going recklessly on to destruction, it has been ingeniously derived from the letters R. I. P. (*requiescat in pace*), often seen on gravestones. Also to swear, curse.

While I was cooking supper the old man took a swing or two, and got sort of warmed up, and went to *ripping* again.— *Adventures of Huckleberry Finn.*

Rise (common), to take a *rise* out of a person is to outwit, quiz, or make him the subject of a jest. A metaphor from fly-fishing.

Gig-lamps, I vote we take a *rise* out of the youth.—*C. Bede: Verdant Green.*

According to the author of "Sam Slick," to get or take a *rise* out of any one is specially

American; but it is very seldom heard in the United States, while it is common in England. It means simply the vulgar and almost obsolete practice of quizzing, or rendering a man ridiculous, sometimes by directly mortifying him, at others by drawing. him out. It is not to be found in Bartlett's Dictionary of Americanisms; but it is given in Hotten as English, specially as Oxford University slang.

Rise a barney, to (patterers, Punch and Judy), to collect a crowd.

River rats, men who plunder the bodies of drowned persons.

"It pays better, if a man has got the heart to do it, to rob a body and let it drift."

"Or rob it first, and take it ashore afterwards and claim the reward," I suggested.

"But you'll never find the regular *rat* doing that, unless it was a body there was a reward offered for. . . . If it's only half-a-crown they find in the pockets, it's best for them to be satisfied with that, and have no more to do with it."—*J. Greenwood: Rag, Tag, & Co.*

Rivets (popular), money.

Road agents (American), highwaymen.

They went up into Virginia, and formed a band of sixty or seventy *road agents*, or highwaymen.—*O'Reilly: Fifty Years on the Trail.*

Roaf (back-slang), four; as *roaf gen*, four shillings; *roaf yanneps*, fourpence.

Roam on the rush, to (racing), is said of a jockey who does not ride well, who swerves from the straight line at the finish when the rush takes place.

Roaring-boys, an old term still used to signify a boisterous, rowdy gang.

A group of *roaring-boys* comes staggering up to the door.—*Thor Fredur: Sketches from Shady Places.*

Roaring forties (nautical), a term applied by sailors to the degrees of latitude between 40° and 50° N.—the zone of storms as far as the Atlantic is concerned. Also sometimes applied to the same latitudes in the Southern Sea.

Roast brown, to (thieves), said of a detective who watches a man.

I was taking a ducat to get back to town
(I had come by the rattler to Dover),
When I see as a reeler was *roasting me brown*,
And he rapped, "I shall just turn you over."
　　　　　—*The Referee.*

Roasting, to give a (thieves), to watch as one watches meat which is being roasted. This seems to be connected with the phrase "to give hot beef," to pursue.

I see a reeler giving me *a roasting*, so I began to count my pieces for a jolly.—*Horsley: Jottings from Jail.*

Roast, to (common), to expose a person to a running fire of jokes for the amusement and with the assistance of a whole company. (Hotten), to severely take to task.

Another letter received from one W. T. Nelson, of Cleveland, severely *roasts* both.—*Daily Inter-Ocean.*

(Thieves), said of a detective on the watch. (Pugilistic), *to roast* the ribs is to strike on the sides.

Robert (common), a policeman. Also *Roberto.*

When coroners sit upon corpses galore
Of people who killed on the sly are,
The guilt of one person is well to the fore,
For our *Roberts* so terribly fly are.
The verdict is always conclusive enough,
And the facts in a nutshell all shown are;
The peelers can prove in ways ready, if rough,
These the deeds of "a person unknown" are.
 —*George R. Sims: An Awful Character.*

Robin Red-breasts, explained by quotation.

Officers attached to the Bow Street police-office, and who were otherwise known as Bow Street "runners," and sometimes, from their scarlet vests, as *Robin Red-breasts.—Daily Telegraph.*

Roby Douglas (nautical), the posterior.

Rock bottom (American), properly basis or foundation. Also "hard pan." Metaphorically ruin.

Other freight wars, covering much less territory than the present, have gone to *rock bottom* before any attempt has been made to restore rates.—*American Newspaper.*

Rock bottom dollar, last dollar.

Rocked, half (popular), half-witted; also, "had a *rock* too much."

Rocker, off one's (popular), mad.

Rocker, to (gypsy), to understand.

Can you *rocker* Romany,
Can you patter flash?
 —*Hindley: Life and Adventures of a Cheap Jack.*

Correctly *rācker.*

Rock of eye and rule of thumb (tailors), refers to doing anything which requires scientific treatment by guesswork.

Rocks (American), small stones or pebbles are called *rocks* in the Southern States.

One rash philologist essayed to prove that "nugget" was simply an American corruption of the word "ingot;" but a Californian digger at once sternly negatived this idea by informing Europeans that he had handled a few "lumps" of gold, and had seen some sacks full of *rocks*, but that "nuggets" had never been heard of in the auriferous West until the word was imported from Australia.—*Globe.*

The term is used in some parts of England.

Rock, the (army), Gibraltar.

Rocky (popular), bad, queer, shaky. Much used by printers.

"Just my usual *rocky* luck," groaned the Conkster.—*Sporting Times.*

(Common), tipsy.

Roglan (tinker), a four-wheeled vehicle.

Rogue and pully (thieves), a man and woman going out to rob gentlemen.

Rogue and villain (thieves' rhyming slang), a shilling.

Rogue's yarn, a thread of red or blue worsted, worked into the ropes manufactured in the Government dockyards, to identify them if stolen (Hotten).

Roker (schools), a ruler, generally a flat one. Scandinavian *rak*, straight, even. On the east coast a skate is called a *roker*.

Roller (Oxford), or roll call, a substitute for compulsory attendance at chapel.

Rollers (Stock Exchange), United Rolling Stock.

Rolleys (popular), vehicles.

> Yet you, with *rolleys* and the like,
> No sympathy can feel, sir,
> But dare a crushing blow to strike
> Against the common-wheel, sir !
> —*Funny Folks.*

Rolling Joe (old cant), a smartly dressed fellow. Also " flashy blade."

Roll of snow (thieves), a piece of Irish linen (Ducange Anglicus).

Roll on (Shrewsbury School), explained by quotation.

Anything approaching swagger is severely rebuked; there is no more objectionable quality than that understood by the expression " He's got such a horrid *roll on.*"—*Pascoe : Everyday Life in our Public Schools.*

Roll your hoop (tailors), go ahead, you are all right.

Rom (gypsy), a gypsy, one of the Romany race. The etymology of the word is uncertain. It would appear to have some affinity to the Hindu *ram-na*, of Sanskrit origin, "to roam." VOL. II.

These wanderers are now generally admitted to have come from Northern India, and probably a mixture of the Jãt, Dom, and other wanderers who, being driven out of India, about the tenth century coalesced and went to the West.

The writer believes that the ancestors of the gypsies must be sought, so far as name at least is concerned, among the Dom, a very low caste in India. But in the north of India, in the hill country, there are the D̩omar or D̩om allied to them who are not by any means so degraded. D and R are convertible in Indian tongues, and *doi*, a wooden spoon in Hindu, is *roy* in gypsy. The writer has met with a Hindoo who declared that he once belonged to a tribe of Indian gypsies who called themselves *Rom*. He said that in their peculiar language *mãro* or *mãnro* was bread. This is the word for bread in all gypsy dialects, but it is not found in any Indian tongue. Mr. Grierson, however, following the indication as to the Dom, discovered in India that among the Bihar Doms, *maro* means wheat.

> " As mandy was pirryin' pre the drom,
> I dicked the patteran of a *Rom*,
> Of a Romany chal as I did know
> And the nav o' the mũsh 'os Petúlengro "—

> " As I was going along the way
> I saw the sign where a gypsy lay,
> Of a gypsy man whom I did know,
> And the name of that man was Petúlengro."

M

Roman fall (common), another of the absurdities of posture in walking which seem to run periodically like an epidemic through the ranks of the shallow-witted and idle members of the community. It consisted in throwing the head well forward and the small of the back well in while walking.

Romany (gypsy and thieves), a gypsy.

And here I am, pals, merry and free,
A regular rollicking *romany*.
          —*Ainsworth: Rookwood.*

A *romany* rye, a gentleman who talks Romany, who associates with gypsies, and is familiar with their ways.

Rome-vile, Rum-ville (old cant), London.

A gage of ben Rom-bouse
In a bousing ken of *Rom-vile*.
          — *The Roaring Girle.*

From *rum*, great (which see), and French *ville;* or old English *vill*, a village.

Rook (common), a cheat, cardsharper. In opposition to "pigeon," a dupe. John Bee, in his dictionary of the turf, ring, &c., gives the following definition of *rooks* of the period —" Fellows about gambling-houses who are employed in plucking well-fledged pigeons, of every quality, from the thorough-paced gent down to the marker. They may be engaged either in actual play, in acting the confederate, in procuring loans, in forcible robbery, in breaking

the pigeon's neck downstairs, or, finally, fighting him with pistols by way of finish."

Daincourt would fain be thought both wit
    and bully,
But punk-rid Radcliffe's not a greater
    cully,
Nor tawdry Isham, intimately known
To all pox'd whores, and famous *rooks* in
    town.
          —*Earl of Rochester: Works.*

The papers give an account of the " International pigeon shooting at Monte Carlo." This is very curious. We should have thought that there were no "pigeons" to shoot at, considering the number of *rooks* there.—*Funny Folks.*

Also a clergyman. In French *corbeau*. (Tailors), a very badly-dressed or dirty person.

Rookery (common, formerly thieves' cant), thickly-populated courts and alleys inhabited by very poor people, as in the East End.

He owns the *rookery* whence, by roguish
    sleight,
From bodily ill and spiritual blight
Greed sucks a rich subsistence.
          —*Punch.*

Rookey (army), a recruit; from the black coat some of them wear. (Common), rascally.

Rook, to (common), to ease a player of his money; without any particularly offensive meaning. Also to cheat.

Roorback (American), a canard, a humbug. Chiefly used in politics. Said to be derived from one Rohrbach, a famous impostor.

" If dey say a candydate am all right dat's a *roorback;* if dey say he am all wrong dat's anoder ? "
" Exactly."—*Detroit Free Press.*

Roost (common), a dwelling.

Rooster (American), a cock.

Go ahead! cock-a-doodle-doo! and he crowed like a real live *rooster.*—*Sam Slick.*

(Old cant), queer *rooster,* a person who shams sleep.

Roosting ken (thieves), lodging-house, inn.

Roost over one, to (American), to get the better of.

Roost, to (common), to cheat. (Military), explained by quotation.

To be *roosted* is to be placed under arrest.—*A. Barrère: Argot and Slang.*

Rooter (popular), anything good or of first quality.

Rooti (Indian army), soldiers thus term their ration bread. Hindu *roti,* bread.

Root, to (schools and London), to give one a kick behind.

Ropes (schools), one who plays "half-back" at football. (Nautical), on the high *ropes,* angry. (Common), to know the *ropes,* to be conversant with the minutiæ of metropolitan dodges, as regards both the streets and the sporting world (Hotten).

Rope, to (turf), to *rope* one's horse, to hold him in in a race in such a manner as not to be perceptible to lookers-on. This is done when a man is betting against his own horse.

Though we are as deaf as posts, and as dumb as the jockey with orders to *rope* his mount.—*Bird o' Freedom.*

Ropper (popular and thieves), a comforter.

Hulking, heavy-jawed gentlemen, with a great deal of the lower part of the face hidden in the thick folds of a *ropper,* and with close-fitting caps and seafaring-looking jackets, into the side pockets of which the hands are thrust deep as the wrists, as though in guard of the neat and elegantly finished tools of his trade —the "jemmy," the skeleton keys, the life-preserver.—*Greenwood: In Strange Company.*

Rorty (costermongers), a complimentary adjective indicating rarity. It is more likely to have come from the German Jews, who continually speak of anything choice as a *rorität,* than from the English rare.

Still, this 'ere blooming Hanarchy, Charley, won't do at no figger, dear boy,
A bit of a *rorty* romp round in the open a chap can enjoy,
But brickbats and hoyster-knives? Walker!
Not on in that scene, mate, not me !
And a bash on the nob with a baton is not *my* idea of a spree.
—*Punch.*

A *rorty* toff, an out-and-out swell costermonger ; a *rorty* dasher, a fine fellow, great swell.

Yah! marriage is orful queer paper ; it's fatal, dear boy, as you say,
It damps down the *rortiest* dasher, it spiles yer for every prime lay.
No; gals is good fun, wives wet blankets, that's wot my egsperience tells,
And the swells foller me on that track, though *you* say as I follers the swells.
—*Punch.*

Rose (Punch and Judy), a bitch.

Rose in judgment (tailors), turned up.

Roses (Stock Exchange), Buenos Ayres and Rosario Railway Ordinary Stock.

Rosh, roush, to (Royal Military Academy), to push about, to indulge in horseplay. Probably from *rush.* Stop *roshing* also means hold your noise, hold your jaw.

Rosin (popular), beer or other drink given to musicians. This is perhaps derived from "rosin up," or refresh the bow, but it may be observed that in Dutch slang *ros* means beer. To give *rosin,* to give a beating.

Rosser, rozzer (thieves), a new term for a detective. From the slang term to "roast," to watch, or more probably from the French *rousse, roussin,* a detective, police.

It was stated that the prisoner, being in Holborn, and seeing a detective watching him, called out to a companion, "There's a *rosser !*" The term is, as the magistrate opined, a new one.—*The Globe.*

"Another wrong un," says the carman. "Hi, Mr. Grabham!"—and up walks a *rozzer* and buckles me tight.—*Sporting Times.*

Rosy (common), wine.

In the attempt to be picturesque, the device of poetry is adopted, and an object is represented not by the ordinary word representing it, but by some epithet or periphrasis. Thus wine has been called the *rosy.*—*St. James's Gazette.*

Rotan (old), a carriage of any kind, originally a cart ; Anglo-Saxon *ruotan.* "Hence Rotten Row," says John Bee.

Rot gut (army), the cheapest, commonest, and, as shown by the word itself, the most unwholesome kind of drink. Termed also "rotto." In America rough whisky.

These thieves fuddling about in the public-houses, and drinking bad spirits, and punch, and such *rot-gut* stuff.— *Hughes : Tom Brown's School Days.*

Rotten (printers). This term is used to denote a weak or uneven impression in the printing of a sheet.

Rotten Row (naval). Men in the navy say of an unserviceable ship, "she belongs to *Rotten Row.*"

Rot, to (common), explained by quotation. From *rot,* rubbish, nonsense.

She kindly introduced me to the expressions "chic," "too-too" (which, however, she said, were now obsolete); the verb *to rot,* which she explained meant to humbug or ballyrag.—*St. James's Gazette.*

Rot was originally circus and acrobats' expression for anything bad.

Rough luck (Royal Military Academy), an ejaculation of disappointment, meaning "no luck."

Roughrider's wash-tub (army), the barrack water-cart, so called because it is used to lay the dust in riding-schools.

Rouncher, roncher (American), a word expressing something extreme, powerful, superlative, as, for instance, a violent wrench or blow. Also anything large, fine, or remarkable. Probably a modification of the old English *rounceval,* strong, large, to which is allied the Northumberland *roundge,* a violent push or blow, also a great noise.

Roundabout (thieves), a female thief's pocket, which encircles her body and reaches down to the knees, with two apertures. It will stand an ordinary search—spoons, a watch, or money sliding round from side to side ; and if the wearer be bulky, much larger articles pass undiscovered. Also the treadmill, invented about 1823.

Roundabout, round robin (American thieves), an instrument used by burglars to cut a large round hole into an iron chest or door. It is said to have been invented by a noted American burglar, known as " the Doctor." Whenever he cut a disk of iron from a " safe," he always kept it, and when he was finally arrested, forty or fifty of these trophies were found in his house.

Round betting (turf), those who bet upon or against several horses in a race are said to *bet round.*

Rounder (American thieves), a man who hangs around faro-banks, but who does not play.

A loafer who travels on his " shape " (*i.e.,* trusts to dress and personal appearance), and is supported by a woman, but who does not get enough money to enable him to play faro. Gamblers call such men *rounders,* outsiders, loafers.

Round on, to (thieves and popular), to inform on, give evidence against a comrade or accomplice, although it is used also of prison officials.

Mary Anne *rounded* on her royal lover, and made the most damaging statements against him.—*Ross's Variety Paper.*

Yesterday the news was announced that one of the men arrested had *rounded* on his accomplices.—*Daily Telegraph.*

Perhaps from an idea of turning round upon one treacherously, or from the old English *to round,* to whisper, a corrupt form of *roun* or *roune.* Anglo-Saxon *rúnian* (German *raunen*), akin to Icelandic *rún,* a secret, a whispering (Rev. A. Smythe Palmer: Folk Etymology).

Round 'un (popular), an unblushingly given and well-proportioned lie (Hotten).

Round up, to (West American), gathering sheep, cattle, or pigs into a compact flock or herd. The metaphor of rounding in the sense of massing is very ancient. The Romans used " globus " in the sense of a mass.

As soon as the *round up* was completed, the herd was taken down to the hacienda, where the branding was to take place.—*F. Francis: Saddle and Moccasin.*

Used also in Australia.

Now they are well away from the scrub,
round them up, if possible, and let them
stand a few minutes to breathe.—*A. Grant:
Bush Life in Queensland.*

Roupy (American), hoarse.

She plays upon the pian-o,
And twirls the light fantastic toe,
And sings just like a *roupy* crow.
　　　　—*Negro Minstrel Song.*

Rouseabout (Australian up-country), a drudge. A *rouseabout* on
a station, like a "super" at a
theatre, is a man who has to
make himself generally useful—
to do any job that may turn up,
such as chopping wood, cleaning
out, &c.

It may be that the *rouseabout* swiper who
rode for the doctor that night,
Is in Heaven with the hosts of the Blest,
robed and sceptred, and splendid with
light.
　　　　—*New South Wales Paper.*

Rouster, roustabout (American),
originally any very powerful fellow, now applied to a rough who
hangs about anywhere for work,
and specially to a deck hand,
stoker, rough fellow. Swedish
rustar, a powerful rowdy, a
roisterer.

A fight occurred on the steamer between
a negro *rouster* and the second mate.—
American Newspaper.

Rovers, fish-hawks (American),
women, often young and good-
looking, who go about every
and anywhere, into brokers'
shops, law-offices, stores, universities, or wherever men may
be met, soliciting subscriptions
or contributions for charitable
purposes. Many of them are
really employed by churches,
hospitals, &c., others are cheats,
who have many ingenious devices to obtain money. One of
these is to inquire if Mrs. ——
is at home (having previously
ascertained the name of the
occupant of the house), and send
up a card. While in the draw-
ing-room, as soon as the servant
is gone, the *rover* steals a few
cards from the receiver. Having
interviewed the hostess, she
goes to the ladies whose names
and perhaps addresses are on
the cards, and states that she
was sent to them by the one
from whom they were taken,
and that she takes a special
interest in the charity for which
money is solicited. There are
many men engaged also in
this infamous business. Women
also largely employ the "collection dodge" for purposes of
intrigue, and to make the
acquaintance of men. Even
when undertaken in good faith,
"roving" has a demoralising
effect on young ladies, as the
soliciting money from "all sorts
and conditions of men" always
must. "When I first went about
collecting for our charity," said
a young lady, "I was ready to
faint whenever anybody looked
at me, but now I shouldn't be
afraid to ask the Old Boy himself for a dollar, and not let him
go till he paid it."

Rowdy (popular), cash, money.
Probably a corruption of *ruddy*,
a gold piece. *Vide* RUDDY.

What gives fools wit?
What beautifies the dowdy?
Hear it and blush,
Ye servile! 'tis the *rowdy.*
—*Punch.*

Rowdy-dow (common), low, vulgar.

Rowing man (University), (pronounce *row* as in bough), one who lives a fast life, a spreer.

Rowl, to (American University), to recite lessons well. Provincial English *rowl*, to rush.

Royal scamp (old cant), a gentleman highwayman, in opposition to "foot scamp."

Rubbed about (tailors), being *rubbed about* is being made a convenience of.

Rubbed out (common), dead.

Rubbs (old cant), hard shifts.

Rub down, to (prison), explained by quotation.

Such searching causes trouble, and it soon degenerates into a mere form even by the strictest officers. The *modus operandi* is as follows: the prisoner stands at attention with his vest unbuttoned—he raises his arms, holding his pocket-handkerchief in one hand. The officer passes his hand over his body, and then proceeds to the next man. This is called *rubbing down.* —*Evening News.*

(Popular), to rate a person soundly, or take him to task.

Rub in, to (American), persevere in teasing or annoying, aggravation without cessation, or what in French is called *monter une sue.*

Rub of the paper, a (army), when any soldier wants to borrow the newspaper in the reading-room he asks for a *rub* of it.

Rub out a pattern, to (tailors), to cut a pattern.

Ruby, the (pugilistic), blood.

They had heard of the "tapping of the claret" and the flow of the *ruby.*—*Punch.*

Ruck (common), common, undistinguished crowd. German *rücken*, to crowd together; Icelandic *hraukir*, probably the true origin.

But I'm quite another guess sort; penny plain, tuppence coloured, yer see,
May do all very well for the *ruck*; but they'll find it won't arnser for me!
—*Punch.*

(Turf), to come in with the *ruck*, to arrive at the winning-post among the unplaced horses.

I once knew a chappie not famed for his luck
Who to punting was muchly addicted;
But the horses he backed to a place "in the *ruck*"
Were with scarce an exception restricted.
—*Bird o' Freedom.*

Ruck along, to (Oxford), to go or make one go along at a great pace.

Ruck on, to (popular), to tell of, to inform. "She's such a sneak, she is, always *rucking* on me."

Ruction (popular), commotion, disturbance. Swedish *ryck*, attack, row, convulsive excitement.

Sure never obstruction
Raised half such a *ruction.*
—*Punch.*

Hotten gives the definition "an Irish row, faction fight."

Ruddy (thieves), a gold piece. Icelandic *roda*, red and gold.

Ruffian, ruffin (old cant), the devil, alluding to the rough hair covering his body (as its synonym "old Harry)." *Vide* HARRY.

The bube and *ruffian* cly the Harman beck and harmans. — *T. Dekker: Lanthorne and Candle Light.*

Ruffian once denoted, not so much roughness of behaviour, as roughness of appearance, especially in the matter of hair. The English ruffian, in its usual sense, is from the Italian *ruffiano*, a pimp; but *ruffian* and *ruffin* are confused in old cant.

Ruffler (old cant), a mendicant who shammed the wounded soldier or maimed sailor, but who robbed on the highway when opportunity offered. Harman has the definition "outcast of serving-men who robs inferior beggars."

Now in the crib, where a *ruffler* may lie, Without fear that the traps should distress him.
— *Lytton: Paul Clifford.*

This seems to be derived, like the old French cant term *rouffier*, soldier, from the Italian *ruffare*, to seize, lay hands upon.

Ruffles (old cant), handcuffs.

Ruffle, the, the production of the crackling sound of a pack of cards, used as a flourish to a trick (" Modern Magic").

Ruffmans (old cant), woods or bushes.

Now bynge we a waste to the hygh pad, the *ruffmans* is by.—*Harman: Caveat.*

From *rough*, and the frequent affix *mans*, as in "darkmans" night, "lightmans" day, &c.

Ruffpeck (old cant), bacon.

Red-shanks then I could lack, *Ruffpeck* still hung on my back, Crennam ever filled my sack.
— *The Scoundrel's Dictionary.*

Rugger (schools), the Rugby game at football.

Ruggins (old cant), to go to *Ruggins*, to go to sleep. From *rug*.

Ruggy (popular), fusty, frowsy (Hotten).

Rug, it's all (old cant), it is all right.

Ruin (popular and thieves), gin; called also "blue ruin."

Rum, rom (old cant). This word, which signified great, excellent, superior, clever, best, &c., came from *rum, rom*, a gypsy. As in *rom*-booze, good drink.

Piot, a common cant word used by French clowns and other tippling companions; it signifies *rum*-booze, as our gypsies call good guzzle. — *Urquhart: Rabelais.*

Rum clan, a silver or gold mug; *rum* cod, a well-filled purse, a purse full of gold; *rum* cole, a new coin; *rum* cull, rich man, lover, best man.

I, Frisky Moll, with my *rum* cull, Would suck in a boozing ken.
— *Frisky Moll's Song, from Harlequin's Sheppard, a Play.*

Rum doxy, best girl, mistress, wife; *rome*-mort, lady, queen; *rum* pad, the highroad; *rum* quick, large booty; *Rom*-vile, the great town, London.

A gage of ben *Rom*-bouse
In a bousing ken of *Rom*-vile.
—The Roaring Girl.

This signification survives in *rum* beak, justice of the peace; *rumbo*, good, and *rum* cull, manager of a theatre, used by actors and showmen, whose slang phraseology is mainly from the gypsy and Italian; also in *rum*-mizzler, one clever at effecting his escape.

The modern *rum* is a word of many meanings, generally implying something strange, queer, difficult, or out of the way.

"What a *rum* chap you are, Tom!' said Master Bales, highly amused.—*Dickens: Oliver Twist.*

He came not to luncheon, all said "it was *rum* of him!"
—Ingoldsby Legends.

A rider unequalled—a sportsman complete,
A *rum* one to follow, a bad one to beat.
—Whyte-Melville: Songs and Verses.

It has been said that this word, with its present signification, was first applied to Roman Catholic priests, and subsequently to other clergymen. Thus Swift spoke of a "rabble of tenants and rusty old *rums*" (country parsons). Swift simply uses the old gypsy cant term here, which meant "queer," hence odd.

Rum or *rom*, as a gypsy word, was applied not only to whatever concerned sport, the ring, and turf, but to what is "queer," and is still used commonly as such, *e.g.*, a "regular Roman" (Borrow), or *rum* 'un, *i.e.*, a Romany. There are other old instances proving that the word, as applied to *rum*, a liquor, was regarded as a gypsy word.

Rum beak (old cant), a synonym of "queer cuffin," a justice of the peace.

Rum bing (thieves), a full purse. From the old canting *rum*, which see, and *bong*, a purse.

Rum bit (old cant), a rogue.

Rumbler (thieves), coach; now more generally a four-wheeled cab.

I first held horses in the street,
But being found defaulter,
Turned *rumbler's* flunky for my meat,
So was brought up to the halter.
—Charles Hindley: The Life and Times of James Catnach.

Also a cart.

The *rumbler* jugged off from his feet
And he died with his face to the city.
—Burrowes: Death of Socrates.

A running *rumbler* was a confederate of thieves, who rolled a grinding stone, to give an opportunity to his accomplices.

Rumbo (theatrical), good. *Vide* RUM.

Rumbo ken (theatrical), a pawnbroker's shop.

Rum boozing wells (old cant), bunches of grapes.

Rum bowling (nautical), anything inferior or adulterated.

Rumboyl (old cant), the watch.

Rumbumptious, rumbustious (popular), haughty, pompous, boisterous, making great fuss and careless of the comfort of others.

Rum cull (theatrical), the manager of a theatre. *Vide* RUM. The *rum cull* of the casa, proprietor, landlord of lodgings.

Rum-dropper (old cant), a vintner.

Rum duke (old), a half-witted, awkward boor.

Rum-gagger (nautical), a cheat who tells wonderful stories of his sufferings at sea to obtain money.

Rum glimmer (old cant), king of the link-boys, rogues who, under colour of lighting people, robbed them.

Rum-gutlets (old cant), a canary.

Rum homee of the case (itinerants), the master of the show, the mistress being the "rum dona of the case."

Rum-hooper (old cant), a drawer.

Rum-Johnny (Anglo-Indian), a low class of natives who obtained employment on the wharves of Calcutta. Among soldiers and sailors, a prostitute. From the Hindu *rāmjānī*, a dancing-girl (Anglo-Indian Glossary).

Rumley (old cant), well. *Vide* RUM. Whid *rumley*, speak well.

Rúmmer, romer, rūmado, or **romado** (gypsy), to marry, married. From *rom*, a husband, or a gypsyman. In Coptic *romi* has the same meaning.

" Te vel tu sī rummado mishto,
Te vel tu rumessa sīgan,
Latchesa ke mandy shom kushto
Te sar mōrı Romany shan"—

" So if you will marry me early,
So if I'm soon wedded to thee,
You'll find that I really am good
As any real gypsy can be."
—*Janet Tuckey.*

Rum mill (American), a groggery.

Rummy (popular), queer. *Vide* RUM.

True, out in foreign parts parties practise *rummy* starts.
—*Punch.*

Rum ned (old cant), a fool, madman.

Rump, to (popular), to turn the back upon one.

Rumpty or **tooth** (Stock Exchange), a thirty-second part of £1.

Rumpus (popular), a noise, disturbance. From *romp*.

It is very fortunate too, sir, . . . since when the finale comes, there will probably be a bit of a *rumpus* that we are not very full of company just now.—*J. Greenwood: Dick Temple.*

Rum, to come it (popular), to do foolish things.

Rum Tom Pat (old cant), a real clergyman.

" What, are Moll and you adamed?"
" Yes, we are, and by a *rum Tom Pat* too."—*Parker: Variegated Characters.*

Rum 'un (pugilistic), a blow that fairly settles a man.

Rumy (gypsy), a wife; feminine of *rom*.

Run (common), the success of a play, according to the number of performances.

The penny "gaff" is usually a small place, and when a specially atrocious piece produces a corresponding *run*, the "house" is incapable of containing the vast number of boys and girls who nightly flock to see it. Scores would be turned away from the doors, and their halfpence wasted, were it not for the worthy proprietor's ingenuity.—*Greenwood: Seven Curses of London.*

To get the *run* upon one, to have the upper hand, the advantage over him.

Run a bluff, to (West American), to outwit; in English slang, to "bounce."

"You got the stock, though?" "Oh, yes; I *run a bluff* on 'em. They said they wasn't driving 'em anyhow, but they got started in the trail ahead of 'em, and it wasn't their business to turn 'em."—*F. Francis: Saddle and Moccasin.*

Run against a pill, to (American), to encounter a bullet, to be shot.

He had always told him he'd *run plumb ag'in' a pill* some day if he wan't blanked careful like. — *Drake's Magazine: He Died Game.*

Run big, to (turf), a horse that runs when too fat, not in training.

It is agreed that the colt *ran big*, but the short lapse of time will hardly be sufficient to get the lumber off him.—*Bird o' Freedom.*

Run-down (French *praticable* and *pont*). The sloping carpeted bridge running from a conjuror's stage into the auditorium (Robert Houdin and Hoffmann).

Rung (up-country Australian). The process of being *rung* or "ring-barked" consists in the bark being cut right through all round the tree a few feet above the ground, which is done to kill the large gum-trees which encumber and draw so much moisture from the pasturage. It is much practised in Australia.

Their road at first lay between paddocks interspersed with a few trees *rung* and mostly dead.—*D. B. W. Sladen: A Summer Christmas.*

Run in, to (popular), to apprehend and take to the police station.

Occasionally some unfortunate is pounced upon, rudely handled, and *run in.*—*Saturday Review.*

It's bad enough to get *run in* even of one's own free will;
But to get *run in* for some one else it makes me sick and ill.
And my boss'll get to know it, since the oof I cannot raise,
And I shall get the blooming *chuck* as well as fourteen days.
     —Sporting Times.

This phrase is not recent, but it was seldom heard out of policemen's circles until the chorus of gendarmes in Offenbach's "Geneviève de Brabant" made it familiar to the public. It may have been derived from the old Bow Street runners, the predecessors of modern constables. The process varies according to the offender. Some need the "policeman's grip," whereby the left hand of the prisoner, palm upwards, is grasped by the left of the constable, whose right passes under the upper part of the prisoner's arm, grasps his waistcoat, and being straightened, forms a lever which makes him helpless, and would even dislocate his shoulder or break his arm if he resisted. Then there is the "frogs' march" (which see). French policemen sometimes use a process by which even the strongest man is rendered quite helpless. The officer's left hand is fixed at arm's length from behind on the prisoner's coat-collar, while his right lifts him slightly by the seat of his trousers. The man, being thus placed out of the perpendicular, and almost on tip-toe, can then be forced on at a swift pace.

Run it, to (American cadet), to go beyond bounds without having previously obtained permission to do so.

Runner (popular), a wave.

All of a sudden I get on a *runner* mountains high, and bang on the beach goes her bow.—*Brighton Beach Loafer.*

(Stock Exchange), a man in the employ of a broker, who having a private connection, spends his time running from client to client in quest of orders.

Running glazier (old cant), a thief who pretended to be a glazier.

Running rumble, the (old cant), going about with a grinding-stone as a pretence to give accomplices an opportunity for picking pockets.

I shall go upon the *running rumble* if you will go with me, Cock-a-brass.—*Parker: Variegated Characters.*

Running snavel (old cant), a thief who watched children going to school to rob them. A form of *snaffle*, which see.

Run of your teeth (Canadian), board; as in the phrase, "I pay so much for the *run of my teeth*," *i.e.*, my boarding expenses are so much. The *run* generally refers to keeping, managing, carrying on.

Run one's face, to (common), to get credit. *Vide* FACE.

Since all my money now is gone,
And I have naught to live upon;
Grant me, O Lord, the special grace
For meat and bread *to run my face.*
—*Harper's Magazine.*

Run one's week, to (American university), to trust to chance for success.

Run rigs, to (old cant), to play pranks.

Run straight, to (society). This is one of the commonest expressions in society as applied to ladies, and it means that a lady is virtuous and faithful to her husband. It is borrowed from racing parlance, where a horse is talked of as running straight.

These foolish ones are content to do what is considered the smart thing, knowing as they do that many in our gossiping and scandal-mongering society will attribute to them the worst of motives, and class them with those who do not *run* straight.—*Saturday Review.*

Run the rule over (prison), to search a person for stolen property or contraband articles.

I was going through Shoreditch, when a reeler from Hackney, who knew me well, came up and said, "I am going to *run the rule over* you."—*Horsley: Jottings from Jail.*

Run through, to (American thieves), when gamblers play with a "sucker" (*i.e.*, a novice), and do not give him a chance to win a single bet, and clean him out without loss of time.

Run, to. This verb is applied in England to several meanings besides the legitimate one, but in the United States it has taken a much wider range. Thus a man *runs* a grocery, a shop, a bank, or a church ; and if he be a mayor, or a very influential person in a community, he is said *to run* the town. "I am *running* Latin just now," said a schoolboy, meaning that he was studying it.

Last week a horse in Duluth found a keg of lager with the head knocked in, and being thirsty, he drank it almost dry. In ten minutes he was waltzing about on his hind-legs, and remarking to every one whom he met, that if he didn't *run* that turn, he would like to know who the d——l did.—*Minnesota Newspaper.*

> Some beople *runs* de beautiful,
> Some works philosophie ;
> Der Breitmann solve de infinide
> Ash von eternal spree !
> —*Breitmann in Kansas.*

The term is being used in England.

> To have a big boom was the general rage,
> And every man's dream was *to run* or to "boss" all.
> —*Punch.*

(American), the term is often applied to keeping of a household. "How much does *running* your house cost you ?"

(Common), *to run* the show, to be the manager of any place of entertainment, theatre, circus, &c.

These two boys that *run* the shows in Argyle Street and elsewhere.—*Bird o' Freedom.*

Run up, to, explained by quotation.

Anyhow there they were, and it required no uncommon degree of penetration to discover that their chief aim was to take note of every bid that was made by an unfortunate whose goods had been seized and *run him up* most villainously. I feel quite convinced that many persons who had come to repurchase their furniture might have got it, taking it at its market value, at half the sum they had to pay.—*Greenwood: In Strange Company.*

Rūp (gypsy), silver ; *rūpeno*, of silver. From the Hindu *rup*, silver. Hence the French slang term *rupin*, rich, handsome, splendid. In Danish slang *rup* signifies gold.

Rush (Australian), the opening of a new gold-field, from the rush which is made to new diggings. (Up-country Australian), a stampede of cattle.

A confused whirl of dark forms swept before him, and the camp so full of life a minute ago is desolate. It was a *rush*, a stampede.—*A. C. Grant.*

(Common), on the *rush*, *i.e.*, in a hurry.

The lumberer's lurch, as he roams on the *rush*.
—*Sporting Times*.

Rushed (up-country Australian) charged by an animal. (American), very busy, hurried.

Some day when Uncle Sam isn't *rushed*, we hope he will melt over his old mail boxes and cast some new ones big enough to stick a paper into.—*Detroit Tribune*.

Rushers (football), the members of a football team who run with the ball.

American football teams are made up as follows—one full-back, two half-backs, one quarter-back, and seven *rushers.*—*Sporting Life*.

Rush, to (common), to *rush* a person, to hurry him.

Do, but try and make it Japanese if you can; it's just possible he might twig if we *rushed* him, don't you know, and then I should suffer.—*Bird o' Freedom*.

(American), to *rush* a bill, to hurry through a bill.

To *rush* a bill is an expression well known in the American Senate, and occasionally also used here.—*Cornhill Magazine*.

Russer, rusher (American), a heavy player, a "plunger," a dashing, sensation-causing man; applied to politicians, clergymen, &c.

Rust (popular), to nab the *rust*, to take offence, get angry, turbulent. For derivation *vide* RUSTY.

Rustler (American), explained by quotation.

I just tell you, he's a *rustler*. Now a *rustler* is a great Western word, and ex-

presses much. It means a worker, an energetic man, and no slouch can be a *rustler.*—*Morley Roberts: The Western Avernus.*

A rowdy, rough.

The habit of removing the hat at restaurant tables, which came some years ago, has been followed by other reforms no less notable, and what may be called the atmosphere of the street has clearly less of the *rustler* about it.—*Letter from Chicago.*

A desperado, cattle lifter.

Then, the *rustlers* had congregated there in force, the locality affording exceptional advantages for their chief occupation, namely, running off cattle and horses from either side of the frontier. Many a spot is pointed out as the scene of a sanguinary skirmish between these modern moss-troopers and the owners and their followers.—*F. Francis: Saddle and Moccasin.*

These men, however, must not be confounded with another class of desperadoes, *i.e.*, those who would not work, and were what is termed *rustlers* or house thieves. —*O'Reilly: Fifty Years on the Trail.*

Rustle, to (American), to go about seeking work. "I set to work, *rustling* for a job." *To rustle* up or along, is to hurry, hasten, as in this phrase, "*rustle* the dinner along."

Rust ringing (American university). "At Hamilton College, the Freshmen," writes a correspondent, "are supposed to lose some of their verdancy at the end of the last term of that year, and the *ringing off* their *rust* consists in ringing the chapel bell—commencing at midnight—until the rope wears out. During the ringing, the upper classes are diverted by the display of numerous fireworks, and enlivened by most beautifully discordant sounds, called 'music,' made to issue from tin kettle-drums, horse-fiddles, trumpets, horns, &c."

Rusty (thieves), to turn a *rusty,* to betray.

Blow me tight, but that cove is a queer one; and if he does not come to be scragged, it will only be because he'll turn a *rusty,* and scrag one of his pals.— *Lytton : Paul Clifford.*

From the colloquial phrase, " to turn *rusty,*" used of a person who becomes stubborn, surly, disobliging. *Rusty* is an old Saxon and Icelandic word, meaning stubborn or rebellious, restive. To cut up *rusty, vide* CUT UP RUSTY.

Ry (Stock Exchange), any sharp or dishonest practice. "It originated," says Dr. Brewer, "in an old stock-jobber, who had practised upon a young man, and being compelled to refund, wrote on the cheque, 'Please to pay to R. Y.,' &c., in order to avoid direct evidence of the transaction."

Ryder, a cloak; gypsy *ruder,* to clothe.

Rye (gypsy), a gentleman; (Hindu), *rae* or *rai* (*rye*), a petty nobleman. *Ryéskro,* gentlemanly. *Romany rye,* a gypsy gentleman, but generally meaning a gentleman who has learned or who speaks Romany. *Gūdlo rye,* a nice (sweet) gentleman. Hotten says this is gypsy for a young man. It is nothing of the kind, *rye* meaning invariably a gentleman or superior person, and nothing else. *E.g.,* "the Romany *rye,*" the gypsy gentleman.

" And the *rye* and the rawnie
A-pirryin āp o drom "—
" The gentleman and lady
A-walking up the road."

Young man in gypsy is *tano mūsh* (*i.e.* manūsh), or *juvo,* or *raklo.*

Ryebuck (American), all right, it will do, I am satisfied.

S

SACK (common), to give the *sack,* to dismiss, discharge from one's employment. To get the *sack,* to be dismissed, discharged.

I wonder what old Fogg 'ud say, if he knew it; I should get the *sack,* I s'pose. —*Dickens : Pickwick Papers.*

He is no longer an officer of this gaol; he has got the *sack. —Reade : Never too Late to Mend.*

Said to be from the practice of putting into a *sack* and throwing into the Bosphorus certain members of the Sultan's harem ; also generally supposed to be from the Spanish *sacar,* meaning to dismiss, and also to "bag," just as in English; but it originated in the old practice of giving a man a *sack* when sending him forth. Hence (St. Luke x. 4) Christ specifies that His disciples, by *not* taking a *sack* or scrip, should not consider themselves as dismissed, *i.e.*, not make provision for themselves. The French have the corresponding expressions, "donner son *sac* à quelqu'un," "avoir son *sac* ; " formerly, "donner son *sac* et ses quilles." French workmen will say, "il a eu son *sac* avec une forte paire de bretelles." The Germans have the phrase, "to give the basket." The synonyms are, "to get the bag," the "empty," or the "bullet." "To give the *sack*" is so widely used as to be almost a recognised phrase.

Sack, to. *Vide* SACK.

We had fixed one day *to sack* him, and
  agreed to moot the point,
When my lad should bring our usual re-
  gale of condered joint.
—*T. B. Stephens : My other
  Chinee Cook.*

Saddle (theatrical), an additional charge made by the manager to a performer on his benefit night.

Saddlebacks (popular), lice. Also Yorkshire greys.

Safe 'un (turf), a horse which will not run, or will not try in a race. Synonyms, "dead 'un," " stiff 'un," " stumer."

Sagaciate (American), a slang word which seems to be mysteriously employed more for sound than sense, as in " How does your corporosity *sagaci-*

ate ?"—"How are you?" In the following extract from one of the "Bre'r Rabbit" stories, it seems as " segashiashun " to mean suggestion.

"Dem ez wuz tuk by Bre'r Buzzard's *segashiashun*, wuz ter drop en er chicky-pin " (chinkapin).

Sailors' waites (nautical), the second mates of small vessels.

Salamon, salomon (old cant), the mass. " I swear by the *salomon*."

And as I keep to the fore-gone,
So may help me *Salamon*.
—*Oath of English Gypsies.*

Salmon, a corpse, in the slang of water-rats, that is, low rascals who ply the river for drowned bodies to rifle. They have different names for them, one with poor ragged clothes being a "flounder" if a man, and a "dab" if a woman. French undertakers call the body of a well-to-do deceased person " un *saumon*."

I knowed a rat . . . who was bit over a job of the kind in a way he isn't likely to forget in a hurry. Just as them two chaps in the sailing boat we saw a while ago might be doing, him and his mate were tacking about on the chance, when they hauled a *salmon*, as they say.—*J. Green-wood : Rag, Tag, &* Co.*

Salt (Eton), money.

Salt-box (thieves), the condemned cell in Newgate. (Naval), a case for keeping a temporary supply of cartridges for the immediate use of the great guns.

Salt cat (bird fanciers), explained by quotation.

Busily concocting a horrid mess, which he called a *salt cat*, and of which old mortar, cumin seed, and urine were the chief ingredients. When he had mixed it all up like cement, he proceeded to fill sundry old pots and kettles, and to place them in various parts of the loft, for the birds to peck at at their pleasure.—*J. Greenwood: Undercurrents of London Life.*

Saltee, solde (costermongers, itinerants, &c.), a penny. A corruption of the Italian *soldo*, plural *soldi*.

It has rained kicks all day in lieu of *saltees*, and that is pennies. — *Reade: Cloister and Hearth.*

This term was originally used by strolling actors, showmen, and became common among other classes of people.

Salting the Freshman (American university). In reference to this custom, which belongs to Dartmouth College, a correspondent writes—"There is an annual trick of *salting the Freshmen*, which is putting salt and water on their seats, so that their clothes are injured when they sit down. The idea of preservation, cleanliness, and health is no doubt intended to be conveyed by the use of the wholesome articles salt and water."

Salt, to (commercial), making fictitious entries in the books to simulate that the receipts are greater than they really are, when about to sell a business connection, is called *salting*

the books. (Mining), sprinkling some gold-dust in an unproductive mine or hole, or a few diamonds, to deceive intending purchasers or investors.

Stymer, long experienced in the mines, set them down for a pair of sharps, and understood their game. He divined that Mose had *salted* the claim.—*Bird o' Freedom.*

In French, *saler* is to overcharge, to make one pay roundly. A similar expression is used in Swedish.

(Stock Exchange), *to salt* down stock, to buy stock and keep it for a considerable period.

Same old crowd (society), same set of people, as applied to society gatherings.

Same there (tailors). The phrase means, "What you say applies equally to yourself."

Sammy - house, swamy - house (Anglo-Indian), an idol temple or pagoda.

Sampsman (old cant), a highwayman. *Vide* RENT.

Now Oliver puts his black nightcap on,
And every star its glim is hiding,
And forth to the heath is the *sampsman* gone,
His matchless cherry-black prancer riding.
—*Ainsworth: Rookwood.*

Literally a collector, from a very old English word *sam*, to collect things together (Halliwell). German *sommeln;* Swedish *samla*, implying money in one sense, also union or being together. Hence to stand *sam*, to treat all the party. *Sam,* the lot. "*Sammed,* assembled together" (Halliwell).

Sam, stand (popular), to be surety for a person, to treat to drink, pay the reckoning. *Vide* SAMPS-MAN.

But not to be baulked of the night's entertainment, he had perforce to *stand Sam* for the lot.—*Hindley: Life and Adventures of a Cheap Jack.*

But the scapegoats must not kick up shindies, and stop up our streets and our squares,
That's a moral. Perhaps there is grabbers as wants to swag more than their shares.
I ain't nuts on sweaters myself, and I do 'ate a blood-sucking screw,
Who sponges and never *stands Sam,* and whose motto's "all cop, and no blue."
—*Punch.*

Sand (West American), courage. An equivalent for "grit."

"Doc would get away with him," said Joe.
"Would he!" ejaculated Squito hotly.
"Yes, he's got all Sam's *sand,* and is cooler."—*F. Francis: Saddle and Moccasin.*

Sand-rat (engineers), a moulder in a foundry.

Sand, to have (American), to be brave.

SHE HAD THE SAND.—Mrs. Lizzie Cook, of No. 18 Clark Street, demonstrated her personal courage and thorough muscular development in rather an odd manner last evening. Without weapon of any kind, she seized and held a strong man, whom she asserts is a horse-thief, until a servant had been despatched to the Central Police Station.—*Daily Inter-Ocean.*

Sandwich boat (university). In bumping races, rowed in two divisions, it is the boat head of

one division and last in the other. It has to row two races each day.

Sandwich-men (general), called also board-men. Poor fellows who for a scanty reward walk the pavement in single file, with advertisement boards on chest and back.

He stopped the unstamped advertisement—an animated *sandwich,* composed of a boy between two boards.—*Sketches by Boz.*

"Declined with thanks; with thanks declined,"
This is the burden of my song :
These words are ever in my mind,
I see and hear them all day long.
I envy every man I see—
Sweeps, *sandwich-men,* and clerks in banks ;
Their services, whate'er they be,
Are not always "Declined with thanks!"
—*Sporting Times.*

Sank-house (tailors), an army clothier's establishment. From *sank,* a great quantity, wholesale.

Sap (Eton), one who works hard. *Vide* TO SAP.

He remembered in English schools and colleges the many epithets applied to those who, not content with doing their work, committed the heinous offence of being absorbed in it. For this purpose schools and colleges had invented phrases, semi-classical or wholly vernacular, such as *sap,* "smug," "swot," "bloke," and "mugster."—*Daily News.*

If a boy did anything more than the regular school-work for his own improvement, he was called a *sap.*—*C. T. Buckland : Eton Fifty Years Ago.*

Sap the tlas (common), back-slang for pass the salt, used when the drink does not go round freely.

Sap, to (public schools), to work hard. It is in common use at Eton. Said to be of circumlocutory derivation from the Latin *sapere*, but more probably *to sap*, taken figuratively, *i.e.*, to dig. The French *piocher* is used in both senses.

These incentives to industry prevent the early years of a boy in college being entirely wasted; but those who, toward the end of their school time, at length begin to value and to practise studious habits, often think regretfully upon the advantages secured by those who *sapped* from the beginning.—*Pascoe: Every-day Life in our Public Schools.*

Sarahs (Stock Exchange), Manchester, Sheffield, and Lincolnshire Railway Def. Stock.

Sarah's boots (Stock Exchange), Sierra Buttes Gold-Mine Shares.

Saratoga walk (American), a fashionable "fad," fully explained in the following elegant extract from an American newspaper:—

" The *Saratoga walk* is said to be the latest fashionable gait for women. One who describes it says that ' the first requisite is to throw your shoulders back, the chest forward, chin up, and stomach in, and then walk, wriggling head, limbs, body, and especially bustle. The aim is to secure a series of revolutions which shall be simultaneous but opposite. In simple brevity, if your head moves right your body must move to

the left, and before your foot reaches ground you must describe a circle with the entire limb. The gait is practised in a night dress before the mirror. The part of the business most difficult to master is the proper position of the stomach.' "

Sardine (American), a man who has nothing distinctive or characteristic in him; a mere average person; a provincial who has always been shut up in some small place among men . like himself. Obviously derived from the *sardine*, which being all of the same size, and packed in tin boxes, suggested to some poetic orator the simile.

Sardines (Stock Exchange), Royal Sardinian Railway Stock.

Sa soldi (strolling actors, &c.), sixpence.

Sass (African coast). When a chief or other person becomes too bold, or powerful, or wicked, he is said in English negro slang to "get too much *sass*." The remedy for this is to make him drink " *sass* water."

According to news from the West Coast of Africa, there have been some human sacrifices in consequence of the death of a son of the King of Grand Jack. Selected victims were obliged to drink " *sass* water," a poisonous liquor, and were then pitched into the surf on the seashore. When the rollers dashed them ashore, men, women, and children cut at them with knives until they were dead. The chief of the tribe flies the British flag, and the captain of a trading vessel remonstrated with him in vain.—*St. James's Gazette.*

Sat. (printers). This is an abbreviation of the word "satisfaction," and is very often used to express a revengeful feeling, *i.e.*, to have *sat.* or to be "even" with any one.

Satin (popular), gin ; a yard of *satin*, a glass of gin.

> Some of them love *satin*, as a softening
>   for the throat,
> While others with dry Heidseck you
>   must woo.
>   —*Bird o' Freedom.*

Sauney, sawney (popular and thieves), bacon, pork. The gypsies, who never confound or mix their own language with canting, say that *sani* for pork is old Romany. *Sawney* hunter, one who steals bacon. A *sawney* (provincial), a fool.

Sausage game (billiards), a German game.

Sawbones (common), a surgeon.

Sawder, soft (popular), properly *solder*, cajolery, plausible words; flattery easily laid on, and received with pleasure, like "butter" and "soft soap."

> You've got *soft sawder* enough, as Frank calls it in his new - fashioned slang.—*Lytton : My Novel.*

> And I also maintain, without any *soft sawder,*
> That Orde is an oar of the very first order ;
> And whichever crew wins, we may safely foretell
> That the crew of Light Blues will this year " bear the Bell."
>   —*Globe.*

Sawdust (American), counterfeit gold-dust or money.

A man, charged with a violation of the postal laws, committed in the pursuit of the *sawdust* or counterfeit money swindle. —*New York Mercury.*

(Popular), not genuine, cajoling.

> The palaver was *sawdust* and treacle.
>   —*Punch.*

Sawdust bloke (circus), a circus rider.

> At the recent performance at Passy, M. Molier was the most conspicuous among the amateurs. To adopt the technology of the ring, M. Molier, by all accounts, approved himself a most accomplished *sawdust bloke.*—*Daily Telegraph.*

Sawdusty (popular), cajoling, using flattering and soft words ; probably same as " sawder."

> Me doing the *sawdusty* reg'lar, and following swells on the stump.—*Punch.*

Saw your timber (common), be off ; equivalent to " cut your stick."

Say it again (tailors), I heartily endorse your sentiments.

Scab (American), an opprobrious epithet applied to a mechanic or workman who does not belong to the trades' union of his calling. Shakspeare uses the term with the meaning of paltry, mean fellow.

> It was a very novel and effective warfare that the wives of the coal strikers used against the imported *scab* labour on Tuesday. If the bread was as hard as some that is baked in the Pennsylvania bakeries, the loaves must have hurt as well as humiliated the unwelcome intruders.—*New York Sun.*

Scabby (printers). In printing, uneven colour, through bad distribution of ink, is thus called *scabby.*

Scab raiser (army), obsolete. A drummer, as formerly one of the duties of his office was to apply the cat.

Scabs (tailors), button-holes.

Scad (American), abundance, large quantities, plenty. Hence *scad* used for money or means. Possibly from Icelandic and Swedish *skat*, tribute money, tax. Hence " to pay one's scot ; " the word *scot* is, however, generally derived from French *écot.*

His mother wishes to impress him with life's sober realities.

" Johnny, yesterday is gone, never to return."

" Oh, that don't matter, mamma ; there are *scads* of to-morrows just like it."— *American Newspaper.*

Scadger (public school), a mean fellow, a corruption of " cadger."

Scaldings (popular), a cry meaning " look out," " get out of the way," " by your leave." A warning that some one is coming along with a bucket of hot fluid, soup, tea, or water, which may scald all who impede progress. (Winchester College), used with same meaning.

Scaldrum dodge, a dodge among begging impostors of burning the body with a mixture of acids and gunpowder, so as to suit the hues and complexions of any accident to be deplored by a confiding public (Hotten).

Scalla-wag (American), a scamp, a scapegrace.

I hev travelled o'er this cont'nent from Quebec to Bogotáw,
But setch a set of *scallawags* as these I never saw.
—*The Ballads of Charity.*

Skall occurs in all the northern tongues as an opprobrious term, and *scalla-wag*, in the sense of wight, a person, is good old English, from *scall* (Anglo-Saxon), a scale or scab.

Scalp, to (American), to sell under price.

Scaly (popular), shabby, mean, disreputable, of dubious character ; a variation of " fishy."

Sister of L. E. L., of Mrs. Stowe, too ;
Of E. B. Browning, Harriet Martineau, too ;
Do theologians know where fibbers go to?
Of dear George Eliot, whom I worship daily ;
Of Charlotte Brontë, and Joanna Baillie.
Methinks that theory is rather *scaly.*
—*J. B. Stephens : To a Black Gin.*

Scammered (popular), intoxicated. From *scammered*, disgraced. Anglo-Saxon *scamn*, shame ; Swedish *skämma*, to put to shame.

Scamp. *Vide* ROYAL SCAMP.

Scamp, to (popular), to give short measure or quantity. Also to hurry through a task and do it badly. (Old cant), *to scamp on the panny*, to be a highwayman.

Scan. (printers), an abbreviation used to describe a Scandinavian printing machine invented by a native of Stockholm.

Scandal water, slang word for tea, dating from the hard-drinking days of a bygone generation, when it was fashionable to get drunk, when "drunk as a lord" was a proverbial expression, when a man was accounted the best in a convivial company who first fell senseless from his chair by excess of liquor, and "a three-bottle man" was considered a king of good fellows.

> Who first shall rise to gang awa,
>   A coward cuckold loon is he ;
> Who first beside his chair shall fa',
>   He shall be king among us three.
> —*Robert Burns.*

Tea was considered so effeminate a drink that the vulgar bacchanals exerted all the ingenuity they possessed to invent feebly contemptuous names for it—among others "cat-lap," "scandal broth," "water bewitched," "tattle water," "kettle-brandy."

Scapali (theatrical), to go away. Also "scaper," "bunk." From the Italian *scappare*, to escape, run away.

Scarecrow (thieves), explained by quotation.

> "Never take up with a fresh hand till you've shopped your *scarecrow.*" The *scarecrow* is the boy who has served him until he is well known to the police, and is so closely watched that he may as well stay at home as go out. Now, perhaps, you understand. — *The Little Ragamuffins.*

Scare up (American), to obtain, get. "See if you can't *scare up* five dollars."

Scarlet fever (common), the passion for military society. In allusion to the colour of English regimentals. Ladies who run after military society are said to have *scarlet fever.* So in Australia people who flock to every new-rush (gold-field), in the hopes of finding an El Dorado, are said to suffer from "yellow fever."

Scarper, to (thieves and Seven Dials), to run away. From the Spanish *escapar*, or Italian *scappare*.

Scat (tailors), signifies "go away and tell it some one else." Sometimes it is used to express utmost disgust or contempt. *Scat* is in imitation of trying to frighten away a cat.

Scene rats (theatrical), extras engaged in ballets or pantomimes.

Schism-shop, cant Anglican for dissenting chapel.

School (popular), a set of regular passengers by a particular train, travelling as a rule in the same carriage, to and from town. From *school* of fishes (for shoal). Any small gathering of people generally bent on pleasure, as a *school* of drinkers in a public-house or canteen. Much used by soldiers. (Thieves and streets), a gang of thieves, a body of idlers or street gamblers, also a number of "patterers" working together.

Schooling (thieves), a term of detention in an industrial school or reformatory.

She is young—just come home from a *schooling.*—*Horsley : Jottings from Jail.*

Schoolman (thieves), a companion, one of a gang termed "school," which see.

The knucks in quod my *schoolmen* did play.
                Fake away !
                —*Ainsworth : Rookwood.*

Schools (Oxford), any university examination at Oxford.

Schooner (American), a large glass of lager-beer, supposed to hold double the quantity of a five-cent glass, but generally a delusion in this respect. A three-masted *schooner*, a beer *schooner* of extra size. Originally *skew* (provincial English), a cup, changed to *skew-ner*, which is a common Yankee pronunciation of *schooner*.

Every time he wiped out an Indian or strung up a greaser a dude would order a round of beer, and this fellow invariably called for a *three-masted schooner.*—*American Newspaper.*

Schoony-orgy (naval), a schooner; termed also hermaphrodite brig, bastard brig, &c.

Schroff (Anglo-Indian), a banker, treasurer, or confidential clerk.

Scob (Winchester College), box spelt backwards (phonetically).

A large box for college men to sit at and keep their books in.

When all is ready, the prefect of hall enters school, and takes his seat facing the stove, followed by the members of the three " sixes," and then by all the scholars, who sit on their *scobs.*—*Pascoe : Everyday Life in our Public Schools.*

Scoff (South African), food. The term is used by natives in the service of Europeans in South Africa. *Skofoor* (*skoffer*), Swedish, is applied to common food, *i.e.*, scrapings.

Scoff away, scuff away (American) to blow away, to drive away, impel. Probably from Swedish *skuffa*.

Scoff, scorf, to (South African), to devour, eat voraciously.

A prospector, with ten donkeys and a waggon, had " outspanned " for the night, during the course of which a hungry lion *scoffed* (*Anglicè*, ate) one of the Jerusalems, and, being filled to repletion, was disinclined to wander from the scene. In the early morning, it being rather dark and the prospector and his niggers half asleep, Mr. Leo was " inspanned " as wheeler in mistake for the missing moke. The eight in front beat their record in the travelling line, and were glad to have the error rectified at dawn.—*Sporting Times.*

Sconce (public schools), a tin candlestick.

Sconce, to (Oxford University), to fine for any breach of etiquette at hall dinner, such as wearing a coloured coat, swearing, or making Latin or Greek quotations. The *sconce*, or fine, is generally levied in beer. The customs vary at different colleges. Hotten says that if the offender could, however, floor the tankard of beer which he was *sconced*, he could retort on his *sconcer* to the extent of twice the amount he was *sconced* in.

... was *sconced* in a quart of ale for quoting Latin, a passage from Juvenal; murmured, and the fine was doubled.— *The Etonian.*

The term is used by Milton with the meaning of to mulct, fine.

Scoop, on the (popular), on the drink. A metaphor derived from *scoop*, a ladle for liquors.

"You seem to forget, George, that when I married you I could have had young Plutus!"
"A nice sort of husband he'd have made. The blackguard goes home drunk in a cab every night."
"Well, if he does, that's better than returning on the top of a penny 'bus, as you do."
He went *on the scoop* that night.—*Topical Times.*

Scoop, to (American). It has become common of late to speak of any one who has been turned out of office, or been rejected, as *scooped*. This agrees exactly with the Dutch phrase,"Jemand den schop geven," to give a man the *scoop*, or a kick, "to cashier one," as Sewell says. Also "Jemand op den schop zetten" (*schop* here means "swing," as well as *scoop*), to take to one's self the liberty to cashier a servant or workman at any time, without being bound to employ him any longer. And also "Een schop in 't gat geven," to give one a kick, or *scoop*, in the breech. All of

which agree marvellously well with the cases of countless "cashiered" Republicans recorded by the *Chicago Tribune.*

Scoot, to (American), to move fast, to run. A corruption of scud; from the Dutch *schut* and *schot*, a shot. "Dat schip makt schot," that ship goes a great pace, or sails fast.

The fellow sat down on a hornet's nest, and if he didn't run and holler and *scoot* through the briar-bushes, and tore his trousers.—*Bartlett: Hill's Yankee Stories.*

Used also in English sporting circles.

I saw that he wanted to serve me out toko,
But I swiftly and carefully thwarted his plans,
For I *scooted*. His blow fell on somebody's boko.
—*Bird o' Freedom.*

Scorcher (society), a fast or very lively person. Derived from to scorch, burn up, consume. (Cyclists), one who always goes at racing speed. (Tailors), properly an iron at burning heat; figuratively, an individual of peculiar, eccentric, or hasty temperament.

Score off, to (common), to get the best of one, especially in wordy warfare. From scoring up the points at billiards.

I say, old man, that was a stuck-up set of prigs at old Brown's the other night! By Jove, though, I did manage *to score off* them a bit, eh?—*Punch.*

Scot (popular), a lot, share. Anglo-Saxon *sceat*, or French *écot*. Also temper or passion; from the irascible temperament of the

Scotch, says Hotten. To be in a *scot*, to be in a passion.

Scotch chocolate (common), milk with brimstone.

Scotchman (South African), a florin.

Scotch peg (roughs' rhyming slang), a leg.

Scout (old cant), a watchman. (Oxford), a college servant. (Thieves), a watch. From the old provincial *scout*, a spy, a play on watching and spying.

Connor then asked what the article was, to which the answer returned was, " A *scout.*" This he understood to mean a watch.—*Scottish Newspaper.*

Scout, to (sporting), to *scout* for pigeons, to shoot pigeons outside the inclosure of a gun-club. Compare scouting for tennis-balls and cricket-balls that have been hit away.

Scrag (popular and thieves), the neck. Derived from *scrag*, a raw - boned piece, especially a neck-piece of meat. The *scrag*, the gallows. He is down for his *scrag*, he is going to be hanged. (Shrewsbury School), explained by quotation.

The highest mark is twenty with a cross . . . and so down to a huge duck's egg and a rent across the paper entitled a *scrag.*—*Pascoe : Everyday Life in our Public Schools.*

Scrag-end, explained by quotation.

There is a long and sinuous thoroughfare situate in the heart of London-in-the-East, the real name of which will not be here given, but which, probably because

of the chronic impecuniosity of those who patronise it as a market-place, is popularly known as *Scrag-end.* It flourishes all the week through, but the time to see it at its busiest is Saturday night, when the glaring jets of gas have just been lit to illuminate the butchers' shops, and the countless costermongers have set their naphtha lamps blazing.—*J. Greenwood.*

Scragging (popular), an execution. *Vide* SCRAG.

Scraggy, from the old Norse *skrukka*, to shrink, shrivel ; hence applied to a lean neck.

Scrag, to (popular and thieves), to choke, throttle. *Vide* SCRAG.

" Pooh !" says his pal, "you great dunce ! You've pouched the good gentleman's money,
So out with your whinger at once,
And *scrag* Jane, while I spiflicate Johnny !"
—Ingoldsby Legends.

To be *scragged*, to be hanged.

"Do you vant to have us *scragged*, fool ?" cried the Sandman, springing into the vault.—*Ainsworth : Auriol.*

For synonyms in English, French, Italian, &c., slang, *vide* Barrère's " Argot and Slang."

Scran (popular), food ; much used in the army. A *scran*-bag is a food wallet ; a *scran*, a meal. A common Irish phrase, "bad *scran* to you," *i.e.*, I wish you bad food.

But ere for the *scran* he had left the Cole,
The Harman he came in.
—Harlequin Sheppard.

His club, Charlie, 'ad a reception,
Which means a big crowd and cold *scran*.
—Punch.

(Beggars), food or pieces of meat, broken victuals. *Scran-*

ning, or out on the *scran*, begging for broken victuals. The term *scran* was originally used in a deprecatory sense, from *scrans*, provincial English for refuse, or more probably from to *scranch*, to grind crackling food between the teeth. Dutch *schransen*, a greedy feeder; *schransen*, to eat greedily. These Dutch words indicate that there is a Teutonic as well as a Celtic original for *scran*, food, if the act of eating may be assumed as of the same origin with that which is eaten.

Scranning (beggars and tramps), begging for food.

Scrape (common), a shave.

Scraper (common), a razor.

Scrapper (popular), a pugilist; given in Jon Bee's dictionary of the turf, 1823. Also used in America. Probably from the movements of a pugilist, who appears to *scrape* with his feet.

People who have of late been playing at pugilism have their own organs, which are not only organs, but partisans also. Thus they, the players, don't want me to break a lance in their behalf; and yet I note that those who have taken upon themselves the rôle of advisers and directors of the toy pugilism which has so aroused Mr. Howell's wrath, have said never a word in defence of the queer thing about which they have for months been making so much vapour. Has the spirit of Bombastes affected the directors and controllers as well as the Lowther Arcade *scrappers?*— *The Referee.*

Scrap, scrapping (popular), a fight, boxing, a rough and tumble row. Also used in America. Suggested to be from

Swedish *skrap*, a difficulty, which has given the English "scrape." *Vide* SCRAPPER.

Tom O'Connell and Bob Banner had a *scrap* on last Tuesday afternoon at Chipeta Park. Six rounds were fought, and from the appearance of the gloves, which were covered with blood, some hard hitting was done.—*The Solid Muldoon, Otway, Colorado.*

Scrap, to (popular), to fight or box. Also used in America.

Scrap up (popular), having a *scrap up* is having a quarrel, a row.

Scratch (common), a *scratch* crew, team, or eleven, consists of men who have not practised together and are collected on the spur of the moment. To come up to the *scratch* is a colloquialism, meaning to meet the point of issue, to enter the contest.

Sir Bingo . . . eyed his friend with a dogged look of obstinacy, expressive, to use his own phrase, of a determined resolution to come up to the *scratch.*—*Scott: St. Ronan's Well.*

In debate, to be brought up to the *scratch*, to be compelled to come to the point. Technically the *scratch* is a line at the starting-point of a race, or the mark which is *scratched* or chalked on the ground in the middle of the "ring," hence the expression coming up to the *scratch*. Also toeing the *scratch*, being ready at the post in time. The rules of the prize-ring require each man to have his toe on the *scratch* within eight seconds of "time" called on pain of losing the battle. He must walk to the *scratch* unaided. This rule was adopted after the fatal fight between Owen Swift and Phelps in 1838, when the latter died of exhaustion, having been brought up to the *scratch* by his second under the older rule. *Vide* OLD SCRATCH, to which add, *Scrat* is the house-demon of the North. In Lancashire "owd Scrat."

Scratching rake (popular), a comb.

Scratch, no great (popular), of little worth. The allusion is to a fowl scratching for food.

Scratch-race (turf), a technical expression, meaning a race without any restrictions. To *scratch* is a technical turf term, meaning to strike a horse's name out of the list of runners in a particular race. Generally to eliminate the name of any candidate from a list in any kind of competition.

A series of *scratchings*, most unpopular, will leave unpleasant memories clinging round each of the big handicaps named above.—*Sporting Times*.

Scratch your wool (tailors), try to recollect.

Screamer (American), an extraordinary person, a great swell; from a metaphor similar to that from which arose the expression *screaming*, which see.

Screaming (common), first-rate, splendid. A *screaming* farce, one that makes the audience scream with laughter.

Scream, to (thieves). When a thief is robbed by another and he applies to the police, he is said to *scream*. More commonly in America to *squeal*.

Screen (thieves), a note. *Screen* is apparently an old term for money. Provincial *scrin*, a small vein of ore. Scandinavian and Teutonic *skrin*, a little box for money. Swedish *skrin-lägga*, to lay up money.

Readily the queer *screens* I then could smash,
Fake away!
—*Ainsworth: Rookwood.*

Screeve (thieves and beggars), a begging petition. *Vide* To SCREEVE.

Screever (street), a street artist and beggar who ornaments the pavements with drawings in coloured chalks. *Vide* To SCREEVE.

Screeve, to (thieves and beggars), to write; to *screeve* a fakement, to write a begging-letter. From provincial *scrive*, obsolete English, to *scribe*, to write. To *screeve* also means to draw on the pavement with coloured chalks.

Ah! once I could *screeve* a fakement or cooper a monekur with any man alive.
—*Mayhew: London Labour and London Poor.*

Screw (general), salary, wages. The metaphor implies efforts on the part of the employer to diminish the rate, or the efforts of the employé to enforce unwilling payment of, the salary, which has to be *screwed* out.

> If I got any practice he would have an excuse for knocking £100 or so off my *screw.*—*Truth.*

> 'Twas Monday morn,
> And he had wasted all his weekly *screw,*
> And was in debt some sixpences besides.
> —*Australian Printers' Keepsake.*

> Drat those clerks, they always want holidays. I'll stop it out of their *screw* though.—*Ally Sloper's Half-Holiday.*

(Popular), explained by quotation.

> That would have interfered with the order for *screws,* penny papers of tobacco.—*Mayhew: London Labour and the London Poor.*

(Thieves), a key, skeleton key.

> It was a good job I did, or else I should have got lagged, and my pal too, because I had the James and *screws.*—*Horsley: Jottings from Jail.*

A jailer, turnkey, prison warder.

> My next neighbour, who had been a bank manager, asked, "What implement in a carpenter's shop does the chief warder look like?" The response was, "A *screwdriver.*" The officers were always designated *screws,* so the description was not improper.—*Evening News.*

To put the *screw* on, to extort money by threats. In allusion to the old torture of the finger-screw.

> Is it true you was pinched for *putting the screw on* an omnibus conductor?—*Sporting Times.*

In common parlance, to apply pressure by threats or otherwise so as to enforce acquiescence. (Common), used in the phrases "a *screw* loose somewhere," something wrong. "He has a *screw* loose," he is slightly deranged. (American University), a searching or strict examination of a student by an examiner or instructor.

Screwed (general), intoxicated, a synonym of "tight," the metaphor being the same.

> By Jove, you must have been *screwed.* Then, I dare say, you don't remember wanting to have a polka with him.—*C. Bede: Verdant Green.*

> An unsexed woman shouting a song at the top of a brazen voice, with an imitation "how her old man got *screwed.*"—*Evening News.*

Screwing up (Oxford University), explained by quotation.

> At present friction occurs between unpopular "Dons" and rowdy students. The Don finds himself *screwed up,* or, in other words, imprisoned to his room by a gimlet thrust into the door in such a way that it requires the aid of a carpenter to unfasten it.—*Daily Telegraph.*

Screwsman (thieves), a burglar; a *screw* being a skeleton key.

> One day after this I asked a *screwsman* if he would lend me some screws, because I had a place cut and dried.—*Horsley: Jottings from Jail.*

Screw, to (common), to extort. (Thieves), to enter a house by means of skeleton keys.

> So we went and *screwed* his place, and got thirty-two quid, and a toy and tackle which he had bought on the crook.—*Horsley: Jottings from Jail.*

(American University), *vide* SCREW.

Scrimshandy (nautical), an Americanism, signifying the objects in ivory and bone carved by whalemen during their long voyages. Synonymous with "scrimshaw," which see.

Scrimshanker (army), one, whether officer or soldier, who is not over keen for danger, whether on active service or at home. One who has avoided his turn of foreign service, who malingers or feigns illness to escape duty. *Scrimshanker*, or idle shuffler, is also used at some public schools to signify a lazy, good-for-nothing fellow. Probably from *scrimp*, to shorten, to stint or contract, and *swanker*, labour; Danish *skrumpe*, German *schrumpen*, Dutch *krimpen*.

Scrimshank, to (military), to shirk one's duty. *Vide* SCRIM-SHANKER.

Scrimshaw-work (nautical), anything made by sailors for themselves in their leisure hours.

Scroby or **claws for breakfast** (prison), whipping while in prison.

Scroof, to (thieves), to sponge, to live with a friend at his expense. Thieves are in the habit of *scroofing* with an old pal when they first come out of prison, till they can steal something for themselves. This seems to be a form of *scoff*, *scorf*, which see.

Scroofer (thieves), a sponge, a parasite.

Scrouge (American University), an exaction, a specially hard task.

Scrouge, to (American University), a term applied to an exacting tailor or master who extorts a maximum quantity of work from his pupils. (Popular), to crush, crowd, or squeeze. "This term was made familiar in the language of literature by Dickens' Ebenezer Scrooge. It is the old English *scruze*, to squeeze or crush, and seems to have no native origin. It is perhaps from Spanish *estrujar*, to press, strain or thrust, which is derived from Latin *extorculare*, to press out (as wine from grapes) ; *torculum*, a press, from *torqueo*, to twist " (Smythe A. Palmer).

Then atweene her lilly handes twaine
Into his wound the juice thereof did *scruze*.
—Spenser : Faerie Queene.

Scrub (American), synonymous with the English " screw " for a horse of little value.

When the regiment was ordered to charge, they raised the rebel yell and rushed forward ; but the colonel's horse— an old *scrub* he had borrowed—" bucked " and refused to move.—*Harper's Magazine.*

The English *scrub* is expressive of meanness. A " scrub-race " is a race in which low and contemptible animals are made to run. (American University), a servant. (Australian), shrubbery, low underground.

Scrubbers (Australian), explained by quotation.

The captain was getting in the *scrubbers*, cattle which had been left to run wild through the mountains. — *H. Kingsley : Geoffry Hamlyn.*

Scrubbing (Winchester College), a flogging in which four cuts were administered.

Scruff, to (Australian), to seize as if seizing by the *scruff* or back part of the neck.

In crossing the Fitzroy River I once had a narrow escape of being *scruffed* by an alligator.—*Finch - Hatton : Advance Australia.*

Scruling (Westminster College), the inquiry made on the first day of election week by the warden and posers of the F. seniors and F. juniors in college as to whether they have any complaint to make as to the state of things in college.

Scrumptious (popular), nice, select.

Ow are yer, my ribstone? Seems *scrumptious* to write the old name, I 'ave quite lost the run of you lately. Bin playing some dark little game?
—*Punch.*

Scrumptious or *skrumshus* is a Suffolk word for stingy, close, or very particular, from the same root as *scrimp*, and it does not mean so much pleasant or agreeable as select or choice, something which is scrimped.

Scruncher (American and English), one who eats greedily. *Scrunch,* to crunch (Wright).

Scuddick (old cant), halfpenny ; from Italian *scudi,* crowns, change.

Scuds (American), money ; English *skids,* sovereigns. Possibly in the sense of shiners ; from

the Dutch *schit, i.e., skit, schitter,* to shine, glitter, or sparkle ; or from the Italian *scudi,* crowns.

Scuff (thieves), a crowd. A pickpocket may have a companion whose sole function it is to "get up a *scuff,*" to provide opportunity and to conceal the operations of his friend. This is done by feigning a fit, by a sham quarrel, &c. Also "push." The derivation is evidently from *scuffle,* a tumultuous broil ; Saxon *soufian,* to push.

While we was there we saw a *scuff* : it was a flat that had been welshed.—*Horsley : Jottings from Jail.*

Scug (Eton and Harrow), a boy who is not distinguished in person, in games, or social qualities. One of untidy, dirty, or ill-mannered habits ; one whose sense of propriety is not fully developed. Provincial *scug,* one who hides or sneaks away.

Bathing was always in great favour with the Eton boys. A boy who did not bathe was called a *scug.*—*C. T. Buckland : Eton Fifty Years Ago.*

Scumble, to (studios), to glaze pictures with an opaque colour.

Scurf (costermongers), a term applied to mean, close-fisted costermongers by their fellows.

"There's a scurf," said one.—*London Labour and the London Poor.*

Scuttle - mouths (Billingsgate), very large shelly oysters.

Scuttle, to (roughs and thieves), to stab, rip a man open. From the ordinary meaning of the word, or gypsy *scattle,* to kill.

Three persons were charged with being accessory to the murder of John Brady in a *scuttling* affray.—*Scotsman.*

Sea cunny (Anglo-Indian), a steersman or quartermaster. Persian *sukkāni,* from the Arabic *sukkān,* a helm.

Sea-grocer (nautical), the purser.

Seal, a religious slang term for a convert. In the phraseology of Mormons, a wife.

Sealed (American), originally used by the Mormons to intimate that wives are appointed or united by eternal destiny to a man. A source of many slang phrases, and not a few unseemly puns and jokes.

A young Mormon wife, in a fit of absent-mindedness at the post-office, dropped herself into the box, and let the letter walk home, nor did she find out her mistake till the clerk asked her if she were double or single ? " Young man," she replied, "don't you know that I'm *sealed?* " —*Newspaper jokes.*

" My wives, Mr. Ward," sed Yung. "Your sarvant, Marms," sed I, as I sot down in a cheer which a gal brawt me.

" Besides these wives you see here, Mister Ward," sed Yung, " I hev eighty more in varis parts of this consecrated land which air *sealed* to me."

" Which ?" sez I, gittin' up and starin' at him.

" *Sealed,* sir ! *sealed !* "

" Wharebouts ? " sez I.

" I sed, sir, that they was *sealed.*" He spoke in a traggerdy voice.—*Artemus Ward.*

Seas over, half. *Vide* HALF-SEAS OVER, to which may be added the following explanation :—

Dr. S. G. Green, in his life of William Wilberforce, the philanthropist, states that he (Wilberforce) would say, " I have often heard that sailors on a voyage will drink ' friends astern ' till they are half-way over, then ' friends ahead.' Could this custom be the origin of the phrase ? . . . Though the phrase is never used, I believe, to denote a person completely drunk, it originally implied semi-intoxication."—*Notes and Queries.*

Sea, to be at (common), to be lost, to know nothing about a matter ; to be uninformed, uncertain.

Second-hand daylight (popular), the light of another world. Apparently a vulgar version of the light that never shines on sea or land.

The other night she came with a candle in one hand and a sixpenny dagger in the other, and started on me in this style—" Where is the old kangaroo ? Let me get at him, and I'll treat him to two-pennyworth of *second-hand daylight ?*"—*Music Hall Song : Why don't you be steady, Maria ?*

Second timer (prison), a man convicted and sentenced for the second time.

I have known hundreds of men who were *second timers,* who in a ten years' sentence had got twenty-seven months' remission, who were compelled to do the whole of this time in addition to what they got in the second sentence.—*Evening News.*

See (American), a sight. " She determined that the world should have an opportunity of seeing her three babes, or trins, or triplets, at twenty-five cents a *see,*" says an Illinois newspaper.

See a man, to (American), to go and have a drink at the bar.

Seedy (common), unwell. The metaphor refers to a plant run to seed, and consequently withering. Also shabby.

Would it not be better for you to receive part (perhaps all) of your money by a wise concealment? for however *seedy* Mr. Bagshot may be now, if he hath really played the frolic with you, you may believe he will play it with others. — *Fielding: Jonathan Wild.*

Little Flanigan here is a little *seedy*, as we say among us that practise the law. — *Goldsmith.*

Sei. *Vide* SOLDI.

Selection (Australian), a kind of farm. The principle of free-*selection* is established in all the self-governing Australian colonies. The Government throws open such and such an area of the crown lands for free-*selection* and then any one is allowed to *select* or *take up* so much land, usually 320 or 640 acres, paying at the rate of a pound an acre, the payment being spread over a number of years, residence on the area selected for so many years, and certain improvements within a prescribed time being conditions attached. As these *selections* are generally taken up for farms, a *selection* has come to mean pretty much the same as a farm, though it has this technical meaning.

Here they can breed a sturdy family
To help them farm more highly, as more
    mouths
Demand subsistence from the same
    selection,
And when they grow too many for its
    means

And have acquired a rife experience,
Send sons forth one by one to found
    fresh hives.
            —*Douglas B. W. Sladen : Home*
                        in Australia.

Selector, free (Australian), a farmer.

I venture to differ from my correspondent when, in telling me that "cocky" is Australian argot for a small farmer, he adds, "By-the-bye, you never hear the word 'farmer' over there; it is always *selector* or 'squatter.'" But I beg to state that many scores of times at the Antipodes I have heard agriculturists whose holdings were small, spoken of, not as "cockies" but as "cockatoo farmers;" while to the term *selector* was generally prefixed the adjective "free." — *Illustrated London News.*

Sell (common), disappointment, deception, practical joke.

Mr. Verdant Green having swallowed this, his friend was thereby enabled not only to use up old *sells*, but also to draw largely on his invention for new ones. — *C. Bede : Verdant Green.*

Sell, to (common), to deceive, swindle, play a practical joke upon a person. Said to be from a cheap Jack's phrase, "sold again," after selling his goods. To *sell* a pup, to make a fool of one.

Send a man up Green River, to (American), *i.e.*, to kill him. The phrase, on De Vere's authority, had its origin in a once famous factory on Green River, where a superior kind of large knife was made, very popular among hunters and trappers. On the blade the words "Green River Works" were engraved, and hence the mountaineers, using the knife to despatch an adversary, literally sent his blood *up Green River*.

Send - off notice (common), an obituary notice.

After the funeral Huggins behaved handsome ; he put the Scalper into deep mourning, and wrote a beautiful *send-off notice* saying what a loss the community had suffered in Scrimmy's untimely end.—*The Golden Butterfly.*

Sensation (popular), a quartern of gin.

Sent down (University), rusticated, sent away for a certain lapse of time.

When "Billy" Wykeham gave to his colleges at Winchester and Oxford the motto "Manners makyth man," we wonder if he considered the publication of skits upon "dons" to be a breach of scholarly manners. The trustees of University traditions at Oxford have, however, no doubts upon the subject, and yesterday an undergraduate of New was *sent down* for irreverent jibes, published in an undergraduate paper for which he was held responsible.—*Globe.*

Sentry go (army), properly the cry made by the sentry nearest the guard-house when it is time for him to be relieved, and which reminds the sergeant or corporal to turn out the next relief. *Sentry go* has come to be accepted as the term for any kind of active military duty. A *sentry go* soldier is one who is always at duty, and in the lesser sense always at the most ordinary form of duty.

Sep (American cadet), a cadet who joins the academy in September.

VOL. II.

Separates (prison), the first nine months of a sentence of penal servitude, which are passed in separate and solitary confinement in Pentonville or Millbank prisons before going to a convict prison.

Serang (Anglo-Indian), a native boatswain or chief of a Lascar crew, the skipper of a small native vessel. Persian *sarhang*, a commander or overseer.

Serene, all (popular), all right.

So fur *all serene* ; but this joker, I tell yer,
　runs slap orf the track
Wen he says that my togs and my talk are
　"the fashion of sev'ral years back."
　　　　　　　　　　—*Punch.*

She saw he needed friendly aid,
To grant it she was not afraid,
　　Thought she, "It's *all serene* !"
　　　　　　　　　—*Sporting Times.*

Sergeant - major (butchers), an expression used by butchers in garrison towns to denote a large piece of mutton in the rib part. So called obviously from the white stripes like sergeants' stripes.

Sergeant - major's brandy and soda (army), a stable jacket gold laced.

Sergeant - major's wash cat (army), a new kit. The troop store man ; a term in the cavalry where the troop sergeant-major has an orderly man or assistant who looks after the stores.

Servante, the concealed shelf at the back of a conjuror's table.

O

Serve, to (thieves), to undergo penal servitude.

He laid claim to have *served* both in Maidstone gaol and the prison of Wandsworth. — *Greenwood : In Strange Company.*

Serving out slops (nautical), punishment on the gangway.

Se, sey, say (costermongers, shows, &c.), yes. From the Italian *si.*

Sessions (popular), an exclamation of surprise.

Set about, to (popular), to chastise, beat, thrash.

This got to my father's ears. When I went home he *set about* me with a strap. —*Horsley : Jottings from Jail.*

Set 'em up, to (American), to treat with drinks.

They threaten to make him *set 'em up* every time he tumbles in hereafter.—*T. Stevens : Around the World on a Bicycle.*

Set her up again! also, **set 'em up again!** (American), try again, begin once more. An encouraging exhortation to any one. Taken from the game of tenpins, where it is a cry to the boy when all the "men" are down.

Rip Sam ! *set her up again !*
Set her up again, set her up again !
Rip Sam ! *set her up again !*
We're all of the Choctaw tribe !
—*Old Song.*

Setter (old cant), a spy. (Thieves), a policeman in disguise or a man in the employ of the police (the French "indicateur") who points out the thief for others to arrest. (Costermongers and others), sevenpence ; from Italian *sette.*

Set up (American), conceited. "You needn't be so *set up* about it," is a very common expression.

Seven pennyworth (thieves), seven years' penal servitude.

Sewed up (popular), *vide* SEWN UP.

Sewer (London), the Underground Railway.

The *sewer*, as it was called by the old school, would be sure to monopolise all traffic.—*Graphic.*

Sewn up (common), exhausted, or simply *sewn.* *Sewn up* is probably only one of slang's ingenious variations of "finished," "done," &c., also intoxicated.

He . . . has twice had Sir Rumble Tumble . . . up to his place, and took care to tell you that some of the party were pretty considerably *sewn up* too.— *Thackeray : Shabby-Genteel Story.*

(Popular), having no work to do, drunk.

Shabash! (Anglo-Indian), well done! bravo! From the Persian *shāh-bāsh, rex fias,* thou shalt become a king! The authors of the Anglo-Indian Glossary very happily and ingeniously illustrate this interjection with the following quotation.

" At pueri ludentes, *rex eris*, aiunt,
Si recte facies."
—*Horace,* Epist. I., i.

So boys in play cry out, " Thou shalt be king,
If thou dost rightly ! "

Used also in America.

Shack (West American), a hut.

It happened one Sunday afternoon that I, Scott, Davidson, Hank, and Mitchell were in one of the *shacks* or huts, and they were idly listening to me. — *R. Morley: The Western Avernus.*

In Canadian society the word is used for a house dwelling. In America a vagabond, provincial English. In Norfolk a mendicant is termed a *shackbag;* to *shack*, or go at *shack*, to wander about.

Shad-belly (American), a Philadelphia term for a Quaker, in special reference to the dress worn by the Friends. The Quaker coat in its outline from the neck to the end of the skirt is cut in a curve exactly corresponding to that of the ventral line of a *shad*, whence the term.

Shadder, for shadow, a woman who watches prostitutes termed dress-women.

She's a dress-woman, that's what she is . . . one of them that they tog out that they may show off at their best and make the most of their faces . . . they can't trust 'em . . . you might tell that by the *shadder.* — *J. Greenwood: Seven Curses of London.*

Shade, to (thieves), to conceal, keep secret.

I felt 'alf inclined to dance, till I remembered as I must *shade* it from Jem, and the boys, or they'd be wanting their corner, and I didn't bloomin' well feel inclined to cut up my luck. — *Sporting Times.*

Shadkin (American), a marriage broker. From the Yiddish *shadchen*, also called a "chasseremschlupfer." "A chasseremschlupfer is ahner der a Hoch-

zich zamine brengt un Chusen und Kalle mocht " (D. H. L.).

The *shadkin* business has received a bad set-back in Brooklyn. A *shadkin* is a marriage broker. He is a very useful man. He finds out spinsters who have money and then he makes a bargain with some fellow who wants a wife with money and gets the couple introduced. Ten per cent. of the dowry goes to the *shadkin* when the others become kin. — *American Paper.*

Shadow (thieves), a first-class detective, one who possesses to a high degree the power of remembering the peculiar features and characteristics of persons, added to indomitable perseverance in following those whom he has spotted.

Shadow, to (popular), to dog a person.

The immediate cause of the present case was that for some months past the male defendant had *shadowed* him wherever he went. — *Daily Telegraph.*

S h a d y (common), dishonest, questionable, of doubtful propriety.

Although it may be *shady* when you wish
　　to mash a lady,
To wink at her and simply whisper,
　　" Tottie ! "
　　　　　—*Bird o' Freedom.*

A *shady* trick is a mean one or a contemptible one, from the want of ability displayed.

Shag back, to, to hesitate and hang back in the field before the enemy, or in a lesser degree, when hunting or riding a steeplechase, to crane at and refuse a fence. From a provincial term (Gloucestershire), to *shag*, to slink away.

Shah (popular), a great swell.

"Guessed it in once, old Ogsland!" went on Posh. "Perish me pink if it wasn't a bloomin' copper, all as blue as mould! And wasn't he a *shah*, neither!" —*Sporting Times.*

Shake (popular), a prostitute; probably from the provincial *shake*, futuere. In the north *shakes* means a bad character. (Printers), an expression used to describe a "slur" or "maekle" in a printed sheet, caused by uneven impression or "drag."

Shake a stick at, to (American), a very common expression, meaning "more than can be counted." Thus, "there are more people there than you can *shake a stick at.*" Another meaning is "worthless," as for instance, "there was nothing there to eat, worth *shaking a stick at.*" As regards the former, it has always seemed to the writer that it must have been of New York Dutch origin, and perhaps in its first form was "more than you can shake" or "hit with a stick." In Dutch *schok* (like *stoot*) is, according to Sewel, not only to shake but to hit. And it would be a very likely thing for a Dutchman endeavouring to say that there was more fruit or nuts on a tree than you could strike with a stick, to say, "more than you could strike at with a stick" and translate the word with "shake." Such an ex-

pression is too natural not to have occurred, and too quaint not to catch the American fancy for odd sayings. Thus "tie the dog loose," from some German's version of *losbinden*, "tar him mit fedders," for "tar and feather him," and "trow him mit ecks," pelt him with eggs, have all become "household words in the street."

Shake-lurk (old cant), a letter prepared for a vagabond stating that he has incurred a great loss, such as sickness or shipwreck. As it is a lying letter, it is probable that the term owes its origin to the Yiddish *shakar*, a falsehood. Also *scheiker*. But it is quite as possible that *shake* is the provincial "shack," a vagabond.

Shipwreck is called a *shake-lurk*, loss by fire is a glim.—*Mayhew: London Labour and the London Poor.*

Shaker (popular), an omnibus, a shirt.

Shake, shakes (American), a fair *shake*, a good opportunity, offer, bargain or chance. Provincial English *shakes*, a bargain.

Shakes (common), no great *shakes*, not much, of a poor description, not up to much.

Will Douglas, *no great shakes* at metre, did write these lines.— *T. Carlyle: Cromwell's Letters.*

And though the acting was *no great shakes*, yet the singing was, and her last note took us and everybody else by surprise.—*Punch.*

"Well, he's *no great shakes*," returned the coal-whipper's wife, in relenting tones;

" he's had a homin', as he calls it, and that always upsets him."—*J. Greenwood: Tag, Rag, & Co.*

" It is probable that *shakes* here is identical with the provincial word *shake*, to brag, which must be of ancient usage, as we find ' *schakare*, or cracker, or booste maker, Iactator, philocompus,' in the Promptorium Parvulorum, about 1440. These words are near akin to Danish *skogger*, noisy, roaring (in *skogger-latter*, roar of laughter, &c.), Icelandic *skak*, *skakr*, a noise. For the change of meaning from ' making a noise,' to ' boasting,' compare *crack*, old English *crake*, any loud noise, a boast, a brag (*cf.* ' a *crack* regiment,' one to boast of); *brag*, to make a loud noise (akin to *bray*, Latin *fragor*), to boast. Thus *no great shakes* would mean nothing to make a noise or brag about. Otherwise we may look for it in the provincial *shakes*, a bargain, comparing Danish *skakkre*, to peddle, or huxter; Icelandic *skakka*, to balance. These latter words seem to be cognate with Anglo-Saxon *scacan :* Icelandic *skaka*, to shake or wave (of the balance), just as weigh and wag are related " (A. Smythe Palmer). It has also been suggested that no great *shakes* may possibly be attributed to the expression to *shake* the elbow, *i.e.*, to play at dice, thus, no great *shakes*, a bad throw.

Shakes, in a brace of (popular), in an instant. Also " in a couple of shakes." Supposed to be from a *shake* in music, but really from provincial English *shake*, a quick motion. Compare with the French " en deux temps," in an instant; literally in two motions, from a fencing term.

Now Dragon could kill a wolf *in a brace of shakes.*—*Reade: Cloister and Hearth.*

I'll be back *in a couple of shakes,* So don't, dears, be quivering and trembling. —*Ingoldsby Legends : Babes in the Wood.*

Shakester, shickster (popular), a female. " Amongst costermongers this term is invariably applied to ladies or the wives of tradesmen, and females generally, of the classes immediately above them " (Hotten). In America a *shakester* is a lady, and *shickster* a woman. Derived from the German-Hebrew *shigsel*, *shixen*, *shichsle*, a girl. In Yiddish vocabulary it is defined as a Christian girl.

Shakes, the (theatrical), a synonym for stage fright. No actor or actress, worthy of the name, ever goes on the stage for a new part, without suffering from this most terrible of all complaints. Most actors feel it more or less every night for a few moments previous to making their appearance before the public. The emotional temperament, and the tendency to hysteria, which are the distinguishing characteristics of all great artists, render them peculiarly susceptible to *the shakes.*

Shake the ghost into one, to (popular), to frighten one.

Shake the red rag, to (tailors), to threaten to discharge. The *red rag* here probably means the tongue.

Shake, to (Australian popular), to steal. Originally imported by convicts into New South Wales, this word has passed into universal use among schoolboys, bushmen, shepherds, &c. When "taking" is stealing, it is called *shaking*. When "taking" is only a breach of etiquette, it is called "jumping;" you would *shake* a person's watch, but you would only "jump" the seat which he had engaged in a railway carriage.

Shake up (American), to obtain, get, procure. As if one had got game by shaking up or beating the bushes or coverts.

I never saw such magnificent weather for drying clothes. They don't *shake up* any such climate as this in Italy.—*Max Adeler.*

Shaking a cloth in the wind (nautical), slightly intoxicated, a drunken man being unsteady, like a sail that trembles in the wind.

Shallow (popular), a barrow used by costermongers.

And here they are after it—in vehicles for the greater part; in carts and "half-carts," and *shallows* and barrows. — *J. Greenwood: Low-Life Deeps.*

Also basket.

The square and oval *shallow* fastened in front of the fruit-woman with a strap round the waist.—*Mayhew: London Labour and the London Poor.*

(Beggars), the *shallow* dodge, explained by quotation.

It may be here mentioned that the "shaller," or more properly *shallow* dodge, is for a beggar to make capital of his rags, and a disgusting condition of semi-nudity; to expose his shoulders, and his knees, and shirtless chest, pinched and blue with cold. A pouncing of the exposed parts with common powder blue is found to heighten the frost-bitten effect, and to excite the compassion of the charitable.—*J. Greenwood: Seven Curses of London.*

The *shallow* brigade, the fraternity of "shallow coves," which see.

People got fly to the *shallow brigade.*— *Mayhew: London Labour and the London Poor.*

Shallow cove, shivering Jemmy (popular), a beggar of the male kind, half naked, who goes about telling frightful tales about shipwrecks, hairbreadth escapes from houses on fire, &c. ; "*shallow mot*" is the female. Also *shallow bloke.*

"What do you call a *shallow bloke?*" "He is a cove that acts the turnpike sailor; pretends he has been shipwrecked and so on."—*Temple Bar.*

A beggar of this description is said to go on the *shallows.* This word is possibly connected with to *shale*, to shell, take the shell or coat off.

Shandy-gaff (common), a drink composed half of beer, half of ginger beer. Sometimes stout or other liquors are used instead of beer.

This functionary has a staff of natives under him for the purpose of serving out the beer, rum, soda water, and lemonade, the latter cooling drinks, which are always kept in ice, being very much used by some of the thirsty souls for the purpose of making *shandy-gaff.*—*Brunlees Patterson: Life in the Ranks.*

Shaney, shanny (popular), a fool. Probably from the expression *shanny*-pated, giddy-pated, *i.e.*, with no more brains than a *shanny*, a small fish that lurks under stones and weeds.

> And out ran every soul beside,
> A *shanny*-pated crew.
> —*Bloomfield: The Horkey.*

Or perhaps from the Yiddish *scheïna*, meaning the same. *Vide* SHEENY.

Shanghai (Australian), a boy's catapult. Small birds are not favourite quarry of the small Australian catapulter ; like his rival, the larrikin, his special prey is the Chinaman. In the writer's memory, even the sons of high police officials found themselves in the dock charged with *shanghai-ing* Chinamen. Perhaps the instrument is so called in delicate allusion to those whom it is used to execute. (American), a dandy.

Shanghai-ing (nautical), explained by quotation.

> I fail to find the term *Shanghai-ing* in either slang or other dictionary, although, amongst sailors, it is a common word, denoting a common occurrence. Anglicised, it means, " Catching an unsuspecting landsman near a ship wanting hands ; drugging and robbing him ; shipping him as an A.B., and securing his first month's wages in advance." The authors of this villainy rely for security principally on the chance of death at sea, and then, should the improvised sailor succeed in reaching land safely, on

his silence regarding the affair, owing to its apparent improbability and a desire to escape exposure.—*Evening News.*

Shank, the (American), the balance, what remains ; as, for example, one friend might say to another, "Suppose you come in and spend the *shank* of the evening with me ? " *i.e.*, the lesser or later part.

> The old Kentuckian who in the *shanks* of the evening was wont to maintain there was no such thing as bad Kentucky whisky, admitted with extreme reluctance, even in the early sermons and soda-water period of the day after, that it might be possible some Kentucky whisky was better than others.—*W. A. Paton: Down the Islands.*

Shant of gatter (vagrants), explained by quotation.

> They have a *shant of gatter* (pot of beer) at the nearest boozing-ken. — *Mayhew: London Labour and the London Poor.*

Shan't play, I (Australian popular), I am annoyed, I don't like it. A metaphor taken from children peevish over a game saying, *I shan't play.* If a person is being chaffed, or if he finds a thing difficult, such as climbing up the soft ashes near the top of Vesuvius, he would say, *I shan't play.*

Shanty (circus and showman), a public-house is always called by this name. Properly *shanty* is a mean dwelling-hut, temporary building or erection, said to be from Irish *sean*, old ; and *tig*, a house (Webster). The word is, however, claimed to be of American origin, from Canadian

French *chantier*, meaning the same. (Nautical), a song.

It was a tough pull, as the shark was over fifteen feet in length, until the mate suggested a *shanty*, or sea-song, a corruption of the French word *chanter*, which a fo'cs'le Mario commenced, and the rest joined in vigorous chorus. So *Carcharias vulgaris*, as naturalists call the white shark, left his native element to the rousing strains of—

> " Were you ever in Quebec,
>   Ho, la! ho, la!
> Hoisting timber on the deck!
>   Ho, la! ho, la!
> With a will now—Heave, oh!"
>   —*Detroit Free Press.*

A contributor to a London journal declares that this is not a true sailor's word, but of literary origin, and only of late years.

Shape (American), "to travel on one's *shape*" is to get on, or pay debts, or live or succeed by the virtue of prepossessing looks.

> He has no more sense than a shad, you
>   know,
> Nor half the wit of an ape;
> But he'll get on while here below,
> By travelling on his *shape*.
>   —*Ballad: Beautiful Billy.*

Shaps (American), leather leggings. Probably from *shap* (provincial English) tight-laced, shapely, fit, comely. *Shapes*, a tight-laced, jaunty girl.

A pair of *shaps* or leather overalls, with tags and fringes down the seams.—*Alex. Stavely Hill: From Home to Home.*

Shark (army), a recruit. (Yale University), reckless absence from college, or shirking of its duties. Applied both to the thing itself and to the person.

(Common), a sharper, rogue, or cheat. "Commonly supposed to be a figurative use of the word *shark*. It is really a slightly disguised form of German *schurke*, a cheat or knave; Dutch *schurk*, a shark, rascal" (Sewel). The French "requin de terre," for an attorney, seems, however, to support the figurative use of *shark*, the fish.

Shark, to (nautical), to purloin.

In the mess I was in, we took up our full whack of provisions, comprising three tins of preserved Fanny Adams, a certain amount of flour, fat, and figs, which we had saved, and of course, salt horse, and salt pork; well that, and what we *sharked*. We were determined to have a grand flare-up, as regards our bread-baskets.—*Tit-Bits.*

Sharp. "A similar expression to 'two pun' ten,' used by assistants in shops to signify that a customer of suspected honesty is amongst them. The shopman in this case would ask one of the assistants, in a voice loud enough to be generally heard, 'Has Mr. *Sharp* come in yet'" (Hotten).

Shave (common), a narrow escape. Hotten has "a false alarm, a hoax, a sell. This term was much in vogue in the Crimea during the Russian campaign— that is, though much used by the military before then, the term did not, until that period, become known to the general public." Almost invariably heard as a close *shave*.

Shaver (popular), a very short jacket. A cunning fellow, one keen in making bargains, close-*shaving* being sharp dealing. A little, insignificant man.

> And yet, wi' funny, queer Sir John,
> He was an unco' *shaver*,
> For monie a day.
>
> —*Burns: A Dream.*

Among all the characters which he bears in the world, no one has ever given him credit for being a cunning *shaver* (be it here observed in a parenthesis that I suppose the word *shaver* in this so common expression to have been corrupted from *shaveling*, the old contemptuous word for a priest).—*Southey: The Doctor.*

> Much did Aunt Fan disapprove of the plan ;
> She turned up her dear little snub at " the man."
> She " could not believe it " — " could scarcely conceive it
> Was possible." What ! such a place ! and then leave it !—
> And all for a " shrimp " not as high as my hat !—
> A little contemptible *shaver* like that !
> With a broad pancake face, and eyes buried in fat !
>
> —*Ingoldsby Legends.*

In the latter meaning the word is possibly from the gypsy *shavie*, *chavy*, or *chavo*, a child or son. In old provincial English, however, a *shaving* is anything small, and *shaver* a small child.

Shave, to (drapery trade), to charge a customer for an article more than the marked price. When the master sees an opportunity of doing this he strokes his chin as a signal to his assistant (Hotten). Ladies are the chief customers at drapers', and this process is facetiously described as " *shaving* the ladies."

Shaving through (common), just escaping failure at an examination, or in anything.

Shebang (American), a shanty, or small house of boards. No one has ever explained the origin of this term, but it may be noted that there are exactly seven board-surfaces in a shanty, the four upright sides, the two sides of the roof, and the floor, and that the word *shebang*, in Hebrew, means seven.

> For last night we had a tempest—while the mighty thunder rang,
> Up there came a real guster, which blew down the whole *shebang*.
> *Shebang* is a word from Hebrew, meaning seven sayeth Krupp,
> And applied to any shanty where they play at seven-up.
>
> —*The Story of Mr. Scroper, Architect.*

Shed a tear, to (common), taking a glass of spirits. In the early part of the eighteenth century, in the days of Allan Ramsay, the Scottish poet, the phrase for a dram was a " bender," from the action of bending the elbow to raise the glass to the lips. The modern phrase applied to a drunkard, " he crooks his elbow," is synonymous. French "lever le coude." The Americans call a dram of alcohol a *smile;* and the question, " Will you smile ?" signifies " Will you drink ? "

S h e e (Charterhouse), a plum-pudding or cake.

S h e e n (Scotch), bad money. Probably alluding to the " glitter," or possibly from German *schein*, a bank-bill.

Sheeny (Yiddish and popular), a common and not very respectful word for a Jew, used principally in the slang of the Goyim or Gentiles, but also to be heard in jest among Jews. It is probably taken from *scheïna* —" *scheïna* jaudea līschkol "—a stupid fellow who does not know enough to ask or inquire. *Schien*, a policeman, and *schiener*, a house-thief, may have contributed to form this rather obscure word.

Benny is a smart boy. The lesson was bein' read to him about Joseph bein' sold by his brothers into bondage. Vhen it vas concluded the master asks, "Vat moral do ve draw from this?" Benny didn't need to think for a minute. "Steer clear of *sheenies*," says he, "if you don't vant to get sold." By my blessed gezundt, the boy's right.—*Sporting Times.*

Also used by thieves.

Took the daisies to a *sheeny*, and done them for thirty blow.—*Horsley: Jottings from Jail.*

In America a pawnbroker is sometimes called a *sheeney.*

Sheepskin fiddle (theatrical), the big drum. Also used by soldiers.

Sheepskin fiddlers (army), drummers.

Sheep wash, to (Winchester College), to throw a man into the water.

Sheffield handicaps, well-known sprint races in which there is no scratch man, the real scratch man receiving an enormous start from an imaginary flyer. It is possible that originally the idea was that when each man was told his start, he would not know the exact distance he had to run, but the whole affair is shrouded in mystery.

Shekels (London), money, coin. Properly an ancient Jewish coin, in value about 2s. 6d.

When you've been racing, and raked in the *shekels*, and you come back to Romano's and order a "Noisette de Brébant," you get a mutton-chop with the bone taken out.—*Sporting Times.*

Shelf, on the (popular), in pawn. (Army), under arrest.

Shell-back (nautical), a sailor; also "old shell."

Shell out, to (common), to pay, disburse; a metaphor, the pocket being likened to a pea pod, or literally out with one's *shells* or money, possibly alluding to the cowries or shells used in Southern Asia, on the coast of Guinea, and in the Philippine Islands.

Will you be kind enough, sir, to *shell out* for the price of a daacent horse?—*Miss Edgeworth: Love and Law.*

Come, fork out, old Flint ! . . *shell out*, old fellow !—*Waters: Recollections of a Detective.*

Also used in America.

It may be imagined I had to *shell out* pretty freely. In all I reckon it cost me more than 25 dollars.—*O'Reilly: Fifty Years on the Trail.*

Shells, brown (popular), onions.

In these ways may the enormous demand for *brown shells* and "big 'uns" be to some extent accounted for; but as one contemplates men, women, and children busy among the heaps as ants on an ant-hill, and bearing off, with satisfaction beaming in their faces, onions enough to garnish steak or tripe through all the days in the year.—*J. Greenwood : In Strange Company.*

Shelving (printers), a man in writing his weekly bill is said to have *shelved* it if he does not fully charge up the work done by him—in contradistinction to " horsing," or charging in advance of work done.

Shenanigan (American), humbug, deceit.

Jim took his bill, two days' board, $2.62, and eyeing the puzzled landlord as though he suspected some *shenanigan*, he broke out : " I want to see them ar books ! "— *New York Mercury.*

Bartlett says, " Foolery or nonsense when advanced to cover some scheme." This indicates, accurately, the beginning or commencing of something disgraceful. In Dutch this would be expressed by *schen-aangaan,* to begin anything disreputable. *Schen* is the root of both. *Schenden* and *schende,* violence and shame. This is only offered as a merely possible derivation of the word.

Shepherd, to (English and Australian popular), to watch, to play the spy on, to guard, to pay court to. The metaphor is obviously taken from shepherding sheep. Adversaries opposite each other at football are said to *shepherd* or watch each other. A man may *shepherd* a rich uncle or rich heiress, a detective *shepherds* a criminal whom he suspects of planning a felony. A man *shepherds* one of his own side at football by keeping off adversaries while he is running or kicking.

Sherbet (popular), a glass of any warm alcoholic liquor, as grog, &c. A misapplication.

Sherry-fug, to (Universities), to spend the afternoon indoors drinking sherry.

Shice, shicey, shicer (popular and theatrical), nothing, no good. *Vide* SHICER. (Thieves), counterfeit, specially counterfeit coin.

Shicer, shyster, the lowest and vilest kind of a man. The term is supposed to have been first used in England among the lowest order of Jews. It is said to be derived from the German *scheisser* (Lat. *cacator*), but may be influenced by the Yiddish *sheiker,* a lie, falsehood, or liar (Heb. *shakar*). " *Sheiker* we kisun," lies and falsehood. In New York the word *shyster* is specially applied to the lowest type of criminal lawyer — " a Tombs lawyer." (Diggings), a hole that yields nothing.

Shicksas (London), a certain class of the demi-monde. From the Jewish slang *shicksel,* a girl.

Shickster. *Vide* SHAKESTER. *Shikster* crabs, ladies' shoes or boots.

Shig (Winchester), a shilling.

Shiggers (Winchester), white football trousers costing 10s.

Shikar (Anglo-Indian), shooting and hunting game. Sport and game.

Shikerry (popular), shabby, bad, shaky, doubtful. Used in Australia. From provincial English *shickle*, fickle, doubtful.

But as the hedge-crocus is *shickerry* togged, he makes poorly out.—*Mayhew : London Labour and the London Poor.*

Shillagalee (American), a low, tricky, sinister fellow. New York Dutch, *scheeloog*, one that is squint-eyed, associated with *scheelen*, to want, ail. Possibly Irish.

Shilling shocker (common), explained by quotation.

The *shilling shocker* is too much given to a beggarly setting forth of its title in plain, fat, black letters, on simple white paper. Even when it aspires to a picture cover, the illustration is generally done in black and white, which unwisely ignores the noble and still unslaked thirst for blood which consumes the consumers of those Belshazzar's feasts of the imagination.—*Globe.*

Shindy. Most probably from the gypsy *chindi*, literally a cut, or cutting up, which is again confused with *chinger*, which has the same meaning and also signifies a quarrel. *Shines*, as applied to noisy deeds, mischief, rioting, &c., may be from the same root, a conjecture which is supported by the fact that it is always associated with *cut*, e.g., "He is cutting up shines."

Shine-nag (costers), a token of bankruptcy, or being "cracked up." "You'll ruin the *shine-nag* if you go on like that."

Shiner (popular), a sovereign; *shiners*, gold coins, money.

'Twas Isobar—this goodly tip—
And Epsomwards I hurried,
Expecting to recoup my trip
When safely home he'd scurried,
But when, at length, 'twas plain to see
That I had lost each *shiner*,
My jubilation struck a key
Comparatively *minor*.
—*Sporting Times.*

To let a lord of land want *shiners*, 'tis a shame.—*Foote : The Minor.*

(Tailors), a *shiner*, a boastful fellow.

Shines. *Vide* CUT UP SHINES.

Shine, to (tailors), to boast. (Popular), to take a *shine*, to be partial to a person or thing, to take a fancy.

Shiney (popular), gold.

We'll soon fill both pockets with the *shiney* in California.—*Reade: Never too Late to Mend.*

Shingle (American), hanging out a *shingle*, i.e., to put up one's sign or name over a shop or office. Of Western origin, *shingles* having been used there for the purpose named.

Shingle short, having a (Australian), equivalent to "having a tile loose," i.e., being slightly crazy or idiotic.

Shingle tramper (nautical), a coastguard.

Shinning around (American), explained by quotation.

"Fossicking about" is now used as a general term for what the Americans call *shinning around*, or what we should qualify as "ferreting about."—*Illustrated London News.*

To *shin* means also to walk.

Shinny on your own side ! (provincial and American). *Shinney* is the game termed hockey in England, and the exclamation is a suggestion to a person to attend to his own personal interest in anything. *Shinney* is provincial English for hockey.

Shin out, to (popular), to pay up money. Probably from the phrase, "to break one's shins," to borrow money from him.

Shin-plaster (American), a term applied ever since the revolutionary war (1776) to depreciated currency.

The House Committee on Banking and Currency will to-morrow make a favourable report to the House upon the bill providing for the issue of $25,000,000 in fractional currency. The demand for these small notes for transmission through the mails has increased within the past year, and numerous petitions asking for a return to the convenient *shin-plaster* have been received during the present Congress.— *New York World.*

Also used in England for a cheque or bank-note.

Mr. —— gave —— a cheque for a monkey . . . he was flourishing the *shin-plaster* in question at Sandown.—*Sporting Times.*

Bartlett tells the familiar tale as to the origin of the word, that after the old continental currency had become almost worthless, an old soldier used a quantity of it to make plasters for a wooden leg. It is, how-

ever, worth noting that the German and Dutch words *schein* or *schyn*, approach very nearly to *scheen*, *shin*, in the latter, and that they mean paper currency. A German proverb speaks of money as a *plaster* for every ill, and the peasants call a great price "a hot *plaster*." There is reason to believe that the phrase a *shin-plaster* will be found to be a translation from the German. The term is sometimes applied to "fractional currency," or notes of small value. Again it may be derived from the slang phrase "to break shins," to borrow money. The term *shin-plaster* is used in England. *Sheen* (which see), Scotch for bad money, is much older than the American Revolutionary War.

Shins (common), to break one's *shins*, to borrow money from one. A corresponding French phrase is, "Donner un coup de pied dans les jambes."

Shin-scraper (prison), explained by quotation.

The treadmill *shin-scraper* (arising, it may be assumed, on account of the operator's liability, if he is not careful, to get his shins scraped by the ever-revolving wheel).—*J. Greenwood: Seven Curses of London.*

Shin up a tree, to (common), to climb up a tree.

'Ship (printers), abbreviation for "companionship"—a body of compositors that work together and share alike all round, as regards the rate of pay per hour, a clicker being appointed to take charge and write the general bill.

Shipped (American University), expelled.

Ship, to (Shrewsbury school), to be unsuccessful in repeating lessons.

Shirking (Eton), explained by quotation.

Shirking was a marvellous invention. Fellows were allowed to boat on the river, but all the approaches to it were out of bounds; we might walk on the terrace of Windsor Castle, but it was unlawful to be caught in the streets of Windsor which led to the terrace. . . . If, happening to be out of bounds, you saw a master approaching, you had to *shirk*, which was done by merely stepping into a shop. The master might see you, but he was supposed not to see you ; the *shirking* was accepted as tantamount to a recognition that you knew you were breaking rules, and this was enough to disarm magisterial resentment. The absurdity of this system was, that to buy anything in the shops in High Street, where all the school tradesmen dwelt, we were obliged to go out of bounds.—*Brinsley Richards : Seven Years at Eton.*

Skeat derives the English word *shirk* from shark ; but *shirk*, a slinking rascal, has a direct affinity with the German *schürke* both in sound and meaning.

Shirt (turf), "to put one's *shirt* on a horse," to lose all one's money on a horse. The French say of a man in extremes, " il a vendu jusqu'à sa chemise."

" Now the word *shirt*," said the pedagogue, " is a common noun, and means an undergarment for men."

" And for horses, sir," put in a sharp youngster.

" For horses ? What do you mean ? "
" Father says he is going to put his on Friar's Balsam for the Derby, sir ! "
There was trouble in that class.—*Bird o' Freedom.*

(Common), to lose one's *shirt*, to lose one's temper. Also " to lose one's hair."

Shirt out, to have one's (used in England, but more in Australia), to be angry. Probably this expression has arisen from the shirt working out between the breeches and waistcoat during a struggle. *To have one's shirt out*, therefore, denotes excitement and thus anger. Another possible derivation is from the provincial *shurty*, to bustle about.

Shirty (common), angry. Used more in Australia and America.

Shivereen, a (Canadian), explained by quotation ; a word imitated from the French *charivari.*

The second night of my stay in Chehailis we had a wedding celebrated according to local custom by a *shivareen*, which is a performance of the following description : When the fond bridegroom and his blushing bride have supped and gone to roost, their friends and well-wishers, mostly males, arrive from the neighbouring ranches, bringing with them guns, rifles, drums, horse-fiddles, and other musical instruments. With these they commence a lively serenade, firing volleys, and working the horse-fiddle, a big wooden box, with a very active stick inside, until the unhappy pair turn out and drink the healths of their untimely visitors. Should the husband turn rusty, his callers may possibly pull his roof off, pour water down his chimneys, or forcibly extract him *in statu quo* from his nuptial couch.—*Phillipps-Wolley : Trottings of a Tenderfoot.*

Shoe-goose (Anglo-Indian), a term which shows how many Anglo-Indian words are manufactured. It is applied to the lynx, and is a corruption of the Persian *siyah-gosh*, literally "flock ear."

Shoe-leather (thieves), a thief's warning cry when he hears any one coming. French thieves, in a like circumstance, will say, "chou! chou!" or "acresto."

Shoe-string (American). When a man bets a small sum and runs it up to a large amount, it is called a *shoe-string*.

Shoes, another pair of (popular), quite different.

We'll show 'em *another pair of shoes* than that, Pip, won't us?—*Dickens: Great Expectations.*

Said to be a corruption of the French *chose;* but that is improbable, as the French have a corresponding and kindred phrase, "c'est une autre paire de manches."

Shoe, to (popular), a variation of making one "pay his footing."

S h o f u l (costermongers and thieves), counterfeit, base coin, sham jewellery. A *shoful*, an impostor. "This cant term originated among the Jews, and is the Hebrew *shâfâl* (or *shâphâl*), low, base, vile, the word which David applied to himself when he danced before the ark (2 Sam. vi. 22). Mayhew quotes *showfuls*, bad money, as a piece of costermongers' slang. It is curious to find the word once used by the King of Israel still living in the vocabulary of a London costermonger. Compare showful, showy" (Smythe-Palmer). (Popular), a hansom cab, *i.e.*, in the shape of a *shovel*, the original appellation. It is said, however, that they were at first despitefully called *shofuls, i.e.,* bad ones. *Schoful* appears in Dutch slang as *sjofel,* bad. The word is common all over Germany, Belgium, and Holland.

Shoful-pitcher (thieves), a passer of base coin. *Vide* SHOFUL.

Shoful-pitching. *Vide* SHOFUL-PITCHER.

Shoful-pullet (popular), a gay girl. *Vide* SHOFUL.

Shoke (Anglo-Indian), a hobby, a whim, a favourite pursuit. Arabic *shank.*

Shoon (thieves), a fool, a lout. Probably from the Hebrew. *Vide* SHEENEY.

Shoot (American), a slang phrase equivalent to "bother that!" "stop it!" "keep that out!"

Once in a while a man may take
A little holiday;
Don't talk to me about the shop!
Oh *shoot* the shop, I say!
—*Song.*

Miss Mabel Brown has jilted me, and that is nothing new of her;
Oh *shoot* Miss Mabel Brown, I say! Miss Wilkins is worth two of her.
—*Western News.*

Shoot is a Lancashire term, to get rid of, reject, eliminate.

I'll gie ya fifteen shillin apiece for those hundred cows, and ya'll let me *shoot* ten on 'em.—*Peacock: Lonsdale Glossary.*

The parallel phrase, to get *shut* of, is still used in Ireland and provincial English. In the Cleveland dialect, to get *shot* of. (Popular), a lot collected for sale.

Mr. —— had a big show of useful harness and hack horses, and as they were all sound and good-looking in appearance, it is needless to state that the Midland dealer got rid of nearly the whole *shoot*, at prices ranging from a "score" to fifty guineas.—*Sporting Life.*

Shooter (old), the guard of a mail coach, from his being armed with a blunderbuss.

He had a word for the hostler about that grey mare, a nod for the *shooter* or guard.— *Thackeray: Shabby-Genteel Story.*

(Printers), short for shooting-stick, an implement used for tightening up the quoins of a forme.

Shooting-irons (American), fire-arms.

The jurors—good, grandfatherly men—took a different view of the matter, and did not seem to think that it was any harm for an injured female to go about the streets with *shooting-irons*, ready to deal, probably, promiscuous destruction around her. —*Daily Telegraph.*

Shooting on the post (sport), to catch your opponents and win just before the tape.

Shoot off your mouth (American), to talk much, or talk in a boasting manner.

If he could kill Indians *shooting off his mouth* at them he'd soon clean them out all there is.—*F. Francis: Saddle and Moccasin*

Shoot one's linen, to (common), to jerk one's sleeves in order to show the shirt wristbands.

And as for the garment I wear next my skin,
To be "shirty" with that after years would be sin,
I could once *shoot my linen* so spotlessly white,
But now I am thinking 'twere best out of sight.
　　　　　—Song: Gone to Smash.

Shoot one's star, to (popular), to die.

Shoot, the (London Railway). Walworth Road Station, on the London, Chatham, and Dover Railway, is called, *par excellence, the Shoot*, because of the large number of passengers who alight there, thus relieving the enormously congested traffic from the city stations. This is especially noticeable at certain times of the evening when those engaged in the city are returning from business.

Shoot the cat, to (common), to vomit. (Army), the bugle-call (in infantry) for defaulters' drill, so called from the onomatopoetic sound of the call which it is fancied follows the words "shoot the cat—shoot the cat." Nearly all bugle-calls have their synonymous words, as the dinner call, which runs "officers' wives have puddings and pies. Soldiers' wives have skill—ee!" and the second watch setting, or tattoo roll-call, which begins "Wiggins, Wiggins, Private Wiggins, come home to barracks," and so on to the end of a long tune.

Shoot the crow (American), explained by quotation.

An ancient sinner was recently charged with *shooting the crow, i.e.,* obtaining alcoholic stimulant at public-houses, and making an artful retreat without paying for the cool, refreshing moisture. His method was charmingly simple. After strolling into a coffee-room, he would order a six of whisky. On the liquor being brought, he usually remarked, " The water in the bottles looks rather cloudy, waiter. Just fetch some fresh, if you please." Then, while the gentle garçon retired, the A. S. invariably drank the spirit with rapidity, and made tracks as speedily as possible. Fifteen days' "hard."—*Fun.*

From an allusion to *crow-whisky,* or the best kind.

Shoot the moon, to (common), to leave a house or lodgings by night, and generally removing the furniture without paying the landlord.

My uncle's got the broker's man,
My cousin's got a month ;
My brother's joined a regiment.
The hard-up ninety-oneth.
My aunt she's gone to Colney Hatch,
To spend the afternoon,
And all our blessed family
To-night *will shoot the moon.*
—*We are a Merry Family* (*Francis and Day*).

Synonyms "move in the blind," "go between the moon and the milkman," &c. In French, "déménager à la cloche de bois." *Vide* MOON.

Shoot, to (Stock Exchange). "To make a man a close price in a stock without knowing if there would be a profit or loss on the bargain" (Atkin, "House Scraps ").

VOL. II.

(Turf), to be *shot* is to make a disadvantageous bet which is instantly accepted.

Then a plucky fielder, who does not perform in London every day, offered "nine monkeys," and was instantly *shot* by the very dealer who had backed.— *Bird o' Freedom.*

(Popular), to be *shot,* to be photographed.

Shop (general), a house, place, establishment, and club. The French use the word *boutique* as a disparaging term for any ill-managed house or establishment. "All over the *shop*" implies a general disturbance, confusion, or commotion of any kind ; to talk *shop,* explained by quotation.

There was another symptom of a parallel feeling in the widespread censure involved in the common reproach that a man talks *shop.* What was talking *shop?* It meant talking of the interests of the work which they did, or the profession to which they belonged. But injustice lay in the word, and a snare in the thought. Too often it meant the exclusion from lively conversation and pleasant discussion of that which formed the dearest intellectual interest of a man's life.—*Daily News.*

A lay guest at a clerical dinner, hoping to ingratiate himself with his neighbour, a well-known London parson, and beginning some rather unctuous talk, was met with the rebuke, " Sir, when I dine with Jack Ketch, I don't talk about hanging." (Army), the guard-room. The Royal Military Academy is termed the *shop.* (Turf), to get a *shop,* to secure first, second, or third place in a race.

P

"My boy," said an eminent bishop to his eldest son, "truth will always triumph in the long run ; for this reason let your guiding principle in life be Veracity." "I don't think your tip will quite win, pa," said the boy ; "but I shall certainly back it for a *shop.*"—*Referee.*

(Theatrical), explained by quotation.

Sometimes one may meet in the Strand an actor who has been out of a *shop*—all engagements being called *shops*, as well as the play-houses—a long time, who having run through, or run in to Attenborough, his ordinary wardrobe, will be wearing his "props" to keep up an appearance.—*Globe.*

Shop-bouncer (popular), generally a well-attired thief, who appropriates articles while being served with other articles of less value.

Shopkeeper (trading), an article which remains long in hand in a shop is always known as an old *shopkeeper.*

Shop-lift (old), a thief who robs at shops.

The tenth is a *shop-lift.* that carries a bob When he ranges the city, the shops for to rob.
—*Pedlar's Pack of Ballads and Songs, collected by W. H. Logan.*

Shopper (trade), one much addicted to "shopping."

The plan is to distinguish between the two classes of *shoppers.*—*Daily Telegraph.*

Shoppy (common), to be *shoppy*, to talk of nothing but about one's calling or profession, or on sporting subjects.

When golfers get together their talk is more unutterably *shoppy* than even that of hunters, cricketers, or racing men.—*Daily Telegraph.*

Shop, to (army), to put under arrest in the guard-room.

If we enter the army, joining the light infantry, we will become a "light bob," and our first contravention of military law will ensure our being *shopped.*—*Morning Advertiser.*

(Royal Military Academy), to put under arrest. (Pugilistic), to punish a man severely, knock him "all over the *shop.*" (Trade), to discharge a shopman. (Thieves), to send to prison.

She looks up in his face. "Jim," says she timidly, and cowering close to him the while, "if you was took and *shopped*, like him in the long boots, I'd go to quod with you, if they'd give me leave—I'd go to death with you." — *Whyte-Melville : M or N.*

Shop-walker (trade), a kind of foreman who walks about the shop.

Short (common), without money.

Barber—"Pretty *short*, sir ?" *Customer*—"Well, yes, I am. Just put it down on the slate, will you ? Much obliged to you for speaking of it."—*Lowell Citizen.*

(Costermongers), neat gin. Originally unsweetened or shortened gin, then *short* gin, then any neat spirit. "Let's have something *short.*"

Old men will swathe their gouty limbs,
And talk of sound old port ;
Converted thieves will sing loud hymns,
Then take their drops of *short.*
—*Fun Almanac.*

(Banks), upon presenting a cheque, the clerk asks, "How will you take it ?" *i.e.*, in gold or notes. If in notes, "long or *short ?*" Should it be desired to receive it in notes for the largest possible amount the answer is, *short* (Hotten).

(Tailors), he bit him off *short*, he abruptly closed the interview or instantly dismissed his appeal.

Shortage (American), a deficit in accounts.

" Let's see," he mused. " You are in some bank down town, aren't you ? "
" Yes, sir."
" And don't all these robberies, embezzlements, and *shortages*, make the directors a little nervous."
" Well, perhaps."
" Any talk of giving the cashier a vacation so as to slyly examine his books ? "
" Not that I have heard of."
" Then you must have confidence in him ? "
" I—I think so. That is, I presume so. That is—I'm the cashier myself."—*Wall Street News.*

Short ear (American University), a rowdy.

Shorter (thieves), a rogue who clips and files coin. From a crown-piece a *shorter* could gain 5d. Chemical means are also resorted to.

Short-hairs, silk stockings (American), the names of two branches of thé Democratic party in the Western States. They appear to have been first used, or at least to have first come before the public, at the Democratic State Convention, held in Springfield, Illinois, August 26, 1886.

They did not resign, as had been hoped by the *short-hairs*, but desired to retain control of the fall campaign, and until December, when their terms expire. This was a disappointment, but their opponents got satisfaction by preventing the re-election of any of them. The *silk stockings*, as they are freely called, made an attempt in the committee meeting when the election of members at large took place to crowd out the Cook County *short-hairs* altogether by a motion that only four members at large be elected.—*Chicago Tribune.*

The *short-hairs* appear to be discontented with the administration, while the *silk stockings* approve of it.

Short of a sheet, to be, the Australian equivalent of a tile loose, crazy.

Shorts, the (Stock Exchange), said of brokers who are minus stocks which they have contracted to deliver.

Shot (popular), reckoning. From Danish *skat*, Anglo-Saxon *sceat.* Hence scot-free. Old French (*escot*), *écot.*

There's three more of 'em, waiter—three more jolly blue boys, give it a name, my Britons ; I'll pay the *shot.—J. Greenwood: Dick Temple.*

(Old cant), explained by quotation.

The " Charley " winked at the robberies committed by nocturnal footpads on drunken wayfarers, he black-mailed the unfortunate female night-prowlers, and especially did he lend aid and countenance to the resurrection-men or body-snatchers, who often found the watchman's box convenient as a temporary receptacle for the *shot*, or corpse, which they had just disinterred.—*Daily Telegraph.*

Shot in the locker (nautical), a metaphor signifying money in the pocket.

Shot, shot in the neck (American), drunk. German, "Er ist geschossen," he is *shot*, *i.e.*, drunk.

Shot, to (horse-dealers), to *shot* a horse, is to give him a quantity of small shot, the result being that for a short time he appears sound in wind.

Shoulder shams (old cant), confederates of a pickpocket who press round the victim.

Shoulder, to (popular), when a servant steals his employer's money he is said to *shoulder* him.

Shouting. *Vide* To **Shout.**

It is the custom in the colonies, or, at all events, in the parts I have visited, to "stand" drinks most profusely at the village or township bars. They call it *shouting.—Blackwood's Magazine.*

Give me the wealth I have squandered in
    shouting,
  Scattered in sixpences, paid by the
    pound,
Ladled out glibly, no grudging or doubting,
  Never a thought of the use to be found.
      —*D. B. W. Sladen: The Sigh of the
        Shouter.*

Shout, to (Australian), to treat, to frank ; *shouter*, one who treats.

He had felt bound, according to custom, to *shout* for them all. I said, " But why do you give in to the practice ? " He replied, " It is not for the drink that we care, but for the expression of friendly feeling."—*C. T. : Impressions of Australia* (*Blackwood's Magazine*).

To *shout*, perhaps, gets this meaning as being equivalent to giving the order. I *shout*, therefore, I call out the order. The custom of *shouting* is universal in Australia. No one

ever voluntarily drinks alone. He *shouts* his friend and his friend *shouts* him back, or each one of a company in turn *shouts*. If there is no one else to *shout* to, the customer generally invites the barman to take a drink. This custom is one of the curses of Australia. A publican knows that, however many there are in a party which enters his house, there will be the same number of "*shouts* all round."

Shove (thieves), to pass bad money ; "*shoving* the queer," passing counterfeit coin. In all probability a combination of the gypsy *chiv*, with the English *shove*, as *chiv* comes much nearer to putting, or placing, or disposing of, than *shove*, *i.e.*, to merely push. A *shove* of the mouth is a glass of gin.

Shovel (nautical), an opprobrious term applied to a marine engineer who knows little or nothing about his work.

Show (theatrical and common), any performance or entertainment. In the quotation reference is made to a cricket match.

And have I " been bored or been weary " ?
  Oh, gracious me, no !
  There is plenty of go
About these broad-chested and cheery
  Young fellows come up for the *show*.
        —*Bird o' Freedom.*

" Many words of stage slang can be traced to Shakspeare's days and Shakspeare's plays. The word *show*, to begin with, meaning the performance and the play indifferently, is to be found in the tragedy of young Pyramus and his love Thisbe in the comedy of the 'Midsummer Night's Dream':—

'The actors are at hand, and by their *show*
You shall know all that you are like to know.'"
—*Globe.*

Used also in such phrases as boss the *show*, run the *show*, to direct, manage.

We determined to run the *show* ourselves, or, in theatrical parlance, by "commonwealth."—*Tit-Bits.*

Over goes the *show*, explained by quotation.

It's all very well to say you won't
Take another of 'em on, but oh!
When a pretty little widow winks at you,
Why, over goes the *show*.
—*Music Hall Song.*

(American), a chance, an opportunity, a turn.

Flanigan hesitated for a second; then he saw he had no *show*, and with an oath he let his rifle drop.—*Century Illustrated Magazine.*

It is often heard in the form, "give a fellow a *show*." "My friends," said a Baptist preacher, "if ever the devil has anything to say for himself, you ought to give him a *show*." It has become one of the commonest of slang words in Australia. The expression probably comes from giving a person a chance of showing his cards, which, for example, he cannot do at écarté if his opponent shows the king, and only requires one point. Australians talk of giving a man a *show*, not having a blessed *show*, a mortal *show*. He hadn't

a *show*, he was altogether outmatched.

Show-box (theatrical), the theatre.

Showing a front (army), a term used when short notice of a parade is given, and a soldier has to turn out without proper time to prepare himself by cleaning up his accoutrements and kit.

Show Sunday, the Sunday in Commemoration week at Oxford. On this day most of the University and their friends used to be seen in the Broad Walk of Christ Church, but of late years, owing to the influx of town's-people, very few of the University are seen there. (Studios), the Sunday before pictures are sent in for the Academy Exhibition, when studios are visited by the artists' friends.

Shrieking sisterhood, the (journalistic), an opprobrious term applied to women who take the lead in matters of reform connected with their sex. This phrase is of American origin.

Shroff (Anglo-Oriental), a money-changer, a money-broker or agent, a banker. Arabic *sarrāf. Shroffage*, a money-broker's commission. To *shroff* is to assort money, pick out uncurrent coins and determine the agio or discount on them. Hence it has come in Oriental-English to mean sifting, choosing, or valuing men, horses, or anything whatever.

"*Shroffing* schools are common in Canton, where teachers of the art keep bad dollars for the purpose of exercising their pupils, and several works on the subject have been published there with numerous illustrations of dollars and other foreign coins, the methods of scooping out silver and filling up with copper or lead, comparisons between genuine and counterfeit money, &c." (Giles' Glossary of References, Anglo-Indian Glossary.)

Shroffing dollars (Anglo-Indian), sorting dollars, selecting them. Among settlers in China, *shroffing* means seducing.

Shucks (American), "don't amount to *shucks*," it is less than nothing. *Shucks!* an exclamation signifying nonsense! or expressive of refusal. In America *shucks* are the husks or shells of nuts and Indian corn. It is an old provincial word for shell or husk. The pods of peas are still called pea-*shucks*, and being worthless have given rise to the slang phrase. The Confederate "blue-backs" or bank notes were also called *shucks*, probably for a twofold reason, because they soon became worthless through the failure of the Southern cause and from the circumstance of money being sometimes designated as dust, pelf, filthy lucre, &c.

Shucks, and stay fooling around here! —*Huckleberry Finn.*

Shulwaurs (Anglo-Indian), trousers or drawers.

Shunter (Stock Exchange), explained by quotation.

One who buys or sells stocks on the chance of undoing his business, on one of the provincial Stock Exchanges, at a profit.—*Atkin: House Scraps.*

Shunt, to (popular) to move, turn aside. From the railway term. To *shunt* any one, to get rid of him.

He started in life as a welsher. Not a respectable welsher, one who snatches your brief when you present it for payment, or punches you in the jaw and tells you to *shunt.*—*Sporting Times.*

Shut of. *Vide* SHOOT.

Shut up! a vulgar but very common phrase used as a forcible request to another to keep silent or quiet. French slang has the expression "ferme ta boîte." The Greeks said, "Keep an ox on your tongue." *Shut up*, also exhausted, done for; "that *shut* him up," that entirely stopped his speech or action.

Shut up your face (American), be silent. Also, "cork up your whisky-bottle."

Shy of the blues (thieves), explained by quotation.

I happened to know that in criminal circles to describe a person as being *shy of the blues*, is equivalent to saying that he has particular reasons for keeping out of the way of the police.—*J. Greenwood: Tag, Rag, & Co.*

Shyster (American), a louting, swindling attorney, or a low fellow who pretends to be an attorney—though possibly he had here no connection with the law except to sweep out an attorney's office, or run an errand, or who hangs about police offices, or courts of justice, to cheat prisoners or suitors on pretence of sending them legal assistance. Derivation uncertain, but probably from the German *scheisser* (cacator), allied to *scheuen*, to avoid, to be in fear of, and *scheusslich*, abominable.

When a man is thrown into prison a *shyster* leech gets access to him, and extorts from him his last cent under the pretence of obtaining his liberation.—*New York Tribune.*

Shysters are a set of turkey-buzzards whose touch is pollution and whose breath is pestilence.—*New York in Slices.*

There is more deep-hued and earnest ingenuity in three hairs of the Counsellor's Londonderry beard than in the Pompadour mop-heads of all the dude *shysters* of the day. The Counsellor knows a dollar when he sees it, and no dollar ever coined had intelligence enough to get out of the way of that astute practitioner.—*San Francisco News-Letter.*

Sick (Australian popular), without trumps. In playing a nap, if the player's trumps are exhausted, he will say *sick*, and if he have a hand full of trumps, and challenges the board, to see if any one has any left, he will ask " All *sick* ? "

Sick market (Stock Exchange), a *sick market* is one in which sales of stock are difficult to place. As a rule this is usually the result of hazardous and reckless speculation.

Side (common), a man is said to put *side* on when he gives himself airs, swaggers, or assumes unusual dignity. This expression is now much in vogue in England and America. It seems at first sight to be a metaphor either taken from the habit of dogs when they are given things to carry, when they invariably put their side out in a curve, like a horse when buckjumping, or from a billiard term meaning making a ball revolve on a perpendicular axis by striking it on the side, or again from a ship that shows its side when sailing fast with a side wind ; but in reality *side* is old provincial English. Bailey gives it as a north-country term, meaning long, steep, proud.

The young men of the present day, who think it is the right thing to put on a lot of *side.—Saturday Review.*

(Cambridge University.) At the larger colleges there are several college-tutors amongst whom the students are apportioned. Those attached to each are called his *side.*

A longer discourse he will perhaps have to listen to with the rest of his *side.—Westminster Review.*

Side degrees are test degrees by lecturers. (Thieves), used in the cant language of the Northern towns as an affirmative. Probably abbreviated from the phrase, " I *side* with you."

Side-board, stick-up (common), a collar.

Side-pocket (American thieves), a drinking saloon in an out-of-the-way place. A quiet resort for out-of-the-way people, fancy women, private gamblers.

Side-show (American). Where there is a large exhibition, as, for instance, a "mammoth circus," or Barnum's "Great Menagerie," there are generally established about and near it a number of trumpery little cheap exhibitions of fat men, tattooed young women, the human fish or dancing dogs, generally charging a dime or fivepence admission. These are called *side-shows*, but the term is extended in popular slang to signify anything not in the expected order of things.

The supper at the party was good, but on temperance principles, and I was beginning to feel doleful after my fried oysters, and terrapin, and chicken-salad, and soft-shell crabs, when Enos came up and whispered softly, " Now you've seen the Great Moral Circus, suppose you step into the *side-show.*" The *side-show* was in the back dining-room, where he had a bottle of fine old brandy.—*Philadelphia Newspaper.*

Side - wheeler (American), a paddle-steamer.

Sight, to take a (American), to take aim.

Another Indian had turned and was getting a bee line on us when Frank *took a sight* at him in return. — *O'Reilly: Fifty Years on the Trail.*

Sil (thieves), a spurious bank-note, especially one drawn on the Bank of Elegance or Bank of Engraving, to avoid the consequences of a more accurate imitation of the genuine note. Much used by welshers and confidence - trick men. In all probability *sil* was originally a forged document used by a "silver beggar" (which see), and abbreviated from silver.

Silencer (pugilistic), a crushing blow.

Sam planted such a *silencer* on his knowledge-box that Neal went down quite stupefied.—*Pierce Egan : Book of Sports.*

Silk, to take (law), to be made a Queen's Counsel.

Sillikin (popular), a silly person.

I don't know where I came from,
And I don't know where I'm going,
They think I am a *sillikin*
But I am rather knowing.
—*H. Wilson: The Blessed Orphan.*

This term is used by Australian thieves.

Silly season (journalistic), the period when there are no parliamentary debates to report, or any interesting events. Newspapers to fill up their columns are then compelled to insert "silly" matter.

Silver beggar (beggars), a beggar who travels through the country with letters containing false statements of losses by fire, shipwrecks, accidents. Forged documents are exhibited with signatures of magistrates and clergymen. Accompanying these are sham subscription-books.

The former in beggar parlance is termed a "sham," whilst the latter is denominated a "delicate." Formerly a pickpocket was termed a silly cheat, corrupted from silver (siller) cheat.

Silvers (Stock Exchange), India-rubber, Gutta-Percha, and Telegraph Works Company Shares.

Sim, in clerical talk, a follower of the late Rev. Charles Simeon, a well-known Cambridge evangelical clergyman, died 1836.

Simkin (Anglo-Indian). Formerly, when Anglo-Indian slang was more prevalent than now-a-days, champagne was called *simkin*, probably in imitation of the native way of pronouncing the word.

The dinner was good, and the iced *simkin*, sir, delicious.—*Oakfield.*

(Theatrical), the fool in comic ballets.

Simmer down! (American), an exclamation to exhort one to silence. Also, "give your tongue a vacation!" "dry up!" "put up."

Simon (circus), a trick horse, or one trained to perform tricks. (Popular), a sixpenny piece.

Simon-Pure cussedness, an American combination of Simon Pure, the character in Mrs. Centlivre's comedy of "A Bold Stroke for a Wife," now a proverbial expression, and "pure cussedness."

They (the mules) very quickly developed a capacity for *Simon-Pure cussedness* that

caused the officers of the ship no little anxiety from day to day.—*T. Stevens in the "Boston Herald."*

Simply throwing up buckets (Australian popular), very vexed or disappointed. When a person means to say that he is as disappointed as ever he can be, he sometimes says, "Oh! I am *simply throwing up buckets,*" this being of course a play upon the Australian use of sick (*q. v.*).

Simpson, water, as applied to its mixture with milk for adulteration. Mrs. *Simpson,* the parish pump.

These authorities know best the average quantity of *Simpson*—the technical term in dairydom for water—used by unscrupulous cow-keepers to debase their milk. —*Daily Telegraph.*

Sinbad (nautical), an old sailor; the allusion is obvious.

Sinch (American), a saddle-girth. Spanish *sincha.*

You can show him the way they corral a train
In an Indian raid on a pinch;
You can show him the bravest son of the plain,
That knotted a broncho's *sinch.*
        —*William Devere : The Great Wild West.*

Sines (Winchester College), bread, which commoners generally went without (*sine,* without).

Sing it, don't (popular), don't exaggerate. Another variation of this is, "Don't chant the poker."

Sinkers (popular), bad money.

Sink, to (tailors), to fall down the *sink*, to take to drinking and forsake work.

Sipper (popular), gravy.

Sir-ree! (American), generally heard as "Yes—*sir-ree!*" A low expression which is said to have originated in this anecdote. A grim, taciturn individual came to a tavern, and was asked if he wanted something to eat? He replied, "No, sir!" "Will you have anything to drink?" "No—*sir-ree!*" "Perhaps," suggested the complaisant landlord, "the gentleman would like a lady companion?" To which the reply, with a glad smile, was, "Yes—*sir-ree*—bob!"

Sit. (printers), an abbreviation of the word "situation." For instance, "out of *sit.*" or "collar."

Sit under. In Evangelical and Nonconformist circles, to *sit under* a preacher is to attend his ministry.

Sit-upons (common), trousers.

But I should advise you, old fellow, to get your *sit-upons* seated with wash-leather.—*C. Bede: Verdant Green.*

Sit up, to (familiar), to make any one *sit up* is to punish him severely at a game. At billiards, for instance, when one is making a break, he is said to make his antagonist *sit up.*

Sivey, sivvy, 'pon my (popular), upon my honour. Corruption of "asseveration."

'Pon my sivey, if you was to see her pecking you'd think she was laying on

pounds' weight in a day instead of losing.—*J. Greenwood: Tag, Rag, & Co.*

Sixer (thieves), explained by quotation.

"Neddie, from City Road, smugged for attempt up the Grove, expected a *sixer*," means that a misguided Edward has been apprehended while promenading outside Whiteley's, and investigating the contents of ladies' pockets, and is reconciling himself to an absence from his oriental home for half a year.—*Horsley: Jottings from Jail.*

Also a six-ounce loaf of bread given to prisoners.

Six quarter or **swop, to get** (city), to be dismissed from one's employment.

Six-shooter horse (West American), a swift horse. A six-shooter is a revolver or repeating rifle.

I'd get on one of the *six-shooter horses* —a *six-shooter horse* is a heap better than a six-shooting gun in these cases.—*F. Francis: Saddle and Moccasin.*

Six-water grog (nautical), very weak grog.

Size, to (American), *to size* a man up means to understand him, to perceive or understand what he is, or to mentally take his *size*, which is a common American equivalent for his whole bodily and mental condition.

I'm a clerk at the Palmer House and *sized* you up the minute you spoke to me. If you show your face again in the house I'll see that you are kicked out of the door in the highest style of the art. Ta-ta!— *A Bunko-Steerer Taken In.*

Also a West Indian expression.

We landed at a quay of well-formed masonry, in the presence of a crowd of blacks who evidently took stock of us, *sizing* us, no doubt, with the design of engaging us in pecuniary transactions more or less connected with fruit.—*W. A. Paton: Down the Islands.*

(Cambridge University), to send for extra victuals in Hall ; *e.g.*, an undergraduate will *size* for a tankard of Buttery ale, instead of the small beer or " swipes " that is placed on the table.

Skedaddle (common), of American origin, to run away, to be scattered in rout.

He raises such a rumpus,
" He's a rum puss out and out,"
That the other cats *skedaddle*,
Quite dismayed they're put to rout.
—*Detroit Free Press.*

" The Scotch apply the word to milk spilt over the pail in carrying it. During the late American war the New York papers said the Southern forces were *skedaddled* by the Federals. Saxon *scedan*, to pour out " (Dr. Brewer). In addition to this it may be suggested that *sketdaddle* in English provincial dialects means to go quickly but unsteadily. *Sket*, quickly, and *daddle*, to walk irregularly or unsteadily (Wright). Though this may not be the true origin of the word it corresponds to the definition of retreating rapidly yet in a confused irregular manner. *Sket* corresponds with *skeet* (which see), to go quickly or run. Dutch *schieten ;* Anglo-Saxon *scaótan*. Schoolboys generally derive the word from Greek σκεδαννυμι, to put

to flight, or the substantive σκεδασμος.

Skeet (American, New York and Philadelphia), to dart, run along rapidly. " Now then, *skeet !* " From the Dutch *schiet, schieten*, to dart, cast, shoot, throw. Hence probably a *skit*, a flippant sarcasm, *i.e.*, a shot. The word is sometimes confused in Philadelphia with *skeet*, the local vulgar pronunciation of skate.

Skeezicks, skeesicks (American). Bartlett defines this as a mean, contemptible fellow. The writer has always understood it to rather mean a fidgety, fussy little fellow. Both may be right. In Cornwall, *skeese* means to frisk about. *Skicer* is " a lamb which kills itself by excess of activity " (Wright).

Sket (thieves), a skeleton key or pick-lock. From provincial *sket*, a latch, bolt, &c.

S k e w (Harrow), a dunce or ignoramus. Probably from provincial *skew*, one-sided (for *askew*), awry, irregular, as *skew*-brained, odd, fanciful, idiotic ; to *skew* is to fail in construing a lesson. (Old cant), a cup, porringer. Probably old French *escuelle.*

Skid, skiv (popular), a sovereign.

S k i d s (American), volunteers, militiamen. Swedish *skyda*, a guard, protector.

Oh brighten up your uniforms !
Put sweet ile on your har !
Go tell yore culled neighbours,
Go tell it everywhar ;

Dis great organisation
De cream la cream, dey say,
March on for decoration,
De *skids* are out to-day!
When! when! dandies!
Now ain't we hat-que-hay
Sweet goodness' sake!
We take de cake!
De *skids* are out to-day!
— *Negro Minstrel Song.*

Skied (artists), said of a picture which is hung on the upper line at the Exhibition of the Royal Academy.

Had a similar course of conduct been pursued with respect to the disposition of pictures in the actual Salon, many loathsome daubs that disgrace the "line" there would have been sternly *skied*, or, still better, peremptorily rejected. — *Daily Telegraph.*

"The Three Graces," now well placed, had been previously *skied*. But didn't this show that Sir Joshua's work ranked uncommonly high in the opinion of the former hangers.—*Punch.*

Skill (football), when the ball is kicked between posts and thus procures a goal, it is termed a *skill.*

Skilly (common), water-gruel, in the workhouse and prisons.

So much the better for you, I say,
So much the better for you.
If you never act silly, you'll keep off the *skilly*,
That's so much the better for you.
— *Music Hall Song.*

A Lincolnshire term, *skilly*, oatmeal - gruel, from obsolete English *skelly*, thin and light, applied to thin, poor food; also sailor's soup of many ingredients.

Skilly and toke (popular), applied to anything mild, insipid.

The mugs and the jugs never joke, never gag, never work in a wheeze; no, their talk is all *skilly and toke.*—*Punch.*

Skilts (American). "A sort of brown tan trousers, formerly worn in New England, very large and reaching below the knee" (Bartlett). Probably from *kilt, kelt,* undyed cloth made from black and white wool.

Skimmer (public schools), a dive into the water in a slanting direction without going down deep.

Skimmery (Oxford), St. Mary's Hall.

So I swopped the beggar to a *skimmery*-man for a regular slap-up set of pets of the ballet.—*C. Bede: Verdant Green.*

Skin (American cadet), a report; hefty *skin*, a rigorous report. (Popular and thieves), a purse. The term is much used by strolling actors, showmen, &c.

Skin a razor, to (common), to drive a hard and close bargain.

You be blowed, you young Jew sharper! You'd *skin a razor*, that you would. I'll back you for drivin' bargens agen Joe hisself. Now, Mo, boy, fair dealin' with an old customer.—*Savage London.*

Skin disease (popular), four ale, *i.e.*, ale at 4d. a quart.

Skin game (American), a swindle.

Skinned (American and Australian), to keep one's eye *skinned*, to be on the look-out, to have an eye to the main chance. *Skinned*, open. *Cf.* also, "to have one's weather eye open."

Kept his eye *skinned,* an eye that never missed a chance of gain. — *New South Wales Paper.*

Skinner (turf). *Vide* SKIN THE LAMB.

Skinners, a variety of a class of persons in confederacy who make a living by attending at sales. *Vide* KNOCK-OUT.

So they themselves modestly describe their avocation, should a stranger venture to make inquiry; but amongst themselves they are *skinners,* "knock-outs," and "odd-trick men," and they work together in what the elegant language of their profession calls a "swim."—*Greenwood: In Strange Company.*

Skin of the teeth, by the (common), just or barely escaped. Of Biblical origin.

Just *by the skin of its teeth* the Manchester New Year's Meeting was brought to a satisfactory finish, but it was a desperately near thing.—*Sporting Times.*

Skin the lamb (turf), when a nonfavourite wins a race, bookmakers are said to *skin the lamb,* under the supposition that they win all their debts, no person having backed the winner. This has been corrupted into "skinner."

"*Skinned the lamb* through you, old chap," yelled the Coke, grasping the lucky jockey's hand.—*Sporting Times.*

It was at the "colonel" that Mr. B——, in sporting parlance, *skinned the lamb* to the extent of some £1200.—*Saturday Review.*

Also a game at cards; a corruption of *lansquenet.*

Skin, to (Yale University), to obtain a knowledge of a lesson by hearing it read by another.

Also to borrow another's ideas and present them as one's own, to plagiarise, to become possessed of information in an examination or recitation by unfair or secret means. "In our examinations," says a correspondent, "many of the fellows cover the palms of their hands with dates, and when called upon for a given date, they read it off directly from their hands." Such persons *skin.* To *skin* a head, to read a lesson over just before going into class. (Common), to pull off a jersey, to pull off one's bed-clothes. More used at colleges and universities.

Skin your own skunks (American). This highly expressive phrase is applied to any man when he is exhorted to do his own dirty or difficult work without involving another in it.

As a last proof of the absence of characteristic individuality in Mr. L.'s style, we take a sentence from a story of two Indians who were by the ears. "To which Marten replied that Moose might *skin his own skunks,* and fish for his own minnows, and also paddle his own canoe to the devil if it so pleased him"—all of these being approved Indian sayings of high and racy antiquity.—*Review of the Algonquin Legends of New England,* 1884.

Skip a cog (American), to make a mistake in planning machinery, metaphorically to commit any error by want of foresight.

A Virginia preacher who believes in prayer met a bear in the woods the other day, and instead of putting his remedy into effect he jumped from a bluff into Cheat River and swam half a mile. He had never tried prayers for bear, and was a little afraid they'd *skip a cog* some-where.—*American Newspaper.*

Skip out, to (American). This means, like "light out," to escape. It is probably only a variation of that word. To *jump*, to evade, to dodge. Both *skip* and *jump* occur in the fol-ing extract.

A woman who keeps a boarding-house on Larned Street called at police head-quarters yesterday to complain that a gen-tleman boarder had *skipped* her house, leaving a bill unpaid. . . . A man who'll *jump* a board bill and a marriage engage-ment, too, is an outlaw who should be locked up.—*Detroit Free Press.*

It is sometimes said when a man dies that he has *skipped out.*

Skipper (old cant), a barn.

Now let each tripper
Make a retreat into the *skipper.*
—*Broome : Jovial Crew.*

Hotten derives this from Welsh *ysgubor,* pronounced *scybor* or *scibor,* a barn. (Strolling per-formers, &c.), to *skipper* it, to sleep in the open air, or in a rough way. *Skipper,* properly master of a small vessel, is often used to designate a chief or manager, or captain of a ship.

Skipper-birds, keyhole-whistlers (beggars), beggars who have their night's lodging in a barn or outhouse. *Vide* SKIPPER.

Skip the gutter, common phrase. In old cant, a *skip-kennel* was a lackey or servant. *Skip the gut-ter* seems to be only an expres-sion equivalent to "Houp la ! " or " Over she goes ! "

Skip the gutter, tra la la ! Tottie, do you love me?
Ting-ting, *au revoir,* girls there's none above me.
If you like me, tell me so—do not let me linger ;
Tottie, if you love me, oh ! squeeze my little finger !
—*Music Hall Song.*

Skip, to (University), to shirk ; not to attend a lecture, for instance.

Skirk out, to (Winchester Col-lege), to go up town without leave.

Skirk, to (Winchester College), to go into the water without jumping in.

Skitting dealers (old cant), in George II.'s time beggars who professed to be tongueless.

Skittles ! (popular), nonsense !

" Stop, sir ! " shouted the jeweller ; " it's four shillings altogether."
"*Skittles !*" observed the customer.—*Bird o' Freedom.*

S k u l d u g g e r y (American), rascality, treachery. A Western word. From Low Dutch slang (thieves), *schooldogerey, schoel,* a villain.

Skull (American), the head man anywhere. The allusion to *skull* as the brain-case. The Presi-dent of the United States, or a governor.

S k u n g l e (American), a word which "had a run " at the end of the civil war. It meant many things, but chiefly to dis-appear, or to make disappear. Thus a deserter *skungled,* and sometimes he *skungled* a coat or watch.

> Dey shtripped off his coat, and *skungled*
> his boots.
> —*The Breitmann Ballads.*

Skunk, used by all English-speaking people, but originally American. Properly an animal nearly allied to the weasel on the one hand and to the otter on the other, which secretes an extremely fetid liquor as a means of defence. Figuratively a paltry, mean wretch, a contemptible creature.

> Mr. —— (jumping to his feet and speaking very excitedly), "I'd knock your two eyes into one. You're a big fellow, and just come over here." Mr. ——, "Go along." Mr. —— (loudly), "Come over here, you common blackguard; you low *skunk.*" Mr. ——, "Go along out of that." Mr. —— (very excitedly), "You dirty low mean skut. I'd ram my fist through you." (Laughter). Mr. ——, "Go to the coal pits, where you were in England."—*Evening News.*

> He was one of those down-lookin *skunks* I was a-speaking of, and a more endless villain, p'r'aps, there ain't between the blessed poles than he was.—*Sam Slick.*

Sky (thieves and popular), a pocket. Abbreviation of "sky-rocket," which see.

> How little of fun do they have in the main
> At the same old haunts again and again;
> When the Oof Bird's scarce and the land-lady's fly,
> And there isn't a mash with a mag in his
> *sky.*   —*Sporting Times.*

(Westminster School), a blackguard. Said to be from the old gown and town rows in which the Westminsters styled themselves Romans, and their antagonists *volsci*—hence *sky.*

Sky-blue, formerly gin, or London milk.

> Oh ! for that small, small beer anew,
> And (heaven's own type) that mild *sky-blue*
> That wash'd my sweet meals down.
> —*Hood: Retrospective Review.*

Sky farmers (old cant), rogues who go about the country with a false pass extorting money.

Sky-larker (old cant), a journeyman bricklayer that belongs to a gang of housebreakers.

Sky-rocket (thieves), rhyming slang for pocket.

> A slavey piped the spoons sticking out of my *sky-rocket*, so I got smugged.—*Horsley: Jottings from Jail.*

Sky-scraper (common), a tall man. In nautical language, a triangular sail set above the sky-sail.

Skyser, skycer (thieves), a low, mean, sponging fellow. *Vide* SHICER and SHYSTER.

Skyte (Shrewsbury School), explained by quotation.

> At one time there used to be a strong feeling against the day boys, who live or lodge in the town ; and the designation of *skytes* was formerly applied to them.—*Pascoe: Everyday Life in our Public Schools.*

Also used by Scottish schoolboys with the meaning of fool.

> They vituperated the dominies as "auld shoon," "coofs," "blasties," "blethering bellums," "blunties," "chuffies," "gowks," "grunzies," "maggot's meat," *skytes*, and "staumris."—*Daily Telegraph.*

Possibly from Σκυθής, a Scythian, but more probably from provincial English *skite* (literally *cacator*), *skite*, and *skitter*, merdis aspergere(Halliwell). (Popular), a fool. Also "kite."

Sky, to (popular), or *sky* a brown, to toss up with pence. (Cricket, lawn-tennis, &c.), to *sky* a ball, to hit a ball up in the air.

Sugg, with his score at twelve, *skied* a delivery from the Oxonian.—*Sportsman.*

Vide SKIED.

Slab-sided (American), straight, without contour or curve. Generally applied to persons of a prim, stiff, "up and down" figure.

Jack Downing says that Maine is the middle and kernel of real Yankeeism, Rhode Island and Connecticut point to each other as the focus of the article; while the Massachusetts man will tell you that the real *slab-sided* whittler is indigenous to Varmount and New Hampshire. —*New Sloper Sketches, by C. G. Leland (Knickerbocker Magazine*, March 1856).

Slack (nautical), to hold on the *slack*, to skulk, as if holding a slack rope.

Slacks (popular), fatigue trousers drawn over others to keep them clean.

Sailors of all nationalities, and almost every shade of colour between white and black, some smart and attired in their best clothes, others as though but just released from ship duty, unwashed and in their working *slacks* and guernseys.—*James Greenwood: Odd People in Odd Places.*

Slack 'un (pugilistic), a smashing hit, on the *lucus a non lucendo* principle, *i.e.*, a blow *à la* Slack. Jack Slack (champion from 1750 to 1760) was renowned for the force of his hits.

Slam, to (popular), to talk fluently—"he is the bloke to *slam.*" From a term in use among low singers at the East End, by which they denote a certain style of note in chaffinches (Hotten). (Army), to simulate drunkenness. The swaggering soldier whose funds are at a low ebb, and who cannot buy drink, often returns with the symptoms of intoxication, assumed, and a maudlin story of the friends he found who liberally stood treat till he was made thus glorious.

Slaney (thieves), a theatre. Probably a variation from "slang," which see.

Slang (showmen, circus, &c.), a performance, a travelling show of any kind. The *slangs*, however, is the more usual expression, meaning any collection of such shows, or generally the showman's profession. Also a gymnast's performance; a performance at penny "gaffs," *i.e.*, low theatres or music halls. A first *slang*, second *slang*, are respectively first and second performances given the same evening. (Thieves), this or that particular kind of thieving. The word is old.

" How do you work now ?" ".Oh, upon the old *slang*, and sometimes a little bully-prigging."—*Parker: Variegated Characters.*

A watch chain.

Fullied for a clock and *slang.*—*Horsley: Jottings from Jail.*

(Prison), the *slang*. Leg-irons worn by convicts as a special punishment inflicted by the superior authority of one of the Board of Directors, and for one of two offences, an assault upon a prison officer or an attempt to escape. The irons consist of a chain weighing from 7 to 8 lbs., attached to ankle basils, which are rivetted on to the leg ; the chain is some three feet in length, and is carried between the legs, being suspended from a leather waist-belt. The noise the chain makes in walking is evidently the origin of the expression *slangs*. These irons may be carried, according to sentence, from three to six months. They are worn with a parti-coloured dress, alternate stripes of yellow and drab for an escape, of yellow and black for an assault, and the dress is continued for a longer period after the chain is removed. These chains are never taken off day or night, when once rivetted. (Costermongers), counterfeit weights and measures. A *slang* quart is a pint and a half.

There are not half so many *slangs* as there was eighteen months ago.—*May-hew: London Labour and the London Poor.*

Out on the *slang*, going about with a hawker's license. Of gypsy origin.

Matty's got his *slangs* . . . now a *slang* means, among divers things, a hawker's license.—*Charles G. Leland: The English Gypsies.*

The term *slang*, as connected with any kind of theatrical performance or show, is of gypsy origin. The gypsies modified the Hindu *swangia* (*w* easily passes to *l, e.g.*, very, London swells, *vewy;* children, *velly*) into the English *slang*. One thing is certain, it has always been regarded as a gypsy word and used as one of them. It may be remarked that while many of the words such as "multee kerteever," "fake," &c., are to be found in common slang, they are used "on the *slangs*," or among showmen, with special application, and a large proportion of them actually originated in shows whence they passed to common slang. The word, in the sense of language or lingo, has been hitherto used to mean "argot," "vulgar language," "abuse." It is clear that in the sense of argot it is gypsy, the *slang* language originally meaning the language of the *slangs*, or shows, just as "langage de l'argot" meant the language of the brotherhood termed "argot," being afterwards shortened into argot and generalised. But *slang*, as "abuse" or "vulgar language," is of an Anglo-Saxon and Scandinavian source, and while there appears to be every reason to believe that the word *slang*, as tradition asserts, is of gypsy origin, there is also ground to believe that it has drawn something from another source. "*Slang* or vulgar language," according

Q

to Skeat (Etymological Dictionary), "is from the Norwegian *sleng*, a slinging, a device, a burden of a song. *Slengja*, to sling; *slengja kieften*, to *slang*, abuse (literally to sling the jaw); *sleng-jenanm*, a *slang* (*i.e.*, an abusive name); *slengjeord*, an insulting word; all from *slengja*, to sling." This is all, however, based on the assumption that *slang* means nothing but abuse, or "the slings and arrows" of vituperation, while it has never at any time meant that, or even "vulgar language," so much as what in Hindu is called *bhât*, a tongue used for purposes of concealment. A man may be abused to the utmost, and in vulgar language at that, without a word of *slang* being employed; while on the other hand, one might translate the New Testament into Romany, which is the very slang of slangs, or Shelta, or even canting itself, with the utmost propriety. Yet it is very probable that while *slang*, in the sense of *bhât*, or jargon, is of gypsy origin, it owes something in the meaning of "abuse" to a northern source. It may, however, be fairly admitted that the Anglo Saxon *slanga* (*circumactio*), and *toislanga* (*dubietas*) (not noticed by Skeat), somewhat favours the association of *slang* with "double meaning" (Glos. Alf.). To conclude, it should be noticed that the common English word sling is

allied to *slang* as abuse, or depreciatory language. *Slinging off* is much used among the lower orders with the signification of casting insinuations, making innuendoes.

Slangander (American), to slander in a silly manner. *Slangoosing*, women's tittle-tattle, backbiting, or gossip.

There are points on which we disagree,
And I will state the facts,
I don't go round *slangandering*
My friends behind their backs.
—*The Breitmann Ballads.*

Slang and pitcher shop, a (popular), a shop where they sell the commonest and cheapest toys, &c., for Cheap Jacks—knock-'em-downs, prizes to give away, &c. From *slang*, a show, performance, and *pitch*, street performance, or place selected by itinerants of all kinds, Cheap Jacks, &c.

Slang boys (old cant). "Boys of the slang, fellows who speak the slang language, which is the same as flash and cant" (Parker, "Variegated Characters").

Slang cull (cant), master of a show.

Slanging (cant), explained by quotation.

To exhibit anything in a fair or market, such as a tall man, or a cow with two heads, that's called *slanging*, and the exhibitor is called the "slang cull."—*Parker: Variegated Characters.*

The term has now a more extended meaning. *Vide* SLANG.

Slang-tree, the, the stage, the trapeze. *Vide* SLANG. To climb up the *slang-tree,* metaphorically, to make an exhibition of oneself in public.

When I was a girl, and a nice girl I was,
  At least so the young men asserted,
Society then was far better than now,
  If now it's correctly reported.
The ladies of fashion felt no sudden passion
  To flash their good looks on the stage,
No Lily or Langtry would climb up the
    slang-tree,
  In hope to become all the rage.
          —Catnach Broadside.

Slang us your mauley (thieves and roughs), shake hands. A variation of "sling your daddle."

Slang-whanger (common), a scurrilous or abusive person.

The personal disputes of the miserable *slang-whangers.—Irving: Salmagundi.*

Americanism for one who makes too constant a use of slang expressions, more especially applied to members of Congress, and of other legislative assemblies, who are addicted to vulgarity of speech, or are incapable of expressing themselves in refined or decorous language.

Parson Brownlow is a local preacher and editor in Tennessee, and one of the *slang-whangers* of the south-west. *—Harper's Magazine.*

Slant (Australian popular), a chance. An Australian M.P., who had the very unenviable nickname of Rogue, was addressing the electors of Ballarat East, a constituency which included the rough mining population of Bungaree. The miners were there in great force, and would not allow him to get a hearing, until one of their number persuaded the rest "to give the old brute a *slant,*" when the speaker had the courage to address them as "Gentlemen of Ballarat East, and savages of Bungaree."

Slant, to (thieves), to run away.

We have collared the swag—let us *slant.*
          —Sporting Times.

(Nautical), *to slant* across, to sail. "We had a good *slant* across the bay," *i.e.,* a good passage.

Slap, paint for the face, rouge or vermilion to colour the face. In allusion to "slapping," a rough, cheap way of colouring walls in a house. Hence to apply rouge in a hurry.

As a suitable commencement to the vengeful machinations
Directed against Maudie and her "chap,"
She nullified the virtues of her toilet preparations;
Or, in other words, she doctored Maudie's *slap.*
          —Sporting Times.

It is said that when Bath Montague, a famous light comedian, who had had the misfortune to lose his hair when a youth, presented himself to the elder Macready, manager of the Bristol Theatre, the latter was very much disappointed at the appearance of his new recruit. Montague, although a gentleman, had been a brother "faker" with Edmund Kean in

Richardson's show, and amongst other bad habits had accustomed himself to the showman's slang. "When I get my *slap* on," said he, "you'll see that I shall be all there!"

"Good heavens! what does the man mean by *slap*?" inquired Macready, who was as great an autocrat as his famous son.

"Wait till night, Guv'nor, and you'll see!"

When at night an elegant, rosy-cheeked youth, with the limbs of Antinous and the head and front of Apollo, bounded on the stage for Mercutio, the manager was amazed.

"Good God!" he exclaimed, "can this be Montague?"

"No, Guv'nor," replied the airy youth, "I'm Mercutio. It's the fakements—the wig and the *slap*, that does it."

Slap-bang (popular), a low eating-house where you have to pay down money with a *slap-bang*.

They lived in the same street, walked into town every morning at the same hour, dined at the same *slap-bang* every day.— *Sketches by Boz.*

Slap up (common), first-rate, excellent, fine, spruce, fashionable.

Might not he quarter a countess's coat on his brougham along with the Jones arms; or, more *slap up* still, have the two shields painted on the panels with the coronets over. — *Thackeray: The Newcomes.*

"Do you think he's one of our perfession?" inquired the Sandman.

"Bless you! no—that he ain't," re-

turned the Tinker. "He's a reg'lar *slap-up* svell." —*Ainsworth: Auriol.*

A poodle they will play with, just to aggravate their mash;
Their fan is more a weapon than a toy.
They'll sport a *slap-up* carriage if he's not hard up for cash,
And they glory in a much-bebuttoned "boy."
—*Bird o' Freedom.*

Slash (thieves), an outside pocket. Properly a cut in cloth.

Slashers (army), the 28th Foot. The name is accounted for as follows:—"A Canada merchant refused to provide the women and children of the regiment with quarters. This happened in winter, and several persons died in consequence from exposure. Some of the officers of the 28th, however, resolved to exact vengeance. They donned the garb of 'red men,' and bursting in on the merchant while he was at dinner, 'slashed' off one of his ears" (*Chambers's Journal*).

Slate (common), abuse, quarrel.

Really these things are ordered much better in England. After a mutual *slate*, a meeting generally takes place in Prossers' Avenue, or some equally lively location, and the results are somewhat deadly; but not until the next day after the encounter.—*Fun.*

(American political), the list of people recommended to office by a political party. (Old canting), a sheet. In Dutch slang *slaatje, klein linnengood*, small linen.

Slate off (common), to have a *slate off*, to be slightly deranged.

A synonym for "to have a tile loose."

Slater (common), a criticiser. Frequently an airy and uneducated youth, who endeavours to be facetious at the expense of the play and the players.

Slate - smasher (American political), a President or leading statesman who will not attend to the nominations or recommendations of a party.

> If there be anything I like, it is to see a *slate* smashed, or a caucus broken up.— *Cincinnati Weekly Inquirer.*

Slate, to (common), to pelt with abuse, to criticise, to "cut up" in a review. From provincial *slate*, to ridicule, to be angry.

> Wy, it's worth a fair six *d.* a week jest to see 'em a *slating* Old Chips.
> —*Punch.*

> "Don't think much of that," says the pit: "I expect it'll be *slated* all round." The pit was right. The piece was *slated*, *i.e.*, written down by the Press.—*G. Sims: Social Kaleidoscope.*

Also to knock a man's hat over his eyes, or to knock him. (Sporting), to lay heavily against a man or horse in a race.

Slathers (American), abundance, superfluity, "no end of."

> Come along, old fellow, you're looking seedy; I'll tog you out—I'll stand a new rig for you, from a red feather in a new hat all the way down to high-heeled boots. I've got *slathers* of money, and I'm goin' to git more. It's high old times with me now—*slatherin'* old times, I tell you.— *Newspaper.*

In the Midland counties *slatter* means to waste or spill, but the principal meaning of the word is rather slovenliness or carelessness.

Slaughterer (booksellers), a man connected with the book trade, who buys up large cheap lots at sales and reduces the material back to pulp. Also furniture dealers, shoemakers, &c., who buy their goods of poor workmen without having given orders for them, at "starvation prices."

> One East-End *slaughterer* used habitually to tell that he prayed for wet Saturday afternoons, because it put £20 extra into his pocket! It was owing to the damage sustained in the appearance of any painted, varnished, or polished article by exposure to the weather. . . . Under such circumstances . . . the poor workman is at the mercy of the *slaughterer.—Mayhew : London Labour and the London Poor.*

Slaughter-house (popular), the place of business of a "slaughterer," which see.

Slavey (general), maid-servant.

> Or even if I was a *slavey*,
> I'd rather be that than a man,
> I'd get the first dip in the gravy,
> I'd get the first sop in the pan.
> —*Song.*

Applied sometimes to a male.

> Then the boy Thomas, otherwise called *slavey*, may say, there he goes again. . . . The *slavey* has Mr. Frederick's hot water.—*Thackeray : The Newcomes.*

Slaving gloke (old cant), a servant.

Sleeper (American), money which lies unclaimed on a gambling table.

Sleeve - board (tailors), a hard word to pronounce, a jawbreaker.

Slewed (common), intoxicated. A maritime phrase employed by sailors to denote the uneven course of a ship in the act of changing her tack or angle of progress, and thence supposed to describe the attempts made by a drunken man to walk straight. The word was very generally used in America when it was much less known in England. It is, however, of old Yorkshire origin.

I feel my head begin to swim,
I see a knock-kneed Seraphim,
I hear old Nick—I know it's him—
    I'm drunk !

I cannot feel my feet at all,
I cannot see the nearest wall,
I cannot hear the missus call—
    I'm boozed !

I feel that I have lost my purse,
I see my wife—that's much worse—
I hear the echo of my curse—
    I'm *slewed !*

I cannot feel my way upstairs,
I cannot see to say my prayers,
I cannot hear my own choice swears—
    I'm screwed !

I feel a thump upon my head,
I see a bedroom full of bed,
I hear the naughty word *she* said—
    She's drunk !
        —*Sporting Times.*

Also *slued.*

He came into our place one night to take her home ; rather *slued*, but not too much.—*Dickens : Martin Chuzzlewit.*

Slewer (American), a servant-girl ; a vulgar word, only heard among fast young men. *Sloor, slure,* Dutch slang, a poor, common woman.

Slick (studios) is synonymous of rapid, bold, dashing. A picture which is dashed off is some-

times said to be too *slick.* (Popular), fast, an Americanism.

Never trust me if I ever seed a dinner go so *slick !* Yer don't need to carry a nosebag when yer goes out of a night, for yer can stow away enough for a week at wonst.—*Savage London.*

Slick-a-die (thieves), a pocket-book. *Vide* DEE.

Slicker (American cowboys), a coat, greatcoat. From *slick,* old form of *sleek. Slick* is in universal use in New England with the meaning of smooth, shining, hence applied to anything nice, neat, apt, or appropriate.

Now, I'll wear this *slicker* and have a red handkerchief around my neck, and also wear this white hat, and for God's sake don't you shoot me.—*St. Louis Globe Democrat.*

Slick, to (American), to swallow ; *slick it down,* swallow it. Dutch *slikken,* to swallow down. Also, " *slick* it up." Dutch *slik-op,* " one that will lick up, or swallow down, almost everything that's edible " (Sewel, 1757). Swedish *slika,* to lick.

Slide (American), "oh, let it *slide,*" or "let it rip," never mind. Though claimed as an Americanism it is a very old English phrase. Shakspeare in the " Taming of the Shrew " has, " Let the world *slide ;* " Chaucer in the " Clerke's Tale " uses, "Well-nigh let all other cures *slide.*" To " let her rip " is of Western river origin. Steamboats when racing were liable to come to grief on sunken trees and quays, but in the mad excitement of a race no account was taken of these dangers—it was all happy-go-lucky—"let her rip," if it so chances, so long as we out-run the rival boat.

Slim (old cant), punch. "A bob-stick of rum *slim*, a shilling's worth of rum" (Parker, "Variegated Characters"). (American), a *slim* chance, a poor chance.

Slingers (popular), bits of bread floating in tea.

Slinging off (popular), casting insinuations, making innuendoes.

Sling, to (thieves), to throw away so as to get rid of and escape detection. Thus a stolen handkerchief or any ill-gotten gains are "slung" or thrown away when pursuit is close. Also to pass to a confederate.

Watching the "screw," getting his dyspeptical neighbours to *sling* him surplus "eighters" with "puddings" on a Thursday.—*Evening News.*

(Popular), *sling* your daddle, give me your hand, shake hands. To *sling*, to blow the nose with the naked fingers; generally to talk, to fling, as to *sling* patter, *sling* abuse.

But Jack could always *sling* touching patter, you never heard such a crying tongue.—*New South Wales Paper.*

To *sling* one's Daniels, to move on, to run away.

He flung up his window with a furious bang . . . swore in horrible terms that if

we did not that instant *sling our Daniels*—which the Trombone informed me was an equivalent for moving off—he would shy at us every heavenly article of crockery his apartment contained.—*Greenwood: In Strange Company.*

Sling your bunk, go away. Literally "sling up your hammock." Hence to *bunk*, to go. To *sling* one's hook, to be-gone.

I used to go horse-racing once,
At last I made a book.
Though lots of men took people's coin,
And then would *sling their hook*;
I paid my losses like a man,
Till I'd lost about a "thou,"
But I haven't (sym :) haven't (sym :)
I haven't for a long time now!
—*Broadside Ballad.*

Probably originally a sailor's expression, as "sling your bunk," and the phrase would explain itself as the intimation to let go one's hold of a boat by means of a boat-hook.

(Theatrical), to jerk or *sling* a part is to fill a part; to *sling* a nasty part is to play it so well that another performer has a difficulty in rivalling it. (American), to *sling* oneself round on the loose, to go about in a hurried, reckless manner. "*Sling* yourself," "let her *sling*," used in the same slangy way by the Dutch *slingeren*, to hurry about. *Slings* a nasty pen is said of a scurrilous writer. *Slings* a nasty foot, is a good dancer.

"I have rather a notion of Jenny. She *slings a nasty foot*," meaning that she danced very well.—*Sketches Attributed to Davy Crockett*, 1834.

Also to give, deliver.

Teach singing geography school for a change, *sling* a lecture sometimes.—*Mark Twain: Huckleberry Finn.*

Slippery (thieves), soap. Termed by French thieves *glissant*, that is, *slippery*.

Slip, to (popular), to *slip* any one, to give him the *slip*.

He told the other policeman that I had been with another girl, who *slipped* him. —*Standard.*

To *slip* into any one, to attack him.

Slither, to (Australian popular), to hurry away. Old provincial. Also "sliter." *Slither* is probably only another form of "slide," and so may be taken to mean slide off, slip off.

Slither, you and your brother, or they'll nab you both.—*New South Wales Paper.*

Slobber (printers), badly distributed ink is expressed thus. The effect is to show a "rotten" or "scabby" appearance.

Slog (popular), a blow, a fight with the fists. (Public schools), a large slice of anything.

Slogger (cricketers), one in the habit of slogging ; that is, playing in an unscientific manner, striking the ball recklessly ; for instance, hitting to leg or long off a ball which ought to be cut at point. (Popular), a quick worker. (Common), a prizefighter.

The great *slogger* had offered, per advertisement, 1000 dollars to any enterprising boxer who would stand up "foreninst" him for four rounds.—*Evening News.*

Also slugger.

Muse, sing of the merriest mill, between two pugilistic rivals,
That yet has been seen in the ring, in this season of fistic revivals,
Don't warble of Smith and Kilrain, or of Sullivan, known as the *Slugger.*
　　　　　—*Punch.*

Sloggers (Cambridge University), *i.e.*, "slow-goers," the second division of race-boats at Cambridge. Called "torpids" at Oxford.

Slogging (popular), a beating, thrashing, and fight. *Vide* To SLOG.

Slog on (printers). A compositor is said to have a *slog on* when he is making a spurt either for the purposes of making a good bill, or because the work he is engaged on is urgent.

Slog, to (popular), to strike hard, thrash. From the German *schlagen*, or Gaelic *slogan*. *Vide* SLOGGER.

This would produce the immediate entry of the night-officer, while the gentleman who occupied the apartment overhead would shower down sanguinary adverbs, and threaten *to slog* the jealous watchmaker the following day.—*Evening News.*

Slop (popular and thieves), a policeman, from back-slang, *esilop*, police.

I wish I'd been there to have a shy at the *esilops.*—*Mayhew: London Labour and the London Poor.*

They found out as you're the parson as 'tices the gals away,
They say it's through you they peaches, and goes on the "Christian lay."
I dragged you in here and saved you, and sent out a gal for the *slops*,
Ha, they're a-comin', sir !
　　　—*George R. Sims: Ballads of Babylon.*

Then the magistrate rose in a roaring
rage,
And said he, "You may think it fun
The feelings of *slops* to thus outrage ;
Just see what you've been and done."
—*Topical Times.*

Slope (alleged American). Of this
word Hotten says, "It means
to decamp, to run, or rather to
slip away. Some persons think
it came originally from *lope*, to
make off, and that the *s* probably became affixed as a portion of the preceding word, as
let 'slope, let us run. It is purely
an Americanism, and is possibly
but an emendation of our own
word *elope*. Lope, leap, and
elope are kindred." It is a
pity to spoil so much ingenious
guess-work, but *slope* is only
American in being old New
York, or Hollands Dutch. "Hy
sloop weg," he sneaked away, is
given by Sewell (1754) as the
perfect tense of *sluypen*, to
sneak or slink away, and *weg-
sluyping*, an evasion or sneaking off. Lope, leap, and elope
may be near kindred, but they
are only fourth cousins to *slope*.

The defendant came up to him and told
him to pack up and *slope*. He obeyed the
constable's order.—*Standard.*

Sloper's Island (London), the
artisan's village near Lough-
borough Junction was and is
still so called from the frequency
with which tenants "sloped"
without paying their rent. This
was more especially the case at
first, when the houses were let
out as weekly tenements. The
"village" was at one time surrounded by fields, hence its
being called an "island ;" now
it is in the midst of a densely-
populated neighbourhood.

Slop over, to (common). "To
slop over one's talk" is to exhibit exaggerated effusiveness
of manner and words—to draw
the long-bow with caddish
servility or effrontery. A very
subtle expression, and used in
a variety of meanings, all of
them, however, with something
or all of the foregoing in them.

Yes, to judge from the opening chapters,
"When we were Boys" is an admirable
essay in the art of *slopping over*. . . . The
sentimental parent and the schoolboys who
allude to their fathers as "pa" are bad
enough, but the picture of the "unspoiled
London *ingénue*," with her warbling voice,
"luminous figure," and insufferable arch
conversation, is calculated to make the
angels weep.—*Globe.*

The expression is attributed
to Artemus Ward.

Slops (thieves), chests or pack-
ages of tea. "He shook a slum
of *slops*," stole a chest of tea.
(Popular), garments. Anglo-
Saxon *slop*, a covering ; Dutch
sloove. Shakspeare uses this
word with the meaning of
breeches. Old English *slop*,
gown or cassock.

Slosher (Cheltenham College) is
synonymous with "driver," an
assistant in one of the board-
ing-houses whose functions consist in superintending evening
work, dormitories, &c.

Slosh, to (American), to frequent grog-shops in a half-tipsy
state.

Tim isn't good for much now; all the good he ever had in him is fast oozing out; since he's taken to *sloshing* about he hasn't done a lick, and isn't worth a red cent.—*Flush Times of Alabama.*

Slouch (American), no *slouch* on the shoot, an excellent marksman. From English *slouch*, Danish *sloff*, stupid, clumsy man.

Slour, to (thieves), to lock up, fasten up. A *sloured* hoxter, a buttoned-up inside pocket.

No *sloured* hoxter my snipes could stay.
        Fake away !
            —*Ainsworth : Rookwood.*

From provincial *slore*, to grasp, or hold fast.

Slug (American), ingot of gold or silver ; twenty-dollar piece. (Common), glass of spirits.

He ordered the waiter to . . . bring alongside a short allowance of brandy or grog, that he might cant a *slug* into his bread-room.—*Smollett: Sir L. Greaves.*

S l u i c e - h o u s e (pugilistic), mouth.

Sam's *sluice-house* was again severely damaged.—*Pierce Egan : Book of Sports.*

S l u i c e r y (popular), a public-house.

Sluicing one's bolt or **one's gob** (popular), drinking.

Slum (New England), explained by quotation.

That noted dish to which our predecessors of I know not what date gave the name of *slum*, which was our ordinary breakfast, consisting of the remains of yesterday's boiled salt beef and potatoes, hashed up and indurated in a frying-pan.—*Scenes and Characters at College.*

Also known as apple *slum*, a broken-up dish of meat, from its resemblance to *slum* or *slump*, broken, boggy earth, mud, dirt, which used metaphorically in a depreciatory sense seems to have given birth to some of the cant significations of *slum*, as *slum* fake; *slum*, formerly a cant word for a muddy, dark alley; *slummy*, a servant-girl, &c. ; to *slum*, to hide ; *slum*, bad money, *i.e.*, dirt, &c. (Thieves), a chest or package, a package of bank-bills, a trick.

That was his leading *slum*, and pretty well he sponged them too.—*Mayhew: London Labour and the London Poor.*

To fake the *slum*, to do the trick ; up to *slum*, knowing. Also nonsense.

And this without more *slum* began.
            —*Jack Randall's Diary.*

(Prison), a room, a letter. (Punch and Judy), the call. *Slum* fake, a coffin.

Slumgullion (American), a servant, one who represents another.

Should in the Legislature as your *slumgullion* stand,
I'd have a law forbidding Dutch through all this 'varsal land.
            —*The Breitmann Ballads.*

Slumguzzling (American), deceiving, humbugging.

But when Breitmann heard de story
    How de fillage hot peen dricked,
He schwore by Leib und Leben
    He hot rader hafe been licked
Dan pe helpt mit soosh *slumgoozlin;*
    Und 'twas petter to be a schwein
Dan a schwindlin honeyfooglin snake,
    Like dat lyin' Yankee Twine.
            —*The Breitmann Ballads.*

Slummy (popular), a servant-girl.

Slump, to (American), to recite badly, fail, bungle. Properly to sink in mire, hobble, and go about in an awkward manner.

Slum, to (common), to go about low places, in *slums*.

It is stated that for some reason or another this person was in the habit of *slumming;* he would visit the lowest parts of London, and scour the *slums* of the East End.—*Globe.*

(Common and gypsy), to follow. Also to fill, crowd, overdo. A gypsy's remark to C. G. Leland, "This here gav is *slummed* up"—*i.e.*, this town is over full (of gypsies). (University), to keep to back streets to avoid observation. (Theatrical), to act in *slums*, or low pieces, or very small towns. (Thieves), to hide as if in a *slum* or dark alley, pass counterfeit coin, pass to a confederate. To *slum* the gorger, to cheat on the sly.

Slung (tailors), *slung* out on his hands and knees, instantly dismissed.

Slush (American), editorial slang for any kind of indifferent matter, poetry, &c., to fill up with.

Slushy (nautical), the cook; termed also "drainings," and "doctor." From *slush*, grease obtained from boiling salt pork —generally the cook's perquisite. *Slush* or *sludge* is also a term used in Australia.

Sludge-lamps are largely used in back-block stations.—*Keighley Goodchild.*

Smack (tailors), to have a great *smack* for one, to have a great liking for him.

Smack calf's skin, to, to kiss the Book, on taking an oath in a court of justice. "It is held by St. Giles's converts," says Bampfylde Moore Carew, "that to kiss the thumb instead of the calf-skin, or book, is to escape the guilt of perjury."

Small cap O (printers). This is an epithet used to define an under or sub-overseer — from the fact that SMALL CAPS are subordinate to the CAP, but superior to the smaller or lower case letters, *i.e.*, the rank and file.

Small cheque (popular), to take a *small cheque* is to take a dram of liquor. Very common among sailors.

Small potatoes (American), an expression of contempt, small potatoes being of little value, as Bartlett remarks, except for feeding hogs and cattle. The full phrase is, "Very *small potatoes*—few in a hill, rotten in the middle, pithy at both ends— mighty stringy at that—the hills a great way apart—a great way to go and dig them—and nobody to do it!" The man who fulfils all these conditions may be set down as of the minimum quality of *small potatoes.*

Smalls (Oxford University), the first examination at Oxford, one of little difficulty.

Mr. Bouncer pointed to Mr. Four-in-hand Fosbrooke . . . on his way from the schools, where he was making a very laudable (but, as it proved, futile) endeavour to get through his *smalls*, or, in other words, to pass his little-go examination.—*C. Bede: Verdant Green.*

Cramming for *smalls*. . . . Julia reminded her that *smalls* was the new word for little go.—*Reade: Hard Cash.*

(Theatrical), explained by quotation.

Minor companies with "fit ups," that is, companies carrying their own theatre, comprising scenes, props, curtains, wings, &c., who visit small towns and villages for one-night performances, are said to be "doing the *smalls*."—*Globe.*

Smash (prison), tobacco. Probably so called from being passed in surreptitiously. *Vide* To SMASH. To sling the *smash*, to bring in and give tobacco. *Smash*, also loose coin or change. (General), a *smash* means a break-up, and is generally applied to monetary affairs; sometimes it means to come to grief generally. (Popular) mashed potatoes.

The sweep asked him what he was going to have. "A two-and-half plate and a ha'p'orth of *smash*."—*Mayhew: London Labour and the London Poor.*

(American), *vide* quotation of SMILE.

Smashed (army), cashiered, reduced to the ranks. In general parlance bankrupt, ruined.

Smasher (thieves), one who passes counterfeit money or forged notes. *Vide* To SMASH.

And then he proceeded to inform me that the individual mentioned on the paper was a *smasher*, or in other words, a dealer

in counterfeit coin or "sours."—*J. Greenwood: Tag, Rag, & Co.*

A cadee *smasher*, formerly a rogue who professed to be a tout to innkeepers, but who occasionally acted as a *smasher*. There is a well-known proverb, "Once a *smasher* always a *smasher*," showing how difficult is the reclaiming of this class of criminal.

Smash feeder (thieves), a Britannia metal spoon, from which the best imitation shillings are made.

Smash, to (thieves), explained by quotation.

Take the base coin, for example—he is always in want of recruits. Old hands, however skilled in *smashing—i.e.*, passing bad money—will not do for him, they are known to the police.—*Thor Fredur: Sketches from Shady Places.*

To *smash*, literally to break coin by changing it. (Hence *smash*, change.) In French slang "casser une pièce," to change a coin. (Lawn-tennis), striking the ball hard.

Lobbing, too, has been greatly improved, and altogether the back-court player, if he possesses the power to *smash* a short return, can more than hold his own against the volleyer.—*Pastime.*

Smear gelt (old cant), bribe money, synonymous with "palm oil."

Smeller (popular and thieves), the nose.

Come on, half-a-dozen of ye, and let me have a rap at your *smellers*.—*C. Bede: Verdant Green.*

Also a blow on the nose. German cant has *schmecker* (lit. "smeller"), for nose. Italian cant, *odoroso*, lit. "full of smell," or *soffiante*, blowing.

Smelling cheat (old cant), nose, garden, nosegay. *Vide* CHETE.

Smelling committee (American). " Persons appointed to conduct an unpopular investigation. The phrase originated in the examination of a convent in Massachusetts by legislative order" (Bartlett). To which may be added, that those who went "smelling about" the convent did not find the slightest trace of the alleged immoralities which they sought, while it came immediately to light that one of them was accompanied on this excursion by a kept mistress.

Smelt (thieves), half-a-guinea. (American), half-eagle, five dollars. In Dutch slang *smelt* is tin.

Smiggins (thieves), formerly the soup given on board the hulks.

Smile (American), a drink of any alcoholic liquor.

Your confirmed cock-tail drinker is not to be confounded with the common sot. He is an artist. . . . With what exquisite feeling will he graduate his cap, from the gentle *smile* of early morning to the potent "smash" of night.—*F. Francis : Saddle and Moccasin.*

Smile, to (American), to take a drink of wine, beer, or spirits.

Because men generally smile while so doing.

"Say, stranger! won't you *smile?*" (I had been smiling unremittingly, I could not help it. But in America *smiling*, "seeing a man," and "liquoring up," are all one.)—*Richard A. Proctor: Notes on Americanisms.*

Smish (old cant), a shirt or chemise.

Smiter (old cant), the arm; a sword, corruption of *scimitar*.

Then, Basket, put thy *smiter* up and hear; I dare not tell the truth to a drawn sword.—*B. Jonson: Tale of a Tub.*

Smock-face (popular), a white face, a face without any hair.

Smoke (popular), an appellation given to London for obvious reasons.

I say, chum, do you know red-headed Jim, in your party? He is from the *smoke.—Evening News.*

Smoker or **smoke - shell** (Royal Military Academy), a chamber-pot.

Smouch (popular), one who obtains anything by unfair means, a cheat, a Jew.

Vhile I, like de resht of ma tribe, shrug and crouch,
You find fault mit ma pargains and say I'm a *smouch.*
—*Ingoldsby Legends.*

From Dutch *smous, smousje*, a German Jew. "So called because many of them being named Moses, they pronounce this name *Mousyee*, or according to Dutch spelling *Mousje*" (Sewell). *Smouch* seems to be allied to the Boer's term *smous* or *smouse* for a trader.

Smouch, to (old cant), still used in America. *Vide* SMOUCH. To obtain by cunning, to steal; also to take unfair advantage of one.

"Why, Aunty, I don't think there's ten." "You numbskull, didn't you see me count 'em?" "I know, but"—— "Well I'll count 'em again." So I *smouched* one, and they come out nine, same as the other time. Well, she was in a tearing way—just a trembling all over, she was so mad.—*The Adventures of Huckleberry Finn.*

Smous (thieves). *Vide* SMOUCH.

Smouting (printing), casual work away from office—now called "grassing." "Workmen, when they are out of constant work, sometimes accept of a day or two's work or a week's work at another printing-house; this by-work they call *smouting*" (R. Holme, 1688). The fine for *smouting* was half a benvenue.

Smouze, to (American), "to demolish as with a blow" (Bartlett). To smash, German *schmeissen.*

Smug (schools), an untidy (properly *smug* means tidy) fellow who does nothing but work. At the university an ill-mannered, ill-dressed, probably poor and generally unpopular student. (Popular and thieves) explained by quotation. From boy's term meaning to steal playthings when the game is out.

After that he used to go *smuggling,* running away with other people's things. —*Mayhew: London Labour and the London Poor.*

Smuggings, snatchings, or purloinings; shouted out by boys when snatching the tops, or small play property, of other lads, and then running off at full speed (Hotten).

Smuggled (schools), pencil sharpened at both ends.

Smug, to (schools), to keep indoors, hard at work. (Thieves), to steal, to apprehend. From the meaning of *smugged,* comfortably hidden.

Then two or three more coppers came up and we got *smugged* and got a sixer each.—*Horsley: Jottings from Jail.*

Smut (popular), a copper boiler.

Snabble, to (old cant), to steal, plunder, sometimes to kill. *Snabble,* as if snapping up with the bill of a bird. *Snabel,* Swedish and Norse; hence Yorkshire, a bird's bill.

From prigs that *snabble* the prancers strong
To you of the peter lay,
I pray now listen awhile to my song
How my bowman he kick'd away.
—*Harlequin Sheppard, acted at Drury Lane,* 1724.

Also to apprehend, imprison.

But filing of a rumbo-ken,
My bowman is *snabbled* again.
—*Frisky Moll's Song, from " Harlequin Sheppard," acted at Drury Lane,* 1724.

Snack (Winchester College), a racket ball.

Snaffled (popular and thieves) arrested, as if by the application of the snaffle-bit.

Snaffler (old cant), a highwayman. From old provincial *snaffle*, to steal, rob.

Snaffling-lay (old cant), highway robbery.

I thought by your look you had been a clever fellow, and upon the *snaffling-lay* at least, but I find you are some sneaking-budge rascal.—*Fielding: Amelia.*

Snag-catcher (common), a dentist.

Snaggling (thieves), angling for poultry.

Snag on, to (American), to attach oneself to anybody.

Two ladies had just *snagged on* to me. —*Howells: April Hopes.*

Snake (tailors), a skein of silk. (Popular), to give one a *snake*, to vex him.

Snake in his boot, a (American). One of the horrible symptoms of *delirium tremens* is the fancy that the sufferer is surrounded by snakes and reptiles, among other horrors.

For instance, alcohol, which produces the phenomena humorously designated by our American friends as *snakes in one's boots*, on the other hand, if used medicinally, is death on snakes, or rather on snake poison.—*Globe.*

Snakes (society), "a caution to *snakes*," something very singular.

Snakes in Virginny, as sure as there's (American), equivalent to declaring the absolute certainty of anything. "As sure as death or taxes," "As sure as I'm a sinner," "As sure as green corn in July," are synonymous.

Snakesman, little (thieves). "A boy thief, lithe and thin, and daring, such a one as housebreakers hire for the purpose of entering a small window at the rear of a dwelling-house" (Greenwood). Most probably a corruption of *sneaksman*, which see.

Snake, to (London slang), to steal in a wary manner. A metaphor on supposed wariness of snakes. More probably a corruption of *sneak*, which see. This term probably was imported from America, where it is used also with the meaning of to take.

Well, it beats me, and *snaked* a lot of letters out of his pocket.—*Mark Twain: Huckleberry Finn.*

(Billiards), to *snake* the show, to win the pool at billiards.

Snam, to (thieves), to snatch, rob from the person. Also stealing anything that may be lying about and making off rapidly.

Snap (American), in England *snaps* is a share or a chance in a job; in the United States the word is applied to a scheme, plan, project, or device.

Free rides to brides is the latest "advertising *snap*" of Canada railways. Brides encumbered with "children over four years of age," however, have to weigh out the full fare.—*Bird o' Freedom.*

Snap company, a small, indifferent theatrical troupe. One

gathered for an occasion, as if at a *snap*. An itinerant troupe.

One night, during the engagement of a *snap* company at the Chestnut Street Theatre, a little boy came down the stairs from the gallery during the first act, and inquired for the manager. The manager was not in at the time, and the doorkeeper inquired why he wished to see him. "Because," returned the lad, "I want my money back." "Aren't you satisfied with the play?" was asked. "Oh, yes," he replied. "The play's good enough, but the fact is I'm afraid to stay up there all by myself."—*Chicago Tribune.*

To give the *snap* away means to betray a plot, so as to lose the profits.

When Dowling heard of Joe's stubbornness he knew there would be a raid. He removed his furniture, and when the "cops" came around they found nothing. Harrison blamed Dumphy for giving the *snap* away to Dowling, and determined to get even with the latter.—*Chicago Tribune.*

A soft *snap*, a profitable affair, an easy position, a good thing, anything worth having. From provincial English *snap*, catch, piece, share.

Frank, old pard! I just want fifty dollars for an hour or two—give it to you again to-night. I've got a soft *snap* on, can't miss it.—*F. Francis: Saddle and Moccasin.*

(Popular), on the *snap*, or looking out for *snaps*, watching for windfalls or odd jobs. In the quotation it refers to eating and drinking.

I sorntered about *on the snap.—Punch.*

(Parliamentary), *snap* division, a division taken by surprise in a thin or unprepared House.

Snapped (American), drunk; probably from *schnapps*, often pronounced *snaps.*

Snapper (American), an impudent tattler. *Snaps vocren*, to be full of impertinent talk; *snappen*, to chatter impudently. Snippish, snappish, and snobbish have much in common, and the Dutch *snappery*, idle, foolish gossip, is very suggestive of snobbery in a colloquial sense. Feeble as this etymology may be, it is worth as much as that which would derive snob · from *sine obolo* and *sine nobilitate*, which as feats of philology may be ranked with Horne Tooke's extraction of Fo-hi from Noah. Also "the snapping turtle."

Snapper soup, pepperpot, tripe and oysters, chicken salad. Be pleased to have you call.—*Philadelphia Press.*

Snapperhead (American), an impertinent fellow, one who snaps or answers too quickly or impudently.

"Don't you 'woman' me, you young *snapperhead*," said Mrs. Wayback, eyeing him with disfavour. "I'm a lady, an' don't you forget it," and she flounced out.

Snapps (East End), spirits; German *schnapps.*

Snarler (popular), a dog.

Snatcher (thieves), a thief of the younger and less experienced type.

Snatcher, body (journalistic), a reporter or special correspondent of a newspaper who fastens on any eminent man whose actions are prominent, &c.

The *Body Snatcher* of the *D. T.* (*Daily Telegraph*) has, we hear, been closeted with his "Peerage" and "Lemprière" ever since.—*The London Figaro.*

Snavel. *Vide* RUNNING SNAVEL.

Sneak (cricket), a *sneak*, "daisy trimmer," "grub," "daisy cutter" or "undergrounder," is a ball bowled all along the ground instead of with a fair pitch. Though perfectly allowable, they are considered bad form. *Vide* AREA-SNEAK.

Sneaking-budge (thieves), thieving, pilfering.

Wild . . . looked upon borrowing to be as good a way of taking as any, and, as he called it, the genteelest kind of *sneaking-budge.*—*Fielding: Jonathan Wild.*

Sneaks (thieves), explained by quotation.

That way, and in less time than it takes a healthy pulse to beat thirty, we are in the regions of gloom, and our footsteps (or rather mine are—my guide wore a pair of what, in criminal phraseology, are known as *sneaks*, and are shoes with canvas tops and indiarubber soles) are trespassing on a stillness instantly suggestive of death in the midst of life.—*Greenwood: In Strange Company.*

Sneaksman or **sneak-thief** (thieves), a petty thief, a shoplifter.

Until at last there was none so knowing,
No such *sneaksman* or buzgloak going,
Fake away !
—*Ainsworth: Rookwood.*

Sneak, to (general), to steal; usually applied to pilfering, stealing in areas, linen from lines, in shops, &c.

VOL. II.

He was always hungry, and every time he acted as orderly managed to *sneak* from the tray the particles of food returned by prisoners whose appetites were not of the usual ravenous nature of the ordinary convict on "public works."—*Evening News.*

"You're the bloke as *sneaked* the kicksies," says he.—*Bird o' Freedom.*

Sneeze-lurker (thieves), a thief who throws snuff in a person's eyes in order to rob him. Hence probably the expression "to give snuff," beat, ill-treat.

Sneezer (thieves), snuff-box, but become obsolete with the common use of the article. A pockethandkerchief.

Fogles and fawnies soon went their way
To the spout with the *sneezers* in grand array.
—*Ainsworth: Rookwood.*

(Pugilistic), the nose, a blow on the nose. (Tailors), anything that puzzles. (Army), a very strict officer or martinet. (American), a dashing, thoroughgoing fellow. Alluding to a horse's snorting. Compare with SNORTER.

Snell-fencer (streets), a streetsalesman of needles. *Vide* SNELLS.

Snells (popular), needles; from the English *snell*, brisk, piercing.

Snick-fadge (thieves), petty thief. From to *snick*, to cut, hence to steal, and *fadge*, a farthing.

Snicktog (thieves), to go shares. To *snick*, to cut, and *tog*, clothes, coat.

R

Snid (thieves), a sixpence.

Sniddy, snidey (popular and thieves), bad, unfavourable. A form of " snide."

Since Bill George was nabbed for liftin' them sax things is been very *sniddy*, so you'll be glad to learn as I have got on a new hook.—*Evening News.*

(Army), dirty.

Snide (common), bad, base, spurious, false, mean ; as *snide* coin, *snide* fellow. Also, "he's a *snide.*"

Sometimes the police will help the thieves by getting *snide* witnesses . . . who will swear anything according to instructions.—*Rev. A. Mursell : Shady Pastorals.*

But no matter how often they sold him,
He failed to perceive that their motives were *snide*,
For he always believed what they told him.
—*Sporting Times.*

" Say ! you, look here, now ! " he would explain to a native, " these 'ere men don't want none of your *snide* outfits, but just good bronchos, and a waggon, and strong harness."—*F. Francis : Saddle and Moccasin.*

In Dutch, *snyden* means to swindle, "as some inn-keepers do," meaning that they cut, or, as Americans would say, "chisel" or "gouge" strangers. "Men *snydt* de luyden lustig in die herberg," that tavern is a swindling shop. *Snood*, in Dutch, means base, sordid, villainous ; German *schnöde*.

Snide-pitcher (thieves), one who gets a living by passing base coin. Such are looked down upon by thieves as of the lowest rank of the criminal fraternity.

Snide-pitching (thieves), passing base coin. *Vide* SNIDE.

Up comes old Andy, too, and says, " This 'ere young man's bin a *snide-pitching* with me, too," and he fishes out the duffer as I'd give 'im unbeknown.—*Sporting Times.*

Snifter (American), to take a *snifter*, to take a drink ; from *sniff*, to smell something, to take a sniff at some perfume. We find in English *snift*, to snuff.

I would sooner *snift* thy farthing candle mad.—*D'Arblay : Camilla.*

Snip (general), a tailor. From to *snip*, to cut with scissors.

"Alton, you fool, why did you let out that you were a *snip?*" " I am not ashamed of my trade."—*C. Kingsley : Alton Locke.*

(Turf), information as to the certainty of a horse winning a race.

D. is in glorious form with his wires, and is certain to keep it up next week at the above meetings, for which he knows of several *snips.*—*Sporting Life.*

Common), to go *snip*, to go shares. Literally to divide, as with scissors.

(American), a small boy or girl, a small person. Generally in a contemptuous sense, as if the *snip* were conceited and ignorant. The writer supposed at first that this was derived from *snip*, a tailor's cutting ; but he finds that in Bargoensch, or Dutch thieves' slang, the word means not only a young person, but also a heedless or foolish one. Shakspeare uses the word *snipe* with the meaning of fool, blockhead. In French *bécasse* (snipe) is a stupid girl.

Snipe (common), a long bill, or account. Evidently a play on a snipe's long bill. Also an attorney, possibly because of his "comptes d'apothicaire," or very long bills.

(London), gutter-*snipe*, a street arab.

Snipes (thieves), scissors for cutting off pockets. From to *snip*, to cut off with scissors.

Snipe, to (American), to pilfer.

Yes, it is bad indeed in some respects. I have to buy my own tobacco now; Or beg it when I can from other boys, In place of *sniping* it from the old man's box.
—*New York Sentinel.*

Snippeny, snippy, sniptious, snippish (American), used in several ways; vain, conceited.

Snippeny folks are not popular, and E. P. Roe says that almost anything will be forgiven sooner than thinking one's self better than other people.—*Detroit Free Press.*

Also given to petty criticism, mincing and pert observation.

Snitch (old cant), nose.

Snitched (horsedealers), explained by quotation.

A horsedealer . . . was showing a farmer a horse that was *snitched*, that is, glandered. It was a fine-looking animal and made up for sale. It was jigged, digged, and figged.—*Hindley: Life and Adventures of a Cheap Jack.*

Allied to provincial English to *snite*, to blow the nose, or the cant term *snitch* for nose,

the allusion being to the running from the nose. (Thieves), caught, arrested, *i.e.*, tied up. To *snitch* is provincial English.

Snitcher, snitch (thieves), an informer, one who turns Queen's evidence, one who causes one to be "snitched," *i.e.*, arrested, more probably from cant *snitch*, nose, a "nose" being a spy, informer.

Then your blowing will wax gallows haughty,
When she hears of your scaly mistake,
She'll surely turn *snitch* for the forty
That her Jack may be regular weight.
—*Lord Byron: Don Juan.*

"In Scotland," says Hotten, "*snitchers* signifies handcuffs."

Snitch, to (thieves), to give information to the police, to turn approver. Hence to arrest.

Snivel, done a (tailors), wept, or told a pitiful tale.

Snob (University), a townsman as opposed to a gownsman. (Common), a shoemaker.

A shoemaker charged with removing a front tooth belonging to a brother *snob*, against his will and consent, was ordered by a bench of magistrates to pay the complainant 10s. as compensation for the loss of the ivory.—*Jack and Jill.*

(Marlborough College), game of *snob*, a kind of rough game of cricket, such as playing two together or at tip and run.

Snobbery, hiding the (tailors), covering up the bad trade. Snob is a journeyman shoemaker, also one who works for lower wages in a strike; hence bad work is expressed by the term *snobbery*.

Snob's-boot (tailors), sixpence.

Snob's-duck (popular), stuffed leg of mutton.

Snob-stick (popular), a workman who refuses to join in strike. Also termed a " snob."

Snob, to (tailors), to do work badly, or in a slovenly manner. *Snob* is a shoemaker or cobbler, the phrase therefore exactly corresponds to the French *saveter*, which means to do work badly.

Snock him on the gob, to (American), to hit him on the mouth. *Gob* is common English slang for mouth. *Snock*, provincial English for a blow.

Snoddy (popular), a soldier.

Snooker (Royal Military Academy), a newly joined cadet-student of the fourth class. Possibly from to *snook*, to lean the head forward in walking, in allusion to awkwardness in drill.

Snooks (common), the name of an imaginary person given as a derisive reply to an idle question, or when the name of the perpetrator of some action is refused.

Snooping, to snoop (American), to pry into, to go about picking up bits of food. " I think it may be granted by everybody that of all petty presumers there are none like those who are habitually given to what New York Americans call *snooping*, a word derived from the Dutch *snoepen*, and meaning the going about and sticking one's nose into all kinds of places where it has no business to be."

Snooze (thieves), a bed.

Snoozey (old cant), a night constable.

Snoozing-ken (old cant), lodging-house or brothel.

Snopsy, snops (American), *schnapps*, *i.e.*, gin.

Oh, I can jump, an' I can hop, an' take a little *snopsy*,
Oh, I can sleep just like a top, bekase my name am Topsy.
                              —*Topsy's Song.*

Snork (Shrewsbury School), to do the whole of a paper in an examination. To beat another in argument or repartee.

Snorter (society), a man who excels in anything. From the snorting of a high-mettled horse. (Cricket), a *snorter*, "corker," "stringer," or "clinker," a very hard ball to play; one that puzzles the batsman. (Popular), the nose, a blow on the nose; a regular *snorter*, great hurry.

Snort, to (Australian), to be enraged at a thing, to refuse to do a thing. This is a metaphor taken from observing the horse. If a horse is afraid to do a thing—such as to swim a river, to go too near the edge of a precipice, to carry "game," or the like, he starts back and *snorts*, hence the expression. The French *renâcler* (to snort) is used metaphorically in like manner, and supports the explanation.

Snot (thieves), a gentleman. (Popular), a term of opprobrium. Much used by schoolboys.

Snot-rag (popular), pocket-handkerchief.

Snotted (popular), being reprimanded, hauled over the coals. This corresponds to the French *mouché*, used in the same metaphorical sense.

Snotter (thieves), a pickpocket whose specialty is stealing silk handkerchiefs. *Snotter*-hauling, stealing pocket-handkerchiefs.

You could make a fair thing by *snotter*-hauling even if you cannot get on at fly-buzzing.—*Temple Bar: Six Years in the Prisons of England.*

Snottie (naval), a midshipman.

Snottinger (popular), a pocket-handkerchief.

Snout (prison), tobacco; a playful allusion to "pig-tail," roll of twisted tobacco. Prisoners will brave all risks to get it. The most elaborate and Machiavellian plots are always in progress in a convict prison to suborn officers, and to tempt them to become the intermediary between the caged bird and his friends outside. The officer who yields becomes "Mr. Wright" (which see), and the bearer of a clandestine letter or "stiff" (which see), his credentials; and armed with this he calls when off duty on the prisoner's friends, who, if they are well-to-do, pay cash down as a bribe. The traitor warder buys tobacco at the market rate, charging the prisoner about £5 per pound, over and above the personal douceur he receives. The tobacco is smuggled into the prison in small quantities, and passed by means of "trafficking" (which see) from the wholesale possessor to purchasers in exchange for food. Tobacco has also a price current in prison in food, generally bread, but meat, cheese, potatoes are also passed. It is always used in chewing. The term is also used by itinerants with the meaning cigar.

Snow (thieves and tramps), linen hung out to dry on hedges or lines. The allusion is obvious.

Snowball (popular), a negro. In French, "boule de neige."

Snow-dropper or **gatherer** (thieves and tramps), a thief who steals linen hung out to dry.

Snow-dropping (thieves), explained by quotation.

"What do you mean by *snow-dropping*?" "Oh," said he, "that's a poor game. It means lifting clothes off the bleaching line or hedges. Needy-mizzlers, mumpers, shallow blokes and flats may carry it on, but it's too low and paltry for you."—*Temple Bar: Six Years in the Prisons of England.*

Also "going *snowing.*"

Snowy (thieves and tramps), linen.

My pals used to send stiffs to the schoolmaster, saying that I was wanted at home ; but instead of that we used to go and smug *snowy* that was hung out to dry.—*Horsley: Jottings from Jail.*

Snuff-box (popular), the nose.

There's a crack on your *snuff-box.*—*C. Bede: Verdant Green.*

Snuff it, to (popular), to die, like a candle snuffed out. In French slang "moucher sa chandelle" means the same.

And I mean to live a good bit longer yet. Josh Heckett isn't going to *snuff it* just for a crack on the head.—*G. R. Sims : Rogues and Vagabonds.*

Snuffler (common), a religious canter.

You know I never was a *snuffler;* but this sort of life makes one serious, if one has at all any reverence at all in one.—*T. Hughes: Tom Brown at Oxford.*

Snuff, to give (popular), to ill-treat, thrash. Possibly alluding to the pain caused by snuff thrown into the eyes of a person for a felonious purpose. French slang has the corresponding phrase, "foutre (donner) or coller du tabac," and the police expression, "passer au tabac," that is, ill-treat a prisoner so as to make him confess, or from obsolete *snuff,* resentment, anger, used in the phrase to take *snuff,* to be angry like a man snorting with vexation.

Snuff, up to (general), knowing, expert, experienced in the ins and outs of life. Literally "up to scent," like a good dog. *Snuff* is equivalent to scent, smell.

He knew well enough
The game we're after : zooks, he's *up to snuff !*
—*John Poole : Hamlet Travestie.*

Queer start that 'ere, but he was one too many for you, warn't he? Up to *snuff* and a pinch or two over.—*Dickens : Pickwick Papers.*

I am pretty well up to newspaper *snuff,* as it is, sir.—*Sporting Times.*

To put *up to snuff* is to initiate into mysteries of any kind, and generally to instruct in, make expert.

He was some ten or eleven years my senior . . . but having travelled all my lifetime, was better *up to snuff* than an ordinary man would be at fifty.—*Hindley : Life and Adventures of a Cheap Jack.*

The thieves knew where to draw the line, and chucked the lot away in the garden, among the other weeds. They were *up to snuff,* but not to tobacco in this form.—*Punch.*

Snuffy (popular), tipsy.

Snuggeries (London), explained by quotation.

Generally at one end of the hall is a long strip of metal counter, behind which superbly - attired barmaids vend strong liquors. Besides these there are *snuggeries,* or small private apartments, to which bashful gentlemen desirous of sharing a bottle of wine with a recent acquaintance may retire. — *Greenwood: Seven Curses of London.*

Soaker (popular), a pelting downpour of rain.

That countryman was right when he prognosticated a *soaker.* The only individual I met on the road going my way was a timid-looking old gentleman in a phaeton, who was well protected from the rain with a mackintosh, knee-wrap, and a gig umbrella.—*J. Greenwood: Tag, Rag, & Co.*

Also a confirmed tippler.

An old *soaker* who was a pretty frequent attendant at the Bell, at Bromley.—*Sporting Times.*

Soak, to (American), turn, change gradually. This is old English.

Said Turpin, " It is time to go,
I've a very fine plant, boys, I know ;
While Oliver *soaks* pale,
We will rob the royal mail,
Before the cock begins for to crow."
—*Broadside: Dick Turpin.*

Hence to exchange, barter, pawn.

The two youths made a call and the watch was *soaked* with a pawnbroker, and $20 obtained on it.—*Daily Inter-Ocean.*

Soap (common), explained by quotation.

Flattery is the confectionery of the world. In polite society it goes by the name of *soap*, and in general is designated "soft sawder."—*Diprose: Laugh and Learn.*

(American), money. (Royal Military Academy), cheese.

Soap-and-bullion (nautical). A
sailor's food is oftentimes of the poorest, not to say revolting description, and Jack has not been slow to signify his disgust thereat. The following are some of his choicest terms for such dainties : — " Lobscouse, dandy funk, dogsbody, sea-pie, choke-dog, twice laid, hishee-hashee, *soap-and-bullion*, dough Jehovahs, tommy, soft tack."

A thin watery soup served out on some vessels.

I have known many a strong stomach, made food-proof by years of pork eaten with molasses, and biscuit alive with worms, to be utterly capsized by the mere smell of soup-and-bouilli. Jack calls it *soap-and-bullion*, one onion to a gallon of water, and this fairly expresses the character of the nauseous compound.—*Clark Russell: Sailor's Language.*

Soap-crawler (popular), a sycophant.

Stale, too, orful stale, my young josser.
It's wot all *soap-crawlers* say,
If a party 'as " go " and " high sperrits "—
percise wot you praise me for, hay ?—
If he " can laugh aloud," as you say I can,
better than much finer folk,
Will you ticket 'im " vulgar," for doin' it ?
Oh, you go 'ome and eat coke !
—*Punch.*

Soapers (American thieves), men
who practise the soap trick. " It is a simple conjuror's trick, and it is not difficult to understand. A number of cakes of soap are wrapped each in a piece of paper, and mixed up together in a travelling-bag, suspended by a strap round the neck of the operator. A five-dollar bill is wrapped around one of the cakes, and enveloped in the paper, like the others. It is then thrown into the bag, after having been marked by the thumb-nail, and the crowd are invited to pick it out of the lot at the cost of one dollar. Of course, the cake containing the money is not thrown into the bag at all, but is palmed (substituted by sleight of hand) by the head of the firm, who gives another cake, similarly

marked. When the capper (confederate) buys a cake, he draws a prize " (Confidence Crooks, *Philadelphia Press*).

Soap, to (common), to flatter.

And the tailor and robemaker, between washings with the invisible soap, so visibly *soaped* our hero in what is understood to be the shop sense of the word.—*C. Bede: Verdant Green.*

(American), to bribe.

If a knock down were needed in a case, Griffin would perform it promptly and expertly. The bloods paid the fine, and *soaped* Griffin besides.—*New York Herald.*

Soc (printers), this is an abbreviation of the word "Society." To be a member of the *Soc.* (compositors'), hence not a "rat."

Sock (Eton), edibles of various kinds privately imported.

The consumption of *sock*, too, in school was considerable, and on occasion very conspicuous.—*Pascoe: Everyday Life in our Public Schools.*

Hotten says the word is still used by the boys of Heriot's Hospital School at Edinburgh, and signifies a sweetmeat, being derived from the same source as "sugar," "suck." Swedish *sock*, sugar. (Popular), credit. (Common), to give one *sock* or *socks*, to thrash him. From provincial English to *sock*, to strike.

Sockdolager (American), a word inadequately explained by its imperfect resemblance to doxology. A *socdolager*, says Bartlett, is a conclusive argument, a "settler," and as that ends

everything, and as the doxology is sung at the end of the religious service, ergo, they are the same. As it is very commonly applied to a settling blow—two out of three of Bartlett's illustrations of it refer to such—it probably owes its beginning to *sock*, to strike. In Dutch a *zaakdadelyk* (or *dadelyke-zaak*) means "a plain case," admitting no further argument ; but it is very doubtful whether this has anything to do with it. A *zakdualertje*, a bag of dollars, would come much nearer than "doxology"—and as it is an effective settler to most disputes, a great deal might be said in its favour, but similarity of sound and even of meaning is not always conclusive. The most probable derivation is *sock*, a hard blow, and *dole*, to give. It is, however, possible that the origin of the much discussed word is the Iceland *saukdolgr*, which Jonæo, in the glossary appended to the Latin version of Nialls Saga, defines as meaning, among other things, *dwellum*, a sudden attack, also a bad affair, evil, and another authority gives it as impetus. *Saukdolgr* is pronounced almost exactly like *sockdolager*. It probably came from the Swedes of Philadelphia, as it is an old word in America.

And the thunder would go rumbling and grumbling away, and quit—and then rip comes another flash and another *sockdolager*. — *Mark Twain: Huckleberry Finn.*

Sam caught him a tremendous blow, clean bang in the left eye, one that nearly knocked him off his pins. Every man in the room heard that *sockdolager* as plainly as he saw it.—*Bird o' Freedom.*

Socker (public schools), football played according to the Association Rules.

Socketer (popular), one who obtains money, "socket-money," by threats of exposure. In French *chanteur.*

Socket-money (popular), a kind of black-mail extorted by threats of exposure, especially by accusations of an unnatural crime. Probably from *soke*, a payment made to the lord by his tenant for the privilege of being a sockman or freeholder. Anglo-Saxon *soke*, a toll.

Sock, sock down, to (American), to pay money down, to *slap* down money. A common expression in Philadelphia. To *sock* it into a man, to press hard on him, to beat or strike, thrash or "larrup." Also applied metaphorically on the Stock Exchange.

If any feller dares to sport with my Eliza Jane, I'll let him have it hot and short till death shall end his pain; and if I find in any way that she is in the swim, I'll take a fence rail ten feet long, and *sock it into him.—American Jokes.*

To *sock* into, for to beat, thrash, is a common expression in England.

Sock, to (Eton), to eat. *Vide* Sock.

We Eton fellows, great and small, "socked" prodigiously. By the way, I do not know whence that term *sock*, as applied to what boys at some schools call "grub," and others "tick," is derived? for I question the theory which makes it spring from "suck." I am rather disposed to accept the story that at the beginning of this century, one of the men, who sold fruit and tarts at the wall, got nicknamed "Socks," in consequence of his having discarded knee-breeches and stockings in favour of pants and short hose. The man's nickname might then have spread to his business and to his wares by a process familiar to etymologists, till "socking" came to mean the purchase of good things not from "Socks" only, but from any other vendor.—*Brinsley Richards : Seven Years at Eton.*

"To *sock* a fellow, was to give him something to eat or drink, outside his regular meals. Sometimes a boy might say, ' My governor has *socked* me a book.' . . . A boy has also been heard to ask another to *sock* him a construe of his lesson" (C. T. Buckland, "Eton, Fifty Years Ago ").

(Winchester), to hit hard, especially at cricket. It also means to beat, or defeat in a game. *Sock* is a provincialism meaning to hit hard, but much used by slang-talking people.

And then he proceeded, in manner most spry,
In his muscular arms to enfold him,
And said, "Dub up, or else you'll get *socked* in the eye ! "
—*Sporting Times.*

Sodom (Oxford), Wadham College. From a similarity of sound.

Soft (thieves), paper money. To do *soft*, to pass bad notes.

I would cut that game of snotter-hauling, and do a little *soft.*—*Mayhew: London Labour and the London Poor.*

(General), foolish ; a *soft,* a fool.

It'll do you no good to sit in a spring-cart, if you've got a *soft* to drive you.—*G. Eliot : Adam Bede.*

Soft ball (Royal Military Academy), tennis.

Soft down on (common), in love with.

Soft horse (turf), a horse with little stamina.

Soft-sawder (common), flattery.

Soft-sawder by itself requires a knowledge of paintin' of light and shade, and drawin' too. You must know character.—*Sam Slick.*

Soft soap (common), flattery.

He and I are great chums, and a little *soft soap* will go a long way with him.—*Hughes : Tom Brown at Oxford.*

Soft soap over, to (popular), to flatter, to wheedle.

Soft tack (nautical), bread. *Vide* TACK.

Spotless calico bags containing quarts and pints, and which were as eagerly purchased almost as the *soft tack* and the green vegetables the bumboat folk bring alongside ships that have been long absent on sea service.—*J. Greenwood : Odd People in Odd Places.*

Soft tommy (common), bread. Originally a sea-phrase. *Tommy,* food, provisions (various dialects), Halliwell.

I've treacle and toffee, and excellent coffee, *Soft tommy* and succulent chops ;

I've chickens and conies, and pretty polonies, And excellent peppermint drops.
    —*W. S. Gilbert : H.M.S. Pinafore.*

" Gringue," known to the polite as bread, has its duplicates in *soft tommy* or prog.
—*Morning Advertiser.*

Softy (popular), silly person, half-witted.

She were but a *softy* after all. —*Mrs. Gaskell : Sylvia's Lovers.*

S o g (American), dulness, a swoon, lethargy. East Anglian *sog,* to decline in health ; *sog,* to hang down as oppressed with weight. To *sogg* on, to walk heavily ; *soggy,* wet, swampy ; hence the association of dropsical, heavy, stupid.

So help me tater (popular), oath or adjuration in common use, and of no definite signification. Synonyms, " So help me bob," " S' help me, Bill Arline," " So help me greens."

Soiled doves, prostitutes.

Soiled doves from the shades of the Evangelist, *alias* strumpets from St. John's Wood.—*Saturday Review.*

Solace (printers), a penalty or fine inflicted by the " chapel," according to Moxon, 1683 — a term rarely met with now. If the offender would not pay he was *solaced* by his companions, *i.e.,* whacked on that part (according to Shakspeare) " on which we sit down."

Soldier (popular), a red herring. *Vide* COMING THE OLD SOLDIER.

Soldiering (army), cleaning accoutrements, doing the routine and irksome part of a soldier's duty.

Soldier's wind (nautical), one that blows both ways—east and west.

Sold up (common), poor or distressed.

Sole-slogger (popular), a shoemaker.

Solid dig (printers). A compositor is said to have a *solid dig* when the copy in hand is very close, *i.e.*, few short lines or whites and usually without leads.

Sollamon, Solomon (old cant), altar, the Mass. By the *sollamon*, by the Mass; on my oath, on my word.

Oh, I would lib all the darkmans,
By the *sollamon*, under the Ruffemans.
    —*The Roaring Girl.*

In the sense of oath it is probably due to the gypsy "Pré mi *sauloben !*" on my oath! In the sense of altar, Mass, it is no doubt a corruption of *sowlemas* (soulmass), "Sowlemas Day" being an old name for the Feast of All Souls. Compare with Solomon's-Avon, *i.e.*, Solomon's Even, a Shetland name for the 3rd of November, and for a superstition of ill-omen connected with that day, a corruption of Sowlemas Even.

Some pumpkins or **some punkins** (American), description of an important person; the contrary to small potatoes, applied to persons of little or no account.

Franklin was a poor printer boy, and Washington only a land-surveyor, yet they growed to be *some pumpkins.*—*Sam Slick: Nature and Human Nature.*

I took to attendin' Baptist meetin's because the Presbyterian minister was such *small potatoes* that it wasn't edifyin' to sit under his preachin'.—*Widow Bedott's Papers.*

Something short (popular), spirits neat, short of water.

When he thought of his friends who'd grown portly on port,
Who never on ale appeared ailing;
If only he might dare to take *something short*,
Would the teetotal ghosts all start wailing?
A pub! Yes, he will! He's hopped in like a bird—
But the curtain shall fall on our brother;
We'll only record that the last words we heard,
Were, " Now, dear, let'sh 'ave jus' another ! "
    —*Judy.*

Generally " summat short."

And as to the benjamin . . . he would keep it long enough, unless the owner stood a drop of *summat short. —J. Wight: Mornings at Bow Street.*

Sonk, sonkey (popular), a stupid fellow. From *sunket*, a foolish fellow. Norfolk dialect.

Son of a gun (popular). " An epithet conveying contempt in a slight degree, and originally applied to boys born afloat, when women were permitted to accompany their husbands to sea; one admiral declared he literally was thus cradled, under the breast of a gun-carriage " (Admiral Smyth).

You may fancy his rage, and his deep de-
spair,
When he saw himself thus befooled by
one
Whom, in anger wild, he profanely styled,
"A stupid, old, snuff-coloured *son of a
gun !*"
—*Ingoldsby Legends.*

Son of wax (American) a cobbler
or shoemaker. Professor S. S.
Haldeman is said once to have
addressed a party of these men
with, "How are you, my *sons
of waxes ?*" The term is not regarded as uncomplimentary.

Soogun (Irish tinkers), a hay
rope.

Soor (Anglo-Indian), an abusive
term. Hindostanee, a pig.

Soot-bag (thieves), an obsolete
term for a reticule.

Sop (popular), a foolish, soft man.
Provincial *sope*, a simpleton.

Soph, abbreviation of *sophistes ;*
second year men are termed
"junior *sophs*," third year men
"senior *sophs*."

Sore fist. *Vide* WRITING A POOR
HAND.

Sore leg (army), German sausage ;
an unsavoury allusion to its
appearance. (Popular), explained by quotation.

"These puddings, I believe, have nicknames ?"
"Yessir. The spotted is called *sore leg*,
and the plain 'sudden death.' "—*Bird o'
Freedom.*

Sort (popular), that's my *sort*,
that is my nature, character,
that is my way of proceeding ;
that's your *sort*, this is the
course for you to adopt. A good
sort, or a good old *sort*, a good-
natured person.

Sorts. *Vide* OUT OF SORTS.

Soundings (printers). Pressmen
are said to be in *soundings* when
they get near the bottom of
their heap. In taking the last
few sheets off the "horse" their
knuckles would touch or rap
against the wood, hence the
term.

Soup (legal), the prosecutions
which are given out to the
junior bar in court by the clerk
of the peace or arraign as the
case may be. The custom is
to give them out whether the
prisoner pleads guilty or not,
but in some places only pleas
of "not guilty" are given out.
They frequently form the first
"brief" which a young barrister
gets. (Printers), bad and sloppy
ink is thus termed. (Burglars),
melted plate ; it is sometimes
called white *soup*.

S o u p e r (popular), one who
pretends conversion to obtain
soup-tickets. (Thieves), *souper*
or *super*, a watch.

Soup-shop (burglars), a place
where melting-pots are always
kept ready, the price not being
paid to burglars and thieves
who have come to dispose of
plate till the recognition of the
plunder is no longer possible.

Sour on, to (American), to treat unkindly, to act unamiably.

"How's your girl, Charley?" "Oh, it's all up with us!" "How's that?" "The hot weather was too much." "What had that to do with you?" "Well, she *soured* on me."—*New York Sun.*

Arthur—"My best girl *soured* on me yesterday." *George*—"I don't wonder. I always said she was a little pickle."—*Almanac.*

Sour planters (coiners), rogues who pass off counterfeit coin.

Publicans, we were given to understand, are usually the unfortunate tradesmen fixed on as a mark, barmaids being easily thrown off their guard by the customer's innocent appearance and manner. But a safer plan, and one more admired by the *sour planter* herself, is to perambulate streets of tradesmen's shops with her companion, with a sharp look-out for spoony shopmen and hobble-de-hoys entrusted with the till.—*J. Greenwood: Rag, Tag, & Co.*

Sours (coiners), counterfeit coin. Roman coins and such old money are called onion-pennies, or *onions* (provincial), onions are also *sours*, and the connection between bad money and *sours* appears evident. The phrase "to plant the *sours*," *i.e.*, to pass bad coin, strongly supports this explanation, further strengthened by the Italian cant term *argume*, literally *onions*, and French slang *oignon*, both meaning money, coin. Again, the term may owe its origin to the acids used in electro-plating. But that is mere conjecture. "Sometimes when coiners are hard pressed, if there is no other way of getting rid of the *sours*, they secretly swallow them. The shilling *sour*, in the opinion of 'smashers,' is the handiest, and pays better than the florin or half-crown, because when it comes to that value people examine it more closely. Shilling *sours* of a superior kind generally cost four shillings a dozen first hand."

And then he proceeded to inform me that the individual mentioned on the paper was a "smasher," or, in other words, a dealer in counterfeit coin or *sours*.—*J. Greenwood: Tag, Rag, & Co.*

To plant the *sours*, to pass base coin.

Southerly buster (Australian), a piercingly cold southerly wind.

The climate of Sydney, always a detestable one, is never the same for more than a few hours. I have often seen a day there open with a hot scorching wind, which lasts perhaps until one o'clock. Suddenly a fierce, cold wind, a *southerly buster* as it is called, sweeps up from the ice-fields of the Southern Sea, and blows perhaps for two days, perhaps only for a few hours.—*Finch Hatton: Advance Australia.*

Sov (general), a sovereign.

Sow's baby (popular), a sixpence, *hog* being a shilling.

S p a n g e (Royal Military Academy), new, as a *spange* war hat, war helmet. Elegant swell, "you look *spange*." Perhaps from provincial *spanged*, shiny, glittering. *Spange* is probably an importation from public schools, whose slang terms are often provincial words or old English.

Spangle (old cant), a seven shilling piece.

(Theatrical), *spangle*-shaker, harlequin. Also *spangle*-guts.

Spanish, or Spanish blunt. Hotten defines this as money, and suggests that it is a relic of buccaneering days. In America it is correctly limited to silver coin. It is a relic of the old word Spanish-boards, or dollars.

> Indeed there's not one in the language that I know
> Save its synonyms, *Spanish blunt*, stumpy, and rhino.
> —*Ingoldsby Legends.*

Spare a rub (tailors), oblige me with some, or after you with it ; possibly alluding to ironing.

Spark (American), a lover, a "beau." Flame is an old English word for a sweetheart ; in America it is more peculiarly applied to a lady-love. "Where there is flame, there will be *sparks*," originated the application of the latter word to men. From this is derived "to *spark* it," and "to go a *sparking*."

> When the dew is just a sprinkling,
> And the stars begin their twinkling,
> And the day dies into darking,
> That is just the time for *sparking*.
> —*Broadside Ballad.*

I was about eighteen years of age, when, for the first time, I took it into my head to go a *sparking*. One of my neighbours a few miles off had a pretty daughter that, I thought, would just suit me.—*Youth's Companion.*

A *spark* in England was formerly applied, like beau, rather to a gay and stylish fellow than a lover.

Our attention has been called to them and their doings by an indignant "Stall-holder," whose plaint we publish in another column. "Stall-holder" is exercised in spirit, and with reason, by the behaviour of certain *sparks*, or "bucks," or "bloods," or "Corinthians." or "Macaronis" (their name changes with the centuries, but their nature is eternally the same), who make too much noise in stage-boxes and stalls, together with their "female companions." —*Globe.*

The Rev. A. Smythe Palmer, in his "Folk Etymology," remarks : "*Spark*, as a name for a self-sufficient fop or conceited coxcomb, has probably no direct connection with the glittering particle of fire which we call a *spark*, any more than flunkey has to do with German *funke*, a spark. Mr. Wedgwood connects the word with provincial English *sprag*, *sprack*, quick, brisk, as of a lively young man (compare *spraic*, vigour, sprightliness), and clearly further points out a connection with Icelandic *sparkr*, *sprakki*, lively, sprightly, also a dandy. See also Professor Skeat's notes to ' Piers Plowman,' p. 398."

> Oft has it been my lot to mark
> A proud, conceited, talking *spark*.
> —*J. Merrick : The Chameleon.*
> No " double entendres," which you *sparks* allow,
> To make the ladies look—they know not how.
> —*Dryden : Love Triumphant.*

According to Skeat, from same root with *spark*, a small particle of fire. Originally noisy. Icelandic *spraka*, to crackle.

Sparkle (thieves), a diamond. In French (not slang), *brillant*.

> I got her purse and found the ring. I saw it was a big *sparkle*. I noticed the size, and

at once went in front of a jeweller's window to compare those in the window with my prize.—*Evening News.*

Also *spark.*

Jack's conversation is essentially diamondy, and he speaks casually of having seen, whilst over yonder, a trifle of a quarter of a million's worth of *sparks* in a bucket.—*Sporting Times.*

Spark prop, diamond breast-pin.

My pal said, "Pipe his *spark* prop." So my pal said, "Front me, and I will do him for it."—*Horsley: Jottings from Jail.*

Sparkle up, to (popular), to hasten, be quick.

Sparring bloke (popular and thieves), a pugilist.

It was while using one of those places I first met a *sparring bloke*, who showed me how to spar.—*Horsley: Jottings from Jail.*

Sparrow catching (popular), going out *sparrow catching* is for a girl to go out for the purpose of finding a lover.

Spec (common), a venture.

Off I posted to the fam'ly lawyer fit to break my neck,
And he philanthropically took the matter up on *spec.*
                    —*Funny Folks.*

(Popular), an occupation generally with an idea of uncertain profits.

They were "little doll" men; poor deluded wretches, three of thrice as many hundred who, quite new to the Epsom game, had heard that little dolls were the best *spec* out.—*Greenwood: In Strange Company.*

Other meaning explained by quotation.

Throughout lower London, and the shady portions of its suburbs, the window of almost every public-house and beer-shop was spotted with some notice of these *specs.* There were dozens of them. There were the "Deptford *Spec*," and the "Lambeth *Spec*," and the "Great Northern *Spec*," and the "Derby *Spec*," but they all meant one and the same thing—a lottery, conducted on principles more or less honest, the prize to be awarded according to the performances of certain race-horses. —*Greenwood: Seven Curses of London.*

Specklebellies (provincial), Dissenters.

Specks (costermongers), damaged oranges.

Specs (common), spectacles.

No matter for that. He had called for his hat,
With the brim that I've said was so broad and so flat,
And his *specs* with the tortoiseshell rim, and his cane.
                    —*Ingoldsby Legends.*

Speech (turf), private information on a horse. In French turf slang *tuyau, i.e.,* private information whispered, "dans le tuyau de l'oreille." *Speech* is used in such phrases as "get the speech," "give the speech."

Speeler (American), a gambler. German *spieler.*

Speel, to (thieves), to run away, to decamp. Probably an abbreviation of "*speel* the drum," to make off to the highway, take to the highway. *Speel* is from German *spielen,* to play, and "drum" is cant for highroad, so that the phrase is a play on these two words, and corresponds to the French cant "jouer des trimoires," *trime*, road, being from the same root as "drum," which see. It has been suggested that this term is from provincial English *speel*, to climb.

Spell for (popular), to long for.

Spellken, spielken, or spell (cant), a theatre. Probably from the German *spielen*, to play, and *ken*, a place.

Who in a row like Tom could lead the van,
Booze in the ken, or at the *spellken* hustle.
—*Byron: Don Juan.*

Spell oats, to (American). "He can't *spell oats*," said of an ignorant fellow. This originated in a practical joke about 1848. One man would leave a grain of oats with another, who was in the joke, and then meeting another friend, would say, "Have you seen Jones? He has *an oat* for you." The victim, not understanding the sell, would go to Jones and ask for a note, the result being, of course, a treat.

When men couldn't *spell oats*, they were
      not given votes,
    Their place was to work, not to worry,
And Brummagem Rads didn't pander to
      cads,
    For office there wasn't such hurry.
The friends of rebellion were one in a
      million,
    They injured no woman or child,
E'en traitors were Trojans, dreamt not of
      explosions,
    And Parliament was not defiled.
  —*Song: In the Good Old Times Long
      Ago* (*published by Francis Bros.
      & Day*).

Sphere (football), the ball.

Spice, to (old cant), to steal, rob, from an obvious metaphor like "salt," referring to overcharge; "pepper," to ill-treat, &c. "To *spice* the swell," to rob a gentleman; *spicer*, a footpad; the *spice*, highway robbery.

On the high-toby *spice* flash the muzzle,
In spite of each gallows' old scout.
        —*Byron: Don Juan.*

Spicey (popular), first-rate.

They live, when doing well, on the best fare, at the *spiciest* cook-shops.—*Mayhew: London Labour and the London Poor.*

Spiff, spiffy (common), first-class, fashionable, spruce. Provincial English *spiff*, dandified.

But, my gracious! if I ain't got the *spiffiest* lot o' items for you about the French church outfit, 'n as usual I haven't left myself enough room to do 'em full justice, so must put it off till next week, when look out for a screamer.—*San Francisco News Letter.*

A *spiff*, a swell. (Trade), a small commission on sales.

Spiffed (Scotch slang), slightly intoxicated.

Spin (Anglo-Indian), abbreviation for spinster. *Vide* PUCKA.

Spindigo (American), said of one who has come out badly, as from an examination at college or a speculation on the Stock Exchange. Probably from the English army slang *spin*, to reject from an examination; *spindle*, the third swarm of bees from a hive; *spinny*, thin, slender. To this some facetious person has probably added *indigo*, to give it a sufficiently blue tone.

Spink (Royal Military Academy), milk, or condensed milk.

Spinning-house (University), the ordinary prison of the Vice-Chancellor's court at the universities of Oxford and Cambridge.

Spin, to. *Vide* SPUN.

Spit (popular), a facsimile. "He's the very *spit* of his father or mother." "Er ist seiner Mutter wie aus dem gesichte geschnitten" (*Londonismen*). French "c'est son père tout craché."

> Emma has a baby boy,
> To own it I decline ;
> But people cry and wish me joy
> Because they think it's mine.
>
> Oh, James, whoa James !
> Whoa James, for shame on you !
> Oh, James ! whoa James !
> James, it's the *spit* of you !
> *—Song.*

Spit curls (American). *Vide* BOW-CATCHER.

Spithead nightingales (naval), boatswains, and boatswains' mates, on account of their calls.

Spit sixpences, to (common), to have one's mouth parched up, be thirsty. French "cracher des pièces de dix sous."

He had thought it rather a dry discourse ; and beginning to *spit sixpences*, he gave hints to Mr. Wildgoose to stop at the first public-house they should come to.—*Graves: Spiritual Quixote.*

Splash (common), complexion powder, as rice powder, &c. To *splash*, to paint the face. Provincial English *splatch*. VOL. II.

Splatchy, painted ; said of a woman's face. (Popular), to do it *splash* up, to do it in fine style.

Splashing (popular), talking without sense or talking too much.

Splathers, hold your (tailors), hold your tongue.

Splathever (tailors), one who talks much of himself or anything.

Splice, to (Winchester College), to throw or fling. (Common), to marry.

The moral obligation of matrimony was fulfilled, and they were indissolubly *spliced.—Savage London.*

Imagine his feelings, if you are human (and *spliced*), pity him.—*Bird o' Freedom.*

(Nautical), to *splice* the main brace, to serve out an extra allowance of grog in bad weather, or after severe exertion ; drinking.

Split (thieves), a detective ; from to *split*, to inform.

Two *splits* (detectives) got into the train, and I got ready to have a go for it if they put their hands upon me, but I got out all right.—*Daily Telegraph.*

(Common), abbreviated from two brandies or whiskies, and a soda *split, i.e.*, shared.

So he sought him a bar where the thoroughbred tart
Regaleth itself on the longest of *splits.*
—Bird o' Freedom.

Split fair (popular), tell the truth ; a variation of to *split*, to divulge, inform.

Split-fig (popular), a grocer.

S

Split out, to (thieves), to separate.

There is a reeler over there who knows me, we had better *split out.*—*Horsley: Jottings from Jail.*

Split, to (common), to let out a secret, to inform against one's accomplices.

If I tell you all about it, will you pro-mise that you won't *split ?*—*Greenwood: The Little Ragamuffins.*

On the hold business. Just to have a chat. When are you going to *split* on your old pal ?—*G. Sims : Rogues and Vagabonds.*

" You needn't think I'm going to *split,* she said indignantly.—*Fergus W. Hume: The Mystery of a Hansom Cab.*

To go at full *split,* or to go as hard as one can *split,* means to go as hard as ever one can at full pace. Used by slangy Aus-tralians as well as in England. Old English *split,* force ; " to make all *split,*" an old phrase implying great violence of ac-tion.

We had run him for seven miles and more, As hard as our nags could *split.* —*A. L. Gordon: Wolf and Hound.*

Splodger (popular), a lout, awk-ward countryman.

Splodgy (common), coarse, re-ferring to complexion, with pimples.

Splurge (American), a dashing, brilliant display. At Princeton University a student who re-cited a lesson badly was said to "fizzle," when he did it credit-ably he " rowled," but to show a perfect mastery of the subject was to *splurge.*

A new wrinkle at seaside resorts is the *splurging* of fair women on borrowed dresses. They only differ in degree from many other fair women who own their dresses, but whose fathers and husbands sometimes have to borrow the money to pay for them.—*St. Paul Globe.*

To cut a *splurge* is synonymous with " cut a dash."

Spoffskins (society), a lady of an accommodating disposition, who makes morganatic arrangements of a temporary character.

Spoffy (common), applied to a bustling busybody, a fussy " finick." From provincial Eng-lish *spoffle,* to busy oneself over-much about a matter of little consequence.

Spondulicks (American), a term for specie or money. It would appear to have some connection with Dutch *spaunde,* "chips," also slang for money, and there is also a word *oolik,* bad, wretched. The term probably originated in New York, in some confusion or perversion of these words. This term has become common among English turf-ites.

I'm derned if I'd live two mile out o' town . . . not for his *spondulicks.*—*Mark Twain : Huckleberry Finn.*

If the essence of slang be the misuse of words, some of the terms in circulation amongst many journalists, chiefly Ameri-can, are slang of the most brilliant type. The following amusing " Proscription," which appeared in the *Chicago Post,* instances a few of the more glaring examples:—

"Hereafter every reporter in this office shall be personally decapitated, and shall lose his situation who shall be guilty of the use of any of the following barbarisms of language:—Postmortemed, for dissected; suicided, infanticided, accidentated; indignated, for got mad; disremembered, disrecollect, disforgot, &c.; abluted, for washed himself, herself, or itself, as the case may be; sporn, for spared; *spondulicks*, for ducats; catastrophed, scrumptious, recepted, planted, or funerated, for buried. And any editor, reporter, correspondent, scribe, or dead-beat shall, as an additional penalty, be put on half pay who shall write 'on last evening,' 'on this morning,' 'on yesterday,' or 'on ten o'clock this forenoon.'"

Sponge, throwing up the (common), to give up, submit, acknowledge one's defeat; from the custom in the prize-ring. The principal second keeps a sponge during the fight, wherewith to cleanse and refresh his principal's face between the rounds; thus his *throwing up the sponge*, as it were, because it has become useless, is taken to be indicative of his side giving up the struggle. This is an almost recognised phrase.

The party . . . told him that he must either return to France or *throw up the sponge*. General Boulanger refused to do either.—*Daily Telegraph.*

Spoof (turf), deception, swindle, sell. Properly a childish kind of game like "tiddlywinks."

Next day I put all my oof
  On to Gold (sixteen to one),
And now I hear the cry of *spoof*,
  The race is o'er, and he's not won.
      —*Bird o' Freedom.*

Spoof has been defined by Sir P. Colquhoun as "an unintelligible shibboleth, invented to indicate an idiotic game—a sell. Exactly as 'the loud laugh proclaims the empty mind,' so, to be an adept in the *spoof* cult, indicates, as the first qualification for that dubious distinction, softening of the brain." It no doubt owes its origin to the game of *spoof*, played on a draught-board with counters, which have to be whisked on the top of the adversary's own counters by means of a small stick. It has been suggested, however, that "*spoof* is from provincial English *spoffle*, to busy oneself overmuch about a matter of small consequence, to rage over a trifle, as a 'great cry and little wool,' *i.e.*, a cheat or sell. Hence disappointment, deceit."

Love he used to think, I've said before, a
  riddle;
To-day he says the *mot d'énigme* is oof,
And that lovers play a very second fiddle
To markers at the noble game of *spoof*.
      —*Sporting Times.*

'Tis oh! to be the people's "pug,"
  Who is paid at halls to spar,
Who's a lovely, unscratched, scarless mug,
  Who lives like a La-di-da!
Big battles he fights which are always
  drawn,
  But draw much golden oof,
He boasts of his biceps and "Boston"
  brawn—
'Tis oh! for the game of *spoof*.
      —*Bird o' Freedom.*

Also the confidence-trick swindle.

Also to play *spoof*.

The alligator and crocodile are just in the prime of life at 100. There are parrots in the gardens who are seventy-five years old, and still cheerful, and the swan begins to think about putting away youthful follies at 200. I hope the keeper who told me all this knows that it is wicked *to play spoof* on Sunday. I believed all he told me, and kept saying "Really" in such a sweetly innocent way, that he may have been tempted to put the pot on.—*Referee.*

Spoof, to (turf). *Vide* SPOOF.

"T," said the Wicked Nobleman, having previously arranged to *spoof* the crowd with the word "taint."—*Sporting Times.*

His railway carriage he will choose and pick,
Till he spots a likely lot,
To royally *spoof* at the three-card trick,
And to lift of a cosy "pot."
And he patters the while of mysterious tips
And dollars he cops for "stable" snips.
—*Bird o' Freedom.*

Spoon (common), courtship; *spoons* together, much in love with one another. *Vide* SPOONEY.

She and I, dontcher know, are great *spoons*.
—*Punch.*

(American), "to do business with a big *spoon*" is the same as "to cut a big swath" (Bartlett); that is to say, on a large scale. Also to help oneself fully, which is the origin of the German phrase, "Er isst mit grossen Löffel"—"He eats with a large spoon."

Spooney. There appear to be two separate or distinct words of this spelling, probably with different roots. A case of spoons, or of two persons who spoon on one another, is a term existing out of English, in Welsh, Arabic, and German (*löffeln*, to play the gallant, also

eat with a spoon; *löffel*, gallantry, and spoon), without any reference to weak-mindedness or folly. It is usual in Wales, Norway, and Sweden, as in Algeria, to make a newly-married couple a present of two spoons both carved out of one piece of wood joined, or a kind of double, and the writer has in his possession specimens of several kinds. The idea in this seems to be that as spoons in a set match and fit together exactly, so should man and wife. A *spooney*, meaning a silly person, had originally no connection with love, though it became natural enough to associate silly fondness with affection. *Vide* TO SPOON.

You don't mean to say you have been doing the *spooney*—what you call making love — have you?—*C. Bede: Verdant Green.*

The original meaning of *spooney*, foolish, possibly owes its origin to the phrase "not past the spoon," *i.e.*, childish, that is, spoon-fed.

"Can't you see it ain't open yet, *spooney!*" demanded the irascible landlady.—*J. Greenwood: Dick Temple.*

Spoons (American), equivalent to money, means, or a fortune. "She has the *spoons*," indicates an heiress.

Spoon, to (common), to court, make love, to woo. Sometimes with an idea of foolish fondness, which was the original meaning.

"You're not a bad-looking fellow. *Spoon* some woman, you'll soon be all right.'

Some short time passed on, when the two met again, the broker in fine feather. " Took your advice, old man. *Spooned* a deuced ugly woman. Doing well. Look at my coat."—*Bird o' Freedom.*

"To *spoon*, borrowed probably from some of the provincial dialects, seems to be akin to Anglo-Saxon *sponere* (*spanere*), an allurer or persuader; *sponung* (*spanung*), persuasion, seduction; *spanan* (past participle *sponen*), to entice, or solicit; the primitive form of which was probably *spunan*, implied by Teutonic *un-spunalih*, inexorable. Thus the original meaning of *spoon* would be 'to be seductive or alluring' in one's looks and manner, to woo'" (A. Smythe Palmer).

(Cricket), to strike the ball in such a way with a slack and almost horizontal bat that it rises up in the air.

They "pulled," they *spooned*, they, in short, committed every fault of which the cricketer can be guilty.—*Daily Telegraph.*

Spoops, or **spoopsy** (American), a soft-brained fellow, or one whose manners are objectionable.

Seniors always try to be dignified. The term *spoopsey*, in its widest signification, applies admirably to them.—*Yale Tomahawk.*

Spoopsy is from English provincial *poop*, a puppy. The ending *sy* is very often irregularly applied in America, as Jimsy for Jim.

Sport (popular), a man who gives himself up to sport, a betting man, turfite. Originally American.

Leastways I don't mean that exackly; I like you too well; you're my sort; But you ain't took my measure kerrect, I'm a Tory, a patriot, a *sport.* So wy should you round on me thusly? I call it a little mite mean. If I took and turned Radical now; but oh! no, 'Arry isn't so green.
—*Punch.*

Sporting door (University), outer door of chamber. Also "oak." *Vide* To SPORT.

Sport, to (common), to exhibit, wear, as "*sport* a new tile." "To *sport* one's oak," to shut the door against visitors. *Vide* OAK.

Mr. Verdant Green had for the first time *sported* his oak. Under any circumstances it would have been a mere form, since his bashful politeness would have induced him to open it to any comer.—*C. Bede: Verdant Green.*

Spot (common), to have a vacant spot, to be crazy; to be *on the spot*, or to be "all there," to be thoroughly *au fait* of some business, occupation, or game. To be in form, or lucky, to be smart. An officer is said to be *on the spot* when he is thoroughly acquainted with his duties. "Off the spot" is the reverse. The metaphor is from a billiards phrase, on or off the spot stroke, the most paying stroke at billiards. To be *on the spot*, therefore, is to be doing the spot stroke skilfully or luckily.

Spotted (army), *spotted* mysteries. Potted preserved beef, which may contain unknown ingredients, or be made of bad meat.

But what do I care? Not a pennorth of *spotted;* and when customers come in and ask for a fourpenny plate with plenty of gravy, I take the money—always look after the coin, you know.—*Broadside Ballad.*

(Army), *spotted* dog, sometimes applied to a currant pudding, but by soldiers used for a sausage or saveloy.

(Popular), *spotted* donkey, coarse plum-pudding, sold at cook-shops.

Spotter (American), spy in the employment of the police. French *indicateur.*

It is shrewdly suspected that there are regularly paid *spotters* who watch in the Paso del Norte establishments and note the customers who go with their purchases into the street cars, and point them out to the United States inspectors when they reach American territory.—*Globe Democrat.*

Spot, to (common), to see, notice, make a note of anything, pick out, identify.

But I preferred pecking and prowling, and *spotting* the mugs making love.—*Punch.*

The next tipster avows he will forfeit a large sum of money unless he *spots* the identical winners, "first and second." Of course, nothing can be more transparent than bombast of this sort; but here it is in black and white.—*Greenwood: Seven Curses of London.*

There are certain movements of individuals, as the extension of a hand, the methods of carrying a cane or a parasol, that mark the persons, so that, disguise themselves as they may, a trained detective would *spot* them anywhere, or under any circumstances. They are involuntary, and all the training in the world would not change them an iota.—*Illustrated Bits.*

Also to lay money down for gambling, setting it on the spots.

Spouter (popular), orator or preacher. Also a whaling term for a South Sea whale.

Spout, to (common), to pawn. *Vide* POP.

He went out one Monday morning and *spouted* his watch to raise funds.—*J. Wight: Mornings at Bow Street.*

The dons are going to *spout* the college plate.—*T. Hughes: Tom Brown at Oxford.*

I hold it truth with him who says
That sometimes 'tis as well *to spout*
One's watch, and not to get it out
Till after lapse of many days.
  —*Bird o' Freedom.*

To shout as a street vendor.

I was out with the missis and the moke a *spoutin'* my wares.—*Bird o' Freedom.*

To *spout* also refers to noisy talking or oratory.

At its case, of an "uncle" of his, who'd a *spout,*
That horrid word *spout* no sooner came out
Than Winifred Pryce would turn her about,
And with scorn on her lip, and a hand on each hip,
Spout herself till her nose grew red at the tip.
  —*Ingoldsby Legends.*

In the following quotation a play is made on the word.

A very interesting article on sponges has been written by one of our Consuls on the Syrian coast. It appears that these interesting, but lowly organised creatures, exist only by *spouting,* in fact they are the Grand Old Man of the sea.—*Moonshine.*

Spout, up the (common), in pawn.

And his pockets, no doubt, being turned
inside out,
That his *mouchoir* and gloves may be put
up the spout.
     —Ingoldsby Legends.

In America there is a poetical paraphrase of this term in very common use. It is "where the woodbine twineth," because in country houses there is generally a woodbine growing on the water-spout. It was invented by the notorious Fiske in reference to bonds hypothecated.

Up the spout is in allusion to the spout up which pawnbrokers send the articles ticketed. When redeemed, they return down the spout, *i.e.*, from the store-room to the shop.

As for spoons, forks, and jewellery, they are not taken so readily to the smelting-pot, but to well-known places where there is a pipe (*spout*) which your lordships may have seen in a pawnbroker's shop. —*The Times.*

There were three of these floors, and the *spout* from the shop penetrated to the topmost. On every floorway a sharp and active youth, whose business it was to discover and send "down the *spout*" the ransomed bundles.—*Greenwood: In Strange Company.*

Sprat (popular), my *sprat*, *i.e.*, my young man, my sweetheart. Swedish *spratt*, beau, coxcomb, dandy. (Popular and thieves), a sixpence.

I got more pieces for the wedge. I got three and a *sprat* (3s. 6d.) an ounce.—*Horsley: Jottings from Jail.*

Sprats (popular), effects, furniture, *i.e.*, "sticks," from provincial English *sprats*, small wood.

Spread (popular), butter. (General), a meal, banquet.

At the conclusion of the exercises on class days all adjourned to the *spreads* (as the cold collations are called) in the various rooms and halls.—*Life at Harvard (U.S.) College.*

Next day I was present at a *spread* at the Mission Hall of a much more gratifying description. Next day was Wednesday, and for a very long time past, on this day, the good missionary among the savage tribes of St. Luke's has somehow contrived to raise from the charitable money enough to give the children—poor, neglected, literally half-starved little fledglings of the surrounding rookeries—a hot dinner, a smoking-hot dinner, and as much as they can eat of it.—*Greenwood: In Strange Company.*

(American), a bed covering.

Spread eagle (nautical), a person seized in the rigging; generally a passenger thus made to pay his entrance forfeit. (Cambridge), pulled and grilled fowl, a fowl opened down the back, and served up with mushrooms, &c. (American), as an adjective it applies to oratory.

The king was satisfied; so the duke got out his book and read the parts over in the most splendid *spread-eagle* way, prancing around and acting at the same time, to show how it had got to be done; then he gave the book to the king, and told him to get his part by heart.—*The Adventures of Huckleberry Finn.*

Spread eagle, the operations of one who buys an amount of stock on time, and then bargains to sell the same stock within the same time at a higher rate, expecting to receive a profit from the difference, without expenditure of capital, but who, as by his bargain the option neither of reception nor delivery is in his hands, is at the risk of being obliged both to buy and sell at a disadvantage in order to fulfil his bargain.

Spread-eagle-ism, an American phrase, first applied to exaggerated, extravagant, and vulgar patriotic speeches in laudation of the American Union, its present greatness and its future probabilities; first suggested by the eagle as the personification of the country, in the same manner as the lion is the heraldic emblem of England, the unicorn of Scotland, the cock of France, the double-headed eagle of Austria, and the black eagle of Prussia. According to the definition in the *North American Review,* as quoted by Bartlett, "A compound of exaggeration, effrontery, bombast, mixed metaphors, platitudes, defiant threats thrown at the world, and irreverent appeals to the Supreme Being."

Spread oneself, to (West American), to boast.

Now he was another man, and for the benefit of the "tenderfoot" he *spread himself.—F. Francis : Saddle and Mocassin.*

Spread, straddle (Stock Exchange), Americanisms for "options."

Spree (Winchester), said of one giving himself airs. "He's *spree*" means he is a conceited person. Applied to dress or other articles it means smart,

stylish, in good form. (General), on the *spree*, on a frolic, bent on amusement generally involving feasting. This word, both as a substantive and adjective, is provincial English, used slangily. Said to be from Welsh *asbri*, a trick, mischief, understood as *a sbri.*

She shouted out "Hansom"—I thought she meant me,
For I'd never rode in one before—
She said to the cabman—"We're out on the *spree*."
—*J. Anthony : The Girl at the Park.*

In Dutch, *spreifest* is a betrothal or marriage feast, which was of old in Holland the great spree of all others in a man's life. *Spreifeest, trouwfeest, spreien, trouwen, huwen; ook vrijen* (Wordenboek van Bargoensch and J. Teirlinck). *Spreiing,* the act of betrothing or wedding (*trouving, daad van trouwen; vrijage*), is both in sound and in fact very nearly an equivalent to "spreeing."

Spreeman (Winchester College), a junior who is permitted to work hard, generally one who has been there some time.

Springers, the. In America the 62nd got this name from their rapid pursuit of the enemy after the battle of Trois Rivières.

Springer up (tailors), a tailor who sells cheap ready-made clothing. The clothes are said to be "sprung up" or "blown together."

Sprint (sporting), a short distance race. Provincial English, *sprint*, lively, such a race being run at full speed. Also *sprint race*. A *sprint* is a professional walker.

Sprinter (American), one who is making great exertion in running.

The young desperado ran like a *sprinter*, but the young lady kept well up with him. Finally, after a chase of about eight blocks, a gentleman jumped from his buggy and stopped the thief.—*Kansas City Times.*

Sprint, to (sporting), to walk in matches, and to run in short distance races. *Vide* SPRINT.

" Now that your son has returned from college, do you feel repaid for your outlay for his education. Did he take any prizes?" "Oh, yes, mum, yes, indeed. He got a medal for what he calls *sprinting*, and he must be high up in mathematics, for he says he's learned four new curves."—*Scranton Truth.*

Sprout (Yale University), any department of knowledge is so called, *e.g.*, botany, mathematics, classics, are each and all of them *sprouts*. (American), a bunch of *sprouts*, the five fingers of the closed fist. Also the chambers of a revolver.

Sprug (Scottish), a sparrow.

Sprung (naval), a man in liquor is "*sprung*, slewed, or half-seas over " or "dead-oh!" according to the stage of intoxication. *Sprung*, like a boat full of water, which springs a leak.

As she went along, the boys bid her be of good cheer, for she was only a little *sprung.—Dickens.*

Spry (American), active, nimble. From provincial English *spry*, nimble ; Swedish *sprygg*, very active (Skeat).

He rejoiced, for he said, "My blackguards will be *spry* and busy, and full of work."—*Sporting Times.*

Spud (American thieves), base coin, bad money. From *spud*, a bad or raw potato. *Vide* SPUDS. (Popular), a dwarfish, round, potato - shaped person. Also a baby's hand, so called because round and plump.

Spuddy (costers), a street seller of potatoes.

Spudgel (American), to move or run away speedily. Same as West of England *spuddle*. *Spudgy*, quick, speedy. Dutch *spoedig*, speedy ; *spoediglyk*, rapidly.

Spuds (popular), potatoes. Query from the implement, the *spud*, with which they are dug up. *Spud* is used by Swift with the meaning of " short knife."

Spun (medical students), having failed at examination.

Spunk-fencer (popular), a lucifer-match seller. *Vide* SPUNKS.

Spunks (popular), lucifer matches. *Spunk* is an excrescence on the bark of trees, used sometimes for tinder.

Spur, to (thieves), to annoy.

The only thing that *spurred* me was being such a flat to bring them home.— *Horsley : Jottings from Jail.*

Squabash, to (popular), to kill. From *squab* and *bash*, both meaning to beat, ill-treat.

Harry the Sixth, who, instead
Of being *squabash'd*, as in Shakspeare we've read,
Caught a bad influenza, and died in his bed.
—*Ingoldsby Legends.*

Squabble (printers). This is a term for the more technical one "broken." Type when disarranged and mixed, as if quarrelling, is said to be *squabbled*, *i.e.*, in "pie," or "squashed."

Squad, defined in quotation.

Squad, applied generally to little parties, of little sense—as an awkward *squad*, a blackguard *squad*, a squandering *squad*, &c.—*J. Wight: Mornings at Bow Street.*

(Public schools, &c.), the *pi-squad, i.e.*, pious *squad*, a set who profess to be very pious and good.

Squaddle (American), to depart rapidly, begone, cut and run, or skedaddle.

And at once released the prisoner,
Sternly bidding him to *squaddle*,
Just as fast as he could make it,
Ere the starry night came on.
—*In Nevada.*

Squantum (American), a common expression in New England is, "She looks as if she came from *squantum*," *i.e.*, from some rustic, out-of-the-way place. Bartlett suggests that the term is probably derived from some Indian place-name, and states that *squantum* was a Massachusetts Indian name for the devil. Also a picnic.

Square (thieves and popular), honest, straightforward.

They considered themselves much better than many *square* (honest) people who practise commercial frauds.—*Greenwood: Seven Curses of London.*

"Take my tip and turn *square*, from a hook who's going to be lagged," would be in common parlance, "Take my advice and get your living honestly, says a pickpocket who is expecting penal servitude."
—*Horsley: Jottings from Jail.*

This word has recently acquired extensive currency among the criminal classes, and the functionaries whose business it is to cope with them ; to *square* is to adjust, to settle, to make straight, to discharge a liability. "On the *square*," fairly and satisfactorily, honestly. The derivation has long been known as coming from the freemasons,

When I was an apprentice, I lived upon the *square*,
My boss gave me no money, which I thought was hardly fair
(*The Cross Boy's Song*);

and the phrase, in its metaphorical sense, would not be justly liable to the reproach of being slang, were it not for its use by the dangerous and disreputable classes to describe the kind of honour that is supposed to exist among thieves and law-breakers in their intercourse with each other. (Society), *square*, to run on the, to be straight, honest, reliable.

Square backdown (sporting), a shuffle of more than usual palpableness.

The fight to a finish between Killen and Conley, which was to have taken place on March 1, is off. Killen made the plea that, owing to the bad condition of his hands, he could not fight until a later day. An agreement was reached January 4 to withdraw the forfeits and declare the fight off. Killen's action is regarded by all sporting men as a *square backdown.—New York Police Gazette.*

Square, to (general), to bribe, conciliate. "Squaring his nibs," silencing anybody by a bribe.

There was in the Manchester detective service one man who could not be *squared*, and had an inconvenient habit of keeping information to himself, and Smith was frequently employed by other detectives to get up bogus cases in order to throw discredit upon this official. — *Evening News.*

Squarehead (thieves), explained by quotation.

"Honesty among thieves" is undoubtedly the production of a *squarehead* or sham thief; a good thief will rob anybody.—*Confessions of Joe Bragg.*

Also Australian prison slang.

Square meal (common), solid, complete meal. Originally American.

I hear that when the members of the Metropolitan Asylums Board visited Leavesden a few days ago, they were regaled with a *square meal* of the most sumptuous description.—*Truth.*

Square rigged (nautical), well dressed.

Square round, to (Winchester College), to make room at the fire for some one.

Square up, to (general), to put oneself in a fighting attitude, to pay a debt.

Square with, to be (common), to be even with him, or to be revenged.

Squarson (clerical), a combination of "squire" and "parson" —a squire in holy orders who works his parish, or rural parson of means and position not overshadowed by resident squires.

Squattle away, to (American), to depart. Probably suggested by ducks *squattling* or "splashing" as they hurry off.

Squatty, squaddy (American), short, stout, small, and fat. *Squat*, a short, stout person in several English dialects.

Tombólin's wife being a very small *squat*,
Out of the water soon she got.
  —Old Ballad of Tombólin.

Squawk (American, but of English origin), to squeak or squall in a loud, harsh tone. Generally associated with the sounds uttered by poultry in rage, pain, or fear. A wretched failure, an abject "fizzle."

Jokes may be divided into the first-rate good, the first-rate bad, and *squawks*. A *squawk* awakens in you a sense of horror, or of shame for the man making it, and causes you to be thankful that you are not in his moccasins.—*Henry P. Leland.*

Squeak, a narrow (common), a narrow escape. Metaphor from a pig escaping through a small opening.

It was *a narrow squeak* for me, as the bullet cut off a lock of my hair, and passed clean through my hat.—*O'Reilly: Fifty Years on the Trail.*

Squeaker (bird fanciers), a young pigeon.

Squeakers — young pigeons — and you take 'em to the public - house, and you enters 'em for the race.—*J. Greenwood: Dick Temple.*

(Popular), a pig.

Squeak, to (thieves), to confess, inform.

I never will whiddle, I never will *squeak*,
Nor to save my colquarron endanger thy
　　neck.
　　　　—*Retoure, my dear Delle.*

This verb is obsolete for to break silence, to speak for fear or pain.

If he be obstinate put a civil question to him upon the rack, and he *squeaks*, I warrant him.—*Dryden.*

Squealer (Wellington College), a small boy. (Thieves), an informer, one who gives information that may lead to detection.

" Somebody saw him ? "
" Yes."
" And that somebody has been arrested and confessed ? "
" No ; oh, no ! "
" No *squealer* yet ? "
" No ; that's straight. I see you doubt it, but it's true."—*Chicago Daily Inter-Ocean.*

Squeal, to (thieves), to lodge information with the police. A " State's evidence " man is a " squealer." The term is, however, becoming quite common as expressing the imparting of knowledge of any kind. Variants are—to blow on, to give away, to let out on, to go back on, to scream, wheeze, whiddle.

A pal *squeals* on his chum, and detectives will capture him in short order.—*Sub-head in Abilene (Kansas) Gazette.*

Squee - gee (American ; English, *wee-jee*), aristocratic, refined, extremely elegant and fashionable.

No minister in the city, not even the one who officiated at the church where the family attended, was *squee-gee* (*squee-gee* is a Gothic word meaning high - toned) enough to conduct the services.—*American Newspaper.*

Squeeze (thieves), the · neck, a crowd, silk. In the sense of neck the allusion is obvious ; compare with the synonym "throttle." *Squeeze* probably acquired the meaning of silk from *squeeze*-clout, a (silk) neckerchief.

After the place got well where I was chived, me and another screwed a place at Stoke Newington, and we got some *squeeze* (silk) dresses, and two sealskin jackets, and some other things.—*Horsley: Jottings from Jail.*

The latter asked Fife if he had been to see the *squeeze* (silk) that morning. Fife answered "Yes."—*Daily Telegraph.*

Squeezer (thieves), gallows.

For Larry was always the lad,
　When a friend was condemned to the
　　squeezer ;
But he'd pawn all the togs that he had,
　Just to help the poor boy to a sneezer.
　　　　—*The Death of Socrates.*

Squelcher (pugilistic), a settling blow. Old provincial. We find *squelch* for a heavy fall in Hudibras.

There's a *squelcher* in the bread-basket that'll stop your dancing, my kivey !—*C. Bede : Verdant Green.*

Figuratively a settler in argument or vituperation.

This last retort would have been a *squelcher.*—*Evening News.*

In that position he used to write his leading articles. *Squelchers*, some of them. —*The Golden Butterfly.*

Squib (costermongers), a head of asparagus. (Painters), a paintbrush.

Squibob (American), a term applied usually in contempt, but sometimes in indifference to anybody. From provincial English *squybobble*, a fuss, a needless ceremony. Hence a man who is finicky and fussy.

Squiffed (common), slightly intoxicated.

He never tells his wifelet what the nature
of the "biz" is ;
And when he rolls home rather *squiffed*,
just as the day is dawning,
Do you think he ever tells her what has
kept him out till morning !
—*Sporting Times.*

Also *squiffy.*

It was melted so soon, I am rather afraid
That our hero was *squiffy*, or worse :
And some might have fancied that most of
it laid.
—*Sporting Times.*

Squinny (American), to cause a laugh, to laugh, wink, and smile. *Squinny*, provincial English, to squint ; *squin*, a wink.

Squinny-eyed (common), a modern street phrase of general application in an offensive sense, but rather out of vogue.

Squinting (tailors), being without food or anything requisite. The French say of anything longed for, " cela le fait loucher."

Squirm or **squirt** (public schools), small obnoxious boy. (Ameri-

can), to get a *squirm* on, to begin moving, to bestir oneself. Properly to wriggle.

Turn out your bundle quick, get a *squirm*
on you !—*Detroit Free Press.*

Squirt (Harvard University), a showy recitation. Hall says : " From the ease and quickness with which the words flow from the mouth, being analogous to the ease and quickness which attend the sudden ejection of a stream of water from a pipe. Such a recitation being generally perfect, the word *squirt* is very often used to convey that idea. Perhaps there is not, in the whole vocabulary of college cant terms, one more expressive than this, or that so easily conveys its meaning merely by its sound. It is mostly used colloquially." Also a fop.

If they won't keep company with *squirts*
and dandies, who's going to make a monkey
of himself?—*Magazine : Jones's Courtship.*

(Stock Exchange), a man who hangs about the market with a paltry order, and who will not deal fairly. (Common), a doctor or apothecary (nearly obsolete).

Squirt your dye (American). This means, " Now, do your best, your turn for action has come ! " A phrase borrowed from the dyer's workshop. It is generally heard as " Now then, *squirt your dye !* "

Squish (University and public schools), marmalade. The term is used at the Royal Military Academy.

Stab (billiards), to make a *stab* shot is to cause your own ball to stop dead on the spot occupied by the object ball, or only to run through it a very little way.

'Stab, on the (printers). A man employed on regular work, and at a fixed weekly wage, is said to be on the " establishment," and this word is very commonly shortened to *'stab.*

Stab rag (popular), a tailor.

Stab, to (theatrical). "*Stab* yourself, and pass the dagger." A jovial synonym for "Help yourself, and pass the bottle."

Stag (Stock Exchange), a man who applies for shares or stock in a new company with the intention of selling as soon as possible at a premium.

> A *stag* there was—as I've heard tell,
> Who in an attic used to dwell,
> Or rather—to use a fitter phrase—
> Who in an attic used to gaze ;
> And being blest, like many I know,
> With little conscience, and less rhino,
> Took to that frailest of all frail ways.
> —*Atkin: House Scraps.*

(Thieves), one who has turned State's evidence, an informer. To turn *stag*, to peach, betray, turn informer, from the meaning of to *stag*, to watch, hence to spy and inform. Also, a shilling.

Stag dance (American), a peculiar buffoon dance performed by men alone. *Vide* STAG PARTY.

> After supper a universal *stag dance* of not less than fifty couples came off. This

is a peculiar kind of affair, in which the dancers arrange themselves in two long lines, facing each other, inside of a lane of candles, half buried in the ground, and above these three muskets forming a tripod, and each bayonet having a candle spluttering on its point. Drums, fifes, and violins formed the orchestra. The cadets started with a simultaneous bound, involving themselves inextricably, and at last it became a mere competition who should work his legs and feet most excruciatingly. —*The West Point Scrap-Book.*

Stage-dooring (theatrical), hanging about the scenes or doors reserved for actors.

> Mr. —— refused to put the chorus ladies into tights, and the public was gently but firmly made to understand that *stage-dooring* was not allowed, that supper parties were forbidden.—*Evening News.*

Stage wait (theatrical), keeping the stage waiting so as to suspend the progress of the play.

> One night, some years ago, there was what we call a *stage wait*—the next performer had not arrived.—*Sporting Times.*

Stagger (popular and thieves), one who looks, watches.

Staggerer (common), applied to anything wonderful, astounding, that *staggers* one.

> Jobson showed me what he rightly called a *staggerer.* Highland scene, cattle life-size . . . "Had to get a Pickford's van to take it to the Academy."—*Moonshine.*

> Considering the slowness of the wicket yesterday, this in itself was a notable feature of the innings, but the greatest *staggerer* was that one man made more than half of the total.—*Star.*

Staggers, hungry, explained by quotation.

> Shall I let the chances of stealing a turnip off a stall, or a loaf out of a baker's barrow, go past me, while I keep straight

on, looking out for an honest way?—straight on, and straight on, till I get the *hungry staggers* (*you* never had the *hungry staggers*, Mr. Magistrate), and tumble down on the road? I'm not such a fool, thank'e. I don't see the pull of it. —*Seven Curses of London.*

Stag mag (theatrical), stage manager.

Stag party (common), a party of men. A simile obviously borrowed from the groups of younger stags who are driven away to associate by themselves, when the stronger and older males monopolise the females.

" I have observed," remarked Cyn, " that among animals it is the strongest, bravest, and best who monopolise the favours of the females. A *stag party* of deer consists of the feebler bachelors, the fools, so to speak, of the herd. But in humanity the rule is reversed. Nineteen out of twenty of the ladies' darlings, the regular mashers, the dear Berties, are the very refuse of our sex, so far as brains are concerned. You may find *stag parties* of the most manly and intelligent men, in which there are some who never had a *bonne fortune*, and those who have enjoyed them had to work hard enough for their happiness; while a drivelling fool of an opera-singer, or a small actor half idiotic with vanity and ignorance, will be overwhelmed with love-letters from all sorts and conditions of belles."—*The Stag Club.*

I lose myself in a little party of old bricks, who, under a pretence of looking at the pictures, are keeping up a small *stag party* at the end of the room. — *Mace Sloper (C. G. L.) in the Knickerbocker Magazine.*

Stag, to (popular and thieves), to look, watch. Alluding to the fixed, intent staring of a stag. Suggested to be from Swedish *staga*, to stop, as staying to listen.

Lest the transaction may have been *stagged* by some impertinent bystander or a trap, he mounts his box and drives away. — *Jon Bee: A Living Picture of London for 1828.*

So you've been *stagging* this gentleman and me, and listening, have you?— *H. Kingsley: Geoffry Hamlyn.*

Stairs without a landing(thieves), the treadmill.

Well, I'll tell you. Our last lodger—about two years older than you he was, and as clever a little fellow as ever turned his hand to diving—he lasted as a lodger of mine only nine weeks. He's lodging now at Coldbaths Fields—getting up the *stairs without a landing.* Three months of it, and twice privately whipped. Bad for him, isn't it?—*The Little Ragamuffins.*

Stakes (thieves), stolen handkerchiefs.

Stake, to (American), to provide for. A phrase derived from the picketing or staking out of horses and mules in frontier life.

There is no doubt that he had plenty of money and plenty of clothing when he left, for his family *staked* him. It is known that he had $55 on the night preceding the murder.—*Chicago Herald.*

Stale bear (Stock Exchange), a man who has sold stock which he does not possess, and has not bought it back. A bear who has been short of stock for a considerable period. *Vide* BEAR.

Stale bull (Stock Exchange), a man who has held stock for a long period without profit.

Stale drunk (common), is said of a man who has been drunk at night, and has taken too much stimulants in the form of spirits the following morning.

Stale whimer (old cant), a bastard.

Stalk, the (Punch and Judy men), the gallows.

Stall (popular), trick, excuse, defence, humbug, pretence. Early English, a snare, or decoy. Also *stale*.

For two pins, wretches, I'd smash you all.
It's nice, on my word, such things I ne'er
   heard,
You've been hiding my bird for a *stall*.
   —*Broadside Ballad: The Masher
      and the Parrot.*

(Thieves), explained by quotation.

" Little Burks (as he was called), the police detective, who was discharged for acquainting the thieves with all that was transacted in the detective department, wouldn't mind acting as a *stall* in a robbery."
"What's that?"
"Why, cover a robbery. If he saw a mob of thieves at work he would get his brother policeman away on some pretence till the job was over, and then claim his share in the swag."—*Evidence given by an old Police Officer.*

Stalling ken (old cant), a broker's or receiver's place.

Stallion (circus), a piebald horse (doubtful or varied in its application). (Common), a lascivious man.

Stallsman (thieves), an accomplice who takes charge of the plunder ; from to " stall off," take away.

Stall, to (theatrical), to act a part. (Popular), to lodge or put up at a public-house. (Thieves), to screen a robbery while it is being perpetrated, to surround an intended victim in a crowd while a confederate operates. (Old cant), to make, arrange ; "*stalling* to the rogue," admitting a new member. Also to conceal, to carry off, put by as booty.

I met a dell, I viewed her well,
   She was benship to my watch ;
So she and I did *stall* and cloy
   Whatever we could catch.
      —*The English Rogue.*

Stall your mug (popular), go away, make yourself scarce. Thieves use this expression generally with the meaning of go home, take shelter.

Stamp (printers), separate types are commonly called—especially by outsiders—*stamps.* (American), a peculiar way of throwing dice out of a box. " I have seen three sixes thrown thrice in succession by *stamping.*"

Stamp-backs (gambling cheats), explained by quotation.

It is absolutely and utterly impossible to distinguish the microscopic dots and lines of the ordinary marked card while it is being dealt off the pack, and no man ever lived who could use them to advantage. The first of the kind produced were the old-fashioned *stamp-backs*, but players soon found out that no system of marks were eligible while the cards were in motion, and they dropped them.—*Star.*

Stampers (thieves), feet, shoes.

Strike up, piper, a merry merry dance,
That we on our *stampers* may foot it and
   prance.
      —*Broome : Jovial Crew.*

Stamps (old cant), legs. "*Stamps in the Harmans,*" legs in the stocks.

Stander-up (American thieves), a man who robs intoxicated persons under pretence of aiding them to go home.

They gave Chandler the name of being a *stander-up* of drunken men. The proper mode of *standing-up* a tipsy man, according to the rules, is to place your right arm under the left arm of the sleeper close to the shoulder, placing the hand on his waistcoat, just above his left vest pocket. As you raise him with the right hand, press your hand hard against his body so that he will not feel the watch slipping from his pocket into your left hand. — *Philadelphia Press.*

Standing dish (society), a common expression for any one who is constantly lunching, dining, or calling at a house. "Mr. —— is always lunching here, he is quite a *standing dish.*" Generally speaking applied to any one or anything which often makes its appearance before the public.

Lottery started with the call of Cigar and Peter Simple (the grey), whose opponents also included those *standing dishes,* Charity and Seventy-four. — *Sporting Times.*

Stand in, to (general), to have a share in a bet or any speculation.

Here, hand me the flimsies, and *stand in* with me,
I'll do a good turn to a friend of old Flo's.
    —*Bird o' Freedom.*

Mr. ——, I believe, was asked to *stand in* with him, but the Jove of the Lyceum declared that the prices were ruinous. The result, however, was an enormous success. —*Star.*

Take a side in a dispute. (Thieves), have a share of the proceeds of a robbery.

If I lend you these I shall want to *stand in*; but I said I can't *stand* you at that; I will grease your dukes if you like.— *Horsley: Jottings from Jail.*

Stand-offish (society), a *noli me tangere* manner.

A hundred years since Versailles was almost divided into two camps. The quarter of Notre Dame almost proudly assumed the title of the patriotic quarter. Its denizens gave the first deputies of France a cordial welcome, while those of St. Louis stood aloof. It is solemn and respectable, one might almost say *stand-offish.* Its doors keep people at a distance, and its windows seem to look with a kind of contempt on the passers-by.—*Evening News.*

Stand off, to (American), to put off by means of a trick.

Loop-holed! Well, the man who built this place expected occasionally to have to *stand off* irate Mexicans who had followed stolen stock into the valley.—*F. Francis Saddle and Moccasin.*

Stand on one's hind legs, to (popular), to show anger, to take a thing in bad part, or to lose one's temper. French *se cabrer.*

Stand on velvet, to (racing), to have all your bets secured, and on the winning side.

Stands on his ears (American), an expression which, like standing on his head, or throwing somersaults, denotes exhilaration of spirits.

Man springeth up as the toad-stool, and *standeth upon his ears* when he is young, but as he groweth older he wrinkleth up with worry, and his beauty fadeth away. —*Thomas P. Montfort.*

Stand to (common), to treat to.

If you like *to stand* a can of beer, you may enter the smithy and have a chat with them ; but idle only on your part. —*Greenwood : In Strange Company.*

Stand me a drink before I go; it is an arduous task I have to perform.—*Bird o' Freedom.*

(Thieves), to *stand* the patter, to be tried.

Star (auction), an article not properly belonging to the sale introduced into an auction of goods.

Starcher (common), stiff white necktie.

Star-gazer (popular), a horse that keeps its head high when trotting or galloping. Also a hedge prostitute.

Star-gazers (American), " ladies of the pavement, who walk by night, not so much, however, to study the heavenly bodies, as to dispose of their own." " Bats, night - hawks, owls, astronomers, nocturnes, moonlighters, moths, nightlies, nymphs of darkness."

Stark-naked (popular), raw gin. So called from being undiluted and unsweetened, being raw, like meat which is not dressed. Also " strip-me-naked," " unsweetened." " Strip-me-naked " is a variation, or possibly a pun, on the phrase "sip me naked."

His " bingo " was unexceptionable ; and as for his *stark-naked*, it was voted the most brilliant thing in nature.—*Lytton : Paul Clifford.*

Starling (police), a person marked for the police. From a play on *spotted*, marked out.

Star-queller (theatrical), is a term applied to an actor whose imperfect acting mars that of better actors.

Starring (prison). " Some crack a pane in a shop-front and by passing the wet thumb along, they can direct the crack as they please ; then removing the glass they can remove the goods " (Chesterton's " Revelations of Prison Life "). A lump of putty is sometimes placed on the window and then struck with a life-preserver. The glass is thus broken without noise, even that of falling glass.

Star the glaze, to (popular and thieves), to break a window pane ; to star in that sense is provincial English.

So, in fractional arithmetic, it is considered highly improper to *star the glaze*, in falling through the sashes of a grapery, when on the look-out for grapes.—*Diprose : Laugh and Learn.*

Start, the (thieves and tramps), London, as having the *start* of (being superior to) all other towns. Also Newgate Prison, as being the most important. (Popular), a rum *start*, an odd circumstance.

I got fullied. I was tried at the Start (Old Bailey).—*Mayhew : London Labour and the London Poor.*

Starting (popular), a reprimand or beating.

Star, to (theatrical), to perform as a *star* with inferior actors. Also to *star* it.

To use a bit of theatrical slang, Mr. —— is *starring it* with success in Wales, and is not likely to forget the extraordinary moonlight demonstration at Singleton Abbey.—*Pall Mall Gazette.*

(Billiards), to *star* is to receive one or more additional lives in the course of the pool game, on payment of an additional entrance fee.

Staruben (gypsy), imprisoned.

Where is Anselo W.? He that was *staruben* for a gry?—*C. G. Leland: The Gypsies.*

Vide STURIBEN.

Starve 'em, Rob 'em, and **Cheat 'em,** slang names for the contiguous or united towns of Stroud, Rochester, and Chatham. "So called," says Grose, "by soldiers and sailors, and not without good reason."

Stash, to (common), to cease, stop, stay, leave off. As this word agrees in every particular as to meaning with the gypsy *hatch,* it is possibly an anagram of it, or a corruption of to *stanch,* which formerly had the limited meaning of to stop.

What to the heel do you *stash* at? I'll chive you.—*Jon Bee: A Living Picture of London.*

Stationery (theatrical), paper, or orders in a theatre.

Staving, rip-staving, rip-stavering (American), to *stave, i.e.,* to break into, as to stave a cask, is correct. From this comes to *stave,* to burst through, or press onward. "The world will *stave* right on," "Where are you *staving* to?" Hence *staving,* dashing on, proceeding brilliantly, doing well, as a *staving* business. "*Ripping* and *staving* along" may be heard sometimes. "*Rip-snorter, rip-staver,* a tearer, driver, dasher" (Bartlett). *Vide* RIP.

Stay (American). "To be *stayed* with is to be courted by a man" (Bartlett). To *stay* with a woman is to carry courtship to the extreme. (Common), to *stay* is said of a horse or man with powers of endurance.

M. Carnot . . . has been unquestionably the most hard-worked citizen in this country; yet he has amazed his entourage by his *staying* powers.—*Daily Telegraph.*

Stayer (sporting), one not to be discouraged. An athlete or horse who has powers of endurance.

The distance was half-a-mile, and considerable interest was taken in the race, in which a fine contest was expected to ensue between the holder, H. C. S., and J. N., who has previously been known as a short-distance swimmer rather than a *stayer.*—*Pastime.*

Gonfalon is stopped by his penalty, and is nearly certain to give way to Theophrastus, who is a rare old *stayer.*—*Referee.*

Stay out (Eton), meaning the reverse.

Sometimes Blazes had a lazy fit, and put himself on the sick list for a day. This was called *stay out,* for the reason that one had to stay in.—*Brinsley Richards: Seven Years at Eton.*

Many things at Eton were called by misnomers, in the construction of which the *lucus a non lucendo* principle came out very strong. Thus, when we stayed in, we said we were *staying out ;* when "absence" was called, we had to be *present ;* a *third* of a year was called a *half,* &c. &c.—*Sketchy Memories of Eton.*

Stay-tape (trade), a dry goods clerk or salesman.

Steak, a two-eyed (popular), a bloater, or "soger," or red herring.

Steamer (American), a tobacco-pipe.

Steaming (popular), a pudding steamed. In Manchester a potato-pie is called a steam-engine. The term is much used in the army.

Steel, prison slang for Coldbath Fields, from the Bastille. A name it earned rightly from its abominable management in the early part of the nineteenth century, and wrongly from the ignorant outcry which greeted the introduction of the separate (or silent and solitary) system of imprisonment.

" And the *Steel*—the place to which Mr. Eggshells alludes in connection with his retirement ?"

"Coldbath Fields," responded Mr. Badger, promptly, "quod — gaol — prison — that's the *Steel.*"—*J. Greenwood : Dick Temple.*

The term has been extended to any prison, lock-up.

He pitched into the policeman, was lugged off to the *steel,* had up before the magistrate, and got a month.—*Thor Fredur : Sketches from Shady Places.*

Steel-bar drivers (popular), journeymen tailors. Termed also " flingers."

Steel-pen (common). A *steel-pen* coat is a dress coat.

As regards the coat, the Emperor has sternly set his face against the "swallow-tail," "claw-hammer," or *steel-pen* garment which, for the last sixty years, has been mercilessly inflicted on civilised society all over the world.—*Daily Telegraph.*

Steep (American), extreme. " A *steep* price." *Steep* grade, a rather difficult undertaking. De Vere remarks that *steep* is not only used in its literal sense, but by a kind of bold hyperbole applied to things generally. Men speak of " a *steep* price for a farm," and complain of " a *steep* tax to be paid." The French have *raide* (steep), for anything difficult to perform, to believe, or to stomach.

At the election in Minnesota one hundred and ten Winnebago Indians, wearing their blankets, voted the Democratic ticket ; but the agent thought this was rather *steep,* so he afterwards crossed that number from the list.—*Chicago Tribune.*

Steeple-house, Puritan for church.

Stems (popular), the legs.

Stem-winder (American), applied to anything quite perfect and finished, " with the latest improvements."

" Denver."

" Yes, sir, you're right, Denver. Now, there's a booming city—regular *stem-winder.* Ever been to Denver ?"

" Yes, siree. Denver is a pretty slick sort of a place. Didn't stay there long, eh ?"—*American Newspaper.*

Step down and step out ! (American), an intimation to cease, or a hint that a man has the worst of it.

Step it, to (common), to run away.

Mr. Curtis slipped into his pockets nine silver knives, and some dessert spoons and forks, and then we regret to say he *stepped it*, but he did so like a gentleman.—*Daily Telegraph.*

Stepper (prison), the treadmill.

Stepping it (army), desertion. When a soldier absents himself with no intention of returning, he is said to have *stepped it* by his comrades.

Stepping ken, a dance-house. English, but now more used in America, where the dance-house is much commoner than in England. It is a dancing-hall frequented by sailors, and the lowest classes of men and women of all kinds.

Stereo (printers), any one relating stale news to his companions, would be told it was *stereo, i.e.,* already " cast." *Vide* GEORGE HORNE.

Steven (thieves), money. *Vide* STEVER.

I rather fancies that it's news,
How in a mill, both men should lose ;
For vere the odds are thus made even,
It plays the dickens with the *steven.*
—*Ainsworth: Rookwood.*

Stever (popular), a penny ; Dutch, *stuiver.* English stiver.

But now I've grown to man's estate, for work I've never cared,
I've " prossed " my meals from off my pals, ofttimes I've badly fared ;

Last night I had a single brown, a faggot thought I'd buy,
I dropped the *stever* down the sink, and then said with a sigh,
" I can't get at it."
—*Catnach Press Broadside.*

Stew (old English), not wholly obsolete as a slang word for a brothel ; we find it in Chaucer :

In Flaundres whilom was a companye
Of yonge folks, that haunteden folye
As ryot, hasard, *stywes*, and tavernes.
—*The Pardoner's Tale.*

The name of *stew* originated from such establishments being generally held in conjunction with places where hot baths were kept, and where the men who frequented them, if afraid of infection, might resort to the hot bath and induce copious perspiration, by way of possible purification. A prostitute was often called a *stew*, in the seventeenth century.

Steward (American cadet), the doctor at West Point, United States Military Academy.

Stick (general and American), an inefficient person.

If you've got any *sticks* working in this office I want them discharged at once. I can't allow any but first-class men in this department.—*Chicago Tribune.*

An awkward and uninteresting actor is often called a *stick*. (Thieves), a crowbar ; of more recent creation than its synonym the historical "jemmy." Burglars that "work with the *stick* " are looked down upon by those that " work with the 'screws.'"

"What tools will you want?" "We shall want some twirls and the *stick*."—*Horsley: Jottings from Jail.*

(Silver trade, &c.), *stick*, for candlestick, also a candle.

Sticker (popular), a butcher or slaughterer.

> Sporting with feelings, 'tis too bad,
>   Although a butcher's boy,
> For *stickers* may be made to smart
>   With love's cruel alloy.
> —*W. B.: Sporting with Young Kill Bull's Heart.*

Stick-hopper (sport), hurdle-racer.

First Fiddler is being taught hurdle-jumping at Richmond, where they are reported to have two or three very promising *stick-hoppers.*—*Evening News.*

Sticking (theatrical), or "dead stick," when all concerned get muddled.

Stick in, to (cricket), or to keep up one's wicket, is to avoid getting out by careful play without attempting to make runs.

Stick it up, to (popular), to put a charge down to any account, to score.

> The old man has died and left in his will
> That all is for me so I'll pay every bill,
> Though some *stick it up*, now I'll pay money down,
> And ride in my carriage all over the town.
> —*Charles Sheard: I'm a Millionaire.*

Sticks (common), furniture.

To the individual whose average earnings are perhaps half-a-crown a day, furnished lodgings are of course out of the question, and so none will permit him to occupy a room in a private house, unless he has at least a few *sticks* by way of security for the payment of a week's rent. —*J. Greenwood: Tag, Rag, & Co.*

To tide over till then is a work of some difficulty, but the *sticks* and the "wardrobe" of the family have paid the rent up to now.—*George R. Sims: How the Poor Live.*

A poor woman owed 11s. 3d. for rent. A broker distrained on her goods. They were sold at auction for £2, 1s. 9d., the expenses amounting to £2, 4s. Among other items 10s. had been charged for advertising her miserable *sticks.*—*Daily Telegraph.*

(Printers), another slang term for bad or hard printing rollers. (Racing), hurdles.

Some little time back Trap was smart over *sticks*, but now, I fear, he is no flyer; and of the others, Lowestoft, if he can jump, might have to be reckoned with, while both Never and Windsor did better at Croydon than is imagined.—*Evening News.*

(Cricket), the stumps.

> Every ball on the *sticks*,
> And the wicket playing vilely up to all kinds of tricks.
> —*Bird o' Freedom.*

(Old cant), pistols.

Sticks and stones (popular), one's *sticks and stones* are one's household goods and possessions, equivalent to Lares and Penates.

Stick, to cut one's. *Vide* CUT ONE'S STICK.

"That lad," said he to the sergeant, when the lad had gone out, "that lad's apprentice to a customer of mine. I suppose he's *cut his stick.*"—*The Gaol Cradle.*

Stick, to stick, to be stuck. This word, in the sense of to cheat, to be taken in, or as signifying loss, is English, but like many slang terms it has been very much extended and developed in the United States. Thus any and every kind of miscalculation, or error, or mistake, involves or results in being *stuck*, or in a *stick*. A man left with a certain number of unsaleable articles is *stuck* to that amount, and so on. There is a story of a country fellow, who, having gone into an auction, was told after it was over that he must pay for an immense quantity of goods which he had purchased. "Why, I didn't buy no goods," he replied. "Yes, you did," replied the auctioneer. "Every time I winked to you, you nodded again, and that was a bid." "'Twan't no bid," cried the countryman. "You kep a winkin' at me, as much as to say, 'Yes, you see how I'm goin' to *stick* somebody this time,' and I nodded back, meanin' 'I'm darned if you don't, mister.'" (Popular and thieves), to *stick* up, to deceive, cheat, disappoint.

Now don't *stick me up* (disappoint); meet me at six to-night.—*Horsley: Jottings from Jail.*

(Australian), to rob, to entrap, to take violent possession of. To *stick up* literally signifies to stop. "Stop," in the days of highwaymen in England, had a similarly disagreeable connotation. Australians talk of a bank being *stuck up*, *i.e.*, robbed, of being *stuck up* by bushrangers, &c.

Why, they *stuck up* Wilson's Station there, and murdered the man and woman in the kitchen; they then planted inside the house, and waited until Wilson came home at night with his stockman. Then they rushed out, and knocked old Wilson on the head, and drove a spear through the man's side.—*A. C. Grant: Bush Life in Queensland.*

A man talks of being *stuck up* when he does not see how to score at billiards, when he is puzzled for an answer, in fact, when he cannot get on in any matter.

Sticky-fingered (popular), thievish or covetous. The metaphor is obvious. In French cant *poisser* (to make sticky, clam), signifies to steal; *poisseur* or *poisse*, a thief.

"You're as *sticky-fingered* as a Scotchman."

"Why a Scotchman in particular?"

"Because he keeps the Sabbath, and everything else he can lay hands on."

A dialogue heard after the joke came out in *Punch.*

Stiff (general), paper of any kind, so called from its stiffness; a promissory note, used in contrast with "hard," which signifies cash, or hard money. To do a "bit of *stiff*" is to accept or endorse a bill.

Could not otherwise obtain his share of the plunder than by taking paper from P., *i.e.*, *stiff*, in the form "I promise to pay."—*Jon Bee: A Living Picture of London.*

(American turf), literally corpse; explained by quotation.

"What do they mean by a *stiff* in the race?"

"That means generally a horse that on public form should win the race, and that either the jockey, trainer, or horse has been 'fixed' so that he will not win. I have heard the term 'bookmaker's *stiff*' used, and it means about the same thing, and is played at the expense of the public and in the interest of the bookmakers."— *St. Louis Republican.*

(Popular and thieves), a letter, a secret or clandestine communication between a prisoner and his friends outside, or between one and another. It is written on a sheet torn out of a library book, or on whitey-brown, with a scrap of pencil picked up and cautiously secreted, or a piece provided by an officer in connivance.

" You've got a ' new chum ' in your party ? "

" Yes ; he's got a fiver. He is a draper, from Leicester. He says you used to be his lawyer."

" Ask him to write me particulars of his case."

" Oh, yes ; I'll swag it in. I have a piece of ' cedar' which I'll lend him to write the *stiff*."—*Evening News.*

(Popular), a *stiff*, a corpse.

I've been terribly scared myself. I recollect one night, something like this, I had gone out about eleven o'clock to get the *stiff* of a man who had died of consumption.—*Globe Democrat.*

Stiff-fencer (streets), a street seller of notepaper. *Vide* STIFF.

Stiff for (sporting Australian), certain for. The metaphor here is something that cannot be diverted (or averted). After the Melbourne Derby and Cup of 1880, Grand Flaneur was considered *stiff for* every race for which he was entered.

Stiff on (tailors). *Vide* DEAD-HORSE.

Stiff 'un (popular), a corpse. (Turf), a horse certain not to run. In America "stiff."

The shilling you sent me, dearest mother,
Has caused your boy some weeks of mental pain,
I backed a *stiff 'un* with it, dearest mother,
You shall have it when the Gee-gees run again.
    —*When the Gee-gees run Again.*

The latter, seeing how sensitive the market is nowadays, and how inclined racing men are to follow what is done by layers who have the reputation of living out of *stiff 'uns*, kept his place in a way that can only be regarded as miraculous. —*Referee.*

There are two bookmakers in Melbourne nicknamed " the Undertakers," because of their fondness for laying against *stiff 'uns*, which, in this case, means horses that are certain not to run.

Stilting (thieves), synonymous with " high flying," explained by quotation.

" Don't say another word," said he : " am I anything in the police, indeed ! You are a nice sort of chap to try your hand at *stilting!* (first-class pocket-picking). " Why, what d'yer mean by it ? How long have you been about ? "—*The Little Ragamuffins.*

Stilton (common), that's the *Stilton*, a rendering of " that's the cheese."

Stinger (common), a hard blow.

Stingo (popular), strong ale, ale.

. . . to prove his trust in native *stingo* quaffed off a flagon of it. — *Daily Telegraph.*

Stink cupboard, a cupboard in a chemical laboratory through which a strong upward draught passes, and into which any evil-smelling and noxious preparation is placed during the process of its manufacture.

Stinkious, gin; a word in use in the early part of the eighteenth century.

Stinks (schools, &c.), chemistry, a lecturer on physical science, especially chemistry. When a man took his degree in natural science, he used to be said at Cambridge to "go out in *stinks*."

Stinky (army), a farrier or shoeing smith. Query so called from the unpleasant smell of burning hoof, &c., so often accompanying the fitting of new shoes to a horse.

Stir (thieves), prison. Abbreviation of "sturiben" (which see).

I was in Brummagem, and was seven days in the new *stir.—Mayhew: London Labour and the London Poor.*

Stock actor (theatrical), an artiste who is a regular member of a stock company.

Stock cards, to (cardsharpers), to arrange cards for cheating purposes.

Stock, long of, explained by quotation.

Long of stock is an American term for a holder of securities who anticipates ability to sell at a higher price than that at which he purchased.—*St. James's Gazette.*

Stodge (Charterhouse), the inside of a roll or the crumb of new bread. (Popular and thieves), food. *Stodge* is pro-

vincial for soft food, pottage, &c., of any kind. From *stodge*, thick, slimy mud.

Stodger (common), a great eater, gormandiser. (Charterhouse), a penny bun.

Stodge, to (common), to gorge oneself with food.

Stolen ken (old cant), a broker's shop. *Vide* KEN.

Stomp drawers (old cant), stockings.

Stone broke or **stoney** (general), term in very common use among men in the fashionable world to express that they are in extreme financial difficulties and on the verge of bankruptcy, if not already bankrupts. Perhaps derived from "stone-breaking," in that the solid mass of rock, broken up into small fragments, and only useful for mending roads with, is a decided come-down for a granite rock. Probably a miner's phrase. Again, possibly from the idea that a man's last resource is breaking stones in the workhouse or on the road. Originally American.

At your mute call the people flock,
The banker for his pounds pawns stock;
The widow for the mite pawns frock;
The milkmaid sweet, she pawns a crock;
All *stoney broke*—with not a "rock,"
  Ye three brass balls.
      —*Detroit Free Press.*

We shall see scores of punters who went *stoney* over Manchester working away at Croydon this afternoon.—*Evening News.*

Stone-jug, the, originally Newgate Prison. Now any prison.

In a box of the stone-jug I was born.
—Ainsworth: Jerry Juniper's Chant.

"The elders of the Kirk in Glasgow used of old to go out of church and make a sweep round for absentees and idlers, who on Monday were placed in the stocks or pillory, which being called (from the Latin *jugum*, a yoke), the *jougs*, the treatment was styled 'clapping them in the *jougs*,' hence stone *jougs* or *jug*. Parish *jugs* in Scotland consisted of an iron collar fastened by a chain and padlock to one of the entrance piers of the churchyard gate. This was the iron *jug*, and a prison in which the offender is confined bodily becomes, by an easy association of ideas, the *stone-jug*." "It is remarkable that the use of the phrase *stone-jug*, for prison, finds a parallel in Greek. The Scholiast on the Iliad, on the word Keramos, gives the meaning, a prison, as a Cyprian usage" (*Notes and Queries*). Grose calls it a "stone doublet."

Stone-fence (common), brandy and ale. A variation of "breaky leg."

Stook (thieves), pocket-handkerchief. Probably Yiddish, from the German *stuck*, a piece. *Stook-hauler*, a pickpocket who steals pocket-handkerchiefs.

Stoop, the (old cant), the pillory.

Stop, on the (thieves), explained by quotation.

You have heard of working *on the stop*, most likely, which means picking pockets when the party is standing still.—*Temple Bar.*

Stop-lay. Two or more well-dressed pickpockets promenade singly, until they select a person that will answer their purpose. One then inquires of him the direction to a place somewhat distant. On being told, he pretends not to understand his informant, who, becoming interested in his desire to be explicit, draws closer to the inquirer. At this instant one or both the others walk up, and in an instant the obliging man is relieved of a part of his property. This is called the *stop-lay*.

Stormen (society), a hot member of society, a man who is extremely proficient at anything, a lady who is fast and peculiar in ways and language; the origin of the word is a storm which bears down everything before it.

Stotor (old cant), a heavy blow, Dutch *stoat*, a blow, thrust, or push. "Het schip stiet op en onder schip"—"The ship fell foul upon another ship."

Stouts (Stock Exchange), Arthur Guinness, Son & Co. Shares.

Stove-pipe (popular), a silk hat. French "tuyau de poële."

A big white fur *stove-pipe* hat on the back of his head.—*Huckleberry Finn.*

Stow, to (thieves), to live.

> You may have a crib to *stow* in,
> Welcome, my pal, as the flowers in May.
> —*W. Maginn: Vidocq's Slang Song.*

(Popular), stop, cease.

> "*Stow* that gammon," interposed the robber.—*Dickens: Oliver Twist.*

> *Stow* it, Emma . . . It's only a lark . . . Lark or linnet, you *stow* it, or I shall have to show you downstairs.—*J. Greenwood: Low-Life Deeps.*

Stow that kid, stop that nonsense, humbug.

> I am a Devonshire clergyman's daughter, and just left my home with an officer—oh, *stow* that kid. Here's half a dollar, which is precious near the last.—*Sporting Times.*

To *stow*, not to talk about.

> You maunders all *stow* what you stall,
> To rum coves what so quire.
> —*Song: Clear Out, Look Sharp.*

Stow magging, *stow* your whids, *stow* your gab, hold your tongue.

> "Oh! *stow* your gab, now, old 'un, do;
> Oh! *stow* your gab," said she;
> "And, though it's nowt to do wi' you,
> I'll tell what's ailin' me."
> —*Scraps.*

(Nautical), to *stow* one's jawing tackle, to hold one's tongue.

> But 'tain't for a British seaman to brag, so I'll just *stow* my jawin' tackle and belay.—*Gilbert: Ruddigore.*

To *stow* comes from old English *stewen*, to restrain; akin to stay, stop, stand. Compare Shetland *stow!* hush! silence!

Straddle, spread (American), a Stock Exchange term for "options."

The well-understood operation of put and call is in danger of being henceforth known as *straddle* or *spread.*—*St. James's Gazette.*

Straddle, to (American). When a candidate for office, "or any other man," in America does not take sides distinctly with one party or the other, he is said to be "on the fence," or to *straddle* it.

Their view of the message is that the President has convictions on the subject, but lacks the courage to give expression to them in a fighting way; so he *straddled.*—*Chicago Tribune.*

Straight (American). In the United States a *straight* drink means one of unmixed spirits, *e.g.,* whisky *straight* is the same as neat. But Mr. Hotten is quite wrong in saying that it is peculiar to dram-drinkers. It is used in many strange ways. Thus, if cigars are labelled, "Ten cents apiece, *straight*," it means that no deduction will be made for buying a number of them. To vote the *straight* ticket at an election is to do so without scratching, that is to say, without taking off the name of any candidate and substituting another.

In molasses, mixtures are relatively cheaper than *straight* goods.—*New York Price Current.*

> But refusing to take e'en a moment of rest,
> He exceedingly rapidly fell,
> By dint of disposing of glass after glass,
> Into that Bacchanalian state,
> Into which you will almost be certain to pass
> If you go in for taking Scotch *straight.*
> —*Bird o' Freedom.*

Straighten the screw, to (thieves), to bribe the jailer.

I've knowed what it was to go starvin on skilly and toke for a month, and then 'ave a cold mutton chop, as was sent in by a pal as 'ad *straightened the screw*, shoved in through my trap.—*Sporting Times*.

Straight griffin, the (popular), "the *straight* tip," or hint.

The Old Temple Bar was to London a cuss,
But I think the new griffin's a jolly sight worse,
Our sage city-fathers grandmothers appear
To raise such a griffin, at which people jeer,
Now here's the *straight griffin*—it won't long be here.
—*Ballad: Oh lor, oh lor, oh dear.*

In explanation of this verse it may be said that Old Temple Bar was removed because it was considered ugly by all who regard everything ugly which is not brand-new, but chiefly because it was in the way. A monument, representing a *griffin*, was raised on its site, to commemorate it—which monument is quite as much in the way as "the Bar" ever was, and, in the opinion of everybody, except perhaps its manufacturer, twice as ugly.

Straight racket, on the (thieves), leading an honest life.

Plenty of cases might be cited where wrong 'uns who were wanted went to a chief of police, demanded truce on promise of amendment, and most scrupulously observed the conditions of the treaty. "Will you leave me alone if I take *on the straight racket?*" is a question often answered in the affirmative.—*Referee.*

Straight tip (racing), *straight* is probably only a slang form of "right." Latin and Greek have each a word meaning both *straight* and *correct*. *Straight tip* originally meant correct information as to what horse would win a race, but is used slangily for "good advice" or "correct information about anything."

He was a real good fellow, and would give them the *straight tip.*—*A. C. Grant: Bush Life in Australia.*

Strain your taters, to (common), to urinate. The play is on *kidney potatoes*. Also "to scatter."

Strap (popular), credit at a public-house or other place where drink is retailed. The word is common among small dealers, but has not yet extended to the classes immediately above them.

I was once told by a brassfounder that out of thirty-six men in the factory where he was employed no fewer than thirty-two were on the books of a public-house to which the men regularly resorted, as there they could get *strap, i.e.,* credit.—*Daily Telegraph.*

I've tried to get fried fish on *strap*,
But found it was no use,
For when I said she was a duck,
She said I was a goose.
—*T. W. Barrett: Blow Me up an Apple-Tree.*

Strap is a Yorkshire term. The idea is probably that of a man in debt, metaphorically bound by a *strap* or tightening his belt as if hungry. The French use the term *serré* for needy. (American), hard *strapped*, in great trouble, much distressed for money. *Vide* BLACK-STRAP.

Straw boots (army), the 7th Dragoon Guards. A nickname gained during the suppression of agricultural riots in the South of England. Called also "Black Horse," and "Virgin Mary's Bodyguard."

Strawer (public schools), straw hat.

Strawing (patterers), explained by quotation.

Strawing, or selling straws in the street, and giving away with them something that is really or fictionally forbidden to be sold, as indecent papers, political songs and the like. *—London Labour and the London Poor.*

Straw, in the, to describe a woman in childbed. "Halliwell and Wright give the expression as an archaism, but without instances of its use. It is not found in the older phraseological dictionary. Hotten derives it from the uses of the farmyard, Webster from the supposed practice of making beds of straw. The more probable derivation is that given from the practice of laying down straw before a house in which a lady is confined. I believed that the expression was only applied to persons of condition. I am reminded of a characteristic witticism uttered by a celebrated judge, many years ago, in connection with this practice. He was on circuit, and going in state with the high sheriff to the courthouse, the street in front and round the court was found covered with straw. Some curiosity was expressed by the sheriff to know why this was done. The learned judge said he supposed it was on account of the *gaol* delivery " (G. B. B., *Notes and Queries*).

Streaked, streaky. Bartlett gives this as American : " To feel *streaked*, is to feel confused, alarmed ; " Hotten as English slang for irritated or ill-tempered, and derives it from its being "said of a short-tempered man who has his good or bad times in *streaks*." The Dutch say, " Daar loopt met hem een *streek* door," *i.e.*, a *streak* runs through him, which Sewell translates as, " He has a weak place in his head."

Streaks, to make (American), to decamp ; also "make tracks."

Street ganger (thieves), a beggar.

Street pitchers (popular), any of the class of people who make a "pitch" or stand in the streets to sell articles or give an entertainment or performance of some kind.

Stretch (thieves), a year. Compare with "length" (six months' imprisonment).

I did not fall again for a *stretch*. This time I got two moon for assaulting the reelers when canon. — *Horsley: Jottings from Jail.*

" All right, Sam." " How much, Toby?" "Three *stretch*," by which the sympathetic Sam knows his friend means "three years." *—Greenwood: Under-currents of London Life.*

One of them called out, "We may get a *stretch* (twelve months) for it," and another replied, "No, we can't, for loitering." One then called out, "We may get 'a drag' (three months), after the remand."
—*Daily Telegraph.*

(University) a walk.

Stretched (thieves), hanged.

The night before Larry was *stretched*,
The boys they all paid him a visit.
—*Death of Socrates.*

Stretcher (common), a falsehood.

He's told some *stretchers*, I reckon, and I said I wouldn't swallow it all.—*Huckleberry Finn.*

Stretcher fencer (streets), a street seller of braces.

Stretch-hemp (common), a candidate for the gallows.

Stretching match (thieves), an execution by hanging.

A long, an audible breath of relief passes like a wave over the crowd. They look at one another. After all, Billy would be saved his *stretching match*, and the girl would die game.—*Savage London.*

Strides (theatrical), trousers.

Strike a bright, to (popular), to have a piece of good fortune.

Strike a jigger, to (thieves), to break open a door, or pick a lock.

Strike a light, to (popular), to open an account of the minor sort, generally applied to ale-house scores. This is said to have originated with printers.

Strike me blind (nautical), rice.

Strike me lucky! (popular), an exclamation used when concluding a bargain; from the old custom of striking hands and leaving a luck or earnest coin in that of the seller, formerly termed God's penny. In France, when letting apartments or a house, it is customary to give the concierge a silver or gold coin as *denier à Dieu.*

Strike oil, to. A metaphor borrowed from an American phrase, to come upon, discover oil. Hence to be very lucky, to hit upon a fortune.

Dr. Stanford has undoubtedly *struck oil* with this novel adaptation of our national melodies.—*London Figaro.*

Strike, to (old cant), to steal money.

The cutting a pocket, or picking a purse, is called *striking.*—*Greene : Art of Coney-catching.*

(American), to borrow or extort money. From provincial *to strike*, to tap a barrel. Compare with French slang *taper.*

I may *strike* you for $10 next week.—*The Judge.*

To find.

I said, "Don't do nothing of the kind; it's one of the most jackass ideas I ever *struck.*"—*Huckleberry Finn.*

To *strike* it rich (American), to find a rich vein.

To increase the unfounded enmity against the boy-miner, and give it such basis as envy would rate enough, he found a vein, *struck it rich*, as the saying goes.—*H. L. Williams : Buffalo Bill.*

Strikers (American), persons who in politics and elections simply aim at personal profit.

My dear boy, you do not understand these matters yet. The mugwumps do not form a party or nominate a ticket. They sit in judgment on the other fellows. They are not political *strikers*. They are political kickers. They want no offices for themselves, but they demand the best services for the State.—*Boston Herald.*

Stringer (cricket), a very hard ball to play, one that puzzles the batsman. Possibly alluding to a ball that comes in direct on the *stringed* handle of the bat, consequently one hard to play.

String, to (printers), to mislead, or put one on the wrong scent; to hoax a person would be to *string* him, *i.e.*, to lead him. (Provincial), to get in a *string*, to deceive. (Billiards), players *string* at the commencement of the game for choice of balls and option of breaking, by playing both together from the two corner spots in the D. They play to hit the top cushion, and rebound back into baulk. The winner is he who gets his ball nearest to the bottom cushion when the balls have come to a rest. To *string* is therefore to play up and down the table, literally to put on a line (as to *string* beads). A common expression in America is "to get in a *string*," applied to any kind of fortunate series. The French have the slang term "se faire enfiler" (literally to get strung or stringed), meaning to have an unlucky series at cards, hence to lose much money.

Strip-me-naked. *Vide* STARK NAKED.

Strippers (gambling cheats), explained by quotation.

Strippers were also great favourites—that is to say, packs in which the high cards were a little wider than the rest, and cut slightly wedge shape, so that they could be drawn out at will.—*Star.*

Struck all of a heap (popular), astounded.

For a second he stood *struck all of a heap*, as he explained to his wife afterwards. Then he burst into a roar of laughter. — *George R. Sims: The Doll's Secret.*

Strummel (old cant), straw. Gypsy *strammel*.

The bantling's born; the doxy's in the *strummel*, laid by an autumn (autem) mort of their own crew that served for midwife.—*Broome: Jovial Crew.*

Hair, called also "thatch."

With my *strummel* faked in the newest twig.
—*Ainsworth: Rookwood.*

Strummel or **strummel faker** (cant), a hairdresser, barber.

Stubble your whids (thieves), hold your tongue.

Stubble your whids,
You wants to trick I.
Lend you my quids?
Not one, by Dickey.
—*Lytton: Paul Clifford.*

Stuck, to be (popular), to be moneyless. ' *Vide* STICK, TO STICK. (American), to be at a disadvantage, to lose in trade, to lose by miscalculation.

We're the only Eastern folks in the Yonkville Stock, unless Mr. Sloper will take a few shares—and, of course, anybody else may be *stuck*, and be darned.— *Mace Sloper, by C. G. Leland: Knickerbocker Magazine,* March 1856 (cited by J. R. Bartlett).

Stuckling (Winchester College), explained by quotation.

Stuckling was a kind of flat pastry made of chopped apples and currants. And the speciality of it was that the apples must be that year's apples. They used to be sent up from Devonshire or Cornwall, and sometimes were with difficulty obtained.—*T. A. Trollope: What I Remember.*

Stuck on it (American), fond of, addicted to. To get *stuck on* a girl, to fall in love with her.

Spring's the best time to buy stock. Turn 'em on to your range when the grass is green, and there's plenty of it ; they get *stuck on it* then, and stop there — you don't have no trouble locating them.—*F. Francis : Saddle and Moccasin.*

Stuff (American), a *stuff*, a weak, worthless person, one without energy. In low slang used for an honest, respectable citizen. (Common), drink, money.

Has she got the *stuff?* Is she rich?— *Sheridan : The Rivals.*

(Prison), tobacco.

When was I at the steel? Had I got any *stuff?* That screw was all right. He would sling some *stuff* for a quid.—*Evening News.*

Stuff-gownsman (legal), a junior or barrister under the degree of Queen's Counsel is so called.

Stuggy (public schools), thickset.

Stumer (London slang), a fictitious or dishonoured cheque. From German *stumm, stumme,* dumb, in imitation of the English "dummy," meaning both "dumb" and "sham."

My collection of writs, pawn-tickets, unreceipted bills, *stumers,* letters from tarts, unpublished operas, and correspondence.—*Sporting Times.*

Stump (old cant), strength.

Now my kinching-cove is gone,
By the rum-pad maundette none ;
Quarrons both for *stump* and bone,
Like any clapperdogeon.
—*The Rum-Morts' Song.*

Stumped (common), defeated in argument, nonplussed, puzzled, confused. Literally bowled out.

To be all "abroad," to be *stumped,* not to know where
To go, so disgraced as not to be "placed,"
Or, as Crocky would say to Jem Bland,
"to be nowhere."
—*Ingoldsby Legends.*

Also bankrupt, in poverty.

Stumper (cricket), wicket-keeper.

Since then he has enjoyed the reputation of being one of the finest *stumpers* that England has ever produced.—*Sportsman.*

Stump, on the (common), or to *stump,* to go about speech-making on politics or other subject. Originally American, alluding to an orator who harangues the populace from the *stump* of a tree or other elevation.

The temptation, in short, would be far too severe, and would, too, so often prevail,
That members, as 'tis far too much on the *stump,* would be always henceforth on "the rail."
—*London Figaro.*

Stumps (common), the legs, synonymous with "pins."

See—see—the fine fellow grows weak on the *stumps.—Lytton: Paul Clifford.*

"Shove on more coke!" yelled the engine-driver. "Shovel it up, shovel it up, you butter-fingered bungler! Move your *stumps*, I say, or I'll help you!" and he did, with a heavy boot.—*C. H. Ross: The Husband's Boat.*

Stump-spouter (Canadian), an itinerant "orator."

They were downright Tories—thought most things would grow better and stronger in the long run for being let alone a bit. If a constitution was to grow up strong,.it didn't want forcing with a lot of *stump-spouter's* rubbish, and so on, and so on.—*Phillipps-Wolley: Trottings of a Tenderfoot.*

Stump, to (common), to defeat, literally bowl out.

He was determined, he said, to *stump* the examiners.—*C. Bede: Verdant Green.*

(Popular), to pay, or *stump up.*

Why don't you ask your old governor to *stump up?—Sketches by Boz.*

Only a pound! it's only the price
Of hearing a concert once or twice,
. . . .
But common prudence would bid you
stump it.
—*Hood: Tale of a Trumpet.*

Why didn't he *stump* up the ochre? —*Punch.*

Also to *stump* the pewter. For derivation *vide* STUMPY.

Stumpy (popular), cash, coin, money.

Reduced to despair, they ransomed themselves . . . till they was reg'larly done over and forked the *stumpy.—Sketches by Boz.*

Down with the *stumpy*; a tizzy for a pot of half-and-half.—*C. Kingsley: Alton Locke.*

Stumpy is that which is paid on a *stump*, synonymous with
VOL. II.

"paid on the nail." "In the centre of Limerick Exchange," says O'Keefe, "is a pillar with a circular plate of copper about three feet in diameter, called the *nail*. On this metal desk the earnest of all Stock Exchange bargains has to be paid." A similar custom prevailed at Bristol, where were four pillars called *nails* in front of the Exchange for a similar purpose.

Stunner (common), splendid, excellent, quite out of the way; applied to a person or thing.

Who's the buyer of coat? Here's a *stunner* for three-and-six, half-a-crown, two bob, anything.—*J. Greenwood: Low-Life Deeps.*

(Popular), a surpriser.

A six-and-thirty tonner
Not inaptly called a *stunner*,
And known as the Woolwich Infant.
—*Punch.*

Stunning (common), astonishing, excellent.

You were justly reproved. The word *stunning* is decidedly slang.—*Household Words.*

She certainly was a *stunning* girl.— *Punch.*

Stun out of the regulars (thieves), to *stun* a man out of his regulars, is to cheat him out of his rights, deprive him of his share in the plunder.

Sturiben (thieves). In America *sturbin*. In England any prison, in America the State-prison. The common canting *stir* or *stur* is an abbreviation of this. It is a pure gypsy word, from the root *star-ava*. Correctly

U

staripen in gypsy. *Stardo* in gypsy means "imprisoned."

My mush is lelled to *sturiben*,
To *sturiben*, to *sturibon*,
My mush is lelled to *sturibon*,
To the tan where mandy jins.
—*Gypsy Song.*

Sub (popular), to do a *sub* is to borrow money, probably an abbreviation of subtraction. Also a small advance of pay in this sense from subsidy or sub-sistence. (Anglo-Indian), all.

Suck (common), a swindle. (University), a parasite. (Old cant), beer, a breast-pocket.

Suck-casa (costermongers and itinerants), a public-house.

Suck egg (popular), a silly person. "Go along, you *suck egg*."

Sucker (American), a greenhorn, a gullible person, a dupe. A term much used by thieves and gambling cheats.

Such men always take it for granted that an Englishman is a *sucker*. It is as well to foster the belief, for the amusement of hearing them ingeniously unfold their magnificent schemes. — *F. Francis: Saddle and Moccasin.*

Perhaps I'd better buy land, waiting for a rise and a *sucker*, buy horses with defects, sellin' 'em for sound; buy shares of railroad stock, or mines, anything to beat some one else and get the better of them.— *Bird o' Freedom.*

From *sucker*, a fish which is a synonym for stupidity, or from *sucking*, young, new to.

My enemy are but *sucking* criticks, who would fain be nibbling ere their teeth had come.—*Dryden: All for Love.*

I suppose you're a young barrister, a *sucking* lawyer.—*Thackeray: The Newcomes.*

Also a sponger, a sycophant, same as English suck. A person who ingratiates himself into the favour of the landlord of a large hotel, praises or puffs the establishment in the newspapers and makes himself agreeable to the guests, does odd jobs for his patron, and lives rent-free and board-free at his expense. The same sort of person was once called a sponger in England, and a sorner in Scotland, though both were confined to private practitioners, and unknown to hotel-keepers.

Sam . . . you're a nigger, but thar's more real white man under your black skin than could be found in an acre of such varmints as that *sucker.*—*Americans at Home.*

Suck in, to (common), to cheat, swindle.

I up wid a rock and I hit him on de shin,
And dat's de way I *sucked* him in.
—*Negro Song.*

Sucking the monkey. *Vide* MONKEY. To which add, sailors thus call a cocoanut on account of the three peculiar spots which give it a striking resemblance to a monkey's countenance.

Suck, to (American University), to make use of cribs and helps to translation. (Common), to sponge, draw information from a person. (Society), to *suck* up to, to toady, flatter, make up to. This word has been borrowed by society from schoolboy slang.

Sudden death (Anglo-Indian), a fowl served as a spatch-cock (*i.e.*, a split and grilled chicken). It was so called because it was often killed and cooked within half-an-hour. *Sudden death*, as food, recalls the German proverb, "Tod ist des Lebens Bothenbrod." (Popular), in tossing, to be decided by the first call, is to go *sudden death*. (University), a crumpet. *Vide* SORE LEG.

Suds, in the (thieves), embarrassed, nonplussed, at a loss to know what course to take.

Suety Isaac (popular), a pudding of only duff, and without plums.

Sugar (common), money. (American), flattery, praise, gammon.

Sugar-bag (Australian blackfellows), a nest of honey; also "chewgah bag." This is the name the blackfellows give to the honey-stores of the wild bee, of which they are inordinately fond.

The regular sharp chop-chop of the tomahawk could be heard here and there where some of them had discovered a *sugar-bag*, or a 'possum on a tree.—*A. C. Grant: Bush Life in Queensland.*

Sugar off, to (American), to amount to, used when speaking of a large fortune.

Josh Billings comes of a wealthy family, Shaws of Lanesborough in Massachusetts, and it is estimated that his estate would *sugar off*, as they say in Vermont, about $200,000.—*Harper's Bazaar.*

Sugar, to (rowing), pretending to row hard but in effect shirking.

Suit (thieves), a watch and seals.

Near to these hopeful youths sat a fence, or receiver, bargaining with a clouter, or pickpocket, for a *suit*, or, to speak in more intelligible language, a watch and seals.—*W. H. Ainsworth: Jack Sheppard.*

(Popular), *suit* of mourning, a pair of black eyes. (American), Whiskers or moustachios, as being a pair or a match, are often in the United States called a *suit*. Hence a head of hair has received the same name. "A full-blown *suit* of whiskers and moustachios, with head to match." Very naturally derived from *suite* as a series, a *suit* at cards, a *suite* of rooms, a *suit* of cards, *suite* being frequently pronounced *suit*.

Sukey (servant-girls), a kettle. A servant-girl is frequently addressed as *Sukey* by the lower classes.

Sulky (common), a one-horse chaise, with only room for one person. Used now only in trotting matches.

Summer game (American gamblers), playing merely for amusement or benefit of another person, but with his money.

Sumpsy (legal), an action of *assumpsit*.

Sumpsy is a pet word among lawyers for an action of *assumpsit*.—*Morning Advertiser.*

Sun (common), in the *sun*, having too much drink. (Naval), " getting the *sun* over the foreyard," taking a forenoon cup of grog at six bells, or eleven o'clock.

Sunday - face (popular), the behind.

Sunday-man (low), the lover of a street girl, her bully. Formerly a man in debt, who went out on Sundays only, for fear of the bailiffs.

Sun dog (nautical), the name given to the phantasmic mirage of a mock sun shining near the real sun—a phenomenon observed in some latitudes.

Sundowner (Australian), a tramp.

The Australian shepherd, like the *sundowner*, is almost a thing of the past.— *The Graphic.*

Vide OVERLAND MAN.

Sunshades (Stock Exchange), Sunehales Extension of the Buenos Ayres and Rosario Railway Company Shares.

Super (theatrical), supers, or supernumeraries. In the dictionaries a supernumerary is described as "a person or thing beyond the number stated, or beyond what is necessary." If this description be accurate, then the word supernumerary is utterly inappropriate to describe the humble but valuable auxiliary popularly known by the name of *super*. The *super* is as essential to the business

of the historical, the melodramatic, or the operatic theatre as the actor or the vocalist. The *super* is the valiant soldier, the faithful follower, the grotesque retainer of the pantomime. He it is who seizes the hero, and loads him with chains, and drags him to the deepest dungeon beneath the castle moat ; or presently leads him to storm the castle, to cut off the giant's head, or the dragon's tail, and anon quaffs his health from a gorgeous empty goblet of *papier mâché* what time he comes crowned with triumphant laurels to rescue the lady of his love, to marry her, and to live happy ever after. He it is who carries the " wood of Birnam " on his shoulders to "high Dunsinian Hill," who patiently bears "the blows and buffets of outrageous fortune " at the hands of that rascal Joseph Rumbuster, the clown. The *super's* work begins with the rehearsal, and ends with the performance, and he keeps the wolf from the door (though God knows how he does it !) at eighteenpence or half-a-crown a night. Amongst the *supers* you will find the idle, the dissolute, and the drunken; but amongst them you shall also find the modest, the gentle, the industrious—the broken gentleman, the disbanded soldier, the disappointed author, the ruined tradesman, bearing their fallen fortunes with equanimity. Most of these poor fellows are unpretentious, uncomplaining ; and very few are unwilling, or un-intelligent. Upon all important occasions, by special permission, detachments from Household troops, the Grenadiers, the Coldstreams, and the Guards officiate as *supers*. During the run of Henry V., at the Queen's Theatre, the actor who played the king had the honour of having amongst his body-guard four stalwart six-footers for his squires, gallant gentlemen who, although reduced to the ranks from adverse circumstances, had all held commissions in Her Majesty's service, and fought in famous battles.

He is only an amateur *supe*, who goes on in the "angry populace" scenes.— *Greenroom Jokes.*

At the Philadelphia Academy of Music, at the close of the performance, the *supers* and ballet - girls demanded their wages, but they were not forthcoming.—*Boston Journal.*

(Thieves), watch.

You must know where to dispose of a *super*.—*Temple Bar.*

(Thieves and popular), *super and slang*, watch and chain. Also used by itinerants, strollers, &c. &c. (Australian up-country), the superintendent of a station or run. Colonial slang is addicted to abbreviations—*e.g.*, prof. for professor, comp. for compositor; and so uses *super*, not in its ordinary sense of supernumerary at a theatre, but in the sense of superintendent of a sheep or cattle station.

Curly Johnson, the *super*, despised him,
and never neglected a chance,
To annoy and degrade the poor wretch,
who replied with not even a glance.
—*New South Wales Paper.*

Super master (theatrical), the superintendent of the *supers* at a theatre.

Supers (medical), explained by quotation.

Dr. Oliver Birnie's consulting-room was generally pretty full in the morning, and always with paying patients. He had long since passed the *super* stage of the profession. Lest any intelligent reader should be unacquainted with this phase of medical practice, let me explain that it is the custom when young doctors are anxious to work up a reputation for being fashionable, for them to engage a few *supers*, that is, to give advice gratis to a few selected persons, on condition that they come once or twice a week and help to make a crowd in the waiting-room.— *G. Sims: Rogues and Vagabonds.*

Super-screwing (thieves), stealing watches.

Supplejacks (up-country Australian), creepers, lianas. The derivation is obviously from the toughness and pliancy of these lianas, which in Victoria are rare, but are commoner in the warmer parts of Australia and New Zealand.

Supplejacks, cyclopean,
Binding huge tree to tree, with strength
of mesh
No apic elephant could tear apart ;
While up the bank, in their spring glory
fresh,
The blue lobelia with yellow heart,
And waratah with flame-hued royal crown
Proclaim the beauties round Australia's
own.
—*D. B. W. Sladen : A Poet of Exiles.*

Supple twelfth (army), the 12th Lancers.

Sura (Anglo-Indian), this is commonly called toddy, the fermented sap of several kinds of palm, such as the cocoa, palmyra, and wild date. Sanskrit *sura*, vinous liquor.

Surat (popular), an adulterated article of inferior quality. From the mixing of cotton with *surat*, an inferior article.

Surf (theatrical), a fourth or fifth-rate actor or musician who blends some other daily occupation with his nightly employment at the theatre. (Popular), *surf*, or *serf*, a sycophant.

Sut (tailors), satisfactory; said of anything gratifying, fortunate.

Swab (naval), an epaulet.

Swack-up (common), a falsehood.

Swad (American), a crowd, a number, a mass, or bunch. Dutch *zwad*, a swath, a row of mown grass; *swod* (Sussex), a bushel basket for measuring fish; a *swod* of fish.

Swadder, swaddler (old cant), a pedlar.

Swaddler. In America this term is specially applied to men who are paid by pickpockets to preach in public places and collect a crowd in which they may ply their craft. In England any street-preacher. In America men who pick a quarrel with a man and at the same time beat and rob him. Originally a contemptuous term for Methodists used by Roman Catholics. "It happened that Cennick, preaching on Christmas Day, took for his text these words from St. Luke's Gospel, 'And this shall be a sign unto you; ye shall find the babe wrapped in *swaddling*-clothes, lying in a manger." A Catholic who was present, and to whom the language of Scripture was a novelty, thought this so ridiculous that he called the preacher a *swaddler* in derision (Southey, "Life of Wesley"). In old cant a *swaddler* was a pedlar. Hotten gives the definition "a Roman Catholic who pretends conversion."

Swaddy (popular), an opprobrious name for a soldier; in old cant *swad*, *swadkin*. *Swad* is a Lancashire term, thought to be from pea-*swad*, used by old writers for a silly fellow, a country bumpkin.

> Did sweare that he would kill and slay,
>   I, mary, would he doe,
> If any *swad* besides himselfe faire madam
>   owle did wowe.
>   —*Warner: Albion's England*, 1592.

Again, it is possible that it owes its origin to the cant term *swadder*, a pedlar, alluding to the soldiers tramping about with a knapsack like a pedlar's pack, or to the provincial *swad*, a sword.

Swag (old cant), a shop. (Costers), a large collection of

miscellaneous goods. Hence
swag-shop (also termed a *swag*),
swag-barrow. (Thieves), booty,
plunder. *Swag*-shop, a receiver's place, also *swag*-chovey.

"It's all arranged about bringing off
the *swag*, is it?" asked the Jew.—*C.
Dickens: Oliver Twist.*

'Twas awful to hear, as she went along,
The dark allusion, or bolder brag
Of the dexterous dodge, and the lots of
swag.
—*Hood: Tale of a Trumpet.*

"We must do it to-night, Doss," said
the elder, soon after dusk. "The *swag's*
all in jewels, and a grab'll collar the lot."—
G. R. Sims: Rogues and Vagabonds.

A mess of sausages may apprise a remanded dog-stealer, "it is all right; the
animal is dead, and his body effectually
disposed of;" "toad in the hole" may
convey to a suspected burglar the glad
tidings that the hidden *swag* has not at
present been discovered.—*J. Greenwood:
Undercurrents of London Life.*

Speak to the tattler, bag the *swag*,
And finely hunt the dummy.
—*C. Hindley: Life and Times of
James Catnach.*

Swag is provincial for a
quantity or lot, a portion of property. Scottish *swag* or *swack*,
from old German *sweig*, a flock.
The Australian *swagman, i.e.,* travelling artisan or journeyman,
"humps his *swag*," *i.e.,* carries
his tools and luggage in a bundle
on his back.

I feel in the race of life of late,
I've been handicapped badly by careless
fate,
Who has put on my back a *swag*.
—*Keighley Goodchild: Through
the Fence.*

Also a small valise.

I would advise anybody to take as little
as possible in the way of articles of toilet,
I mean brushes, combs, &c., as if, later
on, he wishes to travel on horseback, he
will find how little can be squeezed into
a *swag.—Cornhill Magazine: With a
Cockatoo.*

Swagman (Australian), a tramp,
a travelling artisan. *Swag*,
bundle. The *bond-fide* travelling
artisan is properly the *swagman*,
but the word is often used as
equivalent to a *sun-downer, i.e.,*
a tramp. In old cant *swigman*,
a tramp, a mendicant bearing a
wallet, a pedlar.

Swag-chovey bloke (thieves), a
marine-store dealer who buys
stolen goods.

Swaggering Bob (theatrical), an
impudent buffoon.

'Tis the miserable art
Of the vile buffoon, who to please the pit,
Provokes its laughter, but lets down his
part,
Winks at his audience while he slaps his
fob,
And turns Charles Surface into *Swagger-
ing Bob!*
—*Lord Lytton (the present):
Glenaveril.*

Swagsman (thieves), an accomplice who takes charge of the
plunder.

Swag, to (thieves), originally to
carry off as plunder, but extended to carrying off anything.

The next witness is a policeman, who
deposes that he was in a public-house,
where he overheard the prisoner say that
he had had a good haul, and got over a
hundred ounces of plate, which he *swagged*
away.—*Evening News.*

By arrangement they each undertook
to *swag* out their literary treasures, so
that each man would only have the statu-

tory number of books in his cell which were allowed by the authorities.—*Evening News.*

Swallow the cackle, to (theatrical), to learn a part.

Swanker (public and military schools), one who works hard. *Vide* To Swank.

Swankey (West-Indian), a beverage compounded of molasses, vinegar, and water—a favourite drink with fishermen. This term has now become common throughout the States and the Dominion.

"Roll along here," shouted the cook. "Tumble up, and get your *swankey,* boys. It's as good as ever you cocked a lip at." And at the word each man, his face glowing with excitement and exercise, took his turn at the *swankey* pail.—*Newfoundland Fisheries.*

Swank, to (public and military schools), to work hard; old English *swinke,* to labour; *swinked* or *swenkt,* tired with work.

The *swenkt* grinders in this treadmill of an earth have ground out another day.—*Carlyle.*

Swan-slinger (theatrical), a *slinger* of "the sweet Swan of Avon," otherwise a Shakspearian actor.

Swap knives (American), "no time to *swap knives,*" in a moment.

But there warn't no time to *swap knives,* the old man grabbed me by the hand.—*Mark Twain.*

Swapped off (American), cheated, taken in, done, "sold."

Den Brer Fox know dat he been *swap off* mighty bad.—*Uncle Remus.*

That was the time that you got *swapt,* And looked so awfully wambler-cropt.
—*A Poem: Simon Barky.*

Swartwout (American), a verb of local (New York) origin or usage, signifying "to abscond," "to vamoose," "to skip." A Mr. Swartwout once decamped from that city, carrying with him a large amount of public money —hence its origin.

Swat (Royal Military Academy), *i.e., sweat,* work in general, but especially mathematics.

Swatchel (Punch show), Punch. Also the show. *Swatchel* box, the show itself; *swatchel* cove, the showman. *Swatchel* is provincial for "to beat with a switch." Hence probably the nickname given to Mr. Punch, whose principal occupation is plying his stick.

The various slang names used by the Punch and Judy showmen are—"Mozzy" for Judy; "darkey," the negro; "vampo," a clown; "vampire," a ghost; "buffer figure," dog owner; "scrappers," fighting men; "crocodile," a demon; "filio," a baby; "buffer," a dog.

The "frame" is the entire machine; "peepsies," the pan pipes; the "nobbing slum," the bag for collecting money; the "letter cloth," the advertisement; "tambour," the drum; "stalk or prop," the gallows; "slum fake," a coffin; "slum," the call.

Swat, to (University), to *sweat*, to work hard.

Sweat (public schools), fagging. (American), in a *sweat*, in a hurry, impatient.

Besides, he was in a *sweat* to get to the Indian Ocean right off.—*Huckleberry Finn.*

Sweat-box, the cell where prisoners are confined on arrest previous to being brought up for examination before the magistrate.

Sweater (common), explained by quotation.

At the outset Mr. —— is careful to distinguish between a contractor and a *sweater*. Both are contractors, but the *sweater* is a contractor and something more. Both exact from the workmen under them a certain amount of work for a definite wage, but there the likeness ends; for whilst the contractor pays an ordinary wage for an ordinary day's work, the *sweater* "exacts from men employed by him and working under his immediate superintendence the performance of an excessive amount of work in return for an unreasonably low remuneration."—*Evening News.*

The great *sweater* is the public; and as long as the public continues to encourage, or rather to compel, the "unscrupulous employer" to use the over-stocked labour market as he is using it now, so long will the existing evils endure.—*Daily Telegraph.*

(Boating), a thick woollen jersey originally used in boating. (Stock Exchange), a broker who cuts down commissions. A broker who works for such small commissions as to prevent other brokers getting the business, whilst hardly being profitable to himself (Atkin, "House Scraps").

Sweat gallery (Winchester College), the juniors who had to do some "sweat" or fagging. Each prefect had a water-carrier, who brought him cold water on Sunday; a clothes'-brusher, who had to brush his clothes; a valet to bring him his books, and warm water in winter.

Sweating (thieves), a primitive way of scraping gold off coins by shaking them in a bag. Another mode explained by quotation.

By far the most scientific form of smashing is that which is called *sweating*—the modern equivalent for the ruder art of "clipping," so fully described in Macaulay's History. Here the galvanic battery is brought into requisition, the metal being dissolved equally from all the surfaces of the coin operated upon, and that, too, without impairing the sharpness of "image or superscription." Sufficient metal for the *sweater's* purpose being removed, the coin is polished afresh. — *Thor Fredur: Sketches from Shady Places.*

(Schools), working. (Common), extracting money from a person, employing workpeople at starvation wages.

In Bavaria, it appears from the reports of the German factory inspectors, nearly sixty per cent. of the working classes work from ten to eleven hours a day, and over forty-nine per cent. work from eleven and a quarter to sixteen hours daily. It is the immigrants from countries like this who have made *sweating* possible.—*Evening News.*

Sweating shops, establishments where this is practised.

It is the women and children from the factories at the East End and the *sweating* shops in the neighbourhood who are pouring in now.—*Sims: Social Kaleidoscope.*

Sweat one's duds, to (thieves), to pawn one's clothes, that is, extract money from them.

They *sweated their duds* till they riz it.
—*Death of Socrates.*

Sweat one's guts out, a vulgar expression, meaning to work very hard.

Sweep the board, to (common), to take all. (American), to scoop the pool.

Games have introduced others as bandy and *sweep the board.—Standard.*

Sweet (thieves), in thieves' slang, an intended victim is *sweet* if he does not suspect the trick which is about to be practised on him. If he suspects, they try "to sweeten him" and "to keep him *sweet*" until their object is accomplished.

Sweetener (auction), a man who runs up prices at an auction.

Sweetmeat (common), a very young kept mistress, a precocious votary of Venus.

Sweet on (common), in love with.

Swell (general), a showily dressed pretender to extreme fashion.

This isn't the moment, when all *swelldom* is at her feet, for me to come forward. —*Thackeray: Newcomes.*

There were the *swell* and the snob. —*Punch.*

Swell . . . seems to have the greatest amount of vitality; but it is unquestionably moribund.—*Globe.*

This word threatens to be superseded by its more modern synonym of *masher* and *dude.* Both *swell* and masher have had

many predecessors, some of which still linger in popular parlance, such as beau, dandy, brick, macaroni, Bond Street lounger, Mohawk, Corinthian, and bloke. *Swell* survives as an adjective in the sense of showy, brilliant, pretentious, as a *swell* carriage, a *swell* house, a *swell* waistcoat, a *swell* dress, a *swell* turn-out, a *swell* watch-chain, and many others.

Bullingdon Club is the most aristocratic and the *swellest* in Oxford. —*Truth.*

Swell is evidently from the act of being puffed up with pride. French slang *se gonfler*, to feel proud of some achievement, congratulate oneself. It is the exact equivalent in meaning of the Italian *gonfione*, synonymous with *zerbinotto* and *damerino.* It is also used of any one who is proficient in anything, who is high up or excels in his profession. Our distinguished admiral who bombarded Alexandria has the nickname of "*swell* of the ocean."

There was a very large attendance of *swells,* including such magnates of the world of sports as the Dukes of Beaufort and Portland, &c.—*Sporting Times.*

A *swell* at Eton is thus defined by T. R. Oliphant, author of "Eton College":—" It is very hard to define exactly what is meant by a *swell* at Eton; but it usually implies a boy who, brought into notice either by athletic prowess or scholarship, or high standing in the school, by this means becomes acquainted with the leading members of the school, and is found on acquaintance to develop considerable social qualities, which make him hand and glove with all the Eton magnates."

Swell block (American University), a coxcomb and dandy; also those who assume and pretend overmuch.

Swell head (American), a vain, arrogant man, one who gives himself airs. Also a man who is drunk, spirits in excess giving the feeling as if the head were heavy and swollen.

Swell-mob (common), well-dressed, genteel sharpers and swindlers taken collectively.

He is renowned for his acquaintance with the *swell-mob.—Charles Dickens.*

Swell mobsman (common), one of the *swell-mob* (which see).

Swells (Winchester College), services on Sunday, saints' days, &c., when college men used to wear surplices.

Swell, to (Winchester College), to make a *swell* or mess; to bathe, wash, &c.

Swelter, to do a (popular), to perspire.

Athletics ain't 'ardly my form, and a cut-away coat and tight bags
Are the species of togs for yours truly, and lick your loose flannels to rags,
So I let them as liked *do a swelter.*
—*Punch.*

To *swelter* is an old English word used by Shakspeare.

Swift (printers), a fast and expeditious setter of type; quoted by Savage's Dictionary, 1841.

Swill, to (Shrewsbury), to take a shower-bath.

Swim (common), to be in the *swim*, to be in the popular current either in opinion, speculation, or fashion, on the move with the rest. To be one of an association, an affair.

" Look here," said the indignant gentleman in the brown pot hat, " why wasn't I in this *swim?*"
"What *swim?*" asked his Criterion friends.
" Why, this 'ere fight?"
—*Sporting Times.*

One's particular pursuits.

But hus, Charlie, hus? I likes horder,
  and likeways I'm partial to law,
Wen it means keeping my *swim* all clear,
  and a muzzling my henemy's jaw.
Wy, nothink could easy be nicerer, then,
  don'tcher see, dear old pal;
But supposing that game interferes with
  my larks, or my lush, or my gal?
—*Punch.*

(Angling), the section of water one selects to fish in. (Thieves), a good *swim*, a good run of luck, a long time without police interference.

Swimmer (old cant), a guardship on the river. A thief who, to avoid conviction, consented to be sent on board ship to serve the king, was said to have been *swimmered.*

Swimming market (Stock Exchange), in other words, when the *market* is firm and buyers feel no hesitancy in operating; the reverse of a " sick market."

Swim, to (thieves), to make a man *swim* for it, is to cheat him out of his share.

Swindle. This word is used in sporting circles to describe a speculation, or any dealing in which there is an element of chance. When a proposition is made to toss for a drink by spinning a coin, the phrase is generally "let's have a *swindle*." Judge Pigott summed up in a case. "As to the second plea that *swindle* had not a libellous meaning, this was in a great measure carried out by the plaintiff himself, who had advertised that he was getting up a *swindle*. In sporting circles they certainly did deal with an extraordinary vocabulary, and apparently did not use this word *swindle* in Dr. Johnson's sense."

In another case, Davey *v.* Walmsley, the following bit of evidence was tendered.

Mr. Hawkins—"Is the word *swindle* commonly applied to things like 'specs.'"

Witness (Mr. Paul Walmsley, Editor, *Racing Investigator*)—"Certainly! I never heard them called by any other name. It is a regular byword with us as a racing phrase. Lotteries are announced and commonly known as *swindles*."

Swinger (Charterhouse), a box on the ears.

Swing-tail (old cant), a pig.

Swing, to (common), to be hanged.

Whether it be direct infrynging
An oath if I shed waive his *swinging*.
—*Butler : Hudibras.*

If I'm caught, I shall *swing ;* that's certain.—*Sketches by Boz.*

Swipe (popular), at cricket a hard hit with full swing of the bat. Also a blow. Provincial English *swipe*, a blow.

"You might drag me to —— if you liked, if you'd on'y let me get one fair *swipe* at him," growled Mr. Perks, savagely.—*The Little Ragamuffins.*

Swipes (common), the cheapest kind of beer-tap droppings.

We smoked our pipes,
With no such *swipes*,
When we were blithe and bold.
—*Punch.*

At schools, beer good or bad is invariably termed *swipes*. Also tea or weak tea.

Tea! *swipes!* After all, miss, it's your way, and no doubt you don't know no better.—*Golden Butterfly.*

A *swipe*, properly an implement for drawing water for a brewery, hence probably *swipes*, for weak beer.

Swipe, to (American), to appropriate. Frequently said of actors or exhibitors who take the stage jokes of others, and pass them off for their own.

You can't copyright a gag. you know, and as soon as we get off anything good the other fellows *swipe* it and it's all over everywhere before we have time to get clear round.—*Philadelphia Press.*

Swipey (popular), intoxicated. From "swipes."

Swishing (Eton), explained by quotation.

Flogging, or, as it is called at Eton, *swishing*, is to be abolished at that aristocratic seminary. — *Illustrated London News.*

Swished, flogged.

Swiss admiral (naval), a person who personates a naval dignitary at a watering-place. The French have the derisive term *amiral suisse* for a naval officer who has never navigated, who is employed on *terra firma*, or for some suspicious individual who pretends to have held a high rank in army or navy.

Switch in, to (American), to bring in expeditiously, to introduce with promptness, and execute with despatch. "Now's your time, boys ; *switch* in and let them have it ! "

. . . Men were sent to cut out the Chicago, but being denied admittance to the cellar under the pavement went to work and broke through one of the manholes from the street, and were busily engaged *switching in* their own service when the Chicago Company's men appeared on the scene.—*Chicago Tribune.*

Swivel eye (common), squinting eye.

Young Arthur Orkintrooler, him with the *swivel eye* and the pink wart on his blushing brow.—*Sporting Times.*

Swizzle (common), drink.

Humph ! you've turned a teetotaller now, I suppose,
And should I sing "hey! ho! and a bottle of rum,"
You'd not join in the song—or the *swizzle ?*
            —*Punch.*

Also *swiz.*

No, percessions, dear boy, ain't my fad,
But political picnics with fireworks, and plenty of *swiz,* ain't 'arf bad.
            —*Punch.*

To *swizzle* is provincial for to drink, and *swizzle* is ale and beer mixed. (West Indian and Australia.) Mr. Finch-Hatton thus graphically describes a drink which is said to make a man wish he had a throat a mile long and a palate at every inch of it :—

" Never having heard of a *swizzle*, which is a drink peculiar to Mackay, I believe, I watched his proceeding with interest. First of all he put two inches of Jamaica rum into the bottom of a tumbler, into which he shook a few drops of Angostura bitters from a bottle with a small hole in the cork. Next he added a small teaspoonful of brown sugar, and a squeeze of a lemon, and filled the tumbler two-thirds full of water. He then took a small stick with three prongs growing the reverse way up at the end, and whirled it round in the tumbler between his hands, with a dexterity only to be acquired by constant practice, till the decoction was foaming to the top of the glass. Handing it to me quickly with directions to ' drink it while fizzing,' he watched it going down, with one eye shut, and an expression of sympathetic interest on his face. ' How's that for high ? ' he asked, as I set down the glass with a sigh of satisfaction." In America *swizzle* is a mixture of rum, molasses, and water, and the Australian drink described above is nothing but the old American rum cock-tail.

Swizzy, swizzle (nautical), grog.

The drink to be discovered in Dibdin's songs would make a sea large enough for several combined fleets of that age to have floated on. The sailor had nothing to do but to sing in all weathers, beat the French, and drink the *swizzy.—W. Clark Russell.*

Swop (popular), to get the *swop*, to be dismissed from one's employment. Especially used among linendrapers' assistants.

S w o t (University and public schools), explained by quotation.

So much for work or *swot*, as the Harrovian, in common with other boys, somewhat inelegantly terms the more important part of instruction he receives at school. —*Pascoe : Everyday Life in our Public Schools.*

A *swot*, one who works hard. At the Royal Military Academy *swat* or *swot* applies specially to mathematics. (Shrewsbury), in a *swot*, in a rage.

Sycher, zoucher (popular and thieves), a contemptible person. "Sich" is provincial for a bad man.

Sydney-sider (Australian), a convict. There never were any convicts sent to Victoria after its separation from New South Wales, while Sydney was originally a convict settlement. It was therefore natural to talk of a convict as being on the *Sydney.*

T

TAB, the (popular), the Tabernacle of Mr. Spurgeon.

Tabby party (common), a party consisting entirely of women. *Tabby* is a colloquialism for an old maid or gossip.

Tabs (tailors), the ears.

Tack or sheet (nautical), a man's saying that he will not start *tack or sheet*, implies resolution.

Tack or tackle (public schools), food ; sometimes applied to drink. *Vide* HARD TACK. Hard *tack* is properly a large kind of hard crackers much used for food on board ship.

Tackle (old cant), a kept mistress. (Thieves), a watch chain. Red *tackle*, a gold chain.

One day I went to Croydon and touched for a red toy and red *tackle*, with a large locket.—*Horsley: Jottings from Jail.*

(Nautical), clothes.

Tacky (printers), according to printers' vocabulary, a roller is in good condition when it is *tacky*, that is, a little sticky to the touch of the finger.

Tad (American), originally provincial English. In English, *tad* is an excrement (Wright). Hence in the United States, and perhaps in England, it was commonly applied contemptuously to the frequenters of brothels. It is now more widely extended. Bartlett gives "little *tads*, small boys ; provincial *tadde*, a toad, hence applied to any small person. The French have *crapaud* for a little boy ; *les crapauds,* the children ; old *tads,* grey-bearded men."

Taffy (American), flattery, "softsawder," "soap," "gammon," persuasive and unctuous humbug.

Tag (theatrical), explained by quotation.

And the *tag* is the end of the play—the last lines spoken, in rhyme or otherwise—just as this sentence is the end of this article.—*Globe.*

Also the end or catch word of an actor's cue. *Tags,* a species of improvised jokes (called by French actors "cascades"), allied to "tack." Danish *tak,* a supplement, appendix.

Tail (common), to have one's *tail* down, to be discouraged ; to have one's *tail* out, to be angry ; to get one's *tail* up, to pluck up spirits.

Tail-block (nautical), a watch. Properly a rope-stropped block, having an end of rope attached to it as a *tail* by which it may be fastened to any object.

Tail-buzzer(thieves),a pickpocket who devotes his attention to the pockets in the tails of a coat.

Tailed, *vide* LONG-TAILED ONE. A curious coincidence occurs in French cant. *Tailbin* is an accommodation bill, from old word *talle,* tail ; and *tailbin d'altèque,* a bank note, *d'altèque* in this instance signifying superior, genuine.

Tailing (up-country Australian), herding.

Mustering now proceeded with steady vigour, and Desmard was allowed to gain experience in *tailing* those already brought in, along with two old and experienced hands, who were much amused with their companion's eccentricities, and who never tired of relating his peculiar sayings.—*A. C. Grant.*

Tail-piece in the steel (thieves), explained by quotation.

Their conversation, though not the most elegant, was least of all concerning the wretched trade they followed ; indeed, the subject was never mentioned at all, except in melancholy allusion to Peter or Jerry, who had been recently "copped," and was expected to pass a *tail-piece in the steel* (three months in prison).—*J. Greenwood : Seven Curses of London.*

Tail-pulling(publishers), a method of publication explained by quotation.

It came out in evidence yesterday, in the case of Mackay *v.* M'Lean, that the publication of the literary productions of private individuals, who like to contemplate their own handiwork in print, is technically known among those who do it as *tail-pulling.* That seems an odd name to give it, because no animal we are acquainted with likes having its tail pulled ; unless it is on the principle of the little girl who "wagged the dog's tail to give it pleasure."—*Globe.*

Tai-pai (pidgin), a large ticket, a great chop, first, slangily "boss."

Dey lock um up in littee house thlee day till allo done,
An' den Wang-ti come out *tai-pai,* firstchop, an' Numpa One.

Tai-pan, typan (pidgin), literally "great series," *i.e.,* the first of a series, a leader, a head-man, or "boss."

My *typan* must make fun of me,
When all his crowd can see—
Ah! well, perhaps they do not care
For a little clerk like me.
                    —*China Punch.*

Tai-pay (pidgin), great-beer, *i.e.*, porter (Canton).

Take (printers), a synonym used by compositors to signify the portion of copy that falls to their share. A "fat" *take* is considered a good one.

Take a figure (printers). This is an appeal to the ballot instead of "jeffing," or "throwing" with the nine quadrats. To settle shares of good or bad work, or other matter, a man would select a number of figures, according to the number of men concerned, shake them up in his apron, and each individual would *take a figure*, the highest, or *vice versâ*, as agreed on, having the choice.

Take a rise. *Vide* RISE.

Take beef, to (thieves and popular), to run away. *Vide* BEEF.

Take down, to (thieves and popular), to get the best of one, to deceive, humbug.

Well, Governor, I think there is some credit due to me for *taking you down.* Any fool can do an ordinary swindle, but it is not any one who would attempt *to take down* the Governor of a convict prison.— *Evening News.*

Take it in snuff. This old slang phrase, which dates from a time long anterior to the supposed introduction of the tobacco plant into Europe by Sir Walter Raleigh, occurs in plays of the Elizabethan and Shakspearian era. It does not appear to have originated in the habit of snuff-taking, nor would the appositeness or appropriateness of the phrase have been palpably apparent if it had done so. *Sniff*, in its primary acceptation, means a movement of the nostrils, expressive either of annoyance or displeasure at a disagreeable smell, and by metaphorical extension a sign of scorn or anger at any person or thing that is offensive to either the moral or physical sense. It is curious to note how often the consonants *sn* are found as the initial sound of words that express anything disagreeable, and that are manifested by the action of the nose. Among others, sneeze, snore, sneer, snort, snarl, snigger, &c., all more or less suggestive of an unpleasant meaning.

Take it out of him (popular), thrash him well.

Take it out, to (popular), to obtain value for expenditure, labour, &c.

Take my hat (American). In the United States, when any man narrates a story which is so incredible or extravagant that the auditor must confess that he cannot outdo it, the latter often exclaims, "*Take my hat!*" In a pamphlet entitled "Three Thousand Miles in a Railway Car," the author tells us that in a jovial party of men they had a small hat which was made from a champagne cork, and that when one of them told the last best story the hat was given to him, to be retained until another told a better, when it was handed over to the latter. " Saw my leg off " was an equivalent or synonym for the same phrase. When the story was remarkably good it was usual to add " close."

Taken on (turf), another term for welshed.

The old man has been *taken on* to the extent of a fiver.—*Bird o' Freedom.*

Take one's hook. *Vide* HOOK.

She asked him to come in the house,
   Then begged that he would stay
And take some tea along with her,
   And on the Indian drum play.
She told me I could *take my hook*,
   And leave the place at once ;
I was no good—a chump of wood,
   In fact, a perfect dunce.
                              —*Song.*

Takes the gloss off (tailors), it takes away the profit, or materially detracts from its value.

Take the biscuit, to, a variation of "take the cake." *Vide* CAKE and BUN.

I think you will admit this fairly *takes the biscuit* for a detective story.—*Sporting Times.*

Take the cake, to. *Vide* CAKE.

Take the diploma (American), to take the prize, take the cake, to be pre-eminent.

Take the field, to (turf), to stake one's money against the favour-

ite, thus backing all the rest against a single horse.

Take the rag off the bush, to (American), precision and excellence in action or thought. An illustration drawn from the wild life of the Far West, when at improvised shooting competitions the hunters and trappers would hang a rag on a bush as a target, and few of them would miss lifting it.

Take the starch out, to (American), *to take the starch out* of a man is to extinguish his conceit, nerve, or pluck. It is widely applied to weakening, refuting, or deteriorating of any kind.

The forthcoming Women's Bible will *take more of the starch out* of St. Paul, so to speak, in one edition, than the combined assaults of infidels have done in 1800 years.—*Chicago Tribune.*

Take up a collection (American). This is often heard humorously applied to any one who in an emergency, not being able to do any good, nevertheless suggests something which has some shade or colour of a relation to the subject. Also to a man who avails himself of the least excuse to raise money. It is said that when some men were in a boat in a storm on Lake Superior, and expected every minute to go down, as none of them knew a prayer or a hymn, they did the next best thing they could as "a religious exercise," and *took up a collection.*

The President's sole recommendation with reference to the Civil-Service question, is that the salaries of the Civil Service Commission be increased. We suspect Mr. Cleveland of being the man who, in a sinking boat where some religious services were suggested, enthusiastically declared himself in favour of *taking up a collection.* —*Philadelphia Press.*

Take up one's connections, to (American University), to leave college.

Taking the nap (theatrical), making pretence to be struck, by slapping the hands together unseen by audience, *à la* clown and pantaloon. *Vide* KNAP, TO.

Taking the stage (theatrical), assuming a commanding position in the centre of the stage, or crossing from the right hand side to the left, or *vice versâ.* The movement with which a well-graced tragedian, in a burst of passionate emotion, dashes from one side of the stage to the other, or down to the footlights and up again. An almost exploded artifice, and one which requires an artist of great skill to accomplish with precision.

Taking up one's bed (tailors), leaving the shop for good.

Talent, the (racing). The ring is, in racing phraseology, *the talent.* Common in Australia.

And sinks from view for ever, while *the talent*
Declare they never saw a sight so gallant.
                    —*New South Wales Paper.*

Talk a donkey's hind leg off, to (American), to talk to no purpose.

They may *talk a donkey's hind leg off,* and I wouldn't send a single line to the New York papers to tell them what was said nor what they wore.—*The Golden Butterfly.*

Talking through one's neck (Australian), talking foolishly. A young lady, who had been impressing the dangers of football upon her small brother with more ardour than discretion, wound up with, " If you were my son I wouldn't let you go to a boarding-school at all without I had you safe home every night," which was met with a contemptuous " Oh, you're *talking through your neck.*"

Talk, to (stable), said of a horse that roars. (American), tall *talk,* explained by quotation.

The word cheek, as synonymous with conceit or impudence, is, notwithstanding its relative antiquity, still largely patronised by the lovers of argot; but were it not for the obliging correspondent of—if we mistake not—the *Daily Telegraph, tall talk,* a Transatlantic phrase of apparently similar import and of undoubted originality, might never have been naturalised among us.—*Belgravia.*

The expression is now common in England. In quotation *tall* refers to an incredible story.

The new Enoch Arden story which has turned up at East Greenwich is certainly *tall.* It reminds one instinctively of the American tree so high that it took two men to look to the top, one beginning where the other left off, and forty men to believe the tale.—*Daily Telegraph.*

(Pedestrian), the term is applied to a great rate of speed.

Tally (popular), to live *tally* is to live as man and wife though not married. Hence a *tally* wife, " femme de la main gauche."

Talosk (tinker), weather.

Tambour (Punch and Judy), the drum.

Tame cats (society). Thus defined by the *Saturday Review:*— "There is a class of men, who are not at all young by any means, who in society are termed *tame cats ;* these men present rather a ludicrous spectacle for their foolishness. They are by no means vicious, but they are by no means manly. They continue to attend all entertainments till they are well on in the sere and yellow leaf; they have no occupations ; they are neither men of letters nor of arts ; they are not political ; and, last of all, they are in no way sportsmen, neither shooting, hunting, driving, nor fishing. The *raison d'être* of their existence seems hard to define ; their daily occupation is wandering round from house to house, and exchanging gossip and scandal with old ladies and young alike. They have the *entrée* to many houses where they are welcome at all times, and are not looked upon as eligible husbands for the daughters of the house ; they are made use of to fill up vacancies at dinner, theatre parties, &c., and, above all, they are essentially good-natured."

Tame cheater (thieves), a false player.

Tan (gypsy), a tent, a place, a resting-place. A word of very general application. To *tan*, to encamp or rest. "Kek *tan* to hatch "—" No place to rest." " Chiv a *tan* apré "—" Pitch a tent." "Kánná bóro bávol se, huller the *tan* parl the wäver rikk pāli the bor "—" When there is a great wind, move the tent to the other side behind the hedge." (*Tana*, Hindu.)— *Gypsy Saying.*

Tangle - footed, tangle - legged (American), drunk. *Tangle-foot* (from *tangle-footed*), bad whisky or spirits. Derived from the idea that a man when intoxicated has a tendency to entwine or *tangle* his feet together, or to get them locked in every obstacle in the way.

" Drink a pint of *tangle-foot,*
You'll catch your boot
In every root."

Tāni (gypsy), small, young ; *tanirāni*, young lady ; *tanopen*, childhood, youth.

Tanner, a sixpence. Hotten says of it, "Perhaps gypsy *tawno* (*tāno*), little, or Latin *tener*, slender." It is more likely to have been derived directly by the ancestors of the gypsies from the Indian silver coin *tanga* or *tana*, which has been rated from fivepence (Malcolm, 1815), to sevenpence-halfpenny, which is its present value in Turkestan (Anglo-Indian Glossary). This would make its average value sixpence. The obvious derivation is the Sanskrit *tanka*, a weight of silver equal to four moshas, a stamped coin. The word has been in use over a vast extent of territory. The threepenny piece (*ruppeny bitto*) is the only coin which is specially called little in gypsy, and it is most unlikely that a sixpence would be called a particularly small coin while fourpenny, threepenny, and even twopenny silver coins were in circulation.

Old Alec don't like to win with favourites. I shall 'ave my *tanner* on Timothy. —*Sporting Times.*

Tanning (common), a beating.

Tan, to (common), to beat or thrash. Exists in several English dialects, with variations, such as *tan base, tan baste, tancel,* but is used slangily. French slang, *tanner le cuir.* Exists in gypsy as *tanner,* from *tanava,* I beat. Hindu *tan,* abuse.

Tanyok (tinker), halfpenny. (Query *tāni,* little, Romany, and *nyok,* a head?)

Tap (tailors), getting the *tap* of the job, getting the upper hand.

Tape (popular), liquor. Red *tape,* wine. White *tape,* gin. *Vide* WHITE TAPE.

Oh! those jovial days are ne'er forgot!
  But the *tape* lags—
When I be's dead, you'll drink one pot
  To poor old Bags!
      —*Lytton: Paul Clifford.*

(American), explained by quotation.

His white tie was not of lawn, but of that most approved Bond Street pattern known as *tape.*—*American Magazine.*

Tape-worm (Stock Exchange), a nasty name for a man who walks about the House collecting prices of different stock to telegraph on the *tape.*

Tapper (old cant), bailiff, tipstaff. In provincial English it means an innkeeper.

Tapping the admiral, secretly boring a hole through a spirit cask and sucking the contents out through a quill or straw. An admiral died aboard ship some distance from England. He had wished to be buried at home, and to preserve his body the officers placed it in a cask filled with spirits, and securely nailed the head of the cask down. During the voyage home an Irishman of the marines was continually drunk, and it was a great mystery to see where he got his liquor from. For some drunken breach of discipline he was ordered to be flogged, but he was promised forgiveness if he would tell who had supplied him with drink. Upon that he confessed that he had been "so hard up for a dhrink, that bedad he'd *tapped the admiral,*" *i.e.,* made a hole in the cask and sucked out through a tobacco pipe the spirit in which the admiral's body was preserved.

Taps (American). "To be on one's *taps* is to be on one's feet, literally on one's soles; on the move, or ready to move. A metaphor preserved from the shoemaker" (Bartlett). To *tap* is provincial English for to sole shoes.

(American cadet), a bugle-call.

Taps had sounded (at 10 P.M., after which no one is permitted to cross the sentinel's posts without the countersign). —*The West Point Scrap Book.*

Tap the claret, to (pugilistic), to give a blow on the nose which draws blood.

He was thoroughly conversant with the sporting slang of Tintinnabulums Life when he told Verdant that his *claret* had been repeatedly *tapped.*—*C. Bede: Verdant Green.*

Tap the wire, to (American), to obtain surreptitious possession of the electric telegraph wire and extract the information with which it is charged. General Morgan, the Confederate officer, once when *tapping the wire* was in ignorance of the name of the station in the hand of the Federals, and to obtain the information he adopted the following ruse. He telegraphed, "A gentleman in the office bets me two cigars you cannot spell the name of your station." Answer, "Take the bet. Lebanon Junction—is this not right; how did he think I would spell it?" General Morgan replied, "He gives it up; he thought you would put two b's in Lebanon." Answer, "He is a green one." *Vide* TELEGRAM, MILKING A.

Tap, to (thieves), to break into a house.

The most difficult part of all is to dress so as to escape a description which the police have of your usual appearance. Often they will re-dress themselves under a tree, in a field or a barn in the vicinity of the house they are about to *tap*, but as a rule they dress as becomes a poor specimen of the middle class.—*Tit-Bits.*

Tap tub, the *Morning Advertiser,* so called by vulgar people from the fact that this daily newspaper is the principal organ of the London brewers and publicans (Hotten).

Taradiddles (society), falsehoods, travellers' tales or yarns.

Tar brush (nautical), any one of mixed blood is said to have had a touch of the *tar brush.*

Tare, tear (American), a frolic, spree, riot, bender, batter, or rampage.

I'm on a rare (rear),
   I'm on a *tare;*
On a high old circumbendibus,
   Such as will be
   A sight to see,
When the boys pull into the rendyvoos.
                —*American Newspaper.*

Tarryin (tinker), rope.

Tart (common), a young lady, an actress of smart personal appearance and fine manners. There seems some doubt as to whether the term is an aspersion on the lady's character or not, as may be seen from a case of an actress who brought an action against the *Sporting Times* for calling her a *tart,* which created much amusement at the time.

The word *tart* also designates a mistress or girl with whom one has had only casual intimacy, or even a wife. Also any girl or woman. Formerly one's mistress was termed "my jam," or "my little bit of jam." The term is apparently from a simile between a sweet jam *tart* and a girl (compare "cherry-pie" for a girl). It is an old word revived a few years ago by certain sporting journals. *Tart* was originally schoolboys' slang, probably abbreviated from *tartar* in this instance.

I remember, I remember, though Time's
    progress is so fleet,
  How I doated on my juvenile sweet-
    hearts,
And I remember that I thought them so
    superlatively sweet,
  That I spoke of them admiringly as
    tarts.
But *now!* Well, times have altered, and
    I'm not prepared to say
  If a girl's "a *tart*" or not—so here I'll
    pause,
For it's probable that if I called a girl "a
    tart" to-day,
  She would summons me next week to
    show just cause!
                    —*Sporting Times.*

The latest synonym for *tart* is "bun." *Tart* is a word generally recognised and understood in the United States. It is sometimes used as an uncomplimentary epithet, an abbreviation from *tartar*.

Tartlet (London), usually applied to a lady of the demi-monde, or even quart-de-monde. A diminutive of "tart."

E'en *tartlets* are stale, be they ever so
    tasty—
  The magic has fled from their languorous
    looks :

They're but fairies in fake, their com-
    plexions seem pasty—
  I've no wish for a place in their very
    best books.
                    —*Bird o' Freedom.*

Tashi shingomai (tinker), to read the newspaper.

Tasser (gypsy), to suffocate, drown, or strangle. "Beng *tasser* tute!"—"May the devil strangle you!"

Tat-box (gambling), a dice-box : *tats* are dice.

Tatch (popular), a hat ; a corruption of "thatch."

Taters. *Vide* STRAIN YOUR TATERS.

Tater-trap (popular), for potato-trap, mouth.

Up goes the jug to Ginger's *tater-trap.*
  —*Brighton Beach Loafer.*

Tatols (Winchester College), tutors in Commoners who came into course in alternate weeks to be present at meals and Toys, and for names-calling, and to go round galleries at 9.15.

Tats (canting), old rags. Gypsy *tat* or *tats*, not only rags, &c., but coarse sack-cloth. Hindu *tāt*, sack-cloth. Hence *tatters* in English. Milky *tats*, white linen.

Now I'll tell you about the *tat*-gatherers;
buying rags they call it, but I call it
bouncing people.—*Mayhew : London Labour and the London Poor.*

Tatter (tramps), a rag-gatherer.

Tatties (Anglo-Indian), a frame composed of thick jungle grass, the inside being interlaced with layers of slender fibrous roots, on which water is constantly thrown to cool the air.

As a rule, during the very hottest months all the doorways situate on the sides of the buildings towards which the breeze may be blowing are usually fitted with portable arrangements called *tatties.* — *Brunlees Patterson: Life in the Ranks.*

Tattle or **tattler** (thieves), a watch.

A famble, a *tattle*, and two pops
Had my bowman when he was ta'en.
—*Frisky Moll's Song.*

I have made a grab at a bunch of onions to-night, but the jockey wore a guard to his *tattler.—Disconsolate William.*

To speak to the *tattler*, to steal a watch.

Speak to the *tattler*, bag the swag,
And finely hunt the dummy.
—*C. Hindley: Life and Times of James Catnach.*

To nim a *tattler*, to steal a watch. *Tattler*, a dog that barks. In French argot "tambour" or "alarmiste."

Tattogeys (old cant), players who play with loaded dice. *Vide* TAT-BOX. The *tattogey* was the dice-cloth.

Tattoo (Anglo-Indian), a pony.

Taut hand (nautical), a strict disciplinarian, a martinet.

Sir Hannibal regulated his household as he did his ship; he was, in truth, what is termed a *taut hand;* at the sound of his stump cook and housemaid held their peace, while his lady-wife scarcely dared to bless herself without permission.—*Scraps.*

Tav (gypsy), string, thread, fine cord, strip, lace. *Tel*, thread.

Tax collector (old), a highwayman, a bandit. So called from the forcible extraction of money and kind from his victims—a sarcastic reference to the similar tactics of "the powers that be." In America a "road agent."

Tea-boardy (studios), an epithet applied to an inferior picture, which reminds one of the old-fashioned lacquered tea-trays with landscapes on them.

Tea chop (nautical), small craft used to bring a cargo of tea alongside the ocean-going vessel.

Teach-guy (costers), back slang for eight shillings.

The exception to the uniformity of the "gen" enumeration is in the sum of eight shillings, which, instead of "teaich-gen," is *teaich-guy.—Mayhew.*

Tea-fight (society), an evening party.

Tea-kettle (popular), *tea-kettle* grooms, or coachmen, are those who do general work. *Tea-kettle* purgers are scullery-maids.

A decent allowance made to seedy swells, *tea-kettle* purgers, head-robbers, and flunkeys out of collar.—*A Tailor's Advertisement.*

Team (Oxford and Cambridge Universities), the pupils of a coach or private tutor. It frequently, indeed usually happens that a "coach" of reputation declines taking men into his *team* before they have made time in public. (American), it is remarkable that *team*, as now used in America to signify a company or party, or number of people, is old Saxon, or, as Ettmüller defines it, "*Teám, longus ordo cujusvis generis,*" a series of any kind.

"He Nôe bearh and his vîfe and his *teáme* at tham miclan flôde "—" He preserved Noah and his wife and his *team* (*suboles*, offspring) in the great flood." Hence to *team* with, associate. "Godes bearn *tŷmdon* vid manna dohtru*"—"And the children of God *teamed* with the daughters of men" (Ettmüller, Anglo-Saxon Lexicon).

Teapot (American), a mispronunciation of depôt, *i.e.*, a railway station.

> Then outspoke a man unnoted
> Hitherto : " I heard the fellow
> Say just now to the conductor
> Ere we reached the second *teapot*,
> That he reckoned he must hook it
> This here time a little sooner
> If he hoped to get his portion."
> —*In Nevada.*

(Cricketers), a *teapot* stroke, hit up in the air giving an easy catch, a result of " spooning." (Prison), smashing the *teapot*, losing the privilege of tea from bad behaviour, and returning to the third - class. Having one's *teapot* mended, being restored to the higher class and its privileges. Also called "getting it down the spout."

Teapot sneaking (thieves), stealing plate, teapots.

> " *Teapot sneaking* your mark ?'
> " Something better."—*Sporting Times.*

Teapot soak (thieves), a thief who steals plate, teapots, &c.

> *Teapot soaks* will have the twitters,
> Garrotters oft will suffer pain.
> —*Fun Almanack.*

Tearing his seat (tailors), trying to do more than he can.

Tear up, a (criminal), explained by quotation.

> Going a day or two back into the casual ward of my union, I found a policeman standing waiting in the day room. Guessing that he had come to remove a casual to the police court, " What is it this time? Anything serious?" I asked. " Oh no, sir ; only a *tear up*," was the reply. This, of course, was so far satisfactory ; but as it is possible that among the readers of the *St. James's Gazette* there may be some who are unacquainted with the accepted method of obtaining a fresh outfit among the casual poor, it may be worth while to explain a little further. But first let us visit the unfortunate creature that the constable has come for.
>
> In a small room, some seven feet by four, the furniture of which consisted of a bed and a wooden stool (it is usual to call these rooms " cells," and it must be confessed that " cell " is more accurately descriptive of the facts than " room " or " cubicle," which has also been suggested as the proper term), we found a broken-down, dejected-looking man of about forty. He was dressed in a brown cloth coat that had seen better days, a pair of almost new corduroy trousers, and boots which, though not new, were stout and serviceable. At his feet, in a heap on the floor, lay some filthy rags of cloth and cotton, the remnants of what had recently been his garments ; on the top of them the sole and a fragment of the upper part of one of his boots. The heap was the result of the *tear up.—St. James's Gazette.*

Teaser (pugilistic), a maddening blow.

> The latter planted a *teaser* on Sam's mouth, which produced the claret in streams. —*Pierce Egan : Book of Sports.*

Tease, to (prison), to flog; to nap the *tease*, to be flogged.

Teaspoon (sport), five thousand pounds.

Tec or **teck** (popular and thieves), explained by quotation.

> The "detective" was always an untold terror, because he could not see him, and every suspicious man was to him a *teck*. He despised the "bobby" or the "copper," but he had an untold dread of the *teck*.
> —*Evening News.*

> "Hulloh, father!" cried Shakspeare, "look here! Isn't that the *'tec* that we see so often at the races?"—*G. Sims : Rogues and Vagabonds.*

Teck (Harrow school), mathematics.

Teddy Hall (Oxford University), St. Edmund's Hall, Oxford.

Teejay (Winchester College). When a new man comes, he is given by his house-master to an old man to be protected and instructed in notions. From the French *protégé*.

Teek (Anglo-Indian), exact, close, precise, parsimonious. Hindu *thick*.

Teeth (nautical), to have one's "back *teeth* afloat," to be very much intoxicated.

Teeth-drawing (medical students), wrenching off knockers.

Teetotal hotel, her Majesty's (prison), a prison.

Telegram, milking a. A telegram is said to be *milked* when the message sent to a specific party is surreptitiously made use of by others (Dr. Brewer).

> They receive their telegrams in cipher to avoid the risk of their being *milked* by rival journals.—*The Times.*

Telescoped (Australian popular), suppressed, silenced. *Telescoped* signifies "shut up" like a telescope is shut up, *cf.* "shut up" itself. Possibly also when they use it, people may think of it in its railway-accident sense of one carriage being forced into another.

> At first the widow flew into a rage and used indignant language to her pastor, who felt quite *telescoped.*—*New South Wales Paper.*

Té-li-man (pidgin), tailor.

Tell-box (American gamblers). The *tell-box* is an improvement on the "gaff" (*q.v.*), and has a fine spring attached to it. The object of it is to cheat the dealer. The dealer plays with a pack of cards which the player has had a chance to handle, and he nebs the backs of certain of them with sand-paper. The rough card adheres to the smooth one, and the fact that it does not move a hairsbreadth in the box enables him to know the card that is covered, and he plays accordingly. He can also play in the same manner with a new pack of cards without sanding them, as certain cards require a greater amount of ink than others (New York Slang Dictionary).

Tell Chapman to crow! (American). About fifty years ago, it was made the subject of a political revelation or scandal that an eminent Democratic politician (we think it was John Van Buren) had written to an associate bidding him "*tell Chapman* (an editor), *to crow*," i.e., to make a bluster and brag in his newspaper. This caused a great deal of laughter, and from that time " *Crow, Chapman, crow !* " became a byword. From this originated the custom of announcing political victories by putting pictures of crowing cocks at the head of the column. Once an editor, named John Du Solle, in Philadelphia, announced a Democratic victory, only unfortunately " a little too previously," as it appeared a few hours after that the Democrats had lost the battle of the ballot. More unfortunately still, Colonel Du Solle had ordered the " rooster " crowing to be put at the head of the " grand victory and overwhelming defeat," but in the haste of " making up," the typo put it in upside down, so that the cock of triumph appeared like that described by Washington Irving as sprawling ignominiously on his back. From that time, perhaps, even here and there to the present day, a defeat is announced by reversing the gallant bird.

Teller (pugilistic), a well-planted blow that tells.

Each cove vos teazed with double duty,
To please his backers, yet play booty,

Ven luckily for Jem a *teller*
Vos planted right upon his smeller.
—*Ainsworth: Rookwood.*

Temples (Winchester College), explained by quotation.

On the last night of term there is a bonfire in Ball Court, and all the *temples* or miniature architectural excavations in " Mead's " wall are lighted up with candle-ends.—*Everyday Life in our Public Schools.*

Temps. For this there is no English equivalent. Hoffman, translating Robert Houdin, writes that it is "the opportune moment for effecting a given disappearance or the like, unknown to the spectators" ("Conjuring and Magic ").

Ten-cent man, a (American), a small, narrow-minded, or trifling man.

You can get more wind out of a ten-cent fan than you can from a $500 one. It's the same way with *a ten-cent man.—Detroit Free Press.*

Tench (thieves), abbreviated from House of Detention.

I fell at Isleworth for being found in a conservatory adjoining a parlour, and got remanded at the *tench.—Horsley: Jottings from Jail.*

Ten commandments (popular), fingers or nails.

Tender-foot (American), one who is new to the country, a greenhorn or " griffin." Applied in the West to those whose feet are not yet accustomed to much walking, or probably to those unused to moccasins.

Stebbins fell an easy victim to the cigarette and smoked incessantly. The effect of the habit on him was not noticed until one day he fired at a *tender-foot* from the East, three times in succession, and missed him every time.—*Detroit Free Press.*

How an American ever expects to digest his food is a problem to a *tender-foot,* as they call us new-comers.—*Phillips-Wolley: Trottings of a Tender-foot.*

A yell as I put my naked foot on a cactus, and thus made my first acquaintance with a noteworthy member of the flora of the sandy prairies, is a reminiscence of that night, and I realised in a substantial form the nickname that is given to the new-comer out West of *tender-foot* or pilgrim.—*A. Staveley Hill: From Home to Home.*

Tenner (prison), a sentence of ten years' penal servitude.

The speaker, in a stage whisper, would continue : " It's all right. Don't turn your head." After another journey round the ring, he would again hiss : " How long have you got ? "

" A *tenner* and my ticket," would be the reply.—*Evening News.*

(Common), a ten-pound note.

" No money ? " " Not much ; perhaps a *tenner.*" — *Hughes : Tom Brown at Oxford.*

Bookie (holding out his hand): " Evens." *M.P.:* " Yes ; a *tenner.* I'll settle after the race."

B.: " All right. What name ? "

M.P.: " Brown-Smith, R.H.A."

B.: " Oh, one of your bloomin' initials is enough ! "—*Sporting Times.*

Ten-strike (American), a *ten-strike* is the highest " count " which can be made at the game of ten-pins. Applied to a very lucky hit at anything, or to an unusual stroke of success.

Oh, vot ish all dis earthly pliss?
Oh, vot ish man's soockcess?
Oh, vot ish various kinds of dings?
Und vot ish hoppiness?

Ve find a pank-note in de shtreet,
Next dings der pank ish preak,
Ve falls und knocks our outsides in,
Ven ve a *ten-shtrike* make.
—*The Breitmann Ballads.*

Ten up ! (Stock Exchange). If a broker's credit is at all shaky, or it is thought he is unable to carry out his contracts, he is required to lodge ten per cent. of any stock bought before the contract can be considered valid. This is called *ten up.*

Terri (tinker), coal.

Terry (tinker), a heating-iron.

Tertians. *Vide* BEJANT.

Teviss (costers and tramps), a shilling.

Thanks, no (society), an expression meaning one does not intend to be taken in. There are variations of this, as " Not in these boots," &c.

Thari (tinker), to talk, language, conversation. Also *bug.* " Can you *thari* Shelta, sublee ? "— " Can you talk Shelta, man ? " " Do you grani the Minklas *thari?* " — " Do you know the tinkers' tongue ? "

Thatch (popular), a person's hair ; well *thatched,* with a good head of hair. Also a straw hat.

That-side (pidgin), there. " *T'hat sidey* sittee he compladore." *This-side,* here. " Hab makee stop *t'his side.*"

That's too rich for your blood (American), too good for any one.

You go a visitin' Miss Perkinblower!
You makin' calls on a judge's daughter!
That's too rich for your blood—why, they'll
jest tell the servant to carry you out on a
chip and heave you into the barn yard.—
*Newspaper Story: MS. Americanisms,
by C. Leland Harrison.*

That's where your toes turn in
(American), one of many popular
expressions, equivalent to "That
is where you make a mistake."

" My frens," continued the speaker, " de
rich man walks on welwet ca'pets, an' he
sots doun on stuffed cheers, an' he has
Saratoga 'taters ebery meal. He jists rolls
in ham an' eggs, an' he walks all ober fri-
cassed chicken. De poo' man walks on a
bare flo', sots on a hard cheer, an' his
'taters am biled wid de hides on. Yet who
am de happiest? You will say de rich man,
of co'se—but *dat's whar' yer toes turn in.*
—*Detroit Free Press.*

Theatre (thieves), a police court.
(Army), Irish *theatre*, the guard-
room.

Theddy, tedhi, thedi (tinker), fire.

**There's no knowing what an
ox may do** (American). This,
which was once a popular expression, may still be heard
occasionally in New England.

"There was once a Yankee
in Montreal who was about to
race horses with an Englishman
for a thousand dollars a side.
Two days before the run was to
come off, the Yankee learned
that his horse had not a ghost
of a chance to win. While
walking about town, he saw an
immense prize ox adorned with
ribbons, preceded by a band of
music. This gave him an idea.
He went to the Englishman,
and proposed a preliminary ex-

amination of both their 'beasts.'
The Englishman assented, and
said, ' Well, show your horse.' "

" ' Horse!' said the Yankee.
' I ain't got no horse. Why,
Squire, don't you know—my
critter's an ox. Didn't you see
him goin' about town this arternoon?'

" The Englishman was bewildered. He *had* seen the ox,
and believed the Yankee. ' The
race is off!' he exclaimed. ' I'll
run my animal against any
horse, but *there's no knowing
what a d——d ox may do!*' "

There you ain't (popular), this
expression expresses a failure.
It is the converse of "There you
are " (*q.v.*).

I saw a lady, I rose my cadie,
  I went like this, and then I did a wink,
I said you're tasty, very tasty,
  Then proposed adjourning for a drink.
But she was stuck up, and turned her
    nose up,
  And tried to look as though she were a
    saint,
I did just what I thought, but she wasn't
    quite my sort,
  *So there you ain't, there you ain't, there
    you ain't.*
—*Music Hall Ballad (Francis & Day).*

There you are (popular), meaning
that you are all right. " Manage
it properly, and *there you are.*"

Nod politely, but do it nicely,
  And if the chance occurs, just do a wink;
Don't be hasty, but if it's tasty,
  Try within your own her arm to link.
While you're talking, and onward walking,
  Be careful that you do not go too far,
And if the girl's the proper sort, and you
    do just what you ought,
  Why, *there you are, there you are, there
    you are.*
—*Music Hall Ballad (Francis & Day).*

Thick (popular), cocoa. Porter is also known as *thick* or "apron-washings," because the water in which the brewers' aprons are washed is supposed to be utilised in its manufacture. This derivation is doubtful. (Common), intimate.

"You haven't been round to see me so often as you used to?"
"No; I've made a new set of acquaintances."
"What's that to do with it?"
"Well, you see, they're very *thick*. The consequence is, I'm either hoodman or getting over an attack of D.T."—*Bird o' Freedom*.

To lay it on *thick*, to flatter in an exaggerated manner. (Winchester College), a *thick*, a stupid fellow.

Thick 'un (common), a sovereign.

"Have you sufficient confidence in me to lend me a sovereign?" "Oh! yes, I've the confidence, but I haven't the *thick 'un*."—*Atkin: House Scraps*.

I forfeited three *thick 'uns* entrance fee at Alexandra Park over a horse which I have never seen, which was sold to me for nothing by a man that it didn't belong to. —*Sporting Times*.

Thieves, murdering (army), formerly the military train.

Thieving-irons (old), scissors.

Bill placed his canister under the *thieving-irons*, while Dick and the barber gave play to their velvets.—*J. Burrowes: Life in St. George's Fields*.

Thilly (tinkers), a make-weight.

"You're welcome to your fun this mornin', Jim," replies Jack, "but wouldn't you have the halt, and that bit of a spavin your baste have, go agin one another? and maybe you'd give us a pair of specs a blind horse could see wud, by way of a *thilly*: for your hunther will soon want that same sort of a spy-glass."—*Sporting Times*.

Thimble. This, in canting, generally means a watch. The gypsies, however, apply it to both watch and purse; and this confusion of terms is also to be found occasionally among thieves in America. It is probable that the Romany word meaning purse is by far the oldest, since in Hindu *zambil* is a purse or wallet. Gypsy is popularly supposed to be a *mélange* of many languages; but in the Anglo-Romany about forty-nine words out of fifty are not merely Hindustani, but to a very great extent indeed Hindi-Persian, approximating often much more closely to an old form than modern Hindu itself. This was the opinion of the late Professor E. H. Palmer.

Thimble-rigger (common), a sharper who practises the *thimble-rig*, a cheating game, played thus: A pea is placed on a table, and the man rapidly covers it successively with three or four thimbles, which are then laid on the table. You are then asked to point out the thimble which is supposed to cover the pea, but which is concealed under the cheat's nail or up his sleeve.

The poor trumpery beggars—converted clowns, and dog-stealers, and tramps, and *thimble-riggers*—a poor out-at-elbows crew.—*J. Greenwood: Dick Temple*.

Thimble-twister (thieves), a thief who steals watches from the person.

Things, the (thieves), base coin.

Thin 'un (popular and thieves), half a sovereign.

Thirteen clean shirts, getting (prison), three months' imprisonment, shirts being changed once a week in prison.

Thoker (Winton), a large, thick slice of bread, baked after being soaked with water.

Thoke, to (Winchester College), to rest. Old provincial English *thoky*, sluggish. A *thoke* is rest, lying in bed. (Winchester), to lie in bed late. But "to *thoke* upon anything" is to look forward with pleasurable anticipation to its enjoyment.

Thomyok, tomyok (tinker), magistrate. Literally great head.

Three-by-nine smile (American), a laugh or smile to the full extent of the jaws. A pun on the word benign.

"Papa, don't you think young Mr. Canter has a benign smile?"
"Yes, my dear, *seven-by-nine.* I never see him do it without wishing to throw a shovelful of corn into his mouth."—*New York Journal.*

I found Mrs. Langtry engaged in practising a new fall, and she smiled a *three-by-nine smile* on me. — *New York Morning Journal.*

Three cheers and a tiger (American). In the United States, after three cheers are given, it is usual to add a howl, called "the *tiger*," in order to intensify the applause. Bartlett gives a very meaningless account of doubtful authenticity as to the origin of this phrase,

saying that a man once cried to the Boston Light Infantry, "Oh, you *tigers*," and that they began to growl. The true origin seems to be as follows: Once the famous wit and politician, S. S. Prentiss, being on a stumping tour, came to a town where there was a small menagerie on exhibition. This he hired for a day and threw it open to all comers, availing himself of the occasion to make a political speech. The orator, holding a ten-foot pole, stood on the tiger's cage, in the roof of which there was a hole, and whenever the multitude applauded one of his "points" with three cheers, Mr. Prentiss poked the tiger, who uttered a harsh roar. From this *three cheers and a tiger* spread over the country. The writer had this anecdote from a relative of Mr. Prentiss, and can vouch for its authenticity.

"Three cheers and a *tiger*" are the inseparable demonstrations of approbation on all festive and joyous occasions in New York.—*Boston Evening Post.*

The phrase, which was new in 1842, has become common since that time, and has extended from New York to every part of the country where political and social gatherings are held.

Three - decker (booksellers), a three-volume novel.

Three draws and a spit (common), a jocular phrase for a cigarette.

Three-legged mare, the gallows, because originally formed of three parts.

For the *mare with three legs*, boys, I care not a rap,
'Twill be over in less than a minute.
—*Ainsworth: Rookwood.*

The gallows was the sheriff's "picture-frame;" or, before it assumed its later improved shape, the *three-legged mare.*—*Globe.*

Was also called the "triple tree."

Three-pair back (popular), a back room on third floor.

So they eloped together from the work-house, and took shelter in a *three-pair back.*
—*J. Wight: Mornings at Bow Street.*

Three-ply (American), a Mormon name for a man with three wives. How the *three-ply* system works is set forth in the following extract.

Other wives again, through policy, and for their children's sake, become good girls, and jog along in misery as best they can. But when the lord after some time—shorter or longer—becomes somewhat cooled off in his affection for the "second," or perhaps sees another woman who strikes his fancy, he at once feels the necessity of his still greater exaltation in both worlds, and becomes a *three-ply.*—*New York Herald.*

Three ride business, the crack way of running over hurdles, in which just three strides are taken mechanically between each hurdle.

Three sheets in the wind (common), originally a sea phrase; intoxicated, or nearly so.

Many of these votaries of Bacchus were *three sheets in the wind.*—*Punch.*

It should be enacted, in addition, that the drunkard should wear a badge, . . .

let the heralds invent a cognizance for *three sheets in the wind.*—*Illustrated London News.*

A woman who scrubs
Over lathery tubs,
Though not of a bibulous mind,
Has no cause to faint
If folks make a complaint
Of her having *three sheets in the wind.*
—*Bird o' Freedom.*

Three X's (army), the 30th Regiment of Foot, from the Roman numerals XXX.

Throttle (popular), throat.

Sam's *throttle* napt a rum one, but the latter put in his one two with heavy effect.
—*Pierce Egan: Book of Sports.*

Through a side-door (common), "the child came *through a side-door*," *i.e.*, is illegitimate.

Some wicked wretches say, but I
My indignation smother,
That I came *through a side-door*,
Into this world from the other.
—*H. Wilson: The Blessed Orphan.*

Throwing off (American gamblers), a term used by gamblers when a capper is the partner of a sucker (dupe). The capper can lose when he pleases, thereby *throwing off* the sucker (New York Slang Dictionary).

Throw off the belt, to (American), to stop a machine, to cause anything to cease. "Oh, just *throw off the belt*, and stop your wheels," *i.e.*, cease talking.

There seems to be a tolerably general demand that the controller of Lord Tennyson's poetical machine should *throw off the belt.*—*Detroit Free Press.*

Throw up a maiden, to (cricket), to bowl an innings without any runs being made by the batsman.

Thrums (costermongers), three-pence.

Thrups (popular), threepence.

Thugs (American). This word is in the United States applied to the adherents of the native American party and others by their opponents, also to roughs and villains generally.

Thumper (common), a gross false-hood.

Thumpers (showmen, itinerants), dominoes.

Thumping (common), very large.

Thunderer, the (journalistic), the *Times* newspaper. This sobriquet was given to the chief London daily because of the unusual force and vigour displayed in a series of articles formerly contributed to its columns by Captain Edward Stirling.

Thundering (common), very large, superlative.

Young women employed in drapery establishments may be interested to learn that if their employer accuses them of telling *thundering* lies, they are justified in leaving their situation without notice. —*Globe.*

He took me into his confidence, with the professed object, as he himself declared, of proving to me "what a *thundering* fool he had been."—*J. Greenwood: Tag, Rag, & Co.*

Thunder-mug (American low), a chamber utensil.

The first place our Sophomore got in his scenic work was on the slab fence opposite the Presbyterian Church. On the topmost slab he traced, in burning letters a foot long, "T. Williams and Son sell Bugs, Jugs, Rugs, and *Thunder-Mugs.*" A few ornamental flourishes that would have made Michael Angelo look about for a place in which to lie down and die, completed the first venture.—*He'd Paint, so He Would: An American Story.*

Tib (old cant), a goose.

On red shanks and *tibs* thou shalt every day dine.
                    —*Retoure, my dear Dell.*

Also "*tib* of the buttery." *Tib* is provincial English for a calf.

Tibby (popular), the head.

I'm a chickaleery bloke with my one, two, three,
   Whitechapel is the village I was born in,
For to get me on the hop, or my *tibby* drop,
   You must wake up very early in the mornin'.
                    —*The Chickaleery Cove.*

It has been suggested that *tibby*, or a thick skull, is discoverable in *tibbad*, thickness, a blockhead, explained in Shaw's Gaelic Dictionary published more than half a century ago. More probably from *tab*, *tib*, end piece. To "drop on the *tibby*" is to startle or alarm any one, to take him unawares.

Tib's Eve, on (popular), on the Greek Kalends, *i.e.*, never, at no time.

Tichborne's own (army), the 6th Carabineers.

Tick (common), credit. "What is the damage of the *tick*," what is the amount of the bill on credit. *Tick* is old English, now used slangily.

I confess my *tick* is not good.—*Sedley: The Mulberry Garden*, 1668.

What, Timon, does old age begin t' approach
That thou thus droop'st under one night's debauch,
Hast thou lost deep to needy rogues on *tick*,
Who ne'er could pay, and must be paid next week?
—*The Earl of Rochester's Works.*

When you've got lots of money
You're a brick, brick, brick;
When you've got lots of money
All your friends to you will stick;
But when you've got no money
All the world has lost its honey,
And you'll find your name is Dennis
When you want *tick, tick, tick.*
—*Broadside Ballads.*

Some dads leave houses to their sons,
Mine ne'er left me a brick,
And so just like my watch, by Jove,
I always go on *tick.*
—*G. W. Hunt: The Custom of the Country.*

In the seventeenth century a *ticket* was a tradesman's bill or written acknowledgment of a debt or score, and hence the phrase on *ticket*, on trust, on account, on credit, on *tick*, signified the same. In French slang the equivalent is "avoir l'ardoise," alluding to the slate on which accounts are recorded at wine shops.

Your courtier is mad to take silks and velvets
On *ticket* for his mistress.
—*Cotgrave.*

No matter upon landing whether you have money or no—you may swim in twentie of their boats over the river upon *ticket.*—*Decker: Gull's Horn Book*, 1609.

Also a watch. Same in German cant. In French cant "tocante."

VOL. II.

You know you'll buy a dozen or two of wipes, dobbin cants, or a farm, or a *tick* with any rascal.—*Parker: Variegated Characters.*

Ticker (thieves), a watch.

For seven long years have I served them,
And seven long years I have to stay,
For meeting a bloke in our alley,
And taking his *ticker* away.
—*Inscribed on a Prison Wall.*

"And always put this in your pipe, Nolly," said the Dodger. "If you don't take fogles and *tickers*—if you don't take pocket-handkerchers and watches—some other cove will."—*Charles Dickens: Oliver Twist.*

As it is, we're doing proper, and nicking our ten or a dozen *tickers* in the course of a single afternoon.—*Funny Folks.*

(American University), one who does not know what he is talking about.

Ticket (common and American), that's the *ticket*, that is the proper thing, exactly what is required. In this sense *ticket* is the equivalent of the French *étiquette*, of which the original meaning is label, notice posted up, hence arrangement, ceremonial.

Quite the real *ticket* if the dons as wholesales the blacklead would make it up to sell in ha'porths and penn'orths.—*Mayhew: London Labour and the London Poor.*

"'Deed, that ain't the *ticket*, Miss Mary Jane," I says, "by no manner of means."—*Mark Twain: Huckleberry Finn.*

"What's the *ticket?*" what is the programme? what is to be done? In French "quelle est la marche du bœuf gras?" alluding to the pageant and procession of the prize ox in the streets of Paris (now a thing of the past). (American), "what's the *ticket* on it?" what is the price of it? what will be the result. (Theatrical), *ticket* night, a night on which the friends of the supers at a theatre are allowed to buy *tickets*, on the understanding that it is some advantage to the supers, who have a percentage on the receipts. (Australian), to go on a *ticket*, to be in favour of, to adopt the policy of. Probably adopted from the United States. It signifies to make a thing one's policy. Thus Mr. Gladstone would be said to be "going on the Home Rule *ticket*."

Tickler (common), a small short poker used to save the ornamental fire-irons. A regular *tickler*, a poser. (Popular), a whip.

I don't recollect whether Mrs. Joe Gargery's *tickler*, which was the terror of Pip's life, was minutely described in "Great Expectations."—*Greenwood: In Strange Company.*

(American), explained by quotation.

The drummer never travels without a *tickler*, which is not, as the name might seem to imply, a sportive term for a bowie-knife, but a small pocket ledger, in which are carefully noted all the debts incurred by the parties with whom the drummer does business; and which consequently enables him to refresh, or *tickle*, the memory of firms who are a little behindhand with their payments.—*Daily Telegraph.*

Ticks (sporting), debts. From *tick*, credit, or written acknowledgment of a debt.

Tick up, to (popular), to put to one's account.

It was handed round, and everybody praised the ale. . . . Some adding that they would *tick it up* this time, but that the next time they happened to be passing they would be sure to call in and rub off the score. — *Household Words: Lodged in Newgate.*

Tiddlywink (provincial), a leaving shop, where money is lent on goods without a pawnbroker's license.

Tied his hair, that (tailors), that puzzled him, he had to give it up, could not do it.

Tied his wool (tailors), *vide* TIED HIS HAIR.

Tie-drive, tie (American), timbers tied together, rafts.

The "boys" are men engaged in landing *ties* thus floated down; and sitting around the red-hot stove, they make the evening jolly with songs and yarns of *tie-drives* and of wild rides down the long "V" flume.—*James Stevens: Around the World on a Bicycle.*

Tied up (popular), given over, finished.

Tied up prigging (thieves), given over thieving.

Tiffin (Anglo-Indian and pidgin), luncheon, at least in English households. Also to *tiff*, to take luncheon. As there is no plausible or possible derivation of the word from any Eastern tongue, the authors of the Anglo-Indian Glossary believe it to be a local survival of our old English colloquial or slang term. Grose (1785) defines *tiffing* as eating or drinking out of meal time, or, as Americans would say, "drinking in between drinks." To take a little *tiff* is an old-fashioned term for such a mere bit and sup (especially the sup) in the United States (*tiff*, old English for a draught of liquor. Also *tift*, common in America), where it has certainly no Anglo-Indian connection. It is probably an old derivation from the same root with "tip" and "tipple." To *tiff* or take luncheon is correct. To *tiffin* is generally used by lady-novelists who have not been in India, and it is denounced as "bad grammar, according to Anglo-Indian use," in the Anglo-Indian Glossary. The Anglo-Indian word *tiffin*, according to G. A. Sala, is in common use in hotel advertisements in South Africa.

Lawn-tennis, picnics, and flirtation fill up the time of the poor expatriated wives and daughters from *tiffin* to afternoon tea.—*Daily Telegraph.*

Tiger (workmen). The navvies call streaky bacon by this name. *Vide* THREE CHEERS AND A TIGER.

(American), to fight the *tiger*, to gamble with professionals. From the stripes on a faro table.

Tiger Bay, one of the slums of London.

As soon as her eyes are open in the morning, the she-creature of *Tiger Bay* seeks to cool her parched mouth out of the gin-bottle; and "—— your eyes, let us have some more gin!" is the prayer she nightly

utters before she staggers to her straw, to snore like the worse than pig she is.—*Seven Curses of London.*

Tigers, Bengal (army), the 17th Foot, from their badge.

Tight (common), drunk.

And I lie in such pose
On my pallet to-night
(With my boots unremoved),
That you fancy me *tight*—
And I rest so at large
On my pallet to-night
(With my head to its foot),
That you fancy me *tight*—
That you frown as you look at me,
Thinking me *tight*.
  —*Funny Folks.*

He's had his day, and had his night,
And now when he did get *tight*,
He used to go it proper right,
Did grandfather!
  —*C. H. Ross : The Husband's Boat.*

In about half-an-hour they were as thick as thieves again, and the *tighter* they got, the lovinger they got.—*Mark Twain: Huckleberry Finn.*

This corresponds to the French slang word "rond," drunk, *i.e.*, distended by drink. Mr. George Augustus Sala tells an amusing story of Macready in connection with this word. To enable the reader to understand the point of the anecdote, it is essential to state that in America there is a harmless bird called a peep, which, in consequence of being purblind, flies in a groggy and erratic manner, continually striking its wings against the branches of trees. Hence it is popularly known as the boozy bird.

While playing in Philadelphia, Macready was much distressed

by the actor who played Horatio being very drunk. Coming off the stage, the star encountered the manager, to whom he pointed out the peccant player.

"Do you see that beast, sir?" inquired the enraged tragedian, pointing to the drunken Horatio. "I do, sir," replied the manager; "and I guess he's *tight* as a peep."

"Oh, indeed!" growled Mac. "I was not aware that that was the gentleman's name; but it's my private opinion, sir, that Mr. Titus Peep is as drunk as a lord!"

(Popular), "blow me *tight!*" an exclamation. A variation of "jigger me *tight!*" which originally was probably obscene.

> " Good people, he disowns me—he's a false, deceitful churl!
> And if that's not right — well, *blow me tight!*" She was a vulgar girl!
> —*Sporting Times.*

Tightener (general), a meal, or a hearty meal.

> Why I've cleared a "flatch-enork "(half a crown), but "kool esilop" (look at the police), nammus (be off), I'm going to do a *tightener* (have my dinner).—*Diprose: London Life.*

(Popular), do the *tightener*, to dine.

Tight fit (Vermont University), a good joke. The one telling it is said to be "hard up."

Tilbury (old cant), a sixpence.

Tile (common), a hat, sometimes also used for any head covering by the lower orders.

> At a few minutes before one, Sam threw his *tile* into the ring.—*Pierce Egan : Book of Sports.*
>
> John, Lord Kinsale,
> A stalwart old Baron, who acting as henchman
> To one of our early kings, killed a big Frenchman :
> A feat which his Majesty deigning to smile on,
> Allowed him henceforth to stand with his *tile* on.   —*Ingoldsby Legends.*
>
> Tried to get to the bottom of the three-card trick, but fellow was too deep a card. Got my new *tile* flattened by a fellow taking me for a welsher.—*Moonshine.*

The comparison of the head to a house or habitation is obviously appropriate and familiar. Thus the metaphor of a *tile*, as the covering of the house or head, is not incongruous. The hat, or *tile*, as used in this sense, is erroneously supposed to be a corruption of pantile or sugarloaf, because hats shaped like a sugar-loaf were sometimes worn. By a similar metaphor the hat, and sometimes the hair, was called the "thatch," and less commonly the "slate." The similarity in idea of many expressions of the slang of different nations, is exemplified in this as in other instances. Thus in French argot, *ardoise*, a slate, stands for hat or cap, as well as *tile*, and in Spanish cant *tejado*, or *techo*, is literally a tile-roof. Dr. Brewer thinks *tile* is from Saxon *tigel*, to cover, to which is due the English provincial *teag*, an article of head-dress.

Tile-frisking (thieves), stealing hats from halls.

" What's the programme?" said the Dude to the Baby Hippo, last Saturday afternoon.

" Going on a circular tour."

" Personally conducted? Black Maria? Case of *tile-frisking*, I suppose?"—*Bird o' Freedom.*

Tile loose (common), to have a *tile loose*, to be slightly deranged. Also a " tile off " or slate loose."

Questioned by Mr. Finlay, witness said the feather came from Mount Calvary. She thought the major had got a *tile loose*. —*Daily Telegraph.*

Till-sneak (thieves), a rogue that robs tills.

Tilt on, to (American), to tumble on, come across, meet. From to tilt up, or tilt over.

If there are any blooming young Beechers, or flourishing clerical cocks, who expect a hen-reward for their devotion, let them beware, lest when they *tilt on* something extra sweet, they tilt up. Tilting on and tilting up, my young friends, is by far too favourite a vanity among you all.—*Sermon by Don the Third.*

Timbers (popular), the legs. Also " stems," "pegs."

Timber-tuned (musical), said of a person who has a heavy wooden touch on the piano, or other instrument.

Time of day (popular and thieves), that's the *time of day*, that's the thing, how matters stand, or ought to stand.

Pop that shawl away in my castor, Dodger, so that I may know where to find it when I cut; that's the *time of day!*— *Dickens: Oliver Twist.*

To know the *time of day*, to be wide-awake; to be put up to the *time of day*, to be initiated,

made expert. Alluding to teaching a child how to tell the time from a clock. Compare with " to know what's o'clock."

Then " Royal " Prescot dares the fray, And teaches us the *time of day*.
—*St. Helen's Lantern.*

" To be fly to the *time of day*," to be initiated, expert.

Who should I meet but a jolly blowen Who was *fly to the time of day*.
— *W. Maginn: Vidocq's Song.*

Timer (thieves), used in the phrase first, second, &c., *timer*.

Time, to do (thieves), to serve out a term of imprisonment.

Tin (general), money. Also " pewter."

We never put *tin* on a horse to win, Lack of oof explains it partly, But the horse that will be in the final three, Is the one that races Smartley.
—*Sporting Times.*

(Pidgin), thin, *i.e.*, light, not heavy, short weight. Probably the origin of the American phrase "too thin," *i.e.*, shallow, wanting in reason. " That excuse is too *thin*." " You talkee my t'at one catty ginger—t'at too *tin* he àllo samee play, pidgin—you wantchee cheatee my, no can do."

Tindal (Anglo-Indian), a native petty-officer of lascars, or the overseer of a gang of labourers.

Tinge (tailors), special percentage allowed to drapers' assistants when old or damaged stock is sold.

Tin-horn lot, a (American, Western), a term used to express contempt, implying that the one "contempted" is a small-minded, mean fellow. In London "tin-pot."

There wasn't none of this small-minded scraping and shaving, and adding up and keeping tally. Them as got it paid, and them as hadn't it didn't, and that's there was to it ; and if anybody said anything ugly about it, you just blowed the top of his head off, and set up the drinks, and there was an end of him. As to these here Californians that's come out since then— they're *a tin-horn lot* compared, half Jew, half Chinaman, on'y fit to take their pleasure in a one-horse hearse.—*F. Francis: Saddle and Moccasin.*

Tinkers' news (common), news that has been heard or told before. In Scotland the term is "pipers' news," the idea being that information supplied by these people soon gets stale on account of their peregrinatory habits.

Tinkler (common), explained by quotation.

"Hark!" cried the Dodger at this moment, "I heard the *tinkler*." . . . The bell was rung again.—*Dickens : Oliver Twist.*

French thieves call a bell "une retentissante."

Tin-pot (common), low, mean, as a *tin-pot* game ; worthless, as in a *tin-pot* company.

I shall have correspondents all over the world, and I shall have information of every dodge goin', from an emperor's ambition to a *tin-pot* company bubble.—*The Golden Butterfly.*

Most of the men whom one met at the Castle had been under the patronage of sportsmen amongst the Upper Ten, and no *tin-pot* heroes could get a footing.— *Sporting Life.*

(Naval), a contemptuous term for an ironclad.

Tip (general), a bribe or gratuity to servants or others, in reward for services or information furnished or expected. From *tipe*, to toss, as money was at one time commonly thrown to servants. The word is so extensively used as to be hardly slang.

Even instances have come to our notice of men in a good position in society being blackmailed when returning home late, and, under the threat of being run in as drunk and disorderly, giving the necessary *tip* rather than have to go to the police-station, and perhaps get their names brought prominently before the public. — *Saturday Review.*

We do not desire to suggest that a judicious *tip* from Miss —— to Constable E——, when he first addressed himself to her, would have released her from the further effects of his zeal.—*The World.*

In the sporting world, *tip* has also the signification of private information, on the chances of a horse winning, supposed to be derived from some trustworthy source. Straight *tip*, direct information from the owner or trainer of a horse, and generally direct information or hint on any subject. From *tip*, a cue, in showman's slang.

I don't know how he knows about horses, but he does ; he is generally right. He's a tout—makes it his living going round giving *tips*.—*Pall Mall Gazette.*

No matter what paper or tout proclaims,
Take only the *tip* from "Truthful James;"
He is up to all the dodges and games,
And money's not wasted by "Truthful James."
    —*Sporting Times.*

(Popular), to sling the *tip*, to give information, give a hint.

Kim here, you confounded young josser, while straight
From the shoulder I *slings you the tip*,
As regards a bad habit you've taken of late.
—*Sloper's Vagaries.*

(Common), that's the *tip*, that is the proper thing to do; to miss one's *tip*, to miss one's opportunity, fail. (Old), a *tip*, a drink. Provincial English diminutive, *tipple.*

Miss (with a glass in her hand)—"Hold your tongue, Mr. Neverout, don't speak in my *tip*."—*Swift: Polite Conversation.*

Tip and a bopatte (provincial), a shop in country villages, where everything may be had from a shirt to a lucifer match.

Tip a stave, to (common), to sing.

Miss Amy —— can also *tip you a stave* with an ability something above the common.—*Fun.*

Tip one's boom off. *Vide* To Tip.

Tipperary lawyer (Irish), a bludgeon or shillelagh.

Next he produced a shillelagh—a real *Tipperary lawyer*—and, taking off his hat and turning back his cuffs, he proceeded to wield it in a defiant manner, finally bringing it down with a sounding thwack on the lid of the japanned box.—*Daily Telegraph.*

Tippery (common), payment.

In plain words, he wished to have the *tippery* for his toggery.—*J. Wight: Mornings at Bow Street.*

Tipping (American). "*Tipping* about on her toes." Used in Philadelphia to mean a mincing

gait. This agrees, certainly by mere accident, with the Yiddish *tippeln*, to come and go (Hebrew *tapoph*), walking with a minced or tripping gait. (Public and military schools), it is *tipping*, it is first-rate, jolly.

Tipster (turf), an agent who procures special information for his clients on the condition of horses, their capabilities, &c.

It is an open secret that *tipsters* pay for their advertisements on an unusually high scale.—*Bird o' Freedom.*

"Sir, I am a *tipster!*" he said proudly. "I seldom bet for myself."—*Sporting Times.*

Tip the double, to (common), to decamp.

In plain words he fairly *tipped 'em the double*, he was vanished. —*J. Wight: Mornings at Bow Street.*

Tip the little finger, to (slangy Australian), to drink. The expression is taken from the position of the little finger in emptying a glass. When a man takes to drink, or injures his position or business by drinking too much, Australians say that he is a little too fond of *tipping the little finger.*

Tip, to (common), to give, convey. There are many applications of this word in English, which may be translated by "give." Thus "*tip* the wink," a silent request to act with caution, or to abstain from crediting all that is said. Very old. In Colley Cibber's "Flora, or Hob in the Well," ii. 2, the servant says, "Know you, sir! Why, I bought one of your ballads for her, and she *tipt the wink* upon me, with as much as to say, desire him not to go till he hears from me."

Sudden she storms! she raves! You *tip the wink;*
But spare your censure: Silia does not drink.　　*—Pope's Moral Essays.*

At which words Sextus *tipped me the wink,* but I did not observe that Licinius was at all displeased with them.—*Valerius.*

As we went by our house I wished I hadn't sent Mary Jane out of town; because now, if I could *tip her the wink,* she'd light out and save me.—*Mark Twain: Huckleberry Finn.*

"*Tip* us your fin," shake hands. Also "*tip* us your daddle," or "your flipper," &c.

Tip us your daddle.
She *tipped* me her sweet little paw.
　　　　　—Punch.

Old Bottleblue *tipped* me his flipper, and 'oped I'd refreshed and all that.—*Punch.*

Tip me the clank like a dimber mort or you are trim a ken for the gentry-cove, he is no lansweardo, or I am a kinchin.—*Beaconsfield: Venetia.*

To give a gratuity.

"Which they're the very moral of Christyuns, sir!" observed Mrs. Tester, who was dabbing her curtseys in thankfulness for the large amount with which our hero had *tipped* her.—*C. Bede: Verdant Green.*

"What's the *tip?*" what is to be given or paid, same as "what's the damage?" (Popular and thieves), to *tip* the cole, to pay money.

For when that he hath nubbed us,
And our friends *tip* him no cole,
He takes his chive and cuts us down,
And *tips* us into the hole.
　　*—The Life and Death of the Dark-
　　　　man's Budge.*

To "*tip* the cole to Adam Tyler," to pass the stolen money to an accomplice. To "*tip* the loaver," to pay money.

. . . Just by sweetening them, and then they don't mind *tipping the loaver.*—*Mayhew: London Labour and the London Poor.*

(Popular), to *tip* one's boom off, to depart, from a sailor's phrase.

Tip-top (common), of the best kind, first-rate.

Tip-top swells used to come among us, and no mistake; real noblemen, sir.—*Mayhew: London Labour and the London Poor.*

Perhaps a *tip-top* cracksman be,
Or go on the high toby.
　　—The Song of the Young Prig.

Tip-topper (popular), a gentleman, one of the best class, first-rate. Also "topper."

Tip up, to (popular), to pay.

"Come on," whispered Mouldy, first looking up and down to see that we were not observed; "*tip up,* Smiffield."
"*Tip up!*" I repeated, in amazement, seeing that he as well as Ripston were looking perfectly serious.
"Fork out," said the boy last mentioned.—*The Little Ragamuffins.*

Tire, to be tired (American), to be afraid of, alarmed at, timid.

"Sir, I thank you for not giving him your gun (revolver). Perhaps you saved my life." Then getting ferocious, "Not that I'm scared at him." Then a short silence, and glaring fiercely at me, "Nor of you either. I've seen cow-boys, bigger men than you, and with bigger hats too —but they didn't *tire* me. No, they didn't *tire* me any."—*Morley Roberts: The Western Avernus.*

Tish (Oxford Military College), partition or cubicle.

Title-page (printers), a face. A well-displayed *title-page* is a handsome, open face.

Titter (popular), a girl.

> Only a glass of bitter!
> Only a sandwich mild!
> Only a stupid *titter*!
> Only she's not a child!
> —*Song: Only a Penny Blossom.*

From *tit*, used by Dryden as a contemptuous term for a girl. Wright gives *tit* as provincial for smart or proud girl ; a light *tit*, a strumpet. Probably from titmouse. Tytmose, the *pud. fem.* (Halliwell).

Tizzy (common), perhaps a corruption from tester, an old English word for a sixpence.

> There's an old 'oman at the lodge who will show you all that's worth seeing—the walks and the toy cascade—for a *tizzy*.— *Lytton : The Caxtons.*

Tizzy Poole (Winchester), an old term for a fives' ball. They cost sixpence, and were sold to the boys by a head porter named Poole.

Toadskin (American boys' slang), a five-cent postage-stamp.

> "Why, ma, don't you know what a *toadskin* is?" said Billy, drawing a dingy five-cent stamp from his pocket. "Here's one, and don't I wish I had lots of 'em !" —*Fitz-Hugh Ludlow : Little Brother.*

Toasting-fork or **iron** (common), a sword.

> If I had given him time to get at his other pistol, or his *toasting-fork*, it was all up.—*Hughes : Tom Brown at Oxford.*

> I served in Spain with the King's troopers until . . . and hung up my *toasting-iron.*—*Thackeray : Pendennis.*

Toast, on (common), to have one *on toast*, to place another in a corner or dilemma. In America a very common phrase for anything nicely served.

Toasty (studios) is said of a picture painted in very warm tints. French painters call this *rôti.*

Tobacco-curers (South Carolina), explained by quotation.

> "Barns" were built or repaired, cheap thermometers—or *terbacker kyorers*, as they are called there—are bought, and the golden-leafed luxury—the bane of the revenue reformer—is cut from a thousand steep and stony hillsides, and hung in "chinked and daubed" air-tight barns. —*Bird o' Freedom.*

Tobur, toba (showmen, &c.), the ground or field at fairs, hired to put the waggons on for show or circuses, or other *al fresco* entertainments, which does not amount to much, so that a man or manager is considered very hard up if he has not enough to pay the *tobur*. Gypsy *tober*, the road, hence ground.

Toby (cant), highroad. This word is as much in use as ever among "travellers," who now call it "tober." "Tober" is probably the older word. See above.

> You are a capital fellow ! and when the lads come to know their loss, they will know they have lost the bravest and truest gill that ever took to the *toby.*— *Lytton : Paul Clifford.*

Toby consarn (old cant), a highway expedition. *Toby*, highway.

Tobyman (old cant), highwayman. *Toby*, the highway.

All the most fashionable prigs, or *toby-men*, sought to get him into their set.— *Lytton: Paul Clifford.*

Toco or **toks** (popular), to give *toco*, to thrash. Possibly from Italian *tocco*, touch, stroke.

The school-leaders come up furious, and administer *toco* to the wretched fags nearest at hand.—*Hughes: Tom Brown's School-Days.*

Dear Charlie,—Ascuse shaky scribble ; I'm writing this letter in bed.
Went down to the Square, mate, last Sunday, and got a rare clump on the 'ed.
Beastly shame, and no error, my pippin !
    Me cop it ! It's too jolly rum.
When a reglar Primroser gits *toko*, one wonders wot *next* there will come.
                                —*Punch.*

Toddle, to (common), to be off, to walk. Provincial English, to walk with short steps.

"Then *toddle* to bed as soon as you like," said Mr. Belcher. "Can you find your way back?" — *The Little Raga-muffins.*

"We're a-going Hitchin way," said the companionable linker, "we'll *toddle* together."—*J. Greenwood: Tag, Rag, & Co.*

Toe-fil-tie (Winton), to tie string or cord to the toes of sleeping boys with the object of waking them by pulling the string.

Toeing (pugilistic), *toeing* the scratch or mark, beginning the fight, that is, placing one's foot on the scratch or line in a prize fight.

Wednesday was "presentation day" at London University. The gentleman who gained the greatest applause on "*toe-ing* the mark" before the Chancellor was William Waterloo Wellington Rolleston Napoleon Buonaparte Guelph Saunders,

B.A., and the clerk of the course was fairly out of breath when he had got to the end of this appalling cognomen. Even the sweet girl graduates smiled.—*Sporting Times.*

(Common), *toeing* one, kicking one behind.

Toff (popular), a dandy, a swell, one who appears well. Also *toffer*, a well-dressed gay woman. Derived from the Yiddish or Hebrew *toff*, *tov*, *tuw*, literally good, and used in an extended sense which perfectly warrants its application to good or a fine appearance. *Toff*, good ; *töffer*, better ; *töffest*, best ; *jom toff*, good day, a festival ; *toff peg*, a good groschen; *tof malluschim*, fine clothes. A probable derivation is from to *tiff*, to deck oneself out, or *toft*, a dressy individual. *Toff*, often applied to an over-dressed clerk or draper's assistant, who apes the swell. An old *toff*, an old beau.

A magistrate recently sentenced a woman, who made her hundredth appearance at the court, to fourteen days' hard labour. "You are an old *toff*," warbled the lady, "and if you sit there long enough, I'll certainly treat you. I am now going to eat some bread and onions I have in my pocket." "Saints preserve us !" groaned the magistrate. "Remove the lady with electric rapidity, gaoler, and get rid of those onions as quickly as possible," he continued. The gaoler obeyed orders, and as he re-entered the court, a powerful aroma floated round, and the worthy beak was heard to ejaculate "pah !"—*Judy.*

The sort of old *toff* as a cove would be proud of for a dad.—*Punch.*

Up ! sport-loving *toffs*, tool your drags o'er the sward,
And, forsooth ! since a coster may elbow a lord,

At Epsom, let coves who from Whitechapel hail,
Drive their nags and their barrow close
up to the rail.
—*Sporting Times.*

Tofficky (popular), dressy, fine,
nice.

Toffishness (popular), explained
by quotation.

Taking the average, it may be set down
at ten for each of the two hundred, or two
thousand slices in all—thick slices, bear in
mind : anything under an inch thick would
be regarded with contempt by the bony
young barrowman, and perhaps with an
uncomfortable suspicion that you have designs to inveigle him into the detestable
ways of gentility. He calls it *toffishness.*
He is peculiar in his views in this respect.
—*Greenwood : In Strange Company.*

Togged (popular), dressed.

He was *togg'd* gnostically enough. —
Scott : St. Ronan's Well.

So I've *togged* myself up to the nines.
—*Punch.*

In London many female servants seldom
remain long in one situation ; just long
enough to get *togged* and fed up. Then
my lady must have a spree for a few days.
— *Thor Fredur : Sketches from Shady
Places.*

Shakspeare has *toged,* gowned.

Toggery (popular and thieves),
clothing.

Next slipt off his bottom clo'ing,
And his ginger head topper gay.
Then his other *toggery* stowing,
Tol lol, &c.,
All with the swag I sneak away.
—*Burrowes : Vidocq's Song.*

But in Edward the First's days, I very
much fear,
Had a gay cavalier thought fit to appear
In any such *toggery*—then 'twas term'd
. "gear"—
He'd have met with a highly significant
sneer,

Or a broad grin extending from ear unto
ear,
On the features of every soul he came
near ;
There was no taking refuge too, then, as
with us,
On a slip-sloppy day, in a cab or a 'bus.
—*Ingoldsby Legends.*

But take a pal's advice, and don't be over
nice,
Though your suit of *toggery* ain't a very
flash 'un ;
You'd better far put up with the rig than
tear it up,
And be measured for the latest " parish "
fashion.
—*J. Greenwood : A Night in a
Workhouse.*

Toggy, togman (old cant), a coat.

Togman (thieves), a cloak or
coat.

I towre the strummel trine upon thy
nachbet and *togman.*—*Harman : Caveat.*

Togs (common), clothes.

Look at his *togs !* Superfine cloth, and
the heavy swell cut ! Oh, my eye, what a
game !—*Dickens : Oliver Twist.*

"It mightn't spoil some sort of *togs,*"
I replied, with a scornful glance at poor
Sam's wretched rags. "I shouldn't like
to get the soot over my clothes wot I wears
of Sundays, so I tell yer. I'm going to
have another suit to follow my trade in."
—*The Little Ragamuffins.*

My friend could play the fiddle and de-
claim, and I can dance, whistle, and sing
with anybody ; so, having obtained my
pension, we bought an old violin and suitable *togs,* and started to do a bit of nigger
minstrel business in the country, where
such things are nearly unknown.—*Thor
Fredur : Sketches from Shady Places.*

Togs was used for garments
in the time of Henry VIII.
From the Anglo - Saxon *tygan,*
or else from the same root with
the Latin *toga,* a covering ; like
tugurium, hut or roof. Indo-

Germanic *teg*, to cover; hence *tego*, *tegere*. German *dach*, a roof. "Thatch," and the Greek στέγη, a roof, are of the same family. This word seems to be the same as the old term *tugs*, same meaning, as in under *tug*, a petticoat. *Tug* clothes, working clothes.

Also possibly from the Anglo-Saxon *teog*, material, stuff, and *tege*, a binding, tying (*ligatura*, *rexus*). *Tygan* (Boswell), to tie together. Togged out reminds us of *teohjan*, from the same root, signifying to adorn, trick out, *exornare* (Beówulf, 5871). Latin *toga*.

Toheno, tohereno (costermongers), pronounced *tocheno* or *tochereno*, very nice; literally a transposition of "hot one."

Toke (popular and thieves), bread. Same as "tack."

One night coming home to the crib where he lived,
Found two cripples a munching dry *toke* as they sat.
—*J. Greenwood: A Night in a Workhouse.*

For breakfast there is bread and scrap,
And something she calls tea;
I only know it's wet and warm
And disagrees with me;
I wouldn't mind so much for that
If the *toke* was not so thick,
For each slice is two inches high,
And hard as any brick.
—*Broadside Ballad.*

Pieces of bread.

He could devour as many surplus *tokes* as an elephant at the Zoo on an Easter Monday.—*Evening News.*

Token (printers). *Vide* BULLOCK'S HEART. Printers in

working off sheets reckon their work by *tokens* of two hundred and fifty impressions.

Tol (old cant), a sword. Evidently abbreviated from Toledo, when the blades manufactured in that town had a world-wide reputation.

Merrily over the common he flies,
Fast and free as the rush of the rocket,
His crape-covered vizard drawn over his eyes,
His *tol* by his side, and his pops in his pocket.
—*Ainsworth: Rookwood.*

(Costermongers' back slang), stock, share, or lot.

How is a man to sell fine cherries at 4d. a pound that cost him 3½d., when there's a kid alongside of him a selling his *tol* at 2d. a pound?—*Mayhew: London Labour and the London Poor.*

Tol lol, happy, pretty well.

Toll-loll-loll-kiss-me-dear (bird fancier), explained by quotation.

"Just the same," put in old Master Nosey Warren; "just the same as the Middlesex finch calls hisself *toll-loll-loll-kiss-me-dear;* it's the nat'ral note of 'em."
—*Greenwood: In Strange Company.*

Toll-shop (provincial), a prison, a variation of *toll-booth*. "The prison was so called in Cambridge, as it still is in Scotland. Corbel uses the word as a verb, and explains it in a note, 'Idem quod Bocardo apud Oxon.' The English Dictionary gives it as meaning custom-house" (Lewis O. Davies).

The Maior refused to give them the keys of the *toll-booth*, or town prison. —*Fuller: History of Cambridge.*

Tolly (public schools), a candle; from *tallow*.

Tolly up, to (Harrow School), to keep a candle alight after the gas has been turned off.

Toloben (old cant), the tongue. Also *tollibon*, *tullibon*. Possibly from *toll*, to ring a bell, and *bene*, well. This derivation is supported by similar metaphors: English slang "clapper," a tongue, especially a busy tongue; French slang "battant" (tongue of a bell), tongue; "avoir un bon battant," to be a great or loud talker; Italian cant "scampanare" (literally to toll), to talk loud. Or from *tal* (tell), and *bene*, well, or gypsy termination *ben* or *pen* to every verbal noun. The gypsies use the term under the form of *tálloben*. Again, the term may owe its origin to *tully*, red silk, "red rag" being the modern phrase for tongue; in French slang "chiffon rouge." *Toloben rig*, fortune-telling.

Tolsery (old cant), a penny. Literally the price of toll. "Tolsey" is provincial for a place where tolls were taken.

Tom and Jerry shop (popular), a low drinking-shop.

Tomarter or **tomato, a** (American), "he caught a *tomarter* that time." A substitute for "a tartar," provided by Artemus Ward.

Tom astoners (nautical), dashing fellows. From astound or "astony," to terrify (Smyth). *Tom* is tinker for great.

Tombstones (popular), large teeth. Pawn tickets, all that remains of the departed property.

The collection for master amounted to 4½d., and a *tombstone* for ninepence on a brown Melton overcoat.—*Sporting Times.*

Tombstone style (printers), a slang term to indicate a particular kind of display in setting up—similar to that used in monumental inscriptions.

Tom-John, tonjon (Anglo-Indian), a sort of sedan or portable chair.

Tommies (popular), a name for tomatoes.

Now that the wholesome "love-apples," with their delicious sub-acid flavour, have become cheap, the masses in their thousands may be seen continually munching them, not only because the *tommies* are nice, but because they are red.—*Daily Telegraph.*

Tommy (popular), bread, food. The usual name for food amongst navvies. Probably from Irish *tiomallain*, I eat.

One finger is what you've got to look out for. The job what Rip's got will get us the coffee; now, if we can find summat else while he's a-doin' of it, that'll be the *tommy*; which I hopes we shall, cos coffee wirrout *tommy* don't make much of a breakfast. So keep your eyes open, Smiffield.—*The Little Ragamuffin.*

Also inferior. *Tom* seems to enter into many disparaging phrases. The exchange of labour for goods. *Tommy*-shop, a place where a variety of articles, mainly food, are sold. From provincial English *tommy*, provisions.

The proprietor keeps a "tienda" or *tommy*-shop on his estate, just as the Australian squatter keeps his store at his station.—*Daily Telegraph.*

Also a baker's shop. Originally a store belonging to an employer whose workmen were obliged to take out part of their earnings in *tommy* or food.

Tommy Atkins (army), a familiar term given by soldiers to their pocket ledger or small account-book. The origin of this name arose from every document, paper, &c., being headed, for convenience sake, "I, *Tommy Atkins*," &c. In general parlance the term is applied to a soldier.

Tommy Dodd, in tossing, when the odd man either wins or loses, as per agreement (Hotten).

Tommy rot (common), rubbish, nonsense.

Wen he sez my god's "go"—well he's 'it it. Great Scott! wot is life *without* "go?"
But "loud, slangy, vulgar"? No, 'ang it, young man, this is—well, there, it's *low.*
Me vulgar! a Primroser, Charlie, a true "Anti-Radical" pot!
No, excuse me, St. J., I admire you; but this is all dashed *tommy rot.*
—*Punch.*

Tom-pats, in canting, shoes. In gypsy, feet. Hindu *tal-pat*, trampled on. To *patter-alay* in gypsy, is to trample on, *alay*, being an abbreviation of *talé* or *tal.* (Old cant), rum *tom-pat*, a real clergyman, in opposition to the "patrico," which see.

Tom Topper (popular), freshwater mariner, ferryman. Also "Tom Tug."

Tongs (American), an old word used for boys' jackets and trousers. Probably a form of the old English *togs*, aided by the resemblance of trousers to *tongs*, in the forked shape.

(Medical), a familiar name amongst medical students for the midwifery forceps.

Tony catchy, tunnyketch, tawnykertch (Anglo-Indian). In Madras the domestic water-carrier, generally a woman. Tamil, *tannir-kassi.*

Too big for his boots (theatrical), a phrase invented by the late F. B. Chatterton, manager of Drury Lane, to denote an actor who, having made a hit, gave himself airs, and became obstreperous and presuming.

Too forth-putting (American), too demonstrative or "too previous."

The Taylor gush in Tennessee is getting tiresome. At the latest "rally" both were presented with pathetic speeches, and Bob got a bass viol of red roses and Alf a ship of white roses, and both were nominated for Vice-President on the next Presidential tickets. These gentlemen are quite *too forth-putting.* The public is fatigued and would fain seek repose.—*Washington Post.*

Toofered (gypsy), mended.

Tacho, true. But an old coat can hold out better than a man. If a man gets a hole in him, he dies; but his chukko (coat) can be *toofered* and sivved apré (mended and sewed up for ever).—*The English Gypsies.*

Tool (studios), artists give this appellation to their brushes. (Popular), a poor *tool*, a clumsy fellow, a bad hand at anything, a whip. (Burglar), a small boy whom housebreakers employ to enter a house by a small aperture.

Tooler (thieves), a pickpocket; moll-*tooler*, female pickpocket. To *tool* is applied to stealing, picking pockets, and burglary; derived beyond doubt from the gypsy word *tool*, to hold, handle, or take. In all the Continental Romany dialects it is *tulliwawa*.

Tool, to (general), to drive, to hold and manage the reins, to "handle the ribbons." Probably from an association with *tools* and skilful handling. To do a thing in workmanlike style. Suggested to be from the gypsy *tül*, indicative present *tullivava* (*vide* TOOLER), I hold, also generally applied to driving. *Tul tiro chib*, hold your tongue; *tul o solivaris*, hold the bridle, *i.e.*, ride.

He could *tool* a coach.—*Lytton: The Caxtons.*

A coach he'd *tool*. You've coaches still,
I've heard that they're not driven ill,
But where's the fun without the spill?
    Says Grandfather.
    —*C. H. Ross: The Husband's Boat.*

Mr. Carnegie was taking the peace gentlemen with him, and he is well known to be a generous host. Who has not read of his coaching tours in England, when he *tooled* Mr. Matthew Arnold, Mr. John Morley, Mr. William Black, and other men of light and leading behind his teams of prancing nags.—*Pall Mall Gazette.*

(University), to *tool* along, to go or cause to go at a great pace.

Too much bag (American), needless disquisition, padding, superfluity.

There is a great deal of *bag* and a strong sense of too-muchness in this tale. It bulgeth.—*Western Newspaper.*

Toother (pugilistic), a blow on the mouth.

I found . . . two knuckles cut to the bone almost, so I must have got in one pretty good *toother.*—*Sporting Life.*

Tooth-music (popular), mastication.

Toot, on a (American), raising the devil, making a noise, on a spree. *Toot*, the devil (English provincial, Wright). *Toot*, to blow a horn; Anglo-Saxon *tutan*, to swell, to grow; *tanta* (*i.e.*, *toot*), to murmur, sound; *getete*, show, ostentation; *totjam*, *eminere*, *micare*, to cut a shine. All agreeing with the modern forms.

Too-too (society), exceedingly, an expletive. Thomas Scott, in his "Philomythia," employs this phrase, which, after an oblivion of nearly three centuries, has been revived. Speaking of the weathercock, he says, "his head was *too-too* great," and again, "his tail was *too-too* weak," referring to its irregularities.

Tootsies (common), feet, those of ladies and children in particular.

Top! a signal among tailors and sempstresses for snuffing the candle. One cries *top!* and all the others follow; he who last pronounces this word has to snuff the candle (Hotten). An abbreviation of "*top* the glim." To *top* is to burn off the long cotton end of a candle. (American), first-rate. An abbreviation of "tip-*top*."

The third suddenly becomes a very swash-buckler of a young woman. Hitherto she has spoken English ; now she falls into an unknown dialect. "How is your mother, Jenny?" she is asked by the visitor. "Oh, *top!*"—*The Youth's Companion.*

Top - dressing (journalistic), a large-type introduction to a report, generally written by a man of higher literary attainments than the ordinary reporter who follows with the details (Hotten). (Common), doing the hair, coiffure.

The Roman Emperor Caracalla, when he made a progress in Germany, tried to conciliate the fierce Teutons by having his sable locks cropped close to his head, and assuming a *top-dressing* in the shape of a tawny rig.—*Daily Telegraph.*

The coarseness of thy tresses is distressing,
With grease and raddle firmly coalescing,
I cannot laud thy system of *top-dressing.*
—*J. B. Stephens: To a Black Gin.*

Shakspeare uses the word *top* for head :

All the starred vengeance of Heaven fall
On her ungrateful *top.*

Topee (Anglo-Indian), a hat of any kind. Hindu *topi*. Incorrectly limited in popular English parlance to the *sola* (not *solar*) helmet.

Top o' reeb (costermongers' back slang), pot of beer.

Top-heavy (common), drunk. Unsteady, like anything having the upper part too heavy for the lower, as of a boat or ship.

Top-joint (thieves' back slang), a pint of beer.

Top-lights (nautical), the eyes. In French slang, "quinquets;" Spanish cant, "lanternas;" Italian, "lampante."

Topped (thieves and popular), hanged, "may I be *topped!*"

Topper (common), excellent, as a *topper* at billiards. The *toppers,* swells, fashionable people.

But I twigged that the *toppers* left early ;
Yours truly ain't 'ooked for a flat !
—*Punch.*

(Thieves), head *topper,* a hat or wig. (Popular), tobacco left in the bowl of a pipe, a tall hat. (Pugilistic), a blow on the head.

Vile Jem, with neat left-handed stopper,
Straight threatened Tommy with a *topper.*
—*Ainsworth: Rookwood.*

Topper hunter (popular), poor men who pick up cigar ends and pieces of tobacco, which they chop up.

Topping (popular), elegant, swell, great. (Nautical), pretentious, as *topping* the officer ; also fine, gallant.

Topping cheat (old cant), the gallows. *Topping,* hanging, and *cheat,* a thing.

Top-sawyer (general), a term denoting excellence, superiority. It is derived from the rule of the sawpits ; the top man has to work harder and is more responsible for the job than the man who stands below. This term is of many special applications. (Sporting), a renowned horse, that excels others in speed and endurance.

There will be at least a dozen runners—more, probably, should the favourite develop more fibrine in the blood—and far more interest attaches to the race than in years past, when there has usually been a *top-sawyer* in the field.—*Bird o' Freedom.*

(Thieves), an expert thief, one who has gained distinction among his fellows by his achievements.

Wasn't he always a *top-sawyer* among you all? Is there one of you that could touch him, or come near him on any scent? —*Dickens: Oliver Twist.*

They planned their work and executed it without any assistance; not because they declined to associate with the old ones—as the candidate for platform employment hastened to add, with undisguised contempt for the whole race of paltry pretenders—but because they were unacquainted with any of the school, being themselves green hands and novices, who were ambitious "to be *top-sawyers* when as yet they were fit for nothing but to pick up chips."—*J. Greenwood: A Converted Burglar.*

(Common), a rich person.

"I'll marry a *top-sawyer*," he used to say, whenever his uncle broached the question of his settlement in life. "Why, bless ye, it's the same tackle and the same fly that takes the big fish and the little one."—*Whyte-Melville: M. or N.*

A great person.

He had paid the postboys, and travelled with a servant like a *top-sawyer.*—*Thackeray: The Newcomes.*

Also applied to a thing.
VOL. II.

"Well then," says I, "I have made a spec, gineral, and such a spec too as ain't often made now-a-days nother. It's a *top-sawyer* one, I do assure you."—*Sam Slick.*

Formerly a dandy, an exquisite.

When the perfumed mane of the Persian lion flowed over his high coat-collar, and in conjunction with an exuberant pointed beard, imparted a formidable ferocity to his strongly-marked lineaments, his contemporary, the London *top-sawyer*, went about clean-shaven, save for a mutton-chop whisker or so, and with hair sedulously curled but symmetrically trimmed.—*Daily Telegraph.*

(Costers), the largest and best fruit placed at the top of a basket. (Tailors), a collar. Also applied to the fore part of a garment.

Top shuffling (gambling cheats), explained by quotation.

He will make up the hand he wants out of the discards, or else hold out the necessary cards until he gets enough, and it is his deal. Then he drops it on the top of the pack, and performs a very neat little piece of work known as *top-shuffling*, which consists in shuffling the lower half of the pack over the upper half without disturbing it. When this is over the hand he wants is still on top. The cut, of course, buries it, but by a very simple movement he gets the cards back in their original condition. This is called "shifting the cut," and can be done with one hand or two. Nothing then remains but to go ahead and deal. Dexterity in over-shuffling and shifting the cut are the two things that modern gamblers cultivate in all their leisure hours, and with these accomplishments, and coolness and nerve, little else is required.—*Star.*

Tops, short for top-boots, also upper garments.

Z

Tom is the one to patter flash,
And make the coveys laugh;
With whites and *tops* he cuts a dash,
And like a beak can chaff.
—*Pierce Egan: Book of Sports.*

Topsman (thieves), the executioner. *Vide* TOPPED.

Topsy - boozy (popular), very drunk.

Yes, that's it, you laughter-loving jokers and corkers! If you get "screwed," *topsy-boozy*, or "three sheets in the wind" in a dedicated road, the blue-coated warriors may nab you.—*Toby.*

Top-yob (thieves' back slang), a pot-boy.

Top your boom. *Vide* BOOM.

To rights (common), in the proper way, completely. *Vide* RIGHTS.

The comedy provides you with hilarity *to rights!*
With Lottie Venne and Penley in the wild Arabian Nights.
—*Fun.*

Torpids, the eight-oared races at Oxford rowed in the spring, in contradistinction to the summer eights. It is in these races that the freshmen are able to distinguish themselves, and qualify for their college boat in the next term.

Torrac (costermongers), back slang for a carrot.

Tortle (American), a Philadelphia expression meaning go or walk away, or "turtle off." In the "Charcoal Sketches," by J. C. Neal, one man advises another to put on his "skeets" (skates)

and *tortle.* Early English, *tortyll*, to twist or wriggle away.

Tortoise, Pump and (army), "the 38th Foot, on account of their great sobriety and equally remarkable slowness when once stationed at Malta" (*Chambers's Journal*).

Tosh (public and military schools), a foot-bath, any bath. Perhaps a corruption of "toe-wash;" but it is curious to note that in Turkish-Persian *tasi* is a copper basin used in the bath, from which "tosher" (which see) is probably derived.

A *tosh* pan, an important utensil for periodical ablutions on stated nights, is also provided.—*Pascoe: Life in our Public Schools.*

(Royal Military Academy), the *tosh*-pond is the bathing-pond.

Tosher (nautical), a man who steals copper sheathing from ships' bottoms, or from dockyard stores. Probably from *tasi*, a copper basin in Turkish-Persian. (Oxford), an unattached student. (Gypsy, obsolete), food, victuals. Hindu *tosha*, provisions.

Toshing (nautical). *Vide* TOSHER.

Tosh-soap (Charterhouse School), cheese. *Vide* TOSH.

Toss (Billingsgate), a measure of sprats.

Tot (popular), a small glass. (South African), a drink.

Tot, or **tots**, **old** (army), old bones, the kitchen refuse which is often bartered to some barrack sutler who supplies in exchange the crockery for the barrack men. One of the slang names of the 17th Lancers—"the Death or Glory Boys"—is the *Old Tots*, because they carry the device of a skull and crossbones. (School), *tots*, addition sums ; to *tot* up, to add up, abbreviation of "total."

Tote (popular), a hard drinker. From old English *totted*, drunken.

> As well we'd another old chum,
> By all of his mates called the *Tote*,
> So named on account of the rum
> He constantly put down his throat.
> —*He Hasn't Got Over it Yet*
> (*Francis & Day*).

A teetotaller, an abstainer from all intoxicating drinks.

> You'll always find the sober *Tote*
> With a few pounds at command,
> He can buy a house to live in,
> Or else a lot of land.
> His home is peace and happiness,
> His children and his wife
> They never know keen hunger,
> Or hear wild drunken strife.
> . . . . .
> I think I've shown, dear friends,
> Drink leads to sin, while Temperance
> To every comfort tends.
> So look upon these pictures :
> The Toper and the *Tote*,
> And see which has most happiness,
> And which the better coat.
> —*Broadside Ballad : The Toper and the Tote.*

Toted (American), led, or more commonly carried, to be made to act not of one's own free will.

I cannot think Mr. Ulysses S. Grant will degenerate into becoming a puppet by wires held in the hand by gentlemen from Illinois, or that he will degenerate into a kind of hand-organ to be *toted* around on the back of a gentleman from Illinois.—*Mr. Donnely's Speech in Congress on the Impeachment of President Johnson.*

Tote, to (American), to carry or bear. Peculiar formerly to the South. Bartlett says that it has been "absurdly enough derived from the Latin *tollit,*" and thinks it is of African origin. Anglo - Saxon *teohan, teon,* to lead, carry, draw. " *Tedh* his nett on lande "—" Drew his net on land." Also to take ; hence *tôtehan, "altrahere,"* and *tohte, "expedito."* Hence in provincial English *tath,* taketh. It is not impossible that the Dutch *tot,* to, or unto, may have influenced the formation of this word.

> Dey say fetch an' *tote* 'stead of bring and carry,
> An' dat dey call grammar !—by de Lawd Harry !
> —*Old Negro Song.*

I *toted* up a load, and went back and sat down on the bow of the skiff to rest.—*Mark Twain : Huckleberry Finn.*

T'other side of Jordan (American), a phrase expressive of nowhere, the Unknown, or "gone into de Ewigkeit." From a popular song of Methodist origin.

> " Oh, I looked to de north an' I looked to de souf,
> And I saw a mighty charret a comin',
> Wid forty grey hosses a-crackin' on de lead,
> To take us to de *odder side of Jordan.*
> Oh, take off yer coat and roll up yer sleeve,
> *Jordan* am a hard road to trabble ;
> Take off yer coat and roll up yer sleeve,
> *Jordan* am a hard road to trabbel, I believe."

T'other-sider (Australian popular, but growing obsolete), a convict. *Cf.* "Sydney-sider," "Van Demonian," &c. There never were any convicts transported to Victoria after its erection into a separate colony ; hence they can afford to speak contemptuously of convicts from the Sydney side, or Van Diemen's Land. The inhabitants of that island, to escape the odious old convict associations, have changed its name to Tasmania.

Tot rakers (popular), men who go about picking up odds and ends from refuse heaps. Also "*tot*-pickers." From *tot*, anything very small.

Tottie (popular), a girl, a fast girl. A term of endearment, from English *tot*, anything small.

Totting (popular), explained by quotation.

P'r'aps he's goin' a-*tottin'* (picking up bones).—*Greenwood : The Little Ragamuffins.*

Vide TOT RAKERS.

Tottle, tottlish (American), from "totter" (Bartlett). To walk unsteadily. Anglo-Saxon *tealt*, vacillating, unsteady ; *tealtrjan mid fótum*, tottering with the feet.

Totty-headed (popular), slow to understand. English provincial *tot*, a fool, *i.e.*, one with little brains ; Suffolk dialect, *totty*, little.

Touch (common), synonymous with cost or "damage ;" a penny ride in an omnibus is a penny *touch*.

At night went to the ball at the Angel, a guinea *touch.—Phillip : Diary.*

(Eton School), a present of money. Formerly a cant word for a slight essay (Swift).

Toucher (coaching), as near as a *toucher*, as near as possible without actually touching. The old jarveys, to show their skill, used to drive against things so closely as absolutely to touch, yet without injury. This they called a *toucher*, or "touch-and-go," which was thence applied to anything which was within an ace of ruin (Hotten).

Touch, to (thieves), to steal or to succeed in getting.

One day I took the rattler from Broad Street to Acton. I did not *touch* them, but worked my way to Shepherd's Bush. —*Horsley : Jottings from Jail.*

(Common), to borrow money.

He was down on his luck altogether, dead broke, his clobber seedy. He was altogether a woeful object when he ran against a wealthy friend whom he thought to *touch*. "No, my boy," said the friend, "I never give or lend money."—*Bird o' Freedom.*

Tough (American), a low ruffian.

The *tough*, his northern appellation changed to "hoodlum," continues to flourish in San Francisco.—*Daily Telegraph.*

Toughs, old (army), the 103rd Regiment. The nickname was gained by hard service in India. Some of the nicknames of other regiments are as follows: — " Royal Goats," or " Nanny Goats," the 23rd; the " Blood Suckers," the 63rd; " Mud Larks," the Royal Engineers. The " Blind Half-Hundredth," " Fighting Fiftieth," or " Dirty Half-Hundredth," is the 50th Regiment. The "Supple Twelfth," the 12th Lancers; the " Dumpies," the 20th Hussars; the "Cherry Pickers," the 11th Hussars; the "Ragged Brigade," the 13th Hussars (not as incorrectly stated under RAGGED BRIGADE); " Pontius Pilate's Bodyguard " (the oldest of British regiments), the 1st Foot; the " Rib-breakers," the 3rd Battalion Grenadier Guards; the "Slashers," the 28th Foot; the " Cheesemongers," the Regiment of Household Cavalry; the "Steel Backs," the 58th; the "Death or Glory Men," the 17th Lancers; the "Excellers," the 40th; the "Bloody Eleventh," the 11th of Foot; the " Die Hards," the 57th; the "Old Dirty Shirts," the 101st. The Military Train were the " Murdering Thieves;" the "Springers," the 62nd; the " Sweeps," Rifles, &c.

Toure, towre (old cant), see.

Bing out bien morts, and *toure* and *toure*, Bing out of the Romevile fine.
                    —*The English Rogue.*

Tout (turf), an agent on the lookout for any information as to any circumstances as to a horse's capabilities or condition, or for anything else, hotels, railways, theatres, &c.

The *tout* being haled before him, said that he had already "got three races " for his master that morning.—*Truth.*

Touting ken (old cant), a bar in a public-house. Probably one frequented by inn touts.

Touzle (popular), the whisker worn bushy, or mass of frizzled, ragged hair. From *tousle*, to tug at, to entangle, rumple.

With spreads of pink shoulders; slim twisters with *touzles* of tow-coloured 'air.
                    —*Punch.*

Tow (Shrewsbury School), a run in " hare and hounds."

After that last " all up," there is a *tow* or continuous run of from one to three miles. — *Everyday Life in our Public Schools.*

Towelling, to give a (common), to thrash. Provincial English *towl*, to beat with a stick. In Norfolk a man who has been cudgelled is said to have been " rubbed down with a blackthorn *towel.*"

Frankly shaking his cane, bid him hold his tongue, otherwise he would dust his cassock for him. " I have no pretensions to such a valet," said Tom; " but if you should do me that office, and over-heat yourself, I have here a good oaken *towel* at your service."—*Smollett: Humphrey Clinker.*

I got a *towelling*, but it did not do me much good.—*Mayhew: London Labour and the London Poor.*

Towels, lead (old cant), pistols, with which to wipe a man out of existence.

Tower-Hill vinegar (old), the block. Executions used very frequently to take place on *Tower-Hill.*

Town bull (old), a bawd, a very licentious man, popular among women.

Townie (army), a comrade who comes from the same town or part of the world. In French *pays*.

Town-lout (Rugby School), a pupil who resides in the town with his parents.

Tow-pows (popular), Grenadiers (Hotten).

Towzery gang (popular), swindlers who have sale-rooms for mock auctions of cheap and worthless goods. From *towze* or *touse*, to make a noise, a disturbance; *towser*, one that makes a bustle or stir. Hence "Towser," a name for a dog.

Toy (thieves), a watch; white *toy*, silver watch; red *toy*, gold watch.

He was very tricky (clever) at getting a poge or a *toy*, but he would not touch *toys* because we was afraid of being turned over (searched).—*Horsley : Jottings from Jail.*

Toy and tackle, watch with chain attached. *Toy*-getter, a watch stealer.

Toys (Winchester College), explained by quotation.

The clock striking seven, each junior retires to his *toys* or bureau for an hour and a half during what is known as "toy-time." — *Pascoe : Everyday Life in our Public Schools.*

Toy-time (Winchester College), evening preparation.

During what is known as *toy-time*, when the work of the next morning and the week's composition have to be prepared. —*Pascoe : Everyday Life in our Public Schools.*

Tracks, to make (common). *Vide* MAKE TRACKS.

You will be pleased *to make tracks*, and vanish out of these parts for ever.—*C. Kingsley : Two Years Ago.*

He said he was a banker, did our smart Teutonic Max,
And many a quid he'd given her, before he *made his tracks*.
'Twas only when the "thick 'uns" proved but Hanoverian Jacks
That she knew he was a "smasher."
—*Sporting Times.*

Track up the dancers, to (thieves), to go upstairs. *Dancers*, stairs, or flight of stairs.

Trade-mark (common), a scratch or wound in the face.

I know what the old woman is when she is drunk,
She pawns everything in the place ;
And if I correct her for what she has done,
She draws her *trade-mark* down my face.
—*C. Cornell : Father, Take a Run.*

(Servant-girls), a servant's cap.

Tradesman, a regular (popular), a term of encomium meaning one who thoroughly understands his business, whatever his profession (honest or the reverse) may be.

Trafficking (prison), the interchange of money, prohibited articles, food, between prison officers and prisoners, and between prisoners themselves. The practice in the former case is an offence at common law, and when prosecution follows may lead to imprisonment. Between prisoners it is a breach of discipline entailing dietary and other punishment.

Prisoners usually volunteer to serve as permanent "orderlies" for *trafficking* purposes. *Trafficking* means giving of food, exchange of books, or passing of letters or writing materials from one prisoner to another.—*Evening News.*

Tragedy Jack (theatrical), a term of derision for a heavy tragedian.

Train up, to (popular), to hurry.

Tra-la-la (popular), the wealthiest and most extravagant class of dissipated men. The "bucks of the very first water"—the music-hall ideals.

I will not sing of city swells,
　　Your La-di-dahs,
At such cheap toffs we've laughed enough
I sing of swells you know so well,
　　The *Tra-la-las!*
The style's the same,—but better stuff,
　　With glossy hat and spotless boots,
From top to toe, quite *comme il faut,*
You know them by their perfect suits
From far-famed Poole of Savile Row.
　　—*Music-Hall Ballad: Tra-lal-la.*

Trampolin (circus), a double spring - board. This seems to be a very old term, from *tram,* a small bench (generally used for setting a tub on), Herefordshire, and *poling,* a plank.

Trampoose (American), to walk or tramp. "*Trampoosing* about all over town," gadding here and there. From *tramp,* and an affix very common in America.

Tranklements, trollybobs (popular), entrails, intestines. Given by Wright as "trolly-bags."

Tranko (circus), the elongated barrel which a performer manages with his feet, and keeps up in the air while lying on his back. It is said to be from the Spanish *tranco,* a threshold, as the shape is almost like that of one. But the ordinary Spanish word for threshold is *umbral.* The trick is very ancient, and was originally performed by kicking a spear in the air.

Translated (popular), second-hand, as applied to shoes or boots repaired and sold by a cobbler.

Baeker had to limp in his socks to the New Cut, and purchase a pair of *translated* crab-shells to go home in.—*Sporting Times.*

(Tailors), is said of a coat which is cut down and turned; also a garment made to fit a smaller man.

Translator (popular), a cobbler, one who turns worn-out shoes into good ones, or "as good as new." It was an established word more than a century ago. Sewell, 1757, gives the Dutch *schoenlappen* as its equivalent; literally shoe-patcher.

It was not likely to occur to me that Sunday morning when I interviewed the kind-hearted old *translator* of old boots into new ones, in his kitchen in Leather Lane.—*J. Greenwood: The Woodchopper's Wedding.*

Translators are also second-hand boots.

He will part with anything rather than his boots, and to wear a pair of second-hand ones, or *translators*, as they are called, is felt as a bitter degradation by them all.—*Mayhew: London Labour and the London Poor.*

(Tailors), a tailor who cuts down and turns coats.

Trap (popular), up to *trap*, wide-awake, not to be deceived or caught easily. The metaphor is obvious.

> Not the least mite *up to trap.*
> —*Punch.*

To smell *trap*, explained by quotation.

They can discover the detective in his innocent-looking smock-frock or brick-layer jacket, while he is yet distant the length of a street. They know him by his step, or by his clumsy affectation of unofficial loutishness. They recognise the stiff-neck in the loose neckerchief. They smell *trap* and are superior to it.—*Seven Curses of London.*

"You do not understand *trap*," "vous n'y entendez pas finesse" (Boyer's Dictionary, 1748). It is worth observing that, in gypsy, *drab* or *trap* (which words were pronounced alike by the first gypsies who came from Germany to England) is used for medicine or poison, and the employment of the latter is regarded, even at the present, as the greatest Romany secret. A gypsy said, "If you know *drab*, you're up to everything; for there's nothing goes above that." (Common), that *trap* is down, the attempt is a failure.

Traps (thieves), a very old term for the police, detective force.

"But where are the lurchers?" "Who?" asked Wood. "The *traps*," responded a bystander. "The shoulder-clappers," added a lady.—*Ainsworth: Jack Sheppard.*

"What's become of the boy?" . . . "Why, the *traps* have got him, and that's all about it," said the Dodger sullenly.—*Dickens: Oliver Twist.*

T r a s h (gypsy), fear, to fear; *trásherdo*, afraid; *trásheno covva*, an awful or fearful thing; *trás-hipen*, terror; *trásherdo mŭllo*, scared to death.

Trash a trail, to, is an expression used in the West, meaning to conceal the direction one has taken by walking in a stream, or in fact taking water in any way. The fox, deer, and other animals understand this mode of escape as well as man (Bartlett's Dictionary).

Trat (popular), a pretty girl, a "tart." Probably an anagram of "tart."

Travel in the market (sport), how backed, what the odds are about a horse.

These are to be found in the well-doing and health of horses, in the way in which they have stood training, or in the manner in which they *travel in the market*, and a host of other things.—*Sporting Life.*

Traveller (tramps), a tramp.

There are many individuals in lodging-houses who are not regular patterers or professional vagrants, being rather, as they term themselves, *travellers.—Mayhew.*

(Thieves), a thief who goes from town to town.

Traveller, to tip the (common), to humbug. This refers to the wonderful tales, like those of "Baron Munchausen," sometimes told by travellers.

Aha! dost thou *tip me the traveller,* my boy?—*Smollett: Sir L. Greaves.*

Traverse the cart, to. *Vide* CART.

Tray (thieves), three months' imprisonment; obviously from the French, possibly *viâ* the lingo of the card-table. Also *tray* of moons.

The other gentleman remained, was discovered, and did a *tray* of moons.—*Sporting Times.*

Tray soddy mits (popular), threepence halfpenny, a corruption of *trois et demi,* used to express the amount of points in whist in Clerkenwell, Saffron Hill, and the districts where there are a mixture of nationalities.

Treacle (popular), to talk about *treacle,* to talk about love and love affairs. (Publicans), thick, bad port.

Treacle-moon (popular), the honeymoon.

Treaders (popular), shoes. Dutch thieves' slang, *treder;* from *treden,* to tread, step. Evidently from "tread."

Tread the boards, to (common), to appear on the scene in order to compete at anything.

Treat (popular), he's such a *treat, i.e.,* he is such a cunning person or animal, such a nuisance.

Treddle, a cant term for a prostitute (Wright); from *tread,* the copulation of fowls.

Tree-moon (tinker), three months, a "drag." *Vide* TRAY.

Trek, to (South African), to move away, depart. The expression "let's *trek,*" *i.e.,* let's go away, is used in England. A figure of speech. Properly to yoke oxen to a waggon.

The Boers of the Transvaal do not like it at all. They are selling their lands and *trekking* away into regions unpolluted by the presence of the miner.—*Pall Mall Gazette.*

Trials (Harrow School), examinations.

Triangles (popular), a corruption of *delirium tremens.*

Trick and tie (sport), to be *trick and tie,* or touch and go, is to be equal in a race, or other athletic performance.

Tricks (Texas), one's personal belongings; thus one has *tricks* instead of things in a house, and similarly *tricks* and not baggage on a journey.

Trick with a hole in it, a (American), an extraordinary device or performance. "When it comes to making a duck-stew, I can show you *a trick with a hole in it.*"

Trike (common), a tricycle; *triking,* cycling. Do you bike or *trike?* do you ride a bicycle or tricycle.

Trim a jacket, to (nautical), to rope-end the wearer.

Trimmer (cricketers), a ball de-livered in very good style. (Common), explained by quo-tation.

What is a *trimmer?*—"A man who runs with the hare and hunts with the hounds," who tries to face two sides, and sometimes several sides at the one time; one who says to-day what he tries to explain away to-morrow, and re-explains away again the day following—a jelly-fish man, who is a reformer, and at the same time a fossil. —*Toby.*

Trine, to (old cant), to hang.

Now toure the cove that cly'd your duds
    Upon the chats *to trine.*
            —*The English Rogue.*

From old English *to trine*, to put in the aspect of a *trine* (old English *trine*, triple), a triad, alluding to the three beams of the gallows, formerly termed the "triple tree," or "mare with three legs." In gypsy *trin* (three) *bongo drums* means the cross or the crooked road.

Trinkerman (nautical), the Thames tidal fisherman.

Trip (theatrical), a dance. *Pas de deux,* by harlequin and colum-bine, so called because they *trip* across the stage from one side to the other, and then make their exit. This dance usually commences each scene in what is called the harlequinade. (Thieves), a prostitute, concu-bine. Possibly in allusion to *tripping* about. The same idea occurs in old English *trapes,* a slattern; from *trape,* to walk about idly and sluttishly (Ger-man *trappen*). "Trot," an old woman, "troll," "trull," &c.

It was at one of these places I palled in with a *trip,* and stayed with her until I got smugged. — *Horsley : Jottings from Jail.*

I was fullied, and then got three stretch
    for the job,
And my *trip*—cuss the day as I seen
    her—
She sold off my home to some pals in her
    mob
For a couple of foont and ten deaner.
            — *The Referee.*

Tripes (popular), the belly.

Triple-tree (old cant), the gallows.

For whether I sink in the foaming flood,
    Or swing on the *triple-tree,*
Or die in my bed as a Christian should,
    Is all the same to me !
            —*Meister Karl's Sketch-Book.*

Tripper up (thieves), a thief.

Troc (London), the Trocadero Music Hall.

He murmured o'er a glass of hock,
    "It's barely nine o'clock—
Shall it be the Royal, Pav., or *Troc?*"
    And echo answered, "*Troc !*"
            —*Sporting Times.*

Trolly-wags (popular), trousers, breeches. A corruption of the word *trousers* by costermongers, who naturally have the *trolly* uppermost in their minds as being the means of their getting a livelihood, and a further face-tious distortion of *bags.* Com-pare the synonym "trucks." Or possibly from provincial "trolly-bags," intestines, tripe.

Tronk (South African). This is a Cape Dutch expression for gaol, just as in English a prison is called a "stone jug."

He informed me that he had just been in the *tronk,* and on my asking why, re-

plied, " Oh, for fighting and telling lies ! "
—*Lady Duff Gordon's Letters from the Cape.*

Tros - dab (costermongers' back slang), " I've had a regular *tros-dab*," *i.e.*, bad sort of day.

Trosseno (costers), back slang for one sort, a " bad one."

" He's a regular scab ! " cried another ; and a coster declared he was " a *trosseno*, and no mistake ! "—*Mayhew.*

Trotter (University), a tailor's man who goes round for orders. In French slang, " trottin " is a young girl employed by dress-makers to do errands.

Trotter boxes (popular), shoes.

Trotter cases (popular and thieves), shoes or boots.

" If the tottering Edifice were to be hanged privately, I presume they would not allow his sorrowing survivors to cling to his *trotter cases*," plaintively murmured Alexandry, the Blue-Eyed Blossom.—*Ally Sloper's Half-Holiday.*

Trot, to (auctions), to run up, *i.e.*, bid against. (Thieves), to steal in broad daylight. (Common), to *trot* out, to draw one out in order to bring into evidence his capability or foibles, the simile being a horse that is trotted up and down by a horsedealer in the presence of a purchaser.

Trout, Nor-loch (old Scottish cant), a leg of mutton. Other quaint terms for different kinds of food are, " German duck," a sheep's head stuffed with onions, a dish much affected by the German sugar-bakers in the East End of London ; a

" Bombay duck " is a species of dried fish in Western India. Shrimps are " Gravesend sweet-meats ; " a red herring is a " pheasant," a " Yarmouth capon," also " Norfolk capon," " Dunbar wethers," or " Gourock ham." Potatoes are " Irish apricots " or " Munster plums," &c. " Albany beef " in America is sturgeon ; " Cape Cod tur-key " is cod. Herrings are " Taunton turkeys " or " Digby chickens."

Truck (nautical), a hat. From the cap on the top of the mast. (American), odd bits and ends, rubbish, plunder of little value. From provincial English *truck*, rubbish.

No use to take *truck* and leave money. —*Mark Twain : Huckleberry Finn.*

It also means by extension bad food, and corresponds in this instance to the English " scran," broken victuals, food ; from *scrans*, refuse.

Trucks (popular), trousers. Syno-nymous with " trolly - wags," which see.

True inwardness (American). It has always been the fashion in Boston to affect a kind of transcendental metaphysical language, and " the *true inward-ness* " of anything is a term pro-bably derived by some Carlyleist from the German *innerlichkeit.* It is also now used in England.

Mr. Gerald Massey, the poet, who knows all the *true inwardness* of the how and the why, the when and the wherefore of Shakspeare's sonnets, announces a course of lectures on all sorts of occult matters.—*Entertainment Gazette.*

Truk, a prostitute of the lowest class, defined by Grose as "a soldier's or tinker's female companion," and in Hotten's Slang Dictionary as "a dirty, slatternly woman and prostitute, the word being a corruption of troll, or trollop." In reality, the derivation can be traced to old English *trug,* a prostitute ; "*trugging*-place," a whore-house.

Trump, a colloquialism signifying an excellent person, a fine fellow, from the card term (French *triomphe*). It verges on slang, but can hardly be classified as such.

He passes by Waithman's emporium for shawls,
And, merely just catching a glimpse of St. Paul's,
　　Turns down the Old Bailey,
　　Where in front of the jail, he
Pulls up at the door of the gin-shop, and gaily
Cries, "What must I fork out to-night, my *trump,*
For the whole first-floor of the Magpie and Stump?"
　　　　　—*Ingoldsby Legends.*

I stands a quart, like the *trump* as I are.—*Bird o' Freedom.*

Trumped (common), defeated by superior skill in a device or scheme.

Gambling supplies many, like "within an ace," "played out," *trumped,* and "euchred."—*Standard.*

Trunks(theatrical), short breeches worn over tights. Also bathing drawers.

Trunk, shove his (old cant), to go away, *trunk* being the body.

Trūppo (gypsy), the body, the trunk.

Trushull (gypsy), a cross. Supposed to be derived from *triçula,* the trident of Siva. *Vide* Pott's "Thesaurus."

Try a smile. *Vide* INVITATIONS TO DRINK.

Trying it on a dog (American), a metaphor, as of anything of a doubtful nature put to the test by first giving some to a dog.

"Bootle's Baby" will on the 7th of May be produced somewhere in the provinces. This is what the Americans call *trying it on a dog;* if the dog don't die, the baby will come up to London and be on view at the Circus later on.—*Sporting Times.*

Tub, very modern slang for a morning bath. The word has been adopted across the Channel.

When I got home, and had my *tub,* and looked at myself in the glass, I found my frontispiece much disfigured.—*Sporting Life.*

Formerly a bath was termed a bathing-tub.

Tubbing (University), boating, generally in a broad boat, called a tub.

If "up" at the University, we will probably pass our time between "grinding hard" and *tubbing* on the river.—*Morning Advertiser.*

So to the river he next day went, and made his first essay in a *tub.*—*C. Bede : Verdant Green.*

Also before a crew take to their racing craft they have

some preliminary practice in a wide pair-oared boat, called a tub pair. This practice is called *tubbing.* The same term is also applied to the coaching given to new oarsmen. (Prison), imprisonment. " Nantes from the Rents (Fuller's or Tullwood's Rents in Holborn), smugged to rites, pilled, expects a *tubbing ;* " inscription in a prison cell.

Tub-man, an appointment given to a barrister practising in the old Exchequer Court, which gave him a precedence in all " motions," or applications to the judge. This was a great advantage to its possessor, and was always given to one who had a good practice in that court.

Tubs (American cadet), a sobriquet for a very corpulent man, one who, so to speak, possesses a self-contained corporation.

Tub-thumper (common), a street-corner parson.

"But I know a lady friend, an awful nice girl, who's out of an engagement"—— But the *tub-thumper* had fled.—*Sporting Times.*

Dr. —— is a frothy *tub-thumper,* whose sermons (they are published in one of the London " religious" weeklies) are models of what pulpit eloquence should not be.— *Evening News.*

" Tub-preacher" is an old term for a ranting, dissenting preacher. Also " tub-drubber."

Business and poetry agree as ill together as faith and reason ; which two latter, as has been judiciously observ'd by the fam'd *tub-drubber* of Covent Garden, can never be brought to set their horses together.—*T. Brown's Works.*

Tub-thumping (common), street preaching.

Another, who waxed rather warm, was requested not to do any *tub-thumping.*— *Funny Folks.*

Tuck (schoolboys), food, especially sweet-stuff, pastry.

The slogger looks rather sodden, as if he didn't take much exercise and ate too much *tuck.*—*Hughes: Tom Brown's Schooldays.*

To *tuck* is a provincialism signifying to eat, hence *tuck ; tuck*-shop, a pastry cook-shop.

Come along down to Sally Harrowell's ; that's our school-house *tuck*-shop. She bakes such shining murphies.—*Hughes: Tom Brown's Schooldays.*

Tuck-'em-fair (old cant), place of execution. From *tuck-up,* to hang.

He was *tucked-up* so neat and pretty.— *Death of Socrates.*

Tuck in your twopenny, a recommendation by boys playing at leap-frog to the one who stoops to bend his head.

Tuck-man (mercantile), the partner who brings the money to a business is so called. From *tuck,* food.

Tuck on, to (popular), to *tuck on* a price is to charge exorbitantly without reference to the real value of an article.

Tuck out, tuck in (boys), explained by quotation.

The understood terms were a *tuck out,* which in Hale's Street is short and simple language for as much as can be eaten.— *Greenwood: In Strange Company.*

Tuft (University), explained by quotation.

The lad . . . followed with a kind of proud obsequiousness all the *tufts* of the university.—*Thackeray: Shabby-Genteel Story.*

As *tuft* and *tuft*-hunters have become household words, it is perhaps needless to tell any one that the gold tassel is the distinguishing mark of a nobleman.—*C. Bede: Verdant Green.*

Tuft-hunter (society), any one who seeks after and hangs on to the society of people of title. The derivation of the word is from the *tuft* or gold tassels the noblemen and fellow commoners used to wear at the University. The expression is now general in society.

He was at no time the least of a *tuft-hunter,* but rather had a marked natural indifference to tufts.—*Carlyle: Life of Sterling.*

At last a lugubrious crew
Rode pensively over the plain,
Composed of the *tuft-hunters,* who
No Jubilee honours could gain.
Levy-Lawson, he headed the train,
And as they moved gloomily by
The band played a sorrowful strain ;
The soldiers were ordered to cry
Boo-hoo !
The soldiers were ordered to cry !
—*Funny Folks.*

Tug (Winchester College), usual, ordinary, common, stale, as *tug*-clothes, every-day clothes. Also stale news. (Eton), a colleger or boy on the foundation. *Tug* was supposed to be short for *tug*-mutton, as the collegers were then allowed by the college statutes to have no meat but mutton.

The long-looked for St. Andrew's Day arrives, when the great match of collegers, or, as the small oppidan would term it, *tugs*, and oppidans is to be played. — *Pascoe: Everyday Life in our Public Schools.*

Tuggery (Eton), explained by quotation.

My interlocutor was a red-headed, freckled little boy of eleven, who had come from Aberdeen, "to try for *tuggery*," that is, to try and pass on to the foundation as a King's scholar. — *Brinsley Richard: Seven Years at Eton.*

Tulip (roughs), "Go it, my *tulip !*" A street phrase during the tulip mania in 1842, when one bulb was sold for £640.

Tum (American), stylish, "in proper form."

By the way, gold spoons and forks for dessert have come in again, and you get them everywhere. Indeed, no table seems to look quite *tum* for a big occasion without them.—*J. W. K., in Chicago Tribune.*

Tumasha (Anglo-Indian), an entertainment, a spectacle, a popular excitement. Arabic *tamāshī.*

Tumbies (University), ablutions.

Our hero soon concluded his *tumbies* and his dressing.—*C. Bede : Verdant Green.*

Tumbler (printers), a synonym for a printing machine, the cylinder of which has a peculiar rocking motion. (Thieves), cart ; to nap the flog at the *tumbler,* formerly to be whipped at the cart's tail. (Turf), a term applied to a worthless horse not steady on its legs.

Its representatives likewise cut a better figure than Tom Fergusson's three *tumblers.—Sporting Times.*

Tumble, to (American), agree to anything, assent. A variation of "fall in," to concur. The French have *tomber d'accord.*

Now as for this speculation which you propose. It may be a very fine thing, but I don't *tumble to* it.—*American Newspaper.*

Also to understand. In this sense *to tumble* is very general in England among turfites, costermongers, roughs and thieves.

" Eh, Johnson, ever see a nicer run o' sleighing ? "
" Yes, Mr. Green."
" When and where ? "
" In the West Indies in 1857."
Three weeks later Mr. Green meets Mr. Johnson and exclaims :
"Ah ! I *tumble!* Of course, it's winter ten months in the year down there. Ha ! ha ! Good joke ! "—*Detroit Free Press.*

" Well, any woman that's dyin' has to be braced up, an' if she's faintin' has to be brought to. Medicine is the thing. Patent medicine *of course.* S'pose you're doin' *Frou-Frou* — last act. Bottle of 'Warner's Certain Cure ' — big label — on the mantelpiece. Husband in tears rushes to bottle and pours out cupful : ' Take this, my darling, my wayward child, it will keep you with us a moment longer, if it does not pull you through.' One line, twenty dollars a night—we divide—*tumble ?* '
" I am not a *tumbler,*" she said, with rising indignation.—*Green-Room Jokes.*

Although I did not *tumble* to the real essence of the business for some minutes, yet I got in at the finish.—*Sporting Times.*

" To *tumble* to barrikin," to understand language.

" I can't *tumble to that barrikin,*" said a young fellow, "it's a jaw-breaker."—*Mayhew: London Labour and the London Poor.*

" I *tumble* to your barrikin," I understand you, I twig. To *tumble* to the dodge, to perceive the trick.

Jack always believed that he had been robbed by one of his former " pals," who, in the language of the profession, had

" *tumbled* to the dodge."—*George R. Sims: The Doll's Secret.*

To *tumble* to it is to allow oneself to be taken in, to believe a falsehood, implying a certain degree of eagerness. (Provincial), to *tumble* to the racket, to get accustomed to a thing.

Tumble to pieces, to, to be safely delivered, as in childbirth.

Tump, to (American), a Maine word meaning to pull or draw. Bartlett thinks it may be Indian. Till this is established, it may possibly be regarded as related to the Anglo - Saxon *teón,* to draw. Also a slang word, to poke, push into ; so used in a song in an obscene sense. From *tamp,* to fill up a hole in a rock for the purpose of blasting ; to plug.

Tum-tum (Anglo-Indian), a dog-cart.

Tund (schoolboys), *tunding* at Winchester School is thrashing, and *Punch* puts into the mouth of a Wykhamist the confession—

I like to be *tunded* twice a day,
And swished three times a week.

Tunding (Winchester), explained by quotation.

It was the prefect of hall who ordered the infliction of a public *tunding.* . . . The following simple and truthful statement of what a public *tunding* was may enable those who take an interest in the matter to form some reasonable opinion whether the infliction of such punishment were a good or a bad thing. . . . Some dozen or so of boys, who had the best capacities for the performance, were appointed by him for the purpose, and the whole assembly stood around the dais, while the hymn *Te de profundis* was sung. When all were thus assembled, and before the singers commenced, the culprit who had been sentenced to a *tunding* stepped out, pulled off his gown, and received from the hands of one deputed by the "prefect of hall," and armed with a tough, pliant, ground-ash stick, a severe beating.—*T. A. Trollope: What I Remember.*

I never heard of any case in Eton like the *tunding* which, some years ago, brought our mother-school into disagreeable notice.—*Pascoe: Everyday Life in our Public Schools.*

From *tund*, to beat, same as "to tan;" "tan," a switch; "tancel," to beat.

Tunker (popular), a street preacher.

Tunny or **turnee** (Anglo-Indian), an English supercargo. Sea-Hindu, and probably a corruption of attorney (Roebuck, cited in the Anglo-Indian Glossary).

Tup, properly a ram, occurs in the slang phrase a "stray *tup* on the loose," *i.e.*, a man looking out for a girl.

Tuppennies (London), women who for twopence will take articles to a pawnbroker's shop, deposit them, obtain the money and ticket, and take them to the owner.

In those parts of London where pawn-shops and poverty abound there is a class of women who go by the name of *twopennies*, and who make it their business to be intermediaries between the lenders and the borrowers of money on articles of property.—*Tit-Bits.*

Turkey merchant (tramps, &c.), a stealer of fowls.

"We'll make a *Turkey merchant* of you yet," said an old gypsy, "never fear that."—*Beaconsfield: Venetia.*

Also a dealer in plundered or contraband silks.

Turkey, to talk (American), *to talk turkey* is to converse on profitable business, to "talk iron" signifies the contrary. "Now you begin *to talk turkey*," said a man in Philadelphia to one who at last told him how much he was to have out of a certain transaction. It is derived from a well-known story. A white man and an Indian went hunting, with the understanding that the game was to be divided piece by piece. The result of the sport was two wild turkeys and three crows. The white man, who took it on himself to count out, began by allotting a crow to the Indian, then a turkey to himself, then another crow to the Indian, appropriating, of course, the second turkey. To which the native demurred, saying: "You *talk all turkey* for you, and only talk crow for Injun" (C. G. Leland).

Turn (theatrical), length of performance of an actor or singer.

'Twas plain that ere her *turn* had ceased, Her talent had, on him at least, Created a most palpable impression.
　　　　　　—*Sporting Times.*

(Stock Exchange), an American term, very common in Wall Street, signifying a method of eluding the risks pertaining to an infringement of the usury laws — for example, when a broker "carries stock" (which see) for a client, in order to pay for it he often has to seek the aid of bankers or private money-lenders, hypothecating the stocks in return for an advance. When money is tight, the bank, in addition to the legal interest which it is empowered to charge, levies also an additional commission. This, in the slang parlance of the Stock Exchange, is called a *turn*. Also the profit on a bargain.

Turned (prison), converted, by abbreviation from *turned* square, the contrary of being crooked, or on the crook. A conversation between two thieves was overheard in Clerkenwell Prison. "That chaplain!" "What of him?" "He's a rum 'un; he come into my cell, and said, ' Look here, you talk straight to me, and I'll talk straight to you.' Ah! and he do talk straight, don't he? I think he's one of us—*turned*, you know."

Turned up (thieves), arrested.

Turning cart-wheels (popular), a feat performed by circus clowns and street boys of rolling over and over in such a manner that only the palms of the hands and the soles of the feet touch the ground. In French, "faire la roue."

The urchin who watches the passing 'bus in order to mount it while the conductor is collecting fares; who gets a gratuitous ride behind growlers and drays; who sells matches, and opens cab doors,

and carries luggage, and directs strangers, and *turns cart-wheels*—precocious bratlings of this sort are well known to the true Londoner, who marvels at their extraordinary sharpness and unquenchable vitality.—*Daily Telegraph.*

Turnips (common), to get *turnips*, to be taken in, to be jilted. To "turn it up."

> One day I got a letter,
>   It came from Betsy Gay;
> She said she'd given me *turnips*;
>   With another she'd run away.
>   —*London: The Prize Songster.*

Turn one's coat, to, explained by quotation. This is an almost recognised phrase. French "retourner sa veste." A man who changes his political opinions is termed a "turncoat."

Thinking men of both parties who have hitherto strenuously opposed the introduction of politics into municipal elections, are beginning, as it has become the silly fashion to designate a change of opinion, to *turn their coats.—St. Helen's Lantern.*

Turn one over, to (thieves), to search on the person.

"What catch would it be if you was to *turn me over?*" So I took him into a pub which had a back way out, and called for a pint of stout, and told the reeler to wait a minute.—*Horsley: Jottings from Jail.*

Turn-out (society), a very favourite word in London society, meaning *entourage*, get up. "A very smart *turn-out*" is often applied to a carriage which is well and smartly got up, with good horses, harness, and everything well done. It is also applied to people who dress well and look smart. "Mrs. —— is always so well *turned out.*"

(Popular), the name given by working girls to the toilette hired by them to go to pleasure gardens.

"And what should you say it would cost a girl on an average who hired a full *turn-out* on Monday and Saturday evenings?"

"If she was a regular customer, it wouldn't cost her more than two shillings, ostrich and all."—*J. Greenwood: Tag, Rag & Co.*

Other meaning explained by quotation.

The 'Delphi was better than it is. I've taken 3s. at the first *turn-out* (the leaving the theatre for a short time after the first piece).—*Mayhew.*

Turn out slap, to (tailors), to execute work expeditiously.

Turnover (trade), an apprentice transferred from one master to another is called a *turnover.*

Turnpike sailor (popular), a vagabond who shams the shipwrecked sailor.

I became a *turnpike sailor*, as it is called, and went out as one of the Shallow Brigade, wearing a guernsey shirt and drawers, or tattered trousers.—*Mayhew: London Labour and the London Poor.*

Turn the game up, to (common), to give up one's occupation or pursuits, generally dishonest ones.

Marston had long ago announced his intention to *turn the game up*; Brook had determined to get out of the country for a bit in case of accidents.—*G. Sims: Rogues and Vagabonds.*

Turn turtle, to (nautical), to capsize.

Turn-up (common), a prize-fight. Also a street fight.

I'd describe now to you as "prime a set-to," and "regular *turn-up*," as ever you knew; not inferior in "bottom" to aught you have read of.—*Ingoldsby Legends.*

A sudden piece of luck. (Sport), bookmakers are said to have a *turn-up* when an unbacked horse wins.

"Ah, well," said young Bob, "I suppose we shall still be allowed to have our private *turn-ups*, and I can tell you it's pretty warm work sometimes."—*Punch.*

Turn up Jack (American), a phrase borrowed from cardplaying.

Mad dogs, mad cows, and mad men are reported as *turning up Jack* in almost every direction.—*Milford (Massachusetts) Journal.*

Turtle-doves (thieves), rhyming slang for gloves.

Tusheroon (tinker, also canting), a crown. Also a "bull," a "cart-wheel."

Tut-work (workmen), piece-work.

Tweak (old), difficulty, perplexity. "He was in a sad *tweak*." Also a prostitute.

Thence to Bantree, as I came there
From the bushes near the lane there,
Rushed a *tweak* in gesture flaunting,
With a leering eye and wanton.
    —*Drunken Barnaby's Journey.*

Tweedle (thieves), a spurious ring, used to swindle jewellers and pawnbrokers.

Twelve apostles, the last twelve men in the mathematical tripos at Cambridge.

Twelve godfathers, a jury who have to decide whether a prisoner has been guilty of manslaughter, justifiable homicide, or murder, *i.e.*, to give a name to crime.

Twelver (thieves), a shilling.

Twicer (printers), a man that professes to work both at case and press or machine, is generally termed a *twicer*. Country hands coming to town are often looked on as such, for in their native places, owing to a limited number of hands and amount of work, they are expected to turn their hands to either. The Cockney printer as a rule follows but one branch.

Twig, in prime (popular), in first-rate condition, in high spirits. *Twig* is provincial for brisk, active.

Twig, to (popular), a Lincolnshire term, to understand, but commonly used in slang with the further meaning of perceive, see, notice, observe. From the Irish *tuigim*, I understand, discern. Whitley Stokes compares Irish *tuigim*, old Irish *tuccu*, with old Latin *tongĕre*, Gothic *thagkjan*, Icelandic *thekkja*, English *think* (Irish Glossaries).

"They're a *twiggin'* of you, sir," whispered Mr. Weller.—*Dickens: Pickwick Papers*.

A landsman said, "I *twig* the chap—he's been upon the mill."—*Ingoldsby Legends*.

I see you *twig*.—*Punch*.

The giant kept dropping in, usually followed by a crowd of ragamuffins, whilst the gamin shouted in French the equivalent of "*Twig* his legs, Bill?" for he was dreadfully in-kneed.—*Moonshine*.

Henceforth we'll speak with common throat,
For common party ends combine.
Here, put this primrose in your coat ;
That orchid I will place in mine.
Henceforth in concert we will jig,
To Solly's piping—eh, my boy ?
We can't afford to tiff, you *twig*,
If we'd the Gladstonites annoy !
—*Funny Folks*.

Also possibly from the Anglo-Saxon *tvig-sprœc*, geminata loqula, ambiguitas (Ettmüller, Lex. Ang. Sax.), an ambiguous, double-meaning speech. Hence *tweógan*, to doubt. "Ne mägic thäs nâ tveogan," I cannot doubt this, *i.e.*, I *twig*. *Vide* HOP THE TWIG.

Twilight (schools), toilet.

It was no use doing the downy again, so it was just as well to make one's *twilight* and go to chapel.—*C. Bede: Verdant Green*.

Twine, to (prison), explained by following extract from *Temple Bar*:—"Suppose you start in the morning with a good sovereign and a snyde half-sovereign in your pocket. You go into some place or other and ask for change of the sovereign; or you order some beer, and give the sovereign in payment. It is likely you will get half-a-sovereign and silver back in change. Then is the time to *twine*. You change your mind after you have rung your snyde half-quid with the good one, and, throwing down the snyde half, say you prefer silver. The landlord or landlady, or whoever it is, will pick up the snyde half-quid, thinking, of course, it is the same one they have given you."

From to *twine*, to twist or complicate.

Twinkler (thieves), a light. The burglar is said to hold three things in abhorrence when found in a house he intends to rob—a *twinkler*, a tinkler, and a tattler, *alias* a light, a bell on the shutter, and a barking dog.

Twins (American), a now almost obsolete New England term, meaning "dinner and tea at one meal. The custom of having *twins* in the short days of winter was formerly very common" (Bartlett). In England such a meal is called by commercial travellers "Box Harry" (Hotten), a term used in Lincolnshire to mean economy of any kind after extravagance. Probably from the idea of beating or robbing "old Harry," or the devil, who dances in an empty pocket.

Twirlers (thieves), sharpers with a round-about at fairs.

Twirls (burglars), skeleton keys.

He was very lucky at making *twirls*, and used to supply them all with tools.— *Horsley: Jottings from Jail.*

Twist (common), a good appetite, alluding probably to the *twisting* or gnawing sensation in a hungry man's stomach—to the pangs of hunger, which is exactly rendered by the French slang phrase "avoir une crampe au pylore." It is curious to note also the term "tortiller," to eat, literally to twist, coil. Formerly "tordre." "Il ne fait que tordre et avaler," said of a glutton. Oliver Twist was apparently so called by Dickens on account of his "hero's" propensity to ask for "more."

"An egg," cried Shakebacon, who has a *twist.* "Bosh!"

"Well," replied Gubb, "I once hunted all day after breakfasting on two-thirds of one, and never felt a pang till night time." Shaky looked incredulous. — *Bird o' Freedom.*

(Low), brandy and gin mixed.

Twister (popular), a falsehood, imaginary story; "he can spin a *twister*," he is clever at telling a falsehood.

Twistical (American), having a twist, tortuous; hence perverse, unfair, dishonest. In Northamptonshire *twister* means cross, perverse.

Twist on the shorts (Stock Exchange), said when the market has been puffed up by irregular and artificial means, and the *shorts* (which see) have been compelled to settle at a ruinous loss, in consequence of being heavily undersold.

Twist, to (thieves), to hang.

Twitch a twelve, to (American University), to get the highest number of marks.

Two d. (popular), twopence. A costermonger will say, "I'll take *two d.* for it."

Two-eighteener (American), a man or woman of the fastest kind, the allusion being to the highest record in trotting matches, about two minutes eighteen seconds being the fastest time for a mile.

Two-er (popular), a florin. Also a hansom cab.

Two - eyed steak (familiar), a dried herring or bloater.

A few weeks ago said my groom to my housemaid, " Wouldn't you like what I am going to have for breakfast?" "What is it?" " A *two-eyed steak*," which turned out to be a Yarmouth bloater. — *The Reader.*

Twofer (common), a term applied to a loose woman.

Two fours (army), the 44th Regiment of Foot.

Two-nick (printers), a vulgar allusion to infants of the female sex.

Twopenny (popular), the tongue. " *Twopenny* red rag."

Why, you're going into Newgate Street, the Lord Mayor bawls, But John said "Tuck your *twopenny* in— I'm going around St. Paul's."
    —*A Ballad: The Lord Mayor's Coachman.*

Twopenny damn, probably analogous to "not worth a curse," "a tinker's curse." The Duke of Wellington is alleged to have said that he did not care a *twopenny damn* what became of the ashes of Napoleon Buonaparte; and a correspondent of *Notes and Queries*, Series iii., 326, anxious to redeem the Iron Duke's

memory from the charge of profanity, thinks that it was a cant reminiscence of his Indian service—a dam being a coin and weight which had become depreciated in value to about twopence ; hence a *twopenny dam* would naturally pass into ordinary speech. This, however, is very problematical.

We don't—we quote, mind you, our contemporary—we don't care a *twopenny damn* for the argument about Probate.— *Star.*

Twopenny hop (thieves), a cheap dance.

The girl is invited to "raffles," and treated to *twopenny hops* and half-pints of beer.—*Mayhew: London Labour and the London Poor.*

Twopenny rope (popular), explained by quotation.

" And pray, Sam, what is the *twopenny rope?*" inquired Mr. Pickwick.
" The *twopenny rope*, sir," replied Mr. Weller, " is just a cheap lodgin'-house where the beds is twopence a night!"
"What do they call a bed a rope for?" said Mr. Pickwick.
" Well, the adwantage o' the plan's obvious. At six o'clock every mornin', they lets go the ropes at one end, and down falls all the lodgers. Consequence is that, being thoroughly waked, they get up very quickly, and walk away."—*Dickens: Pickwick Papers.*

The French have "coucher à la corde," to sleep in such lodging-houses.

Two - pipe scatter - gun (Canadian), a double-bore rifle.

"Oh, durn your rifles!" said an old settler to me. " Give me a *two-pipe scatter-gun* and a spike-tailed smell-damp and I'm fixed." And this gentleman's neatly expressed opinion seems to be pretty generally received. — *Phillipps - Wolley : Trottings of a Tenderfoot.*

Two pun' ten (trade), an expression used by assistants to one another in shops when a suspected customer enters. The phrase refers to "two eyes upon ten fingers," shortened as above.

Two sevens (army), the 77th Regiment. Also "Pot-hooks."

Two-thirty. *Vide* FULL DRIVE.

Two to one shop, the pawnbroker's ; in allusion, says Grose, to the three blue balls, the sign of that trade ; or, perhaps, from its being *two to one* that the goods pledged there are ever redeemed. The balls are not now of necessity blue, as they appear to have been in Grose's time. The slang of the present day for this convenient banker of the poor, is "my uncle" (in France it is "my aunt," *ma tante*), and the act of pledging is to "spout" or to "pop."

Two twos (army), the 22nd Regiment of Foot, formerly known as the "Red Knights," from being once served out with complete suits of scarlet.

Tyburn (old), *Tyburn* blossom, a young thief. To preach at *Tyburn* cross, to be hung, alluding to the penitential speeches made on such occasions.

That soldiours sterne, or prech at *Tiborn crosse.—Steele Glas.*

Also to fetch a *Tyburn* stretch. *Tyburn* show, hanging, hanged.

If I'm not lagged to Virgin-nee,
I may a *Tyburn* show be.
 —*The Song of the Young Prig.*

A *Tyburn* tippet, a halter.

Tyconna, tyecana (Anglo-Indian), an underground room or cellar, in which people can take refuge during the hottest part of the day. Persian *tah-khāna,* nether house.

Tyke, a dog. This is old English, from Icelandic *tik,* a bitch, but only used now by slang-talking classes. Shakspeare uses the word (*Henry V.*).

There sat auld Nick, in shape o' beast ;
A towsie *tyke,* black, grim, and large,
To give them music was his charge.
 —*Burns: Tam o' Shanter.*

When I got there I found it so hot, because there had been so many *tykes* poisoned, that there was a reeler at almost every double, and bills posted up about it.—*Horsley : Jottings from Jail.*

Also a countryman, clodhopper.

Tyker, a man who takes charge of dogs.

"Put some in your pocket, you'll want 'em on the course," observes my guide. And I sigh for the capacious pockets of the gamekeeper or the "kick" of the *tyker,* yet manage to stow a dozen or so about my person.—*Bird o' Freedom.*

Tyler, Adam. *Vide* ADAM TILER, to which may be added : This probably has no reference to a man's name, *adam* being short for *adamed,* married, united ; hence in confederacy. A "mason and tyler" were swindlers in close association, the first being also called "masoner" (which see), a Yorkshire term for a bricklayer.

Type - lifter (printers), a term generally applied to fast composers of type.

Type-slinger (printers), an expeditious but slovenly compositor, who composes rapidly regardless of errors and blunders.

Typhoon (maritime), a storm. It is not generally known that the exact Hindu word *tufan,* a storm, is used in the same sense by English gypsies.

T y p o (printers), a term of familiarity applied by one typographer to another, the abbreviation being apparent. Also French.

Tzing tzing (London), excellent, elegant, dashing, synonymous with "slap up," "chic," but seldom heard now.

U

UGLIES (theatrical), *delirium tremens.*

Uhlan (tailors), a tramp.

Ullages, a nautical term, meaning the remainder in a cask, which has leaked ; hence the wine of all sorts left in the bottom of glasses at a public dinner. Hotten suggests Latin *ullus,* any, but it is more probably from the French *coulage.*

Ultramarine (London), "blue," that is, more or less indecent.

Woe to the cracker of a "risky" wheeze ; pity the dancer of an *ultramarine* step, for the order of the boot is kept ready behind the bar for these offenders.—*Sporting Times.*

Ultray (Punch show), very ; *ultray* cativa, very bad.

"How are you getting on?" I might say to another Punch-man. "*Ultray* cativa," he'd say.—*Mayhew.*

Unbleached American (American), a negro, a man of colour.

An expression which sprang up during the war. "Am I not a man and a brother ? " was converted about the same time into "Am I not a man and a bother ? "

Uncertainties (printers), a vulgarism applied to babies of the female sex.

Uncle (common), pawnbroker.

"Dine in your frock, my good friend, and welcome, if your dress-coat is in the country." "It is at present at an *uncle's.*" —*Thackeray : The Newcomes.*

We find him making constant reference to an *uncle,* in respect of whom he would seem to have entertained great expectations, as he was in the habit of seeking to propitiate his favour by presents of plate, jewels, books, watches, and other valuable articles.—*Dickens : Martin Chuzzlewit.*

Woe ! woe ! to that jock,
My watch is in soak,
More aid from my *uncle*
I vainly invoke.
I'm a wave on the sea of misfortune,
And—what's frequent with breakers—
I'm broke !
　　　—*Turf, Field, and Farm.*

It has been suggested that *uncle* is from *uncus*, a hook (French *au clou*, in pawn), but it is evidently derived from a jocular allusion to a fond uncle or a mysterious rich uncle —" oncle d'Amérique "—as in Dickens's quotation. Uncles have always been considered as the natural prey of spendthrift nephews. The French term the pawnbroker " ma tante " or " ma tante Dumont " (du mont-de-piété). Also " mon oncle Du Prêt." " Oncle " is a very old term for a usurer, and also means a jailer, prisoners considering themselves as being in pawn.

Uncork the swag (American), deliver ! literally, unlock the portmanteau.

Once more, you bloke, will you *uncork that swag ?—Detroit Free Press.*

Unction, blue (popular), mercurial ointment. Also " blue butter."

Undergraduates (turf), horses that are being trained for steeple-chasing.

It seems to me that the *undergraduates* comprise far better material than what is generally drafted from the ranks of the flat racers . . . the best of the lot are in the hands of trainers who lay themselves out for the preparation of jumpers.— *Referee.*

Undergrounder (cricket). An *undergrounder*, a " daisy cutter," a " daisy trimmer," or " sneak," is a ball bowled all along the ground, without a proper pitch.

Understandings (common), shoes, feet, in opposition to *tops*, upper garments or tops of boots, and bottom clothing.

The massive Kadoudja found a fitting exponent in Miss ——, whose short Circassian skirt admitted of the display of a pair of shapely *understandings.—Modern Society.*

Understudy (theatrical), an actor or actress engaged to understudy, and to act, if necessary, the parts of principal performers—so that, in the event of accident, or indisposition, the run of a piece may not be suspended.

Her voice was no fortune, but it sufficed for the chorus in comic opera, and she was offered an *understudy* of a few lines in the preceding farce.—*Society Times.*

Unguentum aureum, explained by quotation.

To call a bribe *unguentum aurem* shows that slang-makers have not been altogether unlettered.—*Globe.*

Unicorn (thieves), two men and one woman, or two women and one man associated to steal. From *unicorn,* two horses abreast with a leader.

Universal staircase (thieves), the treadmill.

Well, the beaks got up to the dodge, and all the Spanish lurksmen in their turns got to work the *universal staircase.* — *Mayhew: London Labour and the London Poor.*

Unlimber (American), deliver ! out with the money.

No monkeying ! *unlimber !* produce the scads.—*Detroit Free Press.*

Unload, to (Stock Exchange), to sell. (American), *unload* your boodle, empty your pockets, deliver up the property.

Cheese your patter! Don't you see I've got the drop? *Unload* your boodle.—*Detroit Free Press.*

Unmentionables, a silly euphemism for trousers. Also "unutterables, unwhisperables, ineffables, inexpressibles."

Unregenerate chicken-lifter (American), a petty thief beyond all hope of reform. Mr. Stevens applies this beautiful term to an Austrian gypsy.

Unrigged (thieves and popular), naked; *rigged out,* dressed.

Unsalted (American), fresh, green, "young," or inexperienced.

He was an *unsalted* young man at the oyster festival given the other night by the Dorcas Aid Society of Christ Church, and he was seated in front of half-a-dozen fried.—*Washington Critic.*

Unsweetened (popular), gin.

Those who are partial to the *unsweetened* or "Old Tom."—*Bird o' Freedom.*

Up and down place (tailors), a situation where a man is required to cut and fill up time in sewing. *Up and down* is old for "in every respect."

He was euen Socrates *up and downe* in this pointe and behalfe, that no man euer sawe þym either laughe or weepe.—*Udal: Erasmus's Apophthegms.*

Up a tree, treed (American), in difficulty, cornered, unable to do anything.

A Something, apparently intermediate between man and monkey, now ornaments Bowery museum. This Something is believed to be a primeval m—gw—mp. The modern m—gw—mp, it will be remembered, has long ears, and he is arboreal in his habits. That is, he's always *up a tree.*—*New York Sun.*

Also much used in England.

How he lived I can't conjecture; he was
  always *up a tree,*
Though 'tis fair to state he often borrowed
  half-a-crown of me.
                    —*Funny Folks.*

Uphill player (cricketers), a player who plays a good losing game under disadvantage, one who never says "die."

Up in his hat (Irish), drunk, corresponding to English slang "elevated."

Upon my Sam (common), upon my soul. A piece of slang at one time very common in the mouths of women.

Upper Benjamin (popular), a topcoat.

A greatcoat, a sort of *upper Benjamin,* hanging on loosely and unbuttoned.—*Sporting Times.*

Originally a cloak or upper garment was a "Joseph." The connection is obvious.

Upper crust (common), the higher society. Originally American. *La haute.*

Since then our nearest synonym to *chic* has been "good form," a later outgrowth of British *upper-crust* slang.—*Daily Telegraph.*

(Pugilistic), the skin.

Sam's nob had been in pepper alley, and his *upper crust* was rather changed.—*Pierce Egan: Book of Sports.*

Upper Roger (Anglo-Indian), young king. "This happy example of Hobson-Jobson dialect occurs in a letter dated 1755, from Captain Jackson, at Syrian in Burma. It is a corruption of the Sanskrit *yuvah-rajah*, 'young king,' the Cæsar or heir-apparent" (Anglo-Indian Glossary). In a similar way Surajah Dowlah was commonly called by the soldiers Sir Roger Dowler.

Upper shell (old cant), a coat. "Under shell," a waistcoat.

Upper storey (popular), the head ; rats in the *upper storey*, crazy. Also "upper works."

Upright man (old cant), the head of a gang of mendicants.

Upset his apple-cart (American), generally heard in this form— "Look out, or you'll upset your apple-cart and spill the peaches," *i.e.*, "Take care, or you'll come to grief."

Up stakes (American), "*up stakes* and off," meaning the same as "to cut stick," *i.e.*, to depart in a hurry.

Jemmy Jed went into a shed,
And made a ted of straw his bed.
An owl came out and flew about,
And Jemmy Jed *up stakes* and fled.
Wasn't Jemmy Jed a staring fool,
Born in the woods to be scared by an owl?
　　　　　—Mother Goose.

The reference appears to be a pulling up of tent-pegs or stakes before decamping.

Up the spout (common), in pawn. Hence imprisoned.

With our energetic hero he at once commenced to play,
　And then left him on the pavement, in the rain ;
And his notes on the inquiry were not statements *à la mode*,
　But a message worded, "Vine Street *up the spout*),

There is barrack room in plenty to be found in this abode,
　Only send along some oof to bail me out ! "
　　　　　—Sporting Times.

Up to Dick (popular), a phrase which has become very popular of late years, having very extensive application to many circumstances. A man who is clever is *up to Dick*, as is one who is gifted with presence of mind. One who is well off, or rich, or generous, or wise in managing matters ; also one who is quick and ready to please is quite the same. It also means to be well, satisfied, or jolly. There is a popular comic song in which all of these applications are made to the phrase. It is very evidently derived from the gypsy *dick* or *dikk*, which is also common in ordinary slang, meaning to see, to perceive. "He is dressed *up to Dick*," *i.e.*, so that it is worth while to see him, is an old popular phrase borrowed from the Romany.

When, lo ! a dear relation died,
　Who left me lots of tin.
I often think with gratitude
　About the dear old flick,
Who left me cash to cut a dash,
　And set me *up to Dick*.
　　Up to Dick, boys, *up to Dick*,
　　At trifles never stick.
Be like me, a jolly brick,
That's the style, boys, *up to Dick*.
　　　—Catnach Press Ballad.

Also in good health.

Up to dictionary (popular), learned.

Up to his blue china, living (common), living up to or beyond his income. The phrase originated at a time when blue china was a rarity.

He was the possessor of the largest fortune in the empire, and is now scrupulously living up to his blue china.—*Daily Telegraph.*

Up to sample (common), equal to anticipation, of sufficiently good quality.

This combat is *up to sample.* —*Punch.*

Up to snuff. *Vide* SNUFF. *Up to snuff* appears to be literally "up to scent," and a metaphor like "smell a rat," "up to trap," &c.

Up to the door (popular), to the last degree, as fine as possible. Probably a variation of "up to the knocker."

Yes, and we goes out respectable, I can tell you. None of your half-and-half turn-outs. I'm togged *up to the door,* a pair of respectable "round my owsers," a two quid "I'm afloat," a silk "wipe" tied round my "top-deck," and a "bruiser's cady" on the top of the nob.—*T. Browne: Coster Joe ; or, the Happy Trio.*

Up to the knocker. *Vide* KNOCKER. This term usually occurs in the phrase "dressed up to the knocker," *i.e.,* very elegantly dressed, which probably arose from the practice of tying a glove to the knocker of a house when a lady was in childbed, the idea of the height of elegance being, in the popular mind, inseparable from the wearing of gloves, specially kid gloves. Hence, *up to the knocker,* supremely elegant, completely, to the last degree, proficient. "Up to the door" appears to be a variation of this. "Kid," in its meaning of "swell," and "kiddily," fashionably, in fine style, skilfully, probably arose from a like appreciation of the use of kid gloves. Again, it is possible that *up to the knocker* owes its origin to the "knocker" or breast-pin which was formerly in fashion, and which was like a knocker on a door.

I shall have 'em all on to-morrow—tidy sort of weskit, cuffs, collar, and dicky—all *up to the knocker.*—*J. Greenwood: Under the Blue Blanket.*

Up to the mark. *Vide* MARK.

Up to the ropes (London), sagacious, knowing.

Her style and her talk were decidedly "gay,"
And any one *up to the ropes,*
Will guess that, of course, in the usual way,
I took her to supper at "Pope's."
—*Bird o' Freedom.*

U.S. cove (American thieves), a soldier, a man in the service of the American government. "U.S. plate," handcuffs.

Use at, to (thieves), frequent.

I got in company with some of the widest people in London. They used to *use at* a pub in Shoreditch.—*Horsley : Jottings from Jail.*

Very common in Western America. To *use* round a place, to haunt it.

Usher (thieves), yes ; from the Yiddish *user,* it is right, it is so.

When I got into Shoreditch I met one or two of the mob, who said, "Hallo, been out to-day? Did you touch?" So I said *usher.—Horsley: Jottings from Jail.*

Utilities (theatrical), minor parts for beginners. "Responsible *utilities*" are somewhat more important parts than ordinary *utilities.*

Utter (society), excellent, most elegant.

Uzar (gypsy), by chance. (Hindu *usar*, by chance.)

V

VĂCCASHO (gypsy), a calf, also a lamb.

Vag. (American), a vagabond. The Vagabond Act is always called in police circles the *Vag.* Act.

By the way, Billy, why ain't I in with the other *vags.* or the S. D.'s (Simple Drunks)? You're treating me as royally as a murderer.—*Bird o' Freedom.*

Vakeel (Anglo-Indian), a barrister.

Valley tan (American), a kind of whisky sold in the Mormon country is known as *valley tan.*

Valleys (pantomime, &c.), explained by quotation.

Cascades and *valleys* are trundling and gymnastic performances, such as tumbling across the stage on wheels and catching hold of hands and twirling round.—*Mayhew : London Labour and the London Poor.*

Vamos (American). The soldiers who returned from the war with Mexico brought with them several Spanish phrases, such as *vamos*, let us go, which they speedily changed to *vamo*, very properly described by Bartlett as "a curious grammatical perversion." With this came

ranch, a farm ; hence the popular saying, "Let us *vamos* the *ranch.*"

Vamose, vamoose, to (common), to depart, run away. *Vide* VAMOS.

And he *vamosed* with that clear conscience that belongs to him that giveth away his fellow-man.—*Bird o' Freedom.*

Vamp (thieves), a robbery. In for a *vamp*, convicted of stealing.

Vamper, a horse-dealer that "vamps" up, cobbles up a horse ; that is, makes him appear sound by certain tricks and devices. *Vide* To VAMP.

By what process of diabolical conjuration it is contrived, it is, of course, impossible for me to say, but it is beyond dispute that in the hands of the experienced horse-*vamper* the most wretched used-up screw in existence may, for a brief hour or so, be made to exhibit an amount of fire and spirit that if persisted in for a longer period would inevitably shake its ramshackle carcass all to pieces.—*J. Greenwood: Undercurrents of London Life.*

Also a thief.

Vamping (musical), a musical term, introduced from America. "It means a plan of playing an accompaniment at sight, by simply knowing the key and the time to which the song is set. In the Western States men make a good living by teaching it in eight lessons, for which they charge ten dollars (£2) " (*Tit-Bits*).

The man at the shop had no guitar to sell,
So I purchased a banjo, which did just as well;
The hour it was late, and the night it was damp,
But my mind was made up, and I started to *vamp.—Song by Jas. Tabrar.*

Vampire (American), a man who lives by following men and women about until he has proof of their undue intimacy, and then blackmailing them. (Punch and Judy), the ghost.

Vampo (theatrical), the clown.

Vampoose, to (popular and thieves), to decamp. Obsolete English, *vamp*, to go, to travel, influenced by *vamoose*.

Has he *vampoosed* with the contents of a till?—*Kingsley: Two Years Ago.*

Vamp, to (popular), to leave in pawn, to do a thing carelessly, slovenly, anyhow, so that it will pass muster for the time being. *Vamped* is said of anything falsified, arranged so as to make it appear genuine.

Vanish, in conjuring, used almost invariably as a verb active. To *vanish* an object is to make an object disappear from sight of the audience.

Van John, a common corruption of the game of *vingt-et-un.*

Vantage (printers). *Vide* FAT. An old term, according to Moxon, 1683, for good paying work—"fat" being the modern equivalent.

Van-ts'ang-koon-sz (pidgin), the Pacific Mail Steamship Company of Shanghai. An American who heard this name remarked that the *Van Zang coons* must be of the Knickerbocker Kuhn family to judge by their name.

Vardo, wardo, a waggon. According to Hotten this word is "old cant," according to fact it is old Romany, *wardo* being in some form or other found in all gypsy dialects. It is also applied to cards, and to a wheel, from the old gypsy *wortin,* a vessel.

" Awer bíkdom dovo *wárdo* léski
Pátserdo, te yúv te vél kek pessur "—

" But I sold him that waggon on credit, and he will not pay (for it)."

(Roughs, itinerants, strollers, &c.) *Vardo !* or *varder !* look see. From Italian *vedere.*

Varmint (University), spruce, natty, good all round.

A *varmint* man spurns a scholarship, would consider it a degradation to be a fellow.—*Gradus ad Cantab.*

The handsome man, my friend and pupil, was naturally enough a bit of a swell, or *varmint* man.—*Alma Mater.*

Varmint men (University), those who used, like Jemmy Gordon, to write themes for Cantabs too idle to do it themselves.

Varnister (thieves), an utterer of false sovereigns.

Varsity (Oxford and Cambridge), a common pronunciation of university.

With Le Maitre only half a yard worse than 50¼ sec. for the Quarter, it doesn't look as if the Cantabs will have a smell at the Quarter, the Half, or the Mile, at the next '*Varsity* contest.—*Sporting Life.*

Vaseline (Royal Military Academy), butter.

Vássavo, vessavo (gypsy), bad, naughty.

" Awer tu shan *vassavi* lūbbeni
  Sār gorgiko rāt to be kambli "—
" But thou art a bad harlot to be with child with Gorgio blood."—*George Borrow : Lavengro.*

Vaulting-house (common), a house of ill fame. See "Ballads and Songs," seventeenth century.

Velvet (thieves), the tongue; "especially," says Hotten, "the tongue of a magsman." This circumstance would support the derivation of magsman from to *mag*, to talk persuasively. (Common), men, especially racing men, who have succeeded in their speculations, are said "to stand on *velvet.*"

Ventilator (theatrical), a piece, or an actor who ventilates, *i.e.*, empties the house. An amusing story is told of a certain tragedian, who was popularly known as the champion *ventilator.* While acting Othello in the Cork theatre, he became disgusted with the coldness and want of sympathy on the part of the audience. Being extremely short-sighted, the poor fellow could not distinguish whether the house was a good or a bad one, so he sent his dresser—a native of the Emerald Isle—into the pit to discover the state of the land. During his rendition of the crucial scene in the third act, his performance was of such a character that the few people who were in the pit began to straggle out. When the dresser came round at the end of the third act, his master opened fire with, "Well, Larry, I think I had them in that act."

"Faith, you may say that, sor."

"Yes, I flatter myself I moved them in the farewell."

"You did, sor; you moved them so, that, begorra, they've all moved out, and there's nothing lift but the binches to play to."

That was the champion *ventilator's* last engagement in Cork, or anywhere else for that matter. He has now retired, and lives on his means—"a prosperous gentleman."

Verge (thieves), a gold watch.

Vert, frequently used during the Tractarian Controversy, is a per*vert* or con*vert* from the Church of England to that of Rome.

Vertical case-grinder, the (prison), the treadwheel.

There is humour in the description of the treadmill as the "everlasting staircase" or the *vertical case-grinder.—Globe.*

Vest (common), to lose your *vest*, to lose your temper.

Vestas (Stock Exchange), Railway Investment Company Deferred Stock.

Vet., an abbreviation for veterinary surgeon. In the United States it is a common term for a veteran.

I had hired a trap from an innkeeper who was also a *vet.—Chambers's Journal.*

Vice, the (University), obvious corruption of Vice-Chancellor.

Victim (society), a very common expression for any one who is desperately in love.

Victualling department (pugilistic), the stomach. Also "victualling office," "bread basket," "dumpling depôt." In French slang "panier au pain;" in Italian cant "fagiana," literally the bean box.

Vile (thieves), a town; from the French *ville*. In ancient cant London was termed Rome-*vile*, the fine town. *Deuce-a-vile*, the country.

And prig and cloy so benshiply
All the *deuce-a vile* within.
 —*The English Rogue.*

In old English "vill," a village.

Vile child (Eton), explained by quotation.

Being called a *vile child*, the which I subsequently learnt was a very frequent term of mild reproach, and had no particular reference to the age of the individual to whom it was addressed. As a proof of this I may add that, being at Eton for the Winchester Match in 1883, I (*moi-qui-vous-parle*, height 6 feet 2 inches, and weight 14 stone 7 lbs.) was called a *vile child* for being on a committee to oppose a certain obnoxious Indian Bill! I wasn't sorry when tea was over, although many most pleasant evenings did I afterwards spend in that room.—*Polytechnic Magazine.*

Village bustler (old cant), an active thief, that steals anything.

Village, the (London), a playful appellation for London.

Vim, from the Latin, claimed as American, but well known to English schoolboys,—strength, spirit, activity, pluck.

Virginia city is sobering down with the ebbing tide into substantial legitimate business, but Helena has all the *vim*, recklessness, extravagance, and jolly progress of a new camp.—*Tour through Rocky Mountains.*

Vincent's Law, the act of cheating at cards.

Vinegar on his oysters (American), applied to men not perfectly familiar with the minor refinements of highly civilised life.

"What kind of man is he—a gentleman?" "Oh yes, he believes himself to be one, calls himself 'an Amurican,' takes *vinegar on his oysters* instead of lemon-juice, very often skips his daily bath, and never mentions a picture, or a horse, or a human being, without telling you how much it, or he, or she is worth."—*Newspaper Letter.*

Violets (common), an euphemism for sage and onions.

Virgins (Stock Exchange), Virginia New Funded.

Virgin Mary's Bodyguard, a nickname for the 7th Dragoon

Guards, from having served under Maria Theresa of Austria. Also "Black Horse," and "Straw Boots."

Vocaller (American), a singer.

Let things alone, and presently that young lady discovers that she is not likely to get cracked up as a *vocaller.—The Golden Butterfly.*

Voker, a word found only in Hotten, who says that it is the gypsy to talk ("Can you *voker* Romany ? "), and derives it from the Latin *vocare.* He was probably misled by a misprint or mis-writing of *rōker, rāker,* or *rākker,* being the true word. It is true that *verākava* or *verākkerava* is found in continental gypsy dialects, but it is very doubtful whether it exists in England.

Vongar, wongur (gypsy), coals. Also *hangars* and *angars* (Sanskrit *angara*), money ; *angarengro,* a tinker or smith. "It came out in the course of an examination at the Guildhall that receivers of stolen goods are in the habit of carrying small pieces of coal about with them. When they see a thief who seems to be rather shy, they will walk up to him, take out a purse, and innocently show him a bit of coal. It has been suggested that this proceeding is analogous to taking salt together among the Arabs as a sign of good faith and mutual hospitality. In several languages "glowing coals" is a

slang synonym for money, *e.g.,* French *braise.*

Voucher (old cant), a rogue who passed base coin.

The first was a Coiner, that stampt in a mould ;
The second a *Voucher,* to put off his gold.
     —The Twenty Craftsmen.

Vowel mauler (common), one who pronounces his words incorrectly.

Vowel, to (common), to *vowel* a debt is to acknowledge with an I.O.U.

Vulgus (Winchester College), explained by quotation.

The mention of a *vulgus* requires some explanation. Every inferior, *i.e.,* non-prefect in the school was required every night to produce a copy of verses of from two to six lines on a given theme—four or six lines for the upper classes, two for the lowest. This was independent of a weekly verse task of greater length, and was called a *vulgus,* I suppose, because everybody— the *vulgus*—had to do it.—*T. A. Trollope : What I Remember.*

Vum (American), a form of swearing. "'I *vum !*' for 'I vow !' is a euphemistic form of oath often heard in New England " (Bartlett). As the writer has heard "I *vum !*" innumerable times in his boyhood, he always understood it to be much more strongly expressive than "I vow." It is worth observing that, in Anglo-Saxon, *vomm* or *vamm* (*peccatum, crimen,* horror), and *vom,* full of evil, formed a malediction or curse, *e.g.,* *vome,* malediction (Caedmon).

W

WAD, straw. A common abbreviation for *wadding*, which, as padding, means the stuffing of a bed, and dates from the times when straw and hay were used for the purpose for which cotton or other wadding is now employed.

> Moll in the *wad* and I fell out,
> I'll tell you what 'twas all about ;
> She had money, I had none,
> That was the way the row begun.
> —*Old Popular Song.*

(American), a roll of bankbills, hence a fortune.

> Many scores of these philanthropists, who have spent their lives in looking for men to enrich, whilst anxious only to make a small *wad* for themselves, have I encountered.—*F. Francis : Saddle and Moccasin.*

Waddle out of the alley. *Vide* DUCK.

Waddler (popular), a duck.

Waddy (Australian), the Australian natives' club, a native word adopted by the whites.

> Nulla Nullas, *waddies*, or clubs, used chiefly for hand-to-hand encounters, but also for throwing ; the sharpened points cause terrible stab-wounds. The timbers chosen are the hardest and heaviest obtainable in the forests of the different districts, iron bark, myall, swamp myrtle, &c.—*New South Wales Catalogue.*

> Dear Peter from my threshold went
> One morning in the body,
> He " dropped " me, to oblige a gent,
> A gent with spear and *waddy*.
> —*H. Kendall : Peter the Piccaninny.*

Waddy is also slang for any kind of stick. A young colonial

VOL. II.

will speak in joke of his walking-stick as his *waddy*.

> Thanks, generous colonial,
> Thou art very, very kind ;
> Now pick a thickish *waddy* up
> And plug my wound behind.
> —*J. B. Stephens : The Headless Trooper.*

Waffle (printers), to *waffle* is to be endowed with the "gift of the gab," or talk of any kind to an excess ; popular equivalent would be to " jaw."

Wagon (American), a bicycle.

Wag-tail, a prostitute, a harlot.

Wailo, wylo (pidgin-English), go away ! away with you ! to go, depart, gone, departed, went.

> There was an Englishman in Canton who kept a cow, with a maid to milk it, and a dog to guard it. One morning there was no milk, and the gentleman scolded his comprador or steward, who in great agitation burst into poetry and said :—

> T'at cow hab die-lo,
> T'at dog hab *wylo*,
> T'at woman catchee chilo—
> How can hab milk?
> —*The Cow and the Comprador.*

Waistcoat, fœtid, a term current in 1859 for a low, flaunting, vulgar pattern.

Wake up the wrong passenger, to (popular), a phrase of American origin, and derived from railroad terminology. On long distance journeys, when travellers sometimes spend several days and nights on board a car, it occasionally happens that the

2 B

attendant, not being sure of the identity of a passenger, wakes up the wrong man. The expression therefore. indicates uncertainty as to identity, always meaning to catch a Tartar.

Walk (bankers), the round of a banker's collecting clerk is so called. A rich *walk* is one where a large sum of money is got in.

Walk down a person's throat, to (common), to rate or scold any one soundly. Sometimes for "walk," "jumped " is used.

Walker, a vulgar exclamatior to express incredulity.

All this in her ear, he declared, but I fear
That her senses were wandering—she
    seem'd not to hear,
Or, at least, understand—for mere unmeaning talk her
Parch'd lips babbled now, such as " Hookey," and *Walker!*
She expired, with her last breath expressing a doubt
If "his mother were fully aware he was
    out."
            —*Ingoldsby Legends.*

The remark which was made, after perusing the book by that eminent botanist, my friend Professor Hookey, was *Walker!* —*Punch.*

(Popular), *walker,* a postman. "There is nothing inherently humorous, for example, in the name *Walker,* and yet there was a time when it could set a whole crowd roaring with laughter. Occurring in a popular song, it was at first coupled with the prefix *Hookey,* but it soon came to be employed alone, and for a season was in every mouth. It was considered an excruciatingly funny thing to say, and upon its use at some unexpected moment many a reputation for wit was founded. Even now, though it has grown feeble with age, it is sometimes found serviceable by small boys, the tip of the finger pressed against the nose at the time of utterance. Even elderly politicians have not disdained to conciliate the masses with a delicate use of *Walker !* —*Globe.*

Walking mort (old cant), a concubine, the *autem mort* being the lawful spouse.

Walking papers (American), to dismiss one is to give him his *walking-papers.*

Walk into, to (common), to strike, thrash.

When he told Verdant that . . . his bread-basket *walked into,* his day-lights darkened.—*C. Bede : Verdant Green.*

(Metaphorically), to demolish.

A hungry man *walked into* a pigeon-pie. —*Punch.*

To *walk into* the affections, to scold or thrash ; also to run into debt.

Walk one's chalks, to (popular), to walk straight, to be compelled to behave well, to go away, abscond.

That artist was a keen observer, as all true artists should be, so finding the corner was getting too hot for him he simply *walked his chalks.—Moonshine.*

Hotten gives the explanation, "An ordeal for drunkenness used on board ship, to see if the suspected person can walk on a *chalk* line without overstepping it on either side" (the device in the army is putting a man suspected of drunkenness. through his facings); another explanation of the phrase is "a person who has run up a score or *chalk* at a public-house or shop, walking off without paying for it."

And if you want fresh liquor, you must pay,
For *chalks* too often walk themselves away.
—*Albert Smith : Alhambra.*

Walk over (society), when any one wins or succeeds very easily it is called a *walk over.* It is borrowed from racing language. When a horse *walks over* the course, not having any opponents in the race.

Besides his monetary advantage and personal gifts, he could sing well and talk admirably, and he was considered sure to "*walk over* the course."—*H. L. Williams: Buffalo Bill.*

The latest batch we have received are from W. Hazelberg, of Berlin and London Wall, who evidently does not intend that the English manufacturers shall have a *walk over.—Sporting Times.*

Wallaby track, to go on the (Australian), to go on foot, up-country, in search of work.

Wallflowers, second-hand garments exposed for sale in Seven Dials. A common expression for ladies in a ballroom who, either from choice or otherwise, sit looking on without dancing.

Wall, to (Oxford University), confining a student to college.

(Popular), *to wall* it, to post the account for drink on the wall at a public-house.

Waltzing about (tailors) is said of a man who makes himself a nuisance.

Wanky (printers). This expression is used to denote a spurious or wrong article. A bad sixpence given amongst change for a larger coin would be described as a *wanky* sixpence.

Wanted (common), *wanted* by the police for an offence, or by one's creditors.

The police, on their part, caused it to be understood that until he was really *wanted* on a specific charge, a thief should in no case be interfered with, nor any measures be taken to put the public on their guard against him.—*J. Greenwood: Tag, Rag, & Co.*

The landlady's certain to peach
When she finds not a thing do I own.
The Bobby's come into the lane,
And somebody's *wanted*, I see,
They pass me again and again,
But haven't found out that it's me.
—*Bird o' Freedom.*

Wapping. *Vide* To WAP.

Wap, to (old cant), futuere. *Wappen* is provincial English.

Ward-heeler (American), the *ward-heeler* is a power in American politics. He raises the money by which city elections are carried, and when some "prominent politician" is sent to prison, the *ward-heeler* represents to the magistrate or judge the inexpediency of weakening "the party" by withdrawing an "influential" partisan from his sphere of activity. Chiefly applied to men who solicit money, generally without authority from candidates, for electioneering purposes.

Ware hawk! (old cant), a cry of warning, especially when the police are espied. Sir Walter Scott puts the term in the mouth of De Bracy in "Ivanhoe."

Warehousing (society), taking to the pawnbroker's. The more genteel are called "warehouse-men," and their shops "ware-houses."

War-hat, or **war-pot** (army), the new helmet with a spike.

Warming-pan. In clerical circles a *warming-pan* is an incumbent who accepts a benefice on the condition of resigning it in favour of some other presentee so soon as the latter shall be able to assume its duties. He keeps the place "warm" for the son or other friend of the patron. (Common), a large watch.

Warm member (society), a fast man or woman. Also a "hot 'un," a "scorcher."

Warm 'un (common), one who is immoral, fast, dissipated.

> They call me Salvation Sarah,
>   A *warm 'un* I have been;
> But now I am converted,
>   I'll never go wrong again.
> So come and join our army,
>   And better you'll all be;
> And instead of beer,

> Then live on prayer,
>   Peace, sherbet, love, and tea.
>   —*Song of Salvation Sarah.*

War-paint (theatrical), *paint* for the face.

> Stickin' on a few feathers an' a bit o' *war-paint!—Sporting Times.*

Also a common expression for official costume or evening dress, a phrase originally used by some women who dressed, as the Americans say, to kill, determined to make conquests at evening parties.

> *She*—"Have you seen the hero of the evening?"
> *He*—"Who? Do you mean the Portuguese governor in his *war-paint?*"—*Rider Haggard: Dawn.*

War-pot. *Vide* WAR-HAT.

Wash (printers). When a printer "slings the hatchet," that is, exaggerates or tells a falsehood, his companions proceed to *wash* him in a somewhat emphatic and noisy manner, by banging or knocking on their cases. This is another and older expression for "whack," which see. An apprentice coming out of his time would receive a "washing" or "jerry." See Hansard's "Typographia," 1825.

Washing (tailors), to get a *washing* is to have one's workmanship or conduct criticised in language more forcible than pleasant. In French "laver la tête." *Washing* day, dinner at the shop. (Stock Exchange), a fictitious bargain or sale, in which one broker agrees with another to purchase a given stock when put up for sale, the object being to keep it on quotation. If the deal is a large one it may send up the price, in which case the object is sometimes so to increase its value as to form a basis for a genuine deal.

Wash one's ivories, to (society), to drink. In French slang " se rincer la dent."

Wash - outs (American), ragged, stony sides of hills.

Where scraggy - looking latitudinous *wash-outs* are awaiting a chance to commit a murder, or to make the unwary cycler who should venture to " coast," think he had wheeled over the tail of an earthquake. — *T. Stevens : Around the World on a Bicycle.*

Wash, to (common), in the sense of to do, to serve.

The conversation, as a rule, ended in Charley's giving them an order too. Of course this little " caper " would only *wash* once.—*Hindley : Life and Adventures of a Cheap Jack.*

This will not *wash*, this will not stand test, as of colours that will not bear washing.

Waste-butt (thieves), an eating-house.

Wasters (gypsies), hands. (Pronounce *a* as in glass.)

" And as they were gillerin' and huljerin' him, Samson chivved his *wasters* kettenus the boro chongurs of the sturaben, and bongered his kokerus adrée, an sār the ker pet a lay with a boro gudli, an' sār the pooro mushis were mullered an' the ker poggered to bitti cutters "—
" And as they were making fun of him and teasing him, Samson threw his hands around the great pillars of the prison, and

bowed himself in, and all the house fell down with a great noise, and all the poor men were killed and the house broken to small pieces."—*C. G. Leland : The English Gypsies.*

Waste, to (sporting), to reduce one's weight by certain means which bring on profuse perspiration.

He had often heard Archer say that he was so exhausted at the end of the season that he could not ride. But he had to *waste :* that was different from Wood.— *St. James's Gazette.*

Watch and seals (popular), a sheep's head and pluck.

Watcher (special meaning), explained by quotation.

So I do, but not alone. Dress lodgers are never allowed to do that, sir. I haven't been one long, but long enough to find that out. There's always a *watcher*. Sometimes it's a woman—an old woman, who isn't fit for anything else—but in general it's a man. He watches you always, walking behind you, or on the opposite side of the way. He never loses sight of you, never fear.—*Greenwood : Seven Curses of London.*

Watchmaker (thieves), a thief who steals watches.

Water (Westminster School), explained by quotation.

Boating, or *water*, as it is called at Westminster, is in a very flourishing condition. —*Pascoe : Everyday Life in our Public Schools.*

Water a stock, to (Stock Exchange). *Watering* is generally resorted to by companies whose fortunes are on the down grade. It consists in enhancing the total of capital stock by new issues, on the ground that the profits already accrued, or in anticipation, justify such a course.

Waterloo-day (army), pay-day, a day of victory and rejoicing.

Watersman (costers, pugilistic, &c.), a sky-coloured silk pocket-handkerchief.

Water the dragon, or **water one's nag,** a hint for retiring (Hotten).

Wattles (popular), the ears.

Wavy in the syls (theatrical), unsteady in the syllables, loose in the words, imperfect in the text.

Wavy-rule (printers), an inebriated person is said to be making *wavy-rule* ~~~~~ if his gait is unsteady.

Wax (general), in a *wax,* in a rage.

She is in a terrible *wax,* but she'll be all right by the time he comes back from his holidays.—*H. Kingsley: Ravenshoe.*

" *Wax,* to be angry or vexed, . is evidently identical with Scottish *wex,* i.e., *vex* " (A. S. Palmer).

And mak thi self als merry as yhoue may, It helpith not thus fore to *wex* al way. —*Lancelot of the Laik.*

Waxed (tailors), to have him *waxed,* to know all about one, alluding to a thread well waxed before it is used.

Waxy (common), angry. *Vide* WAX.

It would cheer him up more than anything if I could make him a little *waxy* with me ; he's welcome to drop into me right and left, if he likes.—*Dickens: Bleak House.*

Wayzgoose (printers). Essentially a printer's term for the annual dinner or " beanfeast." Derived from the old English word *wayz* or stubble, when the dinners were usually held at the season of the wheat-stubble, the head dish at these entertainments being a *wayz-goose* or stubble-goose. Bailey gives *wayz-goose,* a stubble-goose, and *wayz,* a bundle of straw. Old English *wase,* a wisp. These festive occasions are usually celebrated earlier in the year now—generally July.

The master-printer gives them a *way-goose,* that is, he makes them a good feast. —*Moxon: Mechanick Exercises.*

After the *wayzgoose:* a moment immense ! Gargantuan the feasting has been. —*Bird o' Freedom.*

Weak (popular), tea is so called in the low coffee-shops.

Weaver, query *wheezer,* a broken-winded horse, a "roarer." The definition given to the writer by a stable-keeper was, "a horse that over-gorges himself," probably the cause for the effect, as over-feeding, in the case of horses, often produces thick wind.

T" horse was a *weaver,* if iver one was, as any could ha' told as had come within a mile of him.—*Mrs. Gaskell: Sylvia's Lovers.*

Again, it is possible that *weaver* refers to a horse that rolls from side to side when trotting, one that rocks. *Vide* TO WEAVE, and WOBBLER.

Weave, to (American), to work along from one side to the other, as a shuttle flies right and left in a loom. A drunken man "*weaves* along."

He began in earnest too; and went *weaving* first to one side of the platform and then the other. — *Mark Twain: Huckleberry Finn.*

Hence to get into a *weaving* way, to walk or stagger along recklessly, not to care what one is doing.

When I git in a *weaving* way,
I spend my money free ;
Oh den I hab a merry time,
And Jenny am de girl for me.
— *Old Negro Song.*

Weaving (cardsharpers), a trick performed by keeping some particular cards on the knee and using them when required.

Wedge (thieves, itinerants, strollers, &c.), a very old term for silver or silver money.

He had twice been pull'd, and nearly
lagg'd, but got off by going to sea,
With his pipe and quid, and chanting
voice, potatoes he would cry,
For he valued neither cove nor swell, for
he had *wedge* snug in his die.
— *P. Egan: Book of Sports.*

Wedge-feeder, a silver spoon ; *wedge*-hunter, one who purloins plate from unguarded kitchens. Spelled *wage* in some old cant vocabularies, which perhaps gives a clue to the origin as meaning pay.

Wedge now applies more particularly to silver plate than in the early days of the century.

I succeeded in getting some *wedge* and
a kipsy full of clobber.—*Horsley: Jottings
from Jail.*

Weed (common), a cigar.

A cigar is figuratively styled a *weed*, an innovation applicable enough to the anomalous compounds of nastiness retailed at the Derby, the Boat Race, and other public gatherings, but an evident misnomer as regards the fragrant samples issuing from Mr. Benson's emporium.—*Belgravia.*

So you see, Mr. S., that the modest request
on which you so coolly insist,
Would probably to the establishment tend
of a kind of gigantic free list,
On which would be found every law-maker's
name, and which in its limitless scope
Would ensure him free shaving, free papers,
free *weeds*, free candles, and pickles
and soap.
—*London Figaro.*

Weenie (telegraph), the inspector is coming, used in the same sense as "cave."

W ej e e, a chimney-pot; often applied to any clever invention, or to anything elegant, as "that's a regular *wejee*" (Hotten).

Welsher (common), a race-course swindler who makes bets, takes the money if he wins, and absconds if he loses.

Does the reader know what is a *welsher*, the creature against whose malpractices the sporting public are so emphatically warned? Probably he does not. It is still more unlikely that he ever witnessed a *welsher* hurt ; and as I there have the advantage of him, it may not be out of place here to enlighten him on both points. A *welsher* is a person who contracts a sporting debt without a reasonable prospect of paying it. There is no legal remedy against such a defaulter.—*Greenwood: Seven Curses of London.*

The word has no connection with the natives of Wales, who are quite as honest as other people. *Welsch* in German argot signifies a foreigner, and *roth-*

welsch or *red-welsh*, is the name applied to the canting language which thieves use among themselves. It is supposed with probability that the name was given to the brown or red-skinned gypsies or foreigners, who first swarmed into continental Europe from Central Asia. An account of *roth-welsch* appears as a supplement to the Dictionnaire d'Argot Français, by Francesque Michel. The word *welsher*, as used originally in England and borrowed from the Germans, meant nothing more than an outsider, a foreigner, one who did not conform to the established laws of honest betting, and thus shared the double odium of being a stranger as well as a rogue. *Wälscher* is used in German slang in a discreditable sense, being derived from *wälsh*, Italian, or one of Latin race, and it is extremely probable that it came into English slang through the German Jews.

Westphalia (London), the behind, alluding to Westphalia hams.

Wet (common), a drink.

Many are the schemes, contrivances, and devices of some of the old topers to obtain a *wet* or reviver, first thing in the morning, especially with some of those thoroughly saturated worthies who have had rather " more than 'nuff " the night previous.—*Brunlees Patterson: Life in the Ranks.*

> The gas-glare—the horse-play—
> The fume and the fret—
> Have ceased, with the fever
> That asked for a *wet*—

> With the Jubilee fever
> Demanding a *wet.*
> —*Funny Folks.*

> Oh, come,
> We have no Wilfrid Lawson in Sicily yet ;
> All my Cyclops would strike. Yes ! I'm game for a *wet.*   —*Punch.*

A *wet* night, a night of hard drinking.

As he knew he should have a *wet* night, it was agreed that he might gallop back again in time for church on Sunday morning.—*Thackeray: Vanity Fair.*

Wet-bob (Eton), explained by quotation.

It was the ambition of most boys to be a *wet-bob*, and to be "in the boats." The school was divided between *wet-bobs* and dry-bobs, the former taking their pleasure on the river, and the latter in the cricket-field.—*C. T. Buckland: Eton Fifty Years Ago.*

Wetherall, general in command (army), a term used when inclement weather prevents a parade. The health of the troops, from economic and prudential reasons, is always closely watched, and medical officers are always ready to interpose even when the commanding officer does not of his own motion yield before cold and wet.

Wet quaker, a man who pretends to be religious, and is a dram-drinker on the sly (Hotten). In America a *wet quaker* is a quaker who is limp or loose as regards observing the rules of the sect—one who is worldly-minded, not "dry" in religion.

Would you buy any naked truth, or light in a dark lanthorn? Look in the *wet quaker's* walk.—*T. Brown's Works.*

Socinians, and Presbyterians, Quakers, and *wet quakers*, and merry ones. — *Ward: England's Reformation.*

Wet, to (common), to have a drink. The same idea occurs in French slang " se mouiller."

Greatly as I stared to see him, my surprise
 I cannot forget,
When he paid me all he owed me, and
 invited me to *wet*.
     —*Funny Folks.*

Also *wet* one's whistle or throttle.

" Well, as we have nothing to eat," said
 old Brooke,
" I move that each man *wet* his throttle ;
My hand I can place in a snug little nook,
And fork out the housekeeper's bottle."
  —*H. J. Whymark: The Bachelor's
   Dinner.*

(Navy), *wetting* a commission, giving an entertainment to shipmates on receiving promotion. Among French soldiers "arroser ses galons " is treating one's comrades on being promoted to the rank of non-commissioned officer. Some of the synonyms for " to drink" are " to have a gargle, a *wet*, a dram, a quencher, something damp," " to moisten one's chaffer," " to sluice one's gob," " to lush," " to liquor up," and the American phrases " to smile," " to see a man," &c.

Whack (general), a share. Scotch *sweg* or *swack*.

This gay young bachelor had taken his share (what he called his *whack*) of pleasure.—*Thackeray: Shabby-Genteel Story.*

He complains of the food, and that he doesn't get his *whack*.—*Moonshine.*

So when we got there, there was some reelers there what knew me, and my pals said, " You had better get away from us ;

if we touch you will take your *whack* just the same."—*Horsley: Jottings from Jail.*

To go *whacks*, to share.

"You agreed that we should go *whacks* in everything," I pleaded, appealing to his sense of justice, since I could not succeed in touching his generosity.—*Greenwood: The Little Ragamuffins.*

(Printers), *whack!* a very common and decided expression of doubt or query to a companion's assertion. Generally a polite way of giving the lie direct.

Whacker (common), anything very large, identical with "whopper."

" Look what *whackers*, Cousin Tom, said Charley, holding out one of his prizes by its back towards Tom, while the indignant cray-fish flapped its tail.—*Hughes: Tom Brown at Oxford.*

(American), driver, drover.

There were only eight *whackers* left, and they were obliged to work day and night to keep the stock together. —*O'Reilly: Fifty Years on the Trail.*

Used in the phrases mule-*whacker*, bull - *whacker*, bush-*whacker*.

Whacking (popular), large.

" How kind of them," says he, " to gi'e
 me 'em,
Since they're at such a *whacking* premium."
   —*Atkin: House Scraps.*

Whack, to (general and American), to share.

As far as he was able to speak, it was the " new hands" who went in for revolvers, and not the old ones, who worked in " co.," and on the sound, old-fashioned principle of " sharing the danger and *whacking* the swag."—*J. Greenwood: A Converted Burglar.*

To *whack* up on the square, to share fairly.

He was trying to beat them out of their share of the swag. He ought to have *whacked* up on the square.—*Wall Street News.*

Whack up, share or hand up.

Clap a stopper on your gab and *whack up*, or I'll let 'er speak!—*Detroit Free Press.*

Whacky (tailors), one who does anything ridiculous.

W h a l e (Cheltenham College), codfish. Sardines are called *whales* at the Royal Military Academy. (Common), anchovies on toast. " Very like a *whale !*" very much like a cock and bull story. From Shakspeare, *Hamlet.*

Whale away, to (American), to preach, talk, or lecture away continuously or vehemently. Probably from provincial English *to whale* (wale), to beat soundly, as of an orator's animated gestures, or by association from the common saying, " Going ahead like a *whale.*" The association of greatness and strength with a *whale* led in the New England seaport towns to many comparisons and origins of this kind. Thus a powerful and large man was called " a regular *whale,*" and " a whaler," while anything large and overwhelming was " whaling."

Whaler (American), anything of great or unusual size. Provincial English *whaler*, one that beats, a big strong fellow.

Whang-doodle (American). This eccentric word first appeared in one of the many " Hard-Shell Baptist" sermons which were so common in 1856. " Where the *whang-doodle* mourneth for her first-born." It refers to some mystical or mythical creature. It was subsequently applied to political subjects, such as the Free Trade, Lecompton Democracy, &c.

Whare (New Zealand), a hut. The word is used by the settlers in New Zealand, and is a native term.

What's the ticket on it? *Vide* TICKET.

Wheeler (cycling), a cyclist.

Wheel of life, the (prison), the tread-wheel. *Vide* EVERLASTING STAIRCASE.

Wheels (cycling), a bicycle or tricycle.

Wheeze (common), a comic gag, a funny bit of "business," a joke. Possibly from *wheaze*, a puff.

Alas ! at times on nights like these
Poor is the plot and weak the *wheeze*,
And the only pleasure one extracts
Is 'tween the acts—yes, 'tween the acts.
—*Fun.*

" Swell vernacular"? *Swells* don't invent it ; they nick it from hus, and no kid.
Did a swell ever start a new *wheeze*? Would it 'ave any run if he did?
Let the ink-slingers trot out their kibosh, and jest see 'ow flabby it falls.
Bet it won't raise a grin at the bar, bet it won't git a 'and at the 'Alls.
—*Punch.*

To crack a *wheeze*, explained by quotation.

To crack a *wheeze* is to originate something smart, or to say something at the right moment, whether original or borrowed. —*Globe.*

Wheeze, to (thieves), to say, inform, as of one speaking under one's breath, in husky tones. The synonyms for inform are "to squeal, to scream, to blow, to whiddle."

Connor then asked if they (meaning the police) had got "the scout." To this she replied, "He didna *wheeze*," by which he understood her to mean that he (the superintendent) had given no indication whether or not. —*Scottish Newspaper.*

Whid (old cant), word; stubble your *whids*, hold your tongue; to cut *whids*, to talk, speak.

What! stowe your bene, cofe, and *cut* benat *wydds.* —*Harman: Caveat.*

To cut *bien whids*, to speak soft words.

This doxie dell can cut *bien whids*, And drill well for a win.
—*English Rogue.*

Also a falsehood.

Even ministers they have been kenn'd, In holy rapture, A rousin' *whid* at times to vend, And nail 't wi' Scripture.
—*Burns: Death and Dr. Hornbook.*

In the first edition of Burns the word *whid* did not appear, but instead of it—

"Great lies and nonsense baith to vend."

"This was ungrammatical, as Burns himself recognised it to be, and amended the line by the more emphatic form in which it now appears" (Dr. C. Mackay, "A Dictionary of Lowland Scotch"). Burns also uses the word with the meaning of frisking about, gambols. "Hence," says Drennan, "it is obvious how *whid* applied to statements could come to mean a lie." The transition to "word" is easy, and the origin of *whid* might be thus traced; gambols (akin to said, as in the line "an arrow *whidderan*," *i.e.*, scolding), hence a lie, hence a word. It is now-a-days used with the signification of word, falsehood, joke.

The *whids* we used to crack over them. —*Hindley: Life of a Cheap Jack.*

Whiddle, to. To Hotten's definition, to enter into a parley, or hesitate with many words, must be added, to divulge; "he *whiddles* the whole scrap," he tells the whole secret. *Whiddler*, an informer, who betrays the secrets of the gang. *Vide* WHID.

Whip (parliamentary), a contraction of *whipper-in*, a member of the House of Commons whose duty is to collect his party and bring them to divisions.

Dickens, in "Sketches by Boz," tells us how "Sir Somebody Something, when he was *whipper-in* for the Government, brought four men out of their beds to vote in the majority, three of whom died on their way home again."— *Cornhill Magazine.*

They curse the nation that declines to believe their lies or to be influenced by their cant, they curse their *whips*, they curse their leaders, and they curse their fate.—*Truth.*

Also a notice requesting attendance at a division.

A four-line *whip* has been issued by the Government in opposition to the second reading of Lord Dunraven's Bill for the reform of the House of Lords.—*Standard.*

(Printers), quick setter of type. (Army), after the usual allowance of wine is drunk at mess, those who wish for more put a shilling each in a glass handed round to procure a further supply (Hotten).

Whip-belly (popular), bad beer. Also *whip-belly-vengeance.*

I believe the brewer forgot the malt, or the river was too near him. Faith, it's meer *whip-belly-vengeance.* — *Swift : Polite Conversation.*

Whip-jack (old cant), a vagabond who begged for alms as a distressed soldier. Also freshwater sailor.

Swaddlers, Irish toyls, *whip-jacks.*— *Oath of the Canting Crew.*

Whipper - snapper (popular), a youth, stripling, or youngster of precocious tendencies.

Whipping. *Vide* WHIP.

Whip-round (common), a subscription for a man in distress, or for a drink.

Whipster (thieves), a sly, cunning fellow.

Whip-sticks (Stock Exchange), Dunaberg and Witepsk Railway Shares.

Whip the cat, to (old cant), has reference to mechanics idling their time, "derived from the practice of bricklayers' men, who, when repairing the pantiles, sneak into the adjacent gutters, pretending to be in pursuit of and *whipping the tom cats* and their moll rows" (Jon Bee). It is worthy of remark that the French use the phrase "il n'y a pas de quoi fouetter un chat," referring to a trivial offence ; hence "j'ai d'autres chats à fouetter," I cannot waste my time on matters of such little importance. But the true derivation is from idling the time away at "whipping the cat," *i.e.,* playing tip-cat. To *whip the cat* is modern working-men's slang for shirking work and enjoying oneself on a Monday. (Carpenters), one who does private work by the day. (Tailors), working at the houses of the people for whom the garments are being made. This custom is now almost obsolete, owing to the cheapness of ready-made garments. It is very prevalent in France in the case of sempstresses.

Whip the devil round the stump, to (American), probably older English also, to evade, equivocate, say one thing, and virtually do another. Very common in New England, particularly in Maine, where the devil is whipped around the temperance stump in innumerable ways. There are several English uses of the word *whip,* all implying something roundabout, equivocal, or dishonest.

Thus *to whip* is generally used to express anything dishonestly taken. It may be observed that there is an old negro camp-meeting hymn in which these lines occur—

Oh, *whip de debil roun' de stump,*
Prayer and gospel make him jump.

In this the reference is to justifiably and properly deceiving the devil himself. It is possible that this may be the original source of the expression.

Whip, to (popular and thieves), to swindle.

It was I who got the money, and I swindled one of my confederates, pretending I got only a few shillings. This is a common practice amongst thieves, and is called in criminal parlance *whipping.* I have *whipped* many and have been *whipped* a few times myself.—*Joe Bragg: Confessions of a Thief.*

A naïve confession was made by a woman in the Thames Police-court to-day. The prisoner by way of defence said it all arose out of what happened a fortnight ago, when she and Scully robbed a sailor in Devonshire Street, and Scully was guilty of what is known in Billingsgate as *whipping*—that is, keeping part of the plunder.—*Pall Mall Gazette.*

Whishler (circus), the man with the whip, or the ring-master. The one who superintends the performances, who starts the horses, and acts as interlocutor with the clown.

Whisker-bed (pugilistic), the cheeks or face.

His wories rattled, his nozzle barked, his *whisker-bed* napped heavily.—*C. Bede: Verdant Green.*

Whispering gill, or **syl** (*i.e.*, syllable) **slinger** (theatrical), the prompter.

Whisper, the angel's (army), the defaulter's bugle, the call to turn out to be mustered, or for pack or fatigue drill.

Whisper, to (popular), to borrow, generally a small sum ; to *whisper* for a bob, to borrow a shilling. A *whisperer* is a man in the habit of borrowing.

Whist (Hibernian). "Hold your *whist*," *i.e.*, hold your tongue, is an Irishism which has passed into English slang. In gypsy *whishters* mean lips.

This plea, for "little games" like chess and cards,
The Speaker hath (not chess-tingly), dis-carded,
And so the Members whom St. Stephen's guards
Are doomed, it seems, to pine all disregarded.
But though with chess they mayn't the hours improve,
They still to "hold their *whist*" are not commanded ;
Moreover, they're still up to many a "move,"
And are not for a "nap" entirely stranded—
Besides, while bent on legislation's aims,
In "rowing" they keep up their "little games." —*Fun.*

Whistle, a very ancient slang word for the throat or gullet. "To wet one's *whistle*," is to take a dram, or a drink. More correctly "to *whet* one's *whistle*," which phrase has its exact counterpart in the French slang expression "s'affûter le sifflet." The expression is found in Chaucer, who says of the Miller of Trumpington's wife in his "Canterbury Tales" :—

"So was hir joly *whistal* well y-wet.

Whistle and ride (tailors), work as well as talk.

Whistle-belly-vengeance. *Vide* WHIP-BELLY.

Whistler (horse-dealers), a horse that breathes hard.

He therefore excited plenty of bidding when put up for sale afterwards, and although a *whistler*, is worth the 520 guineas at which he was knocked down.— *The County Gentleman.*

"That horse of mine is the best I ever had. Very fast and a perfect fencer. I had very bad luck the other day, he over-reached himself, and I had to turn him out on the grass."
M.—"Is he a *roarer?*"
A.—"No ; nor a *whistler* either."
M.—"I suppose that's the reason you have to make all the noise for him?"—*Bird o' Freedom.*

Whistling Billy, or puffing Billy (popular), a locomotive.

Whistling breeches (popular), corduroys.

Whistling-shop (popular), a place in which spirits are sold without a license. Explained by Sam Weller.

Whit (old cant), prison.

He broke through all rubbs in the *whit*,
And chiv'd his darbies in twain.
        —*Frisky Moll's Song.*

And when we come unto the *whit*,
    For garnish they do cry ;
We promise our lusty comrogues
    They shall have it by and by.
Then ev'ry man with his mort in his hand,
    Is forced to kiss and part ;
And after is divorced away
    To the nubbing-cheat in a cart.
        —*The Life and Death of the Dark-man's Budge.*

Originally Newgate Prison.

There are three housebreakers that are lately come out of the *whit.*—*Hitchin: A True Discovery.*

Probably a form of *white*, as in Whitsuntide.

White, "as a slang term for blame or fault (Grose), as in the phrase 'You lay all the *white* off your-self,' or to *white*, to blame, is a corrupted form of the old Eng-lish and Scottish *wite* or *wyte*, Anglo-Saxon *witan*, to know (something against one), to im-pute ; O. H. German *wizan.* Cf. *twit*, from Anglo-Saxon *edwitan*, old English *wite*, a fine or punish-ment ; Anglo-Saxon *wite*, Ice-landic *víti*" (A. S. Palmer). To *white*, to blame.

"You lean all the *white* off yoursel," *i.e.*, you remove all the blame from your-self.—*Ray: North Country Words.*

Alake ! that e'er my Muse had reason,
To *wyte* her countrymen with treason.
        —*Burns : Poems.*

White-boy, a term of endearment in the seventeenth century for a favourite child or young man.

I am his *white-boy* and will not be gull'd.—*Ford: 'Tis Pity, &c.*

The name was assumed in Ireland early in the present century, during the agrarian outbreaks, prior to the days of Daniel O'Connell, Smith O'Brien, Mr. C. Stuart Parnell, and the dynamiters. (American), dis-interested, whole-souled.

A good fellow is Rayner, as *white* a man as I ever knew. — *The Golden Butterfly.*

Whitechapel (common), anything mean or paltry. (Billiards), to do *whitechapel*, to pot your opponent. (Cards), *whitechapel* play. At whist playing off all the winning cards without skill or plan. It used to be called bungay play in Norfolk. "Bungay," says Forby, "was a corruption from *bungar*, old English, synonymous with bungler." (Popular), *whitechapel* is a term used in tossing when "two out of three wins." *Whitechapel* fortune, a clean gown and pair of pattens. *Whitechapel* brougham, a costermonger's donkey-barrow.

White choker (common), a white tie.

Not only were *white chokers* seen in every part of the house, including the topmost gallery, but ladies in low dresses were content to brave the draughts of the pit.—*Daily Telegraph.*

A parson, from the white tie. On the resignation of his benefice by a divine still in the prime of life, he said at a farewell meeting that he had no intention of giving up the white tie. This a local journal printed as the white *lie.*

White eye (American), maize whisky, so called all over the United States.

White-horsed in (tailors), having procured a place by influence.

White jenny (popular), a silver Geneva watch, or any silver watch of foreign manufacture.

Called by thieves a "white clock," or "white 'un."

White man's hansom woman (West Indian), a black mistress.

White Mary (blackfellows' lingo). The Australian blackfellows who come in contact with "stations" of the white men have a regular slang of their own. *White Mary* is their generic name for all female cooks, just as it is always "Mary, the maid of the inn," in England.

Blucher, as usual, had marched into the room on the morning in question, coolly ignoring the remonstrances of the irritated woman, when, her passion getting the better of her, she made a rush at him with the poker, which perhaps she had heated on purpose, and touched him on the bare leg —for, like all his race, when not on horseback, he doffed his trousers and boots, and wore nothing but a Crimean shirt. The pain of the wound was as nothing to the indignity. With a bound he rushed into the "Cawbawn Humpy," his eyes flashing with insulted pride, exclaiming, "Missus Fitzgell, *White Mary* cook, 'un me," pointing to his leg.—*A. C. Grant.*

White mice (pidgin), Chinese babes of the poorest class. When blind they are called blind mice. It is very generally believed in China, and often said by Chinese who know better, that European missionaries buy *white mice* in order to make medicines or charms for sorcery out of their eyes.

White-poodle, a woolly, shaggy kind of cloth.

Peter wore a *white-poodle* upper Benjamin of his own make.—*J. Wight: Mornings at Bow Street.*

White prop (thieves), a diamond pin. Also "sparkle prop."

White, smooth (popular), a shilling.

> With him half-crowns were half-bulls, and shillings *smooth whites.*—*Living Pictures of London.*

White stuff (street, strollers, &c.), silver. Also "white wedge."

White tape (popular), gin. Also "white satin." These terms for spirits, *white tape,* "red tape," "lace," &c., most probably originated in the practices of some of the "driz fencers," or sellers of cheap lace, who carried about their persons "jigger stuffs," or spirit made at an illicit still. "They sold it, I've heard them say, to ladies that liked a drop on the sly. One old lady used to give three shillings for three yards of 'driz,' and it was well enough understood, without no words, that a pint of brandy was part of them three yards" (Mayhew).

> Jack Randall, then impatient, rose,
> And said Tom's speech was just as fine
> If he would catch that first of goes.
> By that genteeler name " white wine."
> —*Randall: Diary.*

White trash (American), used by negroes to a white man as a term of opprobrium.

White 'un (popular and thieves), a silver watch, a shilling.

> Then her eyes fell on the present, and she felt a most unpleasant
> Sort of shock, which made her rave, and swear, and sob.

> And her heart began to sicken, for, alas!
> it was no " thick 'un,"
> Twas a *white 'un*—or, in other words,
> a bob!
> —*Sporting Times.*

Whitewashed and fenced in (American). This is a very common phrase applied sarcastically not only to towns whose inhabitants are vain of the beauty or other merits of their "place," but even to people themselves. It implies a sense of exclusiveness, pride, and hauteur, which is of all things most detestable to the Western American. Thus Bostonians, from their noted conviction of the superiority of "the Hub" as regards culture, are often asked if it is not yet *fenced in.* To explain the following illustration taken from the *Pittsburg* (Pennsylvania) *Dispatch,* it must be understood that the dwellers in the "Birmingham" of that state are supposed to be extremely ambitious.

> "A few days since a verdant Oleander was searching through the city for a purchaser for a raft of lumber which he had tied up near Saw Mill Run. On the wharf he learned, much to his gratification, that the Burgess wished to buy a very large quantity of lumber. But when he had found that official he was informed that he was certainly mistaken, the Burgess wanted no lumber. 'Why,' replied the Oleander, 'a man in Pittsburg told me that you wanted all that could be had to *fence in* the town.' And he left, not understanding why there was a roar of laughter from all present."

White wine (old slang), gin. In "A Picture of the Fancy," the old slang names for gin are thus amusingly grouped together. "The squeamish fair one, who takes it on the sly, merely to cure the vapours, politely names it to her friends as *white wine.* The swell chaffs it as *blue ruin,* to elevate his notions. The laundress loves dearly a dram of *Ould Tom,* from its strength to comfort her inside. The drag fiddler can toss off a quartern of *max* without making a wry mug. The costermonger illumines his ideas with a *flash of lightning.* The hoarse Cyprian owes her existence to copious draughts of *jackey.* The link-boy and mudlark, in joining their browns together, are for some *stark naked.* And the out-and-outers, by the addition of bitters to it, in order to sharpen up a dissipated and damaged victualling office, cannot take anything but *fullers' earth.*"

Whittled (American), drunk.

Unquestionably Americans may evince a disposition to whittle without first getting *whittled.—Cowboys and Colonels.*

Also used in England.

Whole boiling. *Vide* BOILING.

Whole-footed, whole-hearted, and whole-souled are now cant, though once possessing a legitimate meaning. Says the *Philadelphia Age,* "Any devising man who invites a crowd to 'drinks all round' is instantly praised as a *whole-footed* man, and the calculating man who gives a piece of land for a church, VOL. II.

with a view to the enhanced value of the adjoining lots which he retains, appears in the newspapers as a noble, *whole-souled* gentleman, whose liberality will earn him the thanks of his countrymen and the gratitude of coming generations."

Whole kit and biling (American), all, all the company.

Go 'long now, the *whole kit and biling* of ye, and don't come nigh me again till I've got back my peace of mind.—*Mark Twain: Adventures of Huckleberry Finn.*

Whole team, and a little dog under the waggon (American). This synonym, for completeness in every detail, is equalled by "a six-storey house—and a lightning rod." *Vide* TEAM.

Whoop it up (American), to keep up an excitement, such as hurrahing, gambling, or drinking.

Midnight is called the whiching time of night, because at that hour it is sometimes difficult to determine which to do, go home or *whoop it up* larger.—*Life.*

Whopper (colloquial and vulgar), anything large, applied especially to a monstrous lie. *Whop,* to beat ; hence a *whopper,* one that beats anything. Originally "whapper."

When once you've passed the door—"Was you ever here before?"
Is the question that the cove on duty asks you ;
But you've got your answer pat, and you won't be such a flat
As to let a little crammer flabbergast you.
Check it proper—tell a *whopper.*
    —*J. Greenwood: A Night in a Workhouse.*

Whop-straw (popular and thieves), a countryman.

Who's your hatter? Formerly a street catchword.

I shall not be surprised if the arrangement in black—this decorative tile which you describe—does not revive the now almost forgotten slang question, the sport of a bygone day, "*Who's your hatter?*" —*Punch.*

Whyos (American), a name for a large gang or class of the lowest villains and vilest desperadoes in New York.

The young men against the walls in the street were *Whyos*—that is to say, members of the most desperate gang of thugs and thieves in town—and Baxters, which is the name of the band from which the *Whyos* are recruited, a mob of boys between fourteen and seventeen, too young to have the nerve needed to be a *Whyo*. . . . They were *Whyos*, also — pickpockets dressed to mingle in the crowds at the best up-town hotels and at the races and on the avenues, so as to drain fatter pockets than ever stray into Park Street, unless they bring them there after a night's work. They did not look like villains. . . . Bezie Garity was a typical *Whyo* girl. She was almost worshipped by the gang, she was so strong and coarse and violent and depraved. . . . When she felt amiable she gave exhibitions of what she called her "nerve." At such time she planted herself squarely on her feet and challenged the strongest *Whyo* to hit her in the face with all his might.—*Philadelphia Press.*

Wide (thieves), well-informed, clever, short for wide-awake.

It was while I was with him that I got in company with some of the *widest* people in London.—*Horsley: Jottings from Jail.*

The bookies had been *wide*, and the plunger homeward hied,
O'erladen he with champagne cup and sorrow.   —*Sporting Times.*

Cabby has none— cabbies are far too *wide*,
So, after lots of hunting, and much bobbery,
I pay two shillings for a half-mile ride.
I call it robbery.
                        —*Punch.*

Wide-awake (common), a broad-brimmed felt or stuff hat. "So called," says Hotten, "because it never had a nap, and never wants one." This word is so universally used as to be almost recognised.

Widdle, to (thieves). "Oliver don't *widdle*," the moon does not shine. Literally, does not inform upon us. *Vide* WHIDDLE.

Widow, the gallows. In French slang "la veuve," now the guillotine, was formerly the gallows. "Epouser la veuve." *Widow* and "veuve" originally were terms to designate the rope or halter, in allusion to a metaphorical marriage knot, or wedlock with a widow of many husbands. However, the Rev. A. S. Palmer thinks that *widow*, as a slang term for the gallows, is no doubt the same as Scotch *widdie*, a halter made of a flexible branch of withes, but this is very doubtful indeed.

(American), a grass *widow*, a wife a long time separated from her husband, or who has been deserted. Used in England.

Wife (prison, old), a fetter fixed to the leg.

Wife in water-colours (society), a wife "de la main gauche." The French talk of an unmarried couple living as man and wife as "un collage à la détrempe," which is a very close rendering of the English phrase.

Wig-block (popular), the head.

Wigger. *Vide* WIG, To.

Wigging (common), a rebuke. When in private it is an "ear-wigging." Also "combing one's hair." In French "laver la tête" is to rebuke, scold; "donner une peignée," to thrash.

Wigster (theatrical), a wiggy actor—an actor whose theory of art is bounded by the idea of making his head a wig block.

Wig, to (pigeon-fanciers), to post a scout on the route of flight in a pigeon race with a hen pigeon, to attract the opponent's bird and retard his progress. Probably a form of "to wool," to discomfit, which see.

"If I *wigs*, I loses," replied Tinker, evidently much hurt at the insinuation. Instructed by Mr. Stickle, I learnt what *wigging* was, and no longer marvelled at Mr. Tinker's indignation. It is a fraudulent, and lamentably common practice amongst the vulgar "fancy."—*Greenwood: Undercurrents of London Life.*

Wild (old cant), the country, a village. *Wild* is frequently used by old authors for the "weald" (old English *woeld, wald,* open country) of Kent, as if it meant a *wild* or uncultivated region, a wilderness (Palmer).

I was borne in the *wylde* of Kent.
                    —*Lyly: Euphues.*

There's a Franklin in the *wylde* of Kent hath brought three hundred markes with him in gold.—*Shakspeare: 1 Henry IV.*

Wild-cat villages (American), places with odd names. The following are all in existence :—

A. B. C.	Jump off Joe.
Accident.	Kiss-Me (Fla.)
Axle-Town.	Long-a-Coming.
Babylon.	Macphelah.
Beef-Hide.	Mad Indian.
Big-Bag.	Matrimony.
Braggadocio.	Mount Hugging
Chicory.	(N.H.).
Coffee.	Nine Times.
Cowboy.	Number One.
Crab Tree.	Obligation.
Dammit.	Our Carter.
Dirt Town.	Oz.
Door-Way.	Pat's Store.
Frozen Creek.	Patta Gumpus.
Good Land.	Plevna (several).
Good Luck.	Quiz-Quod.
Good Night.	Rabbit Hash.
Gunpowder.	Rat.
Hat Off.	Shirt Tail Bend.
Hat On.	Squantum.
High Up.	Swopetown.
Hobbie.	U. Bet.
Jingo.	Yuba Dam.
Johnny Cake.	

Wilfreds (popular), teetotallers.

Fill the bumper, crack the joke,
We're not *Wilfreds.*
                    —*Punch.*

This has reference to Sir Wilfred Lawson, M.P., the great teetotal champion.

William (common), a jocose term for a bill. To meet "sweet *William,*" to meet a "bill."

Willow (cricket), a bat; from the material.

Wilt, to (London), to run away.

Win, wyn (old cant), a penny. Suggested to be connected with Welsh *gwyn*, white, *i.e.*, the silver penny. Some thirty years ago in France pennies were termed "blancs" or "rouges," according to their more or less dark hue.

If we niggle or mill but a poor boozing-
   ken,
Or nip a poor bung with one single *win*,
Or dup but the gigger of a country-cove's
   ken,
Straight we're to the cuffin queer forced
   to bing.
    —*T. Decker: The Beggar's Curse.*

Wind-jammer (popular), a player on a wind instrument.

But hold, there's another, a puffer of fame,
A noted *wind-jammer*, young Conlan's
   his name.
—*R. Blades: The Charing Cross Party.*

(Nautical), a sailing-ship.

Wind one's cotton, to (popular), to give trouble purposely.

Window fishing (burglars), burglarious entry at a window.

Windows (popular), the eyes.

Wind, raise the. *Vide* RAISE. To slip one's *wind*, to die.

Wind-sucker (stable), a term applied to a horse with the heaves. In gypsy "bavolengro," *i.e.*, "air or wind master;" *wind sucker* is provincial for a kestrel.

Wine, a (University), a wine-party. A *wine* consists of dessert, wine (usually only port, sherry, and claret, but at very big *wines* champagne), and tea and coffee later on. *Wines* are generally confined to men of the same college. It is unusual to ask out-college men to a *wine* without asking them to dinner also.

Wing (prison), a small piece of tobacco.

A piece as large as a horse-bean, called a "chew," is regarded as the equivalent for a twelve-ounce loaf and a meat ration, and even a morsel—a mere taste that can only be laid on the tongue and sucked like a small sweetmeat (it is called a *wing*, and is not larger or of more substance than a man's little finger-nail), is "good" for a six-ounce loaf.—*J. Greenwood: Jail Birds at Large.*

Also a "*wing* of snout," "*wing* of stuff."

I had a screw who would sling a *wing* of stuff, and so long as I had a bit of tobacco and did not hear a woman's jawing, I was werry comfortable.—*Evening News.*

Winging (theatrical), taking a part under exceptional circumstances, at a moment's notice, and studying it in the wings.

Winkers (pugilistic), the eyes.

Wins the button (tailors), is the best, and is therefore entitled to the *button, i.e.*, medal.

Winter-cricket (popular), a tailor.

Wipe (popular and thieves), a pocket-handkerchief.

"How many *wipes* did you nibble?"
"Only two, a bird's-eye and a hingy.'—
Disconsolate William.

Cold, callous man !—he scorns to yield,
   Or aught relax his felon gripe,
But answers, "I'm Inspector Field!
   And this here warmint's prigg'd your
    wipe."
    —*Ingoldsby Legends.*

To see him splitting away at that pace . . . and me with the *wipe* in my pocket crying out arter him.—*Dickens : Oliver Twist.*

" As a matter of fact, I had my handkerchief in my pocket all the time, and I have it still," he said, producing a bloodstained *wipe,* with which he had sopped up the blood from his face on Bloody Sunday.— *Pall Mall Gazette.*

Also a blow, as a *wipe* on the kisser, across the chops, &c.

Wipe out, to (American), signifying to extinguish, is taken from the Pawnee Indian language. It means to defeat, to destroy. Imported from America. " To *wipe* one's eye," to shoot game which a person has missed, as if correcting defective vision by wiping watery eyes. Hence to obtain an advantage by superior skill.

She had what is called a bow-gun when she was six years old, a rifle when she was nine, and from that time she has gone on shooting turkeys, red - heads, wild cats, cotton - tails, and pigeons, " *wiping* the eyes " of the boys along the Pacific Coast, and making her name celebrated, until Colonel Cody secured her for his show.— *Bailey's Monthly Magazine.*

Wire (popular), a telegram.

The boots' brother knowed him in Birmingham, and 'as got the tip direct from the stable. He is going to send us a *wire* from the course.—*Bird o' Freedom.*

(Harvard University), a trick or dodge. A pickpocket.

His fingers were very long, and no lady's could have been more taper. A burglar told me that with such a hand he ought to have made his fortune. He was worth £20 a week, he said, as a *wire,* that is, a picker of ladies' pockets.—*Mayhew: London Labour and the London Poor.*

Wirer, wire, or **wire-hook** (English and American), a pickpocket.

Wire, to (common), to telegraph.

It cannot be called the most startling piece of intelligence ever *wired.* —*Pall Mall Gazette.*

(Popular), to *wire* in, to go ahead, push on, go in with a will. Also to join, unite with.

And when larks and loyalty jine, I say *wire* in and bust the expense. —*Punch.*

Wire-worm (Stock Exchange), a man who collects prices to " wire," *i.e.,* to telegraph to country clients.

Wisty-castor (pugilistic), a serious blow. Seems to be from *wistly,* earnestly.

Neal was always dangerous, and now and then put in a *wisty-castor,* which rather changed the look of Sam's frontispiece.—*Pierce Egan : Book of Sports.*

Wobbler (cavalry), an infantry soldier. (Common), a horse that swerves from side to side when trotting. French, " un cheval qui se berce."

Wobble-shop (popular), a shop where beer or spirits are sold without a license.

Wolfer (common), a man with a large appetite, or a hard drinker.

And a great, sad silence fell upon the crowd ; for then, and not till then, did they realise what unwarrantable liberties they had been taking with their internal organisations, and everybody wished that they had been born an elephant or a megalosaurus, or something with a similar capacity for the storage of liquors, until confidence was restored by the reassuring remark of an adjacent whisky *wolfer*, "But it stretches, gentlemen, it stretches ! "—*Bird o' Freedom.*

Wolf, to (common), originally to ingurgitate ravenously, but now with extended meaning of simply to eat.

· And then it transpires that Skipper Hammett is chewing bacca, and that Shifter has *wolfed* all the brandy. This is a cold world.—*Sporting Times.*

I've tasted *bouillabaisse*, and I've *wolfed* roast hare and pickled pork.—*Bird o' Freedom.*

Also to steal, to cheat out of.

It was generally considered that Custance, who was on Comforter in the City and Suburban of 1860, was *wolfed* by Wells on Lord Nelson, who made a dead heat of it, Comforter winning the decider. —*Bird o' Freedom.*

To *wolf* is said to be of American origin. The derivation is obvious.

George.—"Quite a snug pile."
Tom.—"Yes. The boy was only seven years old, and, of course, there was a guardian, or rather a set of them, appointed for him and to take charge of the estate. Well, they *wolfed* him."
George.—"Got away with it all?"
Tom.—"Nearly all."
　　　　—*Missouri Republican.*

Wolloping (popular), thrashing, beating.

"Porliceman, father's giving mother such a *wolloping*, will you come?"—*Music Hall Song.*

Wood (clerical), the pulpit.

Wood-and-water Joey (Australian), a hanger about hotels.

Wood-butcher (tradesmen), workmen who have not thoroughly learned their business as carpenters or joiners.

Counting carpenters and *wood-butchers* together, it is estimated that about 20,000 men make their living in London as carpenters and joiners. Of these nearly 5000 are of the *wood-butcher*, or inexpert workmen class, and therefore do not belong to the trade societies.—*New York Herald.*

Woodcock, a tailor, from an association with a long bill.

Wooden fit (popular), a swoon.

Wooden overcoat (thieves and popular). Wearing a *wooden overcoat* and being put to bed with a shovel, being dead and buried.

Wooden ruff, explained by quotation.

To wear a *wooden ruff* was what plain people called being put in the pillory.—*Globe.*

Wooden spoon, the last man in the mathematical tripos at Cambridge is generally referred to as the *wooden spoon* of his year ; a common wooden spoon is often actually presented to him by the undergraduates in the gallery of the Senate House. When two or more " last " men are bracketed together, the group is termed the *spoon* bracket.

Winning perhaps eventually the *wooden spoon*, or worse, being utterly ploughed.— *Morning Advertiser.*

Spanish undergraduates wear a *wooden spoon* in their hats when in full costume, perhaps an allusion to the intellectual food provided by *Alma Mater*, but more probably from a custom of poor students in the Middle Ages, who often, like the old French poet Villon, associated with vagabonds, such as are depicted by Teniers, with a spoon stuck in their hats. In France the practice still exists among tramps or other low class of people. This would tend to show that the university custom has been handed down from the Middle Ages. In the sixteenth century the " Chevaliers de la Cuiller " were an association formed by noblemen of Vaud who had boasted of eating up their enemies the Genevese, but to this of course is not due the origin of the ornamental spoon.

Wooden wedge (Cambridge University), the last name in the classical honours list at Cambridge. From the name of a wrangler named Wedgewood, who was the last on the list of the first classical tripos in 1824.

Wood merchant (streets), explained by quotation.

> When he can't get on that racket he'll turn mumper and *wood merchant* (which means a seller of lucifer matches).—*Temple Bar.*

Wood-sawyer's clerk (American), employed to indicate a man in the lowest possible or poorest employment. A clam-butcher is applied scornfully to one who is in similar circumstances.

Wool (popular), hair. "Keep your *wool* on," don't get angry, literally an intimation not to tear one's hair ; or, more probably, to keep one's **wig** on. Compare

" Dash my wig ! " expressive of disappointment or angry excitement, which must have originated in the frequency of persons dashing their wigs in anger to the ground when it was the fashion to cover the shaven pate with that ornament, an act far more convenient than tearing the hair. (Pugilistic), pluck, courage. "*Woolled* 'un," or a rare "*wool*-topped 'un," a man of great courage. Said to be in allusion to coloured heroes of the prize-ring.

Wool-bird (popular and thieves), a sheep or lamb. French thieves call a sheep *lainé.*

Wool-hole (popular), a very old synonym for the workhouse. Perhaps more used by printers than any other class of workpeople. Savage, 1841, quotes this term.

Wool is up, times are good ; **wool is down,** times are bad (used by up-country slangy Australians). Wool being the staple of Australia, it is easy to see how a phrase, which at first was applicable only to the fortunes of the wool-growers, gradually passed into a metaphor.

> Bother ! how can I go steady,
> I'm worth thousands—*wool is up.*
> —*Garnet Walch.*

> I go where *wool* has gone—*down*, ever *down.*
> —*Garnet Walch.*

Woolly (studios), a *woolly* painting is one painted in slack touches. (Common), irritable, angry. *Vide*

WOOL. (Popular and thieves), a blanket.

Woolly - headed boy (tailors), a favourite.

Wool-splitter (tailors), a renowned tailor.

Wool, to (common), to get the better of, to discomfit. This phrase, allied to blinding a man in the sense of deceiving him, probably gave rise to the saying so common in America, "To pull the *wool* over one's eyes." German, " Er macht ihn mit sehenden Augen blind "—"He blinds him while he sees with his eyes," is very old, and to be found in the *Hildebrandslied.*

Working the shells (American thieves), a variety of thimble-rig, in which walnut shells are used, instead of thimbles or little cups.

I was pinched for *working the shells* at Atlantic City last summer, and got two months for it. A gent in the crowd offered to bet me ten dollars he could tell which shell the ball was under, and of course I went him on it. As soon as I showed my money, he put his hands on me, and said he was a special officer in plain clothes. Low trick—wasn't it? They brought the *shells* into court, and they've got my table there now.—*Confidence Crooks (Philadelphia Press).*

Works, the (prison), a convict establishment, such as Portland, Portsmouth, or Dartmoor.

Work the bulls, to (coiners), to get rid of bad crown pieces.

Work the pea, to, to swindle one's employer by skilfully appropriating small sums off the takings at the bar of a public-house, alluding to a conjuror's trick. A phrase much used by barmen.

Work, to (thieves), to steal. French slang, *travailler;* Spanish slang, *trābajar.*

Worm (popular), a policeman. *Worm* is provincial for any venomous vermin.

Worm-crusher (cavalry), a foot soldier.

Worm-eater, a man who sells as authentic articles of spurious historical value, manufactured for the purpose, or otherwise.

Now and then, it is true, he picked up some article to which the attached legends were a trifle apocryphal. That industrious artist, who is technically known as the *worm-eater,* was at times too much even for the editor of the *Architect.—Standard.*

Worms (Winchester College), explained by quotation.

Across the two ends of the ground a small trench is dug, about four inches wide and two deep, and a goal is obtained when the ball is fairly kicked across the trench (Wiccamicé *worms).—Pascoe.*

Wrap-rascal (old cant), a cloak.

Wrens, prostitutes who " squatted" amongst the furze of Curragh Common.

These creatures are known in and about the great military camp and its neighbourhood as *wrens.* They do not live in houses or even huts, but build for themselves "nests" in the bush.—*Greenwood: Seven Curses of London.*

Wright, Mr. (prison), a faithless prison officer, the intermediary between an incarcerated criminal and his friends outside. The title is so given in the clandestine letters sent out surreptitiously, in which the prisoner says *Mr. Wright*, who is all right or safe, will call.

Wring oneself, to (thieves), to change one's clothes.

I went home and *wrung myself*, and met some of the mob and got very near drunk.—*Horsley: Jottings from Jail.*

Wrinkle (common), properly a whim, fancy. Used slangily for a cunning trick or artful dodge.

I can put you up to a *wrinkle*. Tollit has got a mare who can lick Tearaway into fits. She's as easy as a chair and jumps like a cat. All that you have to do is to sit back.—*C. Bede: Verdant Green.*

Implying artfulness, this word was probably associated with *wrinkle*, a fold or plait, as if it meant an involved proceeding, a piece of "duplicity" (*duplex*) or double-foldedness, as opposed to what is plain or "simple" (Latin *simplex*, one fold) (Palmer).

Palmer as he was a man symple and withoute all *wryncles* off cloked colusyone, opened to hym his whole intent.—*Narratives of the Reformation.*

I know you're a little bit artful, old boy,
And up to a *wrinkle* or two ;

You know this from that without any doubt,
And many old fakements can do.
—*Ballad: You're More Than Seven.*

Writing a poor hand (tailors), is said of one who sews badly ; also " sore fist."

Wrong (common), *wrong* in the upper storey, crazy. In the *wrong* box, out of one's element. "You'll find yourself in the *wrong box*," refers to being completely mistaken and finding oneself in embarrassment or jeopardy. "We are indebted for this to George Lord Lyttelton. He was of a rather melancholy disposition, and used to tell his friends that when he went to Vauxhall he was always supposing pleasure to be in the next box to his, or at least that he was so unhappily situated as always to be in the *wrong box*" (R. W. Hackwood, *Notes and Queries*).

Wrong 'un (common), anything or anybody that is artful or bad. (Turf), a horse not supposed to be meant to win. (Popular), a prostitute, a spurious coin or note.

Wusser (bargemen), a canal boat.

X

X, or letter *x*, a method of arrest used by policemen with desperate ruffians, by getting a firm grasp on the collar, and drawing the captive's hand over the holding arm, and pressing the fingers down in a peculiar way—the captured person's arm in this way can be more easily broken than extricated.

X, Y, Z, an (literary), a common literary caterer, so called from an advertiser under these initials in the *Times* offering to perform all descriptions of literary work at very moderate and unprofessional prices.

Y

YACK (thieves), a watch. From the gypsy *yack*, an eye or watch. Watches were at one time commonly known as bull's eyes. "To church a *yack*," or "christen a *yack*," to take the works out of the case, to avoid detection.

Yaffle (old cant), to eat.

Yam (West Indian negro, sailors, &c.), food.

Yam, to (popular), to eat. This is provincial English.

Ya-mun, ya-men (pidgin), a mandarin, a prefect's residence.

Yank (American), nickname for Yankee. A quick pull, snap; of very wide application.

No kid. I didn't get home till three o'clock, and the missis would have it I was boozed. I assure you, it rained tea-cups and hailed fire-irons for about half-an-hour, and I've felt like struck by lightning ever since. No; that *Yank* was about right, I guess.—*Bird o' Freedom.*

Yank, to (American), to remove by a quick motion, or a snap.

He moistens his hands, grabs his property vigorously, *yanks* it this way, then that.—*Mark Twain: A Tramp Abroad.*

A grasshopper sat on a sweet-potato vine,
 A sweet-potato vine,
 A sweet-potato vine,
A great turkey gobbler came running up
 behind,
And *yanked* the poor grasshopper off the
 sweet-potato vine.
    —*Popular Song*

To *yank* the bun, a synonym for "to take the cake," meaning to take the prize, or to excel in some way.

Yannam (old cant), bread. Probably a corruption of "pannam," influenced by first syllable of "yaffle," to eat.

Yarmouth bee (tailors), a herring.

Yarmouth capon. *Vide* TROUT, NORLOCH.

Yarmouth mittens (nautical), bruised hands.

Yarn-slinger, one who writes tales in newspapers.

Yarum (old cant), milk; "poplars of *yarum*," milk porridge.

Yaw-sighted (nautical), squinting.

Yellow belly (nautical), a name given to a person born in the fens along our eastern shores. Also a half-caste. (American), a Dutchman; so called from "yellow belly," a frog.

Yellow boy (common), a gold coin, a sovereign. In French slang "jaunet," German cant "fuchs" and "gelbling," from *gelb*, yellow. Some of the synonyms for a sovereign are "canary," "couter," "gingle boy," "goldfinch," "monarch," "shiner," "quid," "meg," "James," "bean," "foont," "portrait," "thick-un," "skiv," "yellow mould."

The best of all robbers as ever I know'd,
Is the bold fighting Attie, the pride of the road!—
Fighting Attie, my hero, I saw you to-day
A purse full of *yellow boys* seize.
—*Lord Lytton: Paul Clifford.*

We shut the cellar door behind us, and when they found the bag they spilt it out on the floor, and it was a lovely sight, all them *yaller boys.*—*Mark Twain: Huckleberry Finn.*

Yellow dog (American). Dr. O. W. Holmes, in "Elsie Venner," has written an amusing comment on the fact that in the New England States a *yellow dog* is a synonym for all that is contemptible.

" I am looked at as a blackmailer," said he, " and those who believe I have been bleeding that old man hold me in as much contempt as a *yellow dog.*"—*American Newspaper.*

Yellow fancy (costers and pugilistic), silk pocket-handkerchief with white spots.

Yellow fever, formerly a cant term for drunkenness at Greenwich Hospital, where drunkards used to be punished by being made to wear a parti-coloured coat in which yellow predominated. (Australian mining), greed for gold. The expression has practically come to mean " Dreams of an Eldorado." In the same way ladies are said to suffer from " scarlet fever " when they run after military society.

Yellow gloak (old), a jealous man or husband. Formerly "to wear yellow stockings" meant "to be jealous." In France, yellow is the emblematic colour of deceived husbands.

Yellow hammer, one of the synonyms for a gold coin.

Yellow Jack (common), yellow fever.

His elder brother died of *Yellow Jack* in the West Indies.—*Dickens: Dombey and Son.*

Yellow man (prize ring), a yellow silk handkerchief.

Sporting the *yellow man.* The wipe was of bright yellow, made on purpose for him.—*Pierce Egan: Book of Sports.*

Yellow-mould (tailors), a sovereign.

Yellow pine (American), a word frequently used to indicate a quadroon or light mulatto.

Yellow stuff (thieves), gold. In French slang "jaune." Also counterfeit gold coins.

If he can manage to begin every morning with *yellow stuff*, he may make a couple of quid a day ; but if he can only muster white stuff, why, of course he can't make so much.—*Temple Bar.*

Yellows (thieves), counterfeit gold coin ; the silver coin is called blanks before impressed. Many of these are struck at Birmingham, but there was in the beginning of the century a large number made in London.

(Popular), Blue-coat or charity school boys.

Yelper, or **bullet, got** (popular), discharged.

Yennep (costers and thieves), back slang for a penny.

" All a fellow wants to know to sell potatoes," said a master street seller to me, " is to tell how many tanners make a bob, and how many *yenneps* a tanner."—*Mayhew: London Labour and the London Poor.*

Yeute (Punch show), no, not, as in *yeute* lette, no bed.

Yid, Yiddisher, Yeddan, or **Yeddican** (London), a Jew. From the German *Jüdisch.*

I might, if I had poached upon the province of the Pitcher,
Have devoted just a verse or two to love among the *Yids.*
—*Sporting Times.*

Yiesk (tinker), fish (Gaelic *casg*).

Ying-jen (pidgin), Englishman.

Yiu (Punch and Judy), a street. Query French "rue" ?

Yob, boy. An example of back slang largely used by costermongers, which simply consists in spelling (more or less accurately) words backwards. Thus, " Hi, *yob,* kool that enif elrig with the nael ekom. Sap her a top o' reeb or a tib of occabot," is " Hi, boy, look at that fine girl with the lean moke (donkey). Pass her a pot of beer and a bit of tobacco." The art or merit of this form of slang consists in the rapidity, often most remarkable, with which words can be reversed. Thus Mayhew, wishing to test the skill of a professor of the art with a word not in common use in the market, asked a coster friend what was the back slang for hippopotamus. At once he answered " sumatopoppy." Back slang largely mingles with the older and more legitimate argot or thieves' slang.

Yob-gab (costers and thieves), boys' talk. This is a jargon used by costermongers, thieves, and tramps to enable them to talk about their doings without being understood by the uninitiated. It is seldom if ever seen written or printed. The " language " is simple enough, and when the key is known there is no difficulty in talking oneself, or in understanding the talk of others. The simplest form of *yob-gab* is the spelling of words letter by letter, with the addition of a consonant after each vowel, and a vowel after each consonant. Thus *legs* is li-*et*-gi-*si* ; but as any vowel or consonant may be used, the same word may be expressed in several different forms ; thus la-*el*-go-*su*, le-*em*-gu-*so*, lo-*es*-ga-*se*, lu-*es*-ga-*so*. Man is represented by mu-*al*-nu, mi-*at*-ni, mo-*ad*-no, and so forth, through numberless variations, which make the jargon more puzzling to any one who hears it spoken, the same word being varied at the will of the speaker. The jargon is easily learned, and amongst costers and their children it was, a quarter of a century ago, quite common, and teachers in the Ragged Schools in Kent Street, and the Mint in Southwark, and the district visitors got quite familiar with it, through hearing it in use by both parents and children.

Yokuff (thieves), a kind of back slang, or anagram, for coffer, that is, a box, chest.

Yok, yoke (tinker), a man. (English canting and old provincial), a countryman. The *el* final is a common termination (*e.g.*, cockerel), like *er*.

Yorkshire, to, to cheat or cozen. Also to come *Yorkshire* over a person. Used by Dickens.

You bet! (American), an exclamation, a strong affirmative or negative. The writer has also heard it with the meaning of

What next ? Don't you think you may get it ?

"You can be supplied cheaper than that, *you bet!* About ten bob's worth of stephanotis, and half a dollar to the doorkeeper"——
Another friendship severed.—*Bird o' Freedom.*

This slang phrase has actually given a name to a settlement in the north-west. *Vide* WILDCAT VILLAGES.

We at last got straightened up, and the snow came on with a heavy wind, but most fortunately it was behind us, so we kept before the storm, and reached, in the course of another two miles, the settlement of *Ubet*. . . . The name of *Ubet* had been selected from the slang phrase so laconically expressive of "You may be pretty sure I will."—*A. Staveley Hill: From Home to Home.*

You bet your buttons ! (American), said of a man who will play at a gambling-table so long as he has money.

"*You bet your buttons!*" murmured Squito proudly, "Sam'll stay with 'em as long as he's got a check."—*F. Francis : Saddle and Moccasin.*

You bet your sweet life ! (American), meaning you may be assured. Also used in England.

You can find me whenever you do ; and you'll find me heeled, too, *you bet your sweet life.*—*F. Francis : Saddle and Moccasin.*

You fasten on (common), synonymous of " you go on."

You'll do ! (American), uttered with a strong accent on the *you'll*. A strong approval, a declaration that the one addressed can take care of himself or hold his own, a note of admiration. In a police report in a Michigan newspaper, a vagrant brought before the mayor, being asked what caused the wound on his nose, replied, "I fell down and stepped on it." Being required to pay a fine, he produced a bank-bill, which he assured the magistrate was the last fragment of an immense fortune left to him by a fond and devoted uncle. He was, in short, so prompt with his replies, and showed such "a healthy indifference" to his adversity, that the magistrate dismissed him, exclaiming in admiration "*You'll do!*" "I'll do" is also commonly heard when a man is confident of his ability to succeed in anything, or to take care of himself.

> And like a rat without a tail,
> I'll do, and I'll do, and I'll do.
> —*Mackbeth.*

Your uncle (American), an equivalent for "I."

You say you can, but can you? (American). "This was ex-plained by one of my friends as being Chesterfieldian for 'you lie!'" (C. Leland Harrison, MS. Americanisms).

You've fixed it up nicely for me (popular), one of the numerous popular slang synonyms for saying that a man is not to be taken in. "No you don't," "Not for Joseph," or "Do you see anything green in my eye?"

> Now grammar is all very well in its way,
> As taught to young folks in their teens—
> But as for myself I am sorry to say
> That I really don't know what it means.
> There is only one phrase I can safely employ,
> When a widow invites me to tea,
> I wink my left eye and I simply reply,
> *You've fixed it up nicely for me.*
> —*Robert Johnson: Ballad.*

You've shot your granny (American), you've found a mare's nest.

Yoxter (thieves), a convict returned from transportation before his time.

Yum-yum (London), first-rate, elegant.

Z

ZIFF (thieves), a young thief.

Zoo (common), abbreviation for Zoological Gardens.

Zooning (American), used in the South. Humming, buzzing, barking.

> Bre'r Bar, he low dat he kin hear de bees *a-zoonin.*—*Uncle Remus.*

Zoyara (American), an effeminate young man, a lady-gentleman, a "Molly." In 1860-61 there was a young fellow whose name "on the slangs" was *Zoyara*, a circus-rider, who affected the dress and airs of a girl so well that it was the town-question in New York for some time as to what the sex of the "phenomenon" really was. Of course every circus in the United States had for some time after a *Zoyara*.

The London *Globe* having inquired why the stage names of female acrobats and circus-riders so generally begin with *Z*, a correspondent (C. G. Leland) remarked that they are, as in *Zazel, Zaniel, Zoes,* derived from Hebrew or Yiddish words meaning devil or goblin.

THE END.

www.ingramcontent.com/pod-product-compliance
Lightning Source LLC
Chambersburg PA
CBHW031046280326
41928CB00048B/373